Single Asset Real Estate Bankruptcies

Current Developments and Legislative Issues

American Bankruptcy Institute
St. John's University School of Law

Published by the Section of
Real Property, Probate and Trust Law
American Bar Association

Printed in the United States of America.

Single-entity asset real estate / Robert M. Zinman, editor
p. cm.
"Real Property, Probate and Trust Section, American Bar Association and the American Banruptcy Institute."
Includes index.
ISBN 1-57073-390-2 (pbk.)
1. Bankruptcy--United States. 2. Real estate investment--Law and legislation--United States. 3. Partnership--United States.
I. Zinman, Robert M. II. American Bar Association. Section of Real Property, Probate, and Trust Law. III. American Bankruptcy Institute.
KF1535.R43S57 1997
346.7304'3--dc21 96-51818

Discounts are available for books ordered in bulk. Special consideration is given to state bars, CLE programs, and other bar-related organizations. Inquire at Publications Planning & Marketing, American Bar Association, 750 North Lake Shore Drive, Chicago, Illinois 606l1.

00 99 98 97 96 5 4 3 2 1

American Bankruptcy Institute
Board of Directors

Board of Directors

SUMMARY OF CONTENTS

CONTENTS

Part IV

Tax Considerations

Part VI

Impact on Institutional Lenders

Part VII

Single Asset Legislation Reform

FOREWORD

ROBERT M. ZINMAN*

A. Real Estate as a Bankruptcy Hot Button.

Call back those halcyon days of the seventies, when there were approximately 200,000 bankruptcy filings a year rather than the more than a million filings predicted for 1996[1] -- and when the likes of Rich Levin and Ken Klee on the House side, and Harry Dixon and Bob Feidler from the Senate staff, struggled with the complexities of conflicting proposals, sought out comments of all constituencies, and developed that remarkable document known as the Bankruptcy Code. Perhaps the predominant force that drove the direction of the drafting during those formative years was single asset real estate bankruptcy.

At that time, single asset real estate bankruptcy was governed largely by chapter XII of the former Bankruptcy Act. Chapter XII did not contain the chapter X (Corporate Reorganizations) requirement that no plan could be confirmed unless it were "fair and equitable, and feasible"[2] The words "fair

---

* President, American Bankruptcy Institute

1. The average number of filings in the 1970-79 period was 208,618.9. AMERICAN BANKRUPTCY INSTITUTE, BANKRUPTCY OVERVIEW: ISSUES, LAW AND POLICY 76 (3d ed. 1996). The 1996 estimate was prepared by the American Bankruptcy Institute and released on November 30, 1995. *ABI Predicts Bankruptcy Filings to Exceed One Million in 1996* (American Bankruptcy Institute, Alexandria, Va.), Nov. 30, 1995.
2. Bankruptcy Act, § 221, 11 U.S.C. § 621 (1976). "The judge shall confirm a plan if satisfied that -- ... (2) the plan is fair and equitable, and feasible ...." The requirement had been derived from § 77B(1). Section 77B, adopted in 1934 (Act of June 7, 1934, 48 Stat. 913) was the forerunner of chapter X, which was adopted as part of the general revision of the Bankruptcy Act of 1898, known as the Chandler Act. Bankr. Act. of 1898, ch. 541, 30 Stat. 544 (1898),

and equitable" had been defined by the Supreme Court to mean that absolute priority was required.[3] Absolute priority meant that a reorganization plan had to compensate senior debt fully before junior debt could be paid, and that the individual debtor, the stockholders or the partners could retain nothing on account of their prebankruptcy interest unless all creditors were paid in full.

Without absolute priority, cases under chapter XII, beginning with *In re Pine Gate*,[4] permitted the plan to "cash out" the mortgagee for the depressed value of the collateral,[5] thereby allowing the debtor to keep the property free and clear of liens.[6] Obviously real estate people fought fiercely to overcome

---

amended by, Act of June 22, 1938, ch. 575, 52 Stat. 883 (1938), *repealed by* Bankruptcy Reform Act of 1978, Pub. L. No. 95-598, 92 Stat. 2549, 2682 (codified as amended at 11 U.S.C. § 101 *et seq.*)

3. Case v. Los Angeles Lumber Prods. Co., 308 U.S. 106 (1939).

4. *In re* Pine Gate Assocs., Ltd., 2 Bankr. Ct. Dec. (CRR) 1478 (Bankr. N.D. Ga. 1976).

5. This was permitted by an interpretation of chapter XII of the Chandler Act, § 461(11), which required, *inter alia,* that if a class of creditors rejected a proposed arrangement, the arrangement could not be confirmed unless "adequate protection for the realization by them of the value of their claims against the property dealt with by the plan" were provided. Among the permissible steps constituting such adequate protection was appraisal and payment in cash of the "value of such debts". In *Pine Gate*, Judge William Norton concluded that, given the nonrecourse nature of the debt, the value of the debt was equal to the value of the collateral -- in the depressed conditions of the Atlanta area at the time. *In re* Pine Gate Assocs., Ltd., 2 Bankr. Ct. Dec. (CRR) 1478.

   Pine Gate, 2 Bankr. Ct. Dec. (CRR) 1478, was followed by, State Mut. Life Ins. Co. of Am. v. KRO Assocs. (*In re* KRO Assocs.), 4 Bankr. Ct. Dec. (CRR) 462 (Bankr. S.D.N.Y. 1978). In that case the property was encumbered by $14 million in mortgages (the first mortgage was $6 million) and Judge Roy Babitt approved a valuation of $895,000, thereby allowing the debtor to keep the property free and clear of mortgages upon the payment of $895,000 to the first mortgagee.

6. The motivation for this was avoidance of recapture of accelerated depreciation on foreclosure. I.R.C. §§ 1245, 1250 (1970). In response to creditor's argument in *KRO* that such a motivation indicated that the filing had not been in good faith, the court stated "Congress did not intend to except tax-minded investors from the class of debtors for whom chapter XII relief is available." *KRO*, 4 Bankr. Ct. Dec. (CRR) at 468.

what became known as "Pine Gate!" They urged that the new one-size-fits-all chapter 11 should require that absolute priority be a condition to plan confirmation. Given the fact that the usual single asset case hardly involved the preservation of a "going concern" with significant numbers of employees, and largely boiled down to a simple question as to whether the debtor or the unpaid creditors would own the real estate, the angst of the real estate people toward Pine Gate was shared by many.

The suggested solution, however, met with some surprising opposition. It came from those involved in corporate reorganizations under chapter X. They were concerned about the absolute application of absolute priority that had been required under chapter X. Even where all classes of creditors voted to approve a plan that provided some share to experienced old equity, the plan could not be confirmed if any creditor objected to the resultant failure to conform to absolute priority.[7] Thus corporate people fought for a relaxing of the absolute priority standards to facilitate negotiation of a successful reorganization plan while the real estate people fought to expand the doctrine.[8]

Out of this controversy the great compromise that comprises the plan confirmation provisions of the Bankruptcy Code was fashioned. The classes were free to negotiate a plan, and, if approved by the requisite majority,[9] the plan would be confirmed without an inquiry as to whether it provided absolute priority. Absolute priority was, however, required as a prerequisite to imposition (or "cramdown") of a plan with respect to any impaired class that had rejected the plan. The purpose was to prevent confirmation of single asset plans under which the debtor proposed to retain the property without compensating creditors in full.

Other changes were made to cement this solution. For example, nonrecourse debt would be converted to recourse debt under § 1111(b) to give the nonrecourse mortgagee an unsecured claim that might be protected where

---

7. *See, e.g.*, Case v. Los Angeles Lumber Products Co., 308 U.S. 106 (1939).
8. At that time this writer worked with the life insurance industry which had substantial investments in both corporate securities and real estate. The American Council of Life Insurance (then the American Life Insurance Association), nevertheless strongly supported an absolute priority requirement as essential to the fair and proper administration of bankruptcy in the Nation.
9. Two thirds in amount and one half in number of each class is required for approval of a plan. 11 U.S.C. § 1126 (Supp. III 1979).

absolute priority was mandated and, under § 1129(a)(10), no plan could be confirmed unless at least one class of impaired creditors approved it.

While it was expected that the new Bankruptcy Code, with these changes, would solve the pre-Code problems surrounding single asset real estate bankruptcies, it was not long before it became apparent that single asset real estate breeds phoenix-like problems that refuse to go "gentle into that good night."[10] For example, it is now argued that the carefully crafted absolute priority cramdown provisions cannot survive an infusion of "new value" by the debtor; that imaginative classification can create the class that will meet the §1129(a)(10) requirement; and that the Code-created deficiency claim of the nonrecourse secured party is not quite "the same as if" the claim had been recourse.[11]

In addition, new problems not fully considered in the 1970's have surfaced involving good faith, venue, taxation, automatic stay and a host of other bankruptcy issues where different treatment for single asset real estate cases might be justified. Thus it was not surprising in 1993 that the first issue of the American Bankruptcy Institute's new law review was devoted to "Single Asset Bankruptcy". What was somewhat surprising was how overwhelming the response to that issue was. Law firms sent cabs to St. John's to pick up page proofs of the judges' roundtable and advance copies of articles for use in major litigation; the issue itself was sold out in a few months and went to second printing. Well over 7000 copies were distributed, a remarkable circulation for a law review.

Now over three years have passed since that issue was published during which time the problems have only become more problematic. It was in this atmosphere that the Books and Media Committee of the American Bar Association's Section of Real Property, Probate & Trust Law suggested publishing an updated and an expanded version of the issue as a book to be made available to a new audience of real estate professionals. Responding as they always do, the St. John's student editors of the American Bankruptcy

---

10. *Cf.* Dylan Thomas, Do Not Go Gentle into That Good Night, *in* THE NORTON ANTHOLOGY OF MODERN POETRY 911, 911 (Richard Ellmann & Robert O'Clair eds., 1973).

11. 11 U.S.C. § 1111(b)(1)(A) (1994). "A claim secured by a lien on property of the estate shall be allowed or disallowed under section 502 of this title the same as if the holder of such claim had recourse against the debtor on account of such claim, whether or not such holder has such recourse...." *Id.*

Institute Law Review, together with the original authors, and a few new ones, undertook this challenge in addition to their full publication scale. The result is this book.

B. What this Book Contains.

To set the stage, the book opens with a summary of typical single asset real estate bankruptcy cases by Deborah Williamson, a Vice President of the ABI. The extent to which the courts will examine the good faith of the debtor is next discussed, through a roundtable discussion by a group of prominent bankruptcy judges from various parts of the country -- Hon. Lisa Hill Fenning (C.D. Cal.); Hon William Greendyke (S.D. Tex.); Hon. William Hillman (D. Mass.); and Hon. Robert Mark (S.D. Fla.) -- moderated by Professor Karen Gross of the New York Law School.

John McNicholas follows up on the judges' comments and discusses the effectiveness of prepetition workout agreements in which the debtor admits that a subsequent filing will have been in bad faith. Next Catherine Battle and Carollynn Gambino Pedreira analyze venue issues in single asset reorganizations and Albert Cardinali and David Miller consider the tax aspects of single asset bankruptcy.

Two major substantive single asset issues follow. The first deals with whether unsecured claims can be imaginatively classified for the purpose of meeting the §1129(a)(10) requirement that at least one class of impaired creditors approve the plan. For this discussion, Professor Linda Rusch has updated her article supportive of freedom of classification and two student editors have contributed a new Note, which reaches an opposite conclusion. The second issue is the so-called "New Value Exception" to the absolute priority rule. Mark E. MacDonald, Sally A. Schreiber and Mark E. MacDonald, Jr. take the position that the exception lives under the Code and is applicable to single asset cases, while Salvatore G. Gangemi has updated the student Note that he and Stephen Bordanaro wrote for the original issue, taking the opposite point of view.

Adding a new perspective to the subject, James Lipscomb, Senior Vice President, and Alan J. Robin, Associate General Counsel at Metropolitan Life Insurance Company, have teamed up to discuss the effect of single asset bankruptcy on institutional investors.

Finally, recent and current legislative initiatives to correct some of the problems discussed by Messrs Lipscomb and Robin, are discussed by Hon.

Roger Whelan in a critical analysis, and Scott Carlisle, Assistant General Counsel at UNUM Life Insurance Company and father of the single asset amendment proposals, looks at the 1994 amendments from a secured creditor's perspective.

* * * *

The publication of this book leaves many people to whom much thanks is due. To the authors who again strove to meet our deadlines; to the ABI staff and Advisory Board; the ABA Media and Books Committee, especially Alan Robin and John Hollingshead; to Jerry Luckman, Lori Webber, Rick Viola and their original band of editors and staff without whom there would have been no ABI Law Review; and to Doug Deutsch and his dedicated and wonderful group of current editors and staff whose efforts, like the original group almost four years ago, continue to amaze this writer, as they again define the meaning of commitment -- to all of them our most sincere appreciation.

CHAPTER I

DEFINING SINGLE ASSET REAL ESTATE BANKRUPTCIES

DEBORAH D. WILLIAMSON

In 1986, Fifth Circuit Judge Edith Jones was a panel-member at a question and answer session at the 1st Annual Real Estate Reorganization and Foreclosure Seminar conducted by the National Business Institute, Inc. in Houston, Texas. One of the speakers asked the rhetorical question: "Why should lenders be allowed to take advantage of the `aberration' in the Houston real estate market?" The speaker contended that conditions such as low occupancies, diminished real estate values, and other factors were an "aberration" in a market that would soon rebound. The argument was that allowing lenders to go forward with foreclosure was therefore granting an undue benefit. Judge Jones quickly responded: "Who's to say that the high occupancy rates and the high values were not in themselves the aberration and that the conditions existing in 1986 are not the norm or reality?"

Regardless of which aberration view one endorses, it is clear that a fall in regional real estate values results in an explosion of single asset real estate cases. Single asset cases cycle from region to region following trends within the regional real estate markets. They seem to have their origin in Texas and Arizona in 1985 and the current cycle appears to be concluding in California. A single asset case may involve a piece of raw land,[1] a strip center,[2] an apartment complex[3] or a large office building.[4] The precipitating motivations

1. *In re* Lake Ridge Assocs., 169 B.R. 576, 579 (E.D. Va. 1994).
2. Principal Mut. Life Ins. Co. v. Baldwin Park Towne Ctr. (*In re* Baldwin Park Towne Ctr.), 171 B.R. 374, 375 (Bankr. C.D. Cal. 1994).
3. California Fed. Bank v. Moorpark Adventure (*In re* Moorpark Adventure), 161 B.R. 254, 255 (Bankr. C.D. Cal. 1993).
4. First Fidelity Bank v. Jason Realty, L.P. (*In re* Jason Realty, L.P.), 59 F.3d 423, 425 (3d Cir. 1996).

for filing single asset cases are varied; they include protection for general partners, a need for new cash infusion, attempts to force concessions from lienholders, and the simple buying of time.

The purpose of this Chapter is to provide an introduction to the traits underlying many single asset real estate cases. In furtherance of this, Part A details many of the factual settings that spawn these specialized cases. Part B draws upon these settings to construct the factors that compose the atypical single asset bankruptcy case. It is upon this framework that the issues raised throughout this book arise.

A. Spawning Single Asset Real Estate Cases

While the causes underlying single asset cases vary greatly, several recurring settings have taken form. A number of single asset real estate cases are filed for tax reasons. Foreclosures in states such as Texas, which have no right of redemption,[5] force an immediate recognition of the tax consequences of a foreclosure. As a result, there is less time for tax planning than in states with a right of redemption. A large number of single asset bankruptcy cases, particularly in the mid-1980s, were filed in order to allow for tax planning by the limited partners. For example, this extended time would alleviate gains, such as accelerated depreciation, that result from partnership tax strategies.

There are also the bankruptcies that were filed in order to protect general partners from claims by the limiteds. Limited partnerships, particularly those publicly traded, have a history of excessive "soft" costs attributable to management or the operation of the limited partnership. The investors in these partnerships (typically doctors and other professionals looking for the tax advantages of a real estate partnership and hoping for an increase in the value of the real estate when the property is sold) historically did not pay particularly close attention to the actual use of the money being invested in the limited partnership, the proceeds of the loans, or income from the property. However, once the property was faced with foreclosure, their interest level rose dramatically. A bankruptcy filing allowed the generals to show the limiteds that they were doing everything possible to protect the latter's interests. It was

5. Sullivan Cent. Plaza, I, Ltd. v. BancBoston Real Estate Capital Corp. (*In re* Sullivan Cent. Plaza, I, Ltd.), 914 F.2d 731, 733 (5th Cir. 1990).

not unusual for the general (with whom the lenders would be negotiating) to indicate to the lender that perhaps a motion for relief from the stay would not be vigorously opposed, although this position was never on the record. In other situations, the general would fight extremely hard to prevent the foreclosure. This was particularly the case when there was a more active limited partner group. It was often discovered that limited partners were already threatening litigation over alleged securities violations or similar claims and the general partner had far more to lose than its ownership interest in the limited partnership or its management fee. This type of litigation, which usually includes claims for securities fraud, mismanagement, and deceptive trade practices, is currently winding its way through the courts.[6]

There were also bankruptcy cases involving something akin to a pyramid scheme. An individual would act as a general partner for a large number of partnerships, either personally or through affiliates, and would also manage the property, either directly or through a wholly owned subsidiary. It was not atypical to find that all income from these partnerships was commingled and used at the discretion of the general partner, even when there was no identity of limited partners. In this situation, the general partner would take from the aggregate funds to oil the "squeaky wheel." That is, the property that was in the greatest need of repairs, or for which a lender refused to agree to a modification, would receive funds in excess of its net operating income (assuming such income even existed). The attempted foreclosure and subsequent filing of bankruptcy for one or more of these limited partnerships usually triggered the collapse of the entire scheme. Once a court or creditor required segregation of funds and began investigating the prepetition use of money, this affected the other limited partnerships and the resulting lack of funds closed the "shell game."

Another basis for single asset filings involved attempts to obtain modifications from a lender, not infrequently with the lender's tacit consent. This might occur when a particular account officer, unable to receive approval for a modification believed to be a good business transaction, indicated to the

---

6. *See, e.g., In re* E.F. Hutton S.W. Properties II, Ltd., 103 B.R. 808, 813-14 (Bankr. N.D. Tex. 1989) (considering whether limited partners committee has standing to pursue claims against general partners for securities fraud, breaches of fiduciary duty, deceptive trade practices, and RICO violations).

borrower that the modification would be subject to a different review process within a bankruptcy. In these cases, the borrower would often rapidly file—and the lender as quickly accept—a plan that replicated the terms of the desired modification. Even without a cooperative account officer, there was often a need to reduce interest rates and to reduce the principal because few of the properties had sufficient cash flow to keep interest current. A portion of the original investment by the limited partners was intended to fund payments to the lender until the property was sold. Unfortunately, a decrease in rental revenues, combined with a deflating real estate market, would erode all available capital and the partnership simply could not service the debt. These single asset bankruptcies focused primarily on interest rate issues.

In other cases, there was equity in the property to be protected by the filing of the bankruptcy and the borrower was unable to service the debt or find a buyer. This situation often occurred early in an economic downturn when the comparative sales upon which value is based does not reflect a current reality of value. Additionally, there were cases in which equity existed behind the first lender. Unless the lender was able to prove a lack of adequate protection (*e.g.*, through extensive deferred maintenance or similar mismanagement of the property), the equity in the property made it difficult to obtain relief from the stay. These bankruptcies often involved plans where there was negative amortization of the loan with a very low initial interest rate or a very low pay rate with the interest accruing over some term of the plan. The attitude of the lender toward such a plan depended on his or her evaluation of the future viability of the real estate market. If the lender and/or the court believed that the market had stabilized, thus protecting the equity from further erosion, the bankruptcy court often confirmed those plans. In a fully recognized downturn, however, it is increasingly difficult to convince a court that the market has bottomed out or that the lender alone should bear the risk of a further decrease in the market simply to protect the limited partners or a junior lienholder.[7]

Many single asset cases were caused by the difficulties of negotiating a transaction with a particular lender, which difficulties were due more to the nature of the lender than the nature of the obligation. As banks, and

---

7. *See In re* French Quarters E., L.P., 148 B.R. 910, 912 (Bankr. W.D. Mo. 1992) (stating that outside creditor should not bear risk to benefit limited partners).

particularly savings and loan associations, failed and the Federal Deposit Insurance Corporation ("FDIC") and the Resolution Trust Corporation ("RTC") became the owner/lender, negotiations often came to a halt.[8] The bankruptcy courts have, for a variety of historical reasons, generally looked at what are perceived as delay tactics by these governmental entities. The debtors who are aware of this attitude often seek bankruptcy as a method of bringing the governmental entity "to the table" and forcing it to focus on the transaction. One of the borrower's goals was the engagement of experienced outside counsel by the RTC or the FDIC. Debtor's counsel would often file a plan very quickly, forcing the RTC/FDIC to take a position. Outside counsel was sometimes even capable of convincing the FDIC/RTC to enter into a consensual plan.

As stated earlier, once the initial capital was eroded, there was frequently a need for an additional cash infusion. However, given the financial condition of the property, it was difficult for the general partners to convince their limiteds to make a further investment in the property without assurances that this would enable the partnership to retain the property or that the additional investment would be recovered. The filing was thus often seen as a way to protect infusions of additional capital. A plan of reorganization would be proposed with "new value" capital, that is, the loan to the debtor would either be given priority status (depending on the value of the property), be paid from sale proceeds after the secured portion of the lender's debt, or provide for increased ownership in the property for the partners that contributed and thereby eliminate the problem of the noncontributing limited partner.[9] Additionally, the plan would provide for the elimination of the interests of noncontributing partners, rather than simply a reduction in their capital accounts.[10]

---

8. *See, e.g., In re* Landing Assoc., Ltd., 157 B.R. 791, 798-99 (Bankr. W.D. Tex. 1993) (describing cessation of negotiations due to bank failure).
9. *See In re* Greystone III Joint Venture, 102 B.R. 560, 572-81 (discussing components and applicability of new value exception to protect infusion of new capital), *aff'd*, 127 B.R. 138 (W.D. Tex. 1990), *rev'd*, 995 F.2d 1274 (5th Cir. 1991), *vacated in part*, 995 F.2d 1284 (5th Cir.), *cert. denied*, 506 U.S. 821 (1992).
10. *Id.*

Last, but far from least, there is the case of the ever-hopeful debtor. Beginning in Houston, and now in the entire country, are examples of some of the factors that have contributed to the single asset real estate cases. The lowering of interest rates allowed a large number of apartment tenants to buy houses. At the same time, there were also increases in unemployment and, in many cities, actual decreases in population. Thus, the tenants who moved into houses were not replaced. The competition for tenants became extremely heated, which usually resulted in the lowering of lease obligations, thus further aggravating the decrease in gross income for the property. This decrease was further exacerbated by the need for repairs and improvements to the apartment projects. For example, many of the projects built in Houston were "flat roofed," that is, constructed with roofs designed for limited lives. These roofs began to need significant repairs. Additionally, the competition for tenants also drove the need for additional improvements and modernization of projects that had been built in the 1970s and early 1980s, which, as a natural course, were beginning to be dated. Many of the owners did not anticipate long-term involvement with projects, and there was often a history of deferred maintenance that grew into a need for capital improvements. Frequently, owners were faced with decreasing net income and high interest rate loans made when the properties were acquired. These loans typically went through one or two modifications, however, without forgiving any debt or reducing the accrual rate on the interest. These developers always believed that the downturn in the economy was the "aberration" and that if they could hold on long enough, the situation would "turn around," allowing them to sell these properties and, at a minimum, break even. These are the most difficult single asset cases. On the one hand, the representatives of the debtors genuinely believe that a plan permitting them to retain the property for three to five years will be the most equitable result–once the downturn in the economy had passed, they will be able to find new financing or sell the property. On the other hand, there is no guarantee that the economy would recover within the period, and the lenders were entitled to protection.

B. Factors Comprising the Prototype Single Asset Real Estate Case

Having described the many different factual situations that have predicated single asset bankruptcy filings, it would now be prudent to outline the factors that are present in most single asset real estate cases. The typical single asset case is important because it is generally discussed throughout this book and it is also the most likely to attract remedial congressional legislation.[11] A few of these factors are present in a typical multiple asset bankruptcy, however most are unique to the single asset real estate case.

1. Nature of the Debtor

The debtor in a single asset real estate case is typically a limited partnership, but occasionally a corporation.[12] The partnership form is chosen for tax purposes and the limited partners invest to limit personal liability and reap the bounty of partnership tax deductions.[13] The partnership is formed for the specific purpose of acquiring the single asset.[14]

---

11. King F. Tower, Note, *"Cramdown" Confirmation of Single-Asset Debtor Reorganization Plans Through Separate Classification of the Deficiency Claim-How* In re U.S. Truck Co. *was Run Off the Road*, 36 WM. & MARY L. REV. 1169, 1173 (1995) (reviewing proposed bankruptcy reform regarding single asset real estate and noting they typically involve partnerships operating hotels or office buildings facing hardship and foreclosure due to declining real estate market).
12. Michael J. Venditto, *The Implied Requirement of "Good Faith" Filing: Where Are the Limits of Bad Faith?*, 1993 DET. C.L. REV. 1591, 1599 (finding typical single-asset debtor is partnership or corporation); Scott W. Carlisle, III, *Single Asset Real Estate in Chapter 11-Need for Reform*, 25 REAL PROP. PROB. & TR. J. 673, 674 (Winter 1991) (finding single-asset real estate typically owned by "individual, partnership or corporation").
13. David G. Carlson, *Artificial Impairment and the Single Asset Chapter 11 Case*, 23 CAP. U. L. REV. 339, 342 (1994) (noting that in single-asset cases, "real estate firm is likely to be a partnership, because of the pass-through nature of partnership taxation"); John D. Ayer, *Symposium on Bankruptcy: Chapter 11 Issues: Bankruptcy as an Essentially Contested Concept: The Case of the One-Asset Case*, 44 S.C. L. REV. 863, 867 (1993) (indicating typical single-asset chapter 11 case has limited partnership with corporation as general partner formed "in large part to reap the bounty of partnership tax deductions.").
14. *See generally* Carlson, *supra* note 13, at 342 (suggesting sole purpose of forming real estate firm is to purchase property); Ayer, *supra* note 13, at 867 (implying creation of partnerships in single asset cases is to participate in real estate transactions).

2. Nature of the Debtor's Assets

As the term indicates, a single asset bankruptcy typically involves just a single asset.[15] While this asset could be anything, a patent for example, it is generally a piece of commercial real estate.[16] The property is usually in the form of a hotel, apartment complex, commercial building, or shopping center.[17] These single asset real estate bankruptcies are the focus of this book.

It is possible that the debtor does hold some items of personal property, but these are generally de minimis.[18] This absence of any substantial personal property eliminates the possibility of liquidating the personal property assets in order to meet current obligations.

3. Secured Creditors

In the typical single asset real estate case there is only one secured creditor.[19] The secured creditor, a financial institution or insurance company, is the lender that made the acquisition or construction of the real estate

---

15. Allen W. Bird, II, et al., *The Bankruptcy Reform Act of 1994*, 17 U. ARK. LITTLE ROCK L.J. 387, 412-13 (1995) (finding single-asset real estate case is "where the debtor's only business is the ownership of non-residential real estate"); *see also* 11 U.S.C. § 101(51B) (1994) (defining single asset real estate).
16. *In re* Kkemko, 181 B.R. 47, 50 (Bankr. S.D. Ohio 1995).
17. *See* Carlisle, *supra* note 12, at 674 (noting "[e]xamples of single asset real estate include office buildings, apartment projects, shopping centers, nursing homes, hotels and warehouses").
18. Hon. Lisa H. Fenning & Brian Tucker, *Profile of Single Asset Real Estate Cases*, in Advanced Bankruptcy Workshop 1995 (PLI COMM. L. & PRAC. COURSE HANDBOOK SERIES NO. A4-4469), *available in* Westlaw, 709 PLI/Comm 537, *3.
19. Hon. Samuel Bufford, *What is Right About Bankruptcy Law and Wrong About its Critics*, 72 WASH. U. L.Q. 829, 835 (1994) (noting typical single asset case "includes a single secured creditor"); *see also* Kathryn R. Heidt, *The Effect of the 1994 Amendments on Commercial Secured Creditors*, 69 AM. BANKR. L.J. 395, 420 (1995) (recognizing one secured creditor to be paid in single asset case).

possible.[20] There is usually no personal liability on the principals for repayment of the loan obligation. In addition to receiving a mortgage on the property the secured creditor often takes an assignment of rents as additional security.[21]

4. Unsecured Creditors

Generally, there are few, if any, unsecured creditors present in a single asset real estate bankruptcy.[22] A handful of trade creditors typify the insignificant amount of unsecured claims that are typically present.[23]

5. Employees

The debtor partnership or corporation in a single asset real estate case usually has either few employees or none at all.[24] This absence of employees stems from the reality that in most single asset real estate cases the debtor does not really have an ongoing business, simply ownership of the single asset

---

20. Paul J. Hunger, *Prohibiting Multiple Classification and Artificial Impairment in Single Asset Chapter 11 Cases: The Creditor's Veto-Its Power Congress Did Not Intend*, 23 CAP. U. L. REV. 541, 552 n.51 (1994) (noting that "lenders and banking institutions . . . are essentially the only entities who lend money to enterprises wishing to start a single asset business").
21. Bonnie K. Donahue & W. David Edwards, *The Heartbreak Hotel Revisited: Hotel Bankruptcy and Suggested Solutions to the Confusion over the Hotel Income/Receipts Issue*, 111 BANKING L.J. 25, 25 (1994).
22. Little Creek Dev. Corp. v. Commonwealth Mortgage Corp. (*In re* Little Creek Dev. Co.), 779 F.2d 1068, 1073 (5th Cir. 1986) (recognizing typical single asset case has "only a few, if any, unsecured creditors"); Janet A. Flaccus, *Have Eight Circuits Shorted? Good Faith and Chapter 11 Bankruptcy Petitions*, 67 AM. BANKR. L.J. 401, 406 (1993) (same).
23. Gregory K. Jones, *The Classification and Cram Down Controversy in Single Asset Bankruptcy Cases: A Need for the Repeal of Bankruptcy Code Section 1129(a)(10)*, 42 UCLA L. REV. 623, 625 (1994) (recognizing trade creditors can be unsecured creditors of single asset debtors).
24. Brian S. Katz, *Single-Asset Real Estate Cases and the Good Faith Requirement: Why Reluctance to Ask Whether a Case Belongs in Bankruptcy May Lead to the Incorrect Result*, 9 BANKR. DEV. J. 77, 78, 85 (1992).

itself.[25] In many cases the debtor has hired a supplier of management services to run the property.

6. Absence of Cash Flow

Third party use of the premises generates the only income from the single asset property.[26] The bankruptcy filing is typically preceded by a deterioration of this incoming cash flow.[27] The rents or hotel fees have dried-up, usually because of a downturn in the local real estate market.[28] Whatever cash flow remains is insufficient to service the secured debt.[29] However, in some cases it is sufficient to cover the property's operating expenses, allowing the debtor to remain current on these obligations.[30] The debtor is now unable to meet its mortgage payments and its goes into default.

7. Impending Foreclosure

While there may be many underlying causes for a single asset real estate bankruptcy, the immediate cause is almost always imminent foreclosure.[31] The

---

25. *See* Katz, *supra* note 24, at 85 (recognizing typical debtor in single asset cases unable to "provide superior managements ability").
26. Carlson, *supra* note 13, at 343-44 (implying all income for single asset real estate derived from rents).
27. Carlson, *supra* note 13, at 344 (noting that foreclosure proceedings begin usually when cash flow declines to point where debtor cannot meet debt obligations); Katz, *supra* note 24, at 78-85 (finding single asset owners have no cash flow).
28. *See* Thomas J. Meaney, Note, *Bankruptcy-Living in Limbo: Single Asset Reorganizations Within the Financially Distressed Fifth Circuit. In re* Greystone III Joint Venture, 948 F.2d 134 (5th Cir. 1991), 23 ST. MARY'S L.J. 1205, 1226 (1992) (recognizing problems encountered by single asset debtors with onset of depression after booming real estate market in 1980s).
29. Carlson, *supra* note 13, at 344 (declining cash flow prevents debtor from meeting obligations resulting in foreclosure proceedings by secured debtors).
30. Jones, *supra* note 23, at 625-26 (recognizing that money generated by debtor from rents is used to pay short-term debts only thereby causing secured creditor to begin foreclosure proceedings which lead to single asset filing).
31. Katz, *supra* note 24, at 78 (recognizing default and foreclosure proceedings as strong factors in single asset debtors filing for chapter 11); Venditto, *supra*

debtor has defaulted on the secured obligation and the lender is about to complete the foreclosure process. The debtor files the chapter 11 bankruptcy petition on the eve of this foreclosure and the automatic stay halts the foreclosure process before completion.

Conclusion

The causes of single asset filings are myriad. While the volume has decreased in most regions of the country, this type of case will always be a part of the practice. The faster track mandated by Congress in the 1994 Amendments to the Bankruptcy Code will serve to increase the creativity of counsel and speed the time to appeal. For these reasons, the factual circumstances that have spawned these cases in the past and the components of the atypical single asset case will retain future significance.

---

note 12, at 1599 (reviewing factors leading up to foreclosure proceedings and ultimately filing petition to stay proceedings).

CHAPTER II

GOOD FAITH: A ROUNDTABLE DISCUSSION

[Editor's Note: The following Roundtable Discussion on good faith issues in bankruptcy was held in December of 1992. Four distinguished bankruptcy judges, Honorable Lisa Hill Fenning, Honorable William Greendyke, Honorable William Hillman, and Honorable Robert Mark, participated in the Discussion. It was moderated by Professor Karen Gross of the New York Law School, a former member of the Board of Directors of the American Bankruptcy Institute and a current member of the Advisory Board for this Law Review. Although the Bankruptcy Reform Act of 1994[*] contained significant provisions affecting single asset cases and the discussion of good faith, most of the issues discussed herein remain unresolved and of great interest to the bankruptcy community. Moreover, we believed that if we tried to recreate the Roundtable Discussion by reuniting all the participants, we might be left with a discussion that was a shadow of its former self. Therefore, each participant was asked to comment on the Roundtable as it originally was published in the Spring 1993 issue of the ABI Law Review. These comments, updated case citations, and editorial notes have been added to this version of the Roundtable in bold typeface. We hope these additions clearly provide the reader with information on changes in the law while retaining the flavor of what has certainly been ABI Law Review's most successful Roundtable. The editors would again like to express their appreciation to the judges who participated in the Discussion and Professor Gross for their generous donation of time and effort to this project.]

---

* **Pub. L. No. 103-394, 108 Stat. 4106, (the "1994 Amendments"). Specifically, a definition of single asset cases now appears in 11 U.S.C. § 101(51B) (1994). Section 362 also was amended to provide that the stay terminates within 90 days unless certain preconditions are met. 11 U.S.C. § 362(d)(3) (1994).**

PROFESSOR GROSS: Let me begin this Roundtable Discussion by introducing our distinguished participants: The Honorable Lisa Hill Fenning from the Central District of California; the Honorable Robert Mark from the Southern District of Florida; the Honorable William Hillman from the District of Massachusetts and the Honorable William Greendyke from the Southern District of Texas. I want to begin this Discussion by first providing a brief contextual overview.

Issues of good faith are arising with increasing frequency in cases under the Bankruptcy Code.[1] Although the Code contains explicit references to good faith, for example, sections 303, 542, 921, 1129 and 1325, among others,[2] courts have increasingly scrutinized cases to determine if there is an implied standard of good faith in cases which have been filed.[3] Indeed, even the

---

1. **For a good overview of the good faith requirement, see Michael J. Venditto, *The Implied Requirement of "Good Faith" Filing: Where are the Limits of Bad Faith?*, 1993 DET. C.L. REV. 1591.**

2. *See generally* 11 U.S.C. §§ 303(i)(2), 542(c), 542(d), 921(c), 1129(a)(3), 1325(a)(3) (1994); *see also* 11 U.S.C. §§ 109(c)(5)(B), 363(m), 364(e), 548(c), 549(c), 550(b)(1), 550(b)(2), 550(e)(1), 727(a)(9)(B)(ii), 1113(b)(2), 1114(f)(2), 1125(e), 1126(e), 1144(1), 1225(a)(3) (1994).

3. Chapter 7: *See generally* Industrial Ins. Servs., Inc. v. Zick (*In re* Zick), 931 F.2d 1124 (6th Cir. 1991); *In re* Krohn, 886 F.2d 123 (6th Cir. 1989); ***In re* Marks, 174 B.R. 37 (E.D. Pa. 1994); *In re* Houck, 180 B.R. 186 (Bankr. S.D. Ohio 1995); *In re* Khan, 172 B.R. 613 (Bankr. D. Minn. 1994); *In re* Cappuccetti, 172 B.R. 37 (Bankr. E.D. Ark. 1994)**; *In re* Khan, 35 B.R. 718 (Bankr. W.D. Ky. 1984); John A. Majors, In Re Zick: *Chapter 7's Good Faith Threshold Standard*, 23 U. TOL. L. REV. 583 (1992).

   Chapter 9: *See In re* Sullivan County Regional Refuse Disposal Dist., 165 B.R. 60 (Bankr. D.N.H. 1994).

   Chapter 11: ***See generally* Marsch v. Marsch (*In re* Marsch), 36 F.3d 825 (9th Cir. 1994)**; Michigan Nat'l Bank v. Charfoos (*In re* Charfoos), 979 F.2d 390 (6th Cir. 1992); Little Creek Dev. Co. v. Commonwealth Mortgage Corp. (*In re* Little Creek Dev. Co.), 779 F.2d 1068 (5th Cir. 1986); ***In re* Lizeric Realty Corp., 188 B.R. 499 (Bankr. S.D.N.Y. 1995); *In re* Springs Plaza Assocs., L.P., 188 B.R. 48 (Bankr. M.D. Fla. 1995);** *In re* Aurora Invs., Inc., 134 B.R. 982 (Bankr. M.D. Fla. 1991); *In re* Victory Constr. Co., 9 B.R. 549 (Bankr. C.D. Cal. 1981), *vacated as moot*, 37 B.R. 222 (Bankr. 9th Cir. 1984); *see also* cases cited *infra* notes 8-9.

   Chapter 12: *See generally* ***In re* Fortney, 36 F.3d 701 (7th Cir. 1994)**; Schuldies v. United States (*In re* Schuldies), 122 B.R. 100 (D.S.D. 1990); ***In***

Supreme Court has entered into this debate in *Johnson v. Home State Bank*,[4] where sequential filings were deemed to be not, per se, bad faith.[5]

Implied good faith has been raised in a wide variety of contexts, and let me give several examples. One example would be a chapter 11 case where one seeks to obtain relief from tort claims[6] or environmental claims.[7] Another example might be a chapter 13 case which is filed in order to get a discharge of debts which would be nondischargeable in a chapter 7 case,[8] or even a

---

***re* Roth, 167 B.R. 911 (Bankr. D.S.D. 1994);** *In re* Bird, 80 B.R. 861 (Bankr. W.D. Mich. 1987).

Chapter 13: *See generally In re* Love, 957 F.2d 1350 (7th Cir. 1992); ***In re* Jones, 174 B.R. 8 (Bankr. D.N.H. 1994); *In re* Paulson, 170 B.R. 496 (Bankr. D. Conn. 1994); Cardillo v. Andover Bank (*In re* Cardillo), 169 B.R. 8 (Bankr. D.N.H. 1994)**; *In re* Earl, 140 B.R. 728 (Bankr. N.D. Ind. 1992); *In re* Powers, 135 B.R. 980 (Bankr. C.D. Cal. 1991); *In re* King, 126 B.R. 777 (Bankr. N.D. Ill. 1991); *In re* Roberts, 117 B.R. 677 (Bankr. N.D. Okla. 1990); *In re* Gaudet, 95 B.R. 4 (Bankr. D.R.I. 1989).

For an excellent overview of the implied good faith filing requirement, see Lawrence Ponoroff & F. Stephen Knippenberg, *The Implied Good Faith Filing Requirement: Sentinel of an Evolving Bankruptcy Policy*, 85 NW. U. L. REV. 919 (1991). *See also* Brian S. Katz, *Single Asset Real Estate Cases and the Good Faith Requirement: Why Reluctance to Ask Whether a Case Belongs in Bankruptcy May Lead to the Incorrect Result*, 9 BANKR. DEV. J. 77 (1992).

4. 501 U.S. 78 (1991). In *Johnson*, the debtor had defaulted on mortgage notes and filed a petition for liquidation under chapter 7 while foreclosure proceedings were pending. *Id.* at 80. After the state court entered an *in rem* judgment for the bank, but before a scheduled foreclosure sale, the mortgagor filed for reorganization under chapter 13. *Id.*

5. *Id.* at 88. The Supreme Court declined to address the good faith issue (remanding it for determination), indicating that such a sequential filing is not, per se, bad faith. *Id.*

6. ***See In re* EPB, Inc., 172 B.R. 241 (Bankr. N.D. Ohio 1994) (dealing with tort judgment claim against chapter 11 debtor);** *In re* Whipple, 138 B.R. 137 (Bankr. S.D. Ga. 1991) (filing chapter 13 to avoid tort claim); *In re* Johns-Manville Corp., 36 B.R. 727 (Bankr. S.D.N.Y. 1984) (commencing chapter 11 filing to seek respite from class action (asbestos) tort claims).

7. *See* United States v. Environmental Waste Control, Inc., 131 B.R. 410 (N.D. Ind. 1991), *aff'd sub nom.* Supporters to Oppose Pollution, Inc. v. Heritage Group, 973 F.2d 1320 (7th Cir. 1992).

8. *See* Washington Student Loan Guar. Assoc. v. Porter (*In re* Porter), 102 B.R.

chapter 7 case which is filed to obtain relief from a state court judgment which was granted as a result of a debtor's deliberate breach of an employment contract.[9] Most recently,[10] with the growing number of single asset chapter 11 cases, courts are increasingly confronting whether these types of cases should be dismissed because they do not represent a good faith filing.[11]

---

773 (Bankr. 9th Cir. 1989), *aff'd*, No. 89-35701, 1990 U.S. App. LEXIS 20578 (9th Cir. Nov. 26, 1990); Handeen v. LeMaire (*In re* LeMaire), 883 F.2d 1373 (8th Cir.), *vacated*, 891 F.2d 650 (8th Cir. 1989), *and rev'd*, 898 F.2d 1346 (8th Cir. 1990); *In re* Stewart, 109 B.R. 998 (D. Kan. 1990); *In re* Rogers, 140 B.R. 254 (Bankr. W.D. Mo. 1992); *In re* Bush, 120 B.R. 403 (Bankr. E.D. Tex. 1990); *In re* Kosenka, 104 B.R. 40 (Bankr. N.D. Ind. 1989); *In re* Adamu, 82 B.R. 128 (Bankr. D. Or. 1988).

9. *See* Industrial Ins. Servs. v. Zick (*In re* Zick), 931 F.2d 1124 (6th Cir. 1991); Bybee v. Geer (*In re* Geer), 137 B.R. 37 (Bankr. W.D. Mo. 1991).

10. **Surprisingly, the 1994 Amendments did not quash the debate regarding good faith in the context of single asset cases. *See In re* Midway Invs., Ltd., 187 B.R. 382 (Bankr. S.D. Fla. 1995); *In re* Victoria Ltd. Partnership, 187 B.R. 54 (Bankr. D. Mass. 1995). *See generally* Janet A. Flaccus, *A Potpourri of Bankruptcy Changes: 1994 Bankruptcy Amendments*, 47 ARK. L. REV. 817, 836 (1994) (acknowledging good faith standard precludes success of many single asset cases); Karen Gross & Patricia Redmond, *In Defense of Debtor Exclusivity: Assessing Four of the 1994 Amendments to the Bankruptcy Code*, 69 AM. BANKR. L.J. 287, 302 (1995) (noting 1994 amendments allow single asset debtors chapter 11 relief).**

11. ***See* Trident Assocs. Ltd. Partnership v. Metropolitan Life Ins. Co. (*In re* Trident Assocs. Ltd. Partnership), 52 F.3d 127 (6th Cir.), *cert. denied*, 116 S. Ct. 188 (1995)**; Humble Place Joint Venture v. Fory (*In re* Humble Place Joint Venture), 936 F.2d 814 (5th Cir. 1991); **9281 Shore Rd. Owners Corp. v. Seminole Realty Co. (*In re* 9281 Shore Rd. Owners Corp.), 187 B.R. 837 (E.D.N.Y. 1995); *In re* SB Properties, Inc., 185 B.R. 198 (E.D. Pa. 1995); Manhattan King David Restaurant Inc. v. Levine, 163 B.R. 36 (S.D.N.Y. 1993)**; Pleasant Pointe Apartments, Ltd. v. Kentucky Hous. Corp., 139 B.R. 828 (W.D. Ky. 1992); *In re* Denver Inv. Co., 141 B.R. 228 (Bankr. N.D. Fla. 1992); *In re* Aurora Invs., Inc., 134 B.R. 982 (Bankr. M.D. Fla. 1991); *In re* Nesenkeag, Inc. 131 B.R. 246 (Bankr. D.N.H. 1991); *In re* Reiser Ford, Inc., 128 B.R. 234 (Bankr. E.D. Mo. 1991); *In re* 1020 Warburton Ave. Realty Corp., 127 B.R. 333 (Bankr. S.D.N.Y. 1991); *In re* I-95 Technology-Indus. Park, L.P., 126 B.R. 11 (Bankr. D.R.I. 1991); *In re* Campus Hous.

When the good faith issue is raised in single asset cases, most frequently by creditors, although sometimes by the courts sua sponte, there is little consensus among circuits or even districts as to what constitutes good faith and how it should be applied.[12]

Developers, Inc., 124 B.R. 867 (Bankr. N.D. Fla. 1991).

12. ***Compare Trident*, 52 F.3d at 130 (stating debtor bad faith is "cause" within meaning of 11 U.S.C. § 1112(b), warranting dismissal of petition) *with* Heartland Fed. Sav. & Loan Ass'n v. Briscoe Enters., Ltd., II (*In re* Briscoe Enters., Ltd., II), 994 F.2d 1160, 1167 (5th Cir.) (holding good faith requirement under § 1129(a)(3) satisfied where plan proposed with legitimate and honest purpose to reorganize and with reasonable hope of success), *cert. denied*, 114 S. Ct. 550 (1993). *Compare Shore Rd. Owners*, 187 B.R. at 848 (listing specific factors for consideration in bad faith filing determination) *with SB Properties*, 185 B.R. at 205 n.5 (focusing on statutory language and legislative history of § 1112(b) and persuasive authority from other circuits in recognizing good faith filing requirement in chapter 11 cases, while noting that the "laundry list" of bad faith factors may be too rigid and inflexible). *See generally* Janet A. Flaccus, *Have Eight Circuits Shorted? Good Faith and Chapter 11 Bankruptcy Petitions*, 67 AM. BANKR. L.J. 401 (1993), for a discussion on treatment of the good faith filing issue.** *See also Pleasant Pointe*, 139 B.R. at 828 (filing of chapter 11 petition found to be in bad faith for single asset debtor facing state foreclosure action). In *Pleasant Pointe* the court cited indicia of bad faith enumerated in Little Creek Dev. Co. v. Commonwealth Mortgage Co. (*In re* Little Creek Dev. Co.), 779 F.2d 1068, 1072-73 (5th Cir. 1986), and Carolin Corp. v. Miller, 886 F.2d 693 (4th Cir. 1989). *Pleasant Pointe*, 139 B.R. at 832. The court determined that the debtor filed the petition to hold the single asset hostage rather than to reorganize the asset. *Id.*; *see also In re* Landings Assocs. Ltd. Partnership, 145 B.R. 101 (Bankr. M.D. Fla. 1992). In holding that a single asset debtor filed chapter 11 petition in bad faith, the *Landings* court stated:

> A mechanical application of the factors set forth in *Little Creek* . . . indicates that this case has most of the hallmarks of bad faith . . . . However, it is equally recognized that not one single factor set forth in *Little Creek*, . . . is determinative of the issue of the lack of good faith of a debtor seeking relief under [c]hapter 11 of the Bankruptcy Code. While *Little Creek* is still well recognized as persuasive authority, it is equally true that there is nothing inherently improper for a debtor with one single asset, generally an income-producing commercial property, to attempt to reorganize its affairs under

This Roundtable Discussion is intended to elaborate on these issues and more particularly, to probe the meaning of good faith in single asset chapter 11 cases.[13] To get the discussion underway, let me pose my first question.

> the rehabilitative provisions of the Bankruptcy Code. . . . In the last analysis, the key considerations are (1) the Debtor's motivation to file the Petition; (2) the economic vitality of the Debtor; (3) the Debtor's real need to reorganize and (4) the ability of the Debtor to achieve reorganization.

Id. at 103 (citations omitted).

In *In re* Franklin Mortgage & Inv. Co., 143 B.R. 295 (Bankr. D.D.C. 1992), a separate analysis was maintained for ordinary, single asset debtors and those who fit within the "new debtor syndrome." *Id.* at 302. The court noted that the "case has all the earmarkings of the `new debtor syndrome.'" *Id.* at 300. In framing its analysis the court stated:

> Where a "new debtor syndrome" and resultant unfair delay of creditors is present, it makes no sense to require objective futility. The court must be able to protect its jurisdictional integrity. In contrast, other single asset cases not involving the "new debtor syndrome" usually present the question whether the case is futile and hence filed in bad faith. It makes sense to require objective futility before dismissing those cases. That is not what is at stake in a "new debtor" case. In the "new debtor" case the critical inquiry is whether the debtor has gained unfair advantage by employment of the new debtor device.

Id. at 302.

One could argue that the inclusion of provisions dealing explicitly with single asset cases in the 1994 Amendments is evidence of the fact that such cases cannot be *per se* in bad faith, otherwise such cases should have been explicitly prohibited. *See Victoria Ltd. Partnership*, 187 B.R. at 62 (stating that Congress clearly intended chapter 11 recourse for debtors violating good faith filing doctrine). One also can argue that the 1994 Amendments regarding single asset cases benefit creditors and hence *add* to, not take away from, the creditor arsenal. Moreover, whatever the 1994 Amendments do mean for single asset cases, the interpretation is arguably limited to only those cases that fit the new definition contained in 11 U.S.C. § 101(51B) (1994) (defining "single asset real estate"). As such, there is no change regarding the good faith analysis for debtors with secured debts exceeding $4 million. *See Midway*, 187 B.R. at 388 n.8.

13. *See supra* note 12.

A. Good Faith Challenges in Single Asset Cases

Are all of you seeing a large number of single asset cases in your Districts,[14] and are these cases being challenged either by you or by creditors on the basis of good faith?

JUDGE MARK: I would guess that in the Southern District of Florida we may have the highest percentage among the panelists here of chapter 11's that are, in fact, single asset real estate cases. It varies and it may be slowing down a bit, but we certainly see many single asset real estate cases and I would even say it's a substantial percentage of the chapter 11's in total.

PROF. GROSS: How many of those cases are challenged on the basis of good faith?

JUDGE MARK: Virtually all of them sooner or later, unless there is some consensual arrangement that's been negotiated at the start of the case. I am overgeneralizing, of course, but typically the cases are filed right before summary judgment hearing or often right before the foreclosure sale. The creditor/borrower is sophisticated enough, given the state of law in the Eleventh Circuit[15] to come in quickly with a motion for stay relief under

---

14. **One legitimate concern is whether the 1994 Amendments affecting single asset cases are being implemented. Early data show that the amendments are being utilized, suggesting their possible impact on cases. *See* Gross & Redmond, *supra* note 10, at 304-07 (reporting results of empirical study among 71 judges gauging effect of 1994 Amendments after 8 months in effect).**
15. **At the time of this Discussion, courts of the Eleventh Circuit were already hearing motions based on the bad faith of single asset debtors. *See* Phoenix Piccadilly, Ltd. v. Life Ins. Co. (*In re* Phoenix Piccadilly, Ltd.), 849 F.2d 1393 (11th Cir. 1988). The Eleventh Circuit decision in *Phoenix Piccadilly* was followed within the circuit, *see, e.g.*, *Aurora*, 134 B.R. at 990, and in other circuits, *see, e.g.*, *Pleasant Pointe*, 139 B.R. at 832. The law regarding the good faith filing requirement in single asset real estate cases continued to develop after the 1994 Amendments. *See In re* Springs Plaza Assocs., L.P., 188 B.R. 48 (Bankr. M.D. Fla. 1995); *Midway*, 187 B.R. at 382; *In re* Immenhausen Corp., 172 B.R. 343 (Bankr. M.D. Fla. 1994).**

section 362(d)(1) for cause, or for dismissal, arguing bad faith.[16] So we are confronted with these motions early on in many cases.

JUDGE GREENDYKE: Judge Mark, what kind of numbers are we talking about in terms of total number of chapter 11's and what percentage of that might be single asset real estate cases? I really don't have an idea what kind of numbers you are talking about.

JUDGE MARK: I probably have maybe 150 pending chapter 11's. My numbers may be way off. I didn't really do a statistical check. And it may very well be that half of them are single asset real estate cases.

JUDGE GREENDYKE: That's a lot.

JUDGE MARK: South Florida has been over-built with shopping centers, office buildings, and less commonly, residential properties. We have visiting judges coming down to Palm Beach and they could virtually take a chapter 11 golf tour when they are not sitting because we also have a lot of country club developments that are in chapter 11.

JUDGE GREENDYKE: When I started out in 1987 I had given to me 540, 550 chapter 11 cases, and I would say hundreds of them were single asset cases that took years to get rid of. Now I have 125 cases and probably 25 of those are two large conglomerate-type debtors that are not real estate related at all.

---

16. **There is now a special relief stay provision for single asset cases. 11 U.S.C. § 362(d)(3) (1994). This new provision is intended to speed up the progress of these cases or to permit creditors to recover their property or be paid. *See* Allen W. Bird II et al., *The Bankruptcy Reform Act of 1994*, 17 U. ARK. LITTLE ROCK L.J. 387, 414 (1995) (stating "concept that single asset real estate debtor cases should move along more quickly than other types of cases has finally found its way into the Bankruptcy Code in [s]ection 218 of the Act"); *see also* 69TH ANNUAL MEETING OF THE NATIONAL CONFERENCE OF BANKRUPTCY JUDGES 4-8 (1995) (stating § 362(d)(3) intended to protect creditors from lengthy delay in enforcing rights in single asset cases).**

The single asset real estate cases are virtually a thing of the past in Houston. Coincidentally, I was in a hearing for three hours this afternoon with one, but it's been since the springtime since I've had a confirmation hearing in a single asset chapter 11.

We in Houston raise good faith issues sua sponte. Of course, creditors always had good faith on their minds because it was their first punch besides a motion to lift.

JUDGE FENNING: In the seven years I have been on the bench in the Central District, the percentage of single asset filings on my calendar has fluctuated with the real estate economy. And for awhile I had a lot of Texas single asset real estate cases, but those are history.

At the moment, probably about half of my chapter 11 cases are single asset real estate cases.[17] About a quarter of those are "house" cases, that is, where the only purpose for filing a consumer chapter 11 is to try and stave off foreclosure on the house. In the Los Angeles housing market, a lot of fairly ordinary houses are sufficiently costly to put people over the debt limits for chapter 13.[18] Most of our chapter 11 "house" cases are pro se filings.

The single asset cases at this point include apartment buildings, shopping centers and vacant land. Most have been filed by limited partnerships, although recently, more single asset debtors are corporations. In addition to the single asset cases, I have some very large individual chapter 11 cases filed by entrepreneurs in the real estate development or management business who own twenty or thirty or forty apartment buildings within their individual

---

17. ***See* Lisa Hill Fenning & Brian Tucker, *Profile of Single Asset Real Estate Cases*, 1994 AM. BANKR. INST. ANN. SPRING MEETING 1 (Apr. 1994), *available in* WESTLAW 709 PLI/COMM, *reprinted in*, 1 COMM. L. & BANKR. SECTION NEWSL. (Los Angeles County Bar Assoc.), Summer 1994, at 4. Following the Roundtable Discussion, the single asset real estate percentage declined to approximately 33% to 40% of Judge Fenning's chapter 11 cases. *See* Hon. Lisa Hill Fenning & Craig Hart, *Measuring Chapter 11: The Real World of 500 Cases*, 4 AM. BANKR. INST. L. REV. 119 (1996).**

18. *See* 11 U.S.C. § 109(e) (1988) (providing that only individual owing unsecured debts of less than $100,000 and secured debts of less than $350,000 may file under chapter 13). **These limits have been raised to $250,000 and $750,000 respectively. 11 U.S.C. § 109(e) (1994).**

estates. Those chapter 11 cases technically don't qualify as "single asset" cases. The overwhelming bulk of my current pending case load of about 620 chapter 11 cases consists of real estate based cases of one sort or another.

JUDGE HILLMAN: The District of Massachusetts is famous for chapter 11's. The four of us each have more 11's than any other judges in any other district in the country. I think I have 500 right now. Of those, about one-quarter of them are single asset real estate. Of those, very few are residential. Most of them are what we call triple-deckers, small real estate folk who went out and bought themselves — they listened to the lecturers on television at night and they went out and bought themselves one asset and maybe they leveraged it and they are down to one.

PROF. GROSS: How do you get to the name "triple-decker"?

JUDGE HILLMAN: In the working class neighborhoods of the Northeast, three-story houses inhabited by three families were built, my guess is 1900 give or take 20 years, and they are called triple-deckers, and they are investment properties in the older residential areas. You live in one and you rent two, that is, if you can get tenants.

JUDGE FENNING: You also asked whether single asset cases are being dismissed for bad faith. In our district, I don't think any of the judges are raising the issues sua sponte. Bad faith is sometimes an argument that is added onto a relief from stay motion. Almost always we are seeing these cases for the first time on a relief from stay that's filed within the first 60 days or on a cash collateral motion that's filed by one or the other parties.

At the moment, the real estate market is about what it is in Massachusetts. It's entirely dead, but we are still having some evidentiary hearings because the appraisals are drastically in conflict. The outcome of the relief from stay motion usually depends upon valuation, rather than "bad faith."

PROF. GROSS: Is that true for you also, Judge Mark, that good faith is not raised sua sponte?

JUDGE MARK: There is no need for it. You would virtually be committing malpractice as a creditor attorney in the Eleventh Circuit[19] if you did not raise the bad faith issue early on in a chapter 11, if it met the criteria that have led to dismissals in the Eleventh Circuit.

PROF. GROSS: We'll get to the standards in a minute but first, do judges raise good faith concerns sua sponte in Massachusetts?

JUDGE HILLMAN: It's been known to happen from time to time. We very seldom see a motion to dismiss in the first few days. I think that's because the case has been in foreclosure and it's in the hands of a real estate lawyer, not a bankruptcy lawyer. But within two weeks they have bankruptcy counsel and a section 362(d)(1), (d)(2) motion comes tearing in.[20] Whether they say it or not, they are arguing for dismissal on bad faith grounds.

B. What is a Single Asset Case?

PROF. GROSS: I just want to make sure that when we talk about single asset cases that we are all talking about the same thing. For me, there is a definitional question here as to what is a single asset chapter 11 case. The proposed legislation that was part of the Senate bill had a definition of single asset chapter 11 cases.[21] Let me just read you that section and see if you all agree with that definition. Single asset real estate cases involve "real property, other than residential real property with fewer than four residential units, which generates substantially all of the gross income of a debtor and on which no business is being conducted by a debtor other than the business of operating the real property and activities incidental thereto."[22]

---

19. *See supra* note 15 and accompanying text (discussing state of law in Eleventh Circuit).
20. 11 U.S.C. § 362(d)(1),(2) (1994) (providing relief from automatic stay "for cause, including the lack of adequate protection" and where debtor has no equity in property and such property is not necessary to effective reorganization).
21. S. 1985, 102d Cong., 2d Sess. § 211(a)(2) (1992).
22. ***See* 11 U.S.C. § 101(51B) (1994). The new definition of "single asset real estate" specifically provides that there must be a single property or project which provides substantially all of the debtor's gross income. The**

JUDGE FENNING: I think we are talking about a slightly bigger universe. The triple-deckers wouldn't come within the statutory definition. Vacant land wouldn't come within the statutory definition, but I consider those single asset real estate filings because the same issues are present; that is, is there anything to reorganize and what is the value.

PROF. GROSS: Are we all agreeing though that single asset chapter 11 cases involve real estate?[23]

JUDGE FENNING: Yes.

JUDGE HILLMAN: Yes.

JUDGE MARK: But interestingly, the bad faith cases, a lot of the early ones, involved vacant land and it's been an expansion of the concept or

---

debtor's aggregate noncontingent liquidated secured debts must be $4 million or less. Importantly, residential property with fewer than four units is expressly excluded from the scope of the provision. Additionally, the provision specifically notes that the debtor can only operate a real estate business on the property. *Id.* This definition is problematic on a variety of fronts and has already generated litigation. For example, how is the $4 million secured debt calculated? Who makes the valuation and when? Is vacant land (with plans for development) within the scope of the definition if no money has been generated as yet? *See* Kathryn R. Heidt, *The Effect of the 1994 Amendments on Commercial Secured Creditors,* 69 AM. BANKR. L.J. 395, 416-18 (1995); *see also In re* Kkemko, 181 B.R. 47, 49-51 (Bankr. S.D. Ohio 1995) (holding marina not single asset real estate because its business not limited to real estate rental); *In re* Philmont Dev. Co., 181 B.R. 220, 223 (Bankr. E.D. Pa. 1995) (stating that drafters intended to keep common usage of "single asset real estate" to include only entities that "cling to ownership of real property in a depressed market").

23. **The 1994 Amendments make it abundantly clear that the only single asset cases that are "fast-tracked" involve real estate. 11 U.S.C. § 362(d)(3) (1994) (providing for relief from automatic stay in single asset real estate cases unless, within 90 days, the debtor files a plan or begins making monthly payments to creditors with security interest in real estate). It would seem like an unusual negative inference to assume that any other single asset case would *not* be "fast-tracked."**

expansion of the doctrine that's been applied more and more now to income-producing properties. So it is a broader universe than the definition you just read.

JUDGE FENNING: I suspect part of that expansion occurred because a lot more properties started coming into bankruptcy with a negative cash flow. That is, they were income-producing, but with a negative cash flow that raised the question of whether the debtor could possibly confirm a plan.

JUDGE HILLMAN: Then I suppose when you get to vacant land you have to consider as a single asset the acreage that has been platted, broken out into lots and is still undeveloped.

JUDGE FENNING: We get a lot that have tentative tract maps out that are pending final plan.

JUDGE HILLMAN: It's still a single asset case. It's one mortgage on one piece of real estate.

PROF. GROSS: Let me try a hypothetical. What is your view of a corporation that was set up to hold a patent or a contract right. Is that a single asset chapter 11 debtor for purposes of our discussion?

JUDGE MARK: Good topic for law school, but we don't see it much.

PROF. GROSS: Okay, fair enough.

JUDGE GREENDYKE: I think from a practical standpoint, we are all talking about real estate cases whether it's undeveloped real estate or somebody that's got one apartment complex or one shopping center. It can be a patent. My most humorous example of a single asset case arose at a show cause hearing in 1987 where I found out somebody had a model railroad and I inquired about what the scope of the railroad was. He said, "Well, it's about 20 feet by 15 feet," and that was a single asset. It can be anything you want. But by and large we are talking about real estate.

C. Is Imposition of a Good Faith Requirement Appropriate?

PROF. GROSS: Since you have all taken after academics, let me refer to a commentator, who is not an academic, but who has certainly written academic material. He stated the following about good faith: "The imposition of the good faith requirement appears contrary to the statute, illogical, and unworkable in its application."[24] Do you have any views as to the merits of that observation?

JUDGE HILLMAN: That's Marty Bienenstock[25] and he had me two-thirds convinced before I came on the bench, and I thought about it a great deal. Then when I came on, I came into a district where we have a case called *In Re The Bible Speaks*.[26]

PROF. GROSS: An unforgettable name.[27]

JUDGE HILLMAN: The holy writ from Judge Queenan in *In re The Bible Speaks* is that there is a good faith test and there was a good faith test under Roman XI and there is a good faith test under Arabic 11.[28] So the cases in my district are uniform, and there is good faith, Marty to the contrary, notwithstanding.

JUDGE FENNING: I think there is implicit good faith, but we are talking about chapter 11's here. You cannot confirm a chapter 11 plan without a determination that it's being proposed in good faith.[29]

---

24. MARTIN J. BIENENSTOCK, BANKRUPTCY REORGANIZATION 28 (Practicing Law Institute 1987).
25. Martin J. Bienenstock is a partner at the firm of Weil, Gotshal & Manges in New York.
26. 65 B.R. 415 (Bankr. D. Mass. 1986) (denying motion to dismiss chapter 11 case on "bad faith" grounds but noting good faith statutory requirement).
27. **The judge deciding *Bible Speaks* also decided *In re* Victoria Limited Partnership, 187 B.R. 54 (Bankr. D. Mass. 1995) (Queenan, J.) (deciding that good faith doctrine would not apply because it conflicted with Bankruptcy Code, legislative history, and Supreme Court precedent).**
28. *Bible Speaks*, 65 B.R. at 415.
29. **11 U.S.C. § 1129(a)(3) (1994).**

JUDGE HILLMAN: That's back end.

JUDGE FENNING: That's back end, but if there is no way they can clear that hurdle at the end of the case and it's obvious at the beginning of the case, you can address the good faith issue at the beginning.

JUDGE GREENDYKE: That is Leif Clark's *Anderson Oaks* case[30] — if one can find out in a 362 hearing[31] or a hearing on a motion to dismiss[32] that it is impossible to confirm a plan, just stop the case right there.[33]

JUDGE FENNING: In the interest of full disclosure, we should tell you Judge Clark just walked into the room a few minutes ago.

JUDGE GREENDYKE: I figured he'd be here.

PROF. GROSS: I think what Martin Bienenstock is talking about is an implied good faith standard.[34] I think what Judge Fenning is raising is the issue of why we need to focus on this when an explicit good faith standard shows up in section 1129(a)(3)? Can one infer from that you don't think you need —

JUDGE FENNING: I think this is an "angels on the head of a pin" question. You have to pass a good faith hurdle in order to do anything in a chapter 11. So that can be tested at the beginning of the case as well as at the

---

30. *In re* Anderson Oaks (Phase I) Ltd. Partnership, 77 B.R. 108 (Bankr. W.D. Tex. 1987) (granting relief from stay due to debtor's failure to show that effective reorganization was possible).
31. **11 U.S.C. § 362(d) (1994) (providing for relief from stay where creditor establishes certain grounds).**
32. ***Id.* § 1112(b)(2) (providing that on motion of party in interest court may dismiss case because of inability to effectuate plan).**
33. **One of the prongs of the amendment to § 362 provides that the stay remains only if the plan proposed by the debtor "has a *reasonable* possibility of being confirmed within a *reasonable* time." 11 U.S.C. § 362(d)(3)(A) (1994) (emphasis added). There will undoubtedly be litigation over the meaning (in two spots) of the term "reasonable."**
34. BIENENSTOCK, *supra* note 24, at 28-39.

end of the case, if you have enough evidence at the beginning of the case to reach a conclusion on that question.

JUDGE MARK: Although it's not going to apply in the Eleventh Circuit because we have clear Eleventh Circuit authority to dismiss on a finding of bad faith,[35] I think a good argument could be made that in most instances, the same results could be obtained by either stay relief for cause under section (d)(1) of 362 or just a finding under the express provisions of 1112(b) — either (b)(1), that there is continuing loss or diminution of the estate in absence of a reasonable likelihood of rehabilitation or, (b)(2), that there is an inability to effectuate a plan. And it may be that the factors we often look at in determining whether a case is right for dismissal under bad faith just go in a sense to how quickly after the filing of a case do you look at (b)(1) and (b)(2). And part of a way to do it without a separate doctrine of bad faith is just to say that you will look immediately at the ability to effectuate a plan if certain criteria exist. But as I said, in the Eleventh Circuit we have that doctrine that's now well-established and although lawyers alternatively argue 1112(b)(1) and (b)(2), we can plug into the Eleventh Circuit doctrine of bad faith and still proceed in that fashion.

JUDGE HILLMAN: It's a question of how far forward do you want to drag the confirmation issues.

PROF. GROSS: Well, if there is an implied good faith standard, where is it found? Where is the authority to create it?

JUDGE GREENDYKE: I think it's a case law creation and it probably comes in under section 105[36] or just a general inherent ability, at least under the Fifth Circuit case law,[37] to protect our jurisdiction. If you find

---

35. *See supra* note 15 and accompanying text (discussing state of law in Eleventh Circuit).

36. 11 U.S.C. § 105(a) (1994) (providing that bankruptcy court may take any action necessary to "implement court orders or rules, or to prevent an abuse of process").

37. *See* Humble Place Joint Venture v. Fory (*In re* Humble Place Joint Venture), 936 F.2d 814, 817 (5th Cir. 1991) (holding that Bankruptcy Code provision that chapter 11 case may be dismissed "for cause" includes lack of good faith

that somebody is doing something that's inappropriate or that would constitute an abuse of your jurisdiction, you can cleanse your docket, in effect.

I am paraphrasing liberally Judge Jones' words in *Little Creek*[38] and cases that have followed that. That's where we do it and how we do it.

JUDGE FENNING: But you also find it in Rule 11.[39]

PROF. GROSS: Some people find it in Bankruptcy Rule 9011.[40]

JUDGE FENNING: And 28 U.S.C. § 1927,[41] which is an alternative source of sanction law. It's implicit in federal court that you can review all filings to determine whether they have been made in good faith. I just don't think you have to get to all of those more generic formulations where you are

---

in filing); Little Creek Dev. Co. v. Commonwealth Mortgage Corp. (*In re* Little Creek Dev. Co.), 779 F.2d 1068, 1072 (5th Cir. 1986) ("Determining whether the debtor's filing for relief is in good faith depends largely upon the bankruptcy court's on-the-spot evaluation of the debtor's financial condition, motives, and the local financial realities.").

38. *Little Creek*, 779 F.2d at 1072 (discussing bankruptcy court's power to prevent "abuse of the bankruptcy process" and to "protect[] the jurisdictional integrity of the bankruptcy courts" by limiting the "powerful equitable weapons" to those debtors and creditors with "clean hands").

39. FED. R. CIV. P. 11 (allowing court-imposed sanctions against attorneys, law firms or parties that bring actions deemed frivolous or improper).

40. FED. R. BANKR. P. 9011. The Rule provides, in pertinent part, that to the best of the attorney's or party's knowledge, information, and belief formed after reasonable inquiry it is well grounded in fact and is warranted by existing law or a good faith argument for the extension, modification, or reversal of existing law; and that it is not interposed for any improper purpose, such as to harass or to cause unnecessary delay or needless increase in the cost of litigation or administration of the case.
Id.

41. 28 U.S.C. § 1927 (1994). This section provides:

> Any attorney or other person admitted to conduct cases in any court of the United States or any Territory thereof who so multiplies the proceedings in any case unreasonably and vexatiously may be required by the court to satisfy personally the excess costs, expenses, and attorneys' fees reasonably incurred because of such conduct.

Id.

dealing with a statutory requirement that, in order to accomplish what you are supposed to be accomplishing in a chapter 11 case, you have to be proceeding in good faith. I mean, I rely primarily on section 1129.

JUDGE MARK: I think the Eleventh Circuit cases just find that section 1112(b)[42] is not exhaustive and that it allows the court to dismiss in the best interest of creditors for cause and then they say there is another ground for dismissal, not expressly stated, but there is a valid ground based on bad faith — and the doctrine has developed. It's sort of an unnumbered cause now under section 1112(b) in the Eleventh Circuit.

JUDGE HILLMAN: That's exactly how the *Bible* spoke.[43]

JUDGE FENNING: In the Ninth Circuit we have *Victory Construction*,[44] which deals with the badges of fraud in "new debtor syndrome" cases.[45] That is the primary scenario in which bad faith is pled and argued strenuously as opposed to a throw-away alternative argument on relief from stay in the Ninth Circuit. "New debtor syndrome" is the nickname for a new entity created to hold the real property which then is dumped into bankruptcy with no employees, no history, no other source of income.[46]

---

42. 11 U.S.C. § 1112(b) (1994). *See, e.g.*, Natural Land Corp. v. Baker Farms, Inc. (*In re* Natural Land Corp.), 825 F.2d 296 (11th Cir. 1987) (dismissing debtor's petition for reorganization because it was not filed in good faith); Albany Partners, Ltd. v. Westbrook (*In re* Albany Partners, Ltd.), 749 F.2d 670 (11th Cir. 1984) (same).
43. *In re* The Bible Speaks, 65 B.R. 415 (Bankr. D. Mass. 1986) (dismissing on ground of bad faith filing).
44. *In re* Victory Constr. Co., 9 B.R. 549 (Bankr. C.D. Cal. 1981), *vacated as moot*, 37 B.R. 222 (Bankr. 9th Cir. 1984).
45. *Id.* at 568.
46. Scott Carlisle, *Single Asset Real Estate in Chapter 11: Secured Creditors' Perspective and the Need for Reform*, 1 AM. BANKR. INST. L. REV. 133 (1993) ("[T]he debtor is framed for the sole purpose of filing bankruptcy.") (citing H. Miles Cohn, *Good Faith and the Single-Asset Debtor*, 62 AM. BANKR. L.J. 131, 131 (1988)); Venditto, *supra* note 1, at 1611 (discussing "new debtor syndrome cases in which property is transferred to a newly created or revived entity which then files a chapter 11 case").

JUDGE HILLMAN: We have adopted Judge Ordin's test from *Victory*,[47] but we use it also when it isn't a new debtor. If you take the catalogue of events and it just doesn't happen to be a new debtor, it still may flunk the good faith test.

D. What is the Test for Good Faith?

PROF. GROSS: Since we are all talking about what the standard is, let's talk about that specifically. How is it that a court should determine what is good faith in a chapter 11 single asset real estate case? As you answer, I assume you are answering for yourself, but if you have the view of your circuit or the judges in your district, it may be worth identifying that.

Judge Greendyke, do you want to go first?

JUDGE GREENDYKE: I think, at least from my standpoint, it's difficult to say here's the test. It's usually four or five criteria because it is inherently a fact-intensive type of search.[48] One of the best examples that we have had and used down here is a District Court opinion that was penned by a circuit judge who was sitting by designation, Judge Jones.

The case is called *Chemical Research*[49] and it involved two quarreling factions of a joint venture. One of the venturers, Chemical Research filed for relief under chapter 11 to gain advantage in state court. It basically represented a two-party dispute over entitlement to some intellectual property rights. There were virtually no creditors, and the company was solvent, with a wonderfully lucrative, profitable business. Judge Jones just said, look, you all don't have the right kind of attitude toward this case. You are not in subjective bad faith, but you are not in objective good faith. That is, you

---

47. *Victory Constr.*, 9 B.R. at 549 (requiring good faith as "implicit prerequisite to filing or continuation of chapter 11 proceeding").

48. *See* Humble Place Joint Venture v. Fory (*In re* Humble Place), 936 F.2d 814, 817-18 (5th Cir. 1991) (upholding application of faith factors developed in Little Creek Dev. Co. v. Commonwealth Mortgage Corp. (*In re* Little Creek Dev. Co.), 779 F.2d 1068, 1072-73 (5th Cir. 1986)); *In re* Devine, 131 B.R. 952, 955 (Bankr. S.D. Tex. 1991) ("Findings of lack of good faith are based on an overall review of the circumstances on a case by case basis.").

49. *In re* Chemical Research & Licensing Co., No. 85-00210-H1-5, slip op. (Bankr. S.D. Tex. Nov. 13, 1986) (Jones, J., sitting by designation).

meant well but what you are doing is wrong. This is a two-party dispute and it needs to be resolved outside of bankruptcy court.

Well, I don't think I have ever seen a case like that since then, but lawyers like to argue its application in any apparent two-party dispute. If you are presented with a situation in which you have just two creditors fighting, there's lots of case authority to say, "send them out."

If you have a situation like Mike McConnell was confronted with in *Little Creek*,[50] where he found the only reason why they went into bankruptcy court was to dodge a state court judgment and avoid the posting of a supersedeas bond,[51] there's a line of cases that say that constitutes bad faith,[52] but it's really an example by example situation. It's a matter of how offended the bankruptcy judge is that these parties are in front of him or her and whether or not the judge decides that the case is one that is susceptible of reorganization.

PROF. GROSS: Would you say, then, that there is an objective test to determine whether a debtor is reorganizable? Of course, in applying that test, lots of factors must be taken into account.

JUDGE GREENDYKE: Well, it's both. It can be a subjective test or it can be an objective test. My favorite approach is to be objective about it because every debtor "is a bad guy" and they are going to give you lots of evidence about how bad the debtor is and how bad the debtor has been historically. It is very difficult to establish subjective standards and thresholds. It's a lot easier to try the case from an objective standpoint and allow the subjective evidence that comes forth to be kind of a shading on what you find objectively.

While Judge Jones ruled in *Chemical Research*[53] probably on a somewhat subjective basis, she was looking at objective evidence on what the situation was in front of her to make that determination. So, yes, I guess the first

50. *In re* Little Creek Dev. Co., 54 B.R. 510 (Bankr. N.D. Tex. 1985) (McConnell, J.), *rev'd*, 779 F.2d 1068 (5th Cir. 1986).

51. *Id.* at 513-14.

52. ***See In re* Ramji, 166 B.R. 288, 290-91 (Bankr. S.D. Tex. 1993)**; *In re* Roberts, 117 B.R. 677, 677-78 (Bankr. N.D. Okla. 1990); *In re* Ford, 74 B.R. 934 (Bankr. S.D. Ala. 1987).

53. *In re* Chemical Research & Licensing Co., No. 85-00210-H1-5, slip op. (S.D. Tex. Nov. 13, 1986).

approach is objective and then I would allow the subjective evidence to just sort of help you make your decision.

PROF. GROSS: And Judge Greendyke, you also seem to be looking at this issue by categorizing types of cases: single asset cases which are on the eve of foreclosure, single asset cases which are two-party disputes, and . . .

JUDGE GREENDYKE: — the new debtor cases that we mentioned.

PROF. GROSS: Or the new debtor syndrome. In essence, you are lumping single asset cases into various discrete categories.

JUDGE GREENDYKE: Well, the lawyers are going to want to lump them in categories. I guess to a certain extent they are susceptible to some type of categorization. Again, each one is usually so different that it's not fair to the parties to lump them entirely into one group.

JUDGE HILLMAN: The judges in the District of Massachusetts started with *Little Creek* and then developed a list of fourteen characteristics. The best place to find it is *In re Village Green Realty Trust,*[54] which is a Judge Gabriel decision in 1990, and he lists fourteen factors, which I can either read to you, or I can put them in a footnote, however you want to handle it, but they are there.[55]

---

54. 113 B.R. 105 (Bankr. D. Mass. 1990).

55. *Id.* at 115-16. The fourteen characteristics are as follows:

> 1. The debtor has few or no unsecured creditors;
> 2. There has been a previous bankruptcy petition by the debtor or a related entity;
> 3. The prepetition conduct of the debtor has been improper;
> 4. The petition effectively allows the debtor to evade court orders;
> 5. There are few debts to non-moving creditors;
> 6. The petition was filed on the eve of foreclosure;
> 7. The foreclosed property is the sole or major asset of the debtor;
> 8. The debtor has no ongoing business or employees;
> 9. There is no possibility of reorganization;
> 10. The debtor's income is not sufficient to operate;
> 11. There was no pressure from non-moving creditors;
> 12. Reorganization essentially involves the resolution of a two

Now, what most of us seem to be doing with that list is you count up how many of the fourteen they have hit and if they hit enough, they move.

PROF. GROSS: Would seven or more satisfy the test?

JUDGE HILLMAN: I don't know. In *In re Thane Development Associates, L.P.*,[56] which I decided about four or five months ago, I said that ten out of fourteen did it.

JUDGE GREENDYKE: But it's not fair to you on a case-by-case basis to have to set a limit like that to say that it needs to be more than fifty percent. If the case is so egregious, if you will, that one factor outweighs all the others, you just need to consider all the remaining factors or to look at their potential application to make sure of your decision. It is appropriate to give different weight to the various factors.

JUDGE FENNING: I think that laundry list includes pretty much every factor that we look at, but it doesn't tell you what's enough, and that's the hard case. We have inexperienced counsel coming in sometimes arguing dismissal for bad faith filing simply because the case was filed on the eve of foreclosure. Our response is, "Every real estate case is filed on the eve of foreclosure." So by itself, unless we are told that real estate doesn't belong in bankruptcy, that is not enough to make this a bad faith filing. There's no magic formula.

PROF. GROSS: Well, Judge Fenning, do you have an approach that you or your district take?

JUDGE FENNING: Well, the "new debtor syndrome" cases[57] do not

---

party dispute;

13. A corporate debtor was formed and received title to its major assets immediately before the petition;

14. The debtor filed solely to create the automatic stay.

Id.

56. 143 B.R. 310 (Bankr. D. Mass. 1992).

57. *See* California Mortgage Serv. v. Yukon Enters., Inc. (*In re* Yukon Enters., Inc.), 39 B.R. 919, 921 (Bankr. C.D. Cal. 1984); *In re* Victory Constr. Co., 9

last long in our district, but we don't see that many of them filed by experienced bankruptcy lawyers because they know there is no point. You are going to be out of court at the first hearing and probably damage your reputation in the process as a lawyer for filing such a case.

The marginal bad faith cases that we get tend to be somewhat more complex than that. Debtors try and use excuses about how well they really can formulate a plan, if only the following fifteen things happen but most of which would require a miracle.

But as I said, we usually are not litigating the bad faith issue. The bad faith is normally present in our cases as a back drop to relief from stay as an additional factor for relief from stay, or as an additional reason to deny confirmation of the plan, rather than as a free-standing justification to dismiss the case.

Dismissal of a case requires notice to all the creditors and sometimes it's a lot easier to file a motion for relief from stay with a more restrictive notice list under Bankruptcy Rule 4001[58] and get out on relief from stay and not worry about the procedural problems of dealing with a motion for dismissal.

JUDGE MARK: In the Eleventh Circuit we have the authority of several decisions. Most recently and one most often cited is *In re Phoenix Piccadilly,*[59] which is a 1988 case, which sent shock waves through the debtor bar because in that case the court said even if the debtor has equity in the property, bad faith dismissal may be appropriate.[60]

As applied, it hasn't expanded the law greatly, but as a result, we have this shorter laundry list than the District of Massachusetts, with largely the same kind of criteria.[61] The debtor has one asset, few unsecured creditors and their

---

B.R. 549, 565 (Bankr. C.D. Cal. 1981), *vacated as moot*, 37 B.R. 222 (Bankr. 9th Cir. 1984).

58. FED. R. BANKR. P. 4001(a)(1) (referring to Rule 1007(d)).
59. 849 F.2d 1393 (11th Cir. 1988).
60. *Id.* at 1395 (disregarding potential for successful reorganization).
61. The list of criteria includes:

> (i) The debtor has only one asset, the Property, in which it does not hold legal title; (ii) The Debtor has few unsecured creditors whose claims are small in relation to the claims of the Secured Creditors; (iii) The Debtor has few employees; (iv) The Property is the subject of a foreclosure action as a result of arrearages on the debt; (v) The

claims are small in relation to the mortgage, few employees, foreclosure action, essentially a two-party dispute which is pending in the state court and the timing evidences an intent to delay or frustrate the creditors.

It's interesting, because the older Eleventh Circuit authority cases, such as *In re Natural Land Corporation*[62] involved the "new debtor syndrome" and I think the whole concept of bad faith came about in these new debtor cases that were really egregious, but in the Eleventh Circuit it is now argued and applied in the typical single asset real estate case.

As far as how it's applied, though, in this type of test, most of the judges, with varying degrees of flexibility, still look at the feasibility of reorganization as a very important factor. You find, for example, that Judge Paskay dismisses a lot on bad faith grounds,[63] but also has published cases where he has denied bad faith motions or stay relief motions at the outset because there is some possibility of reorganization.[64]

> Debtor's financial problems involve essentially a dispute between the Debtor and the Secured Creditors which can be resolved in the pending State Court Action; and (vi) The timing of the Debtor's filing evidences an intent to delay or frustrate the legitimate efforts of the Debtor's secured creditors to enforce their rights.

Id. at 1394-95.

62. Natural Land Corp. v. Baker Farms, Inc. (*In re* Natural Land Corp.), 825 F.2d 296 (11th Cir. 1987).

63. ***See, e.g., In re* Springs Plaza Assocs., L.P., 188 B.R. 48, 49 (Bankr. M.D. Fla. 1995); *In re* Immenhausen Corp., 172 B.R. 343, 348 (Bankr. M.D. Fla. 1994);** *In re* Landings Assocs. Ltd. Partnership, 145 B.R. 101, 102, 104 (Bankr. M.D. Fla. 1992); *In re* Tampa Medical Tower Ltd. Partnership, 145 B.R. 99, 101 (Bankr. M.D. Fla. 1992); *In re* Colonial Daytona Ltd. Partnership, 144 B.R. 924 (Bankr. M.D. Fla. 1992), *aff'd*, 152 B.R. 996 (M.D. Fla. 1993); *In re* Meadowood Club Apts., Ltd., 145 B.R. 96, 97-98 (Bankr. M.D. Fla. 1992); *In re* Punta Gorda Assocs., 143 B.R. 281, 283 (Bankr. M.D. Fla. 1992); Oliver v. Kolody (*In re* Oliver), 142 B.R. 486 (Bankr. M.D. Fla. 1992); *In re* Aurora Invs., Inc., 134 B.R. 982 (Bankr. M.D. Fla. 1991); *In re* Smail, 129 B.R. 676, 678 (Bankr. M.D. Fla. 1991); *In re* Mohan Kutty Trust, 134 B.R. 987, 989 (Bankr. M.D. Fla. 1991).

64. ***See In re* Scott, 166 B.R. 459, 461 (Bankr. M.D. Fla. 1994); *In re* Clause Enters., 150 B.R. 476, 478 (Bankr. M.D. Fla. 1993).**

JUDGE GREENDYKE: That brings in an interesting question. In a lot of instances when you go through the checklist, you will find many of the factors are satisfied, but that there's a smell somewhere that the debtor has got something to work with. Do you all do anything to manage those cases like requiring, for instance, a capital infusion prior to the time of the disclosure statement hearing, in order to assess–condition the case on proof of some sort of viability? If, indeed, the main argument is this debtor is a dead duck and it won't work, do you say to the debtor or its principals, I am going to find this, unless you can disprove it by coming up with the money to make the deferred improvements or to meet the deferred maintenance costs in the form of a deposit. Do you ever do anything like that?

PROF. GROSS: There is another way of asking that question. How much time do you give a debtor to make the showing that it is feasible that it will file a plan? For me, one of the differences between the good faith standard in the plan context and the implied good faith standard is that of timing. The issue ostensibly comes up later in the plan context but with implied good faith, the issue comes up right on filing. So, there is a critical timing issue in determining good faith.[65]

JUDGE MARK: Well, I have a procedure I have used in three or four cases and it's, I guess, a carryover of giving debtors rope to hang themselves, which I liked to do when I did creditor work before I was appointed. But if you find in a typical case that meets these basic criteria the issue becomes what does a debtor have to show to establish that there's a feasible reorganization. If the debtor hasn't gotten a judgment yet, typically stay relief, at least through the point of judgment, is given. There's usually not a lot of argument against that in these cases, but if it's a case where they already have a judgment and it's a question of delaying the sale, we put them on an extremely fast track where they may have 20 days to file a plan. We'll expedite the hearing on the disclosure statement and I, rather than hearing a lot of happy talk at the first hearing on the motion to dismiss as to what they are going to do, I will say file your plan and at the disclosure hearing, which we are going to have in 10 or

---

65. **The 1994 Amendments make it clear that, whether or not a good faith test exists in respect of filing, the debtor must file a plan within 90 days, or pay the secured creditor, or the stay will be lifted. 11 U.S.C. § 362(d)(3) (1994).**

15 days after you file your plan, we'll have a further evidentiary hearing on the motion to dismiss and you will have to put on a prima facie case that your plan is feasible at the disclosure hearing. Not for disclosure purposes, because it doesn't really fit in for disclosure. What I like to see is the feasibility of an actual plan, not just what they think they are going to do. And that may mean putting up money. If they are going to put in new money to try and reorganize, that will mean putting up money.

PROF. GROSS: So the burden of proof for you, Judge Mark, is on the debtor to prove good faith as opposed to on the creditor to prove bad faith?[66]

JUDGE MARK: I think that overstates it a bit. I think once the case fits what we use as a shorthand sort of the *Phoenix Piccadilly*[67] mold in the Eleventh Circuit; it has these criteria. They have gotten a judgment. It's a two-party dispute. Conceptually, if you still believe there is some purpose to chapter 11 for equity versus mortgagee, and you are giving them some chance, the burden shifts, I guess, for them to prove that there is a feasible plan and to prove it quickly in order to stave off complete stay relief or dismissal for bad faith.

JUDGE HILLMAN: It may be that this entire process we have been discussing is nothing more than factors you look at when you come to a *Timbers*[68] decision. How are we going to get there? What are the evidentiary matters that are involved in reaching a *Timbers* decision?

JUDGE GREENDYKE: I think it's probably more akin to a jurisdictional question. Once the issue is raised, it's going to be the debtor's

---

66. **It is unstated as to which party has the burden of proof under the 1994 Amendments to §§ 101 and 362 to prove a bad faith filing. The case law developed to date does not address this issue either. 11 U.S.C. §§ 101, 362 (1994).**
67. Phoenix Piccadilly, Ltd. v. Life Ins. Co. (*In re* Phoenix Piccadilly, Ltd.), 849 F.2d 1393 (11th Cir. 1988).
68. United Sav. Ass'n v. Timbers, 484 U.S. 365 (1988) (holding that unsecured creditor not entitled to interest on collateral as compensation for delay of foreclosure caused by automatic stay).

burden to prove its entitlement to remain in court. If a creditor shows or if I find in the context of just a review of the documents that there is some question as to whether or not the jurisdiction is being abused because of lack of good faith, it's the debtor's burden and obligation to prove and continue to prove it's entitled to be here. And that's how I support my sua sponte motion to make the debtor do something like what you all suggested such as speeding up the discovery and disclosure process and confirmation process.

JUDGE FENNING: Under section 362, it's the debtor's burden to establish feasibility of the plan[69] and, to the extent that incorporates a good faith standard, the burden is with the debtor. To put that at issue on a motion for relief from stay at the beginning of the case, the creditor has to come forward with sufficient evidence to establish a prima facie case that the debtor can't meet the confirmation standard. That forces the debtor to make its showing earlier in the case than it might otherwise, but whenever raised, good faith is fundamentally the debtor's burden.

I often put single asset cases on a very short leash, though not as short as Judge Mark does, for a plan and disclosure statement. If it appears clear that capital infusion is necessary, I require a showing that the capital will be available. Sometimes I require that money be posted before the confirmation order under Bankruptcy Rule 3020.[70]

PROF. GROSS: Does it strike any of you as the least bit odd that we screen bankruptcy filings on what we could call an abusive process standard that is higher than the standard that is applied *outside* of bankruptcy for ordinary civil litigation?

---

69. 11 U.S.C. § 362(d)(2),(g) (1994).

70. FED. R. BANKR. P. 3020(a):

> In a chapter 11 case, prior to entry of the order confirming the plan, the court may order the deposit with the trustee or debtor in possession of the consideration required by the plan to be distributed on confirmation. Any money deposited shall be kept in a special account established for the exclusive purpose of making the distribution.

Id.

JUDGE GREENDYKE: Well, if you became aware of a Rule 11 violation, we probably are obligated to go ahead and do something about it. I don't think there's a fair analogy outside of bankruptcy court, unless you have a multiple filer, pro se litigant, or something like that. I just don't think there are very many analogies in plain old civil litigation.

JUDGE FENNING: In state court you have demurrers right away. There are equivalents elsewhere.

JUDGE MARK: But in the run of these typical cases, and where I put them on a very short fuse is where they filed on the day or the day before the sale and the sale has been canceled. In Florida, that means at least a 30-day delay.[71] So the mortgagee is losing at least a month and the question is how much time–how much extra time are they going to get by filing a chapter 11, if any?

And I don't think we are setting a tougher standard than the state court. In these cases they have already lost in state court. Those of us who give them some time and have some flexibility still recognize there is a legitimate purpose and right to file a single asset chapter 11 case, even if you have exhausted your remedies in state court, but you better be prepared to do something meaningful very quickly.

E. Do Standards of Good Faith in Single Asset Cases Differ From Other Cases Under the Code?

PROF. GROSS: Let me ask all of you the following: are the standards for good faith in a single asset real estate chapter 11 case any different from the standards for good faith in any other chapter 11 case or any other chapter of the Code for that matter? In other words, is this standard that you have been articulating unique to single asset chapter 11 cases or is it one you would apply to the panoply of good faith issues that are raised in all sorts of other cases and contexts?[72]

---

71. FLA. STAT. ANN. § 197.542(2) (West 1989) (providing that in event of cancellation of sale circuit court clerk may "readvertise sale to be held no later than 30 days from" cancellation date).

72. **There is another area in which determinations involving single asset real estate cases may differ from other cases. The stay is not lifted under**

JUDGE FENNING: I don't think it's unique to single asset cases. The only difference is that we all have a lot of experience with repetitive fact patterns in single asset filings that permit us to draw inferences and see patterns much more readily than, say, in a manufacturing company case. I think the basic standard is the same.

PROF. GROSS: Do the rest of you share Judge Fenning's view that it is the same basic good faith standard for the chapter 11 that involves mass torts, or the chapter 13 filed to get rid of claims that would be dischargeable in a chapter 7 case or the chapter 7 case that is filed to get rid of a state court defamation judgment that you didn't like?[73]

JUDGE HILLMAN: In a broad sense.

JUDGE GREENDYKE: I agree. I think the standards almost have to be the same. It's just that chapter 11 single asset cases are so much different than any other fact pattern. I do not think it is a helpful question or comparison.

JUDGE MARK: I would disagree, in part. In the Eleventh Circuit, as the law developed and as it's been applied, and this goes back to the objective versus subjective analysis of a debtor's filing. I have looked debtor principals in the eye and said, I am not saying you are a bad person. I am not finding that you are evil or that are acting subjectively in bad faith, but objectively, under these criteria, you are gone in shorthand.

JUDGE FENNING: I have been known to say that, too.

JUDGE MARK: So to go back to your question, I don't think that it's necessarily in terms of bad faith or absence of good faith in other sections of

---

§ 362(d)(3)(B) if the debtor makes payments to the secured creditor. 11 U.S.C. § 362(d)(3)(B) (1994). Specifically, the payments must equal the "interest at a current fair market rate." ***Id.*** **This is a different approach to valuation than used elsewhere in the Code, an observation noted in several recent cases.** ***See In re*** **Dingley, 189 B.R. 264 (Bankr. N.D.N.Y. 1995);** ***In re*** **Yrlas, 183 B.R. 119 (Bankr. N.D. Tex. 1995).**

73. *See supra* notes 6-7.

the Code where you may be focusing more on actual proof of bad intent, which we don't really need to find in the Eleventh Circuit under the *Phoenix Piccadilly* test.[74]

PROF. GROSS: The reason I raised this whole line of inquiry, and it may not be one with which you all agree, is that there are cases involving individual debtors as opposed to corporate debtors where the good faith issue is raised early and then the courts say you ought to be *much more* reluctant to dismiss those cases initially on an implied good faith standard since the philosophy of the Code is to let people have access to the system in the first instance.[75] The Courts go on to say, at least in the context of a chapter 13, that good faith can be raised later in the context of the plan — where good faith is specific.[76] What seems to be said here about single asset real estate cases is the opposite: don't be skeptical initially; make the judgment about good faith early, if you can and dismiss cases early if necessary.

JUDGE HILLMAN: I think that should be the same rule in any case. If you can make the determination early, what is the point of waiting until confirmation, when you can tell two weeks into the case that this is a sick puppy that's not going to make it?

JUDGE MARK: In the context, though, it's different. For example, in the chapter 13, you might have an individual that files on the eve of the foreclosure sale and with few unsecured creditors, but in a 13, because it's got

---

74. The *Phoenix Piccadilly* test is a factor test used to find a bad faith filing. "[C]ourts may consider any factors which evidence `an intent to abuse the judicial process and the purposes of the reorganization provisions' or, in particular, factors which evidence that the petition was filed `to delay or frustrate the legitimate efforts of secured creditors to enforce their rights.'" Phoenix Piccadilly, Ltd. v. Life Ins. Co. (*In re* Phoenix Piccadilly, Ltd.), 849 F.2d 1393, 1394 (11th Cir. 1988) (quoting Albany Partners, Ltd. v. Westbrook (*In re* Albany Partners, Ltd.), 749 F.2d 670, 674 (11th Cir. 1984)).

75. ***See* Eisen v. Curry (*In re* Eisen), 14 F.3d 469 (9th Cir. 1993); Robinson v. Tenantry (*In re* Robinson), 987 F.2d 665 (10th Cir. 1993)**; *In re* Love, 957 F.2d 1350 (7th Cir. 1992); *In re* Ristic, 142 B.R. 856 (Bankr. E.D. Wis. 1992); *In re* King, 131 B.R. 207 (Bankr. N.D. Fla. 1991); *In re* Powers, 135 B.R. 980 (Bankr. C.D. Cal. 1991).

76. 11 U.S.C. § 1325(a)(3) (1994).

special rights, they can have a feasible plan.[77] So I would have to find some real abuse and subjective bad faith to knock out a 13 early before we had a chance to really analyze the facts and the trustee had made his recommendations on the feasibility of curing the arrearage.

So you have suddenly a new bundle of rights in a 13 that you don't really have in an 11. There are different rights in 11 than you have in state court obviously, but the context, I think, does affect how you look at the good faith issue.

JUDGE GREENDYKE: I don't think it's the same. I agree with what you are saying. I don't think there's the same need for a judge to monitor 13's or 7's. You have trustees in both those cases and they are watching, and they are on a much quicker fuse — a quicker time track than the 11's are in large part. I can remember years ago actively looking at the 11's to try and find cases I thought were susceptible to a bad faith attack, cases in which we had new businesses or undeveloped real estate, cases that really needed to be looked at and managed actively by me — that's just a different approach than we take in 13's.

JUDGE FENNING: I guess I have a slightly different perspective. This is not the major bad faith issue in the Central District of California. Our principal bad faith problem is with a huge volume of chapter 7's and 13's being filed solely to avoid eviction from a residential tenancy where an unlawful detainer judgment has already been entered in state court.[78]

---

77. *See* 11 U.S.C. § 1325 (1994).

78. ***Report of the Ninth Circuit Ad Hoc Committee on Unlawful Detainer and Bankruptcy Mills*, January 26, 1994, submitted by Geraldine Mund, United States Bankruptcy Judge, Chair of the Ad Hoc Committee on Unlawful Detainer and Bankruptcy Mills. Unfortunately, since the December 1992 date of this Roundtable Discussion, the Central District has been plagued by the emergence of a virulent new form of "bad faith" filing in both chapter 7 and 11 cases. The typical pattern in these cases is the transfer of 10% interests in multiple pieces of real property to a debtor either just before or after the filing of a bankruptcy petition. Some properties have been the subject of ten or more bankruptcy filings. Typically, the debtors do not schedule their interests in these properties, nor do they appear at the § 341(a) meetings of creditors or in opposition to relief from stay motions. *See In re* Cherokee New York Invs., 27**

I haven't put that in the hopper as a single asset real estate case because they don't have any interest in real property, strictly speaking. It's a different category that's more predominant unfortunately in our jurisdiction than anyplace else for a variety of reasons. We examine the "unlawful detainer" cases very closely and if they fit a prima facie bad faith pattern, we grant relief from stay or dismiss them immediately.[79] So our "unlawful detainer" consumer cases are on a far shorter leash than single asset real estate cases.

I don't mean to imply that I am currently confirming a lot of chapter 11 plans for single asset real estate cases. They are not living that long in our jurisdiction at the moment, at least not in my courtroom, because there's no equity[80] in any of these properties and they have no way of repaying the debt or refinancing, given the fact that the bottom has fallen out of our real estate market.

So single asset cases are mostly history on the first relief from stay motion. A few survive, but most of them don't get past relief from stay because there is no equity and no prospect for successful reorganization.

F. What is Different About Single Asset Cases?

PROF. GROSS: Let me play devil's advocate for a minute here. Why is it that these single asset cases where a debtor is seeking to rework secured debt are any different than any other chapter 11 where a debtor is trying to

---

Bankr. Ct. Dec. (CRR) 1010 (Bankr. E.D.N.Y. 1995) (describing impact of these California-based schemes even on cases filed in New York). Judge Fenning has developed a fast track order to show cause procedure to dismiss these cases and annul the stay as to any and all affected properties.

79. *See* Omoto v. Ruggera (*In re* Omoto), 85 B.R. 98 (Bankr. 9th Cir. 1988); Little v. Taylor (*In re* Taylor), 77 B.R. 237 (Bankr. 9th Cir. 1987), *aff'd in part, and rev'd in part*, 884 F.2d 478 (9th Cir. 1989); Centinela Church of Christ v. Calvary Full Gospel Assembly (*In re* Centinela Church of Christ), 16 B.R. 877 (Bankr. 9th Cir. 1982).

80. ***See* 11 U.S.C. § 362(d)(2)(A) (1994) (allowing relief from stay due to lack of equity in the property)**; Albany Partners, Ltd. v. Westbrook (*In re* Albany Partners, Ltd.), 749 F.2d 670, 673 (11th Cir. 1984) (granting relief from stay where debtor had no equity in property and no realistic chance for reorganization).

basically restructure its secured debt? Why are these particular cases being "singled" out for singular treatment as abusive?[81]

JUDGE MARK: I don't think it's implied that they necessarily are. I like what Judge Hillman said earlier, that it's a matter of how far forward you push the analysis of the feasibility of a plan of reorganization. It's easy to say why they are different in terms of restructuring debt.

Well, they are not if they can come up with something in the way of a plan, a feasible plan to restructure the debt. What has caused the courts to look at these early cases is that many of them are simply filed to delay the foreclosure sale and there is no prospect of restructuring the debt.

It is somewhat complicated in courts, including mine, where the possibility of a new value, strip-down plan[82] exists, even where there is no equity. That is a possible argument, even in a no equity case, that a feasible plan is possible, however I don't think we are saying single asset debtors don't have an opportunity to restructure. I think we are saying if certain criteria exists, particularly in the Eleventh Circuit, you have to come to the table very quickly with how you are going to do it.

G. Proposed Legislation

PROF. GROSS: Let me change gears here. As everyone is aware,[83] Congress contemplated legislation specifically to address single asset real estate chapter 11 cases.[84] My first question is: Do you think we need a statutory fix or should we leave things as they are for case-by-case determination? And then more specifically, as you may know, the proposed

---

81. **As an interesting corollary, these cases were also "singled" out in the 1994 Amendments, generating amendments all of their own!**

82. "The phrase stripping down or strip down shall refer to the process of reducing a secured claim to the value of the underlying collateral." Zlogar v. IRS (*In re* Zlogar), 101 B.R. 1, 2 (Bankr. N.D. Ill. 1989).

83. **As noted, the Bankruptcy Code was amended in 1994. *See supra* note *. *See* Myron M. Scheinfeld, *Small Business and Single Asset Real Estate Bankruptcies*, 41 PRAC. LAW. 17 (1995). The wording of the 1994 Amendments does differ from the Senate version of the bill, the Senate version being that set forth *infra* notes 85 and 86.**

84. S. REP. No. 279, 102d Cong., 2d Sess. (1992).

legislation in essence provided a fast track for chapter 11 single asset real estate cases. The legislation contemplated permitting a stay to be lifted to go up to the point of sale in the context of foreclosure, and then allowed for the plan process to be sped up.[85] And, if it didn't speed up or if payment wasn't made to a secured creditor, then the legislation allowed the stay to be lifted and foreclosure to conclude.[86] So my question is: Do you think we need legislation, and if so, what is your view as to what that legislation should be?

JUDGE HILLMAN: I say, first of all, we don't need it. What it's addressing is the attitude of a number of judges that you don't get relief from stay right away. There is one judge who says to me repeatedly, you have to try three times before I grant relief from stay.

---

85. S. 1985, 102d Cong., 2d Sess § 211 (1992). The section provides in pertinent part:

> With respect to a stay of an act against real property under subsection (a), if the property is single asset real estate, and the debtor has not, within 90 days after the filing of a petition under section 301 or section 302 of this title, or the entry of an order for relief under section 303 of this title, filed a plan of reorganization which has a reasonable possibility of being confirmed within a reasonable period of time, or the debtor has commenced payment to the holder of a claim secured by such real property of interest on a monthly basis at a current fair market rate on the value of the creditor's secured interest in such property. The court may extend such 90-day period only for cause and only if an order granting such an extension is entered within such 90-day period.

Id.

86. *Id.* The section provides in pertinent part:

> Upon request of a party in interest in a case under this title in which the property of the estate is single asset real estate, the court, with or without a hearing, shall grant such limited relief from a stay provided under subsections (a)(1), (a)(3), and (a)(4) of this section, as is necessary to allow such party in interest to proceed during the pendency of the case under this title with a foreclosure proceeding, whether judicial or nonjudicial, which had been commenced before a petition was filed under this title, up to but not including the point of sale of such real property.

Id.

JUDGE FENNING: Or you have to wait a year or whatever the formula is, for other judges.

JUDGE HILLMAN: Whatever it is. Those judges who are doing that now are the reason why Congress was asked to act. No matter what Congress does, those judges will still require three motions or a year before they are going to grant relief from stay. So I don't think that the proposed legislation is going to accomplish anything.

JUDGE FENNING: I think it may change some of the practices of the judges that are inclined to extend the stay forever.

JUDGE HILLMAN: You are much more optimistic than I.

JUDGE FENNING: Well, I believe that some of the judges who hold those views and don't grant relief from stay very liberally or very often and certainly not early, strongly believe that that's the job they are supposed to be doing, per Congressional direction. And this will give clear Congressional direction that that's not what they are supposed to be doing. They are supposed to move these cases up and out. And I think it would change practice for some judges. It would not change the practice in my courtroom particularly, because I take a similar approach already and a number of my colleagues do, but not all of them.

JUDGE MARK: I suspect it would slow us down.

PROF. GROSS: You are on a faster track than the legislation?[87]

---

87. **While the 1994 Amendments appear to speed up single asset real estate cases (plan or pay within 90 days), one could envision a situation in which secured creditors could be hurt, and the process could *slow* down (even though there is no evidence to support such a hypothesis at this juncture). For example, a secured creditor might be required to wait 90 days before seeking to get the stay lifted. Moreover, determinations of value of the collateral may need to be made earlier, and that could be to a secured creditor's disadvantage. *See* Heidt, *supra* note 22, at 417-18; Bird et al., *supra* note 16, at 415.**

JUDGE MARK: I suspect so.

PROF. GROSS: Judge Greendyke.

JUDGE GREENDYKE: I don't think there is any need for legislation. Without getting into other subjects, I think there are a lot of other things that need fixing besides this. I think the case law on good faith works fine and we in Texas have worked with it. Massachusetts clearly has. California has known a long time how to do it.

You are never going to iron out the differences between judges and how they practice the art of judging bankruptcy law. I just think there are other things that Congress needs to spend its time doing besides worrying about bankruptcy cases.

PROF. GROSS: One thing that this legislation *would* do is that it would mean that it is not, per se, bad faith to file a single asset chapter 11 real estate case.[88]

JUDGE HILLMAN: It doesn't say that at all.

PROF. GROSS: You don't think so?

JUDGE HILLMAN: No.

PROF. GROSS: You think you could still raise the bad faith, good faith debate if this proposed legislation were in place?

JUDGE HILLMAN: Certainly.

JUDGE FENNING: It's clear from the legislative history currently that it's not per se bad faith to file a single asset real estate case.[89] There's discussion about contemplation of single asset real estate filings. It's not a per

---

88. ***See supra* note 10.**

89. S. REP. NO. 598, 95th Cong., 2d Sess. 5 (1978), *reprinted in* 1978 U.S.C.C.A.N. 5787, 5838-39; *see also* Carlisle, *supra* note 46 at 136-39 (explaining that filing single asset bankruptcy is not per se bad faith).

se situation. You have to have a whole list of different kinds of factors even now.

JUDGE GREENDYKE: I agree, you would have to question the ability of many portions of section 365[90] if we were to get rid of single asset real estate cases.

JUDGE FENNING: I don't think it would be a good idea to get rid of single asset cases. They are a good check on the system in many states that allow creditors to just jump the gun on foreclosures where it's really not warranted. I would not favor an elimination of single asset cases. It would help, however, if there were clear standards about what constitutes confirmability for a plan. Then debtors would not have to play Russian Roulette on assignment of judges. Currently, the luck of the draw on judges can determine case outcome: some judges would let the debtor confirm this plan, but the next judge down the hall wouldn't. I think that clear standards for confirmability would simplify the single asset problem enormously and reduce the litigation.

JUDGE HILLMAN: You are right into the cram down classification issues[91] where there is such diversity between judges. In my district people deliberately file in the Western Division because they like Judge Queenan, as opposed to the Boston judges, who have different views of classification.

JUDGE GREENDYKE: That's what circuit courts are for.

JUDGE FENNING: But the circuit courts aren't getting the cases. Because of the appellate structure in bankruptcy, the appeals are not getting as far as the circuit courts. District court and bankruptcy appellate panel decisions are not controlling precedent in most districts and therefore you don't have clear controlling precedent telling us what to do.

---

90. 11 U.S.C. § 365 authorizes the trustee, subject to court approval and certain limitations (*i.e.*, bad faith) to assume or reject an executory contract or unexpired lease. 11 U.S.C. § 365(a) (1994).

91. 11 U.S.C. § 1129 allows a creditor to confirm or "cram down" a plan over the dissent of secured creditors if the plan does not discriminate unfairly and is fair and equitable. 11 U.S.C. § 1129(b)(1) (1994).

Now, if the Supreme Court had agreed to decide *Bryson*[92] or *Greystone*,[93] a clear ruling would have simplified this whole issue enormously.[94] If the parties knew what ball park they were playing in, knew that, yes, these plans are confirmable under these circumstances, or, no, they are never confirmable where there is no equity, then it would simplify single asset filings, and eliminate a lot of them. The parties would work it out before coming to court because they would know what would happen to them with a reasonable degree of predictability without filing bankruptcy.

H. Forum Shopping In Good Faith Cases

PROF. GROSS: Do you think there is forum shopping as to the good faith issues? Are people choosing where to file, to the extent they can on what a court's reaction will be to their filing?

JUDGE FENNING: Oh, yes. The variance among the judges is so considerable that to the extent debtors can choose, they are choosing.

JUDGE GREENDYKE: I think they will forum shop for anything — for attorney's fees, for docket loads.

JUDGE FENNING: Extensions of exclusivity.

JUDGE GREENDYKE: I think that's true.

---

92. Banner Oil Co. v. Bryson (*In re* Bryson), 187 B.R. 939, 960 (Bankr. N.D. Ill. 1995) (holding debtor's issuance of insufficient funds checks not false pretenses under § 523(a)(2)(A), without positive statement regarding sufficiency of account).

93. *In re* Greystone III Joint Venture, 102 B.R. 560, 574-75 (Bankr. W.D. Tex. 1989), *aff'd*, 127 B.R. 138 (W.D. Tex. 1990), *rev'd*, 995 F.2d 1274 (5th Cir. 1991), *vacated in part*, 995 F.2d 1284 (5th Cir.), *cert. denied*, 506 U.S. 821 (1992).

94. **Of course, the Supreme Court has since granted certiorari to decide a related issue in Bonner Mall Partnership v. U.S. Bancorp Mortgage Co. (*In re* Bonner Mall Partnership), 2 F.3d 899 (9th Cir. 1993), *cert. granted*, 114 S. Ct. 681, *and cert. dismissed as moot*, 115 S. Ct. 386 (1994). Because the case was settled and withdrawn, the substantive issue was not addressed by the Supreme Court.**

JUDGE HILLMAN: Well, the flexibility exists. People look and see what the odds are.

PROF. GROSS: There is a recent article by two law professors, Lawrence Ponoroff and Stephen Knippenberg,[95] who suggested that this good faith debate is really quite misguided and that what we are really talking about is a discussion of how we feel or how we believe that bankruptcy law should function.[96] What Professors Knippenberg and Ponoroff are really saying is that this whole discussion is really a debate about bankruptcy policy, not good faith. I'd like your view as to whether or not what we are really talking about is what is the role and function of bankruptcy law or the role and function of a chapter 11.[97] Alternatively, are we talking about a much narrower issue — good faith?

JUDGE MARK: I think there's policy issues here. The *Phoenix Piccadilly*[98] case I have talked about in the Eleventh Circuit is applied more readily by some judges than others to knock out single asset cases. When applied in the extreme, I think it does get into almost a policy decision by judges that chapter 11 shouldn't be used by equity when it's just equity against a secured creditor. But I think other than when applied in the extreme, I still believe most of us that deal with these single asset cases and put them on a short fuse or require a quick showing that there is a reorganization that's feasible are consistent with what I believe to be the policy of allowing single asset cases to be filed and giving them a chance to reorganize. Again, it's just a matter of timing.

---

95. Ponoroff & Knippenberg, *supra* note 3.

96. *Id.* at 973-74.

97. **Although not phrased as such, the 1994 Amendments on single asset cases do affect exclusivity. Section 1121 is not explicitly amended but the debtor's 120 day exclusive period is narrowed. Stated differently, if no plan is filed within 90 days, the debtor must pay for exclusivity between day 90 and day 120 by allowing for the lifting of the automatic safety after 90 days. *See* Gross & Redmond, *supra* note 10, at 303-04.**

98. Phoenix Piccadilly, Ltd. v. Life Ins. Co. (*In re* Phoenix Piccadilly, Ltd.), 849 F.2d 1393, 1394 (11th Cir. 1988) (affirming dismissal of debtor's single asset filing for bad faith).

I. Sanctions for Good Faith

PROF. GROSS: If there is a finding of bad faith, do you think that sanctions are warranted and if so, what should the range of those sanctions be and against whom should they be brought?

JUDGE HILLMAN: It depends upon the circumstances. There is no hard and fast rule. I have denied sanctions in cases where there was a possible basis for the filing, even though I didn't accept it.

JUDGE GREENDYKE: I think that sanctions are clearly warranted upon a finding of bad faith. The most obvious and appropriate sanction is dismissal of the case. Beyond that, and recognizing that bankruptcy judges arguably do not have the jurisdiction to impose criminal contempt or punitive sanctions, compensatory sanctions in the form of costs and attorneys fees are frequently warranted and granted. The debtor is most often the one against whom the sanctions should be awarded, however, in appropriate circumstances and given the right amount of culpability and/or knowledge, debtor's counsel can and should be held liable for sanctions.

JUDGE FENNING: A finding of "bad faith" would require, in my view, compelling evidence of "subjective" bad faith. Merely filing a chapter 11 to delay a foreclosure is not bad faith. If the debtor happens to get a sympathetic judge, a confirmed plan may result. Another judge might grant immediate relief from stay or dismiss the case. The uncertainty of the legal standards and the wide variation among judges preclude sanctions in the typical case under "objective" Rule 9011 standards.[99]

"Subjective" bad faith may, of course, exist in single asset real estate cases, just as in any other type. The filing of the chapter 11 case may be part

---

99. FED. R. BANKR. P. 9011 (imposing sanctions for bad faith filing). A 1963 amendment to the rule removed the requirement that subjective bad faith be proven. Thus an "honest mistake" was no longer a defense and courts have been more willing to impose sanctions. *See* Scott J. Hyman, *Sanctions in Bankruptcy Court: The Bite of Rule 9011*, 3 LEGAL MALPRACTICE REP. 9 (1992). The Rule was further amended in 1991 to apply to the "unnecessary delay or needless increase in the cost of the administration of the case." FED. R. BANKR. P. 9011.

of an active scheme to defraud creditors. If proven, such factors justify Rule 9011 sanctions. Whether both the debtor and the attorneys should be sanctioned depends upon the circumstances.

After seven years on the bench, I have concluded that litigating a "bad faith" filing claim and imposing sanctions is unproductive. Shortly after I came on the bench, I did fully litigate such a case, entering an order of dismissal on grounds of bad faith and imposing sanctions on both party and counsel because of their outrageous conduct.[100] The amount of sanctions was based upon the attorney fees generated, the ability of the sanctioned attorney to pay, and the need to deter similar conduct in the future. Unfortunately, the cost of that litigation was high. If faced with a similar case today, I would probably just lift the stay for cause at the first hearing, sending the parties back to state court without imposing sanctions or litigating the "bad faith" issue. The chapter 11 filing in such cases is usually just a side-show, and should be simply and economically resolved.

J. Enforceability of Prepetition "Bad Faith" Agreements

PROF. GROSS: There is one more question I would like to ask, namely, has there been some pragmatic change in how lawyers are functioning to address good faith problems? Let me present a hypothetical. Suppose a debtor and a creditor agree in a workout context that should any chapter 11 ultimately occur, it will be deemed to be bad faith. Then, they write that into their out-of-court workout agreement. Suppose then that for any number of reasons, the out-of-court workout agreement either is not consummated or if it is consummated there is a default under it. Do you think those kinds of provisions are enforceable when the single asset chapter 11 case is ultimately filed?

A variation on the theme is that suppose that the debtor and creditor in this context agree that if a chapter 11 case is ultimately filed, the stay can automatically be lifted with no need for a hearing and the lender can just proceed ahead to foreclosure. Is that kind of lawyering now appropriate? Are these types of provisions enforceable?

---

100. *In re* Eighty S. Lake, Inc., 63 B.R. 501, 502-03 (Bankr. C.D. Cal. 1986), *aff'd*, 81 B.R. 580 (Bankr. 9th Cir. 1987).

JUDGE FENNING: I don't think it's enforceable. You are dealing with a different entity once the filing has occurred. Different parties who were not represented at the table at the time that deal was struck, namely other creditors of the estate, have an interest to be protected. Such an agreement is certainly admissible as evidence of the intent of the parties on the issue of whether the filing is in bad faith, but it would be one of several factors to be considered.

And I think it's entirely appropriate to draft agreements with recitals about the intent of the parties and all of that kind of thing as evidence that can later be used, but it's not binding on the court. Such recitals may be awfully persuasive, but they are not binding.

PROF. GROSS: But in a single asset case, where there are very few other creditors, can't you just sort of say, there aren't that many of them to be protected anyway. There may even be none.

JUDGE GREENDYKE: That may be the call. I agree with Judge Fenning, I think it's good lawyering, but I think once the case is filed, it's sort of a public case and it becomes her call or my call as to what's going to happen to it, and I want to look at it and I want to know. The agreement may be a factor in deciding whether or not it's a bad faith filing, but it won't be a per se bad faith filing just because of the existence of this agreement.

JUDGE HILLMAN: I want to look at what the new debtor obtained in exchange for that promise. If there was some sort of reworking of the deal that was very much in the debtor's favor and they had the benefit of that for sometime and they just couldn't go any longer and they now filed, I think I would be inclined to say, you bargained away any rights you otherwise have in 11.

JUDGE MARK: I think there's a danger in saying that you would enforce that kind of stipulation because it will immediately whet the appetite of lenders and lenders' counsel to draft it in and it is already happening in Florida as a result of a couple of decisions that really were typical bad faith dismissals, but also mentioned in passing that there were prepetition stipulations and implied, if not directly stating, that they were enforcing those.

One was the *Citadel Properties*[101] case by Judge Proctor. Another was *In Re Aurora Investments*,[102] which was Judge Paskay. The Paskay decision noting that there was a stipulation that a bankruptcy filing would be deemed to be bad faith and the *Citadel Properties* enforcing, which I think was almost dictum, prepetition agreement for stay relief.

I don't think we can anticipate any expansion of that concept, if that concept is even really implicit in these cases, but I agree with Judge Hillman and with Judge Fenning, that you look at that as another indication of the prepetition misconduct or prepetition conduct. And I have found a case where the debtor or borrower obtained a six-month extension on the eve of a judgment in the state court promising that it will sell off enough property in the development to pay you by December. If not, it will stipulate to judgment in sale.

They didn't. They filed chapter 11. Motion to dismiss on bad faith. What is your plan? Well, now we are going to sell it off over the next four years. I say forget it. You made a deal in state court. You bought six more months. In this instance, you don't get another chance in bankruptcy to change the deal. So I think it does get into what happened prepetition, what consideration was given for these promises, more so than just a stipulation itself.

K. Good Faith 10 Years Ahead

PROF. GROSS: As a way of concluding this Discussion,[103] let me ask the following: if you were all clairvoyant, where would you see the issue of single asset chapter 11 real estate cases and the questions of good faith in that context ten years from now?

JUDGE HILLMAN: If we are lucky, Massachusetts will be over its depression by then.

---

101. *In re* Citadel Properties, Inc., 86 B.R. 275, 276 (Bankr. M.D. Fla. 1988).

102. 144 B.R. 899, 900 (Bankr. M.D. Fla. 1992).

103. **One party has argued that the 1994 Amendments implicitly permit separate classification of a secured creditor's claim. While classification is a pertinent issue, one court has found the amendments nondispositive. *See In re* Gato Realty Trust Corp., 183 B.R. 15, 18 (Bankr. D. Mass. 1995).**

JUDGE GREENDYKE: We'll be paying attention to something else like individual chapter 11 cases or the chapter 13 problems we talked about earlier involving apartments. I think we are going to work through it all. I think once Massachusetts gets rid of all their real estate cases and a couple of second timers around, it will pretty much be done — that has been our experience in Houston.

JUDGE FENNING: I guess I am with Judge Hillman, I am hoping that California is out of its real estate depression by the end of the decade. I believe that norms will develop, just as they have around the "new debtor syndrome" pattern where experienced bankruptcy lawyers have a client come to them and say I want to file this case in the Central District of California. The lawyers respond, "Look at *Victory Construction*.[104] I won't file the case for you. It doesn't make sense. Let's do something else to deal with your problem."

It would help a lot if the Supreme Court will resolve some of the major substantive legal issues surrounding these cases, like the new value exception and the classification issues.[105] If those are resolved, these cases will sort themselves out in the wash and they won't occupy the kind of time on our calendars anymore. A turn in the real estate market will solve 90 percent of it, of course.

JUDGE MARK: With the RTC and FDIC, after fighting like crazy to get stay relief and foreclose in bankruptcy, selling properties for 20 cents on the dollar, there are such bargain prices now being paid by the new owners that they probably won't wind up in chapter 11. So I am–

PROF. GROSS: You are optimistic.

JUDGE MARK: I hope that doesn't cause me to be audited again.

---

104. *In re* Victory Constr. Co., 9 B.R. 549, 565 (Bankr. C.D. Cal. 1981) (granting creditors relief from automatic stay for bad faith), *vacated as moot*, 37 B.R. 222 (Bankr. 9th Cir. 1984) (finding subsequent payments by debtor to creditor, along with other creditors, rendered original issue moot).

105. **The National Bankruptcy Review Commission may also consider statutory revisions to address these issues.**

PROF. GROSS: On behalf of the American Bankruptcy Institute, I want to thank you all. Let me also say that, as an academic, where most scholarship is done in law review articles and those types of articles are viewed as the *sine qua non* of how to address legal issues, I think this type of format works remarkably well. Perhaps it is even better. So, in addition to addressing good faith, maybe we have begun a trend and have come up with a new format for how to think about legal issues.[106]

---

106. **Since the inaugural thematic issue of the *ABI Law Review*, the thematic approach and the use of a Roundtable Discussion have continued. Indeed, this issue and subsequent issues have been cited with some frequency. Michael D. Bruckman, Note, *The Thickening Fog of "Substantial Abuse": Can 707(a) Help Clear The Air?*, 2 AM. BANKR. INST. L. REV. 193, 201 (1994) (discussing references to "bad faith" in Bankruptcy Code); David G. Carlson, *Symposium on Bankruptcy: Rents In Bankruptcy*, 46 S.C. L. REV. 1075, 1076 (1995) (discussing single asset real estate bankruptcies). While I hesitate to jinx things, it does seem as if the ABI approach has been and will continue to be successful.**

CHAPTER III

WORKOUT BREAKTHROUGH? PREPETITION AGREEMENTS MAY LEAD TO DISMISSAL OR RELIEF FROM STAY

JOHN P. MCNICHOLAS

The recurring workout nightmare: Borrower is in default. Lender negotiates in good faith with borrower to restructure the debt with a view to preventing foreclosure. The resultant workout agreement provides for forbearance-reduction in payments of principal or interest or both-and a host of other debt accommodations, perhaps including additional cash infusions by the lender. Borrower continues to manage the property drawing management and leasing fees directly or through affiliated organizations. Six months later when the workout fails, lender commences foreclosure. On the eve of foreclosure sale, borrower files in bankruptcy, stays the sale and continues to manage the property as debtor-in-possession.

Recent developments indicate that bankruptcy courts are becoming concerned about these tactics and may be willing to consider and enforce protective language in the workout agreement under which the borrower admits and agrees that a subsequent filing of the bankruptcy petition would be for the sole purpose of delay and would constitute a bad faith filing, requiring dismissal of the petition or relief from the automatic stay. This Chapter discusses these recent developments and suggests a workout agreement clause that may be helpful in protecting the interests of the lender.

Although not specifically required by the Bankruptcy Code[1] (the "Code"), courts have firmly established that a debtor must file a petition for bankruptcy in "good faith."[2] Lurking behind a court's imposition of the implied good faith

1. 11 U.S.C. §§ 101-1330 (1994).
2. *In re* Aurora Invs., Inc. 134 B.R. 982, 985 (Bankr. M.D. Fla. 1991). "[I]t is now established beyond peradventure that the court may dismiss a [c]hapter 11 case for cause if the court finds that the [p]etition was filed in 'bad faith.'" *Id.*

requirement is the increasing number of filings, ever expanding court dockets

---

(citations omitted). Section 1112(b) of the Code permits dismissal of a case for "cause" and sets forth a list of circumstances warranting dismissal, which fails to mention lack of good faith. 11 U.S.C. § 1112(b) (1994). The legislative history, however, states that the list is "not exhaustive." H.R. REP. NO. 595, 95th Cong., 1st Sess. 405-06 (1977), *reprinted in* 1978 U.S.C.C.A.N. 5963, 6361-62; S. REP. NO. 989, 95th Cong., 2d Sess. 117 (1978), *reprinted in* 1978 U.S.C.C.A.N. 5787, 5903.

A judicially created precept, lack of good faith on the part of the debtor constitutes "cause" for dismissal under § 1112(b). *See* Elmwood Dev. Co. v. General Elec. Pension Trust (*In re* Elmwood Dev. Co.), 964 F.2d 508, 510 (5th Cir. 1992); Humble Place Joint Venture v. Fory (*In re* Humble Place Joint Venture), 936 F.2d 814, 816-17 (5th Cir. 1991); Baker v. Latham Sparrowbush Assocs. (*In re* Cohoes Indus. Terminal), 931 F.2d 222, 228 (2d Cir. 1991); First Nat'l Bank v. Kerr (*In re* Kerr), 908 F.2d 400, 404 (8th Cir. 1990); Carolin Corp. v. Miller, 886 F.2d 693, 698-99 (4th Cir. 1989); 9281 Shore Rd. Owners Corp. v. Seminole Realty Co. (*In re* 9281 Shore Rd. Owners Corp.), 187 B.R. 837, 848 (E.D.N.Y. 1995); *In re* Franklin Mortgage & Inv. Co., 143 B.R. 295, 298-99, 302-03 (Bankr. D.D.C. 1992); *In re* Edwards, 140 B.R. 515, 517 (Bankr. W.D. Mo. 1992); *In re* Coones Ranch, Inc., 138 B.R. 251, 258 (Bankr. D.S.D. 1991); *In re* Reiser Ford, Inc., 128 B.R. 234, 237-38 (Bankr. E.D. Mo. 1991); *In re* I-95 Technology-Indus. Park, L.P., 126 B.R. 11, 13 (Bankr. D.R.I. 1991).

The implied good faith filing requirement also has been read into § 362(d)(1) of the Bankruptcy Code which enables creditors to obtain relief from the automatic stay "for cause." 11 U.S.C. § 362(d)(1) (1994); *see* Lawrence Ponoroff & F. Stephen Knippenberg, *The Implied Good Faith Filing Requirement: Sentinel of an Evolving Bankruptcy Policy*, 85 NW. U. L. REV. 919, 924-25 n.15 (1991). Courts similarly have implied a good faith filing requirement into chapters 7, 12 and 13 of the Code. For chapter 7 cases, see Industrial Ins. Servs., Inc. v. Zick (*In re* Zick), 931 F.2d 1124, 1126-27 (6th Cir. 1991); Cassady-Pierce Co. v. Burns (*In re* Burns), 169 B.R. 563, 567 (Bankr. W.D. Pa. 1994); *see generally* John A. Majors, In re Zick*: Chapter 7's Good Faith Threshold Standard*, 23 U. TOL. L. REV. 583 (1992) (discussing evolution of implied good faith requirement in chapter 7 cases). For chapter 12 cases, *see* Schuldies v. United States (*In re* Schuldies), 122 B.R. 100, 102 (D.S.D. 1990); *In re* Bird, 80 B.R. 861, 863-64 (Bankr. W.D. Mich. 1987). For chapter 13 cases, see *In re* Love, 957 F.2d 1350, 1354 (7th Cir. 1992); *In re* Jones, 174 B.R. 8, 12 (Bankr. D.N.H. 1994); *In re* Earl, 140 B.R. 728, 733-34 (Bankr. N.D. Ind. 1992); *In re* Powers, 135 B.R. 980, 990-91 (Bankr. C.D.

and the general overburdening of bankruptcy judges.[3] One author states that "[s]ince the strategic use of bankruptcy is on the rise, courts are increasingly required to police filings in an attempt to identify those cases that are more appropriately settled in a nonbankruptcy forum."[4] This requirement is frequently applied in petitions filed by single asset debtors due to the courts' underlying efforts to isolate "new debtor syndrome"[5] cases from those that

---

Cal. 1991); *In re* King, 126 B.R. 777, 781 (Bankr. N.D. Ill. 1991); *In re* Roberts, 117 B.R. 677, 678 (Bankr. N.D. Okla. 1990); *In re* Gaudet, 95 B.R. 4, 5 (Bankr. D.R.I. 1989).

In addition to the straightforward statutory construction of §§ 1112(b) and 362(d), courts have offered other justifications for imposing a good faith filing requirement, *viz.*, the presence of FED. R. BANKR. P. 9011 and 11 U.S.C. § 105(a) (1994). *See* Ponoroff & Knippenberg, *supra*, at 924-25 nn.16-17.

3. *See* Ed Flynn, *Bankruptcy by the Numbers*, AM. BANKR. INST. J., Apr. 1992, at 25. "The per judge caseload in the bankruptcy courts continues to soar. . . . Total case filings increased by 185% between 1980 and 1991, but the number of bankruptcy judges increased by only 25% during the same time. The per judge annual caseload increased from 1,427 in 1980 to 3,244 in 1991 (based on 232 judges in 1980 and 291 judges in 1991)." *Id.*

4. Brian S. Katz, *Single-Asset Real Estate Cases and the Good Faith Requirement: Why Reluctance to Ask Whether a Case Belongs in Bankruptcy May Lead to the Incorrect Result*, 9 BANKR. DEV. J. 77, 77 (1992); *see also* Ponoroff & Knippenberg, *supra* note 2, at 919-22 nn.2-10 (describing rise in bankruptcy litigation as indicative of innovative, tactical use of Bankruptcy Code and subsequent judicial response of imposing implied good faith filing requirement on debtors seeking relief).

5. *See* Little Creek Dev. Co. v. Commonwealth Mortgage Corp. (*In re* Little Creek Dev. Co.), 779 F.2d 1068, 1073 (5th Cir. 1986). The "new debtor syndrome" is, by definition, a phenomenon unique to single asset debtors and is characterized by the formation of a one-asset entity (corporate shell) that "has been created or revitalized on the eve of foreclosure to isolate the insolvent property and its creditors." *Id.* Courts are likely to dismiss cases falling into the "new debtor syndrome" for bad faith. *See* Trident Assocs. Ltd. Partnership v. Metropolitan Life Ins. Co. (*In re* Trident Assocs. Ltd. Partnership), 52 F.3d 127, 132 (6th Cir.), *cert. denied*, 116 S. Ct. 188 (1995); *In re* Edwards, 140 B.R. 515, 518-19 (Bankr. W.D. Mo. 1992) ("It appears that this debtor engaged in a form of the 'new debtor syndrome' which is indicative of a bad faith filing."); Ponoroff & Knippenberg, *supra* note 2, at 927-29 nn.29-33. There is even an indication that courts are likely to apply a separate analysis for

truly deserve the protection of chapter 11 of the Bankruptcy Code.[6] The often

---

debtors fitting within the "new debtor syndrome," –a less exacting standard than the hybrid analysis prevalent in most courts. *See Franklin Mortgage*, 143 B.R. at 302. In *Franklin*, the court first determined that the "case ha[d] all the earmarkings of the 'new debtor syndrome'." *Id.* at 300. In framing its analysis of good faith, the court stated:

> Where a "new debtor syndrome" and resultant unfair delay of creditors is present, it makes no sense to require objective futility. The court must be able to protect its jurisdictional integrity. In contrast, other single asset cases not involving the "new debtor syndrome" usually present the question whether the case is futile and hence filed in bad faith. It makes sense to require objective futility before dismissing those cases. That is not what is at stake in a "new debtor" case. In the "new debtor" case the critical inquiry is whether the debtor has gained unfair advantage by employment of the new debtor device. Once bad faith has been established in a new debtor case, based on a finding of unfair delay, the existence of equity in the property and the prospects of a successful reorganization are irrelevant and cannot transform the bad faith filing into one taken in good faith. To hold otherwise would allow the processes of the court to be used as part of an intentional scheme of delay: a court of equity can condition the use of its processes on conduct comporting with the public interest.

Id. at 302 (citations omitted) (footnote omitted).

6. *See* Ponoroff & Knippenberg, *supra* note 2, at 975. Single asset debtor cases are likely to be earmarked by the court as "suspect" due to an "apparent factual remoteness from the prototypical bankruptcy case." *Id.*; *see also* Katz, *supra* note 4, at 78.

> The single-asset debtor is normally structured in the form of a corporation or limited partnership, and usually holds a fully mortgaged piece of real estate as its only asset. With few or no employees and little or no cash flow, the single-asset real estate debtor typically falls behind in debt payments, and the secured creditor initiates foreclosure proceedings. In response, the debtor files a chapter 11 petition, obtaining the benefit of the automatic stay.

Id. (footnotes omitted).

Filing a single asset case under chapter 11, however, is not, per se, in bad faith. *See In re* Colonial Daytona Ltd. Partnership, 144 B.R. 924, 926 (Bankr. M.D. Fla. 1992), *aff'd*, 152 B.R. 996 (M.D. Fla. 1993). "While *Little Creek* is

cited bad faith indicia set forth by *Little Creek Development Co. v.*

---

still well-recognized as persuasive authority, it is equally true that there is nothing inherently improper for a debtor with one single asset, generally an income-producing commercial property to attempt to reorganize its affairs under the rehabilitative provisions of the Bankruptcy Code." *Id.*

A court may raise the threshold issue of bad faith in filing sua sponte. 11 U.S.C. § 105(a) (1994). The statute states:

> The court may issue any order, process, or judgment that is necessary or appropriate to carry out the provisions of this title. No provision of this title providing for the raising of an issue by a party in interest shall be construed to preclude the court from, sua sponte, taking any action or making any determination necessary or appropriate to enforce or implement court orders or rules, or to prevent an abuse of process.

Id. Likewise, the legislative history of § 1112(b) suggests that the court has wide discretion to, on its own, raise the issue of whether a petition has been filed in good faith. S. REP. NO. 989, *supra* note 2, at 117, *reprinted in* 1978 U.S.C.C.A.N. at 5903. Nevertheless, it is cautioned that the court exercise this discretion "sparingly." *Id. Cf.* Colloquy, *Good Faith: Roundtable Discussion*, 1 AM. BANKR. INST. L. REV. 11, 16 (1993) [hereinafter *Roundtable Discussion*] (suggesting that among Eleventh Circuit bankruptcy courts it is unlikely a judge will have to raise good faith issues sua sponte because creditor's attorney will move to dismiss if factors typical of bad faith are present). Judge Mark commented, perhaps tongue in cheek, "[t]here is no need for it. You would virtually be committing malpractice as a creditor attorney in the [Eleventh] Circuit if you did not raise the bad faith issue early on in a [c]hapter 11, if it met the criteria that have led to dismissals in the [Eleventh] Circuit." *Id.*

For an example of a court raising the issue of good faith sua sponte, albeit in the context of § 1129(a)(3), see *In re* Anderson Oaks, Ltd. Partnership, 77 B.R. 108, 111 (Bankr. W.D. Tex. 1987) (Clark, J.).

> Thus, though this Court might normally be reluctant to 'pull the plug' so early in a case, where the determinative facts which would shape a plan are not going to change, the greater injustice is to allow the case to remain on the docket, serving no purpose but to temporarily shelter the Debtors from the inevitable.

Id.

For an interesting discussion of the appropriateness of single asset debtors enjoying chapter 11 protection (absent bad faith), see Chief Judge Paskay's discussion in *In re* North Redington Beach Assocs., 91 B.R. 166, 168-69 (Bankr. M.D. Fla. 1988).

Commonwealth Mortgage Corp. (In re Little Creek Development Co.),

---

7. 779 F.2d 1068 (5th Cir. 1986). *Little Creek* involved an entity with a single asset (two undeveloped tracts of raw real estate) that had no employees, no income, no cash flow, no plan contemplated for the infusion of capital, nor any reasonable prospects for the conduct of future business. *Id.* at 1070, 1074. The bankruptcy court granted the creditor relief from the stay *solely* on the ground of an admission of debtor's counsel that the petition was filed to avoid posting a bond in a pending state court proceeding. *Id.* at 1070-71. On appeal, Judge Jones reversed and remanded the bankruptcy court's decision indicating that findings of bad faith should be made based on a "conglomerate of factors rather than on any single datum." *Id.* at 1072. The court must make an "on-the-spot evaluation of the debtor's financial condition, motives, and the local financial realities." *Id.* The court considered various indicia of bad faith that were categorized numerically in subsequent decisions:

   (i) the debtor has only one asset;

   (ii) the debtor has few unsecured creditors whose claims are small in relation to those of the secured creditors;

   (iii) the debtor's one asset is the subject of a foreclosure action as a result of arrearage or default on the debt;

   (iv) the debtor's financial condition is, in essence, a two party dispute between the debtor and secured creditors which can be resolved in the pending state foreclosure action;

   (v) the timing of the debtor's filing evidences an intent to delay or frustrate the legitimate efforts of the debtor's secured creditors to enforce their rights;

   (vi) the debtor has little or no cash flow;

   (vii) the debtor can't meet current expenses including the payment of personal property and real estate taxes; and

   (viii) the debtor has few, if any employees.

   Id. at 1073; *see also* Phoenix Piccadilly, Ltd. v. Life Ins. Co. (*In re* Phoenix Piccadilly, Ltd.), 849 F.2d 1393, 1394-95 (11th Cir. 1988).

   Little Creek and its progeny, including *In re* Winshall Settlor's Trust, 758 F.2d 1136 (6th Cir. 1985), either implicitly or explicitly (depending on the particular facts of the given case) held that an ongoing business was a requirement for chapter 11 debtors. *Little Creek*, 779 F.2d at 1073; *Winshall Settlor's*, 758 F.2d at 1137. Nevertheless, the Supreme Court recently decided there is no such requirement. Toibb v. Radloff, 501 U.S. 157, 161 (1991). The Court remained silent, however, regarding other good faith considerations and simply stated that an ongoing business is not a necessity. *Id.* The Court's decision not only relies on the plain meaning of 11 U.S.C. § 109 (1994), but along with further refinements established in *Carolin Corp. v. Miller*[8] and *Phoenix Piccadilly, Ltd. v. Life Insurance Co. of Virginia (In re Phoenix Piccadilly, Ltd)*,[9] attempt to provide a framework for determining whether a petition has been filed in good faith. Even with such helpful decisions and a substantial body of accompanying case law,[10] the *precise* standards by which courts arrive at their decisions defy definitive explication because of the intuitionistic, "on the spot" nature of the inquiry.[11]

---

also indicates the Court's desire to provide a forum for those debtors who do not meet the requisite criteria for relief under chapter 13 and yet are entitled to bankruptcy relief. *Toibb*, 501 U.S. at 162.

8. 886 F.2d 693 (4th Cir. 1989). *Carolin* followed a two pronged test to analyze the debtor's good faith in filing a chapter 11 petition: inquiring into both the debtor's subjective bad faith and the objective futility of the debtor's possible reorganization. *Id.* at 700-01. A stringent test for threshold dismissals of chapter 11 filings "contemplates that it is better to risk proceeding with a wrongly motivated invocation of [c]hapter 11 protections whose futility is not immediately manifest than to risk cutting off even a remote chance that a reorganization effort so motivated might nevertheless yield a successful rehabilitation." *Id.* at 701.

9. 849 F.2d 1393 (11th Cir. 1988). In *Phoenix*, the court held that even if there exists the possibility of successful reorganization, a single asset debtor's chapter 11 petition may be dismissed for bad faith in filing. *Id.* at 1394. In response to the debtor's petition filed to delay the exercise of creditor's legitimate rights, the court stated, "[t]he possibility of a successful reorganization cannot transform a bad faith filing into one undertaken in good faith." *Id.* at 1395.

10. *See* Ponoroff & Knippenberg, *supra* note 2, at 929 n.33; *see also* cases cited *supra* note 2 (implying requirement of good faith for filing of bankruptcy petition).

11. *See Little Creek*, 779 F.2d at 1072. "Determining whether the debtor's filing for relief is in good faith depends largely upon the bankruptcy court's on-the-spot evaluation of the debtor's financial condition, motives, and the local financial realities." *Id.*; Ponoroff & Knippenberg, *supra* note 2, at 944. "[I]n spite of the widespread acceptance of a good faith filing prerequisite, the standards by which good faith is to be judged remain ill defined and obscure." *Id.*; *In re* Franklin Mortgage & Inv. Co., 143 B.R. 295, 302 (Bankr. D.D.C. 1992).

There is a split of authority over whether in deciding motions to dismiss for bad faith the courts should apply a subjective motive

This Chapter declines the invitation to recast the continuing evolution of the implied good faith requirement into an archetypal framework.[12] Instead, it evaluates the potential impact of prepetition workout agreements that stipulate that a debtor is acting in "bad faith" or that the debtor waives its right to protection from the automatic stay when it files a chapter 11 petition subsequent to the agreement. Part A introduces the mechanics of such prepetition stipulations as well as cases in which they were found to be enforceable. Part B notes the policy implications of enforcing these agreements. Part C points out tactical considerations of both the debtor in attacking the validity of such stipulations, and the creditor in defending these agreements so as to enforce the prepetition workout. Additionally, a model prepetition agreement is set forth. The discussion concludes by observing that, although providing little solace to single asset debtors already blemished by the indicia of bad faith in filing, the inclusion of these types of prepetition stipulations can only help creditors wishing to avoid the time and expense involved in litigating their claims in bankruptcy court, their inclusion will additionally help lighten the already unbearable caseload of bankruptcy judges.

> analysis, an objective feasibility analysis, or a hybrid analysis. Some decisions require that both objective futility and subjective bad faith be present. Other courts hold that dismissal may be justified when either futility or bad faith is evident.

Id. (citations omitted). See also Professor Gross' introductory remarks in *Roundtable Discussion*, ***supra*** note 6, at 13. Professor Gross states, "there is little consensus among circuits or even districts as to what constitutes good faith and how it should be applied." *Id.*

12. The author respectfully defers to the exhaustive study on the subject prepared by Professors Ponoroff and Knippenberg, ***supra*** note 2, and the authorities set forth therein. *Id.* at 923 n.11. A review of the literature reveals the genuine difficulty in attaining a true paradigm–a reality occasioned by decisions that apparently are not limited to determinations of good faith. Courts seem to be grappling simultaneously with the challenging task of shaping bankruptcy policy, while determining who does and does not qualify for relief under chapter 11 of the Bankruptcy Code. ***See generally id.*** at 923 (illuminating evolution of good faith requirement in filing bankruptcy petition).

A. Prepetition Stipulations

Prepetition clauses classifying a debtor's conduct to be in bad faith in the event of a subsequent filing have been held "enforceable" in the bankruptcy courts of at least one circuit, the Eleventh.[13] The courts in the Eleventh Circuit also have enforced prepetition stipulations entitling creditors to stay relief should the debtor subsequently file for bankruptcy.[14] As for the other circuits,

---

13. *See In re* Aurora Invs., Inc., 134 B.R. 982, 986 (Bankr. M.D. Fla. 1991) (holding debtor filed in bad faith when debtor stipulated in advance that if bankruptcy petition was filed primarily for purpose of delaying foreclosure sale, petition was filed in bad faith); *In re* Orange Park S. Partnership, 79 B.R. 79, 82-83 (Bankr. M.D. Fla. 1987) (dismissing "new debtor syndrome" petition and refusing to allow debtor to escape "binding effect of the [prepetition] stipulation").
14. *See In re* Club Tower L.P., 138 B.R. 307, 311-12 (Bankr. N.D. Ga. 1991) (entitling creditor to relief from automatic stay as result of prepetition agreement between debtor and creditor); *In re* Citadel Properties, Inc., 86 B.R. 275, 277 (Bankr. M.D. Fla. 1988) (enforcing prepetition stipulation granting relief from stay and acknowledging presence of other significant indicia of bad faith); *In re* International Supply Corp., 72 B.R. 510, 511-12 (Bankr. M.D. Fla. 1987) (same). *But see In re* Sky Group Int'l, Inc., 108 B.R. 86, 88-89 (Bankr. W.D. Pa. 1989) (stating prepetition stipulations regarding stay relief are not self-executing and require authorization of bankruptcy court).

    Cases holding prepetition agreements providing for creditors' stay relief should the debtor subsequently file for bankruptcy are discussed in the context of this Chapter because it has been held that a bad faith filing of a bankruptcy petition constitutes "cause" for purposes of Bankruptcy Code § 362(d) justifying relief from the automatic stay. *See Club Tower*, 138 B.R. at 310 (citing *In re* Phoenix Piccadilly, 849 F.2d 1393, 1394 (11th Cir. 1988) and *In re* Natural Land Corp., 825 F.2d 296, 297 (11th Cir. 1987)). This author asserts that if the factual setting (economic circumstances, feasibility of business, etc.) in which the debtor files a subsequent bankruptcy is one which was contemplated by the parties at the time the agreement was executed, there is strong evidence that grounds for stay relief exist. In the single asset context involving only one creditor with no equity in the property, stay relief for the creditor is the death knell of the debtor's chapter 11 petition, thereby having virtually the same effect as a § 1112(b) dismissal. *See In re* Jenkins Court Assocs., Ltd. Partnership, 181 B.R. 33, 37 (Bankr. E.D. Pa. 1995).

it appears that, at the very least, the bankruptcy courts may accept such stipulations as persuasive evidence of the debtor's bad faith in filing.[15]

Many of the cases holding the stipulations enforceable involved debtors that manifested the usual indicia of bad faith: single asset real estate with little or no equity, no employees, relatively few unsecured creditors, and no realistic chance of successful reorganization.[16] Considering the prevalence of these

---

15. *See Roundtable Discussion*, *supra* note 6, at 39-40. Judge Fenning (Bankr. C.D. Cal.), commenting that prepetition agreements may serve as persuasive evidence of the intent of the parties in the Ninth Circuit, stated, "I don't think it's enforceable . . . [but it] is certainly admissible as evidence of the intent of the parties on the issue of whether the filing is in bad faith, but it would be one of several factors to be considered. . . . And I think it's entirely appropriate to draft agreements with recitals about the intent of the parties . . . [which] may be awfully persuasive, but they are not binding." *Id.* at 39. Judge Greendyke (Bankr. S.D. Tex.) commented in the same Roundtable Discussion, "I think it's good lawyering. . . [and it] may be a factor in deciding whether or not it's a bad faith filing, but it won't be a per se bad faith filing just because of the existence of this agreement." *Id.* at 40. Judge Hillman (Bankr. D. Mass.) called for an analysis of the agreement itself, focusing on what the debtor actually received in exchange for the promise. *Id.* at 40. Judge Mark (Bankr. S.D. Fla.) expressed his concern for what is happening in the bankruptcy courts of the Eleventh Circuit regarding prepetition agreements and stated, "I think there's a danger in saying that you would enforce that kind of stipulation because it will immediately wet [sic] the appetite of lenders and lenders' counsel to draft it in and it is already happening in Florida as a result of a couple of decisions that really were typical bad faith dismissals. . . ." *Id.* In any event, Judge Mark did indicate "that you look at [the prepetition agreement] as another indication of the pre-petition misconduct or the pre-petition conduct." *Id.*
16. *See Club Tower*, 138 B.R. at 309-10; *Aurora*, 134 B.R. at 985-86; *Citadel*, 86 B.R. at 275-76; *Orange Park*, 79 B.R. at 81; *International Supply*, 72 B.R. at 511-12. *But see In re* Sky Group Int'l, Inc., 108 B.R. 86, 89 (Bankr. W.D. Pa. 1989) (stating that "[r]elief from stay must be *authorized by the Bankruptcy Court*") (citation omitted). *Sky Group* involved a debtor who entered into a prepetition agreement waiving its rights to the protection of the automatic stay in the event the debtor filed for bankruptcy subsequent to the agreement. *Id.* at 88. The court held that the agreement was not self-executing since the protection of the stay is contingent upon the conduct of the debtors and cannot be compromised unless "there exists good reason to do so." *Id.* Unlike *Aurora*, *Club Tower*, *Citadel*, and *Orange Park*, the debtor's filing in *Sky Group* was

factors, the courts conceivably could have dismissed the cases on an independent finding of "bad faith" without deciding the enforceability of the prepetition agreements.[17] Nevertheless, language from the decisions indicates implicitly, if not expressly, that the courts upheld the enforceability of the stipulations in determining the merits of the debtors' filings.[18]

The factual settings in which these agreements have found application typically involve some form of forbearance on the part of the creditor in return for, *inter alia*, certain stipulations concerning a subsequent chapter 11 filing by the debtor.[19] Ordinarily, the creditor agrees to forebear from proceeding with foreclosure in exchange for a reciprocal agreement by the debtor that, in the event the debtor files for bankruptcy, (a) the filing is deemed to be in bad faith;[20] or (b) the creditor is entitled to relief from the automatic stay.[21] In all the cases, the debtor first breached the workout agreement and subsequently filed for bankruptcy.[22]

---

not surrounded by the traditional indicia of bad faith and the creditor was adequately protected by a sizeable equity cushion. *Id.* at 90-91.

For a discussion of the traditional indicia of bad faith and its application to single asset debtors, see *supra* notes 5-8 and accompanying text.

17. *See Club Tower*, 138 B.R. at 309-10 (stating that delay and frustration of creditor's ability to enforce its rights and remedies as a secured creditor was sole objective of debtor's filing); *Aurora*, 134 B.R. at 985-86 (same); *Citadel*, 86 B.R. at 276 (same); *Orange Park*, 79 B.R. at 81 (same); *International Supply*, 72 B.R. at 511-12 (same); *see also Roundtable Discussion*, *supra* note 6, at 40 (Judge Mark commenting that cases in Eleventh Circuit enforcing these prepetition stipulations are "typical bad faith dismissals"); *see supra* note 2 and accompanying text (discussing implied good faith requirement for chapter 11 filings).
18. *See, e.g.*, *Aurora*, 134 B.R. at 986 (holding debtor could not avoid "legal consequences" of prepetition agreement regarding bad faith in filing); *Orange Park*, 79 B.R. at 82 (same); *see also Club Tower*, 138 B.R. at 312 (enforcing prepetition agreement regarding stay relief as a means of "encouraging out of court . . . settlements"); *Citadel*, 86 B.R. at 276 (enforcing prepetition agreement regarding stay relief); *International Supply*, 72 B.R. at 512 (same).
19. *See supra* note 13 (listing cases where such stipulations found to be enforceable).
20. *Aurora*, 134 B.R. at 984; *Orange Park*, 79 B.R. at 80.
21. *Club Tower*, 138 B.R. at 309; *Citadel*, 86 B.R. at 275.
22. *See Club Tower*, 138 B.R. at 309; *Aurora*, 134 B.R. at 984; *Citadel*, 86 B.R.

The enforceability of prepetition stipulations is, however, unclear and dependent upon the factual settings of the cases involved.[23] The prepetition stipulations enforced in *In re Aurora Investments*,[24] *In re Club Tower L.P.*,[25] and *In re Orange Park South Partnership*[26] were enforced in a filing environment surrounded by bad faith indicia.[27] When, however, there is no showing of bad faith on the part of the debtor at the time of filing,[28] at least one bankruptcy court has found that a prepetition agreement regarding stay relief for the creditor is not self-executing inasmuch as relief from the automatic stay must be authorized by the bankruptcy court.[29]

---

at 275; *Orange Park*, 79 B.R. at 80-81; *International Supply*, 72 B.R. at 511.

23. *See supra* note 14 and accompanying text (discussing bad faith); *infra* note 27 (setting forth paradigm factual settings).
24. 134 B.R. 982, 984 (Bankr. M.D. Fla. 1991).
25. 138 B.R. 307, 309 (Bankr. N.D. Ga. 1991).
26. 79 B.R. 79, 80 (Bankr. M.D. Fla. 1987).
27. In *Aurora*, the court concluded that the debtor was "not a viable economic entity and it [had] no realistic possibility of an effective reorganization and . . . the petition was filed for the sole purpose to frustrate and delay the legitimate efforts of secured creditors to enforce their rights." *Aurora*, 134 B.R. at 986. The court also stated that even if the debtor could successfully reorganize a bad faith filing would not be transformed into a good faith one. *Id.* In *Club Tower*, the court found that the debtor had one fully encumbered asset, few unsecured creditors, "no employees, no cash flow, and no available resources of income to sustain a plan of reorganization . . . ." *Club Tower*, 138 B.R. at 310. The court, therefore, believed that the debtor's only reason for filing was to prevent the secured creditor from enforcing its rights. *Id.* In *Orange Park*, the court stated that it was undisputed that the debtor had no employees, conducted no business, and was "a mere shell entity created on the eve of foreclosure." *Orange Park*, 79 B.R. at 81. In addition, the debtor did not own the property it was seeking to salvage. *Id.*
28. *See In re* Sky Group Int'l, Inc., 108 B.R. 86, 90 (Bankr. W.D. Pa. 1989) (concluding "involuntary petition in this case was not brought in bad faith").
29. *Id.* at 88, 89. The court stated, "[t]he contention that this waiver [of the automatic stay] is enforceable and self-executing is without merit." *Id.* at 88; *see also infra* note 40 and accompanying text.

B. Enforceability and Public Policy

In *In re Club Tower L.P.*,[30] the debtor asserted that a prepetition agreement allowing the creditor relief from the automatic stay violated public policy by requiring the debtor to waive unwaivable rights provided in the Bankruptcy Code.[31] Indeed, any prepetition stipulation that totally prohibits debtors from exercising their right to file for bankruptcy is violative of public policy and unenforceable as a matter of law.[32] In *Club Tower*, the court distinguished the agreement from such a provision reasoning that the debtor was *not* prohibited from filing for bankruptcy since the debtor had, in fact, already filed.[33] The

---

30. 138 B.R. 307 (Bankr. N.D. Ga. 1991).
31. *Id.* at 311 & n.1.
32. *Id.*; *see In re* Madison, 184 B.R. 686, 690-91 (Bankr. E.D. Pa. 1995) (stating that "[e]ven bargained-for and knowing waivers of the right to seek protection in bankruptcy must be deemed void"); Archambault v. Hershman (*In re* Archambault), 174 B.R. 923, 933 n.8 (Bankr. W.D. Mich. 1994) (stating that case law indicates prepetition agreement not to file bankruptcy is against public policy and unenforceable); *In re* Cheeks, 167 B.R. 817, 818-19 (Bankr. D.S.C. 1994) (stating that agreement precluding debtor from filing in bankruptcy is different from agreement waiving stay protection which is enforceable).
33. *Club Tower*, 138 B.R. at 311; *see also In re* Darrell Creek Assocs., L.P., 187 B.R. 908, 913 (Bankr. D.S.C. 1995) (stating waiver of stay is distinguishable from waiver of right to file in bankruptcy and is enforceable); *Madison*, 184 B.R. at 690-91 (distinguishing between prepetition waiver of stay protection and waiver of right to file in bankruptcy); *In re* Atrium High Point Ltd. Partnership, 189 B.R. 599, 607 (Bankr. M.D.N.C. 1995) (same); *Cheeks*, 167 B.R. at 818-19 (same); *Citadel*, 86 B.R. at 275 (suggesting "total prohibition against filing for bankruptcy would be contrary to Constitutional authority as well as public policy"); *In re* Gulf Beach Dev. Corp., 48 B.R. 40, 43 (Bankr. M.D. Fla. 1985) (stating that contractual provision precluding right to file petition in bankruptcy was unenforceable, but prepetition agreement providing creditor relief from stay is enforceable). *But see In re* Jenkins Court Assocs. Ltd. Partnership, 181 B.R. 33, 37 (Bankr. E.D. Pa. 1995) (refusing to enforce waiver of automatic stay because "[a]s a practical matter, there may be little significant distinction between the enforcement of a pre-petition waiver of the automatic stay in a single asset case and the enforcement of a provision prohibiting the filing of a bankruptcy case in the first place"); *In re* Sky Group Int'l, Inc., 108 B.R. 86, 88-89 (Bankr. W.D. Pa. 1989) (stating that automatic stay meant to protect all creditors and therefore relief from stay must be autho-

court stated that the debtor had simply waived one benefit of the Bankruptcy Code,[34] which benefit Congress never intended to be permanent.[35] The court further reasoned that the debtor still retained,

> the benefits of the automatic stay . . . as well as all the other benefits and protections provided by the Bankruptcy Code including but not limited to the right to conduct an orderly liquidation, discharge debt or pay it back on different terms, assume or reject executory contracts, sell property free and clear of liens, and pursue preferences and fraudulent conveyance claims. Debtor still retains the core rights under the Bankruptcy Code and has the ability to make a "fresh start."[36]

In holding the agreement enforceable, the court stated that such stipulations actually "further[] the legitimate public policy of encouraging out of court restructuring and settlements."[37] Furthermore, the court stated that "[i]n order to facilitate this goal, pre-petition agreements should be enforced against a borrower who later files for bankruptcy. To hold otherwise could make lenders more reticent in attempting workouts with borrowers outside of bankruptcy."[38] In enforcing such agreements, the bankruptcy courts in the Eleventh Circuit have either dismissed the petition as having been filed in bad

---

rized by bankruptcy court).

34. *Club Tower*, 138 B.R. at 311; *see In re* Darrell Creek Assocs., L.P., 187 B.R. 908, 913 (Bankr. D.S.C. 1995) (finding prepetition agreement waiving stay enforceable in bankruptcy) (citation omitted).
35. Congress expressly provided a means for creditors to have the stay lifted, *viz.*, for "cause" under § 362(d) of the Code. In this context lack of good faith constitutes "cause" for purposes of 11 U.S.C. § 362(d) (1994). *See supra* note 2 (discussing § 362(d)).
36. *Club Tower*, 138 B.R. at 311-12.
37. *Id.* at 312. "Workouts and restructurings should be encouraged among debtors and creditors, particularly where, as here, there is a debt between two parties and a single asset." *Id.* "The Bankruptcy Code . . . recognizes that the filing of a bankruptcy petition might not always be the most efficient means of restructuring the relations of a debtor and its creditors." *Id.*; *see also* Katz, *supra* note 4, at 77 (noting rise in bankruptcy filings and need for courts to "police filings").
38. *Club Tower*, 138 B.R. at 312.

faith or lifted the stay allowing the creditor to proceed with foreclosure.[39]

A number of bankruptcy courts' decisions, however, have held that these types of waivers of the Code's stay protection by the debtors are neither self-executing[40] nor "per se" enforceable.[41] In addition, courts have also stated that another reason the debtor may not waive the stay in a prepetition agreement is because the purpose of the stay is to protect the creditors as well as the debtors.[42]

Nevertheless, even though courts have found that the prepetition agreement alone is insufficient to lift the stay, courts have used these prepetition agreements, together with other facts and circumstances present in the case, to either establish good cause for lifting the stay or to determine that an evidentiary hearing was needed.[43] These cases have generally consisted of a single asset debtor who files a petition in an environment with indicia of bad faith.[44]

C. Tactical Considerations

1. Debtor's Standpoint

In order to escape the binding effect of prepetition stipulations regarding good faith and stay relief, a debtor may argue that the circumstances under

---

39. *See supra* notes 13-14 and accompanying text.
40. *See supra* note 29 and accompanying text.
41. Farm Creditor, ACA v. Polk, 160 B.R. 870, 873 (M.D. Fla. 1993) (affirming bankruptcy court's finding that prepetition stipulations providing for relief from stay are not "per se" binding on debtor); *In re* Powers, 170 B.R. 480, 483 (Bankr. D. Mass. 1994) (stating waiver not self-executing); Jeffrey W. Warren & Wendy V.E. England, *Pre-Petition Waiver of the Automatic Stay is Not Per Se Enforceable*, AM. BANKR. INST. J., Mar. 1994, at 22, 22 (same).
42. *In re* Sky Group Int'l, Inc., 108 B.R. 86, 89 (Bankr. W.D. Pa. 1989); *see Farm Credit*, 160 B.R. at 873 (denying creditor relief from stay, although prepetition agreement existed, and noting that debtor's business, unlike single asset cases, employed many people and had many secured and unsecured creditors).
43. *In re* Jenkins Court Assocs. Ltd. Partnership, 181 B.R. 33, 37 (Bankr. E.D. Pa. 1995) (ordering evidentiary hearing on bad faith issue); *In re* Powers, 170 B.R. 480, 484 (Bankr. D. Mass. 1994) (same); *In re* Citadel Properties, Inc., 86 B.R. 275, 276 (Bankr. M.D. Fla. 1988).
44. *See supra* note 43.

which the filing occurred were never contemplated at the time the prepetition agreement was executed.[45] In light of the fact that a court may look at the debtor's present conduct as well as the circumstances under which the petition was filed,[46] the debtor may argue "change of circumstances" in attempting to justify to the court its subsequent filing and prove its worthiness of the rehabilitative protection of chapter 11.[47] Additionally, it is asserted that when a debtor is placed in bankruptcy involuntarily, it is unlikely that a prepetition stipulation regarding either good faith in filing the petition or providing for relief from the stay will be enforced.[48]

---

45. James Lipscomb, Address at the *St. John's University Bankruptcy Law Society* Fall Lecture (Nov. 18, 1992). Mr. Lipscomb is Vice President of Metropolitan Life Insurance Company. When questioned on the effect of prepetition stipulations regarding debtors' good faith in a bankruptcy filing following a workout agreement breach, Mr. Lipscomb responded: "They have been effective. Of course the debtor will probably argue 'change of circumstances,' thereby claiming he is not presently filing in bad faith and is a debtor worthy of chapter 11 protection." *Id.* Mr. Lipscomb intimated that the debtor will argue that it is now (at the time of filing) in a position it never contemplated at the time the workout agreement was executed. *Id*; *cf. In re* Glendhill, 76 F.3d 1070, 1081 (10th Cir. 1996) (vacating order granting relief from stay because of debtor's changed circumstances such as increased property value); Monarch Life Ins. Co. v. Ropes & Gray, 65 F.3d 973, 981 (1st Cir. 1995) (reasoning that "changed circumstances" may preclude application of doctrine of collateral estoppel) (citations omitted); Fein v. United States (*In re* Fein), 22 F.3d 631, 634 (5th Cir. 1994) (stating that doctrine of laches precludes party from asserting claim where opponent would suffer severe prejudice due to changed circumstances); Green Tree Acceptance, Inc. v. Hoggle (*In re* Hoggle), 12 F.3d 1008, 1011 (11th Cir. 1994) (reasoning that Code § 1329 permits plan modification to debtor's unforeseeable change in circumstances).
46. *See* Baker v. Latham Sparrowbush Assocs. (*In re* Cohoes Indus. Terminal, Inc.), 931 F.2d 222, 227 (2d Cir. 1991) (recognizing need to review "totality of the circumstances surrounding" debtor's filing to determine if bad faith exists); *In re* Roxy Real Estate Co., 170 B.R. 571, 573 (Bankr. E.D. Pa. 1993) (same); *In re* Sky Group Int'l, 108 B.R. 86, 90 (Bankr. W.D. Pa. 1989) (stating necessary to see "whether any abuses of the provisions, purpose, or spirit of bankruptcy law have occurred").
47. *See supra* note 45.
48. *See generally Sky Group*, 108 B.R. at 91 (stating that dismissal in this involuntary case would not be in best interest of all parties).

2. Creditor's Standpoint

It is suggested that creditors should include in their workout agreements prepetition stipulations contemplating the debtor's conduct for a subsequent filing.[49] A carefully drafted prepetition stipulation provides the creditor with in-hand evidence of the character of debtor's conduct in filing a subsequent bankruptcy petition.[50] Moreover, even if unenforceable, the stipulation can still assist the court in judging the debtor's conduct and facilitate the court's "good faith" determination.[51] Additionally, it is suggested that the stipulation may enable the creditor to meet the initial burden of proof for dismissal under Bankruptcy Code sections 1112(b)[52] or 362(d).[53] At present, exactly what constitutes a carefully drafted agreement is somewhat uncertain. It is proffered that, at the very least, the clause should set forth the relative positions of the debtor and creditor. It should emphasize the benefit conferred on the debtor by the creditor's forbearance as well as the substantial risk involved with such forbearance. A model clause appears below:

---

49. *See supra* note 15 (particularly comments of Judge Fenning and Judge Greendyke).
50. *See supra* note 15.
51. *See supra* notes 14-15.
52. *See generally* BARRY RUSSELL, BANKRUPTCY EVIDENCE MANUAL § 301.78(A), at 333 (1995-96 ed.). "The initial burden of proof for conversion or dismissal of a [c]hapter 11 case under 11 U.S.C.A. § 1112(b) lies with the movant to establish a prima facie showing of the debtor's bad faith in proposing its [c]hapter 11 plan." *Id.* (citing *In re* Wilkins Inv. Group, Inc., 171 B.R. 194 (Bankr. M.D. Pa. 1994) and *In re* Hartford Run Apartments, Ltd., 102 B.R. 130 (Bankr. S.D. Ohio 1989)). "Once the debtor's good faith is placed in question, the debtor then bears the burden of proving its good faith." *Id.* (citing *In re* Copy Crafters Quickprint, Inc., 92 B.R. 973, 985 (Bankr. N.D.N.Y. 1988)).
53. RUSSELL, *supra* note 52, § 301.42, at 287. "A creditor seeking relief from the automatic stay has the initial burden of producing evidence sufficient to establish a prima facie case of entitlement to relief." *Id.* (citing *In re* McGuinness, 139 B.R. 3 (Bankr. D.N.J. 1992); Lazard v. Texaco, Inc. (*In re* Texaco), 81 B.R. 820 (Bankr. S.D.N.Y. 1988); *In re* Compass Van & Storage Corp., 61 B.R. 230 (Bankr. E.D.N.Y. 1986); Setzer v. Hot Prods., Inc. (*In re* Setzer), 47 B.R. 340, 345 (Bankr. E.D.N.Y. 1985)).

The following workout agreement provision is based on circumstances that appear to have influenced courts willing to consider such agreements. It is recommended that firms employing clauses such as the following advise clients of the purpose for which the clause is used and that there is no assurance that a bankruptcy court will enforce its provisions.

In the clause below, brackets indicate provisions that may vary with the facts of the case, negotiating posture of the parties, and provisions of applicable nonbankruptcy law. Terms that are defined elsewhere in the workout agreement are initially capitalized.

XX. Borrower's Representations, Agreements, Acknowledgments, and Warranties; Lender's Reliance

Borrower represents, acknowledges, agrees, and warrants that:

(a) the Loan is in default and has remaining unpaid balance of $ _____;

(b) the Loan is secured by a first mortgage [deed of trust] on the Property;

(c) Lender may under the terms of the Loan Documents commence foreclosure proceedings immediately [and immediately seek the appointment of a receiver] and has had such ability since the initial default on ___;

(d) Borrower has no defenses, offsets or counterclaims to the institution of foreclosure proceedings and has had none during the period of default;

(e) this Agreement constitutes a reorganization plan for Borrower;

(f) Borrower has no equity in the Property and no realistic chance for reorganization other than pursuant to the terms of this Agreement;

(g) [Borrower has no employees who are not partners of Borrower];

(h) Borrower has no unsecured creditors other than those listed, together with the amount of indebtedness owed lenders in Schedule A attached hereto;

(i) Borrower has no assets other than the Property;

(j) at the request of Borrower, and in reliance on this Agreement and on Borrower's expressed good faith attempt to negotiate the terms of this Agreement, Lender (i) has forborne, and agrees to continue to forbear institution [continuation] of foreclosure proceedings or [seeking of the appointment of a receiver] so long as Borrower is not in default hereunder, (ii) [et. seq. Here set forth each additional lender concession to borrower including forbearance of payment, extension of time, additional financing, reduction of interest or constant principal payments etc.];

(k) Borrower, recognizing that Lender has changed its position and will change its position in reliance on the foregoing representations, acknowledgments and warranties of Borrower, further agrees that;

(i) if Borrower should default under the terms of this Agreement [and such default is not cured within 10 days after notice from Lender] Lender may commence [or continue] foreclosure proceedings [, seek immediate appointment of a receiver,] and proceed with the lawful sale of the property thereunder;

(ii) Borrower will not attempt to delay or frustrate the foreclosure process [, appointment of receiver,] or sale of the property, nor raise any defenses thereto;

(iii) in the event Borrower, directly or indirectly, files a petition under the Bankruptcy Code, or any general partner of Borrower, directly or indirectly files such a petition against Borrower, Borrower admits and agrees that such petition shall have been filed to frustrate or delay the foreclosure proceeding, in bad faith, and in abrogation of this agreement and should be deemed to have been so filed by the Bankruptcy court; and in addition to any rights lender may have under this Agreement, the Loan Documents, at law or in equity, Lender shall have the right (and Borrower will interpose no objection thereto and hereby waives its rights with respect thereto) to request and receive from the bankruptcy court or any other court of competent jurisdiction, immediate relief from the automatic stay imposed under section 362 of the Bankruptcy Code or any stay or other restriction on Lender's rights hereunder, under any of the court's equitable powers, a termination of the exclusive period under section 1121 of the Bankruptcy Code, and a dismissal of the bankruptcy case or proceeding;

(l) nothing in this Agreement shall be deemed in any way to limit or restrict any of Lender's rights to seek in a bankruptcy court or any other court of competent jurisdiction, any relief Lender may deem appropriate in the event that a voluntary or involuntary petition under any title of the Bankruptcy Code is filed by or against Borrower;

(m) Borrower will enter a Cash Collateral Stipulation with Lender in the form of Exhibit B attached hereto upon the filing of any petition by or against borrower under the Bankruptcy Code; and

(n) Borrower further acknowledges and agrees that the representations, acknowledgments, agreements and warranties in this Agreement have been made by Borrower as a material inducement to Lender to enter into this Agreement, that Lender is relying on such representations and warranties, has changed and will continue to change its position in reliance thereon and that Lender would not have entered into this Agreement without such representations, acknowledgements, agreements, and warranties.

(o) Borrower has consulted with counsel and relied upon counsel's advice in connection with the negotiation and execution of this agreement.[54]

Conclusion

The circumstances under which a court will enforce prepetition stipulations that either characterize any subsequent bankruptcy filings by a debtor as being conducted in "bad faith" or waive the debtor's right to protection of the automatic stay are as yet indeterminable. However, given that each case thus far recognizing the validity of such stipulations involved factual settings already tainted by indicia of bad faith, it is suggested that such agreements, standing alone, might not have enjoyed court enforcement. Indeed, overcrowded bankruptcy dockets would seem to encourage judges to enforce these types of stipulations since they promote out of court restructuring. Notwithstanding this pressure of case management, the ultimate test for the enforceability of these agreements likely rests on whether the enforcement of the agreement furthers the Bankruptcy Code's policy of providing debtors a chance to reorganize while preserving the value of the estate for creditors, and whether or not the bankruptcy petition is filed simply to forestall, thwart,

---

54. The author wishes to thank the numerous professionals who provided input for the drafting of this clause.

or frustrate the satisfaction of creditors' claims. Judges evaluating petitions for the reorganization of single asset holdings may seldom reach these policy considerations given the propensity for "bad faith" in single asset cases. All things considered, it is suggested that the creditor should include such prepetition agreements in a workout arrangement, and that the debtor understand the potential binding or evidentiary effect of such stipulations in the event the debtor decides to file for bankruptcy.

CHAPTER IV

VENUE ISSUES IN SINGLE ASSET REORGANIZATIONS*

CATHERINE V. BATTLE
CAROLLYNN H. G. PEDREIRA

The proper venue of a bankruptcy case under chapter 11 is the district encompassing the debtor's domicile, residence, principal place of business, or principal assets.[1] The issue of what constitutes proper venue often arises in cases involving a single asset real estate asset[2] owned by a limited partnership

---

* The views expressed in this Chapter are of the authors and do not necessarily reflect the views of their firms.

1. 28 U.S.C. § 1408 (1994). The statute states:

> Except as provided in section 1410 [venue of cases ancillary to foreign proceedings] of this title, a case under title 11 may be commenced in the district court for the district–
>
> (1) in which the domicile, residence, principal place of business in the United States, or principal assets in the United States, of the person or entity that is the subject of such case have been located for the one hundred and eighty days immediately preceding such commencement, or for a longer portion of such one-hundred-and-eighty-day period than the domicile, residence, or principal place of business, in the United States, or principal assets in the United States, of such person were located in any other district; or
>
> (2) in which there is pending a case under title 11 concerning such person's affiliate, general partner, or partnership.

Id.

2. *See* 11 U.S.C. § 101(51B) (1994).

> "Single asset real estate" means real property constituting a single property or project, other than residential real property with fewer than four residential units, which generates substantially all of the gross income of a debtor and on which no substantial business is being conducted by a debtor other

debtor.[3] In these cases, courts have concluded that proper venue for the partnership is either the district in which the partnership's principal place of business is located or the district in which the partnership's principal asset is located.[4] The "nerve center" test is utilized to determine a partnership's principal place of business,[5] while the "bulk of activity" test is used to

---

> than the business of operating the real property and activities incidental thereto having aggregate noncontingent, liquidated secured debts in an amount no more than 4,000,000.

Id.

3. *See, e.g., In re* Pinehaven Assocs., 132 B.R. 982, 983 (Bankr. E.D.N.Y. 1991); *In re* Garden Manor Assocs., L.P., 99 B.R. 551, 553 (Bankr. S.D.N.Y. 1988); *In re* Bell Tower Assocs., Ltd., 86 B.R. 795, 798-99 (Bankr. S.D.N.Y. 1988); *In re* Nantucket Apartments Assocs., 80 B.R. 154, 155-56 (Bankr. E.D. Mo. 1987).
4. *See In re* Washington, Perito & Dubuc, 154 B.R. 853, 859 (Bankr. S.D.N.Y. 1993) (stating that venue may properly lie where partnership has its principal place of business or where principal assets are located); *In re* Greenridge Apartments, 13 B.R. 510, 512 (Bankr. D. Haw. 1981) (same); *In re* Oklahoma City Assocs., 98 B.R. 194, 197 (Bankr. E.D. Pa. 1989); *Garden Manor*, 99 B.R. at 553 (same); *Bell Tower*, 86 B.R. at 799 (stating that when debtor is partnership, only meaningful test for venue is location of principal place of business or location of principal assets); 1 COLLIER ON BANKRUPTCY ¶ 3.02[1][c][ii], at 3-125 to 3-126 (Lawrence P. King ed., 15th ed. 1995) (discussing proper venue test for partnerships in title 11 cases as either location of principal place of business or location of assets in United States).
5. *See* Federal Beef Processors, Inc. v. CBS Inc., 851 F. Supp. 1430, 1433 (D.S.D. 1994) ("The 'nerve center' test locates the principal place of business in the state from which a corporation's decision-making authority and overall control emanate."); *see also In re* Holiday Towers, Inc., 18 B.R. 183, 186 (Bankr. S.D. Ohio 1982) (stating that "nerve center" test focuses on location of general executive offices from which broad management decisions are made). Thus, the "nerve center" test looks to where the major managerial business decisions are made. *See Washington, Perito & Dubuc*, 154 B.R. at 859; *In re* Standard Tank Cleaning Corp., 133 B.R. 562, 564 (Bankr. E.D.N.Y. 1991); *Oklahoma City*, 98 B.R. at 198; *In re* Pavilion Place Assocs., 88 B.R. 32, 35 (Bankr. S.D.N.Y. 1988); *Bell Tower*, 86 B.R. at 800; *In re* 1606 New Hampshire Ave. Assocs., 85 B.R. 298, 302-03 (Bankr. E.D. Pa. 1988); *see also In re* Landmark Capital Co., 19 B.R. 342, 347 (Bankr. S.D.N.Y.) (considering overall coordination, financing and management of

determine where its principal asset is located.[6] Even if venue is found to be proper, a court may transfer a chapter 11 case "in the interests of justice or for the convenience of the parties."[7] In many single asset cases, a limited

---

business), *aff'd sub nom.*, Landmark Capital Co. v. North Cent. Dev. Co. (*In re* Landmark Capital Co.), 20 B.R. 220 (S.D.N.Y. 1982).

But see In re Dock of the Bay, Inc., 24 B.R. 811 (Bankr. E.D.N.Y. 1982). In *Dock of the Bay*, the debtor was a Maryland corporation operating a chain of fast-food restaurants in Maryland, whose president had offices in New York. *Id.* at 813-14. The debtor alleged that New York was the "nerve center" of the business because it was from there that the president directed and controlled the company and provided financing. *Id.* at 814. The court held, however, that the president's activities were insufficient to make New York the debtor's principal place of business. *Id.* at 815.

Another factor which may be considered in determining a partnership's principal place of business is the location of the partners. General partners participate in the decision making process, and their location may be relevant in determining the partnership's principal place of business. *See Garden Manor*, 99 B.R. at 553 (finding venue proper where owners of corporate general partner who made major business decisions for limited partnership debtor were located); *see also Oklahoma City*, 98 B.R. at 197 n.6 (noting that insofar as domicile of general partners is related to where business decisions are made, it is relevant in determining partnership's principal place of business); *Bell Tower*, 86 B.R. at 799 (considering location of general partner relevant in determining proper venue). *But see Nantucket Apartments*, 80 B.R. at 156 (stating that where debtor is a limited partnership, domicile or residence of general partners is irrelevant in determining venue).

6. *See* Kristufek v. Saxonburg Ceramics, Inc., 901 F. Supp. 1018 (W.D.N.C. 1994), *aff'd*, 60 F.3d 823 (4th Cir. 1995). The "bulk of activity" test "looks to 'where the corporation carries out the bulk of its activities as evidenced by the location of its physical assets and daily production or services activities rather than high-level policymaking.'" *Id.* (citing Carolina Carbon & Stainless Prods., Inc. v. IPSCO Corp., 635 F. Supp. 305, 307 (W.D.N.C. 1986)); *see also Holiday Towers*, 18 B.R. at 186 (indicating that "bulk of activity test" emphasizes location of debtor's principal assets, factories, mills and other manufacturing facilities).

7. 28 U.S.C. § 1412 (1994). This section states: "A district court may transfer a case or proceeding under title 11 to a district court for another district, in the interest of justice or for the convenience of the parties." *Id.*

Section 1412 superseded 28 U.S.C. § 1475 in 1984. *See* Bankruptcy

partnership debtor brings a bankruptcy case in the district encompassing the

---

Amendments and Federal Judgeship Act of 1984, Pub. L. No. 98-353, § 1412, 98 Stat. 333, 335 (codified as amended at 28 U.S.C. § 1412 (1994)). Section 1475 provided that "[a] bankruptcy court may transfer a case under title 11 . . . to a bankruptcy court for another district, in the interest of justice and for the convenience of the parties." 28 U.S.C. § 1475 (superseded 1984). This change from "in the interest of justice and for the convenience of the parties" to "in the interest of justice or for the convenience of the parties" suggests that the movant has a lower burden under §1412. *See* 1 COLLIER, *supra* note 4, ¶ 3.02[4][c][i], at 3-155; *In re* Portjeff Dev. Corp., 118 B.R. 184, 192 & n.3 (Bankr. E.D.N.Y. 1990) (discussing replacement of § 1475 with § 1412 in 1984). However, other than this difference, the standard for transfer under §1412 is essentially the same as under §1475, and the case law construing § 1475 is still influential. 1 COLLIER, *supra* note 4, ¶ 3.02 [4][c][i], at 3-155 to 3-156.

Prior to the enactment of § 1475, transfer of venue was governed by Bankruptcy Rule 116(b). *See, e.g.,* Puerto Rico v. Commonwealth Oil Ref. Co. (*In re* Commonwealth Oil Ref. Co.), 596 F.2d 1239, 1241 (5th Cir. 1979) (determining motion to transfer venue of case pursuant to former Bankruptcy Rules 116(a) and (b)), *cert. denied,* 444 U.S. 1045 (1980); *see also In re* Pope Vineyards, 90 B.R. 252, 255 n.1 (Bankr. S.D. Tex. 1988) (stating that standards announced under *Commonwealth Oil* apply under current law); *Holiday Towers*, 18 B.R. at 186 (Bankr. S.D. Ohio 1982) (stating that standards under §§ 1472 (proper venue for corporation), 1475 (change of venue where original venue proper), and 1477 (change of venue where original venue improper) are same as under former Bankruptcy Rule 116(b) and cases decided under Rules 116(a) and (b) remain persuasive).

Rule 1014 of the Federal Rules of Bankruptcy Procedure describes the procedure for transfer pursuant to 28 U.S.C. § 1412, thus implementing that statute. FED R. BANKR. P. 1014, advisory committee notes to the 1987 Amendments. The rule states, in pertinent part:

> If a petition is filed in a proper district, on timely motion of a party in interest, and after hearing on notice to the petitioners, the United States trustee, and other entities as directed by the court, the case may be transferred to any other district if the court determines that the transfer is in the interest of justice or for the convenience of the parties.

FED. R. BANKR. P. 1014(a)(1).

Rule 1014 also governs cases in which the petition is filed in an improper district. FED. R. BANKR. P. 1014(a)(2). The rule provides that:

> If a petition is filed in an improper district, on timely motion of a

partnership's principal place of business,[8] and creditors move to transfer the

---

> party in interest and after hearing on notice to the petitioners, the United States trustee, and other entities as directed by the court, the case may be dismissed or transferred to any other district if the court determines that transfer is in the interest of justice or for the convenience of the parties.

Id.

The majority of courts hold that "[the] Court may not retain an improperly venued case and must either transfer the case where venue is properly laid or dismiss it." *Standard Tank Cleaning Corp.*, 133 B.R. at 563; *see Washington, Perito & Dubuc*, 154 B.R. at 857-58 (holding that court may only dismiss or transfer case if venue is improper); *In re* Petrie, 142 B.R. 404, 405-06 (Bankr. D. Nev. 1992) (holding that court may not retain improperly venued case over objection of a party interest); *In re* Suzanne de Lyon, Inc., 125 B.R. 863, 866 (Bankr. S.D.N.Y. 1991) (recognizing that court must either transfer or dismiss improperly venued case); *Bell Tower*, 86 B.R. at 798 n.4 (same); *see also* 1 COLLIER, *supra* note 4, ¶ 3.02[4][d][i] and [d][ii], at 3-159 to 3-161 (discussing transfer of venue where venue is improper). Discussing the 1987 amendment to Rule 1014, the Advisory Committee stated:

> Formerly, 28 U.S.C. § 1477 authorized a court either to transfer or retain a case which had been commenced in a district where venue was improper. However, 28 U.S.C. § 1412, which supersedes 28 U.S.C. § 1477, authorizes only the transfer of a case. The rule is amended to delete the reference to retention of a case commenced in the improper district. Dismissal of a case commenced in the improper district as authorized by 28 U.S.C. § 1406 has been added to the rule.

FED. R. BANKR. P. 1014, advisory committee notes to 1987 Amendments. *But see In re* Lazaro, 128 B.R. 168, 175 (Bankr. W.D. Tex. 1991) (holding that bankruptcy court may retain improperly venued case).

The party moving for transfer bears the burden of proof and must carry this burden by a preponderance of the evidence. Gulf States Exploration Co. v. Manville Forest Prods. Corp. (*In re* Manville Forest Prods. Corp.), 896 F.2d 1384, 1390 (2d Cir. 1990); *Commonwealth Oil*, 596 F.2d at 1241; Wittes v. Interco, Inc. (*In re* Interco, Inc.), 139 B.R. 718, 720 (Bankr. E.D. Mo. 1992) (quoting *In re Manville*, 896 F.2d at 1390); *In re* Weatherly Frozen Food Group, Inc., 133 B.R. 862, 867 (Bankr. N.D. Ohio 1991); *Pavilion Place*, 88 B.R. at 35.

8. Where venue is proper in more than one location, the debtor's choice of forum is given "great weight," but this is not dispositive. *In re* Delaware & Hudson Ry., 96 B.R. 467, 467-68 (Bankr. D. Del. 1988). Courts will also consider the

case to the district in which the debtor's principal asset is located.[9]

This Chapter suggests that, with certain limited exceptions, a single asset debtor's estate can best be administered in the district in which the asset is located. Part A discusses the factors that courts utilize in deciding motions to transfer under 28 U.S.C. §˙1412 generally. Part B examines the utilization of these factors in single asset cases. Finally, Part C summarizes and evaluates *In re Vienna Park Properties*,[10] an exceptional single asset case decided by a bankruptcy court in the Southern District of New York, wherein the court declined to transfer the case to the district in which the debtor's single asset was located.

A. Factors Utilized in Determining Transfer of Venue Motions

1. Transfer for Convenience of the Parties

In the 1979 decision of *Puerto Rico v. Commonwealth Oil Refining*

---

proximity of the court to the parties, location of assets, and the economics of estate administration. *Id.*

9. *See, e.g., Garden Manor*, 99 B.R. at 555 (creditor's motion to transfer denied); *Oklahoma City*, 98 B.R. at 200 (creditor's motion to transfer granted); *In re* Greenhaven Assocs., Ltd., 93 B.R. 35, 41 (Bankr. S.D.N.Y. 1988) (motion to transfer granted); *Pavilion Place*, 88 B.R. at 36 (same); *1606 New Hampshire Ave. Assocs.*, 85 B.R. at 312 (same); *In re* Eleven Oak Tower Ltd. Partnership, 59 B.R. 626, 630 (Bankr. N.D. Ill. 1986) (same); *In re* Old Delmar Corp., 45 B.R. 883, 885 (S.D.N.Y. 1985) (same).

A motion to transfer a case is a core matter concerning the administration of the estate which bankruptcy judges may hear and determine. 28 U.S.C. § 157(b)(1), (b)(2) (1994); Sudbury, Inc. v. Dlott (*In re* Sudbury, Inc.), 149 B.R. 489, 491 (Bankr. N.D. Ohio 1993); *In re* Ridgely Communications, 107 B.R. 72, 77 (Bankr. D. Md. 1989).

10. 128 B.R. 373 (Bankr. S.D.N.Y. 1991) [hereinafter *Vienna Park III*]. The bankruptcy court initially denied the creditor's motion to transfer on October 23, 1990. *In re* Vienna Park Properties, 120 B.R. 320 (Bankr. S.D.N.Y. 1990) [hereinafter *Vienna Park I*]. On appeal, the district court vacated the order of the bankruptcy court and remanded the action to that court for reevaluation of the transfer motion. *See In re* Vienna Park Properties, 125 B.R. 84, 88 (S.D.N.Y. 1991) [hereinafter *Vienna Park II*].

Co. (In re Commonwealth Oil Refining Co.),[11] the Fifth Circuit determined whether the convenience of the parties warranted transfer of a chapter XI case.[12] The debtor in that case, a Puerto Rican corporation which operated a petroleum refinery and petrochemical facilities in Puerto Rico,[13] filed for bankruptcy in the Western District of Texas.[14] At that time, the debtor's executive offices were located in San Antonio.[15] The Government of Puerto Rico and the Puerto Rico Water Resources Authority moved, pursuant to Rule 116,[16] to transfer the case to the District of Puerto Rico.[17]

The Fifth Circuit, affirming the bankruptcy court's finding that venue was proper in Texas,[18] reviewed the motion to transfer under Rule 116(b)(1)[19]

---

11. 596 F.2d 1239 (5th Cir. 1979), *cert. denied*, 444 U.S. 1045 (1980).
12. *Id.* at 1247 (restating list of six factors enumerated by bankruptcy court and further stating that parties neither questioned these factors nor suggested additional ones).
13. *Id.* at 1241. Before 1971, Commonwealth Oil Refining Company ("CORCO") maintained its physical plant and executive offices in Puerto Rico. *Id.* In 1971, the executive officers were moved to New York City and remained there until 1976. *Id.* at 1241-42.
14. *Id.* at 1240-41 (petition filed on March 2, 1978, in San Antonio Division of Western District of Texas).
15. *Id.* at 1242. In 1975, Tesoro Petroleum, a San Antonio corporation, obtained a controlling share (36.7%) of CORCO's common stock. *Id.* at 1241-42, 1242 n.4. Subsequently, in 1976, Tesoro had CORCO's executive offices moved to San Antonio in contemplation of a merger of the two companies. *Id.* at 1242. Although the merger did not take place, CORCO's executive offices remained in San Antonio. *Id.*
16. *See supra* note 7 (discussing Rule 116). When *Commonwealth Oil* was decided, Federal Rules of Bankruptcy Procedure 116(a), (b) governed transfer of venue. Rule 116 was replaced by 28 U.S.C. § 1475, yet § 1475's standards were the same as those under former Bankruptcy Rule 116. *Id.* Eventually, § 1475 was superseded by 28 U.S.C. § 1412, which effected a minor change in the statute's language ("or" instead of "and") providing an ultimately more liberal standard for transfer of venue. *Id.*
17. Puerto Rico v. Commonwealth Oil Ref. Co. (*In re* Commonwealth Oil Ref. Co.), 596 F.2d 1239, 1241 (5th Cir. 1979), *cert. denied*, 444 U.S. 1045 (1980).
18. *Id.* at 1247, 1249. Focusing primarily on whether the requested transfer would promote the economic and efficient administration of the estate, the bankruptcy court found that because all of CORCO's management personnel were located

by considering the following six factors: (1) the proximity of creditors of every kind to the court; (2) the proximity of the bankrupt (debtor) to the court; (3) the proximity of those witnesses necessary to the administration of the estate; (4) the location of assets; (5) the economic administration of the estate; and (6) the necessity for ancillary administration if bankruptcy should occur.[20] Weighing the factors, the Fifth Circuit concluded that the bankruptcy court did not abuse its discretion by refusing to transfer the case to Puerto Rico.[21] While courts continue to utilize these six factors in the resolution of 28 U.S.C. § 1412 motions,[22] it is well recognized that the ultimate decision of whether to transfer a case rests within the discretion of the court.[23]

---

in San Antonio, the proper venue was Texas. *Id.* at 1247. The Fifth Circuit held that the bankruptcy court's ruling was not "clearly erroneous." *Id.*

19. *Id.* at 1247; *see supra* note 7 (discussing Rule 116).
20. *Commonwealth Oil*, 596 F.2d at 1247.
21. *Id.* at 1249.
22. *See supra* notes 19-20 and accompanying text (citing case using *Commonwealth Oil* factors); *see also In re* Metz, 173 B.R. 280, 282 (Bankr. E.D.N.Y. 1994) (applying factors enumerated in *Commonwealth Oil*); *In re* Finley, Kumble, 149 B.R. 365, 369 (Bankr. S.D.N.Y. 1993) (acknowledging that courts typically balance six factors from *Commonwealth* in determining venue motions).
23. Gulf States Exploration Co. v. Manville Forest Prods. (*In re* Manville Forest Prods. Corp.), 896 F.2d 1384, 1391 (2d Cir. 1990) (relying on Stewart Org. v. Ricoh Corp., 487 U.S. 22 (1988)). *Stewart* held that 28 U.S.C. § 1404(a) was "intended to place discretion in the district court to adjudicate motions for transfer according to an 'individualized, case-by-case consideration of convenience and fairness.'" *Stewart*, 487 U.S. at 29 (quoting Van Dusen v. Barrack, 376 U.S. 612, 622 (1964)); *see also In re* Pope Vineyards, 90 B.R. 252, 255 (Bankr. S.D. Tex. 1988) (maintaining that court must examine particular facts of each case to determine if transfer of venue proper); *In re* Pavilion Place Assocs., 88 B.R. 32, 35 (Bankr. S.D.N.Y. 1988) (same); *In re* 19101 Corp., 74 B.R. 34, 35 (Bankr. D.R.I. 1987) (same); *In re* Waits, 70 B.R. 591, 594-95 (Bankr. S.D.N.Y. 1987) (same); *In re* Pickwick Place Ltd. Partnership, 63 B.R. 290, 291 (Bankr. N.D. Ill. 1986) (same); *In re* Landmark Capital Co., 19 B.R. 342, 344 (Bankr. S.D.N.Y.) (same), *aff'd sub nom.*, Landmark Capital Co. v. North Cent. Dev. Co. (*In re* Landmark Capital Co.), 20 B.R. 220 (S.D.N.Y. 1982).

2. The Interest of Justice Analysis

While the *Commonwealth Oil* court clearly distinguished the factors applicable to the convenience of the parties and the interest of justice,[24] many courts apply the six factors to motions to transfer generally without specifically attributing them to either basis for transfer.[25] Courts that have analyzed the "interest of justice" basis independently have considered whether rulings are required to be in accordance with local law[26] and the court's interest in having localized controversies decided at home.[27] Quoting a Seventh Circuit

---

24. *Commonwealth Oil*, 596 F.2d at 1239, 1247-48 (Bankr. S.D.N.Y.), *aff'd sub nom.* 20 B.R. 220 (S.D.N.Y. 1982). In *Commonwealth Oil*, the court stated that a factor to consider in accounting for the interest of justice is the importance of CORCO to the economic stability and welfare of the people of Puerto Rico. *Id.* at 1248. However, because CORCO's difficulties were financial and could best be dealt with in Texas, the court found that the factors relating to the interest of justice weighed in favor if retaining the case in Texas. *Id.*

25. Although *Commonwealth Oil* was decided under the former chapter XI, the six factor test has been widely adopted by courts for use in chapter 11 cases. *In re* Pope Vineyards, 90 B.R. 252, 255 (Bankr. S.D. Tex. 1988). *See, e.g.*, Consolidated Equity Properties, Inc. v. Southmark Corp. (*In re* Consolidated Equity Properties, Inc.), 136 B.R. 261, 266-67 (D. Nev. 1991) (utilizing *Commonwealth Oil* factors in considering both convenience of parties and interest of justice); *In re* Boca Raton Sanctuary Assocs., 105 B.R. 273, 274-75 (Bankr. E.D. Pa. 1989) (omitting statutory language and solely utilizing *Commonwealth Oil* factors in determining whether to transfer case); *Pickwick Place*, 63 B.R. at 291-92 (reviewing *Commonwealth Oil* factors to determine whether transfer would be in interest of justice and convenience of parties).

    But see In re Portjeff Dev. Corp., 118 B.R. 184, 192 (Bankr. E.D.N.Y. 1990) (noting that phrases "for the convenience of the parties" and "in the interest of justice" give independent authority for transfer under § 1412); *In re* Toxic Control Technologies, Inc., 84 B.R. 140, 143 (Bankr. N.D. Ind. 1988) (stating that two requirements of § 1412 are discrete).

26. *Landmark Capital*, 19 B.R. at 348 (noting that rulings in accordance with Arizona law might be required and that Arizona court was in better position than New York court to make such rulings); *see also infra* note 35 and accompanying text (considering impact of possible application of local law in single asset cases).

27. *Portjeff Dev.*, 118 B.R. at 193 (asserting that state's interest in having local

case construing 28 U.S.C. § 1404(a),[28] one bankruptcy court has noted that "[f]actors traditionally considered in an 'interest of justice' analysis relate to the efficient administration of the court system."[29] In situations where petitions involving the same or related debtors are filed in different courts,[30] the interest in having concurrent related cases adjudicated by the same court also implicates the interest of justice.[31]

B. Transfer of Venue in Single Asset Cases

Notwithstanding a finding that venue is proper, courts will grant a movant's request to transfer the case to the district where the principal asset is located in most single asset cases.[32] In utilizing the *Commonwealth Oil* factors, courts often accommodate single asset cases by according additional weight to the location of the asset.[33] The reasons for this practice include the

---

controversies decided within its borders is significant consideration bearing on interests of justice); *Landmark Capital*, 19 B.R. at 348. The *Landmark Capital* court noted that since the debtor's principal asset and "centerpiece of Phoenix" is located in Arizona and employs thousands of people, there was a significant local interest in the success of a chapter 11 or the proper sale of the assets. *Landmark Capital*, 19 B.R. at 348; *see also infra* note 35 and accompanying text (discussing local interest in having localized controversies at home in context of single asset cases).

28. 28 U.S.C. § 1404(a) (1994). "For the convenience of parties and witnesses, in the interest of justice, a district court may transfer any civil action to any other district or division where it might have been brought." *Id.*

29. *Portjeff Dev.*, 118 B.R. at 192 (quoting Coffey v. Van Dorn Iron Works, 796 F.2d 217, 220-21 (7th Cir. 1986)).

30. *See* FED. R. BANKR. P. 1014(b) (providing that "the court may determine, in the interest of justice or for the convenience of the parties, the district or districts in which the case or cases should proceed."); *see also supra* note 7 and accompanying text (discussing how 1014(b) serves interest of justice).

31. *See, e.g.*, Lemke v. St. Margaret Hosp., 594 F. Supp. 25, 28 (N.D. Ill. 1983) (considering party's interest in avoiding simultaneous related suits in two distant states); *In re* Portjeff Dev. Corp., 118 B.R. 184, 193 (Bankr. E.D.N.Y. 1990) (noting objective of avoiding conflicting decisions).

32. *See supra* note 9 (listing decisions regarding transfer of venue motions in single asset cases).

33. *See, e.g., In re* Macatawa Hospitality, Inc., 158 B.R. 82, 86 (Bankr. E.D. Mich.

following: the case may require rulings in accordance with the law of the state in which the asset is located and the bankruptcy court sitting in that district is in the best position to make such determinations;[34] matters involving real

---

1993) (placing particular importance on location of asset); *In re* Oklahoma City Assocs., 98 B.R. 194, 199 (Bankr. E.D. Pa. 1989) (recognizing that estate of real estate partnership is most efficiently administered where principal asset is located); *In re* Bell Tower Assocs., 86 B.R. 795, 801 (Bankr. S.D.N.Y. 1988) (finding that location of asset plays a "pivotal role"); *In re* 1606 New Hampshire Ave. Assocs., 85 B.R. 298, 304 (Bankr. E.D. Pa. 1988) (recognizing numerous cases holding that venue should be transferred to locus of realty); *In re* Landmark Capital Co., 19 B.R. 342, 348 (Bankr. S.D.N.Y. 1982) (stating that transfer of case is consistent with principle that estate is most efficiently administered at location of principal asset), *aff'd sub nom.*, Landmark Capital Co. v. North Cent. Dev. Co. (*In re* Landmark Capital Co.), 20 B.R. 220 (S.D.N.Y. 1982). *But see In re* Garden Manor Assocs., 99 B.R. 551, 554-55 (Bankr. S.D.N.Y. 1988) (denying transfer of venue to location of asset). The *Garden Manor* court found that the location of the debtor's asset was offset by the nature of the debtor's business (a limited partnership owning one apartment complex in Arizona) and the direction that the reorganization would follow. *Id.* at 554. "[A]lthough the real estate is located in Arizona, it appears from the testimony that more of a custodial function is performed there and that the actual business is operated from New York." *Id.* at 555; *see also In re* Willows Ltd. Partnership, 87 B.R. 684, 686 (Bankr. S.D. Ala. 1988) (stating that in reorganization where goal is rehabilitation and not liquidation, location of debtor's asset is of little consequence) (quoting *In re* Commonwealth Oil Refining Co., 596 F.2d 1239, 1258 (5th Cir. 1979)); *In re* Holiday Towers, 18 B.R. 183, 188 (Bankr. S.D. Ohio 1982) (recognizing that location of debtor's asset is merely one factor to be weighed along with other factors); *In re* One-Eighty Invs., Ltd., 18 B.R. 725, 729 (Bankr. N.D. Ill. 1981) (determining that in reorganization proceeding location of debtor's asset has little significance).

34. *In re* Kona Joint Venture I, Ltd., 62 B.R. 169, 172 (Bankr. D. Haw. 1986); *In re* Greenridge Apartments, 13 B.R. 510, 513 (Bankr. D. Haw. 1981); *In re* Macon Uplands Venture, 2 B.R. 444, 450 (Bankr. D. Md. 1980); *see also In re* Boca Raton Sanctuary Assocs., 105 B.R. 273, 275 (Bankr. E.D. Pa. 1989) (recognizing that Florida courts are in better position to construe difficult issues of Florida law); *Oklahoma City*, 98 B.R. at 200 (asserting that transfer of venue to location of principal asset justified based on issues arising under that state's laws pertaining to secured creditor's motion for order prohibiting

property are traditionally a matter of local concern and should be decided by a local court;[35] the court sitting in the district where the asset is located is in the best position to evaluate appraisals of the property as well as the appraisers responsible for them;[36] and that the debtor has knowingly subjected itself to the possibility of legal action in the state in which he bought the property.[37] In furtherance of this policy of according special consideration to the location of the asset, bankruptcy judges in the Eastern District of Pennsylvania have rejected the *Commonwealth Oil* court's determination that the economic administration of the estate is the most important factor to be considered.[38] These Pennsylvania courts, while attempting to balance the

---

debtor's use of rents without court approval); *In re* Pavilion Place Assocs., 88 B.R. 32, 36 (Bankr. S.D.N.Y. 1988) (stating that transfer of case to Minnesota, site of debtor's sole asset, was supported by fact that issues of Minnesota law had already arisen and would likely continue to arise). *But see* Frazier v. Lawyer's Title Ins. Corp. (*In re* Butcher), 46 B.R. 109, 113-14 (Bankr. N.D. Ga. 1985) (rejecting argument that because questions of state law will arise proceeding should be decided in court where asset located).

35. *See Pavilion Place*, 88 B.R. at 36 (stating that "[i]mproved real estate is a peculiarly local concern often better administered by a court in the district in which it is located."); *In re* Eleven Oak Tower Ltd. Partnership, 59 B.R. 626, 629 (Bankr. N.D. Ill. 1986) (stating that proceeding should be in circuit where land is located and prior foreclosure took place); First Fed. Sav. & Loan Ass'n v. Dew Mortgage Co. (*In re* Dew Mortgage Co.), 10 B.R. 242, 244 (Bankr. M.D. Fla. 1981) (stating that real property matters are of local concern and are traditionally decided at situs of property); *see also Bell Tower*, 86 B.R. at 803 (stating that local courts should decide local disputes such as whether structural damage occurred to property and whether complex complied with local building codes); *In re* Old Delmar Corp., 45 B.R. 883, 885 (S.D.N.Y. 1985) (stating that local court is in best position to meet emergencies and administer real estate property); *Landmark Capital*, 19 B.R. at 348 (recognizing substantial local interest in reorganization because asset involved was "centerpiece" of Phoenix and offices in asset employed over 4,000 people).

36. *See Kona Joint Venture I*, 62 B.R. at 172 (discussing *In re Greenridge* and inherently local nature of appraisals); *Landmark Capital*, 19 B.R. at 348 (noting that local courts are best suited to evaluate local appraisers); *Greenridge Apartments*, 13 B.R. at 513 (finding local court in better position to evaluate appraisal of property and appraisers).

37. *Oklahoma City*, 98 B.R. at 199-200; *Pavilion Place*, 88 B.R. at 36.

38. *In re* Wood Family Interests, Ltd., 78 B.R. 434, 434 n.4 (Bankr. E.D. Pa.

factors enumerated in *Commonwealth Oil*, place greater weight on the location of the debtors principal asset.[39] Other courts have attempted to reconcile the efficient administration and economic administration views by finding that the estate will be administered most economically where the principal asset is located.[40]

There are, however, notable exceptions to the practice of transferring the case to the locale of the asset. For instance, courts usually retain the case where a substantial number of creditors agree to maintain the action in the

---

1987) (stating that court was not bound by fact that some courts deem economic administration of estate most important factor); *Oklahoma City*, 98 B.R. at 199 ("[I]n this district it has been stated that bankruptcy courts are not bound to consider `economic administration' as the `most important' criterion for consideration.") (quoting *Wood Family*, 78 B.R. 434 at n.4); *see also In re* 1606 New Hampshire Ave. Assocs., 85 B.R. 298, 304 (Bankr. E.D. Pa. 1988) (stating that analysis set forth in *Wood Family* provided key to proper resolution of secured creditor's motion to transfer case to locale of asset).

39. *See, e.g.*, *Wood Family*, 78 B.R. at 434 n.4 (finding location of debtor's principal asset and location of local witnesses persuasive in motion to change venue).

40. *Oklahoma City*, 98 B.R. at 199. "The administration of the estate is likely to be most economically conducted where it is in close proximity to the principal asset and witnesses (including creditors). Further, it is generally accepted that the estate of a real estate partnership is most efficiently administered where its principal asset is located." *Id.* (citations omitted)*; see Greenridge Apartments*, 13 B.R. at 513 (favoring rationale that held efficiency foremost among the factors enumerated in *Commonwealth Oil*). The *Greenridge* court followed the *Commonwealth Oil* court's determination that the most important consideration in deciding whether to transfer is whether doing so "would promote the economic and efficient administration of the estate." *Id.* The court held that Washington would be a more efficient place in which to administer the estate in large part because both the nonpartnership creditors and the partnership's primary asset were located there. *Id.; see also Eleven Oak Tower*, 59 B.R. at 629-30 (holding that administration of case involving highrise office tower could most efficiently and expeditiously be administered in court closest to debtor's principal asset); *Landmark Capital*, 19 B.R. at 348 (determining that transfer of case to locale of debtor's principal asset was consistent with principle that estate of real estate partnership is most efficiently administered where principal asset is situated).

district where the management is located.[41] Additionally, if the realty at issue is undeveloped or the locus of the realty is divided (not the usual single asset situations), transfer of the case may be denied.[42] Furthermore, where the movant's motion to transfer is not timely, it will be denied.[43]

---

41. *In re* Boca Raton Sanctuary Assocs., 105 B.R. 273, 275 (Bankr. E.D. Pa. 1989) (stating that court may deny change in venue motion if "substantial number of creditors concur that venue should be retained" by court where filing originally made); *1606 New Hampshire Ave.*, 85 B.R. at 304 (same); *In re* Island Club Marina, Ltd., 26 B.R. 505, 508 (Bankr. N.D. Ill. 1983) (stating that objection of majority of unsecured creditors to motion for change of venue was a relevant consideration); *In re* One-Eighty Invs., 18 B.R. 725, 728 (Bankr. N.D. Ill. 1981) (indicating that opposition to change of venue to locus of realty by secured and unsecured creditors is persuasive); *see also* Puerto Rico v. Commonwealth Oil Ref. Co. (*In re* Commonwealth Oil Ref. Co.), 596 F.2d 1239, 1248 (5th Cir. 1979) (noting that number of creditors and size of claims are factors of equal weight in venue consideration), *cert. denied*, 444 U.S. 1045 (1980).
42. *See In re* Melgar Enters., Inc., 140 B.R. 43, 47 (Bankr. E.D.N.Y. 1992) (stating that when a debtor's major asset is unimproved land, not requiring debtor's attendance in region, location of asset alone is not dispositive); *1606 New Hampshire Ave.*, 85 B.R. at 304 (noting that motions to change venue have been denied where substantial number of creditors agree that court where case is filed should retain venue or realty at issue is undeveloped and, therefore, testimony regarding its value is limited); *In re* Boca Dev. Assocs., 18 B.R. 648, 653-54 (Bankr. S.D.N.Y. 1982) (denying motion to transfer to location of property where property was vacant and no business was operated on property due to zoning restrictions); *In re* Marina Enters., Inc., 14 B.R. 327, 331-32 (Bankr. S.D. Fla. 1981) (denying motion to transfer venue to location of property where property consisted of unimproved parcel); *see also Boca Raton Sanctuary*, 105 B.R. at 275 (ease of administration and economy to the debtor alone may be sufficient to warrant denial of motion to transfer if division in location of realty or location of creditors exists).
43. *See Boca Raton Sanctuary*, 105 B.R. at 275 n.2. In finding that motion was timely brought, the court stated:

    > We would be much less receptive to this motion if [the movant] had delayed until after a significant issue was submitted to this court . . . . We believe that such motions should generally be filed no later than sixty (60) days after the case filing, before the debtor and the original filing court have expended resources in reliance upon the case's

C. The *Vienna Park* Decision

On November 22, 1989, Vienna Park Properties, a limited partnership,[44] filed a chapter 11 petition in the bankruptcy court in the Southern District of New York.[45] The two largest secured creditors filed a motion seeking transfer of the case to the Eastern District of Virginia, the location of the debtor's 300-unit apartment complex.[46] The bankruptcy court held that a "single consideration, the 'learning curve' established in this case, work[ed] to deny" the creditor's motion to transfer venue of the case to the district in which the debtor's sole asset was located.[47]

Although venue was proper, the creditor alleged that transfer was warranted in the interest of justice and for the convenience of the parties pursuant to 28 U.S.C. section 1412.[48] Since the debtor's principal place of business was in Virginia, where on-site managers managed the property, and

---

presence there.

Id; *1606 New Hampshire Ave.*, 85 B.R. at 305 (finding motion timely brought when filed within sixty days of commencement of case and before first major motion decided); *see also In re* Jones, 39 B.R. 1019, 1020 (Bankr. S.D.N.Y. 1984) (denying motion to transfer venue where one and a half years had passed since case commenced because transfer would result in duplication of administrative expenses and delay in reorganization process).

44. *See Vienna Park I*, 120 B.R. 320, 322 (Bankr. S.D.N.Y. 1990). The debtor was a New Jersey limited partnership with 53 limited partners, 47 of whom were located or resided in or near New York. *Id.* The general partners resided in or near New York City and had offices in New York. *Id.* The records and books pertaining to the property were situated in the New York office of the general partner, while the records pertaining to the day to day management of the property were located in Washington, D.C. and Virginia. *Id.* at 326.

45. *Id.* at 321.

46. *Vienna Park I*, 120 B.R. at 321-22. The motion was filed on January 10, 1990. *Vienna Park III*, 128 B.R. 373, 374 (Bankr. S.D.N.Y. 1991). A trial on the motion began on March 13, 1990, continued on March 14, 1990 and April 5, 1990, and concluded on April 25, 1990; after this, post-trial memoranda of law were submitted to the court. *Vienna Park I*, 120 B.R. at 321.

47. *Vienna Park III*, 128 B.R. at 374.

48. *Vienna Park I,* 120 B.R. at 321. The creditor also maintained that venue was improper under 28 U.S.C. § 1408 and that case should be transferred pursuant to Bankruptcy Rule 1014(a)(2). *Id.*

the debtor was merely a passive owner who delegated all managerial functions to local managers, the creditors claimed the "central nerve center" of the debtor was in Virginia.[49] The creditors, however, failed to demonstrate that the debtor's general partners in New York did not make long-range business decisions.[50] Applying the six factors set forth in *Commonwealth Oil*, the court recognized that the case would normally be transferred.[51] The court declined, however, to transfer the case after applying the "efficient administration of the case factor."[52] The secured creditors challenged this ruling,[53] and on appeal,

---

49. *Id.* at 328.

50. *Id.* at 329. The court stated that "[e]ven if the Debtor followed to the letter the suggestions made by either [of its on-site managers], it was the Debtor's business judgment to do so. The decisions not to change anything proposed by the on-site management are major management decisions." *Id.*; *see also supra* note 5 and accompanying text (discussing "nerve center" test).

51. *Id.* at 332.

52. *Vienna Park* I, 120 B.R. 320, 332 (Bankr. S.D.N.Y. 1990). The court stated that it had "decided numerous issues and matters in this case and finds that its imprint on this case is so pervasive that transfer to another bankruptcy judge would not be in keeping with judicial economy." *Id.*

53. *Vienna Park II*, 125 B.R. 84, 86 (S.D.N.Y. 1991). The creditors argued that the following constituted reversible error: 1) the court's finding that all of the *Commonwealth Oil* factors weighed in favor of transfer, yet the court declined to transfer because of the pervasiveness of its "imprint" on the case; and 2) the court's declared desire to avoid reversal on a question of Virginia law by a bankruptcy court sitting in Virginia. *Id.* at 87. The creditors argued that the bases for the decision was improper as a matter of law. *Id.*

On appeal, a trial court's findings of fact may not be set aside unless clearly erroneous. FED. R. BANKR. P. 8013; Crocker v. Braid Elec. Co. (*In re* Arnold), 908 F.2d 52, 55 (6th Cir. 1990); *Vienna Park II*, 125 B.R. at 87. This limitation does not extend to the district court's review of the bankruptcy court's conclusions of law, however, which must be reviewed *de novo*. *See, e.g., id.* (stating that district court must review bankruptcy court's conclusions of law *de novo*); Diamond Gateway Coal Co. v. LTV Corp. (*In re* Chateaugay Corp.), 104 B.R. 637, 642 (S.D.N.Y. 1989) (same); *In re* O.P.M. Leasing Servs., Inc., 79 B.R. 161, 162 (S.D.N.Y. 1987) (stating that district court may review bankruptcy court's conclusions of law *de novo*).

In the instant case, the district court held that "time and effort spent by a court are appropriate factors in determining the venue in which the estate may most efficiently and economically be administered. Thus, the bankruptcy court

the district court vacated the order of the bankruptcy court and remanded the matter to that court for clarification of its reasoning.[54]

---

did not err as a matter of law in considering its 'imprint' on the case." *Vienna Park II*, 125 B.R. at 87 (citing Gulf States Exploration Co. v. Manville Forest Prods. Corp. (*In re* Manville Forest Prods. Corp.), 896 F.2d 1384, 1391 (2d Cir. 1990)).

54. *Vienna Park II*, 125 B.R. at 88. The court found that "the language of the lower court regarding a desire to avoid reversal of its ruling concerning Virginia law suggests that an inappropriate criterion might have colored its decision on the venue motion." *Id.* at 87. The language the court is referring to includes the following:

> This Court has decided numerous issues and matters in this case and finds that its imprint on this case is so pervasive that transfer to another bankruptcy judge would not be in keeping with judicial economy. This is especially true because of my opinion, rendered *sua sponte* and signed and decided simultaneously with this decision, reversing an earlier decision. A bankruptcy judge should not be placed in a position of overruling a decision of another bankruptcy judge.

Vienna Park I, 120 B.R. at 332.

The opinion rendered *sua sponte* is reported in *In re* Vienna Park Properties, 120 B.R. 332 (Bankr. S.D.N.Y. 1990). There the court reconsidered its decision that the rents generated by the apartment complex were cash collateral as of the date of the debtors default on the loans. *Id.* at 335-36. *See In re* Vienna Park Properties, 112 B.R. 597, 598, 600 (Bankr. S.D.N.Y. 1990) (construing Virginia law concerning assignment of rent pursuant to United States Supreme Court guidelines). On reconsideration, the court vacated its previous order and held that the secured creditors "were not entitled to collect rents prior to the Debtor's filing of its petition . . . ." *Vienna Park Properties*, 120 B.R. at 338. The court also denied their "claim to entitlement of the rents prospectively as of the filing of the motion for the sequestration of the rents . . . ." *Id.* at 340.

The secured creditors appealed from the latter decision, and the district court held that the secured creditors were entitled to sequestration of the rents from the date they filed such motion under the cash collateral provisions of the Code. *In re* Vienna Park Properties, 136 B.R. 43, 55, 58 (S.D.N.Y. 1992). Vienna Park appealed from this decision, and the Second Circuit held that the rents were cash collateral, that they were so from the outset of bankruptcy, and that the sequestration motion should have been granted. Vienna Park Properties v. United Postal Sav. Assoc. (*In re* Vienna Park Properties), 976

On remand, the bankruptcy court reviewed its prior application of the *Commonwealth Oil* factors,[55] and again found that the economic administration of the estate, specifically the "learning curve" established in the case supported the denial of the motion to transfer.[56] The court stated that this learning curve factor encompassed consideration of the time and effort the court had expended in the case.[57] Since the court's prior involvement with the case was extensive, the court had already resolved a cash collateral dispute and approved the debtor's attempt to make improvements on the property, the court concluded that the "learning curve" issue warranted a denial of the transfer.[58] Although the court acknowledged that it was inclined to agree that the economic administration of the estate would be better served by a transfer to Virginia, it nonetheless found the "learning curve" factor decisive.[59] In making its determination, the court relied almost exclusively on *Manville Forest Products*.[60] *Manville Forest Products*, however, is arguably distinguishable from *Vienna Park*. First, *Manville Forest Products* involved a motion to transfer a proceeding rather than a motion to transfer a case.[61]

F.2d 106, 114 (2d Cir. 1992).

55. *Vienna Park III*, 128 B.R. at 375-76. The court applied the *Commonwealth Oil* factors to address both bases for transfer under 28 U.S.C. § 1412. *Id.* Both the debtor and creditor cited these factors as the legal standard. *Id.* at 375. *See also supra* note 24 and accompanying text.

56. *Vienna Park III*, 128 B.R. at 378. The court held and the district court agreed that the time and effort expended by a court, or its imprint on the case, are appropriate factors in determining the venue where the estate will be most economically and efficiently administered. *Id.* at 376.

57. *Id.* at 377-78. The court discussed its earlier finding that its progress on the "learning curve" was too far advanced to allow a transfer of the case. *Id.* at 377 (citing Gulf States Exploration Co. v. Manville Forest Prods. Corp. (*In re* Manville Forest Prods. Corp.), 896 F.2d 1384, 1391 (2d Cir. 1989)).

58. *Id.* at 377-78. The court stated:

> A transfer of venue would have imposed on the new court the burdensome task of moving up along the "learning curve" and would have delayed the entire reorganization process. Ultimately, a delay in the reorganization process would not have worked in favor of the convenience of the parties or the interest of justice.

Id. at 378; *see supra* note 56 (discussing court's "imprint" on case).

59. *Vienna Park III*, 128 B.R. at 378.

60. *See id.* at 377-78.

61. *Manville Forest Prods.*, 896 F.2d at 1386; *see also In re* New Hampshire Ave.

Additionally, the district in which the bankruptcy case is pending is presumed to be the appropriate venue for the proceedings within the case.[62] Second, the *Manville Forest Products* court found that the motion to transfer was untimely and denied the motion, in part, for this reason.[63] As of the date of this writing, there are no reported cases which have followed the holding of *Vienna Park*.[64]

Assocs., 85 B.R. 298 (Bankr. E.D. Pa. 1988) (stating that "different consequences ensue when the movant seeks transfer venue [sic] of an adversarial proceeding within a case rather than, as here, transfer of the entire case. We are most reluctant to allow pieces to be severed from a case . . . .").

62. *See, e.g.*, Silverman v. U.W. Marx, Inc. (*In re* Leco Enters., Inc.), 125 B.R. 385, 392 (S.D.N.Y. 1991) (noting strong presumption favoring maintenance of venue where bankruptcy proceeding is pending); Lionel Leisure, Inc. v. Trans Cleveland Warehouses, Inc. (*In re* Lionel Corp.), 24 B.R. 141, 143 (Bankr. S.D.N.Y. 1982) (recognizing "general presumption that all matters involving a bankruptcy should be tried in the court in which the bankruptcy is pending"); First Fed. Sav. & Loan Ass'n v. Dew Mortgage Co. (*In re* Dew Mortgage Co.), 10 B.R. 242, 244 (Bankr. M.D. Fla. 1981) (stating that presumption for deciding all bankruptcy matters in a single forum is not easily overcome); *see also* 1 COLLIER, *supra* note 4, ¶ 3.02[4][a], at 3-153 (discussing transfer of proceedings pursuant to § 1412).

63. *Manville Forest Prods.*, 896 F.2d at 1391. Other courts have also found that a party's failure to file a motion to transfer before the court has decided other issues is a factor to be considered in resolving transfer motions. *See In re* Boca Raton Sanctuary Assocs., 105 B.R. 273, 275 n.2 (Bankr. E.D. Pa. 1989). The court asserted that "[w]e would be much less receptive to this motion if [the creditor] had delayed until after a significant issue was submitted to this court, as in the [Franklin Pembroke Venture] case . . . ." *Id.* at 275 n.2. In *Franklin Pembroke Venture*, the debtor moved to use the rents from its office complex to pay ordinary costs and expenses. *See In re* Franklin Pembroke Venture II, 105 B.R. 276, 276 (Bankr. E.D. Pa. 1989). The debtor's only secured creditor opposed the motion, arguing that it had a valid security interest in the rents under Florida law, which was applicable because the debtor's asset was located there. *Id.*; *see also 1606 New Hampshire Ave.*, 85 B.R. at 305 (discussing factors favoring transfer motion); FED. R. BANK. P. 1014, advisory committee's note (noting that "transfer would result in fragmentation or duplication of administration, increase expense, or delay closing the estate, . . . bear[ing] on the timeliness of the motion as well as on the propriety of the transfer under the [interest of justice or for convenience of the parties] standards.").

64. In *In re* Standard Tank Cleaning Corp., 133 B.R. 562 (Bankr. E.D.N.Y. 1991), the court took note of the "learning curve" factor but found that the facts of the

Conclusion

In conclusion, the factors set forth in *Commonwealth Oil* are accepted as the legal standard in determining transfer of venue motions in single asset cases, with the location of the asset taking on significantly more weight than the economic administration of the estate. Typically, courts reach the conclusion that the bankruptcy court sitting in the jurisdiction in which the single asset is located is best qualified to deal with matters that arise in and are characteristic of single asset cases. Practitioners should bear in mind, however, that a motion to transfer venue should be timely brought, since the timeliness of the motion, in addition to the related consideration of the "learning curve" established in *Vienna Park*, may be taken into account by the court.

---

case made it inappropriate to take such factor into account in determining the appropriate venue of the case. *Id.* at 568-69. The court found that the case was distinguishable from both *Vienna Park* and *Manville Forest Products* insofar as the court's ascension along the "learning curve" was the "result of the Debtor's motion to vacate the prior order transferring venue. Accordingly, this Court's familiarly with this case as a result of the Debtor's actions would not be an appropriate factor in determining that venue belongs here." *Id.* It is noted that *Standard Tank* is not a single asset case.

CHAPTER V

TAX ASPECTS OF REAL ESTATE MORTGAGE FORECLOSURES AND WORKOUTS FOR NONCORPORATE BORROWERS

ALBERT J. CARDINALI
DAVID C. MILLER

In recent years, mortgage defaults, foreclosures and workouts have become commonplace.[1] Many borrowers, already facing the possible loss of their investments, are surprised to discover that they also may incur substantial tax liability despite incurring a loss or successfully restructuring their debt.[2] Not surprisingly, many of these borrowers have resorted to bankruptcy courts in search of relief. Thorough and timely tax planning can often mitigate the financial problems of such borrowers. Conversely, the absence of such planning can result in unexpected and otherwise avoidable costs.[3] This

---

1. *See* Ronald Goldstein, *Reforming the Residential Mortgage Foreclosure Process*, 21 REAL ESTATE L.J. 286, 286 (1993) (discussing recent rush of residential foreclosure sales).
2. Many mortgage defaults, foreclosures, and workouts involve the cancellation of debt because it may be advantageous for the creditor to help the debtor avoid bankruptcy. LYNN M. LOPUCKI, STRATEGIES FOR CREDITORS IN BANKRUPTCY PROCEEDINGS § 3.6 (1985). When a creditor does cancel debt, the borrower realizes cancellation of debt ("COD") income. I.R.C. § 61(a)(12) (1994); *see* discussion *infra* Part A.1. (regarding COD income).
3. A New York State Bar Association report on tax laws governing corporate bankruptcy proceedings, described the area as "complex, inconsistent, and unpredictable. Its underlying policies are uncertain; its applications erratic. There is no first principle to provide direction. The statute–in many instances–simply does not provide coherent answers to the day-to-day questions that arise in planning and consummating bankruptcy reorganization plans." COMMITTEE ON BANKRUPTCY, *Report on Suggested Bankruptcy Tax Revenue Rulings*, NEW YORK STATE BAR ASSOCIATION, 50 TAX NOTES 631 (1991).

Chapter discusses the tax treatment of foreclosures, workouts and bankruptcies involving real estate financing. Real estate financing transactions involving more than one equity investor is usually pursued through a partnership in order to avoid an entity level tax on earnings (*i.e.*, a corporate tax) and generally permit investors to deduct losses.[4] Accordingly, the scope of this Chapter will be limited to individual and partnership investments.[5]

---

4. This includes, for example, losses generated by deductions for depreciation. Such losses are subject to certain limitations, such as the limitation on deductions of "passive activity losses." *See* I.R.C. § 469 (1994).
5. For purposes of this discussion, "partnerships" includes limited liability companies and other entities that are treated as partnerships for tax purposes. *See, e.g.*, Rev. Proc. 95-10, 1995-1 I.R.B. 20; Rev. Rul. 94-6, 1994-1 C.B. 314; Rev. Rul. 93-38, 1993-1 C.B. 233. Other business organizations, such as S corporations, are sometimes used in real estate financing transactions, but have disadvantages for an investor as compared to a partnership. For example, the amount of an S corporation's losses that can be deducted by a shareholder is limited, to the shareholder's basis in the shares of stock in the corporation. I.R.C. § 1366(d)(1)(A) (1994). This is similar to principles applicable to partnerships. *See* discussion *infra* Part A.3.a. However, in the case of an S corporation, basis does not include any portion of loans made to the corporation, whereas loans to a partnership are allocated to the bases of the partners. Estate of Leavitt v. Commissioner, 90 T.C. 206, 212 (stating that loan not included in basis of shareholder even if shareholder personally guarantees loan to S corporation), *aff'd*, 875 F.2d 420 (4th Cir. 1988), *cert. denied*, 493 U.S. 958 (1989). Nevertheless, for various reasons an S corporation can provide substantially more beneficial tax results in a workout situation. A principal reason is that the favorable treatment of COD income for insolvent taxpayers depends on insolvency tested at the corporate level rather than the shareholder level, a rule opposite to that used for partnerships and partners. I.R.C. § 108(d)(7); *see* Richard M. Lipton et al., *Planning for Noncorporate Debt Workouts Outside of Bankruptcy*, C135 ALI-ABA 847, 852 (1995). For an excellent discussion of some of the advantages S corporations and their shareholders have over partnerships and partners when a business is in financial difficulty, *see generally* Richard M. Lipton, *The Story of the Tortoise and the Hare: Workouts Involving S Corporations*, 72 TAXES 163 (1994).

   Although C corporations can also be partners in a partnership and thereby achieve some of the tax results discussed generally in this Chapter, U.A. §§ 2, 6.2 (1914); R.U.A. § 101(8),(11) (1994), this discussion assumes that the

Part A sets forth rules of general application to workouts and foreclosures not involving bankrupt or insolvent debtors. Part B deals with general rules pertaining to insolvency and bankruptcy. Part C focuses more specifically on partners and partnerships in bankruptcy.

A. Tax Treatment of Transactions Involving Distressed Investments in General

The tax consequences of workouts and dispositions of encumbered real property can seem perverse to an ordinary taxpayer. At a time when the debtor's financial world is crumbling and the value of the debtor's property may be well below its cost, a debtor often will realize, or be in danger of realizing, income substantially in excess of both the value of the property and any cash that may be realized by the debtor or the debtor's creditors in the transaction. These results follow from two basic rules of federal income taxation. First, a cancellation or reduction in the principal amount of a debt can result in the realization of income ("COD income") by the debtor.[6] Second, a foreclosure or other disposition of encumbered real property[7] can result in the realization of income by the debtor, in the form of both gain and COD income.

1. Cancellation of Indebtedness

The original authority for the inclusion of a reduction of debt in income is the 1931 Supreme Court decision in *United States v. Kirby Lumber Co.*[8] which held that a corporation realized COD income when it purchased its own

---

partners in the partnerships discussed are individuals. Furthermore, although this Chapter does not deal with the tax treatment of corporations in bankruptcy, the reader should be aware that there is a substantial body of legislative, administrative, and judicial tax law pertaining exclusively to such corporations. For a general discussion of corporate bankruptcy laws, see DANIEL R. COWANS, 3 BANKRUPTCY LAW AND PRACTICE § 16 (6th ed. 1994).

6. I.R.C. § 61(a)(12) (1994).
7. Such as a "deed in lieu," a sale or, possibly, an abandonment. *See infra* Part A.2. (discussing tax treatment of foreclosures, "deed in lieu" transfers and abandonment of property encumbered with recourse debt).
8. 284 U.S. 1 (1931).

bonds from the public at a discount because the purchase resulted in a debt reduction without a corresponding reduction in assets.[9] That rule is now codified in section 61(a)(12) of the Internal Revenue Code (the "IRC")[10] and in the related Treasury Regulations which provide that a settlement of a debt for less than its face amount can result in COD income.[11] Although COD income can arise in many contexts,[12] and in a variety of ways, real estate workouts and foreclosures are most likely to produce COD income in the situations discussed below.

a. Foreclosure of Recourse Debt[13]

When a debt is discharged in a foreclosure or a "deed in lieu" transaction involving recourse liability, the borrower will realize COD income to the extent the outstanding principal balance of the loan discharged exceeds the fair market value of the property securing the loan.[14] In a foreclosure, fair market

---

9. *Id.* at 3.
10. I.R.C. § 61(a)(12) (1994).
11. Treas. Reg. § 1.61-12(a) (as amended in 1980).
12. One example is the repurchase of corporate bonds at a price lower than the issuance price. Treas. Reg. § 1.61-12(c) (as amended in 1980).
13. For a more detailed discussion of the tax treatment of foreclosures *see infra* Part A.2. The following is a preliminary explanation of how foreclosures and workouts can create COD income. There are a number of exceptions and exclusions to COD income. *See* I.R.C. § 108(a)(1)(A) (1994) (discussing discharge in bankruptcy cases); *id.* § 108(a)(1)(B) (discussing taxpayer insolvency). The most important exclusion in the context of depreciable real property used in a trade or business may be the recently enacted election to exclude COD income arising from the discharge of "qualified real property business indebtedness." I.R.C. § 108(a)(1)(D),(c) (1994). These provisions are effective for discharges of indebtedness occurring after January 31, 1992 in tax years ending after that date. Omnibus Budget Reconciliation Act of 1993 ("OBRA 93"), Pub. L. No. 103-66, 107 Stat. 446, 446-48. For a further discussion of the exclusion for qualified real property business indebtedness, see *infra* Part A.1.e. Examples 1, in this subsection, and 2 in subsection A.1.c.(4), are intended to demonstrate how certain transactions can result in COD income, and assume that the taxpayers in question have not elected to use the exclusion of COD income arising with respect to "qualified real property business indebtedness."
14. Rev. Rul. 90-16, 1990-1 C.B. 12.

value is usually determined by the bid price because that is the amount by which the debt is reduced.[15] If the debtor remains liable for a deficiency judgment, there is no COD income unless and until the judgment is discharged for less than the amount of that judgment.[16] The debtor also realizes gain or loss in an amount equal to the difference between the fair market value of the property and the debtor's adjusted basis in the property (which is often below its fair market value).[17] Although some case law suggests that a debtor realizes gain measured by the full amount of the debt discharged and, therefore, has no COD income,[18] the present view of the Internal Revenue Service (the "IRS") is that the transaction must be treated as having two distinct parts: (1) a sale of property, and (2) a discharge of indebtedness.[19] The critical nature of the distinction between COD income[20] and gain from a disposition[21] needs to be

---

15. Treas. Reg. § 1.166-6(b)(2) (as amended in 1967) (stating presumption that bid price of property is fair market value).
16. *See generally* Aizawa v. Commissioner, 99 T.C. 197 (1992), *aff'd*, 29 F.3d 630 (9th Cir. 1994).
17. *Id.* at 202; Rev. Rul. 90-16, 1990-1 C.B. 12; *see* Example 1 *infra* p. 112.
18. *See* Turney's Estate v. Commissioner, 126 F.2d 712, 713-14 (5th Cir. 1942).
19. Rev. Rul. 90-16, 1990-1 C.B. 12; *see also* Gehl v. Commissioner, 95-1 U.S. Tax Cas. (CCH) ¶ 50,191 (stating that transfer by debtor to creditor of property having fair market value in excess of basis but less than unpaid balance of recourse debt results in gain and not COD income), *cert. denied*, 116 S.Ct. 257 (1995); Priv. Ltr. Rul. 91-20-010 (Feb. 14, 1991). In the unlikely event that the fair market value of the property exceeds the debt, there would be no COD income because the entire debt would be satisfied. The treatment of a foreclosure of recourse debt should be contrasted with the results of a foreclosure of nonrecourse debt under which the debtor will realize only gain and no COD income. *See* discussion *infra* Part A.2.b.
20. COD income is ordinary income if it must be currently included in income. I.R.C. § 64 (1994) (providing ordinary income includes any gain from property not characterized as capital asset or property as defined by I.R.C. § 1231(b)). It may, however, qualify for one of the available exclusions at the cost of a reduction in favorable tax attributes. I.R.C. § 108(b) (1994) (providing for reduction in certain enumerated tax attributes equaling amount excluded).
21. In the case of real estate, gain from a disposition will ordinarily be capital gain. I.R.C. § 1221(2) (1994); *see* JACOB MERTENS, JR., REAL ESTATE SALE AND EXCHANGES § 22A.01 (Clark Boardmen Callaghan 1995) (discussing generally when real property is includable as capital gain). This is so except to the extent accelerated depreciation in excess of straight-line depreciation has been

kept in mind when determining the course of action a debtor should adopt to minimize the ordinarily adverse tax consequences of a foreclosure or workout.[22]

> *Example* 1 - Debtor borrows $100,000 on a recourse basis from Lender to acquire property. The loan is secured by a first mortgage on the property. Debtor defaults after taking depreciation deductions of $50,000 and before making any principal payments on the loan. Lender forecloses with a bid price of $60,000 and negotiates a settlement with Debtor under which Debtor is released from liability for the $40,000 deficiency upon making a $10,000 cash payment to Lender. Debtor realizes a gain of $10,000 ($60,000 bid price minus $50,000 adjusted basis) and has COD income of $30,000 ($40,000 deficiency cancellation minus $10,000 payment).

b. Purchase of Debt

COD income also will be realized by a debtor who purchases the debt for an amount less than the balance owed.[23] A similar result will be obtained if the debt is acquired at a discount by a party related to the debtor from an unrelated creditor.[24] In such case, the amount of COD income will depend upon whether there is a direct acquisition of the debt by the related party from the unrelated creditor or an indirect acquisition, *i.e.*, a transaction in which an unrelated creditor becomes related to the debtor if the creditor acquired the debt in anticipation of becoming so related.[25] Subject to certain modifications, a "related" party is one bearing a relationship to the debtor specified in sections 267(b)[26] or 707(b)(1)[27] of the IRC which, in general, includes certain family

---

claimed. I.R.C. § 167 (1994) (allowing depreciation deductions); *id.* § 1250(a)(1)(A) (providing that upon disposition gain shall be characterized as ordinary income).

22. *See* discussion *infra* Part A.2.
23. Treas. Reg. § 1.61-12(a) (as amended in 1980).
24. I.R.C. § 108(e)(4) (1994).
25. Treas. Reg. § 1.108-2(a) to (e) (as amended in 1992) (providing rules and definition for direct and indirect acquisition).
26. I.R.C. § 267(b) (1994) (defining related parties).
27. *Id.* § 707(b)(1) (providing certain partnership losses shall be disallowed).

members and controlled entities.[28] The determination of whether the debt was acquired in anticipation of the creditor becoming related to the debtor is made under a facts and circumstances test.[29] However, a creditor will be deemed to have acquired the indebtedness in anticipation of becoming so related if the creditor acquired the indebtedness less than six months before the date on which the creditor became related to the debtor.[30] In the case of a direct acquisition, or an indirect acquisition where the creditor acquires the debt by purchase within six months before the creditor becomes related to the debtor, the COD income will be an amount equal to the difference between the amount of the debt and the adjusted basis of the debt in the hands of the related creditor[31] (usually, the purchase price). However, in the case of an indirect acquisition, if the original creditor did not become related to the debtor within such six month period, the COD income is measured by the fair market value of the indebtedness on the date the creditor becomes related to the debtor.[32]

c. Modifications

For income tax purposes, a material change in the terms of a debt instrument (a "modification") is treated as an exchange of the debt instrument for a new obligation[33] and can result in the realization of COD income.[34] In

---

28. I.R.C. § 108(e)(4) (1994); Treas. Reg. § 1.108-2(d)(2).
29. Treas. Reg. § 1.108-2(c)(2) (as amended in 1992).
30. *Id.* § 1.108-2(c).
31. *Id.* § 1.108-2(f).
32. *Id.* § 1.108-2(f). Such transactions between a debtor and a related party will also produce original issue discount in an amount equal to the difference between the amount of the debt and either the purchase price or the fair market value of the debt, whichever was used in determining the debtor's COD income. *Id.* § 1.108-2(g)(1). Compare the computations of COD income and original issue discount using the issue price of the debt in the case of the issuance of new debt in satisfaction of a debt under I.R.C. § 108(e)(10). *See infra* Part A.1.c.(4) (discussing original issue discount).
33. Prop. Treas. Reg. § 1.1001-3(a), 57 Fed. Reg. 57034, 57036 (1992) (as amended in 1994). *See* Rev. Rul. 87-19, 1987-1 C.B. 249 (stating that material changes in terms of debt instrument results in a taxable change in income under I.R.C. § 1001). Modifications do not occur solely in workout or foreclosure situations. For example, during periods of high interest rates lenders may try to induce their low rate borrowers to prepay at discounts; such a discount

view of the 1991 United States Supreme Court decision in *Cottage Savings Association v. Commissioner,*[35] changes that previously were not considered material may now result in an exchange of debt instruments. In that decision the Supreme Court held that an exchange of mortgage pools that were considered to be economically equivalent was nevertheless taxable because the pools embodied "legally distinct entitlements" and were, therefore, "materially different."[36] In light of controversy generated by the decision and dicta in *Cottage Savings*, the IRS has issued proposed regulations[37] dealing with the federal income tax consequences of modifications of debt instruments.

(1) Proposed Regulations

The principal purpose of the proposed regulations is to clarify when a modification of a debt instrument will be treated as an exchange of the original instrument for a materially different instrument[38] with the correlated realization of gain or loss by the holder of the debt instrument. In addition, if a modification results in an exchange, such modification could result in the realization of cancellation of indebtedness income to the borrower and the creation of original issue discount with respect to the modified loan.[39] Furthermore, a transaction deemed to be a reissuance of a debt instrument can have other consequences due to the reissuance occurring after the effective

---

would be COD income to the borrower. Sutphin v. United States, 14 Cl. Ct. 545, 551 (1988); Rev. Rul. 82-202, 1982-2 C.B. 35.

34. Prop. Treas. Reg. § 1.1001-3(a), 57 Fed. Reg. 57034, 57036 (1992).
35. 499 U.S. 554 (1991).
36. *Id.* at 566.
37. Prop. Treas. Reg. § 1.1001-3, 57 Fed. Reg. 57034 (1992); *see generally* Laurence H. Brenman, *Tax Oriented Investments-Proposed Regulations Regarding Debt Modification Issued in Response to Cottage Savings Decision*, 10 J. PARTNERSHIP TAX'N 175 (1993); George G. Wolf & Steven C. Molvey, *IRS Proposes Debt Modification Rules in Response to Cottage Savings*, 78 J. TAX'N 140 (1993).
38. Prop. Treas. Reg. § 1.1001-3(a), 57 Fed. Reg. 57034, 57036 (1992) (as amended in 1994). Under existing regulations, gain or loss is realized on an "exchange of property differing materially either in kind or extent." Prop. Treas. Reg. § 1.1001-3(b), (e), 57 Fed. Reg. 57034, 57036 (1992).
39. *Id.* § 1.1001-3(a); Treas. Reg. § 1.1001-1(a) (as amended in 1994); I.R.C. § 1273 (1994).

dates of intervening changes in the tax law since the debt instrument's original issuance.[40] The question of whether a modification is a sale or exchange can arise in connection with a number of common transactions, such as the resetting of interest rates, conversion from fixed to variable or from variable to fixed rates, the substitution or addition of collateral, changes in credit enhancement, the waiver of rights (*e.g.*, accelerations, interest resets), and extensions.[41] Final regulations on this subject were expected to be promulgated in 1995, but have not been issued as of the date of this publication.

Under the proposed regulations, the determination of whether there is an exchange of the original debt instrument for another debt instrument that is materially different involves a two-step test. First, there must be a determination of whether there has been a modification of the debt instrument. Second, there must be a determination of whether such a modification is a "significant modification."[42] Thus, a modification that is not a significant modification is not such an exchange.[43] A significant modification of debt instrument is treated as an exchange of the original instrument for another instrument that differs materially in kind or extent.[44]

(i) Modifications

The proposed regulations define the term "modification" broadly to mean "any alteration in any legal right or obligation (including the addition or deletion of a right or obligation) of the issuer or a holder of a debt instrument, whether the alteration is evidenced by amendments of the instrument, conduct of the parties or otherwise."[45] However, the proposed regulations also provide two exceptions to this broad definition. First, a temporary failure of the issuer to perform its obligations under a debt instrument and a temporary stay of

---

40. *See* Philip S. Winterer, *"Reissuance" and Deemed Exchanges Generally*, 37 TAX LAW 509, 511 (1984). Since Congress frequently changes the law in certain areas, the law may not be the same as when the debt instrument was issued and therefore a deemed exchange may result in unplanned consequences. *Id.*
41. Prop. Treas. Reg. § 1.1001-3(d), 57 Fed. Reg. 57034, 57036 (1992).
42. *Id.* § 1.1001-3(e).
43. *Id.* § 1.1001-3(a).
44. *Id.*
45. *Id.* § 1.1001-3(c).

collection or temporary waiver of an acceleration clause or similar default right by a holder of a debt instrument are not modifications.[46] For example, a holder's waiver, pursuant to negotiations between the parties, of its right to accelerate for three months in order to allow the issues to arrange short-term balancing is a temporary waiver and not a modification.[47]

Second, an alteration of a legal right or obligation that occurs pursuant to the original terms of the debt instrument, including any such alteration that occurs through the unilateral waiver or exercise of a right under the debt instrument by either the issuer or the holder, is not a modification.[48] Accordingly, an adjustment to the interest rate, pursuant to the terms of a debt instrument, is not a modification.[49] A *waiver* is not unilateral, and therefore is a modification, if it represents a settlement of terms among the parties.[50] Thus, the proposed regulations specifically provide that a workout of a debt instrument is a modification even if the workout results only in a reduction in the interest rate or in the stated principal amount of the instrument.[51] In general, a waiver will represent a settlement of terms among the parties and, will, therefore, constitute a modification if the party making the waiver receives a benefit from the other party to the instrument. This is so even though other facts and circumstances may result in a contrary conclusion.[52] An *exercise* is not unilateral if: (1) "it creates a right in the other party to alter or terminate the instrument, or to put the instrument to a third party"; (2) "it requires consent of the other party, unless that consent may not be unreasonably withheld; or" (3) "it requires consideration, unless the amount of the consideration is fixed on the issue date" of the instrument.[53] For example, if the terms of a fixed rate debt instrument allow the holder to convert a variable rate upon payment of an administrative fee, the exercise will be unilateral because the fee was fixed on the issue date.[54] Conversely, if the

---

46. Prop Treas. Reg. § 1.1001-3(c)(2)(ii), 57 Fed. Reg. 57034, 57036 (1992).
47. *Id.* § 1.1001-3(d).
48. *Id.* § 1.1001-3(c)(2)(i).
49. *Id.* § 1.1001-3(d).
50. *Id.* § 1.1001-3.
51. Prop. Treas. Reg. § 1.1001-3(c)(2)(i)(B), 57 Fed. Reg. 57034, 57036 (1992).
52. *Id.*
53. *Id.* § 1.1001-3(c)(2)(i)(A).
54. *Id.* § 1.1001-3(d); *see also* Wolf & Molvey, *supra* note 37, at 141 (discussing proposed application of regulations).

issuer exercises its right to convert to a fixed rate, but the holder gains the right to put the bond to the issuer, the issuer's exercise of the right is not unilateral.[55]

The proposed regulations also provide that the "alteration of the terms of a debt instrument . . . is a modification if [it] results in an instrument or property right that is not debt for federal income tax purposes," even if the alteration occurs by operation of the original terms of the instrument.[56] However, the exercise of a right to convert a debt instrument into stock of the issuer is not a modification if it is pursuant to the terms of the original debt instrument.[57]

(ii) "Significant" Modifications

The second step in testing whether an exchange of the original instrument for a materially different one has occurred is a determination of whether the modification is a "significant modification." In general, this determination is made on the basis of the relevant facts and circumstances. However, the proposed regulations specifically discuss the circumstances under which four types of modifications may or may not be significant.[58] In addition, under the proposed regulations "a ministerial change in the terms of an instrument, such as a change in the mechanics of making a payment, is not a significant modification."[59] The four types of modifications discussed are: (1) changes in yield; (2) changes in timing or amounts of payments; (3) changes in obligors or security; and (4) changes in the nature of the instrument.

Changes in Yield. The same "bright line" tests apply to three different situations involving changes in yield. First, a mere change in the annual rate of an instrument that provides for current interest payments will be "a significant modification if the modified rate varies from the original rate by more than one fourth of one percent" (*i.e.*, twenty-five basis points).[60] Second, in the case of a variable rate debt instrument, a change in the index or other mechanism used to determine the interest rate for each period will be "a

---

55. *See supra* note 54.
56. Prop. Treas. Reg. § 1.1001-3(c)(3), 57 Fed. Reg. 57034, 57036 (1992).
57. *Id.*
58. *Id.* § 1.1001-3(e).
59. *Id.*
60. *Id.* § 1.1001-3(e)(1)(i).

significant modification if it can reasonably be expected to affect the annual yield on the instrument by more than one fourth of one percent."[61] Lastly, a modification that changes the annual yield will be a significant modification if the annual yield after the modification, measured from the date the parties agree to the modification to its final maturity date, varies from the annual yield on the original, unmodified instrument for the same period by more than one fourth of one percent.[62] For this purpose, the annual yield after the modification is computed by increasing the adjusted issue price immediately before the modification by any accrued but unpaid interest or, in the case of any prepaid discount instrument, by any unaccrued discount included in the prepayment, and is also increased or decreased to reflect any payment made to the issuer or to the holder as consideration for the modification.[63]

Changes in Timing and/or Amounts of Payments. With respect to the deferral of payments, a change in the timing or amount of payments will be a significant modification if it "materially defers" payments due under the instrument or if the change is designed to avoid the application of the original issue discount rules.[64] An extension of the final maturity date will be a significant modification if it exceeds the lesser of five years or fifty percent of the original term of the instrument.[65] However, "extensions of the final maturity of an instrument for only *de minimis* payments are disregarded."[66] This would be a significant change from the IRS's position that changes in maturity alone are not "material" modifications under the existing regulations under section 1001 of the IRC.[67] A partial prepayment is not a significant modification.[68] However, the proposed regulations warn that a change in the terms of the remaining portion of the debt could be a significant modification even though a "commercially reasonable" prepayment penalty for the partial prepayment is not a change in the remaining portion and is not to be

61. Prop. Treas. Reg. § 1.1001-3(e)(1)(iii), 57 Fed. Reg. 57037 (1992).
62. *Id.* § 1.1001-3(e)(1)(ii).
63. *Id.*
64. *Id.* § 1.1001-3(e)(2).
65. *Id.* § 1.1001-3(e)(2)(ii).
66. Prop. Treas. Reg. § 1.1001-3(e)(2)(ii), 57 Fed. Reg. 57034, 57037 (1992) (emphasis added).
67. Rev. Rul. 73-160, 1973-1 C.B. 365.
68. Prop. Treas. Reg. § 1.1001-3(e)(2)(iii), 57 Fed. Reg. 57034, 57037 (1992).

considered a modification that affects the yield of the debt.[69] The addition or deletion of a put or call of the debt instrument that has significant value at the time is a significant modification.[70] Alterations in an existing put or call right are similarly treated if the alteration "significantly" affects the right's value.[71]

Change in Obligor or Security. The treatment of a change in obligor or security often will depend upon whether the debt obligation is recourse or nonrecourse. For example, a substitution of a new obligor is a significant modification with respect to recourse debt but not with respect to nonrecourse debt.[72] The addition of a co-obligor is not a significant modification unless it is intended to circumvent the rule regarding the substitution of a new obligor with respect to recourse debt.[73] Also, the addition or material alteration of a guarantee or other form of credit enhancement is a significant modification with respect to nonrecourse debt.[74] However, it is not a significant modification with respect to recourse debt unless the provider of the guaranty or credit enhancement is, in substance, substituted as the obligor and the exchange is designed to circumvent the general rule that the substitution of a new obligor is a significant modification with respect to recourse debt.[75] Similarly, a substantial release of or change in the collateral securing a nonrecourse debt is a significant modification unless the collateral is fungible or is of a nature where particular units are unimportant, such as government securities. "A change in collateral securing recourse debt, [however], is not a significant modification."[76] A subordination of debt to other debt of the issuer also is not a significant modification in the case of either recourse or nonrecourse debt.[77]

Changes in the Nature of the Instrument. The proposed regulations provide that the following changes in types of payments (assuming they are modifications) are significant modifications:

---

69. *Id.*
70. *Id.* § 1.1001-3(e)(2)(iv).
71. *Id.*
72. *Id.* § 1.1001-3(e),-(3)(e)(3)(i)(B), 57 Fed. Reg. 57034, 57037 (1992).
73. Prop. Treas. Reg. § 1.1001-3(e)(3)(ii), 57 Fed. Reg. 57034, 57037 (1992).
74. *Id.* § 1.1001-3(e)(3)(iii).
75. *Id.*
76. *Id.* § 1.1001-3(e)(3)(iv).
77. Prop. Treas. Reg. § 1.1001-3(e)(3)(v), 57 Fed. Reg 57034, 57037 (1992).

(1) a change of a fixed rate instrument to a variable rate instrument or a contingent payment instrument;[78]
(2) a change of a variable rate instrument to a fixed rate instrument or a contingent payment instrument;[79]
(3) a change of a contingent payment instrument to a fixed rate instrument or a variable rate instrument;[80]
(4) a change of the currency in which payment under the debt instrument is made;[81]
(5) a change of a recourse debt instrument to a nonrecourse debt instrument;[82] and
(6) a change of a nonrecourse debt instrument to a recourse debt instrument.[83]

The proposed regulations also deal with certain equity interests and equity conversion rights. For example, a modification is significant if it changes a debt instrument to an instrument or property that is not treated as debt for federal tax purposes.[84] Also, the addition or deletion of a right to convert a debt instrument into stock will be a significant modification if that right has significant value at the time of its addition or deletion.[85] The alteration of an existing conversion or exchange right also will be a significant modification if it significantly affects the value of the existing right or if the corporation whose stock is to be received is changed.[86] There are also exceptions to some of these equity rules in the case of certain "tax-free" corporate transactions.[87]

---

78. Prop. Treas. Reg. § 1.1001-3(e)(4)(ii)(A), 57 Fed. Reg. 57034, 57037 (1992).
79. *Id.* § 1.1001-3(e)(4)(ii)(B).
80. *Id.* § 1.1001-3(e)(4)(ii)(C).
81. *Id.* § 1.1001-3(e)(4)(ii)(D).
82. *Id.* § 1.1001-3(e)(4)(iv)(A).
83. Prop. Treas. Reg. § 1.1001-3(e)(4)(iv)(B), 57 Fed. Reg. 57034, 57037 (1992).
84. *Id.* § 1.1001-3(e)(4)(i).
85. *Id.* § 1.1001-3(e)(4)(iii)(A).
86. *Id.*
87. *Id.* § 1.1001-3(e)(4)(iii)(B).

(iii) Interpretative Rules

The proposed regulations provide that multiple changes to a debt instrument, *e.g.* simultaneous changes in interest rate and maturity, will not collectively result in a significant modification if none of such changes would itself be a significant modification individually.[88] A modification, however, must be tested under each rule contained in the proposed regulations.[89] For example, although an extension of a maturity date may not in itself constitute a significant modification, its effect on the yield of a debt instrument must be tested to determine whether the change in yield is a significant modification.[90] Similarly, even if the yield is not affected by a change in the timing of principal payments, such a change in principal payments may itself be a material modification if it materially defers payment of the amounts due under the debt instrument.[91] Each such change is tested as though all of the other changes had already occurred.[92] Multiple changes that occur over a period of time will be tested on a cumulative basis so that a series of changes will result in a significant modification only if they would have constituted a significant modification had they occurred at the same time.[93] A determination of whether a significant modification has occurred is made at the time the parties to the debt instrument agree to the modification even if the agreed change is not then effective.[94]

(2) Existing Authority

The proposed regulations have resulted in as much controversy as the *Cottage Savings* decision itself,[95] and they may undergo substantial revision

---

88. Prop. Treas. Reg. § 1.1001-3(f)(3), 57 Fed Reg. 57034, 57038 (1992).
89. *Id.* § 1.1001-3(f)(1)
90. *Id.*
91. *Id.* § 1.1001-3(e)(2)(i).
92. Prop. Treas. Reg. § 1.1001-3(f)(3)(i), 57 Fed. Reg. 57034, 57038 (1992).
93. *Id.* § 1.1001-3(f)(3)(ii).
94. *Id.* § 1.1001-3(f)(1).
95. *See generally* Cottage Savings Ass'n v. Commissioner, 499 U.S. 554 (1994); *see supra* text accompanying notes 37-41 (discussing IRS's response to controversy generated by *Cottage Savings*); *see also* Prop. Treas. Reg. § 1.1001-3, 57 Fed. Reg. 57034 (1992). "The decision of the Supreme Court in [*Cottage Savings*] has generated additional controversy regarding the

before they are published in final form. A review of the treatment of certain changes in the terms of debt instruments prior to *Cottage Savings* and the proposed regulations is, therefore, appropriate. A material change (a "modification") is treated as an exchange of the debt instrument for a new obligation and can result in the realization of COD income.[96] Following are some examples which may or may not be affected in varying degrees by *Cottage Savings* despite new regulations.

A reduction in the stated principal amount of recourse debt is a modification,[97] and the IRS has ruled that the same is true with respect to nonrecourse debt.[98] There is, however, case law indicating a contrary result. In *Fulton Gold Cor v. Commissioner*,[99] the Board of Tax Appeals held that the satisfaction of a nonrecourse acquisition debt for less than its face amount where the taxpayer did not dispose of the property resulted in a reduction in the taxpayer's basis in the property in an amount equal to the payment discount.[100] The decision did not discuss the possibility of COD income. However, in Revenue Ruling 91-31,[101] the IRS rejected *Fulton Gold* and stated that the reduction of nonrecourse debt by a creditor who was not the seller of the property securing the debt resulted in COD income.[102]

Although a material change in interest rates is a modification, it is not clear whether an insignificant change of interest rates is a modification or what magnitude of change is required to make the change significant.[103] Generally,

---

treatment of modifications....Questions have arisen...concerning the Court's interpretation of the material difference standard and its possible application to modifications of debt instruments by issuers and holders." *Id.* at 57034.; *see also* Elliot Pisem & Charles E. Valliere, *New Rules Would Impact Debt Modifications*, N.Y. L.J., Dec. 31, 1992, at 5, col. 1.

96. Rev. Rul. 89-122, 1989-2 C.B. 200.
97. *Id.*
98. Rev. Rul. 91-31, 1991-1 C.B. 19. *See* Rev. Rul. 82-202, 1982-2 C.B. 35; *compare* Rev. Rul. 92-53, 1992-2 C.B. 48.
99. 31 B.T.A. 519 (1934).
100. *Id.* at 520.
101. 1991-1 C.B. 19.
102. *Id.*; *see also* Rev. Rul. 92-99, 1992-2 C.B. 35.
103. *See* Rev. Rul. 89-122, 1989-2 C.B. 200 (holding reduction of interest from 10% to 6.25% is material change); Rev. Rul. 81-169, 1981-1 C.B. 429 (holding material difference in bond terms existed when municipal bond with interest rate of 9% maturing in 1996, and subject to sinking fund calculated to

the mere extension of the maturity date will not constitute a modification.[104] Often, in a workout, the current amount of the periodic installment payable currently is reduced and the difference between the reduced payment and the interest computed at the accrual rate is added to principal. This would appear to be a mere change in maturity and, therefore, not a modification. It is more likely to be treated as a modification, however, if the deferred payment does not bear interest so that the yield is changed.

Whether a change in collateral is material appears to depend on the facts in each case. In view of *Cottage Savings*,[105] such a change appears to be material if it is in combination with other changes, such as a change of obligors. However, it also appears that a change in collateral by itself will not be treated as a modification.[106]

---

provide level payments is exchanged for new bond series that bears interest at 8.5%, matures in 2006 and is not subject to a sinking fund provision); Rev. Rul. 57-535, 1957-2 C.B. 513 (holding taxable exchange occurred when marketable Treasury securities plus cash were exchanged for nonmarketable Treasury securities with different maturity date and higher interest rate). However, the IRS has ruled that certain minor rate changes were not material: Priv. Ltr. Rul. 88-35-050 (June 8, 1988) (holding change of yield to maturity less than 3/100th of one percent did not constitute material change); Priv. Ltr. Rul. 89-32-067 (May 17, 1989) (holding yield to maturity changed by less than 1/8th of one percent did not constitute material change). Both of these private letter rulings involved waivers of interest rate adjustments that would have been required under the terms of the debt instrument. On the other hand, the IRS declined to rule that a change of a fixed rate on a tax-exempt bond by 2/10th of one percent was not a material change; the bonds, however, remained tax-exempt and thus, the IRS was not forced to face squarely the modification issue. Priv. Ltr. Rul. 88-34-090 (June 3, 1988).

104. Rev. Rul. 73-160, 1973-1 C.B. 365.

105. 499 U.S. 554 (1991); *see supra* text accompanying notes 35-36 (discussing decisions making exchange of "mortgage pools" a taxable event).

106. *See* Priv. Ltr. Rul. 83-46-104 (Aug. 18, 1983) (holding amendments to mortgage indenture, including substitution as collateral of U.S. Government obligations for real property, release of mortgage lien on real property, extension of mortgage lien and various technical changes, did not constitute sale or exchange under I.R.C. § 1001); *see also* Priv. Ltr. Rul. 80-38-217 (June 23, 1980) (holding stock substituted as collateral for installment sale did not materially alter the rights accruing to the holder and therefore did not constitute disposition of installment obligation for purposes of I.R.C. § 453(d)); Rev. Rul.

A modification may result if a noteholder actually waives a right under the bond or note, at least in cases where such waiver has a direct effect on the yield on such instrument. In Revenue Ruling 87-19,[107] the holder of a tax exempt bond waived the right to receive additional interest triggered by a change in federal marginal tax rates pursuant to an interest modification clause in the original obligation language.[108] The IRS ruled that, although an adjustment to the interest rate pursuant to an interest adjustment clause does not result in an exchange under IRC section 1001, waiver of the right under the bond did create a material change which resulted in an exchange as of the waiver date[109] (and not as of the date the interest change would have been triggered).

(3) Calculation of COD Income

Under IRC section 108(e)(10), a material modification is treated as an exchange of old debt for a new debt, and results in COD income to the extent the issue price of the new obligation is less than the "adjusted issue price" (usually the unpaid principal balance) of the original debt instrument (and, in the case of an accrual basis taxpayer, accrued interest on the debt).[110] For this purpose, the "issue price" of the new obligation is not necessarily its face amount. Rather, in the case of a publicly traded obligation, the "issue price"

77-416, 1977-2 C.B. 34 (holding sale of proceeds given as a substitute security for bonds sold did not affect interest on outstanding bonds as excludable from gross income under IRC § 103(a)(1)); Rev. Rul. 90-63, 1990-31 I.R.B. 5 (holding change in credit support did not constitute impermissible power to vary investment of grantor trust if purpose was solely to maintain credit rating of debt instruments issued by trust); Rev. Rul. 85-42, 1985-1 C.B. 36 (holding that if corporation places property in trust for sole purpose of securing payment of its bonds, this property set aside remains an asset of corporation and is not treated as transferred to bondholders in satisfaction of outstanding bonds).

107. 1987-1 C.B. 249.

108. *Id.*

109. *Id.*

110. I.R.C. §§ 108(e)(10), 1273, 1274 (1994). The "adjusted issue price" would not be the unpaid principal balance if the original loan were made with original issue discount. *See* H.R. CONF. REP. NO. 964, 101st Cong., 2d Sess. 1097 (1990), *reprinted in* 1990 U.S.C.C.A.N. 2802 (relating to I.R.C. § 108(e)(10)).

is the public trading price,[111] and in the case of nonpublicly traded debt, it is the present value of all payments to be made under the new obligation discounted using the appropriate applicable federal rate ("AFR") of interest.[112] It is usually easier to avoid COD income by using nonpublicly traded debt because the AFR is likely to be lower than the rate required to have the fair market price of the publicly traded debt equal its face amount.

(4) Original Issue Discount

In addition to creating COD income, a modification can result in original issue discount ("OID").[113] The lender will have OID income and the debtor will have OID deductions generally to the extent the issue price is less than the "stated redemption price" of the new obligation.[114] OID is deemed to accrue to the maturity date of a debt instrument on a constant economic yield basis[115] so that, regardless of the accounting method used, the borrower must deduct, and the lender must include in gross income, the amount of OID accrued in each taxable period.[116] The accrued but unpaid OID is added to the lender's basis in the debt instrument and also to the adjusted issue price of the debt for purposes of computing COD income.[117]

> *Example 2* - Debtor and Lender agree to reduce the principal balance of an existing ten percent $100,000 loan to $60,000. The loan is not publicly traded, provides for monthly payments of interest only until maturity and has a ten year term remaining. Debtor is treated as having satisfied this $100,000 obligation for an amount equal to the present value of the payments to be made under the $60,000 obligation.[118] Assuming that ten percent is adequate interest (that is, at least equal to the AFR), Debtor will be deemed to have satisfied its $100,000 obligation for

---

111. I.R.C. § 1273(b)(1) (1994).
112. *Id.* §§ 1273, 1274.
113. *Id.* §§ 1271(a)(2)(A), 1272(a)(1), 1273(a).
114. This is usually the unpaid principal amount of the new obligation. I.R.C. § 1272(a)(1) (1994).
115. I.R.C. § 1271(a)(4)(D) (1994).
116. *Id.* § 1272(a)(1).
117. *Id.* § 1272(a)(3).
118. Rev. Rul. 89-122, 1989-2 C.B. 200.

$60,000 and will realize $40,000 of COD income.[119] If, however, interest on the "new" debt is inadequate (because the applicable AFR rate is thirteen percent), Debtor will have satisfied the $100,000 debt for less than $60,000 and will have COD income equal to the difference between $100,000 and the present value (determined by using the AFR as the discount rate) of all payments to be made under the $60,000 low-interest debt.[120] If, for example, such present value were $50,000, Debtor would have $50,000 of COD income, and the new obligation would have $10,000 of OID which would be taxable as interest to Lender and be deductible as interest to Debtor during the ten year term of the modified loan.

Example 3 - Same facts as in *Example* 2 except that the principal amount of the new debt remains unchanged ($100,000) but the interest rate is reduced from ten percent to five percent. Again, assuming the five percent interest is "inadequate" (that is, less than the appropriate AFR) the issue price of the new debt will be the present value of all payments to be made under the new note using the appropriate AFR discount rate (in this example, thirteen percent).

d. Exceptions to COD Income[121]

(1) Deductible Payments

No COD income is realized to the extent that the liability discharged would have been deductible.[122] For example, a cash basis taxpayer will not realize COD income to the extent such taxpayer is discharged from an obligation to pay accrued but unpaid interest, the payment of which, would normally be deductible. This particular exception would not apply to an accrual basis taxpayer who would have already accrued the deduction for such interest, although such taxpayer may have relief available under IRC sections

---

119. I.R.C. § 1274(c)(1),(2) (1994).
120. Rev. Rul. 89-122, 1989-2 C.B. 200.
121. The following exceptions to COD income are of general applicability. An additional possible exception applicable to partnerships is discussed *infra* Part A.3.b.
122. I.R.C. § 108(e)(2) (1994).

108(a)(1)(d) and 108(c) if the indebtedness is "qualified real property business indebtedness."[123]

(2) Purchase Price Adjustment

The reduction of purchase money debt, that otherwise would be COD income, will not be COD income if at the time of the reduction, the debt is still owed by the purchaser to the seller, and if the purchaser is *not* insolvent or in bankruptcy.[124] A taxpayer who *is* insolvent could exclude any COD income resulting from the reduction of the purchase price to the extent of the insolvency.[125] To the extent the taxpayer is solvent, he could rely on the purchase price adjustment exception to COD income.[126] Although the purchase price adjustment exception, by its terms, does not apply if the original creditor sells the obligation, or if the original debtor sells the property securing the debt to a party who assumes or takes subject to the debt, certain transferees of the original debtor may be able to use the exception.[127] It appears that the debtor must reduce the basis of the property by the amount of the purchase price adjustment and, if the reduction exceeds such basis, realize gain or COD income.[128] This remains true unless another of the exclusions from COD income applies, such as that for "qualified real property business indebtedness."[129]

IRC section 108(e)(1) provides that "[e]xcept as otherwise provided . . . there shall be no insolvency exception from the general rule that gross income includes income from the discharge of indebtedness."[130] Section 108(e)(1) was added to the IRC by the Bankruptcy Tax Act of 1980.[131] Prior to that legislation, case law indicated that, when the fair market value of property fell

---

123. *See* discussion *infra* Part A.1.e.
124. I.R.C. § 108(e)(5) (1994).
125. *Id.* § 108(a).
126. *Id.* § 108(e)(5).
127. *See* Priv. Ltr. Rul. 90-37-033 (Sept. 14, 1990) (stating purchase price exception applies to debtor that acquires title to property pursuant to nontaxable transfer under I.R.C. § 351).
128. Rev. Rul. 92-99, 1992-2 C.B. 35.
129. I.R.C. § 108(a)(1)(D) (1994).
130. *Id.* § 108(e)(1).
131. Pub. L. No. 96-589, § 2(a), 94 Stat. 3389.

below the amount of the acquisition mortgage debt secured by the property, including an acquisition where the original purchase money debt is assumed by the purchaser, a settlement of the debt at the fair market value of the property reduces the purchase price and, thus, the basis of the property, resulting in no COD income.[132] This judicial exception to COD income based upon a purchase price reduction is broader than the exception provided in IRC section 108(e)(5) because it applies to subsequent debtors (and, presumably, to subsequent creditors) and is not limited to cases where the debtor is solvent. The continued viability of the judicial exception is questionable in light of the above-quoted language of section 108(e)(1)(D) and the reenactment of IRC sections 108(a)(1) and 108(a). Nevertheless, in *Sutphin v. United States*,[133] the United States Claims Court held that a prepayment by a solvent debtor of a mortgage loan at a discount resulted in COD income. In *dictum*, the court distinguished the cases establishing the judicial exception on the ground that, in the case before it, the value of the property had not fallen below the unpaid mortgage balance.[134] This *dictum* at least permits an inference that the judicial exception to COD income based upon a reduction in the purchase price may still apply when IRC section 108(e)(5) does not. However, in Revenue Ruling 92-99,[135] the IRS ruled that it would not follow the judicial rule where an undersecured nonrecourse purchase money debt is reduced by a holder of the debt who was not the seller of the property except to the extent that the reduction is based on "an infirmity that clearly relates back to the original sale (*e.g.*, the seller's inducement of a higher purchase price by misrepresentation of material fact or by fraud)."[136]

e. Exclusion by Solvent Taxpayers of Discharge of Qualified Real Property Business Indebtedness

Recognizing the difficulties borrowers faced when they attempted to work out distressed commercial real estate loans due to the tax consequences, in

---

132. *See generally* Commissioner v. Sherman, 135 F.2d 68 (6th Cir. 1943); Hirsch v. Commissioner, 115 F.2d 656 (7th Cir. 1940); Fulton Gold Corp. v. Commissioner, 31 B.T.A. 519 (1934).
133. 14 Cl. Ct. 545 (1988).
134. *Id.* at 550.
135. 1992-2 C.B. 35.
136. *Id.*

1993 Congress enacted a new, elective exclusion for COD income arising from the discharge of "qualified real property business indebtedness" in the case of taxpayers other than C corporations.[137] As an operating matter, the section 108(a)(1)(A) and (B) exclusions from COD income for bankrupt and, to the extent of their insolvency, insolvent taxpayers, and evidently the purchase price adjustment rule of section 108(e)(5) as well, apply before the elective exclusion of section 108(a)(1)(D).[138]

"Qualified real property business indebtedness" ("QRPBI") is indebtedness which was incurred or assumed by the taxpayer before January 1, 1993[139] "in connection with" real property "used in a trade or business" and which is "secured" by that real property.[140] In order for such indebtedness to qualify as QRPBI, the taxpayer must elect to treat it as such.[141] If such indebtedness was incurred or assumed (or, undoubtedly, significantly modified) after January 1, 1993, it must have been incurred to refinance pre-January 1, 1993 QRPBI (but only to the extent the amount of such debt does not exceed the amount being refinanced) or was "qualified acquisition indebtedness."[142] "Qualified acquisition indebtedness" is indebtedness incurred or assumed in acquiring, constructing, reconstructing or substantially improving property of the type described above.[143]

No final or proposed regulations have been issued under this now three-year old statute, and practitioners have expressed concern about what it means to require debt to be incurred "in connection with" real property.[144] The term might, for example, connote a tracing of the proceeds borrowed to some property-related purpose, as opposed to unrestricted use by the borrower. Similarly, the term "used in a trade or business" has a variety of potential meanings, some of which could exclude real estate that is inventory in a

---

137. I.R.C. § 108(a)(1)(d) (1994).
138. The requirement of an election is in I.R.C. § 108(c)(3)(C) (1994). The election is currently made by filing IRS Form 982 with the tax return for the year in which the debt discharge occurs. *Id.*
139. I.R.C. § 108(c)(3)(B) (1994).
140. Id. § 108(c)(3).
141. *Id.* § 108(c)(3)(C).
142. *Id.* § 108(c)(3).
143. *Id.* § 108(c)(4).
144. *See* Michael Hirschfeld, *Antacid for the Real Estate Industry: Newly Enacted Debt Discharge Relief*, 79 J. TAX'N 268 (1993).

taxpayer's hands, real estate held for less than one year or even net leased real estate from the relief of the statute.[145] Given the purposes of the statute, the legislative history,[146] and the context in which the phrase appears, one would hope that the proposition the phrase was intended to exclude real property used for personal purposes and possibly inventory,[147] but nothing more, will eventually be reflected in regulations. Further, some have questioned whether a lender's failure or intentional choice not to record a lien or security interest renders the loan not "secured" by real property.[148] Finally, notwithstanding the repeated references to principal in the legislative history and possible arguments the IRS might have available to it under the "tax-benefit" doctrine, the treatment of interest accrued and deducted by an accrual method taxpayer and added to principal is unclear. This doctrine generally requires the reversal of the tax effect of previously accrued expenses that the taxpayer deducted with a "tax benefit," but is ultimately not required to pay.[149]

---

145. *See infra* note 146; I.R.C. § 1221(1), (2) (1994) (stating that "capital asset" does not include inventory or real property used in a trade or business, implying two separate categories); *id.* § 1231(b) (stating that "real property used in a trade or business" does not include property that is held primarily for sale to customers or held for less than one year); Rev. Rul. 73-522, 1973-2 C.B. 226 (finding foreign lessor of real property under a net lease not "engaged in a trade or business" in the United States for purposes of I.R.C. § 871). *Compare* I.R.C. § 172(d)(4) (1994) *with* Hazard v. Commissioner, 7 T.C. 372 (1946), *acq. in result*, 1946-2 C.B. 3.

146. H.R. REP. NO. 111, 103d Cong., 1st Sess., pt. 5, at 622-25 (1993) *reprinted in* 1993 U.S.C.C.A.N. 853-56; Priv. Ltr. Rul. 94-26-006 through 94-26-019 (March 15, 1994).

147. The statute's focus on depreciable real property, together with the basis adjustment rules under I.R.C. § 1017, including the unavailability of the § 1017(b)(3) election suggest that real estate held for sale to customers in the ordinary course of business might not be within the statutory definition of "real property used in a trade or business."

148. *See* Temp. Treas. Reg. § 1.163-10T(o)(3) (1987). To be "qualified residence interest," the interest must be paid on a recorded mortgage. *Id.*

149. *See generally* Hillsboro Nat'l Bank v. Commissioner, 460 U.S. 370 (1983) (discussing history and applicability of tax benefit doctrine); MARTIN M. WEINSTEIN ET AL., MERTENS LAW OF FED. INCOME TAX'N § 7.53.50 (1995) (discussing aspects of tax benefit doctrine).

If QRPBI is discharged, there are two limitations on the amount of COD income that may be excluded. First, the amount excluded under IRC section 108(a)(1)(D) may not exceed the excess of the principal amount of the debt (immediately before discharge) over the fair market value of the property (immediately before discharge reduced by any other QRPBI secured by the property at that time).[150]

> *Example 4*– Assume J owns a building used in his trade or business, worth $150,000 and subject to a first mortgage and a second mortgage securing debts of $110,000 and $90,000, respectively. J is neither bankrupt nor insolvent. J agrees with the second mortgagee to reduce the amount of the second mortgage debt by $60,000. If J's basis in depreciable real property is at least $50,000, J may elect to exclude that amount of COD income from gross income ($200,000 in predischarge debt minus $150,000 property value), but must include the remaining $10,000 as COD income. J is required to reduce J's basis in depreciable real property by an amount equal to the $50,000 of COD income so excluded.

The second limitation on the amount of COD income excluded as attributable to QRPBI is that it may not exceed the aggregate adjusted bases of depreciable real property held by the taxpayer before the exchange, but after any basis reductions required due to the exclusion of such COD income under other provisions of IRC section 108.[151]

The limitations described in the preceding paragraph might be circumvented by making additional real property subject to the lien of the related mortgage (in the case of the first limitation), or by the acquisition of additional depreciable real property (in the case of the second limitation). Accordingly, the statute expressly authorizes regulations to prevent "the abuse of [I.R.C. section 108(c)] through cross-collateralization or other means"[152] to discourage the first tactic. The statute provides that the aggregate adjusted

---

150. I.R.C. § 108 (c)(2)(A) (1994). Presumably, value will be determined without regard to I.R.C. § 7701(g), which ordinarily would require the property to be valued at not less than the principal amount of any nonrecourse indebtedness secured by it. *Id.*

151. *Id.* § 108(a)(2)(B).

152. *Id.* § 108(c)(5).

basis of depreciable real property held by the taxpayer is to be determined without regard to depreciable real property acquired by the taxpayer in contemplation of a discharge of indebtedness in order to prevent the second.[153]

The amount of any COD income excluded under section 108(a)(1)(D) is applied to reduce the basis of depreciable real property held by the taxpayer at the beginning of the taxable year following the taxable year in which the debt discharge took place, under section 1017, but without the election under section 1017(b)(3) to treat inventory as such property being available.[154] If the taxpayer disposes of the real property that gave rise to the discharge or otherwise prior to the first day of the next taxable year, then the basis must be reduced immediately before that disposition.[155]

This procedure raises a number of interesting questions. The current regulations under section 1017 were promulgated in 1956. When the Bankruptcy Tax Act of 1980 was enacted, Congress directed that the Treasury regulations to be adopted thereunder generally accord with the regulations promulgated under prior law.[156] Thus, it remains unclear whether a taxpayer must first reduce the depreciable portion of his or her basis in property consisting of building and land, or may reduce the depreciable and nondepreciable components pro rata. It is also unclear whether under section 1017(b)(3)(F)(iii), the disposition that may cause an immediate basis adjustment during the taxable year in which a debt discharge occurs must be a disposition of the real property securing the discharged debt, or whether any disposition of depreciable real estate may attract cause a basis reduction to the asset.

If the basis of depreciable real property is reduced under this provision, and the real property is subsequently sold, then recapture under IRC section 1250 (*i.e.*, the portion of any gain realized that must be treated as ordinary income, an amount generally equivalent to the excess of accelerated depreciation over straight-line depreciation in the case of real property) should be determined by treating (i) any basis reduction as a deduction allowed for depreciation, and (ii) determining the straight-line depreciation as if there had

---

153. *Id.* § 108(c)(2)(B).

154. I.R.C. § 1017(b)(3)(F)(ii) (1994); H.R. REP. NO. 111, 103d Cong., 1st Sess. 186 (1993).

155. I.R.C. § 1017(b)(3)(F)(iii) (1994).

156. *See* S. REP. NO. 1035, 96th Cong., 2d Sess. 8 (1980), *reprinted in* 1980 U.S.C.C.A.N. 7017, 7023.

been no reduction in basis.[157] Thus, the amount of the basis reduction recaptured as ordinary income is reduced over time, as the taxpayer holds the property and smaller depreciation expenses over time due to the basis reduction than the taxpayer would have if the basis reduction had not occurred.

Finally, for purposes of these rules, the interest of a partner in a partnership that owns depreciable real property is treated as depreciable real property to the extent of the proportionate interest of the partner in such property.[158]

2. Foreclosure or Other Disposition

In general, a foreclosure is treated as a sale of the encumbered property, which can result in the realization of gain or loss by the debtor.[159] Such gain is includable in gross income,[160] and such gain or loss is computed under normal tax rules; gain or loss equals the difference between the amount realized on the foreclosure and the adjusted basis of the encumbered property.[161] However, tax treatment and calculation of gain or loss will differ depending on whether the debt is recourse or nonrecourse.[162] In general, the tax treatment of foreclosures applies equally to other involuntary dispositions of encumbered real property, such as the giving of a "deed in lieu of foreclosure" or a condemnation.[163] Such treatment will also apply to voluntary sales that may occur as part of workouts, with some obvious differences, such as the use of an actual sales price instead of a bid price in determining gain or loss.

---

157. I.R.C. § 1250 (a)(3)(A)(i),(ii) (1994). *See* Holiday Village Shopping Ctr. v. United States, 773 F.2d 276, 280 (Fed. Cir. 1985) (holding recapture of depreciation on liquidating distribution of assets allowable).
158. *See* I.R.C. § 1250(d)(6)(A), (B) (1994); *id.* § 705. *See also Holiday Village*, 773 F.2d at 279 (describing creation of partnership interest percentage). Provisions relating to partnerships will be discussed *infra* notes 190-224 and accompanying text.
159. Helvering v. Hammel, 311 U.S. 504, 512 (1941).
160. I.R.C. § 61(a)(3) (1994).
161. *Id.* § 1001(a).
162. *See infra* notes 172-174 and accompanying text; *see also infra* notes 176-180 and accompanying text.
163. Laport v. Commissioner, 671 F.2d 1028, 1033 (7th Cir. 1982); Freeland v. Commissioner, 74 T.C. 970, 981 (1980).

a. Foreclosure of Recourse Debt

Although there are potentially conflicting judicial decisions regarding the tax treatment of the foreclosure of recourse debt,[164] when the proceeds of the foreclosure are insufficient to satisfy the entire amount of the debt and the resulting deficiency is reduced or canceled through negotiations between lender and debtor, the correct approach (and the IRS's current view) appears to be to treat the foreclosure as a two-step transaction.[165] The first step is a sale of the property for an amount that is deemed to equal its fair market value,[166] and the second step is the reduction or cancellation of the deficiency. Clearly, there will be no deficiency and, therefore, no second step if the value of the property is equal to or greater than the debt.

The first step (the sale) will result in a gain or loss equal to the difference between the fair market value of the property (usually deemed to be the bid price in the case of recourse loans)[167] and the debtor's adjusted basis for the

---

164. *See, e.g.*, Chilingirian v. Commissioner, 918 F.2d 1251, 1253 (6th Cir. 1990) (including entire amount of recourse mortgage loan in computing gain upon foreclosure, without discussion of fair market value or COD income); Diamond v. Commissioner, 43 B.T.A. 809, 812 (1941) (including amount paid in satisfaction of deficiency judgement at a discount in computing loss upon foreclosure, without discussion of COD income).

165. Treas. Reg. §§ 1.1001-2(a)(1), -2(A)(2), -2(c) (1980) *see* Example 8 *infra* p. 138; Rev. Rul. 90-16, 1990-1 C.B. 12. The same treatment results from a transfer in lieu of foreclosure, *id.*, and from an abandonment of the mortgaged premises. Priv. Ltr. Rul. 91-20-010 (Feb. 14, 1991).

166. *See supra* note 165; Aizawa v. Commissioner, 99 T.C. 197, 200 (1992) (recognizing borrowers' amount realized was proceeds of foreclosure sale where borrowers were not discharged from remaining amount owed under recourse debt); *see also In re* Walsh, 5 B.R. 239, 241 (Bankr. D.C. 1980) (holding "value" of property to be judged at "liquidation value").

167. The bid price is usually accepted as the indicator of fair market value even if the lender makes the only bid. *See, e.g.*, O.M.P. v. Security Pac. Business Fin., Inc., 716 F. Supp. 251, 258, n.8 (1989) (explaining that court can adjust prices when lender is only bidder and bids well below FMV); Community Bank v. Commissioner, 819 F.2d 940, 941 (9th Cir. 1987) (same); Southern New England Prod. Credit Ass'n v. O/S My Marie, 611 F. Supp. 757, 759 (D. Me. 1985) (same). The bid price will not control if it does not reflect fair market value. *See, e.g.*, BFP v. Resolution Trust Corp., 114 S. Ct. 1757, 1761 (1994) (explaining illegality of debtor knowingly accepting bid well below FMV). As

property (usually, cost less depreciation).[168] Although it may seem inappropriate for a debtor to realize a gain in these circumstances, such gain can arise when depreciation deductions have substantially reduced the debtor's basis or if, in a refinancing, the proceeds were not invested in the property and, therefore, did not increase its basis.

The second step in the foreclosure of recourse debt (the reduction or elimination of the deficiency for which the debtor is personally liable) creates COD income in an amount equal to the reduction in debt.[169] Unless one or more of the exclusions from gross income under section 108 are applicable, such COD income will be ordinary income to the debtor.[170]

This two-step treatment differs from the treatment of nonrecourse debt foreclosure.[171] There is some uncertainty as to whether a local law prohibition with respect to deficiency judgments would cause recourse debt to be treated as nonrecourse and thereby eliminating the possibility of COD income in such jurisdictions.

> *Example 5*– Debtor borrows $100,000 from Lender and secures the loan with a recourse mortgage on depreciable property. At the time of foreclosure, Debtor's adjusted basis for the property is $40,000, the property has a fair market value of $50,000 and the principal balance remains at $100,000. At foreclosure, Lender acquires property for a bid price of $50,000 and Debtor's deficiency of $50,000 is discharged. Debtor has a gain of $10,000 ($50,000 fair market value less $40,000 adjusted basis) and potential COD income of $50,000, the amount of the deficiency that was discharged.

---

discussed *infra* Part B.1., COD income can be beneficial to an insolvent debtor or a debtor in bankruptcy. On the other hand, a solvent debtor with a large capital loss or capital loss carryover may want to maximize gain or treat the entire amount of COD income as additional gain.

168. *See supra* notes 165-167.
169. Treas. Reg. §§ 1.1001-2(a)(1),(2), -2(c) (1980) *see* Example 8 (1980) *infra* p. 138; Rev. Rul. 90-16, 1990-1 C.B. 12.
170. *See supra* notes 166-69 and accompanying text.
171. *See* discussion *infra* Part A.2.b.

Example 6– Same facts as Example 5 except that fair bid price is $30,000. Debtor has a loss of $10,000 ($40,000 adjusted basis less $30,000 bid price) and potential COD income of $70,000.

Example 7– Debtor borrows $100,000 from Lender and secures the loan with a recourse mortgage on depreciable property. At the time of foreclosure, Debtor has paid down the loan to $50,000, Debtor's adjusted basis for the property is $40,000 and the property has a fair market value of $60,000. At foreclosure, the property is sold for its fair market value. Debtor has a gain of $20,000 ($60,000 sale price less $40,000 basis) and no COD income since the entire unpaid balance was satisfied with the proceeds of the foreclosure sale.

b. Foreclosure of Nonrecourse Debt

A foreclosure of nonrecourse debt is treated as a sale of the encumbered property in a manner similar to the first step in a foreclosure of recourse debt.[172] However, when computing gain or loss for a nonrecourse debt, the *entire* unpaid balance of the debt is treated as having been satisfied and is included in the amount realized by the debtor on the sale,[173] even if the value of the property is less than the amount of the debt.[174] Since there is no personal liability for nonrecourse debt, there is no amount of debt to be forgiven and,

---

172. *See infra* notes 181-89 and accompanying text; *see also* Helvering v. Nebraska Bridge Supply & Lumber Co., 312 U.S. 666 (1941); Laport v. Commissioner, 671 F.2d 1028, 1033 (1982); Freeland v. Commissioner, 74 T.C. 970 (1980).
173. Crane v. Commissioner, 331 U.S. 1, 11 (1947).
174. Tufts v. Commissioner, 461 U.S. 300, 310 (1983); Treas. Reg. § 1.1001-2(c) (1980) *see* Example 7 *supra* p. 137; Priv. Ltr. Rul. 93-02-001 (Aug. 31, 1992) (holding such gain is not COD income). This treatment can create a particularly egregious situation for a debtor who receives the proceeds of a postacquisition nonrecourse loan secured by the property but does not invest such proceeds in the property. As a result, the entire principal amount of the postacquisition loan will be treated as gain because there will be no increase in basis to offset that amount. Of course, since the borrower, in effect, will have "cashed out" the property, a tax cost may not be inappropriate. *See also* I.R.C. § 7701(g) (1994).

therefore, no second step to the transaction. This results in no COD income for the debtor, to his benefit, or detriment.[175]

Example 8 - Same facts as *Example* 5, except that the debt is nonrecourse. In this case Debtor realizes a gain of $60,000 (amount realized, *i.e.*, unpaid principal balance of $100,000, minus adjusted basis of $40,000), and there is no COD income.

Example 9 - Same facts as *Example* 6, except that the debt is nonrecourse. Debtor realizes a gain of $60,000 (amount realized, *i.e.*, unpaid principal balance of $100,000 minus adjusted basis of $40,000), and there is no COD income.

Example 10 - Same facts as *Example* 7, except that the debt is nonrecourse. Debtor realizes a gain of $20,000 ($60,000 sale price minus adjusted basis of $40,000), and no COD income.

There is no COD income in *Examples* 8, 9 and 10 because there can be no COD income upon foreclosure of nonrecourse debt.[176]

3. Foreclosures and COD Income On Loans Made to Partnerships

a. General Rules

For federal income tax purposes, a partnership is not itself taxable.[177] Instead, each partner reports his allocable share of the partnership's items of income and deductions on his personal tax return.[178] A partner may deduct his allocable share of partnership losses up to an amount equal to the partner's basis in the partnership[179] which, in general, is an amount equal to the difference between (a) the sum of the partner's investment in the partnership, share of undistributed partnership earnings and share of partnership liabilities,

---

175. *See* discussion *infra* Part B.1.
176. *See* Example 14 *infra* p. 143. There can, however, be COD income in connection with a refinancing of a nonrecourse debt.
177. I.R.C. § 701 (1994).
178. *Id.* § 702.
179. *Id.* § 704(d).

and (b) the sum of the partner's distributions from the partnership, partnership losses and reductions in partnership liabilities.[180] The portion of a partnership liability that is allocable to a partner is determined by the partner's interest in the partnership and by whether the liability is recourse or nonrecourse.[181] For purposes of determining a partner's share of partnership liabilities, recourse debt is allocable only to partners who bear the economic risk of the debt.[182] The allocation of nonrecourse debt among the partners is more complicated.[183] In general, a partner is allocated a portion of nonrecourse debt that is equivalent to the share of the gain that would be allocated to the partner upon a taxable disposition of the encumbered property.[184] However, nonrecourse

---

180. *Id.* § 705.
181. I.R.C. § 704(b) (1994).
182. Treas. Reg. § 1.752-2(a) (1991). General partners or limited partners who guarantee a portion or all of the loan are those who bear the economic risk of the debt. *Id.*
183. Treas. Reg. § 1.752-3(a) (1991).
184. This includes gain resulting from foreclosure. *See* discussion *supra* Part A.2.b. It appears that only a partner who is personally liable for a partnership debt (i.e., a general partner of a limited partnership) or who otherwise bears the risk of economic loss (i.e., a partner who guarantees all or part of a nonrecourse partnership debt) would realize (i.e., be allocated) COD income since only such a partner would economically benefit from the discharge or reduction of the debt. A foreclosure of such debt would be subject to the two-step treatment. *See* discussion *supra* Part A.2.a. It is unclear the extent to which recourse debt so allocated to a bankrupt or insolvent partner may be required to be reallocated to another, solvent partner. Under I.R.C. § 752 regulations, nonrecourse debt should be allocated among partners for this purpose in the proportions in which partners would share (or have shared) in the related deductions and income (including, under I.R.C. § 704 (b), any "minimum gain chargeback"). To be consistent with the principles of I.R.C. § 704(b), any related COD income should be allocated first in proportion to the partners' shares of any "minimum gain chargeback" (and should reduce such "minimum gain chargeback" until it is reduced to zero) with any additional COD income allocated in accordance with the profit allocation in the partnership agreement. I.R.C. § 704(b) regulations do not specifically address this issue with respect to COD income, but do suggest this treatment is appropriate. Rev. Rul. 92-97, 1992-2 C.B. 124. *See* Treas. Reg. §§ 1.752-2(f)(1), -2(j)(2) (1991).

debt owed to or guaranteed by a partner generally is allocated only to that partner.[185]

Gain or loss and potential COD income are computed at the partnership level even if the partnership is insolvent or has filed in bankruptcy,[186] and each partner reports his allocable share on the partner's individual tax return.[187] Insolvency is tested at the partner level, and elections to exclude COD income attributable to QRPBI[188] discharge are made at the partner level.[189] However, the determination as to whether indebtedness is QRPBI is made at the partnership level as well.[190]

> *Example 11* - A and B are equal partners in the AB partnership. The partnership borrows $100,000 from Lender and secures the loan with a nonrecourse mortgage on depreciable property. At a time when the partnership's basis for the property is $50,000, Lender accepts a deed in lieu of foreclosure. The partnership has a gain of $50,000 ($100,000 unpaid balance of the nonrecourse loan less $50,000 adjusted basis) which is allocated in equal shares to A and B.

> *Example 12* - Same facts as *Example* 11, except that the debt is recourse and the property has a fair market value of $50,000 at the time of the deed in lieu. As a result, the partnership has no gain ($50,000 fair market value minus $50,000 basis equals zero) but it has potential COD income of $50,000, the amount of the deficiency forgiven by the deed in lieu; the COD income is allocated in equal shares to A and B.

In addition, when a partner's share of partnership debt is discharged or reduced, the partner is deemed to have received a cash distribution in the amount of such discharge or reduction.[191] This deemed distribution is treated as a return of capital to the extent of the partner's basis in the partnership

---

185. *See supra* note 184 and accompanying text.
186. I.R.C. § 108(d)(6) (1994).
187. *Id.* § 702.
188. *See* discussion *supra* Part A.1.e.
189. I.R.C. § 108(d)(6) (1994).
190. *Id.* §§ 108(d)(6), 1017(b)(3)(C); H.R. REP. NO. 111, 103d Cong., 1st Sess. 186 (1993).
191. I.R.C. § 752(b) (1994).

interest, and as a gain to the extent it exceeds such basis.[192] Ordinarily, there will be no such gain because the gain or COD income caused by such discharge or reduction in debt and allocated to the partner results in an offsetting increase in the basis of that partner's partnership interest.[193]

A recent case has called that result into question if the reduction occurs in the context of COD income not currently included in gross income by a partner. In *Babin v. Commissioner*,[194] the Sixth Circuit held that a partner was not permitted to increase the basis of his partnership interest by the amount of his share of COD income if he was entitled at the partner level to exclude such COD income.[195] This holding is flatly contradicted by the legislative history to the Bankruptcy Tax Act of 1980,[196] as well as the legislative history to the 1993 enactment of IRC section 108(c).[197] The decision appears to be bad law and bad arithmetic. One basis increase due to excluded COD income, minus one basis decrease due to a deemed distribution

---

192. Conversely, an increase in a partner's share of partnership liabilities is treated as a deemed contribution of money by the partner to the partnership and, therefore, increases the partner's basis in the partnership interest. I.R.C. § 752(a) (1994).
193. *Id.* § 705(a)(1)(A).
194. 23 F.3d 1032 (6th Cir.), *cert. denied*, 115 S. Ct. 421 (1994).
195. *Id.* at 1036.
196. S. REP. NO. 1035, 96th Cong., 2d Sess. 631, n.28 (1980), *reprinted in* 1980 U.S.C.C.A.N. 7017.
197. H.R. REP. NO. 111, 103d Cong., 1st Sess. 186 (1993), states:

> The deemed distribution (under Tax Code § 752) arising from the reduction in a partner's share of partnership liabilities is treated as follows. The allocation of an amount of debt discharge income to a partner results in that partner's basis in the partnership being increased by such amount (sec. 705). The reduction in a partner's share of partnership liabilities caused by the debt discharge also results in a deemed distribution (under sec. 752) which in turn results in a reduction (under sec. 733) of the partner's basis in his partnership interest. This section 733 basis reduction is separate from any reduction in basis of the partner's interest under the provision, i.e., the basis reduction that occurs as a result of treating the partnership interest as depreciable real property to the extent of the partner's proportionate interest in the depreciable real property held by the partnership.

Id.

upon relief from the liability, minus another basis decrease as the price for excluding the COD income, adds up to one basis decrease and no current income recognition. That is clearly the right result. Presumably, at least with regard to the elective exclusion under section 108(c) of the Internal Revenue Code, the legislative history, which is a recitation of the general understanding of the mechanical partnership rules in this area,[198] will be accepted by the courts.

> *Example 13* - A and B are equal partners in the AB partnership which acquires depreciable property with a $100,000 recourse loan secured by the property. As a result of this loan, A and B each has an initial basis in the AB partnership of $50,000. At the time of foreclosure, because of $60,000 of depreciation deductions, the partnership's adjusted basis for the property is $40,000 and the basis of each partnership interest is $20,000. At that time, the property has a fair market value of $50,000 and the principal balance of the loan remains at $100,000. At foreclosure, Lender acquires the property for a bid price of $50,000 and the partnership's deficiency of $50,000 is discharged. The partnership has gain of $10,000 ($50,000 fair market value less $40,000 adjusted basis) and COD income of $50,000, the amount of the deficiency that was discharged, for total income of $60,000. A and B do not make elections under IRC section 108(c) and pay tax on the gain and COD income currently. This income is allocated in equal shares of $30,000 to each of A and B, which allocation causes the basis of A and B in their partnership interest to increase by $30,000. This results in a total basis of $50,000 each, which will then be reduced by $25,000 each due to the cash distribution in that amount that was deemed to occur because of the reduction in each partner's share of the partnership debt. Each partner has a $25,000 basis in his or her partnership interest, and will receive that amount of cash when the partnership is liquidated.

> *Example 14* - Same facts as Example 13, except that the debt is nonrecourse and, instead of a foreclosure, the partnership satisfies the $100,000 nonrecourse mortgage loan with a payment of $50,000 (the FMV of the property) financed with a new loan from another lender. As

---

198. *See infra* note 213.

a result, the partnership has COD income of $50,000 which is allocated in equal shares of $25,000 to each of A and B. Neither A nor B makes an election under IRC section 108(c) and both pay tax on the COD income currently. This causes the basis of A and B in their partnership interests to increase by $25,000, each increase being completely offset by a $25,000 reduction in basis occasioned by the cash distribution that was deemed to made to each of them because of the settlement of the loan at a $50,000 discount. On a net basis, neither the basis of the partnership in its asset nor the bases of A and B in their partnership interests is affected by the workout.

Example 15 - Same as *Example* 14, except that A and B both make elections under IRC section 108(c) and treat their interests in AB as depreciable real property under IRC section 1017(c). Assuming that *Babin* is incorrectly decided, and that the explicit legislative history referred in the discussion above is followed, the basis of A and B in their partnership interests is first regarded as increased by the excluded COD income of $50,000 allocated to them. That basis is then reduced by the amount of the reduction in their liabilities and the accompanying deemed distribution of $50,000. Finally, they reduce the basis of their partnership interests, and the partnership reduces the basis of the depreciable real property, under IRC section 1017 by the $50,000 of COD income excluded by the partners under IRC section 108(a)(1)(D) and 108(c). The basis of A and B in their partnership interests, and of the partnership in the property, is zero after the workout.

While the deemed distribution rules applicable to partnerships should not ordinarily give rise to additional income or gain, a reduction in a partner's share of partnership debt can nevertheless create income in the form of recapture of previously taken deductions.[199] In general, individual partners (and partners in closely held corporations) can deduct their share of partnership losses only to the extent of the amount they have "at risk" in the activity.[200] If the amount at risk decreases, the partner may have to recapture such losses.[201] It is unclear whether in order to effect the purposes for which

199. I.R.C. § 465 (1994).
200. *Id.* § 465(a)(6)(C).
201. *Id.* § 465. Although a nonrecourse loan generally does not put such a partner

the QRPBI exclusion was intended, basis reductions under IRC section 1017 may be ignored in the determination of the amount a taxpayer has "at risk" in an activity.

There are also technical problems that arise under the rules of the IRC relating to allocations of income and deductions among partners, in particular those related to "minimum gain chargebacks."[202] To the extent a nonrecourse liability of a partnership exceeds the adjusted basis of the property it encumbers, any disposition of that property, even in foreclosure, will generate at least that much gain, defined to be "partnership minimum gain."[203] This commonly occurs when property acquired with nonrecourse financing is depreciated more rapidly than the nonrecourse loan is amortized. The allocation of those depreciation deductions to partners will generally only be respected if, among other things, a "minimum gain chargeback requirement"[204] is satisfied, essentially assuring that a partner allocated depreciation of this type will also be allocated the income or gain inevitably recognized in order to retire the loan or when it is foreclosed.[205] In order to assure this, the regulations require that if any partner has a net decrease in partnership minimum gain share, that partner must be allocated items of income for that year equal to such decrease.[206]

A discharge of nonrecourse debt will reduce the "partnership minimum gain" and create technical problems in circumstances involving a IRC section 108(c) election. First, partnership minimum gain decreases are measured at the end of each taxable year, but the IRC section 1017(c) basis adjustment generally is to be made at the beginning of the taxable year following the year

---

at risk, there is an exception to the "at risk" limitation for nonrecourse loans made by institutional lenders that are neither purchase money loans nor loans convertible into equity interests. *Id.*

202. I.R.C. § 704(b) (1994).
203. Treas. Reg. § 1.704-2(b)(2) (1991).
204. *Id.* § 1.704-2(f).
205. *Id.*
206. *See* Treas. Reg. § 1.752-2(a) (1991). The regulations allocate the entire amount of a nonrecourse loan to the partner who makes that loan. *Id.* However, one must bear in mind the safe harbor of Treasury Regulation § 1.752-2(d). This regulation does not make such an allocation if the loan is "qualified nonrecourse financing" under I.R.C. § 465(b)(6), and the lender/partner has a 10% or less interest in each item or partnership income, gain, loss, deduction or credit. *Id.* § 1.752(d).

of a debt discharge.[207] That is, if COD income arises in one year, the decrease in partnership minimum gain, with its concomitant required allocations of income to partners experiencing that decrease, will not occur until the following year.[208] Second, in the absence of a change in, or clarification of, the applicable regulations,[209] rather than COD income alone being used to satisfy the minimum gain chargeback, the partner making the IRC section 108(c) election will be allocated a pro rata share of partnership income items to satisfy the chargeback requirement.[210] To effect Congress's evident intent in enacting IRC sections 108(a)(1)(D) and 108(c), the regulations need to say that COD income from the discharge of a nonrecourse liability will be treated as satisfying the chargeback requirement in the year in which the debt discharge occurs, and that such COD income will be the first item of income used for that purpose. Failing such an interpretation, the benefits of IRC section 108(c) will be substantially adversely affected.

Another area involving the new exclusion election that will need clarification is the method to be employed in computing partnership income and allocations when some partners make the election, either with respect to property held by the partnership or with respect to other property, and other partners have not.[211] While the effect of the basis adjustment is clearly to be felt only with respect to electing partners, it remains to be seen whether the intention is to look to the treatment of basis adjustments applicable to sales of partnership interests under IRC sections 743 and 754, or to use the more flexible, more recently promulgated (and more complicated) regulations under IRC section 704(c).[212]

---

207. I.R.C. § 1017(a) (1994).

208. *Id.* The built in gain problem may not exist if the reduction in basis of property is made under the normal rules discussed in Part B.2. of this Chapter and not under the basis election. I.R.C. § 1017(b)(2) provides that, in the case of the normal reduction, basis shall not be reduced below the aggregate of the taxpayer's liabilities after discharge, a limitation that could prevent the creation of built-in gain. I.R.C. § 1017(b)(2) (1994).

209. Treas. Reg. § 1.704-2(j)(2)(i) (1991).

210. I.R.C. § 703(b) (1994).

211. *See generally* Treas. Reg. § 1.704-3(d) (1993); *see also* I.R.C. §§ 743, 754, 704(c) (1994). These statutes exemplify the various methods available for calculating partners' income and allocation when some partners make elections under I.R.C. § 108 and when some do not.

212. *See generally* Treas. Reg. § 1.704-3(b), (c), (d) (1993). The Regulations

b. An Additional Possible Partnership Exception to COD Income; Exchange of Debt for Equity; Caveat Emptor

The IRC's exception to COD income for the transfer of debt to a corporation in exchange for an equity interest was repealed by the Omnibus Budget Reconciliation Act of 1993 ("OMBRA '93") with respect to transfers after December 31, 1994.[213] There is no similar statutory exception for a transfer of debt to a partnership in exchange for an equity interest in the partnership. Nevertheless, to the extent the corporate debt for equity exception has a common law basis, there is an argument for the existence of such an exception to COD income in the partnership context (which also applies in bankruptcy cases and in insolvency).[214] However, even if this were clear, partnerships and partners would have to consider such proposals with a view to the general rules applicable to partnerships. When the partnership debt is discharged and the lender becomes a partner, to the extent a partner's share of partnership debt is reduced by its discharge or its reallocation to the

---

describe respectively, the "traditional method," the "traditional method with curative allocations" and the "remedial allocation method," as representing three alternative methods for dealing with circumstances in which a partner's proportionate share of basis in a partnership's assets differs from that of other partners and implies "built-in" gain or loss in partnership's assets that should be specifically allocated to that partner. *Id.* I.R.C. §§ 743 and 754 methods are plausibly applicable, too, but are generally written for circumstances in which basis is being adjusted to reflect fair market value.

213. I.R.C. § 108(e)(10) (1988) *repealed by* Omnibus Budget Reconciliation Act of 1993, § 13226(a)(1)(A), Pub. L. No. 103-66, 107 Stat. 312, 487.

214. *See* Richard M. Lipton, *Planning For Noncorporate Debt Workouts Outside Of Bankruptcy*, 70 TAXES 275, 279-80 (1992) ("This leaves open the issue whether there is a partnership-interest-for-debt exception to the general rules concerning C.O.D. income."); *see also* Richard M. Lipton, *The Tax Consequences To A Debtor From a Transfer of Its Indebtedness*, 69 TAXES 939 (1991). But see I.R.C. § 108(e)(7)(E) (1994), which may be read to suggest that partnership interests received in exchange for debt are analogous to corporate stock acquired in exchange for debt which can, and outside of bankruptcy or insolvency will, result in COD income. On the other hand, I.R.C. § 108(e)(7)(E) is part of a subsection that focuses narrowly on the character of gain realized on an equity interest acquired in exchange for debt, treating such gain as ordinary income to the extent of any bad deductions previously claimed with respect to the debt. *Id.*

lender (who is now a partner), that partner will be deemed to have received a cash distribution.[215] To the extent that deemed distribution exceeds basis, the partner will recognize gain and, it appears, such gain will not be COD income eligible for any of the favorable treatments that may be available under IRC section 108.[216]

Moreover, under the "minimum gain chargeback" rules of the regulations under IRC section 704(b),[217] a reduction in the partner's share of partnership nonrecourse debt may, even though it may carry with it gain due to the deemed IRC section 752 distribution, require future income to be allocated disproportionately to such partner in an amount equal to the reduction in such partner's share of the "minimum gain chargeback."[218] Despite the fact that the amount of gain on the deemed IRC section 752 distribution and the reduction in the partner's share of the minimum gain chargeback should be identical in most circumstances, this effective "double counting" (while it appears completely inappropriate) may be required by the literal language of the regulations under IRC section 704(b).[219] Accordingly, existing partners, even if they conclude that the exchange of debt for a partnership interest may not generate COD income, should be very wary of admitting their lender as a partner *per se*. Although beyond the scope of this Chapter, one possibility to be considered is to retain the lender's status as a lender, but also to modify the

---

215. *See* Treas. Reg. § 1.752-2(C)(1) (1991). This regulation allocates the entire amount of a nonrecourse loan to the partner who makes that loan. *Id.* But also bear in mind the de minimis exception of Treasury Regulation § 1.752-2(d), which does not make such an allocation if the loan is "qualified nonrecourse financing" under I.R.C. § 465(b)(6) and the lender/partner has a 10% or less interest in each item of partnership income, gain, loss, deduction or credit so long as it is a partner. Treas. Reg. § 1.752-2(d) (1991).
216. The transaction could even be regarded in some circumstances of a disguised sale under I.R.C. § 707(a)(2)(B) (1994), involving a simultaneous contribution by the lender/new partner and a (deemed) distribution to the old partners. *Id.*
217. *See generally* I.R.C. § 704(b) (1994) (regarding determination of partner's distribution share); Treas. Reg. § 1.704-2(b)-(m) (1991) (outlining rules governing minimum gain chargebacks).
218. *See* Treas. Reg. § 1.704-2(b)(4), -2(c), -2(h) (1991).
219. *See* Treas. Reg. § 1.704-2(f)(1),-2(g)(2) (1991) (stating that net decrease in partnership minimum gain triggers minimum gain chargeback and each partner must be allocated items of partnership income equal to partner's share of net decrease in partnership minimum gain).

loan to a participating or "equity kicker" loan. This carries with it the risk of recharacterization of the loan as equity, however, with all the potential consequences noted above.[220]

4. State and Local Transfer and Gains Taxes

Since the exercise of creditors' remedies can result in one or more transfers of encumbered property, including foreclosures and deeds in lieu of foreclosure, state and local transfer and transfer gains taxes may be of significance.[221] These taxes may apply, not only to transfers of fee interests, but also to transfers of leasehold interests, shares of stock in a cooperative housing corporation and transfers of controlling interests in entities that own real property.[222]

Transfer taxes are generally measured by the consideration received by the borrower upon the transfer of the collateral to the lender or a third party.[223] Consideration will often be broadly defined and may include the principal, interest and late charges due to the lender, any payments made by the lender to discharge obligations of the borrower and the amount of any liens remaining on the collateral after the transfer. Although transfer and transfer gains taxes are usually imposed on the transferor, the transferee may be secondarily liable for payment of the taxes. Therefore, since the defaulting borrower may not have the funds to pay them, these taxes can significantly increase the lender's

---

220. *See, e.g.*, Farley Realty Corp. v. Commissioner, 279 F.2d 701, 704 (2d Cir. 1960) (holding that right to part of appreciation in value of property was equity in property and not deductible as interest on loan when liquidated). *See generally* Feder, *Either a Partner or a Lender Be: Emerging Issues in Real Estate Financing*, 36 TAX LAW. 191 (1983) (discussing debt versus equity question).
221. *See, e.g.*, N.Y. TAX LAW §§ 1440-1449(c) (McKinney 1987 & Supp. 1995) (levying 10% tax on real estate transactions with consideration over $1 million).
222. *See, e.g.*, N.Y. TAX LAW § 1440(1)(c) (McKinney 1995) (defining consideration by apportioning FMV of interest in real property to controlling interest for purpose of ascertaining consideration for transfer of such controlling interest).
223. *See, e.g.*, N.Y. TAX LAW § 1440(1)(a) (McKinney 1987) (defining consideration, in part, as "cancellation or discharge of indebtedness or obligation").

cost of exercising its remedies. For example, a lender taking a deed to New York City commercial property in lieu of foreclosure could become secondarily liable for both New York State and New York City transfer taxes. Moreover, upon the lender's subsequent transfer of the property to a third party, the transfer taxes would again be imposed[224] and the New York State transfer gains tax could apply.[225]

In an effort to reduce transfer and gains taxes, a lender may consider offering a low bid price at the foreclosure sale. Previous doubt as to the availability of such a strategy has been dispelled by the United States Supreme Court decision in *BFP v. Resolution Trust Corp.*[226] which rejected the "Durett Rule".[227] The Court held that a sale will not be set aside in a bankruptcy proceeding solely on the grounds of inadequate price when the property is sold at a regularly conducted, noncollusive foreclosure sale in a commercially reasonable manner because, in such circumstances, the debtor is deemed to

---

224. N.Y. TAX LAW §§ 1400-1421 (McKinney 1987 & Supp. 1995) (Real Estate Transfer Tax); N.Y.C. ADMIN. CODE Tit. 11, §§ 11-2101-2118 (City Real Property Transfer Tax). It may be possible to avoid the imposition of two sequential transfer taxes if the owner of the mortgage sells the foreclosure bid for an amount equal to or less than the bid price rather than take title and then sell the property. A detailed analysis of these taxes is beyond the scope of this Chapter.

225. N.Y. TAX LAW §§ 1440-1449(c) (McKinney 1987 & Supp. 1995)) (Tax on Gains Derived From Certain Real Property Transfers). There is no secondary or transferee liability under the New York State transfer gains tax when the owner of a mortgage takes title to property by foreclosure or by deed in lieu of foreclosure; furthermore, for purposes of computing gain on a subsequent sale of the property, the owner's "original purchase price" will include the amount of the foreclosure judgment, the amount of any transfer taxes paid and certain additional amounts, with the result that the owner is unlikely to realize a gain unless and until there is a significant increase in the value of the property.

226. 114 S. Ct. 1757 (1994).

227. The "Durett Rule" had its inception in Durett v. Washington Nat'l Ins. Co., 621 F.2d 201 (5th Cir. 1980). The Fifth Circuit held that a court might set aside a noncollusive and regularly conducted foreclosure sale as constructively fraudulent where the borrower was insolvent and the price paid at the sale was less than what the court determined to be fair consideration. *Id.* In dictum, the Court indicated that any transfer for less than 70% of the market value of the property would be less than a reasonably equivalent value. *Id.* at 204.

receive "reasonably equivalent value," thereby satisfying the Bankruptcy Code's fraudulent transfer provision.[228]

B. Insolvency and Bankruptcy

The IRC, as well as the Bankruptcy Code,[229] provide relief and planning opportunities to insolvent debtors, primarily by virtue of IRC section 108(a)(1)(A) and (B) which provides certain exceptions to the normal COD income rules for bankrupt and insolvent debtors,[230] and IRC section 1398, which deals with the tax treatment of individuals in bankruptcy.[231]

1. Exclusions from COD Income

Under IRC section 108(a)(1)(A) and (B), COD income is excluded from the debtor's income if the debtor's debt is discharged in a bankruptcy case (the "bankruptcy exception"),[232] or to the extent the debtor is insolvent (the "insolvency exception").[233] If the debtor is in bankruptcy, the bankruptcy exception applies and the insolvency exception does not.[234] This is important because *all* COD income is excluded under the bankruptcy exception[235] whereas, under the insolvency exception, COD income is excluded only to the extent the debtor is insolvent immediately prior to the realization of the COD income;[236] the COD income is includable to the extent that, by eliminating liabilities, it renders the debtor solvent.

---

228. *See BFP*, 114 S. Ct. at 1765; *see also In re* BFP, 974 F.2d 1144, 1149 (9th Cir. 1992) (holding that "the price received at a noncollusive, regularly conducted foreclosure sale establishes irrebutably reasonably equivalent value under 11 U.S.C. § 548(a)(2)(A)"), *aff'd*, 114 S. Ct. 1757 (1994).
229. 11 U.S.C. §§ 101-1330 (1994).
230. I.R.C. § 108(a)(1)(A),(B) (1994).
231. *Id.* § 1398. *See* discussion *infra* Part B.4.
232. I.R.C. § 108(a)(1)(A) (1994).
233. I.R.C. § 108(a)(1)(B) (1994).
234. *Id.* § 108(a)(2)(A).
235. *See* discussion *infra* Part B.4.
236. I.R.C. § 108(a)(3) (1994).

Example 16 - Same facts as *Examples* 1 through 6, except that Debtor is in bankruptcy. In each case, the gain is includable in Debtor's income but, assuming the debts are discharged in bankruptcy, all COD income will be excluded. If Debtor is insolvent but not in bankruptcy, COD income will be excluded to the extent of such insolvency but will be included to the extent it renders Debtor solvent.

Example 17 - If the debt is nonrecourse, as in *Examples* 8, 9 and 10, all the gain is includable and there is no exclusion from income since there is no COD income.

These examples further illustrate the relative benefit of COD income, which is not includable in the gross income of a debtor in bankruptcy or an insolvent debtor (to the extent of insolvency), as opposed to gain, which is always includable and which can result in a tax liability that may survive bankruptcy.[237] In certain circumstances, this may induce insolvent debtors to attempt to convert nonrecourse loans, with respect to which there is no COD income, into recourse loans, or to avoid foreclosure by negotiating a material change in the debt that would result in excludable COD income.[238]

For this purpose, a debtor is insolvent if and to the extent that, immediately prior to the realization of COD, the debtor's liabilities exceed the fair market value of its assets.[239] The determination of solvency can involve questions of contingent liabilities, joint and several liabilities and potential liability as a guarantor. To the extent a debtor is entitled to reimbursement from a co-debtor or a guaranteed party, the debt probably is not taken into

---

237. Gehl v. Commissioner, 102 T.C. 784, 789 (1994), *aff'd*, 50 F.3d 12 (8th Cir.), *cert. denied*, 116 S. Ct. 257 (1995). Priv. Ltr. Rul. 91-20-010 (May 17, 1991). In general, such tax claims are eighth priority, as described in Bankruptcy Code § 507(a)(8), and nondischargeable in bankruptcy. 11 U.S.C. § 523(a)(1) (1994).
238. *But see* discussion *infra* Part B.4.d.
239. I.R.C. § 108(d)(3) (1994); *cf.* 11 U.S.C. § 101(32)(A) (1994). Under the Bankruptcy Code, insolvency of an entity other than a partnership means a "financial condition such that the sum of such entity's debts is greater than all of such entity's property, at a fair valuation . . . ." *Id.*

account in determining solvency unless it can be established that the right to reimbursement is worthless.[240]

It is unclear, in the case of nonrecourse liabilities, whether the full amount of the liabilities is included in the computation of insolvency under IRC section 108, or only an amount equal to the value of the property securing the liabilities. However, in Revenue Ruling 92-53[241] the IRS held that the amount by which a nonrecourse debt exceeds the fair market value of the property securing the debt is treated as a liability only to the extent that such excess nonrecourse debt is discharged.[242] This ruling has been criticized in view of its apparent inconsistency with: (1) IRC section 108(d)(1), which defines the term "indebtedness of the taxpayer" to include indebtedness subject to which the taxpayer holds property; (2) IRC section 108(d)(3), which defines the term "insolvent" to mean the excess of liabilities over the fair market value of assets without distinguishing between recourse and nonrecourse liabilities; and (3) Revenue Ruling 91-31,[243] which held that a reduction of nonrecourse debt results in COD income.[244]

Insolvent debtors with recourse loans would have an incentive to establish a lower fair market value (and lower bid price) since that will decrease the gain portion of the income realized by the debtor on foreclosure and maximize the COD portion, or to negotiate the unpaid principal balance of the loan down to an amount equal to the basis of the property thereby eliminating gain and transforming it into COD income. Of course, such "planning" would be subject to scrutiny by both the IRS and the Bankruptcy Court.

2. Reduction of Tax Attributes

The insolvency and bankruptcy exceptions to COD income are designed to permit only a deferral of tax cost, rather than a permanent benefit, in many

---

240. Consideration of the rules regarding contingent liabilities may soon be an IRS project. *See* HIGHLIGHTS AND DOCUMENTS, Oct. 26, 1992, 1909.

241. Rev. Rul. 92-53, 1992-2 C.B. 48.

242. *Id.*

243. Rev. Rul. 91-31, 1991-20 I.R.B. 1.

244. *See* Richard M. Lipton, *IRS Adopts Inconsistent Positions on Nonrecourse Debt in Loan Workouts*, 77 J. TAX'N 196 (1992).

circumstances.[245] This effect is achieved by requiring a reduction in the "tax attributes" of the debtor, in the case of insolvency, and of the bankruptcy estate, in the case of bankruptcy.[246] A reduction of this type eventually could result in a tax cost roughly equivalent to the tax savings resulting from the exclusion of COD income. Often, the most important tax attribute of individuals and members of a partnership are net operating losses ("NOL") and NOL carryovers.[247] Subject to the basis election described below, these attributes must be reduced before other attributes are reduced.[248] Other tax attributes must be reduced in the following order:[249]

(i) surviving business credit carryover, *e.g.*, investment tax credit under the pre-1986 IRC;[250]
(ii) net capital loss and capital loss carryover;
(iii) the basis of depreciable and nondepreciable assets;[251] and
(iv) foreign tax credit carryovers.

The reduction in tax attributes is made *after* determining the debtor's tax liability for the "taxable year of the discharge."[252] Thus, the debtor (or

---

245. *See* Kentucky & Ind. Terminal R.R. Co. v. United States, 330 F.2d 520, 522-24 (6th Cir. 1964) (finding that provisions relating to exclusions from gross income from discharge of indebtedness do not exempt from taxation gain realized by taxpayer attributable to discharge, but simply provide means whereby taxpayer may elect to defer gain).
246. I.R.C. § 108(b) (1994). *See* discussion *infra* Part B.4.
247. *See* Terence L. Shen, Note, *Tax Consequences for a Tax-Driven Plan of Reorganization Under Section 1129(d) of the Bankruptcy Code and Section 269 of the Internal Revenue Code*, 1994 COLUM. BUS. L. REV. 267, 267 (stating that frequently ability to use NOL carryovers is among debtor's most valuable assets).
248. I.R.C. § 108(b)(2)(A) (1994).
249. *Id.* § 108(b)(2)(B)-(E).
250. Such tax credits are reduced by an amount equal to one-third of each dollar thereof. *Id.* § 108(b)(3)(B) (1994). The reduction of the investment tax credit is of diminishing importance under the Tax Code but could be of greater significance if investment tax credits are restored by future legislation.
251. *See* discussion of the basis election, *infra* p. 157.
252. I.R.C. § 108(b)(4)(A) (1994). In the case of a bankruptcy proceeding, it is not altogether clear in which year the "discharge" occurs, although the better view

bankruptcy estate)[253] has the full use of tax attributes in that year. Clearly, timing can be of great importance. For example, the acceleration of other income into the year of the COD income will permit an offset of such other income with NOLs and passive activity losses carried to that year.[254] A failure to fully utilize such losses in that year may result in a waste of the unutilized losses since they will have to be reduced (unless the basis election is made). In general, if a debtor has NOLs or passive activity loss carryovers, it would be a mistake to realize COD income in a taxable year prior to the year in which taxable gain is realized since that would cause such carryovers to be reduced by the prior year's COD income. Instead, the debtor should strive to recognize the gain either in the same year in which the COD income is realized or in a prior taxable year so as to fully utilize these losses against any gains before they are reduced.[255]

> *Example 18* - Insolvent Debtor has an NOL of $10,000,000 in the current year and an NOL carryover from previous years of $20,000,000. Debtor also has $30,000,000 of COD income for the current year and assets with a basis of $10,000,000 and built-in gains of $20,000,000. The COD income will not be taxable in the current year but will require Debtor to eliminate the current year NOL and the NOL carryforward, resulting in a loss of tax benefits of $30,000,000. However, if Debtor sells assets with a built-in gain of $20,000,000 in the current year, current year NOL and NOL carryovers will be available to offset that gain, resulting in a loss of tax attributes of only $10,000,000.

The "basis election" mentioned above permits a reduction in the basis of depreciable assets before a reduction is made in the other tax attributes.[256]

---

seems to be that it occurs upon conclusion of the bankruptcy proceeding. *See* Kenneth C. Weil, *Effects of Real Property Abandonments in Bankruptcy*, 70 J. TAX'N 358, 359 (1989).

253. *See* discussion *infra* Part B.4.

254. *See generally* BORIS I. BITTKER & JAMES EUSTICE, FEDERAL INCOME TAXATION OF CORPORATIONS AND SHAREHOLDERS ¶ 12.30[5][c] (6th ed. 1994) (explaining I.R.C. § 108).

255. I.R.C. § 108(b) (1994).

256. *Id.* § 108(b)(5). If property transferred to a bankruptcy estate has been

Such an election could be used to protect NOLs and other tax attributes in the current year with the concomitant tax cost (*i.e.*, the built-in gain created by the basis reduction) deferred to some future year in which the assets are sold.[257]

> *Example 19* - Same facts as *Example* 18 except that insolvent Debtor anticipates $10,000,000 net income in the following year. Debtor does not sell the property and elects the basis reduction option. The $30,000,000 of COD income is offset by $10,000,000 basis reduction and $20,000,000 of NOLs, thereby preserving $10,000,000 NOL carryover to offset next year's income.

Although Debtor in *Example* 19 eventually will realize $10,000,000 income because of the basis reduction, a deferred tax is preferable to a present tax. Furthermore, there may be no deferred tax if property is disposed of by sale, foreclosure or otherwise in the same year in which the COD income is realized because the basis reduction is made in the taxable year following the taxable year in which the COD income is realized.[258] Thus, a sale in the year in which the COD income is realized, or in a prior year, would preserve the property's basis, whereas a deferral of a sale to a subsequent year with the reduced basis could result in gain.[259] The deferral of the basis reduction until the following taxable year will also give those taxpayers who are in a position to do so time to acquire assets the basis of which can be reduced and thereby preserve their other tax attributes.

---

transferred by the bankruptcy estate back to the debtor, the election to first reduce basis will apply to the basis of such property rather than to the basis of property continued to be owned by the estate. *Id.* § 108(d)(8). *See* discussion *infra* Part B.4.a.

257. Although the basis election may be beneficial for federal income tax purposes, it may have an adverse state income tax effect since many states do not permit NOL carryovers.

258. I.R.C. § 1017(a)(2) (1994).

259. *Id.* § 1017(a). The built-in gain problem may not exist if the reduction in basis of property is made under the normal rules discussed *infra* Part B.2. and not under the basis election. I.R.C. § 1017(b)(2) provides that, in the case of the normal reduction, basis shall not be reduced below the aggregate of the taxpayer's liabilities after discharge, a limitation that could prevent the creation of built-in gain. *Id.* § 1017(b)(2).

If the COD income exceeds the tax attributes, there is no carryover of the excess to offset tax benefits that may arise in future years; the excess is permanently forgiven and never taxed.[260]

3. COD Income of Partnerships

Since the bankruptcy and insolvency exceptions are applied at the partner level, COD income of a partnership is considered to be realized by the partnership even if the partnership is insolvent or in bankruptcy.[261] For example, if a partnership satisfies a $300,000 debt for $200,000, the partnership has $100,000 of COD income which is allocated among the partners in accordance with their profit shares, a determination that is not always as simple as it might seem.[262] Each partner then must individually

---

260. *See* S. REP. NO. 1035, 96th Cong., 2d Sess. 8 (1980), *reprinted in* 1980 U.S.C.C.A.N. 7017, 7023.
261. I.R.C. § 108(d)(6) (1994).
262. It appears that only a partner who is personally liable for a partnership recourse debt, *e.g.*, a general partner of a limited partnership, or who otherwise bears the risk of economic loss or a partner who guarantees all or part of a nonrecourse partnership debt, would realize (i.e., be allocated) COD income since only such a partner could economically benefit from the discharge or reduction of the debt. A foreclosure of such debt would be subject to the two-step treatment described *supra* Part A.2.a. It is unclear the extent to which recourse debt so allocated to a bankrupt or insolvent partner may be required to be reallocated to another, solvent partner. Under I.R.C. § 752 regulations, nonrecourse debt should be allocated among partners for this purpose in the proportions in which such partners would share (or have shared) in the related deductions and income (including, under I.R.C. § 704(b), any "minimum gain chargeback"). To be consistent with the principles of I.R.C. § 704(b), any related COD income should be allocated first in proportion to the partners' shares of any "minimum gain chargeback" (and should reduce such "minimum gain chargeback" until it is reduced to zero) with any additional COD income allocated in accordance with the profit allocations in the partnership agreement. I.R.C. § 704(b) regulations do not specifically address this issue with respect to COD income, but do suggest that this treatment is appropriate, a conclusion that appears consistent with Revenue Ruling 92-97, 1992-2 C.B. 124. *See* Treas. Regs. §§ 1.704-2(f)(1),-2(i)(2) (1994).

qualify for the insolvency or bankruptcy exclusion, and each partner who so qualifies will be subject to the reduction in tax attributes.[263]

> *Example 20* - The ABC Partnership, which has three partners who share equally in income and loss, realizes COD income of $150,000, $50,000 of which is allocable[264] to each partner. Partner A, who is solvent and not in bankruptcy, recognizes $50,000 of COD income, assuming A makes no election under IRC section 108(c). Partner B is in bankruptcy and, therefore, excludes the COD income; but B's tax attributes must be reduced. If partner C is insolvent to the extent of $50,000 or more, C will receive the same tax treatment as partner B, the bankruptcy debtor. If partner C is insolvent to the extent of less than $50,000, he will be treated like partner B to that extent and like partner A with respect to the balance of his COD income including having the election under IRC section 108(c) available with respect to that balance.

If a partner who must reduce tax attributes elects to reduce the basis of depreciable assets, such partner's interest in the partnership can be treated as depreciable property (*i.e.*, the partner's basis for the partnership interest can be reduced) to the extent of the partner's proportionate interest in the partnership's assets, provided the partnership makes a corresponding reduction in the basis of its depreciable assets.[265] It is not necessary for all of the partners to make the election to reduce the basis of depreciable assets or to elect to reduce the basis of their partnerships interests.[266]

> *Example 21* - Partner A of the AB partnership is in bankruptcy and elects to reduce the basis of his depreciable assets as the price of excluding COD

---

263. *See* discussion of reduction in tax attributes *supra* Part B.2.
264. Assume this, but remember that the allocation of income might not be so easy. *See infra* note 278 and accompanying text.
265. I.R.C. § 1017(b)(3)(C) (1994).
266. *See* William T. Carman & Marc Pinto, *Involuntary Conversion Elections: How Partners Can Make Best Use of the Elections for Involuntary Conversions and Discharge of Indebtedness*, 4 J. PARTNERSHIP TAX'N 73, 77 (1987) (stating that "[s]ince there is no statutory requirement for a formal election, absent regulations to the contrary, a memorandum entry on the partnership books should suffice").

income. The partnership consents to a reduction of the basis of its depreciable assets to the extent partner A reduces his basis in his partnership interest. The tax effect of the reduction of the basis of the partnership's assets will be allocated only to partner A so that partner A's share of future depreciation deductions with respect to such partnership assets will be reduced and the portion of any gain realized by the partnership upon a subsequent sale of such assets that is attributable to the reduction in basis will be allocated and taxable solely to partner A.

COD income usually is preferable to gain when the debtor is insolvent or in bankruptcy.[267] In the case of a partnership, insolvent partners who would like to structure a workout in such a manner as to create COD income may find themselves at odds with solvent partners who prefer to realize gain rather than COD income because of favorable capital gains tax rates or a capital loss carryforward that may result from such realization.

4. The Bankruptcy Estate and Individuals (Including Partners)[268] in Bankruptcy

a. Creation and Taxation of the Bankruptcy Estate

When a chapter 7 or chapter 11 bankruptcy proceeding with respect to an individual is commenced, a new entity, the "estate" or "bankruptcy estate," is created under the Bankruptcy Code,[269] and all of the debtor's assets are deemed

---

267. *See* discussion *supra* Part B.1.

268. The following portion of this discussion does not apply to partnerships. *See* I.R.C. § 1398(b)(2) (1994). For tax purposes, no new entity is created when a partnership files in bankruptcy. *Id.* § 1399. The partnership continues to realize income and loss, including gain or loss and COD income resulting from workouts and foreclosures, all of which continue to be taken into account by the partners. *See* discussion *supra* Part A.3. This should be compared with Bankruptcy Code § 541, under which all partnership assets are transferred to the bankruptcy estate. 11 U.S.C. § 541 (1994) (discussing bankruptcy estates for all cases including partnerships).

269. 11 U.S.C. § 541(a) (1994). In chapter 7, a trustee is appointed to liquidate the debtor's assets and pay the claims of creditors. *Id.* § 701. A trustee may also be appointed in chapter 11, according to 11 U.S.C. § 1104, although the debtor will often continue to operate his business affairs as a "debtor in possession."

to be transferred to this estate.[270] Under IRC section 1398, there are no tax consequences resulting from this deemed transfer[271] and the estate is treated as the debtor would be treated with respect to the transferred assets.[272] In general, the estate is a separate taxable entity,[273] the gross income of which includes the gross income of the debtor to which the estate is entitled in bankruptcy, other than amounts received or accrued by the debtor before the commencement date.[274] Furthermore, the estate is deemed to succeed to the debtor's tax attributes (*e.g.*, NOL and other carryovers, basis and accounting method),[275] including the debtor's passive loss carryovers and losses suspended because of the at risk limitations, but, as of the date of this writing, apparently not including the debtor's suspended S corporation losses.[276] Finally, the estate

---

Id. § 1104.

270. *Id.* § 541(a)(1).
271. I.R.C. § 1398(f)(1) (1994). For example, the debtor realizes no gain or loss and there is no change in basis or holding periods.
272. *Id.*
273. *Id.* § 1398(c). For tax purposes, a separate estate is not created in other types of individual bankruptcies, *e.g.*, chapter 13. *See id.* § 1398(a) (stating that only applies to chapter 7 and chapter 11 cases).
274. *Id.* § 1398(e).
275. I.R.C. § 1398(g) (1994).
276. The Regulations under § 1398 and Treasury Decision 8537 provide that the bankruptcy estate succeeds to losses and credits suspended under both I.R.C. § 469 (passive losses) and I.R.C. § 465 (at risk limitation), and that such attributes, to the extent not used by the estate, revert to the debtor upon termination of the estate. *See* Treas. Reg. §§ 1.1398-1, -2; T.D. 8537, 1994-1 C.B. 230. Since S Corporation losses are not among the attributes enumerated in either the statute or the regulations, they are not among the tax attributes that pass to the bankruptcy estate. Under the regulations, if, before the termination of the estate, the estate transfers to the debtor (other than by sale or exchange) a partial interest in a passive activity or formerly passive activity or a partial interest in an I.R.C. § 465 activity, the debtor succeeds to an allocable portion of the unused losses and credits. Perhaps of greater significance, these regulations provide that such a transfer of these tax attributes from the estate to the debtor before the termination of the estate shall not be treated as a taxable transaction. *Id.* §§ 1.1398-1(d), -2(d). Also important is a statement in the accompanying IRS explanation of the regulations that these provisions are consistent with the decision in Samore v. Olson (*In re* Olson), 100 B.R. 458, 459, 463 (Bankr. N.D. Iowa 1989), *aff'd*, 121 B.R. 346 (N.D. Iowa 1990),

is normally taxed in substantially the same manner as an individual taxpayer would be taxed,[277] except that the estate cannot realize COD income since it is not liable for the debtor's debts even though it must attempt to pay or settle those debts. The tax attributes to which the estate succeeds, however, are reduced by any COD income excluded from the debtor's income under IRC section 108.[278] Any tax incurred by the estate is an allowable first priority claim payable out of the estate's assets.[279] The bankruptcy court may determined the estate's tax liability and the payment of any liability will operate to discharge the estate and the debtor from liability.[280] Upon termination of the bankruptcy estate, any tax attributes of the debtor that have been transferred to but not used by the bankruptcy estate revert to the

---

aff'd, 930 F.2d 6 (8th Cir. 1991), dealing with "midstream" abandonments by a bankruptcy trustee. T.D. 8537, 1994-1 C.B. 230. If a midstream abandonment of a mortgaged property by the trustee is not a taxable event, the debtor stands to realize substantial income upon a subsequent foreclosure without the benefit of related sheltering tax attributes which are retained by the estate. Under the regulations, the situation is mitigated in the case of a midstream transfer to the debtor of property that was part of a passive or I.R.C. § 465 activity because the debtor will also receive an allocable portion of the related suspended losses and credits. In the interest of both consistency and fairness, a similar rule, allocating directly related tax attributes and apportioning other tax attributes with respect to the abandonment or transfer of other property by the trustee, to the debtor would be appropriate. *See also* discussion *infra* Part B.4.c.

277. I.R.C. § 1398(c) (1994). The tax liability of the bankruptcy estate is computed using the tax rates applicable to married persons filing separate returns, one personal exemption and the standard deduction applicable to such persons. *Id.* The first taxable year of the bankruptcy estate commences on the date of the filing of the bankruptcy petition and the estate may elect its own taxable year and change it one time without approval. *Id.* § 1398(j)(1). Amounts paid or incurred by the estate are allowable as deductions or credits to the same extent they would have been so allowable to the debtor had the debtor been engaged in the same trade or business or activities that he was engaged in before commencement of the bankruptcy. *Id.* § 1398(e)(3)(A). The estate may also deduct administrative expenses, court fees, *etc. Id.* § 1398(h)(1).

278. *Id.* § 108(d)(8); *see supra* note 257 and accompanying text (regarding reduction of basis of assets transferred back to the debtor).

279. 11 U.S.C. §§ 507(a)(1), 503(b)(1) (1994).

280. *Id.* § 505(b).

debtor.[281] The retransfer of tax attributes and of other assets of the estate to the debtor also is not a taxable event.[282]

Example 22 - An individual owning real property with a $50,000 adjusted basis and $60,000 fair market value and subject to a nonrecourse mortgage debt of $100,000 is in bankruptcy. The encumbered property is deemed transferred to the bankruptcy estate with no effect on such attributes, and is then conveyed by the estate to Lender in full satisfaction of the mortgage debt. The estate realizes a gain of $50,000 (unpaid balance of $100,000 less adjusted basis of $50,000), resulting in a federal tax liability which is an allowable claim against the estate.

This treatment should be contrasted with the treatment of the debtor if the property had been conveyed to the lender in satisfaction of the debt immediately prior to the creation of the bankruptcy estate. In that case, the tax liability of the debtor, arising from the gain realized on the conveyance, would be a postpetition liability (because it would not be fixed until the end of the taxable year in which the conveyance occurred) and, therefore, would not be an allowable claim against the estate and would not be dischargeable[283] *unless*

---

281. I.R.C. § 1398(i) (1994). If the bankruptcy proceeding is dismissed, however, I.R.C. § 1398 is inapplicable *ab initio*. *Id.* § 1398(b)(1).
282. *Id.* § 1398(f)(2).
283. Moore v. IRS, 132 B.R. 533, 535 (Bankr. W.D. Pa. 1991) (discussing effect on estate for failure to make election); *In re* Eith, 111 B.R. 311, 313 (Bankr. D. Haw. 1990) (noting failure to make election creates tax liability for debtor); Wittman v. United States (*In re* Weir III), No. 85-40456-7, 1990 WL 63072, *2 (Bankr. D. Kan. Apr. 3, 1990) (same); *In re* Gonzalez, 112 B.R. 10, 11-12 (Bankr. E.D. Tex. 1989) (same); *In re* Mirman, 98 B.R. 742, 745 (Bankr. E.D. Va. 1989) (same); *In re* Turboff, 93 B.R. 523, 525-26 (Bankr. S.D. Tex. 1988) (same). If the debt were recourse and a deficiency judgment obtained against the debtor were discharged in the bankruptcy proceeding, any tax liability arising from the resulting COD income would also be postpetition income (even if the two year election discussed in the text were made) since the discharge could not occur until after the bankruptcy proceeding was commenced. Such COD income would result in a reduction of the tax attributes received by the estate from the debtor. *See infra* note 289 and accompanying text.

the two taxable year election is made.[284] Thus, if the assets of the bankruptcy estate will be sufficient to satisfy the tax liability, it could be beneficial to the debtor to delay workouts and transfers until after the initiation of a bankruptcy proceeding. Of course, unsecured creditors may be unhappy with such a delay since tax liability incurred by the estate is a first priority claim,[285] the payment of which could deplete assets otherwise available to unsecured creditors if the taxable income results largely from an unpaid mortgage debt which does not generate cash. In addition, such a delay could cause an unanticipated problem to the debtor if the bankruptcy trustee should seek to avoid the realization of taxable gain without commensurate cash by abandoning the property back to the debtor rather than conveying it to the lender.[286] On the other hand, if the debtor has tax attributes that can offset such gain, and the debtor's other income, he may be better off delaying the initiation of a bankruptcy proceeding in order to use the benefit of such tax attributes, particularly those that otherwise would be transferred to the estate under IRC section 1398(g).[287]

b. The Debtor's Taxable Year Election

The debtor has an option to divide the year in which the proceeding is commenced into two separate taxable periods.[288] The first period, known as the prepetition period, ends on the day before the commencement date of the proceeding.[289] The second period, known as the postpetition period, begins on the commencement date and ends on the last day of the debtor's normal taxable year.[290] Such an election, which is irrevocable, can provide the debtor with two

---

284. *See* discussion *infra* Part B.4.b. (discussing two taxable year election).

285. 11 U.S.C. §§ 507(a)(1), 503(b)(1) (1994); *see supra* note 281 and accompanying text.

286. *See* discussion *infra* Part B.4.c. (discussing trustee abandonment).

287. I.R.C. § 1398(g) (1994) (noting tax attributes of debtor succeeds to estate).

288. *Id.* § 1398(d)(2)(A). The election must be made on or before the due date for filing the return for the first (the prepetition) period, *id.* § 1398(d)(2)(D), and is not available to a debtor who has no assets other than property which the debtor may treat as exempt under Bankruptcy Code § 522. I.R.C. § 1398(d)(2)(C) (1994); *see* 11 U.S.C. § 522 (1994).

289. I.R.C. § 1398(d)(2)(A)(i) (1994).

290. *Id.* § 1398(d)(2)(ii).

benefits. First, the debtor will avoid COD income in the first taxable period to the extent the debtor is insolvent and will be able to use all attributes existing prior to the deemed transfers of assets to the bankruptcy estate to offset other income realized in the first taxable period.[291] Second, the debtor's tax liability for the prepetition period will be an allowable seventh priority claim against the bankruptcy estate,[292] although such a claim, if not paid by the estate, is not dischargeable.[293] Although the tax attributes available to the estate will be reduced to the extent utilized by the debtor in the prepetition period and by the amount of COD income not taxed to the debtor in the prepetition period,[294] any tax liability resulting from that reduction during the administration of the estate will be an allowable first priority claim against the estate.[295]

Example 23 - Insolvent Debtor owns real property with a $50,000 adjusted basis and $60,000 fair market value and subject to a recourse mortgage of $100,000. Debtor has $30,000 of income unrelated to the real estate, and a $50,000 NOL carryover. The encumbered property is conveyed by Debtor to Lender in full satisfaction of the mortgage debt. Debtor realizes a gain of $10,000 ($60,000 fair market value less $50,000 adjusted basis) and COD income of $40,000, the amount of the deficiency that was discharged. Since, however, Debtor remains insolvent after this transaction, the COD is excluded from income. Furthermore, since tax attributes do not have to be reduced until after the determination of tax for the taxable year in which the debt is discharged, the $50,000 of NOL carryover will be available to offset Debtor's other $30,000 of income as well as the $10,000 gain realized in that year. If Debtor then files for bankruptcy and makes the election to create two taxable periods, the

---

291. *Id.* § 108(b)(4)(A). *See* discussion *supra* Part B.2.
292. 11 U.S.C. § 507(a)(8) (1994).
293. *Id.* § 523(a)(1).
294. The estate succeeds to the tax attributes as of the first day of the debtor's taxable year in which the case commences. I.R.C. § 1398(g) (1994). This will be the date of such commencement, if the election is made. *Id.* § 1398(d)(2)(A)(ii).
295. 11 U.S.C. §§ 507(a)(1), 503(b)(1)(C) (1994); *see supra* notes 279, 282 and accompanying text.

bankruptcy estate will not be able to use the remaining $10,000 NOL carryover because of the requirement that tax attributes be reduced because of the exclusion of $40,000 of COD income. Any tax liability that results from this reduction, however, will be an allowable claim against the estate.

If the debtor does not elect to create two taxable periods, the debtor's tax liability attributable to the debtor's (as opposed to the estate's) activity during the entire year in which the bankruptcy commences is a postpetition claim, which is not an allowable claim and remains payable by the debtor.[296] In such a case, the debtor's tax liability will be calculated at the end of the normal taxable year under regular rules, except that the debtor will not be able to use tax attributes that exist on the first day of the normal year.[297] Instead, such attributes will be transferred to the estate and will be used to compute the estate's taxable income.[298] Accordingly, if the debtor will realize taxable income in the prepetition period and wants to use attributes that arose in years prior to the year of bankruptcy to reduce such income, the election should be made.[299] On the other hand, if the debtor anticipates a loss in the prepetition period, the debtor should consider foregoing the two taxable periods election, keeping in mind that any tax liability for that entire year would be a postpetition liability not payable out of the bankruptcy estate.

---

296. Although there is no judicial authority on point, it appears that if a debtor elects to create two taxable periods, any tax liability for the second period would not be an allowable claim against the estate since such liability would be postpetition. The debtor's tax liabilities for years ending prior to the year in which the bankruptcy case is commenced are allowable claims against the estate. Under 11 U.S.C. § 507(a)(8), however, even certain prepetition tax liabilities, which are "seventh priority claims" are not dischargeable. 11 U.S.C. § 507(a)(8) (1994); *see supra* notes 292-95 and accompanying text.

297. I.R.C. § 1398(g) (1994).

298. *Id.*

299. Note, however, that because of the alternative minimum tax imposed under I.R.C. §§ 55-59 (1994), the debtor may not be able to eliminate all tax liability with such tax attributes. The alternative minimum tax, however, would also be a seventh priority claim against the estate, which, although not dischargeable, may nevertheless be paid by the estate.

c. Trustee Abandonment

The Bankruptcy Code permits the trustee to abandon property of the estate that is "burdensome . . . or . . . of inconsequential value and benefit to the estate."[300] A trustee may be inclined (and unsecured creditors may be enthusiastic) to take such action with respect to property that secures a debt in excess of its fair market value, especially if the property has a low tax basis (*e.g.* resulting from depreciation deductions) that would cause the estate to realize substantial taxable gain (but little cash) if the property were sold or if the mortgage securing the debt were foreclosed upon.[301] If the act of abandonment itself is not a taxable event to the estate, the debtor, when the mortgage is ultimately foreclosed upon, would face the prospect of realizing gain and COD income,[302] and postpetition, nondischargeable tax liability. This comes at a time when the bulk of the debtor's assets and tax attributes, including NOLs that resulted from the ownership of the encumbered property which might shelter the gain, are owned by the bankruptcy estate.[303] The debtor's situation will be aggravated if the basis of the property had been further reduced because of an earlier exclusion of COD income.[304] In the event of a trustee abandonment prior to the termination of the bankruptcy proceeding, the debtor would likely take the position that the act of

---

300. 11 U.S.C. § 554(a) (1994).

301. *See* discussion *supra* Part A.2. (regarding calculation of gain on disposition of encumbered property).

302. *See generally* Weil, *supra* note 252, at 362 (describing abandonment as a "dilemma" since debtor may ultimately have to recognize more gain than if not abandoned). *Compare* Gibraltar Fin. Corp. v. United States, 825 F.2d 1568, 1572 (Fed. Cir. 1987) (holding amount realized on sale of foreclosed property taxable as ordinary income) *with* Terjen v. Santoro (*In re* Terjen), 154 B.R. 456, 459 (E.D. Va. 1993) (abandonment by trustee during pendency of bankruptcy not taxable event), *aff'd*, 30 F.3d 131 (4th Cir. 1994).

303. *See generally* Weil, *supra* note 252, at 359 (analyzing timing of tax attribute reductions); Jack F. Williams, *Rethinking Bankruptcy and Tax Policy*, 3 AM. BANKR. INST. L. REV. 153, 180-81 (1995) (recognizing that bankruptcy estate should use debtor's tax attributes to reduce tax liability).

304. *See* discussion *supra* B.2. The situation may be mitigated if the basis reduction were made under the "normal" tax attribute reduction rules. *See also supra* notes 258-60 and accompanying text.

abandonment was a taxable event to the bankruptcy estate.[305] Under general tax principles, an abandonment is treated as a taxable sale,[306] and IRC section 1398(f)(2), which provides that a transfer of assets from the estate to the debtor shall not be treated as a taxable disposition, by its terms, applies only to an abandonment on "a termination of the estate."[307] Although there are conflicting precedents on the question of "midstream" abandonments by a trustee,[308] the IRS's position is that such an abandonment is not a taxable

---

305. *See generally* Mark S. Wallace, *Is a Midstream Abandonment of Property by a Bankruptcy Trustee Taxable to the Estate?*, 77 J. TAX'N 26, 27 (1992) (arguing that § 1398(f)(2) creates exception for sale or exchange as a taxable transaction); Lisa M. Hebenstreit, Comment, *Tying Together the Tax and Bankruptcy Codes: What is the Proper Tax Treatment of Abandonments in Bankruptcy?*, 54 OHIO ST. L.J. 859, 860 (1993) (describing concerns of debtor and estate for tax consequences of abandonment by bankruptcy trustee).
306. Arkin v. Commissioner, 76 T.C. 1048, 1056 (1981) (finding abandonment sufficient to constitute sale or exchange under I.R.C. § 165(f) even if not under state law); Freeland v. Commissioner, 74 T.C. 970, 980 (1980) (interpreting "sale or exchange" broadly); Yarbro v. Commissioner, 737 F.2d 479, 486 (5th Cir. 1984) (labeling abandonment of real property subject to nonrecourse debt as "sale or exchange" for capital loss determinations), *cert. denied*, 469 U.S. 1189 (1985).
307. I.R.C. § 1398(f)(2) (1994).
308. *Compare In re* A.J. Lane & Co., 133 B.R. 264 (Bankr. D. Mass. 1991) (denying bankruptcy trustee's request for authority to abandon mortgaged property when foreclosure was imminent with result that gain realized on foreclosure was includable in income of the bankruptcy estate which also still possessed debtor's tax attributes) *with In re* Nevin, 135 B.R. 652, 653-54 (Bankr. D. Haw. 1991) (holding that IRS petition to compel trustee to abandon debtor partnership's interest to individual partners in bankruptcy results in federal income tax liability following sale of such interests); Samore v. Olson (*In re* Olson), 100 B.R. 458, 463 (Bankr. N.D. Iowa 1989) (stating abandonment by bankruptcy estate during administration has same effect under I.R.C. § 1398(f)(2) as abandonment at termination of bankruptcy estate), *aff'd*, 121 B.R. 346, 348 (N.D. Iowa 1990) (stating abandonment by bankruptcy estate during administration not sale or exchange), *aff'd*, 930 F.2d 6 (8th Cir. 1991); *In re* McGowan, 95 B.R. 104, 107 (Bankr. N.D. Iowa 1988) (holding "termination of the estate" used in I.R.C. § 1398(f)(2) includes termination of estate's interests in property). *See generally* Cook & Beckett, *Bankruptcy Abandonment: Who Pays the Fare-Trustee or the Debtor?*, 10 REAL ESTATE

transaction.[309] If such encumbered property is not abandoned by the trustee during the bankruptcy proceedings, but is returned to the debtor upon termination of the bankruptcy estate, the debtor will have no argument that the transfer was a taxable event to the estate.[310] The debtor will, however, at least have restored at that time any remaining tax attributes that might shelter the income realized upon foreclosure.[311] In either case, the debtor might have been better advised to have disposed of the property prior to the bankruptcy filing and to have made the election for two separate taxable periods.[312] In that event, the tax liability would have been transferred to, and paid by, the estate to the extent the estate had sufficient assets.[313] The bankruptcy trustee and bankruptcy court, however, have substantial authority to avoid (*i.e.*, to set aside) prepetition transactions that were intended to "hinder, delay or defraud any entity to which the debtor was . . . liable."[314]

d. Avoidance of Debtor Action

Recent case law demonstrates that the trustee and the court can also thwart a debtor's plans. In *Official Committee of Unsecured Creditors v. PSS Steamship Co. (In re Prudential Lines, Inc.)*,[315] the bankruptcy court held that the NOL carryforward of a corporate debtor is an asset of the bankruptcy estate within the meaning of Bankruptcy Code section 541.[316] Consequently,

---

TAX DIGEST 83 (Apr. 1992); Richard M. Lipton, *Tax Planning for Noncorporate Bankruptcies*, 70 TAXES 653, 660-62 (Oct. 1992); Weil, *supra* note 254.

309. *Cf.* Priv. Ltr. Rul. 92-45-023 (Aug. 7, 1992); *see supra* note 289 (discussing midstream abandonment and IRS explanation of Treasury Regulations under § 1398).

310. *Supra* note 25, at 8. *See* Lipton, *supra* note 308, at 660-62, 676 (discussing reversion of unutilized tax attributes back to debtor from estate).

311. I.R.C. § 1398(i) (1994); *see supra* notes 294-97 and accompanying text.

312. *See* discussion *supra* Part B.2.

313. *See* 11 U.S.C. §§ 507(a)(1), 503(b)(1)(B) (1994) (allowing first priority claim to taxes incurred by estate). To the extent the taxes are not paid by the estate, the debtor would remain liable for the tax. *See also supra* note 309 (noting that abandonment is not taxable event).

314. 11 U.S.C. § 548(a)(1) (1994).

315. 107 B.R. 832, 836 (Bankr. S.D.N.Y. 1989).

316. *Id.* at 836-37.

the debtor's stockholder was enjoined from taking a worthless stock deduction with respect to its stock in the debtor because such a deduction would have effectively eliminated the NOL carryforwards.[317] In *In re Phar-Mor, Inc.*,[318] the bankruptcy court continued a stay against sales or transfers of the debtor's stock without the Court's approval, stating that "the NOL has a potential value, as yet undetermined, which will be of benefit to creditors and will assist Debtors in their reorganization process. This asset is entitled to protection while Debtors move forward toward reorganization."[319] These decisions appear to have implications for noncorporate debtors who plan to have tax liabilities paid by their bankrupt estates rather than paying those liabilities themselves particularly when they accomplish this by using favorable tax attributes themselves and delaying the use of those attributes to their estates.

In *Gibson v. United States (In re Russell)*,[320] the Eighth Circuit Court of Appeals set aside the debtor-in-possession's irrevocable election under the former IRC section 172(b)(3)(C)[321] not to carry back prepetition period NOLs to prior years but, instead, to carry them forward for the permissible fifteen year period under the former IRC section 172(b)(1)(B).[322] By making this election, the debtor apparently sought to retain at least that part of the benefit of the carryforward that would have been realized in years subsequent to the termination of the bankruptcy proceeding, rather than have the bankruptcy

---

317. *Id.* at 841-42. This is because an "ownership change" would have occurred for purposes of the limitation on NOL carryforwards under I.R.C. § 382(g)(4)(D) (1994).
318. 152 B.R. 924 (Bankr. N.D. Ohio 1993).
319. *Id.* at 927. *See* Robins v. Brandt (*In re* Southeast Banking Corp.), 178 B.R. 291 (Bankr. S.D. Fla. 1995) (enjoining sale of inventory in chapter 7 proceeding where court found it appropriate for the Trustee to hold inventory for possible sale and to consider alternatives to liquidation of the estate under chapter 7 and in connection therewith to preserve the NOL as a potentially valuable asset of the estate for the benefit of creditors and, ultimately, equity security holders).
320. 927 F.2d 413 (8th Cir. 1991).
321. As in effect prior to the Omnibus Budget Reconciliation Act of 1990, Pub. L. No. 101-508, § 11811(a), 104 Stat. 1388-530 to 1388-532. Present I.R.C. § 172(b) is substantially similar to prior § 172(b)(3).
322. I.R.C. § 172(b)(1)(B) (1988).

estate realize all of the potentially substantial tax refund that would have resulted from a carryback of the NOLs.[323] The debtor had made the election with respect to two tax returns, one prepetition and one postpetition.[324] Over the objection of the IRS, the court held that the debtor's election on the postpetition return was a fraudulent transfer of a property interest of the bankruptcy estate avoidable by the trustee under Bankruptcy Code section 549.[325] With respect to the prepetition return, the court, stating that the election could be set aside under Bankruptcy Code section 548, remanded the matter to the Bankruptcy Court to determine whether or not the requisite intent to hinder delay or defraud was present.[326]

e. State Taxes

Although a comprehensive discussion of state and local taxes is beyond the scope of this Chapter, the following is merely a summary of some potentially important differences between federal taxation and state and local taxation of debtors in bankruptcy and bankruptcy estates and of some recent developments regarding local transfer and gains taxes.

(1) State Income Taxes

Bankruptcy Code section 346 provides rules regarding the state and local taxation of debtors and bankruptcy estates[327] that, although substantially similar in effect to the provisions of IRC section 1398,[328] differ from the IRC rules in several potentially significant ways, most of which are detrimental to

---

323. *Russell*, 927 F.2d at 415 (argument of trustee urging avoidance of irrevocable election); *see* I.R.C. § 172(b)(1)(A)(ii) (1994).
324. *Russell*, 927 F.2d at 414-15.
325. *Id.* at 418-19 (remanding case to determine if property was fraudulently transferred). Although the theory of the trustee's suit was based on Bankruptcy Code § 549, the proceeding was a refund suit under 28 U.S.C. § 1346(a)(1), an important procedural distinction since the period of limitations under Bankruptcy Code § 549 had expired. *Id.*
326. *Id.* at 419.
327. 11 U.S.C. § 346 (1994).
328. I.R.C. § 1398 (1994) (discussing rules concerning bankruptcy cases).

the debtor. For example, the Bankruptcy Code has no provision allowing the debtor to make the two taxable period election that is permitted for federal tax purposes under IRC section 1398(d)(2)(A). Instead, the debtor's taxable year will normally terminate at the inception of the bankruptcy proceeding.[329] Also, Bankruptcy Code section 346(g)(1)(B) provides that no gain or loss shall be recognized to the estate by reason of a transfer by the estate of property to the debtor[330] (unless the estate sells the property to the debtor), but does not limit this treatment to transfers that occur upon a termination of the estate as does IRC section 1398(f)(2).[331] Accordingly, the possibility that a "midstream" abandonment by a trustee is a taxable event to the estate[332] is less likely. Consequently, for state and local tax purposes, the debtor is even more likely to incur any tax cost resulting from a foreclosure or other transfer of the property that occurs after such an abandonment.[333]

Another difference is found in Bankruptcy Code section 346(g)(1)(A) which provides that a transfer of property to the estate by operation of law will not result in any "gain or loss."[334] This is a far less comprehensive exclusion than the comparable provision in IRC section 1398(f)(1) which provides that such a transfer shall not be treated as a disposition for purposes of any provision of the IRC that assign tax consequences to a disposition. In addition, under Bankruptcy Code section 346(i)(1), *all* of the debtor's tax attributes are transferred to the bankruptcy estate and not just those listed as examples, whereas the comparable list in IRC section 1398(g) is exclusive except as it may be expanded in regulations not yet promulgated. The lesson to be derived is that it can be hazardous to carry out plans designed with the IRC in mind without first determining their state and local tax law consequences.

---

329. 11 U.S.C. § 728(a) (1994).
330. *Id.* § 346(g)(1)(B).
331. *Id. See also* I.R.C. § 1398(f)(2) (1994).
332. *See* discussion *supra* Part B.4.c.
333. *See generally* Hebenstreit, *supra* note 305, at 888 (suggesting strategies for debtor to mitigate tax liability due to trustee property abandonment).
334. 11 U.S.C. § 346(g)(1)(A) (1994).

(2) Transfer and Gains Taxes[335]

The Bankruptcy Code offers some relief from state and local taxes for transfers that occur in a chapter 11 case, but not for those in a chapter 7 case. The scope of this relief, however, is somewhat uncertain. Bankruptcy Code section 1146(c) provides:

> The issuance, transfer, or exchange of a security, or the making or delivery of an instrument of transfer *under a plan confirmed under section 1129 of this title*, may not be taxed under any law imposing a *stamp tax or similar tax.*[336]

The Second Circuit Court of Appeals has held that the requirement that the transfer occur under a confirmed plan was satisfied when the sale was clearly anticipated in order to carry out the plan that was approved, even though the approved plan did not specifically authorize the sale and a supplemental court approval was required to effect the sale.[337] A "stamp tax or similar tax" includes both the New York City Real Property Transfer Tax[338] and the New York State Real Estate Transfer Tax.[339] However, in *995 Fifth Avenue Associates, L.P. v. New York State Department of Taxation and Finance (In re 995 Fifth Avenue Associates L.P.),*[340] the Second Circuit held that the exemption provided under Bankruptcy Code section 1146(c) does not apply to the New York State Real Property Gains Tax because that is not a stamp tax or similar tax.[341] As discussed elsewhere in this Chapter, substantial gain can be realized upon a sale or exchange of encumbered property even though the value of the property is depressed. Accordingly, the holding in *995 Fifth Avenue Associates,* may be of substantial economic significance. In this

---

335. The potential importance of state and local transfer taxes is discussed *supra* at Part A.4.
336. 11 U.S.C. § 1146(c) (1994) (emphasis added).
337. New York v. Jacoby-Bender, Inc. (*In re* Jacoby-Bender, Inc.), 758 F.2d 840, 842 (2d Cir. 1985).
338. *In re* Jacoby-Bender, Inc., 40 B.R. 10, 14-15 (Bankr. E.D.N.Y. 1984), *aff'd sub nom.* 758 F.2d 840 (2d Cir. 1985).
339. *Id.* at 14.
340. 963 F.2d 503, 513 (2d Cir.), *cert. denied*, 506 U.S. 947 (1992).
341. *Id.* at 513.

connection, it should be noted that the gains tax applies to a transfer or acquisition of a controlling interest in an entity owning New York real property, as well as to a transfer of the property itself.[342] Accordingly, it may not be possible to avoid the tax through the transfer of stock of a reorganized debtor.

C. Additional Considerations Regarding Partner and Partnership Bankruptcy

1. Partnership Filings

A partnership is not taxed as a separate entity, but is a conduit through which its income, deduction, gain and loss are allocated to its partners and shown on their individual tax returns.[343] Unlike individuals, when a partnership files a petition in bankruptcy,[344] no separate taxable entity comes into existence.[345] Despite the bankruptcy filing, the partners continue to have their respective shares of partnership assets allocated to them, including any gain from foreclosure and any COD income.[346] The partnership taxable year

---

342. N.Y. TAX LAW § 1440.7 (Consol. 1994); N.Y. COMP. CODES R. & REGS. tit. 20, § 590.45 (1994).

343. *See supra* notes 177-93 and accompanying text.

344. All general partners must join in a voluntary proceeding, but any one or more of the general partners may file an involuntary petition. 11 U.S.C. § 303(b)(3) (1994).

345. I.R.C. § 1399 (1994).

346. Partnerships, like corporations, are not discharged from debts in a chapter 7 case or a liquidating chapter 11 plan on the theory that the partnership creditors may proceed against the general partners. Partnerships, however, may receive a discharge under a nonliquidating chapter 11 plan. The bankruptcy or insolvency of the partnership is irrelevant to the I.R.C. § 108 relief provisions, because these provisions are based on determinations applied at the partner level, not the partnership level. *Id.* § 108(d)(6); *see* Rev. Proc. 92-92, 1992-2 C.B. 505 (finding that purchase price adjustment under I.R.C. § 108(e)(5) may be made without regard to partnership bankruptcy or insolvency, provided debt reduction otherwise qualifies for such treatment and no partner takes inconsistent position).

continues and the trustee becomes responsible for filing the partnership's tax returns.[347]

The major tax consequence to the partners of a partnership bankruptcy filing is the loss of control over events for which they will have responsibility for tax consequences. Similarly, unsecured creditors of the partners, who may prefer a course of action that minimizes priority tax claims on the bankruptcy estate, may have interests that conflict with those of the partnership's unsecured creditors, who will be able to consider all economic proposals and decisions without regard to their tax consequences, at least as to federal taxes. As this Chapter suggests, there are many delicate timing and characterization questions presented in bankruptcy tax planning. To split the authority to make those decisions, which will be that of the bankruptcy trustee, from their tax consequences, which will be to the partners and their bankruptcy estates, can be devastating.

> *Example 23* – Assume partnership AB with equal partners A and B who are all in bankruptcy. AB has one asset, a building with a basis of \$3,000,000 and a fair market value of \$6,000,000, encumbered by a nonrecourse debt of \$9,000,000. Its other assets are now sufficient to satisfy its trade creditors, but may be reduced if the building continues to operate. The bankruptcy estates of A and B each have assets of \$1,000,000 (other than their partnership interests), recourse debt of \$2,000,000 and no other taxable income. The lender to AB has offered that it will either write the loan down to \$7,000,000 and agree to interest adjustments and deferrals that should probably allow the loan to be carried based on current cash flow from the building or will take the property by deed in lieu of foreclosure. What would the trustee and creditors of the bankruptcy estates of A and B prefer the trustee of AB to do from a tax point of view and can they accomplish it?

In the above example, the creditors of the bankrupt estates of A and B have one objective: to avoid the recognition of foreclosure gain in the bankruptcy estate of the partnership and thus, the bankruptcy estates of A and B. If such gain is recognized, \$6,000,000 of taxable income will be allocated equally to A and B and the estates of A and B will each pay tax on that gain

---

347. H.R. REP. NO. 833, 96th Cong., 2d Sess. 21 (1980); S. REP. NO. 1035, 96th Cong., 2d Sess. 26 (1980), *reprinted in* 1980 U.S.C.C.A.N. 7017, 7040.

as a first priority administrative expense, wiping out their bankruptcy estates. One possible avenue the creditors might follow is to require their trustees to abandon the AB partnership interests back to A and B, respectively, to attempt to shift the tax liability to A and B[348] individually.

The trustees and creditors of the estates of bankrupt partners may attempt to influence or control the actions of the trustee of the bankrupt partnership under the doctrine of *Official Committee of Unsecured Creditors v. PSS Steamship Co. (In re Prudential Lines),*[349] which states that favorable tax attributes of a bankruptcy estate are assets of the bankruptcy estate–here, the estate of the bankrupt partner. *Prudential Lines* held that a parent corporation could be enjoined from claiming a worthless stock deduction with respect to the stock of a bankrupt subsidiary where the effect of such action would be to subject the subsidiary to severe restrictions on the use of its NOLs after it emerged from bankruptcy, presumably to be owned thereafter by its creditors.[350] The court's theory was that the subsidiary's NOLs were "property" of the estate under Bankruptcy Code section 541 that would be dissipated by the parent's proposed action. In the example, this suggests that a partner's creditors might attempt to require the trustee of the partnership's bankruptcy estate to accept the debt writedown alternative, rather than to deliver a deed in lieu of foreclosure, by bringing an action to enjoin delivery of a deed in lieu of foreclosure as violative of the Bankruptcy Codes automatic stay provisions.[351] Such a writedown would generate excludable COD income rather than gain,[352] thus preserving the partner's estate. The trade creditors of AB partnership, on the other hand, will prefer to be paid immediately, thereby avoiding the dissipation of other assets sufficient to satisfy their current claims, even if that involves allowing a foreclosure to proceed.

Although the precise scope of *Prudential Lines* is unclear, the holding was that because the purpose of the automatic stay was to prevent "dismemberment" of the estate, it extended to acts that had tax consequences to, or significantly affected tax attributes that were part of, the bankruptcy estate. To the extent that a partnership's trustee's acts could have such consequences on partners' bankruptcy estates, the trustees of partners'

---

348. *See* discussion *supra* Part B.4.c.

349. 107 B.R. 832, 836-38 (Bankr. S.D.N.Y. 1989); *see supra* notes 317-19 and accompanying text.

350. *Prudential,* 107 B.R. at 837-41. *See* I.R.C. § 382(g)(4)(D) (1994) (providing for treatment of worthless stock); *see generally id.* § 382.

351. 11 U.S.C. § 362(a)(3) (1994) (imposing stay on "any act to obtain possession of property of the estate . . . or to exercise control over property of the estate").

352. *See* discussion *supra* Part B.1.

bankruptcy estates might consider making a *Prudential Lines* argument to avoid "dismemberment" of the estates by taxes.

2. State Taxes and Partnership Filings; Bankruptcy Code Section 728(c)

Bankruptcy Code section 728(c) provides special rules if a partnership and one or more partners are in chapter 7 cases. Under that section, the state or local tax liability of a partner, to the extent such liability arises from the inclusion in a partner's taxable income of "earnings" of a partnership that are not "withdrawn" from the partnership, is a liability only of the partnership and not of the individual partners.[353] Since a partnership's taxable income or taxable gain from a foreclosure or like action, as well as any COD income, could arguably by definition (because it is unaccompanied by cash) not be "withdrawn"[354] from a partnership, the partnership creditors may have an interest in minimizing state or local taxable income, which will often bear at least some conformity to federal taxable income. If Bankruptcy Code section 728(c) operates, it will ordinarily create a first priority state or local tax claim[355] against the partnership bankruptcy estate's assets. While under Bankruptcy Code section 723(c) the trustee will have a corresponding claim against a bankrupt partner's estate, that claim evidently will not have the same priority status.[356] These considerations may, at least in high tax rate state and local jurisdictions, cause partnership creditors' interests to conform to some extent to those of the partners (or their bankruptcy estates).

---

353. 11 U.S.C. § 728(c) (1994).

354. To date, 11 U.S.C. § 728(c) has not been interpreted in any reported cases. It appears to be an anachronism. In 1978, at the time the Bankruptcy Code was last substantially revised, the IRS held the view that partnership bankruptcies, like individual bankruptcies, created separately taxable estates. Rev. Rul. 68-48, 1968-1 C.B. 301. That concept was rejected as to federal taxes when I.R.C. § 1399 was added by the Bankruptcy Tax Act of 1980, but survives in a modified form as to state and local taxes in Bankruptcy Code § 728(c). Arguably, "earnings" and "withdrawn" are ambiguous terms: if taxable income arises due to the recapture of earlier losses, is it "earnings"? If it is, does the use of those earlier losses cause the later "earnings" to be deemed "withdrawn"?

355. *See, e.g.*, 11 U.S.C. § 507(a)(1) (1994) (prioritizing administrative expense claims).

356. *Id.* § 723(c); NOTES OF COMMITTEE ON THE JUDICIARY, S. REP. NO. 989, 95th Cong., 2d Sess. 95 (1978), *reprinted in* 1978 U.S.C.C.A.N. 5787, 5881.

3. Partner Filings

a. Short Taxable Year Election

Determination as to whether to make the short taxable year election is particularly difficult when an individual's assets include partnership interests. A partner's taxable income from a partnership is based on that partner's allocable share of the partnership's taxable income for any taxable year of the partnership ending "within or with" the partner's taxable year,[357] taking into account such partner's varying interests in the partnership during such taxable year.[358] A partnership's taxable year closes as to any partner who sells or exchanges such partner's entire partnership interest.[359]

IRC section 1398 complicates matters in two ways: First, subsection (f)(1) provides that the transfer of property from an individual to the individual's estate "shall not be treated as a disposition for purposes of any provision of this title assigning tax consequences to a disposition. . . ."[360] Second, and perhaps more importantly, under IRC section 1398(d)(2)(A)(i), if a short taxable year election is made, it terminates the debtor's first short taxable year on the day *before* the petition is filed and begins the debtor's second short year on the day the petition is filed.[361] The debtor's partnership interest is not conveyed to the bankruptcy estate until the day the petition is filed and thus the debtor continues to own the partnership interest individually until the first day of the second short taxable year.

The interplay of these rules appears to lead to the following conclusions: (1) the debtor is required to report individually the partnership income "attributable" to the period such partner (as opposed to the estate) is a partner; (2) under IRC section 1398(f)(1), due to the absence of a sale or exchange of the partnership interest, the partnership's taxable year may not close as to such partner until December 31 (assuming a calendar year partnership taxable year); and (3) even if the transfer to the estate is treated as a sale or exchange that terminates the partnership year as to the debtor partner, the earliest date the partnership's taxable year can be so terminated is the day the petition is filed–which is one day too late for the short taxable year election to perform its intended function of having all of the prepetition short taxable year tax liability be a claim against the bankruptcy estate. Instead, no matter what

---

357. I.R.C. § 706(a) (1994).
358. *Id.* § 706(d)(1).
359. *Id.* § 706(c)(2)(A).
360. *Id.* § 1398(f)(1).
361. *Id.* § 1398(d)(2)(A)(i).

action the partner takes, all prepetition taxable income from the partnership will be includable in the partner's individual taxable income for either the full calendar year in which the petition is filed or, if a short year election is made, for the second short taxable year of the partner rather than the first short taxable year. Consequently, in either case the tax against such income is a postpetition claim, which claim is not against the estate, is nondischargeable, and must be paid out of the debtor's postpetition earnings.[362] This is exacerbated by any favorable tax attributes that might otherwise be used to offset such income being available only to the bankruptcy estate and not to the partner individually.

There is an argument, based on the legislative history of IRC section 1398(d)(2), that this negative consequence is unintended.[363] If a short year election is made, to require the debtor partner to treat what is economically prepetition partnership income as giving rise to a nondischargeable postpetition personal tax liability, rather than a prepetition priority tax claim against the estate, is arguably contrary to the purposes of the short year election. The language of the various applicable statutes, however, makes it prudent for a debtor partner making the short year election to consider various self-help remedies.

First, the debtor partner should consider the means of apportioning income under the partnership rules between the two short taxable years. If the transfer of the partnership interest to the estate is treated as a "sale or exchange," there are two available methods, the "pro rata" method and the "closing the books" method.[364] The pro rata method allocates income arising during a calendar year proportionately between the two short taxable years based on the number of days in each. The closing the books method allocates items of income, deduction, gain or loss actually realized through the date the case commences to the partner and allocates items accruing after that date to the partner's estate. Since the partnership agreement determines which method is to be used,[365] a partner contemplating bankruptcy will want to review the partnership agreement to determine whether the allocation method it uses is

---

362. *See supra* Part B.4.b.

363. H.R. REP. NO. 833, 96th Cong., 2d Sess. 21 (1980).

364. Treas. Reg. § 1.706-1(c)(2)(ii) (1987). The regulation allows other reasonable methods as well. One example of another reasonable method might be to use the *pro rata* method for ordinary operations and the exact method for extraordinary events, such as sales, foreclosure, refinancings or dispositions.

365. *Id.* If the agreement is silent, the "close the books" method is used. *Id.* In order to avoid closing the books, a partner's share may, by agreement among partners, be determined on a *pro rata* basis. *Id.*

appropriate to that partner's situation. Ordinarily, the partner will choose the exact method, because of the possibility that significant gain or COD income may be realized by the partnership and allocated under the exact method entirely to the bankruptcy estate after the petition is filed.

A second matter to consider is the timing of filing the petition. Ordinarily, a partner filing for bankruptcy will prefer to do so as early in the taxable year as possible, to minimize the partnership taxable income potentially includable on his individual return. For example, a bankruptcy filing in the first fifteen days of January arguably results in no partnership income for the taxable year being allocated to the partner individually.[366]

Finally, the partner may wish to cause the partnership year to terminate as to such partner prior to making a bankruptcy filing by selling such partner's partnership interest or by transferring it to a newly-formed corporation or, possibly, a newly-formed partnership. Transferring the interest by sale or transfer to a corporation in exchange for its stock will clearly terminate the partner's interest in the partnership as of the date of that transfer,[367] but will also result in gain recognition to the extent that partner's share of partnership liabilities exceeds such partner's basis in the partnership interest.[368] Thus, the cost of assuring that no tax will arise in the second short taxable year due to partnership operations during the first short year may be a significant increase in prepetition tax liability. A possibility to be considered to avoid this result is the contribution of the existing partnership interest to another partnership, which might be treated as a sufficient sale or exchange to terminate the partner's year[369] without significant gain being recognized on the transfer, although this is of doubtful use if no significant beneficial ownership change is associated with the contribution.[370]

---

366. The legislative history to The Tax Reform Act of 1984, Pub. L. No. 369, 98th Cong. 2d Sess. 98 Stat. 494, states that regulations should allow a half month convention under which transactions in partnership interests occurring on or before the fifteenth day of a month are treated as occurring on the first day of the month, while those occurring after the fifteenth day of a month are treated as occurring on the last day of the month. H.R. CONF. REP. NO. 861, 98th Cong., 2d Sess. 858 (1984), *reprinted in* 1984 U.S.C.C.A.N. 1445, 1546.
367. Treas. Reg. § 1.706-1(c)(2) (1992); Rev. Rul. 81-38, 1981-1 C.B. 386.
368. Treas. Reg. § 1.1001-2(a) (1992); I.R.C. § 357(c) (1994).
369. *See* Rev. Rul. 84-115, 1984-2 C.B. 118; Priv. Ltr. Rul. 81-16-041 (Jan. 21, 1981); Priv. Ltr. Rul. 82-29-034 (Apr. 20, 1982).
370. *See* Priv. Ltr. Rul. 88-19-083 (Jan. 12, 1988).

4. Impending Foreclosure-Abandonment of Partnership Interest

Impending foreclosure on a partnership asset presents a debtor partner with the issues discussed above in an especially aggravated form, partly due to uncertainty concerning whether a prepetition foreclosure in the same taxable year as the petition will give rise to a postpetition tax liability of the debtor. In addition, the debtor might be concerned that the trustee, if it receives the partnership interest as one of the assets of the estate, might abandon that partnership interest (with its built-in tax liability and consequent negative "value") back to the partner rather than incurring tax liability in the estate and reducing assets available to the estate's creditors.[371]

The debtor partner might under these circumstances consider abandoning the partnership interest prior to making a bankruptcy filing.[372] Considerable authority supports the proposition that a partnership interest may be abandoned,[373] although controversy has surrounded the question of whether a loss realized on the abandonment is a capital loss or, due to the absence of a "sale or exchange,"[374] is an ordinary loss.[375] In Revenue Ruling 93-80,[376] the IRS ruled that a loss incurred on the abandonment of a partnership interest is an ordinary loss under IRC section 165 if sale or exchange treatment does not apply.[377] However, if there is even a *de minimis* actual or deemed distribution to the partner (or if the transaction is otherwise in substance a sale or

---

371. *See* discussion *supra* Part B.4.c.
372. The term "abandonment" is serving two distinct functions here. First, the trustee's "abandonment" back to the debtor is under Bankruptcy Code § 554 and has the tax consequences described in I.R.C. § 1398(f)(2). Second, the debtor's abandonment of the partnership interest is under I.R.C. § 165(a) and Treasury Regulation § 1.165-2(a) (1992) and is, in the context of this discussion, conceptually quite different.
373. *See, e.g.*, Gannon v. Commissioner, 16 T.C. 1134 (1951); Hutcheson v. Commissioner, 17 T.C. 14 (1951); Cooley v. Commissioner, 52 T.C.M. (CCH) 411 (1986); Rev. Rul. 93-80, 1993-2 C.B. 239.
374. *See* I.R.C. § 1001(a) (1994).
375. *Compare* Gannon v. Commissioner, 16 T.C. 1134, 1139 (1951) *and* Hutcheson v. Commissioner, 17 T.C. 14, 20 (1951) (holding abandoned partnership interest in law partnership to be ordinary loss) *with* Arkin v. Commissioner, 76 T.C. 1048, 1053-57 (1981) (holding abandoned interest in land trust to be capital loss).
376. Rev. Rul. 93-80, 1993-2 C.B. 239.
377. *Id.*

exchange), sale or exchange treatment will apply and the partner's loss will be capital (except as provided in IRC section 751(b)).[378]

If a partner effectively abandons a partnership interest where such partner's share of nonrecourse partnership liabilities exceeds the partner's basis in the partnership interest, the IRS's position and the case law are clear in treating the transaction as a sale or exchange.[379] *A fortiori*, the same result will follow from a decrease in a partner's share of recourse liability.[380] Abandonment of such a partnership interest by a partner prior to filing a bankruptcy petition thus will give rise to gain, allow the deduction of any suspended passive activity losses,[381] cause the partnership taxable year to close as to the partner, and cause any resulting tax liability to be a prepetition tax liability that is a seventh priority claim against the estate. In addition, the trustee, unless it seeks to avoid the partner's abandonment under the Bankruptcy Code,[382] would not succeed to the partnership interest and therefore would not be able to abandon (in a bankruptcy sense) the partnership interest back to the partner during or at the termination of the case.[383]

Under Revenue Ruling 93-80,[384] sale or exchange treatment will result even if the partner's share of nonrecourse liability is less than the partner's basis because any decrease in a partner's share of liabilities is a deemed distribution under IRC section 752(b).[385] Accordingly, in such a case, abandonment of the partnership interest will result in a capital loss (which would be increased by any suspended passive activity losses).[386] It appears that

---

378. I.R.C. § 741 (1994) (recognizing sale or exchange of partnership interest as sale or exchange of capital asset); *but see id* § 751(b) (classifying certain distributions of partnership assets ordinary gain or loss).

379. *See* Middleton v. Commissioner, 77 T.C. 310 (1981) (abandonment of partnership real property treated as sale), *aff'd*, 693 F.2d 124 (11th Cir. 1982); Arkin v. Commissioner, 76 T.C. 1048 (1981) (same); Rev. Rul. 78-164, 1978-1 C.B. 264 (finding transfer of ownership to avoid foreclosure sale); Rev. Rul. 76-111, 1976-1 C.B. 214 (concluding transfer of property to seller in consideration of cancelling indebtedness is sale).

380. I.R.C. §§ 752(b), 731, 741 (1994).

381. *Id.* § 469(g).

382. *See* discussion *supra* Part B.4.d. The trustee would undertake such action presumably in order only to *re*abandon the property to the debtor, thereby attempting to eliminate the tax liabilities associated with the *debtor's* prior abandonment as prepetition, seventh priority claims against the estate.

383. *See supra* Part B.4.c.

384. Rev. Rul. 93-80, 1993-2 C.B. 239.

385. I.R.C. § 752(b) (1994).

386. *See supra* notes 377-78.

a partner abandoning a partnership interest would be entitled to an ordinary loss under IRC section 165 only if there are no actual distributions to such partner, and if such partner does not bear the economic risk of loss for any partnership liability and is not entitled to include a share of partnership liabilities in the basis of such partnership interest so that there can be no deemed distribution under IRC section 752(b).

In addition, anticipating preabandonment manipulations, Revenue Ruling 93-80 states that, for purposes of determining whether or not there is a deemed distribution under IRC section 752(b), liability shifts that take place in anticipation of the abandonment are treated as occurring at the time of the abandonment, and that a partner's receipt of consideration from another partner or a party related to another partner may cause the purported abandonment to be treated in substance as a sale or exchange of the partnership interests.[387] The Ruling applies equally to losses incurred when a partnership interest becomes worthless.[388]

An abandonment must be evidenced by a voluntary, affirmative, overt act of abandonment on the part of the abandoning partner.[389] Ideally, this would be by agreement with the other partners, but intrapartnership communication of an intent to abandon the partnership interest, not to contribute any additional funds to the partnership, not to receive any additional distributions from the partnership and not to participate in any further activities of the partnership have been held sufficient to evidence the partner's intent to abandon the partnership interest.[390] It also would also be helpful for the partner to notify the partnership's lender of the abandonment of the interest, as the IRS has argued that the failure to do so is significant.[391]

Conclusion

It should be clear from the foregoing that careful tax planning, including an analysis of existing and potential tax attributes, income, deductions gains

---

387. Rev. Rul. 93-80, 1993-2 C.B. 239.
388. *Id.*
389. *Id.*
390. *See* Citron v. Commissioner, 97 T.C. 200, 209, 213 (1991); O'Brien v. Commissioner, 77 T.C. 113, 115 (1981).
391. *See* Echols v. Commissioner, 93 T.C. 553, 557 (1989), *rev'd*, 935 F.2d 703 (5th Cir. 1991).

and losses, is essential in planning for a financially distressed debtor. Complicated tax considerations may seem secondary in the tense atmosphere of complex negotiations with various creditors having different interests and goals. Nevertheless, the best advice that a debtor's business and bankruptcy advisors can render to the debtor is to confer with a tax advisor with experience in bankruptcy tax planning as early as practicable in that process.

CHAPTER VI

SINGLE ASSET CASES AND CHAPTER 11: THE CLASSIFICATION QUANDARY*

LINDA J. RUSCH

Recently, the issue of single asset debtors seeking protection under chapter 11 of the Bankruptcy Code[1] (the "Code") has received increasing attention.[2]

---

* Parts A and B of this Chapter are based on Linda J. Rusch, *Gerrymandering the Classification Issue in Chapter Eleven Reorganization*, 63 U. COLO. L. REV. 163 (1992). I am grateful to the editors of the *University of Colorado Law Review* for their permission to use portions of that Chapter in the *American Bankruptcy Institute Law Review*.

Since the original publication of this Chapter in 1 AM. BANKR. INST. L. REV. 43 (1993), there have been many additional court decisions and commentaries on the classification issue and related subjects. Accordingly, the footnotes in this version have been revised to include the new cases as well as the recent writings of several commentators. The only substantive change to the text is the insertion of Part C of this Chapter discussing the amended definition of "impairment" pursuant to the Bankruptcy Reform Act of 1994, and the resulting effect on the classification issue. *See infra* notes 108-13 and accompanying text.

1. 11 U.S.C. §§ 101-1330 (1994).
2. *See* Boston Post Rd. Ltd. Partnership v. FDIC (*In re* Boston Post Rd. Ltd. Partnership), 21 F.3d 477, 481 (2d Cir. 1994) (addressing right of single asset debtor to classify claims separately), *cert. denied*, 115 S. Ct. 897 (1995); *In re* Woodbrook Assocs., 19 F.3d 312, 317 (7th Cir. 1994) (same); Bonner Mall Partnership v. U.S. Bancorp Mortgage Co. (*In re* Bonner Mall Partnership), 2 F.3d 899, 916 (9th Cir. 1993) (recognizing relative bargaining position of debtors and creditors where new value exception is applicable), *cert. granted*, 114 S. Ct. 681, *cert. dismissed as moot*, 115 S. Ct. 386 (1994); Phoenix Mut. Life Ins. Co. v. Greystone III Joint Venture (*In re* Greystone III Joint Venture), 995 F.2d 1274, 1279 (5th Cir. 1991) (prohibiting debtor classification to gerrymander affirmative vote to plan), *vacated in part*, 995 F.2d 1284 (5th

A recurring problem in single asset cases has been the court's willingness to "cram down"[3] a debtor's proposed reorganization plan over the objection of the

---

debtor under chapter 11 to avoid foreclosure); Humble Place Joint Venture v. Fory (*In re* Humble Place Joint Venture), 936 F.2d 814, 817-18 (5th Cir. 1991) (dismissing chapter 11 case filed in bad faith); *In re* Stratford Assocs. Ltd. Partnership, 145 B.R. 689, 691 (Bankr. D. Kan. 1992) (filing by single asset debtor under chapter 11 to avoid foreclosure); *In re* Landings Assocs. Ltd. Partnership, 145 B.R. 101, 102-03 (Bankr. M.D. Fla. 1992) (same); *In re* AWB Assocs., G.P., 144 B.R. 270, 272-73 (Bankr. E.D. Pa. 1992) (finding that bankruptcy court may determine single asset debtor's tax liability); *In re* Franklin Mortgage & Inv. Co., 143 B.R. 295, 298 (Bankr. D.D.C. 1992) (indicating creditors are subject to sanction for violation of automatic stay in single asset case); *In re* Triple R Holdings, L.P., 134 B.R. 382, 391 (Bankr. N.D. Cal. 1991) (preserving incentive to seek bankruptcy protection by disallowing veto power to undersecured creditors), *rev'd on other grounds*, 145 B.R. 57 (N.D. Cal. 1992). *See generally* Alfred G. Adams, Jr., *The Mortgagee's Guide to Single Asset Bankruptcy Reorganizations*, 98 COM. L.J. 350 (1993) (discussing effect of new value exception and artificial classification on lenders); John D. Ayer, *Bankruptcy as an Essentially Contested Concept: The Case of the One-Asset Case*, 44 S.C. L. REV. 863, 865 (1993) (arguing that bankruptcy law does not comfortably encompass single asset bankruptcies); W. Scott Carlisle, III, *Single Asset Real Estate in Chapter 11—Need for Reform*, 25 REAL PROP. PROB. & TR. J. 673 (1991) (proposing revisions to Code for sections affecting single asset bankruptcies); H. Miles Cohn, *Single Asset Chapter 11 Cases*, 26 TULSA L.J. 523 (1991) (discussing confirmation of plan in single asset chapter 11 case); Thomas J. Meaney, *Recent Developments—Living in Limbo: Single Asset Reorganizations Within the Financially Distressed Fifth Circuit:* In re Greystone III Joint Venture, 948 F.2d 134 (5th Cir. 1991), 23 ST. MARY'S L.J. 1205 (1992) (considering advantages and disadvantages of classification); Michael L. Molinaro, *Single-Asset Real Estate Bankruptcies: Curbing an Abuse of the Bankruptcy Process*, 24 UCC L.J. 161 (1991) (discussing burdens of Code provisions on single-asset bankruptcies).

3. Chapter 11 of the Code provides for the confirmation of a reorganization plan over the objections of a dissenting class of claims. *See* 11 U.S.C. § 1129(b) (1994). The basic requirements of cramdown are that the plan and debtor meet all the requirements contained in 11 U.S.C. § 1129(a), except for acceptance by all classes, and the requirements of 11 U.S.C. § 1129(b). *Id.* For a discussion of those provisions and their impact on the classification issue, see Linda J. Rusch, *Gerrymandering the Classification Issue in Chapter Eleven*

major secured creditor whose claim is undersecured.[4] One argument the undersecured creditor has advanced to resist cramdown is the classification argument,[5] which posits that the debtor is not entitled to classify the unsecured portion of the creditor's claim separately from the claims of other unsecured creditors. This argument maintains that the undersecured creditor's unsecured claim is substantially similar to the unsecured claims of other creditors[6] and thus must be classified with them.[7] Most courts have held that dividing substantially similar claims into different classes for the express purpose of creating an accepting class of impaired claims thwarts basic principles underlying the bankruptcy process.[8]

Reorganizations, 63 U. COLO. L. REV. 163, 167-75 (1992); *see also infra* notes 28-61 and accompanying text (discussing § 1129(b) "cramdown" requirements).

4. *See infra* notes 10-18 and accompanying text (discussing importance of undersecured creditor's role in plan confirmation).

5. *See* 11 U.S.C. § 1122 (1994) (classifying claims or interests); *see generally* Rusch, *supra* note 3, at 181-89 (describing classification and explaining cramdown provisions).

6. *See* Rusch, *supra* note 3, at 182 n.96 (citing cases holding that substantially similar means equal legal status vis-a-vis debtor); *see also infra* notes 19-27 and accompanying text (discussing meaning of substantially similar); *see generally* Richard F. Broude, *Recent Developments in Chapter 11 Plan Process*, C638 ALI-ABA 251 (1991); Lewis Kruger et al., *Chapter 11 and Plan Formulation, in* BASICS OF BANKRUPTCY AND REORGANIZATION 1992 (PLI Com. L. & Practice Course Handbook), *available in* WESTLAW, 630 PLI/Comm 223; Michael S. Lurey & Robert J. Rosenberg, *The Battles for Confirmation of Chapter 11 Plans, in* DOING BUSINESS WITH TROUBLED COMPANIES 1991 (PLI Com. L. & Practice Course Handbook), *available in* WESTLAW, 582 PLI/Comm 505; Thomas M. Mayer & David M. Barse, *Basic Bankruptcy, in* WORKSHOP FOR LEGAL ASSISTANTS 1992 (PLI Com. L. & Practice Handbook), *available in* WESTLAW, 619 PLI/Comm 87; Meaney, *supra* note 2, at 1208.

7. Granada Wines, Inc. v. New England Teamsters & Trucking Indus. Pension Fund, 748 F.2d 42, 46-47 (1st Cir. 1984); *In re* Fantastic Homes Enters., 44 B.R. 999, 1000 (M.D. Fla. 1984); *In re* L.G. Salem Ltd. Partnership, 140 B.R. 932, 935 (Bankr. D. Mass. 1992); *In re* Mastercraft Record Plating, Inc., 32 B.R. 106, 108 (Bankr. S.D.N.Y. 1983), *rev'd on other grounds*, 39 B.R. 654 (S.D.N.Y. 1984); Rusch, *supra* note 3, at 164 n.7.

8. *See* Montclair Retail Ctr., L.P. v. Bank of the West (*In re* Montclair Retail Ctr., L.P.), 177 B.R. 663, 665 (Bankr. 9th Cir. 1995) (stating that where treatment

---

of unsecured claims is similar, they cannot be classified separately); Boston Post Rd. Ltd. Partnership v. FDIC (*In re* Boston Post Rd. Ltd. Partnership), 21 F.3d 477, 483 (2d Cir. 1994) (noting key premise of Bankruptcy Code is to give greater voice to creditors holding larger debt), *cert. denied*, 115 S. Ct. 897 (1995); John Hancock Mut. Life Ins. Co. v. Route 37 Business Park Assocs., 987 F.2d 154, 159 (3d Cir. 1993) (stating where sole purpose of creating multiple classes is to ensure confirmation, each class must be sufficiently distinct to justify separate vote); Travelers Ins. Co. v. Bryson Properties, XVIII (*In re* Bryson Properties XVIII), 961 F.2d 496, 501-02 (4th Cir.) (finding classification to gerrymander vote impermissible) (citations omitted), *cert. denied*, 506 U.S. 866 (1992); Phoenix Mut. Life Ins. Co. v. Greystone III Joint Venture (*In re* Greystone III Joint Venture), 995 F.2d 1274, 1279 (5th Cir. 1991) (indicating classification affects integrity of voting process), *vacated in part*, 995 F.2d 1284 (5th Cir.), *cert. denied*, 506 U.S. 821 (1992); Olympia & York Fla. Equity Corp. v. Bank of New York (*In re* Holywell Corp.), 913 F.2d 873, 880 (11th Cir. 1990) (limiting debtor's power to classify claims); State St. Bank & Trust v. Elmwood, Inc. (*In re* Elmwood, Inc.), 182 B.R. 845, 849 (D. Nev. 1995) (stating classification may not be used to manipulate vote); Fairfield Executive Assocs. v. Hyperion Credit Capital Partners, L.P. (*In re* Fairfield Executive Assocs.), 161 B.R. 595, 600-01 (D.N.J. 1993) (same); *In re* Barney & Carey Co., 170 B.R. 17, 24 (Bankr. D. Mass. 1994) (prohibiting classification for sole purpose of gerrymandering vote); *In re* Dean, 166 B.R. 949, 953-54 (Bankr. D.N.M. 1994) (same); *In re* Bloomingdale Partners, 170 B.R. 984, 997 (Bankr. N.D. Ill. 1994) (finding separate classification justified only when claims not "substantially similar"); *In re* Thornwood Assocs., 161 B.R. 367, 372 (Bankr. M.D. Pa.) (finding classification scheme improper because creditors of equal rank placed in separate classes), *aff'd*, 162 B.R. 438 (M.D. Pa. 1993); *In re* One Times Square Assocs., Ltd. Partnership, 159 B.R. 695, 703 (Bankr. S.D.N.Y. 1993) (finding classification permissible where motivation not to create assenting class), *aff'd*, 165 B.R. 773 (S.D.N.Y.), *aff'd mem.*, 41 F.3d 1502 (2d Cir. 1994), *cert. denied*, 115 S. Ct. 1107 (1995); California Fed. Bank, F.S.B. v. Moorpark Adventure (*In re* Moorpark Adventure), 161 B.R. 254, 257 (Bankr. C.D. Cal. 1993) (same); Rusch, *supra* note 3, at 165 n.8 (listing cases which examine separate classification as abuse of bankruptcy process).

Since this Chapter was originally published, several commentators have written on the gerrymandering issue of claim classification. *See generally* David G. Carlson, *The Classification Veto in Single-Asset Cases under Bankruptcy Code Section 1129(a)(10)*, 44 S.C. L. REV. 565 (1993) (arguing that separate classification is necessary and creditor veto power should not be

In most single asset cases, the size of the undersecured creditor's unsecured claim allows the creditor to control the vote of the only impaired class in favor of the plan, namely the unsecured claims class.[9] If the

---

allowed); Bruce A. Markell, *Clueless on Classification: Toward Removing Artificial Limits on Chapter 11 Claim Classification*, 11 BANKR. DEV. J. 1 (1995) (stating that separate classification should be permissible as long as participants have same priority level); Peter E. Meltzer, *Disenfranchising the Dissenting Creditor Through Artificial Classification or Artificial Impairment*, 66 AM. BANKR. L.J. 281 (1992) (indicating that artificial impairment classification not intended by Congress); Scott F. Norberg, *Classification of Claims Under Chapter 11 of the Bankruptcy Code: The Fallacy of Interest Based Classification*, 69 AM. BANKR. L.J. 119 (1995) (arguing that separate classification of similar claims should not be based on interests other than legal status vis-a-vis debtor); Louis S. Robin, *Classification of Claims: An Examination of Disregarded Legislative History*, 98 COM. L.J. 225 (1993) (recommending "re-examination of the ability to classify unsecured creditors in different classes"); Christopher G. Sablich, *Separate Classification of Non-Recourse Undersecured Creditors in Single-Asset Chapter 11 Cases: Forbidden, Permitted, or Mandatory?*, 4 J. BANKR. L. & PRAC. 507, 511 (1995) (suggesting separate classes are necessary); Gregory K. Jones, Comment, *The Classification and Cram Down Controversy in Single Asset Bankruptcy Cases: A Need for the Repeal of Bankruptcy Code Section 1129(a)(10)*, 42 UCLA L. REV. 623 (1994) (suggesting repeal of consenting class requirement to avoid discriminatory motive for classification); Howard M. Neuger, Comment, *The Authority of a Debtor to Place Substantially Similar Claims Into Separate Classes in Order to Cram Down a Reorganization Plan: Should a Bright Line Rule Requiring All Substantially Similar Claims to be Placed into a Single Class be Adopted?*, 9 BANKR. DEV. J. 567 (1993) (proposing bright line rule requiring substantially similar claims to be placed in common class); King F. Tower, Note, *"Cramdown" Confirmation of Single-Asset Debtor Reorganization Plans Through Separate Classification of the Deficiency Claim-How* In re U.S. Truck Co. *was Run Off the Road*, 36 WM. & MARY L. REV. 1169 (1995) (recommending unrestricted classification); Paul J. Unger, Comment, *Prohibiting Multiple Classification and Artificial Impairment in Single Asset Chapter 11 Cases: The Creditor's Veto-It's Power Congress Did Not Intend*, 23 CAP. U. L. REV. 541 (1994) (stating that creditor veto power not intended by Congress).

9. *See* Rusch, *supra* note 3, at 167 n.15 and accompanying text. Section 1126(c) outlines the voting requirements for confirmation and rejection, providing:

A class of claims has accepted a plan if such plan has been accepted

undersecured creditor is successful in asserting the classification argument, the debtor will be unable to confirm its plan without the undersecured creditor's approval, unless an impaired[10] class of claims other than the unsecured claims class approves the plan. Thus, the effect of the classification argument is to allow the undersecured creditor's vote to control the vote of the unsecured claims class, thereby controlling the debtor's ability to reorganize.[11]

At issue in these cases is whether the undersecured creditor should be able to use the classification argument to exercise such control over the reorganization of the single asset debtor. The classification issue becomes important when three requirements are met: (1) the unsecured claims class is the only accepting class of impaired claims, (2) the creditor's unsecured claim carries the power to control the vote of the class if placed in the same class as the other unsecured claims, and (3) the plan otherwise meets all the requirements of cramdown.[12] When these conditions are met, the undersecured creditor's successful classification argument will result in the creditor effectively controlling the debtor's attempts to reorganize.[13] If any one of the

---

> by creditors . . . that hold at least two-thirds in amount and more than one-half in number of the allowed claims of such class held by creditors . . . that have accepted or rejected such plan.

11 U.S.C. § 1126(c) (1994). *See generally* Cohn, *supra* note 2, at 544-46 (describing requirements for consenting class); Daniel M. Glosband et al., *Current Developments on the Automatic Stay, Postpetition Lending and the Use of Section 105, in* REAL ESTATE WORKOUTS AND BANKRUPTCIES 1992 (PLI Real Est. L. & Practice Course Handbook), *available in* WESTLAW, 379 PLI/Real 237.

10. At least one class of impaired claims must accept the plan. 11 U.S.C. § 1129(a)(10) (1994). A claim is impaired if the plan proposes to alter the legal, contractual, or equitable obligations on the claim. 11 U.S.C. § 1124(1) (1994). *See* Rusch, *supra* note 3, at 171 nn.37-39 and accompanying text. The Bankruptcy Reform Act of 1994, Pub. L. No. 103-394, 108 Stat. 4106, amended the definition of impairment in § 1124. For the effect of that amendment on the classification argument, see *infra* notes 108-13 and accompanying text.

11. Unger, *supra* note 8, at 541-42; Glosband, *supra* note 9, at 244; Tower, *supra* note 8, at 1174.

12. *See* Rusch, *supra* note 3, at 167-75 (discussing cramdown requirements).

13. *See id.* at 192-96 (asserting that by controlling reorganization, creditor controls

conditions are not met, the undersecured creditor's classification argument will not defeat confirmation of the plan.

The classification issue raises two key questions. First, what did Congress intend when it enacted the chapter 11 classification provision, and second, what should the rule be in the event legislation is proposed to amend this provision. As discussed, the creditor's classification argument plays a major role in determining whether a single asset debtor will be able to cram down a plan on a major undersecured creditor. Part I of this Chapter explains why the creditor's classification argument affects the debtor's ability to cramdown by examining the concepts of claim bifurcation and substantially similar claims, and by reviewing the requirements of cramdown. Part B analyzes congressional intent concerning the classification issue by discussing legislative history, pre-Code law and the statutory language. Part C examines the Bankruptcy Reform Act of 1994 and its changes to the definition of "impairment" which affect the classification argument. Part D addresses the question of what the classification rule should be in light of two competing theories: the collective bargain theory and the loss allocation theory. Finally, this Chapter suggests that, aside from the requirement that claims within a class must be substantially similar to each other, Congress did not intend to place any further restrictions on the debtor's ability to classify claims. It concludes that under the current Code structure, the debtor should have the ability to classify claims for the purpose of creating an accepting class of impaired claims.

A. Chapter 11 "Cramdown"

1. Bifurcation of the Undersecured Creditor's Claim

When formulating a reorganization plan under chapter 11, the debtor will utilize section 506(a)[14] and divide the undersecured creditor's claim into two

---

debtor's property).

14. 11 U.S.C. § 506(a) (1994). Section 506(a) provides:

> An allowed claim of a creditor secured by a lien on property in which the estate has an interest, or that is subject to setoff under section 553 of this title, is a secured claim to the extent of the value of such creditor's interest in the estate's interest in such property, or to the extent of the amount subject to setoff, as the case may be, and is an unsecured claim to the extent that the value of such

parts; a secured claim and an unsecured claim. The secured claim will equal the value of the collateral, and the unsecured claim will constitute the amount of the creditor's claim that exceeds the value of the collateral.[15]

When the debtor's plan is confirmed, the collateral is freed from all claims against it except as provided for in the plan.[16] Thus, confirmation allows the debtor to write down the amount of the undersecured creditor's secured claim to equal the current value of the property.[17] In the event the debtor defaults, the

---

> creditor's interest or the amount so subject to setoff is less than the amount of such allowed claim. Such value shall be determined in light of the purpose of the valuation and of the proposed disposition or use of such property, and in conjunction with any hearing on such disposition or use or on a plan affecting such creditor's interest.

Id.

15. *Id.*; *see* Michael S. Lurey & Leslie A. Tucker, *Developments in Confirmation Standards for Chapter 11 Plans*, *in* CURRENT DEVELOPMENTS IN BANKRUPTCY AND REORGANIZATION 1991 (PLI Com. L. & Practice Course Handbook), *available in* WESTLAW, 573 PLI/Comm 389; Gerald F. Munitz & Karen M. Gebbia, *Section 1111(b)—Unique Rights for the Undercollateralized Creditor*, *in* BASICS OF BANKRUPTCY AND REORGANIZATION 1992 (PLI Com. L. & Practice Course Handbook), *available in* WESTLAW, 629 PLI/Comm 613; Raymond T. Nimmer, *Negotiated Bankruptcy Reorganization Plans: Absolute Priority and New Value Contributions*, 36 EMORY L.J. 1009, 1025 (1987) (noting bankruptcy laws alter creditors' rights to collect entire debt); Rusch, *supra* note 3, at 166 n.14 (discussing § 506(a)). The time and method for valuation of the property is subject to some debate. *Id.*

16. 11 U.S.C. § 1141(c) (1994). Section 1141(c) addresses the effect of confirmation on the status of the debtor's property and provides:

> Except as provided in subsections (d)(2) and (d)(3) of this section and except as otherwise provided in the plan or in the order confirming the plan, after confirmation of a plan, the property dealt with by the plan is free and clear of all claims and interests of creditors, equity security holders, and of general partners in the debtor.

Id. See Frank R. Kennedy & Gerald K. Smith, *Postconfirmation Issues: The Effects of Confirmation and Postconfirmation Proceedings*, 44 S.C. L. REV. 621, 644 & 645 n.73 (1993).

17. *See* Rusch, *supra* note 3, at 177 n.72 ("In essence, the debtor's obligation to the creditor is 'rewritten' as provided in the plan, and that plan obligation, not the

undersecured creditor will only be able to foreclose on the property for the amount of the secured claim provided for in the plan.[18]

2. Substantially Similar Claims

Section 1122(a)[19] provides that only substantially similar claims may be placed in the same class. The general rule is that claims are substantially similar to each other if they have equal legal status vis-a-vis the debtor.[20]

---

pre-confirmation obligation, is all the creditor can enforce."). The undersecured creditor can choose to have its entire claim treated as a secured claim. 11 U.S.C. § 1111(b)(2) (1994); Cohn, *supra* note 2, at 525 (discussing § 1111(b)); Rusch, *supra* note 3, at 175 nn.58-59 (same). In the event the undersecured creditor elects to have its entire claim treated as secured, the plan would provide that the creditor has a secured claim for the entire amount of its allowed claim and no unsecured claim. *Id.* In the event the undersecured creditor does not elect to have its entire claim treated as secured, the secured claim amount will be the value of the property. *See id.* at 176-77 (explaining consequences of § 1111(b) election). The secured claim, however, will be paid the present value of the lien value of the property, not the face amount of the secured claim. Carlson, *supra* note 8, at 588-89. *See* Dale C. Schian, *Section 1111(b)(2): Preserving the In Rem Claim*, 67 AM. BANKR. L.J. 479, 484 (1993) (discussing valuation of secured claim as including postpetition interest). The analogous situation has arisen in chapter 7 proceedings. Rusch, *supra* note 3, at 177 n.72. The Supreme Court, in Dewsnup v. Timm, 502 U.S. 410 (1992), held that stripping secured claims to the value of the collateral using 11 U.S.C. § 506(d) in a chapter 7 proceeding is not allowed. *Id.* at 417. For thoughtful discussions of *Dewsnup*, see Barry E. Alder, *Creditor Rights After* Johnson *and* Dewsnup, 10 BANKR. DEV. J. 1 (1994); Mary Josephine Newborn, *Undersecured Creditors in Bankruptcy:* Dewsnup, Nobelman, *and the Decline of Priority*, 25 ARIZ. ST. L.J. 547 (1993); *see also* Dever v. IRS (*In re* Dever), 164 B.R. 132, 133 (Bankr. C.D. Cal. 1994) (holding *Dewsnup* not applicable in chapter 11). In a chapter 11 proceeding, however, the Code expressly provides for lien stripping. *See* 11 U.S.C. § 1141(c) (1994).

18. *See* Rusch, *supra* note 3, at 177 n.72.
19. 11 U.S.C. § 1122(a) (1994).
20. *See In re* Thornwood Assocs., 161 B.R. 367, 374 (Bankr. M.D. Pa.) (finding separate classification invalid based upon relationship of creditor's claim to third party, not debtor), *aff'd*, 162 B.R. 438 (M.D. Pa. 1993); Ronald W. Goss, *Chapter 11 of the Bankruptcy Code: An Overview for the General Practitioner (Part II: The Reorganization Process)*, 4 UTAH B.J. 6 (Nov.

Courts have held that each secured claim is considered to have a different legal status, either because secured claims are interests in different property or because each secured claim has a different priority in the same property.[21] Under this reasoning, the undersecured creditor cannot contend that its secured claim is substantially similar to other secured claims. Similarly, the undersecured creditor cannot successfully argue that its secured claim is similar to an unsecured claim, because the claims do not have equal legal status vis-a-vis the debtor and its property.

On the other hand, the undersecured creditor may argue that its unsecured claim is substantially similar to other unsecured claims against the debtor. Courts usually consider unsecured claims to be substantially similar to other unsecured claims, because each claim has the same legal status vis-a-vis the debtor and its property.[22] Debtors disagree with this premise for several

---

1991) (discussing "substantially similar" as it relates to § 1122 (a)); Harvey R. Miller et al., *Formulation and Confirmation of Chapter 11 Plans Under the Bankruptcy Code*, *in* REAL ESTATE WORKOUTS AND BANKRUPTCIES 1992 (PLI Real Est. L. & Practice Course Handbook), *available in* WESTLAW, 379 PLI/Real 469 (same); Gerald F. Munitz & Karen M. Gebbia, *The Chapter 11 Plan, Confirmation and Cramdown*, *in* BASICS OF BANKRUPTCY AND REORGANIZATION 1992 (PLI Com. L. & Practice Course Handbook), *available in* WESTLAW, 630 PLI/Comm 329 (same); Rusch, *supra* note 3, at 182 n.96 (citing cases addressing whether claims have equal status vis-a-vis debtor). For a good overview of the different approaches courts have taken on whether a claim is substantially similar to another, see *In re* Barney & Carey Co., 170 B.R. 17, 22 (Bankr. D. Mass. 1994) (noting that most courts have denied confirmation of plans that separately classify deficiency claims because they are substantially similar in legal nature).

21. *See* Federal Home Loan Mortgage Corp. v. Bugg (*In re* Bugg), 172 B.R. 781, 784 (E.D. Pa. 1994) (stating that courts have consistently held that secured creditors on different pieces of property are not similar); *In re* Holthoff, 58 B.R. 216, 219 (Bankr. E.D. Ark. 1985) (finding "[s]ecured creditors with liens in different property or liens in the same property but with different priorities may not be classified together since their legal rights are not substantially similar") (citations omitted); John C. Anderson, *Classification of Claims and Interests in Reorganization Cases Under the New Bankruptcy Code*, 58 AM. BANKR. L.J. 99, 100-02 (1984) (analyzing Bankruptcy Code § 1122); Miller, *supra* note 20, at 479 (same).

22. *See* One Times Square Assocs. Ltd. Partnership v. Banque Nationale de Paris (*In re* One Times Square Assocs. Ltd. Partnership), 165 B.R. 773, 777-78

reasons. First, the undersecured creditor can elect to have its entire claim treated as secured,[23] thereby creating different voting incentives between the undersecured creditor and the other unsecured claims.[24] Second, the undersecured creditor may be a nonrecourse creditor who is using the Code-created recourse unsecured claim to affect the treatment of its secured claim.[25]

(S.D.N.Y.) (stating that unsecured claims are of equal legal rank and are therefore substantially similar), *aff'd*, 41 F.3d 1502 (2d Cir. 1994), *cert. denied*, 115 S. Ct. 1107 (1995); Fairfield Executive Assocs. v. Hyperion Credit Capital Partners (*In re* Fairfield Executive Assocs.), 161 B.R. 595, 603-05 (Bankr. D.N.J. 1993) (rejecting examination of voting incentive to determine if substantially similar); *In re* Bloomingdale Partners, 170 B.R. 984, 997-98 (Bankr. N.D. Ill. 1994) (stating that relevant issue is similarity of legal rights, not claimholder motive); Cohn, *supra* note 2, at 541 (discussing Bankruptcy Code § 1122(a)); Rusch, *supra* note 3, at 182 n.96 (citing cases holding that substantially similar claims are those that have equal legal status vis-a-vis debtor).

23. *See* 11 U.S.C. § 1111(b) (1994); *see also supra* notes 17-18 and accompanying text.

24. *See In re* Creekside Landing, Ltd., 140 B.R. 713, 715 (Bankr. M.D. Tenn. 1992) (finding different voting incentives enough to justify separate classification); *In re* Bjolmes Realty Trust, 134 B.R. 1000, 1003-04 (Bankr. D. Mass. 1991) (same).

25. *See* John Hancock Mut. Life Ins. Co. v. Route 37 Business Park Assocs., 987 F.2d 154, 161 (3d Cir. 1993) (rejecting debtor's argument that unsecured claims are different because undersecured creditors would be unable to proceed under state law); *Creekside Landing*, 140 B.R. at 715 (stating "[e]vidence that separately classified claim holder has . . . other means for protecting its claim in the reorganization will support separate classification"). For an argument that the nonrecourse undersecured creditor's deficiency claim must be classified separately from the other recourse unsecured creditors, see *In re* Woodbrook Assocs., 19 F.3d 312, 319 (7th Cir. 1994) (arguing for separate classification because § 1111(b) claim exists only in chapter 11, while general unsecured claim exists in all chapters); *In re* Gato Realty Trust Corp., 183 B.R. 15, 21 (Bankr. D. Mass. 1995) (finding that § 1111(b) affords deficiency claims a "different rank, character and status" than other unsecured claims); Principal Mut. Life Ins. Co. v. Baldwin Park Towne Ctr., Ltd. (*In re* Baldwin Park Towne Ctr., Ltd.), 171 B.R. 374, 377 (Bankr. C.D. Cal. 1994) (finding deficiency claim different based on evaluation of kind, species and character of deficiency claims); *In re* Overland Park Merchandise Mart Partnership, L.P., 167 B.R. 647, 650-53 (Bankr. D. Kan. 1994) (finding that nonrecourse,

Third, the debtor may have business reasons, such as wanting to maintain good will with unsecured trade creditors, that will result in divergent voting incentives for the undersecured creditor and the unsecured trade creditors.[26]

---

unsecured claims and other unsecured claims are not substantially similar and must be classified separately); *In re* SM 104 Ltd., 160 B.R. 202, 218-21 (Bankr. S.D. Fla. 1993) (same); Carlson, *supra* note 8, at 587; Sablich, *supra* note 8. *But see* Montclair Retail Ctr., L.P. v. Bank of the West (*In re* Montclair Retail Ctr., L.P.), 177 B.R. 663, 665-66 (Bankr. 9th Cir. 1995); Oxford Life Ins. Co. v. Tucson Self-Storage, Inc. (*In re* Tucson Self-Storage, Inc.), 166 B.R. 892, 897 (Bankr. 9th Cir. 1994) (stating that separate classification of unsecured claims based solely on right to make § 1111(b)(2) election is impermissible); *In re* D & W Realty Corp., 165 B.R. 127, 128-29 (S.D.N.Y. 1994) (holding separate classification of unsecured deficiency claim and other unsecured claims allowed only for legitimate business or Code-based reasons); *In re* Dean, 166 B.R. 949, 953 (Bankr. D.N.M. 1994) (finding "the manner in which unsecured claimants achieved their status, `does not alter their current legal character and thus does not warrant separate classification'"); California Fed. Bank v. Moorpark Adventure (*In re* Moorpark Adventure), 161 B.R. 254, 258 (Bankr. C.D. Cal. 1993) (submitting separate classification of unsecured claim not mandated "where it constitutes an abuse of the reorganization process").

26. Steelcase Inc. v. Johnston (*In re* Johnston), 21 F.3d 323, 328 (9th Cir. 1994) (stating that possibility of debtor and creditor nonbankruptcy litigation resulting in creditor having claim satisfied prior to other unsecured creditors is sufficient reason for separate classification); Heartland Fed. Sav. & Loan Ass'n v. Briscoe Enters., Ltd. II (*In re* Briscoe Enters., Ltd., II), 994 F.2d 1160, 1167 (5th Cir.) (finding city's continuing contribution and interest in project distinct from other creditors' interests and thus proper to separately classify), *cert. denied*, 114 S. Ct. 550 (1993); *In re* Chateaugay Corp., 177 B.R. 176, 186-87 (S.D.N.Y. 1995) (allowing separate classification of employee worker compensation claims because of need for employee cooperation); State St. Bank v. Elmwood, Inc. (*In re* Elmwood, Inc.), 182 B.R. 845, 850 (D. Nev. 1995) (permitting separate classification of unsecured claims because of differing payment methods to each class); *In re* Eddington Thread Mfg. Co., 181 B.R. 826, 833-34 (Bankr. E.D. Pa. 1995) (finding unsecured claimants willing to agree to potential subordination and postponement of payments should be separately classified); *In re* EBP, Inc., 172 B.R. 241, 244 (Bankr. N.D. Ohio 1994) (allowing separate classification of unsecured trade claims and unsecured tort claim based upon continuing relationship with trade claimants); *In re* Pattni Holdings, 151 B.R. 628, 631 (Bankr. N.D. Ga. 1992)

Each of these arguments is based on the identification of different motivating factors of the undersecured creditor and other unsecured claimants. These differences, however, are unrelated to the legal status of the claims against the debtor and its property. Each creditor who possesses an unsecured claim risks nonpayment. The undersecured creditor takes the same risk of nonpayment on its unsecured claim as other unsecured creditors.[27] As long as the test of substantially similar claims is that of equal legal status vis-a-vis the debtor and its property, the undersecured creditor's unsecured claim is substantially similar to other unsecured claims.

3. Section 1129(b) Requirements

To confirm a reorganization plan, the debtor must either obtain the acceptance of each class of impaired claims[28] or satisfy the cramdown requirements contained in section 1129(b).[29] In single asset cases, the undersecured creditor's claims are usually impaired[30] because the plan proposes to alter the original terms of the loan between the debtor and the undersecured creditor.[31] The plan typically will place the undersecured

---

(allowing separate classification of deficiency and trade creditors claims). *But see* Life Ins. Co. v. Barakat (*In re* Barakat), 173 B.R. 672, 681 (Bankr. C.D. Cal. 1994) (finding no business justification to separately classify trade creditors because other trade creditors were available to provide future services); *In re* Cantonwood Assocs., Ltd. Partnership, 138 B.R. 648, 657 (Bankr. D. Mass. 1992) (holding that maintenance of good business relationships insufficient reason for separately classifying trade claims).

27. *See* Norberg, *supra* note 8, at 119-20; Rusch, *supra* note 3, at 182 n.97 (suggesting that undersecured creditor could have protected itself from undercollateralization).

28. 11 U.S.C. § 1129(a)(8) (1994).

29. *Id.* § 1129(b)(1). "Cramdown" allows the debtor to confirm a reorganization plan over the objection of an impaired class if "the plan does not discriminate unfairly, and is fair and equitable with respect to each class of claims or interests that is impaired under, and has not accepted, the plan." *Id.*; *see id.* § 1129(b)(2) (describing "fair and equitable").

30. *See id.* § 1124(1). Generally, a class of claims is impaired unless the "legal, equitable, and contractual rights" of the claim holders are unaltered. *Id.*

31. *See* Acequia, Inc. v. Clinton (*In re* Acequia, Inc.), 787 F.2d 1352, 1363 (9th Cir. 1986) (finding that plan significantly impaired undersecured creditor's shares by modifying shareholder's rights); Rusch, *supra* note 3, at 171 n.38

creditor's secured claim in a separate class and then impair it by changing the interest rate,[32] stretching out the payments,[33] or proposing negative amortization of the claim.[34] If the undersecured creditor wishes to block the debtor's reorganization plan, it will vote its impaired secured claim against the plan. Once the plan has been rejected by an impaired class, the only way for the debtor to confirm the plan is to use the cramdown process.

In order to cram down a plan upon dissenting classes, the debtor must propose a plan that meets several Code requirements.[35] If any one of these requirements is not met, then the plan cannot be confirmed, regardless of how the claims are classified.[36] First, the plan must comply with all applicable provisions of the Code.[37] This includes section 1122 of the Code which provides that substantially similar claims may be classified together.[38] As will be discussed below,[39] this requirement does not support the undersecured

---

(explaining why undersecured claims are impaired).

32. *See* Cohn, *supra* note 2, at 537-40 (discussing interrelationship between interest rates and valuation for cramdown purposes).

33. *See id.* at 534 (discussing effect of extending payments on cramdown).

34. *See* Great W. Bank v. Sierra Woods Group, 953 F.2d 1174, 1177 (9th Cir. 1992) (finding no reason why negative amortization is not fair and equitable); *In re* Bouy, Hall & Howard Assocs., 141 B.R. 784, 791 (Bankr. S.D. Ga. 1992) (finding debtor's negative amortization plan fair and equitable); *cf.* 641 Assocs., Ltd. v. Balcor Real Estate Fin. (*In re* 641 Assocs., Ltd.), 140 B.R. 619, 632 (Bankr. E.D. Pa. 1992) (holding that contract rate of interest must be used with negative amortization feature); Cohn, *supra* note 2, at 535-36 (discussing whether negative amortizations meets "fair and equitable" requirement); *see generally* Barry S. Schermer & Keith W. Bartz, *Negative Amortization and Plan Confirmation: Is It Fair and Equitable Under Section 1129(b) of the Bankruptcy Code?*, 8 BANKR. DEV. J. 1 (1991) (same).

35. *See* 11 U.S.C. § 1129(a) (1994) (listing requirements that must be met before court can confirm plan). For a more in depth discussion of these requirements as they relate to classification, see Rusch, *supra* note 3, at 167-75. Other requirements of § 1129 not discussed in the text are not directly relevant to the classification issue. Rusch, *supra* note 3, at 169 n.21 (listing requirements irrelevant to classification issue).

36. 11 U.S.C. § 1129(a) (1994).

37. *Id.* § 1129(a)(1).

38. *Id.* § 1122(a).

39. *See infra* notes 62-107 and accompanying text.

creditor's argument that all unsecured claims must be classified together or that separate classification of unsecured claims to create one accepting class of impaired claims is abusive.[40]

The second requirement is that the plan must provide all holders of impaired claims with an amount equal to the liquidation value of these claims.[41] The liquidation value of each claim is equal to the amount the creditor would get if the case were liquidated under chapter 7.[42] Thus, the undersecured creditor must receive the liquidation value of both its secured claim and its unsecured claim, no matter how the claims are classified.

The third cramdown requirement mandates that the plan be feasible.[43] The feasibility test requires the court to determine if the debtor can meet the plan payments and whether the plan has a realistic possibility of success.[44] In doing

---

40. *See* Rusch, *supra* note 3, at 169, 181-92 (discussing classification under § 1122); *see also infra* notes 62-107 and accompanying text (discussing congressional intent with respect to classification issue).

41. *See* 11 U.S.C. § 1129(a)(7) (1994) (requiring that each holder of impaired claim or interest must accept plan or receive not less than amount he would have received if debtor were liquidated under chapter 7).

42. *Id.* § 1129(a)(7)(A)(ii); *see* Heartland Fed. Sav. & Loan Ass'n v. Briscoe Enters., Ltd., II (*In re* Briscoe Enters., Ltd., II), 994 F.2d 1160, 1167-68 (5th Cir.) (holding that creditor must receive present value of liquidation value of its claim), *cert. denied*, 114 S. Ct. 550 (1993); *In re* Union Meeting Partners, 160 B.R. 757, 772 (Bankr. E.D. Pa. 1993) (finding that in liquidation creditors would get nothing so payment of 25% to creditors would satisfy § 1129(a)(7)); *In re* Club Assocs., 107 B.R. 385, 407 (Bankr. N.D. Ga. 1989) (finding unsecured creditor would get more in liquidation thereby satisfying § 1129(a)(7)); *In re* Neff, 60 B.R. 448, 451-52 (Bankr. N.D. Tex. 1985) (noting that absent unanimous consent of a class, the class must receive under plan at least what such class would receive in chapter 7 liquidation), *aff'd*, 785 F.2d 1033 (5th Cir. 1986).

43. *See* 11 U.S.C. § 1129(a)(11) (1994) (requiring that it be unlikely that liquidation or further reorganization will take place, unless such is provided for in plan); One Times Square Assocs. Ltd. Partnership v. Banque Nationale de Paris (*In re* One Times Square Assocs. Ltd. Partnership), 165 B.R. 773, 778 (S.D.N.Y.) (affirming rejection of unfeasible plan), *aff'd mem.*, 41 F.3d 1502 (2d Cir. 1994), *cert. denied*, 115 S. Ct. 1107 (1995); *In re* Swiftco, No. 85-07083-H1-5, 1988 WL 143714, at *9 (Bankr. S.D. Tex. Oct. 5, 1988) (rejecting plan because financial future was "unrealistic and speculative").

44. *See* Kane v. Johns-Manville Corp. (*In re* Johns-Manville Corp.), 843 F.2d 636, 649 (2d Cir. 1988) (finding debtor's plan, proposed with intention of

so, the court evaluates the evidence submitted by the parties and decides if the debtor has satisfied its burden of proof that the plan is feasible.[45]

The fourth requirement is that at least one class of impaired claims must accept the plan.[46] In most single asset cases, this class is the unsecured claims

---

accomplishing successful reorganization, satisfactory); *In re* Sound Radio, Inc., 103 B.R. 521, 523 (D.N.J. 1989) (noting that plan must provide reasonable assurance that debtor will remain commercially viable for reasonable time), *aff'd mem.*, 908 F.2d 964 (3d Cir. 1990). Some courts look at the following factors in assessing feasibility:

> (1) the adequacy of the capital structure; (2) the earning power of the business; (3) economic conditions; (4) the ability of management; (5) the probability of the continuation of the same management; and (6) any other related matter which determines the prospects of a sufficiently successful operation to enable performance of the provisions of the plan.

In re Lakeside Global II Ltd., 116 B.R. 499, 506 (Bankr. S.D. Tex. 1989); *accord In re* One Times Square Assocs. Ltd. Partnership, 159 B.R. 695, 709 (Bankr. S.D.N.Y. 1993) (using same factors), *aff'd*, 165 B.R. 773 (S.D.N.Y.), *aff'd mem.*, 41 F.3d 1502 (2d Cir. 1994), *cert. denied*, 115 S. Ct. 1107 (1995); *In re* Landing Assocs. Ltd., 157 B.R. 791, 819 (Bankr. W.D. Tex. 1993) (same); *see* Cohn, *supra* note 2, at 529-31.

In single asset cases there are other possible indications of feasibility: the debtor's equity in the property; the stability of occupancy and rental rates; the debtor's management quality and experience, the amount of capital contributions; and the market need for the particular asset. Cohn, *supra* note 2, at 530-31; *see* Goss, *supra* note 20, at 14; Munitz & Gebbia, *supra* note 20, at *42-44.

45. *See* Rusch, *supra* note 3, at 198 n.182.

46. 11 U.S.C. § 1129(a)(10) (1994). Confirmation of a plan also may be opposed if the single asset debtor "artificially" impaired claims in a class in order to construct one accepting class of impaired claims. *See generally* David G. Carlson, *Artificial Impairment and the Single Asset Chapter 11 Case*, 23 CAP. U. L. REV. 339 (1994) (discussing strengths and weaknesses of new artificial impairment argument); Eric W. Lam, *On the River of Artificial and Arbitrary Impairment: An Erroneous Analysis*, 70 N.D. L. REV. 993 (1994) (disagreeing with Eighth Circuit holding that claim is not impaired where alteration of rights in question arises solely from debtor's exercise of discretion); Meltzer, *supra* note 8 (indicating that classification argument results in "separate but equal treatment" which minimizes vote of largest creditor); *see also* Windsor on the

class.[47] As stated above, the classification argument will allow the undersecured creditor to block plan confirmation only if the unsecured claims class is the only accepting class of impaired claims and the size of the undersecured creditor's unsecured claim is sufficient to enable the creditor to control the vote of that class if its unsecured claim were placed there.[48]

The fifth requirement is that the plan must not unfairly discriminate against dissenting classes of impaired claims.[49] This means that substantially similar claims, even when separately classified, must be treated similarly unless a good reason exists for treating them differently.[50] Therefore, if the

---

River Assocs., Ltd. v. Balcor Real Estate Fin., Inc. (*In re* Windsor on the River Assocs., Ltd.), 7 F.3d 127, 131 (8th Cir. 1993) (holding manipulation of claims under chapter 11 proceeding contrary to purpose of § 1129(a)(10)); *In re* W.C. Peeler Co., 182 B.R. 435, 437-38 (Bankr. D.S.C. 1995) (requiring debtor to show impairment of claim is necessary to reorganize, not to manipulate cramdown); *In re* Dean, 166 B.R. 949, 954 (Bankr. D.N.M. 1994) (explaining that classification permits small unsecured creditor disproportional voting rights). *But see* Mutual Life Ins. Co. v. Patrician St. Joseph Partners Ltd. Partnership (*In re* Patrician St. Joseph Partners Ltd. Partnership), 169 B.R. 669, 678 (D. Ariz. 1994) (finding that since payment of claims is delayed for small unsecured creditors, their legal, equitable and contractual rights are affected as matter of law); *In re* Landing Assocs., Ltd., 157 B.R. 791, 812-15 (Bankr. W.D. Tex. 1993) (denying creditors argument that artificial impairment solely to satisfy requirements of § 1129(a)(10) is bad faith tactic).

47. *See* Carlson, *supra* note 46, at 348 nn.37-41 (stating trade creditors are easily persuaded to vote for plan either to accommodate good customer, receive payment from general partner postconfirmation or to prevent being swallowed by large creditor); Jones, *supra* note 8, at 627 n.17 (indicating that trade creditors will usually consent to plan since they will receive little under liquidation); Kenneth N. Klee, *The Concept of "Impairment" in Business Reorganizations*, C946 ALI-ABA 499, 526-27 nn.58-60 (noting that unsecured creditors generally will consent to plan where there is large oversecured creditor, since liquidation will yield little or no dividends).

48. *See* Rusch, *supra* note 3, at 171 n.39.

49. 11 U.S.C. § 1129(b)(1) (1994). *See In re* Eitemiller, 149 B.R. 626, 629 (Bankr. D. Idaho 1993) (rejecting plan because it unfairly discriminated among classes of creditors); *Landing Assocs.*, 157 B.R. at 822 (stating that unfair discrimination requires plan to allocate value to all classes with similar legal claim) (citation omitted).

50. *See* Oxford Life Ins. Co. v. Tucson Self-Storage, Inc. (*In re* Tucson Self-Storage, Inc.), 166 B.R. 892, 898 (Bankr. 9th Cir. 1994) (finding classification

undersecured creditor's unsecured claim is placed in a class separate from the other unsecured claims, the treatment of those two classes must be the same unless the court determines different treatment is justified.

The final requirement states that the plan be fair and equitable as to dissenting classes of impaired claims.[51] For a plan to be fair and equitable with

---

impermissible where debtors offered no business or economic justification for separate treatment of similarly situated unsecured claims); *In re* Barney & Carey Co., 170 B.R. 17, 25 (Bankr. D. Mass. 1994) (noting that although statute might permit some fair and reasonable differences in treatment among classes, discrimination must be fair and supported by rational basis); *In re* Pattni Holdings, 151 B.R. 628, 631 (Bankr. N.D. Ga. 1992) (finding that although unsecured claims were similar, circumstances from which claims arose justify separate treatment); Rusch, *supra* note 3, at 171-72 nn.41-45. The criteria some courts have used to determine if the discrimination between similar classes is unfair are: "(1) [w]hether the discrimination is supported by a reasonable basis; (2) [w]hether the debtor can confirm and consummate a plan without the discrimination; (3) [w]hether the discrimination is proposed in good faith; and (4) [t]he treatment of the classes discriminated against." *In re* 11,111, Inc., 117 B.R. 471, 478 (Bankr. D. Minn. 1990) (citing *In re* Storberg, 94 B.R. 144, 146 (Bankr. D. Minn. 1988)); *see In re* Buttonwood Partners Ltd., 111 B.R. 57, 63 (Bankr. S.D.N.Y. 1990) (using same test); *In re* Aztec Co., 107 B.R. 585, 590 (Bankr. M.D. Tenn. 1989) (same). For an analysis of unfair discrimination between unsecured classes of claims in the chapter 13 context, William H. Brown & Katherine L. Evans, *A Comparison of Classification and Treatment of Family Support Obligations and Student Loans: A Case Analysis*, 24 MEM. ST. U. L. REV. 623 (1994) (concluding that mechanical test is inadequate to determine classification/discrimination, and all facts and circumstances must be examined); see Marguerite N. Conboy & Michael J. Chmiel, *Preferential Classification in Chapter 13: How Unfair Discrimination Has Created a Murky Body of Case Law*, 98 COM. L.J. 486 (1993) (suggesting amendment to § 1322(b) eliminating "unfair" and specifically providing which claims deserve preferential treatment); Oliver B. Pollak & David G. Hicks, *Student Loans, Chapter 13, Classification of Debt, Unfair Discrimination and the Fresh Start After the Student Loan Default Prevention Initiative Act of 1990*, 1993 DET. C. L. REV. 1617 (stating that student loan debt should receive preferential treatment regardless of fair/unfair discrimination).

51. 11 U.S.C. § 1129(b)(1) (1994); *see In re* Lakeside Global II, Ltd., 116 B.R. 499, 510 (Bankr. S.D. Tex. 1989) (stating that in cramdown analysis, court

respect to a secured claim, it must provide for the creditor to retain its lien on the property for the amount of the secured claim and to receive payments that total the amount of the claim, with a present value equal to the amount of the lien.[52] For example, if the undersecured creditor had a secured claim of $50,000 based upon the property valuation, that creditor would retain a lien for $50,000 and would receive payments during the life of the plan with a present value of $50,000.[53]

---

must consider whether plan is fair and equitable and does not unfairly discriminate under § 1129).

52. *See* Travelers Ins. Co. v. Bryson Properties, XVIII (*In re* Bryson Properties, XVIII), 961 F.2d 496, 500 (4th Cir.) (stating "'fair and equitable' requirement is not satisfied with respect to a secured claim unless the claimholder: (1) retains its lien; and (2) receives 'deferred cash payments totaling at least the allowed amount of such claim, . . . of at least the value of such holder's interest in the estate's interest in such property'") (citing 11 U.S.C. § 1129(b)(2)(a)(i)(I), (II) (1988)), *cert. denied*, 506 U.S. 866 (1992); *see* Federal Home Loan Mortgage Corp. v. Bugg (*In re* Bugg), 172 B.R. 781, 785 (E.D. Pa. 1994) (noting that "fair and equitable" standard requires second claimholder to retain its lien and receive deferred cash payments totalling at least amount of claimant's secured claim and present value equal to value of its collateral); *Landing Assocs.*, 157 B.R. at 821 (stating simply that holder of allowed secured claim must receive present value of its claim on effective date of plan); *In re* Stratford Assocs. Ltd. Partnership, 145 B.R. 689, 700 (Bankr. D. Kan. 1992) (stating that for secured claims to be fair and equitable, it must provide that creditor retain lien); Cohn, *supra* note 2, at 532 (indicating that plan is fair and equitable when it provides for deferred cash payments with present value of lien and creditor retains lien on property); Rusch, *supra* note 3, at 173 nn.47-49 (same). Part of the calculation of present value is the determination of the appropriate interest rate. *See* Aneel M. Pandey, *Determining Interest and Discount Rates Applicable to Secured Claims in the Specter of Bankruptcy Law*, 30 SAN DIEGO L. REV. 549 (1993) (reviewing function of interest rate from macroeconomic perspective). If the undersecured creditor makes the § 1111(b)(2) election, the fair and equitable rule requires the creditor to receive deferred cash payments totaling the allowed amount of the secured claim with a present value equal to the amount of the lien. 11 U.S.C. § 1129(b)(2)(A)(i)(II) (1994).

53. If the undersecured creditor's total allowed secured claim after exercising the § 1111(b) election is $60,000 and the actual property value is $50,000, the total amount of payments must total at least $60,000 but need only have a present value of $50,000. Rusch, *supra* note 3, at 177.

To be fair and equitable to an unsecured claim, the plan must provide for the claim's payment in full, or alternatively, that no junior claim or interest receive any value in the property on account of its claim or interest.[54] Thus, the undersecured creditor's unsecured claim must be paid in full before principals of the debtor can receive or retain any interest in the reorganized debtor's property on account of their ownership interest in the bankrupt debtor. In many single asset cases, the principals desire to maintain an ownership interest in the debtor, but are unable to satisfy all of the unsecured claims in full.[55] If the debtor's principals maintain their ownership interest without paying all of the unsecured claims in full, the fair and equitable rule is violated. In order to avoid violation of this rule and obtain an ownership interest in the reorganized debtor without paying all unsecured claims in full, the principals typically contribute new value to the reorganized debtor.[56]

---

54. 11 U.S.C. § 1129(b)(2)(B)(ii) (1994); *see* Case v. Los Angeles Lumber Prods., Co., 308 U.S. 106, 116 (1939) (discussing priority of claims); Norwest Bank Worthington v. Ahlers (*In re* Ahlers), 794 F.2d 388, 401 (8th Cir. 1986) (stating that absolute priority rule mandates that dissenting class of unsecured creditors be compensated in full prior to junior class receiving or retaining any property), *rev'd on other grounds*, 485 U.S. 197 (1988); *In re* Dean, 166 B.R. 949, 954-55 (Bankr. D.N.M. 1994) (relying on absolute priority rule which mandates that no junior class of creditors may receive or retain property interest in debtor if dissenting class of unsecured creditors has not been provided for in full) (citation omitted); *In re* Batten, 141 B.R. 899, 907 (Bankr. W.D. La. 1992) (holding absolute priority rule cannot be violated to partition land in favor of undersecured creditor); Rusch, *supra* note 3, at 173-74 (testing whether plan is fair and equitable by using absolute priority rule).

55. Cohn, *supra* note 2, at 542-43; Rusch, *supra* note 3, at 174-75 & n.56.

56. The debate whether the new value exception to the absolute priority rule actually exists is ongoing. *See* Bonner Mall Partnership v. U.S. Bancorp Mortgage Co. (*In re* Bonner Mall Partnership), 2 F.3d 899, 907-09 (9th Cir. 1993) (holding that new value exception to absolute priority rule serves purpose of chapter 11 by permitting prior stockholders to contribute new money in exchange for participation in reorganized company), *cert. granted*, 114 S. Ct. 681, *cert. dismissed as moot*, 115 S. Ct. 386 (1994); Charles W. Adams, *New Capital for Bankruptcy Reorganizations: It's the Amount That Counts*, 89 NW. U. L. REV. 411 (1995) (arguing that requiring new value to be reasonably equivalent to ownership interest received in return is merely a tautology); Edward S. Adams, *Toward a New Conceptualization of the Absolute Priority Rule and Its New Value Exception*, 1993 DET. C. L. REV.

As the cramdown requirements illustrate, the Code is protective of the dissenting class interests where the debtor seeks confirmation through the cramdown process.[57] Given this protection, the question arises as to what the undersecured creditor is trying to accomplish by advancing the classification

---

1445, 1479-98 (pointing out potential abuses of new value and suggesting modifications); John T. Bailey, *The "New Value Exception" in Single-Asset Reorganizations: A Commentary on the* Bjolmes *Auction Procedure and Its Relationship to Chapter 11*, 98 COM. L.J. 50 (1993) (discussing problems with new value exception); Mark E. MacDonald et. al, *Confirmation by Cramdown Through the New Value Exception in Single Asset Cases*, 1 AM. BANKR. INST. L. REV. 65, 72 (1993) (acknowledging that there is no consensus among commentators regarding vitality of new value exception); Linda J. Rusch, *The New Value Exception to the Absolute Priority Rule in Chapter 11 Reorganizations: What Should the Rule Be?*, 19 PEPP. L. REV. 1311, 1313 (1992) (arguing value is an essential tool to parties and judges in chapter 11 reorganization process); Charles R. Sterbach, *Absolute Priority and the New Value Exception: A Practitioner's Primer*, 99 COM. L.J. 176, 178 (1994) (providing that new value doctrine "will continue to serve both as a valuable aid for debtors in their struggle to emerge from chapter 11 and an ongoing obstacle to creditors who view the chapter 11 proceedings as an unattractive alternative to prompt liquidation of the debtor"); Julie L. Friedberg, Comment, *Wanted Dead or Alive: The New Value Exception to the Absolute Priority Rule*, 66 TEMP. L. REV. 893, 895 (1993) (concluding that new value exception to absolute priority rule did not survive enactment of Code); Cathy R. Iles, Note, Dewsnup v. Timms: *Reinforcement or Vitiation of the "New Value Exception" To Chapter 11's Absolute Priority Rule?*, 35 ARIZ. L. REV. 489, 490 (1993) (arguing that Supreme Court dicta, legislative history and practical considerations mandate recognition of absolute priority rule). The criteria for the new value exception are that the contribution must be fresh money or money's worth, substantial, necessary and reasonably equivalent to the interest the contributor receives in the reorganized debtor. *Los Angeles Lumber*, 308 U.S. at 121-22; *In re* Woodbrook Assocs., 19 F.3d 312, 319-20 (7th Cir. 1994).

57. Windsor on the River Assocs., Ltd. v. Balcor Real Estate Fin., Inc. (*In re* Windsor on the River Assocs., Ltd.), 7 F.3d 127, 131 (8th Cir. 1993) (stating § 1129 was created to protect creditors' interests in cramdown); *In re* Office Prods. of Am., Inc., 136 B.R. 983, 986 (Bankr. W.D. Tex. 1992) (noting that cramdown provisions reflect congressional intent to further reorganization provided creditors' interests are protected).

argument to block confirmation. There are several possibilities which may explain this phenomenon. First, the creditor may believe that it will be more successful in satisfying its claims through state law remedies.[58] This situation usually arises when the undersecured creditor believes that the property is likely to depreciate after confirmation and the debtor will likely default on the plan, or that the property is likely to appreciate after confirmation and the debtor is not likely to default on the plan.[59] In both cases, the undersecured creditor will utilize the classification argument to block plan confirmation if it thinks state law remedies promise a higher recovery than the reorganization plan. Second, the creditor has an incentive to use the leverage conferred upon it through its ability to block the plan in order to obtain increased payments under the plan.[60] Finally, the creditor may use the classification argument to relieve itself of the onus of dealing with a troublesome debtor, even though blocking confirmation could result in a lower monetary recovery.[61]

The classification argument requires the courts to determine what Congress intended on this issue in light of the protection provided to the undersecured creditor in a cramdown situation. As demonstrated in the next section, nothing in the Code's language, legislative history, structure, or purposes supports the undersecured creditor's use of the classification argument in any one of the aforementioned scenarios.

B. Congressional Intent on the Classification Issue

When ascertaining congressional intent on the classification issue, the following indicators must be examined: the statutory language, the legislative history, the pre-Code law, the Code structure, and the Code purposes.[62] The

---

58. Rusch, *supra* note 3, at 167-68 n.18.
59. *Id.* at 175-80. These two scenarios are the most likely because in the situations where the property is appreciating and the debtor is likely to default or the property is depreciating and the debtor is not likely to default, the creditor can use the election under § 1111(b) to protect itself from harm to its position. *Id.* at 180 n.87.
60. *Id.* at 197 n.172.
61. *Id.* at 167-68 n.18.
62. *See* Rusch, *supra* note 3, at 180-202 (discussing each indicator in detail). The Supreme Court cannot decide the weight to accord these factors in interpreting the Code. *Id.* at 180-81 n.88. For varying viewpoints of the Supreme Court's

initial step in this analysis is an examination of the statutory language of section 1122.[63] This section provides:

> (a) Except as provided in subsection (b) of this section, a plan may place a claim or an interest in a particular class only if such claim or interest is substantially similar to the other claims or interests of such class.
>
> (b) A plan may designate a separate class of claims consisting only of every unsecured claim that is less than or reduced to an amount that the court approves as reasonable and necessary for administrative convenience.[64]

This statutory language provides that the proposed plan may classify claims together if they are substantially similar, but does not explicitly mandate that all substantially similar claims must be classified together.[65]

---

statutory interpretation methodology in bankruptcy, see Peter H. Carroll, III, *Literalism: The United States Supreme Court's Methodology for Statutory Construction in Bankruptcy Cases*, 25 ST. MARY'S L.J. 143, 144 (1993) (commenting that since 1989 "Supreme Court has consistently adopted a narrow textualistic approach to resolving questions of statutory construction arising under the Bankruptcy Code"); Walter A. Effross, *Grammarians at the Gate: The Rehnquist Court's Evolving "Plain Meaning" Approach to Bankruptcy Jurisprudence*, 23 SETON HALL L. REV. 1636, 1639 (1993) (stating it is arguable that Supreme Court has "championed policy over punctuation, and pre-Code precedent over linguistic logic" leaving its decisions susceptible to conflicting interpretations and applications); Thomas G. Kelch, *An Apology for Plain-Meaning Interpretation of the Bankruptcy Code*, 10 BANKR. DEV. J. 289 (1994) (examining bankruptcy cases decided by Supreme Court since 1986 and concluding that Court used a myriad of interpretive concepts which are neither consistent nor interrelated); Bruce A. Markell, *Conspiracy, Literalism, and Ennui at the Supreme Court*, 41 FED. B. NEWS & J. 174 (1994) (arguing that Supreme Court's plain meaning approach to interpreting bankruptcy law lacks consistency); Charles J. Tabb & Robert M. Lawless, *Of Commas, Gerunds, and Conjunctions: The Bankruptcy Jurisprudence of the Rehnquist Court*, 42 SYRACUSE L. REV. 823, 823 (1991) (stating that Rehnquist Court has decided 16 bankruptcy cases without leaving any significant imprint on shape of bankruptcy law).

63. 11 U.S.C. § 1122 (1994).

64. *Id.*

65. Rusch, *supra* note 3, at 182.

Some courts have held that all substantially similar claims must be classified together based on an inference from the language of subsection (b).[66] Those courts contend that the only reason for the explicit authorization of a separate classification for de minimis unsecured claims is that the general classification rule of section 1122(a) requires that all substantially similar unsecured claims be classified together.[67] The language of subsection (b), however, may also be read as authorizing an exception to the rule of subsection (a), that only substantially similar claims may be classified together.[68] Subsection (b) could be construed as authorizing the classification of de minimis claims together even if the claims were not substantially similar to each other.[69] Thus, the statutory language itself does not explicitly support the undersecured creditor's argument that all substantially similar claims must be classified together or that classifying claims to create one accepting class of impaired claims is abusive.

Secondly, the legislative histories of sections 1122 and 1129 also do not support the undersecured creditor's argument. When the new Bankruptcy Code was enacted in 1979, Congress rejected language requiring all substantially similar claims to be classified together and stated that section 1122 codified existing case law on claim classification.[70] Congress amended

---

66. *Id.* at 182 n.95 (citing Phoenix Mut. Life Ins. Co. v. Greystone III Joint Venture (*In re* Greystone III Joint Venture), 995 F.2d 1274, 1278 (5th Cir. 1991), *vacated in part*, 995 F.2d 1284 (5th Cir.), *cert. denied*, 506 U.S. 821 (1992)).

67. *Greystone*, 995 F.2d at 1278.

68. *See In re* Bloomingdale Partners, 170 B.R. 984, 989 (Bankr. N.D. Ill. 1994) (concluding that subsection (b) is exception to general rule of subsection (a) thereby allowing dissimilar de minimis claims to be classed together); Rusch, *supra* note 3, at 182 n.95.

69. *See* Meaney, *supra* note 2, at 1209 (discussing exception contained in subsection (b), where small unsecured claims may be grouped together without regard to similarity); Rusch, *supra* note 3, 182 n.95 (same).

70. *See* S. REP. NO. 989, 95th Cong., 2d Sess. 118 (1978), *reprinted in* 1978 U.S.C.C.A.N. 5787, 5904. The final version of the Senate Judiciary Committee's report on § 1122 provided in pertinent part:

> This section codifies current case law surrounding the classification of claims and equity securities. It requires classification based on the nature of the claims or interests classified, and permits inclusion of claims or interests in a particular class only if the claim or interest being included is substantially similar to the other claims or interests

section 1129(a)(10) to include the requirement that at least one class of impaired claims, as opposed to any class of claims whether or not impaired, must accept the debtor's reorganization.[71] Congress was silent, however, on the issue of whether classifying claims to obtain the acceptance of an impaired class was an abuse of process.[72] Representative Edwards, supporting the added requirement to the confirmation standard, addressed this issue of classifying claims to create an accepting class. In fact, Representative Edwards did not condemn such classification practices; rather, he stated that creditors were protected as long as the one accepting creditor's claim was also impaired.[73]

The only express statement of congressional intent on this issue is that pre-Code practice should be followed.[74] Chapter 11 of the Bankruptcy Code is a consolidation of three different forms of business reorganizations that existed prior to the Bankruptcy Reform Act of 1978—chapter X corporate reorganizations, chapter XI arrangements for undersecured debts, and chapter XII real property arrangements for noncorporate debtors.[75] In all three forms of reorganization the courts allowed unsecured claims to be placed into

---

of the class.

Id. (footnote omitted).

71. Bankruptcy Reform Act of 1978, § 512(a)(9); 11 U.S.C. § 1129(a)(10) (1994).

72. Rusch, *supra* note 3, at 185-89. Section 1129 conforms to the original intention of Congress to counter the pre-Code chapter XII cases that permitted cramdown without the consent of any class of creditors. *See* 5 COLLIER ON BANKRUPTCY ¶ 1129.02 [10], at 1129-59 (Lawrence P. King ed., 15th ed. 1995). From 1979 until the 1984 amendment, Congress considered various approaches to § 1129, during this period no one suggested that this section was intended to require that all substantially similar claims be classified together or that separate classification to create an accepting class of claims was abusive. Rusch, *supra* note 3, at 187-88. In addition, courts which have been unwilling to "venture into the thicket of legislative history" to determine the scope of § 1129 have stated that even if the history is considered, there is nothing that would suggest Congress intended to modify past judicial interpretation. *See, e.g., In re* SLC Ltd. V, 137 B.R. 847, 853 (Bankr. D. Utah 1992) (finding that courts considering legislative history have concluded Congress did not intend change in scope of § 1129).

73. Rusch, *supra* note 3, at 189.

74. *See supra* note 70.

75. *See* Rusch, *supra* note 3, at 189-92 (discussing pre-Code forms of business reorganization).

different classes.[76] This pre-Code practice refutes the undersecured creditor's first argument that substantially similar claims must be placed in the same class.

In addition, nothing in pre-Code practice supports the creditor's argument that classifying claims to create an accepting class of impaired claims is abusive. In chapter X and XII proceedings, courts allowed separate classification of similar claims if there was a need to award the claimants a different payment priority.[77] Under both of those chapters, courts were empowered to confirm plans over dissenting classes of creditors.[78] The acceptance of one class of impaired claims as a requisite to confirmation did not exist.[79] In chapter XI, however, all classes of claims had to accept the plan by a majority vote,[80] and cramdown on dissenting classes of claims was not allowed.[81] The pre-Code practice in chapter XI compositions was to allow classification of claims for the precise purpose of creating accepting classes of claims.[82] Nothing in the legislative history suggests Congress intended to

---

76. *See id.*; *see also* Robin, *supra* note 8, at 239-41.

77. *See* Rusch, *supra* note 3, at 190-91 (describing class arrangements and noting that although presumption was that all creditors of equal rank should be in same class, courts permit separate classes if there is equitable reason to do so).

78. For chapter X, the court could confirm the plan if the dissenting class interest in property were adequately protected, the plan was fair and equitable, and the plan was feasible. *Id.* at 191. For chapter XII, the court could still confirm if the class members' interests were adequately protected. *Id.* at 190.

79. *Id.* at 190-92.

80. "[T]he plan must be accepted by a majority in number and amount of creditors; if creditors are divided into classes, the plan must be accepted by a majority in number and amount of the creditors of each class." 9 COLLIER ON BANKRUPTCY ¶ 9.05[2], at 240 (James W. Moore et al. eds., 14th ed. 1978).

81. *Id.* ¶ 9.15.

82. *See* 11 HAROLD REMINGTON, A TREATISE ON THE BANKRUPTCY LAW OF THE UNITED STATES § 3607 (J. Henderson ed., 6th ed. 1955). The author proposes the following on the issue of debtor's use of classification to create an accepting class of claims:

> Division of the petitioner's unsecured creditors into classes is contemplated as permissible in proposing an arrangement, if the petitioner wishes to approach the problem in that manner . . . . There is also a general provision whereby the court may fix the division of creditors into classes for purpose of the arrangement and its

change this result in the new chapter 11 process.

Third, the structure of the Code does not support the undersecured creditor's arguments on classification. Congress structured chapter 11 to encourage negotiation between the parties, leaving it up to them to resolve the difficult issues implicit in property distribution in reorganization.[83] In order to facilitate successful bargaining, each side needs sufficient leverage, and the Code specifically provides such levers.[84] These levers also protect a dissenting creditor who raises objections to a reorganization plan.[85] For example, in the

---

> acceptance. Thus, claims of merchandise creditors, claims of bank creditors, etc., may be placed in separate classifications and may be treated differently.

Id.

83. *See* H.R. REP. NO. 595, 95th Cong., 2d Sess. 224 (1978), *reprinted in* 1978 U.S.C.C.A.N. 5963, 6183-84; *see also* Rusch, *supra* note 3, at 196 (noting that to encourage parties to negotiate, Code imposes certain requirements to insure sufficient bargaining leverage).

84. *See* Rusch, *supra* note 3, at 196-97.

> The Code gives many clubs to the creditor seeking to block confirmation of a plan. These clubs include the voting requirements, the best interests of the creditors test, the feasibility test, the fair and equitable test, the unfair discrimination test, the [§] 1111(b) election, the one accepting impaired class requirement, and the good faith requirement.
>
> The Code also gives clubs to debtors who seek to confirm plans over the objections of dissenting creditors. These clubs include the exclusive plan filing period for debtors, the automatic stay, the use of property while putting together a confirmation plan, the flexibility to negotiate different payout structures with accepting creditors, and the good faith voting requirement. By far, the most powerful club given to debtors is the ability to cram down a plan on dissenting creditors.

Id. (footnotes omitted).

85. *Id.* at 197-98.

> The Code provides a good faith dissenting undersecured creditor with protection for each of the following objections the creditor could raise regarding a plan:
>
> 1) Objection — The valuation assigned to the property in the plan is inadequate. Code Protection — A valuation hearing;
>
> 2) Objection — The debtor is unable to fulfill the plan. Code Protection — The feasibility test;

event that the undersecured creditor attempts to use the classification argument to block plan confirmation and obtain a larger recovery under state remedies,[86] the feasibility and valuation provisions afford protection to the dissenting creditor.[87] The feasibility test protects this creditor when it thinks that the value of the property is depreciating and it is likely that the debtor will default. Where the likelihood of default is high, the judge should find that the plan is not feasible.[88] Similarly, in the situation where the creditor believes the property will appreciate postconfirmation, a valuation hearing to determine the

---

> 3) Objection — Junior classes are paid before the undersecured creditor's claims are paid in full. Code Protections — The fair and equitable test and the absolute priority rule;
> 4) Objection — Similar claims are paid a more favorable dividend, or in a different manner, than the undersecured creditor's claims. Code Protections — The requirement of no unfair discrimination against dissenting classes and the requirement that all claims within a class be treated equally;
> 5) Objection — The undersecured creditor will get a better recovery if its interest were foreclosed today. Code Protections — The best interests of creditors test and the [§] 1111(b) election;
> 6) Objection — The interest rate payable on the secured portion of the undersecured creditor's claim is inadequate. Code Protection — The present value requirement contained in the fair and equitable test;
> 7) Objection — The debtor is dishonest or otherwise abusing the bankruptcy process. Code Protection — The good faith requirement.

Id. (footnotes omitted).

86. *See supra* notes 58-59 and accompanying text (discussing requirement that plan must not unfairly discriminate against dissenting classes of impaired claims unless good reason exists).

87. The valuation procedure determines the value of property which the debtor holds. *See* Rusch, *supra* note 3, at 166-67 n.14. "The purpose of [§] 1129(a)(11) [requiring feasibility] is to prevent confirmation of visionary schemes which promise creditors and equity security holders more under a proposed plan than the debtor can possibly attain after confirmation." 5 COLLIER, *supra* note 72, ¶ 1129.02[11], at 1129-61.

88. *See* Rusch, *supra* note 3, at 198.

amount of the secured claim will protect the creditor from a high probability of postconfirmation appreciation. If such a high probability exists, this fact typically will be reflected in a higher valuation of the property.[89]

In the situation outlined in the preceding paragraph, it is apparent that the undersecured creditor is attempting to use the classification argument in order to substitute its judgment on feasibility and valuation for the judgment of the bankruptcy judge.[90] If the creditor's classification argument is accepted, the creditor will have enough leverage to force all parties to the reorganization to accept the creditor's determination on the issues of feasibility and valuation. This result would read cramdown out of the Code for single asset debtors.

> Although some might advocate allowing the creditor that power in single asset cases, Congress did not deny cramdown to such debtors even though this precise situation was brought to the attention of the committee drafting the Code provisions and it was recommended that cramdown be denied debtors in single asset real estate cases.[91]

When the undersecured creditor is using the classification argument because of its belief that state remedies will provide a better recovery, the undersecured creditor does not need the classification argument as a

---

89. *Id.* at 198-99 (discussing effect of low probability of postconfirmation appreciation).

90. Some scholars in the law and economics school argue that judges are not competent to make feasibility and valuation decisions. *See* Mark J. Roe, *Bankruptcy and Debt: A New Model For Corporate Reorganization*, 83 COLUM. L. REV. 527, 547-48 (1983). This objection is not based upon empirical evidence of incompetency, but rather a belief that negotiations between parties is the only competent way to determine these issues. *Id.* Judges, who are not parties to the negotiation, are thus apt to make erroneous decisions. *Id.* This belief ignores the fact that in a cramdown the negotiation has failed, and judges or juries commonly make these types of decisions when negotiations have failed. *See* Rusch, *supra* note 56, at 1329-30 nn.74-76. Even though these judgments are difficult to make, the bankruptcy judge is in a better position to make an unbiased decision on these issues than is the undersecured creditor. *Id.* at 1329-30 n.75; *see* David G. Carlson, *Secured Creditors and the Eely Character of Bankruptcy Valuations*, 41 AM. U. L. REV. 63, 78 (1991) (discussing one judge's approach to valuation).

91. Rusch, *supra* note 3, at 199 (footnotes omitted).

negotiating lever because it already has levers to protect its interests.[92] Allowing the undersecured creditor to use the classification argument would in effect undermine the negotiation structure by tipping the balance of power too far in favor of the creditor.[93]

The second structural consideration incorporates Congress's judgment that all of the creditors' and debtors' interests cannot be completely protected if reorganization is allowed as a remedy for financial distress. The Code strikes a balance between conflicting interests of the debtor and its creditors in order to facilitate the reorganization of distressed businesses.[94] Congress has used the concepts of current valuation and feasible reorganization as points of accommodation between the conflicting interests of debtor and creditors. As long as the current valuation of the property is protected and the reorganization is feasible, the Code, through its automatic stay, allows the debtor to use the property in an attempt to structure a reorganization.[95]

---

92. *See id.* at 196 (listing negotiation tools at disposal of creditor).

93. *Id.* at 200; *see also In re* Triple R Holdings, L.P., 134 B.R. 382, 390-91 (Bankr. N.D. Cal. 1991) (reasoning that allowing creditors control over reorganization negotiations would dissuade debtors from filing under chapter 11), *rev'd on other grounds*, 145 B.R. 57 (N.D. Cal. 1992). *But see In re* Main Rd. Properties, Inc., 144 B.R. 217, 220-21 (Bankr. D.R.I. 1992) (holding that "numbers, not policy" should determine outcome of creditor control) (citing *In re* Cantonwood Assocs. Ltd. Partnership, 138 B.R. 648 (Bankr. D. Mass. 1992)).

94. The debtor has an interest in controlling the property to effectuate a reorganization. The creditor has an interest in controlling the property as a way to recover as much as possible on the debt owed. *See* Rusch, *supra* note 3, at 167-68. Both interests cannot be fully recognized and protected at the same time in a reorganization. *Id.* at 201 n.192.

95. *Id.* at 192-95. On June 17, 1992, the Senate passed a bill that contained an amendment to 11 U.S.C. § 362(d) which would allow relief from the automatic stay in single asset real estate cases for creditors with secured claims in the real estate unless, within 90 days after the order for relief, the debtor has filed a reorganization plan that has a "reasonable possibility of being confirmed within a reasonable time" or is making monthly market rate interest payments on the value of the secured claim. *See* S. 1985, 102d Cong., 1st Sess. § 211 (1991), *reprinted in* 138 CONG. REC. S8359, S8365 (daily ed. June 17, 1992). The secured creditor with more than a de minimis secured claim could ask for relief from the automatic stay to continue any foreclosure started prior to bankruptcy. *Id.* The creditor could take foreclosure up to, but not including, the point of

Similarly, in a cramdown, the bankruptcy judge determines whether the proposed reorganization is feasible, and whether the undersecured creditor will receive the present value of its secured claim based upon the property's value.[96] The undersecured creditor who uses the classification argument to block confirmation of a feasible plan requiring payment of the present value of that creditor's secured claim is attempting to claim an interest in property above the current valuation. Such an action is not explicitly or implicitly allowed under the Code.[97] This accommodation of conflicting interests would be thwarted if the undersecured creditor's classification argument prevailed in any one of the three scenarios outlined earlier.[98]

Finally, none of the various purposes of the Code would be advanced if the undersecured creditor's classification argument were allowed to succeed. Some of the Code's stated purposes[99] are to provide debtor relief, facilitate feasible reorganizations, preserve equality among similarly situated creditors, and assure equitable loss distribution.[100] In the three scenarios previously

---

sale. *Id.* (proposed 11 U.S.C. § 362(i)). This proposed bill was not enacted. The proposed amendment confirms the point in the text regarding allowing reorganization to occur if current value is protected and reorganization is feasible. The proposed amendment would merely put a time limit on the debtor's attempt at reorganization.

In the Bankruptcy Reform Act of 1994, Pub. L. No. 103-394, § 218, 108 Stat. 4106, 4128, Congress enacted the provision on allowing relief from the automatic stay for creditors with real estate secured claims in single asset real estate cases. Under current 11 U.S.C. § 362(d)(3) (1994), those creditors can get relief from the stay unless the debtor has filed a reorganization plan that has a "reasonable possibility" of confirmation within a "reasonable time" or is making monthly payments secured by the real estate and equal to market rate interest on the value of the creditor's secured claim.

96. *See* Rusch, *supra* note 3, at 195-96.

97. *Id.* at 196.

98. *See supra* notes 58-61 and accompanying text.

99. A distinction must be made between the purposes that Congress or the courts ascribe to the Code and the purposes that scholars ascribe to the Code. For instance, even though creditor control of reorganization is a working premise of bankruptcy for some scholars, *see infra* notes 116-19 and accompanying text, Congress has not stated that principle or structured the Code in such a way as to support that principle.

100. Rusch, *supra* note 3, at 200 nn.188-91. Some commentators question whether any of these purposes are actually served in chapter 11. *Compare* Hon. Edith H. Jones, *Chapter 11: A Death Penalty for Debtor and Creditor Interests*, 77

discussed,[101] where the undersecured creditor is most likely to use the classification argument to block the plan, allowing the argument to succeed would thwart the Code's objectives. The purposes of debtor relief and promoting feasible reorganizations would be defeated if the classification argument were used to allow the undersecured creditor to substitute its own judgment for the court's judgment on valuation and feasibility or to block reorganization in order to eliminate the troublesome debtor, irrespective of the recovery the creditor would receive. In these situations, the successful use of a classification argument would work to deny debtor relief when reorganization is feasible and desirable, and thus defeat those Code purposes.[102]

The purposes of equality between similarly situated creditors and equitable loss distribution would be frustrated if the classification argument were used to force the debtor to make a larger payment than the minimum required on its secured claim.[103] Using this argument, the undersecured creditor is attempting to use the leverage of its position to recover more on its unsecured claim than the other unsecured claimants.[104] This leverage will reallocate the undersecured creditor's risk of having an unsecured claim to the other unsecured creditors, in spite of the fact that the undersecured creditor took the same risk of being at least as partially unsecured as the other unsecured creditors.[105]

After reviewing the Code's language, legislative history, structure, and purposes, nothing has been found that supports the undersecured creditor's

---

CORNELL L. REV. 1088 (1992) (arguing chapter 11 fails in fact to advance any of these purposes) *with* Elizabeth Warren, *"Why Have a Federal Bankruptcy System?"*, 77 CORNELL L. REV. 1093 (1992) (arguing chapter 11 is better than state law alternatives in spreading losses caused by financial distress).

101. *See supra* notes 58-61 and accompanying text.

102. *See* Rusch, *supra* note 3, at 200-01.

103. *See id.* at 197 n.172.

104. *See id.* at 201 n.196.

105. *Id.* at 201-02 n.197. The difference in leverage and interest is reflected in the argument that the undersecured creditor's unsecured claim is really different from other unsecured creditors' claims and should be separately classified. *See supra* notes 23-27 and accompanying text; *see also In re* Triple R Holdings, L.P., 134 B.R. 382, 387 (Bankr. N.D. Cal. 1991) (recognizing undersecured creditor will vote for both secured and unsecured claims based on interest as secured creditor), *rev'd on other grounds*, 145 B.R. 57 (N.D. Cal. 1992).

classification argument. In reality, the undersecured creditor uses the classification argument to resist what it perceives to be an unjustified level of forced investment in the reorganized debtor.[106] If accepted, the classification argument would give the undersecured creditor complete veto power over the ability of the single asset debtor to reorganize whenever that creditor thought, for any reason or for no reason at all, that it was being forced to accept an unacceptable level of investment in the reorganized debtor.[107] Congress did not explicitly or implicitly give the undersecured creditor this kind of veto power in chapter 11 reorganizations.

C. Bankruptcy Reform Act of 1994

The Bankruptcy Reform Act of 1994 amended the definition of impairment.[108] Prior to the 1994 amendment, a class of claims was not impaired if the plan provided that each claimant in the class would receive cash on the plan's effective date equal to the allowed amount of the claim.[109] The 1994 amendment has deleted this provision, making it possible for an unsecured claims class to be paid in full in cash on the effective date and still be an impaired class for cramdown purposes.[110] Similarly, a secured claimant may be paid the full amount of its secured claim in cash on the effective date and still be impaired. Both of those fully paid unsecured and secured claim classes would be impaired because some of their prebankruptcy contractual rights would have been altered. Examples of those altered rights include not paying postpetition interest to the unsecured claimant or paying the secured claimant earlier than provided for in the contract.[111]

---

106. *See* Rusch, *supra* note 3, at 202-04.

107. *See, e.g., In re* Rivers End Apartments, Ltd., 167 B.R. 470, 478-79 (Bankr. S.D. Ohio 1994) (noting that right to vote does not entail right to control outcome of vote).

108. Bankruptcy Reform Act of 1994, Pub. L. No. 103-394, § 213(d), 108 Stat. 4106, 4126 (amending 11 U.S.C. § 1124).

109. 11 U.S.C. § 1124(3) (1988).

110. Bankruptcy Reform Act of 1994, Pub. L. No. 103-394, § 213(d), 108 Stat. at 4126. This amendment applies to cases commenced after the enactment date, October 22, 1994. *Id.* § 702, 108 Stat. at 4150. For a further discussion of the reason for this amendment, see Linda J. Rusch, *Unintended Consequences of Unthinking Tinkering: The 1994 Amendments to the Chapter 11 Process*, 69 AM. BANKR. L.J. 349 (1995).

111. 11 U.S.C. § 1124(1) (1994) (altering any legal, equitable or contractual right

This change in the definition of impairment undercuts the rationale courts use to argue that gerrymandering to achieve one accepting impaired class is abusive. The alleged purpose of prohibiting such classification is to make sure that a class of creditors, that is truly harmed, agrees to the reorganization that the debtor has proposed.[112] The change in the definition of impairment allows creditors who are not significantly harmed by the reorganization attempt, and are in fact fully paid in cash, to be the one accepting impaired class.[113] The rationale for prohibiting gerrymandering classification has been significantly undermined by the change in the definition of impairment. The Bankruptcy Reform Act of 1994 thus adds another argument in support of the proposition that the attempt to prohibit classification to create one accepting class of impaired claims is unfounded.

D. What Should the Rule on Classification Be?

Although it seems obvious that Congress did not intend to give the undersecured creditor absolute veto power over a single asset debtor's reorganization plan, an evaluation of congressional intent does not address whether creditors should have such a power.[114] This idea should be evaluated in light of the two existing theoretical constructs of bankruptcy law, the creditor's bargain theory and the loss allocation theory.[115]

The creditor's bargain theory is based upon the underlying premise that the creditors' collective monetary wealth maximization is the only justification for

---

is impairment).

112. Meltzer, *supra* note 8, at 302-05 (arguing artificial classification results in disenfranchisement of dissenting creditors).

113. Carlson, *supra* note 46, at 368-71 (arguing courts must not allow lump sum payments to constitute "cure" of claim).

114. *See supra* note 99 and accompanying text (noting difference between scholar's theories and congressional intent).

115. *See* Lawrence Ponoroff & F. Stephen Knippenberg, *The Implied Good Faith Filing Requirement: Sentinel of an Evolving Bankruptcy Policy*, 85 NW. U. L. REV. 919, 948-62 (1991) (outlining and contrasting collective and traditional views toward these theories); Linda J. Rusch, *Bankruptcy Reorganization Jurisprudence: Matters of Belief, Faith, and Hope-Stepping Into the Fourth Dimension*, 55 MONT. L. REV. 9 (1994) (analyzing varying beliefs and values of those two theories).

the alteration of creditors' state law rights in a bankruptcy reorganization.[116] In order to foster the goal of greater collective monetary recovery, the creditors themselves should control the reorganization process.[117] In addition, the

---

116. *See* Donald R. Korobkin, *Value and Rationality in Bankruptcy Decisionmaking*, 33 WM. & MARY L. REV. 333, 338-39 (1992) (discussing economic account's model of bankruptcy decision making); Rusch, *supra* note 56, at 1323-24 nn.51-54; Rusch, *supra* note 115, at 17-19 (discussing creditor's bargain theory). This theory is derived from the law and economics theory. The creditor's bargain theory has been advanced by many commentators. *See generally* Thomas H. Jackson, THE LOGIC AND LIMITS OF BANKRUPTCY LAW (1986); Douglas G. Baird, *The Uneasy Case for Corporate Reorganization,* 15 J. LEGAL STUD. 127 (1986); Douglas G. Baird & Thomas H. Jackson, *Bargaining After the Fall and the Contours of the Absolute Priority Rule*, 55 U. CHI. L. REV. 738 (1988); Douglas G. Baird & Thomas H. Jackson, *Corporate Reorganizations and the Treatment of Diverse Ownership Interests: A Comment on Adequate Protection of Secured Creditors in Bankruptcy*, 51 U. CHI. L. REV. 97, 100-01 (1984) [hereinafter Baird & Jackson, *Corporate Reorganizations*] (arguing that secured creditors should not be deprived of benefit of bargain); Douglas G. Baird & Randal C. Picker, *A Simple Noncooperative Bargaining Model of Corporate Reorganizations*, 20 J. LEGAL STUD. 311 (1991); Thomas H. Jackson, *Of Liquidation, Continuation, and Delay: An Analysis of Bankruptcy Policy and Nonbankruptcy Rules*, 60 AM. BANKR. L.J. 399 (1986); Thomas H. Jackson, *Translating Assets and Liabilities to the Bankruptcy Forum*, 14 J. LEGAL STUD. 73 (1985); Thomas H. Jackson, *Bankruptcy, Non-bankruptcy Entitlements, and the Creditors' Bargain*, 91 YALE L.J. 857 (1982) (arguing that creditors' bargain should be recognized in bankruptcy); Thomas H. Jackson & Robert E. Scott, *On the Nature of Bankruptcy: An Essay on Bankruptcy Sharing and the Creditors' Bargain*, 75 VA. L. REV. 155 (1989) (analyzing original creditors' bargain theory); David A. Skeel, *The Uncertain State of an Unstated Rule: Bankruptcy's Contribution Rule Doctrine after Ahlers*, 63 AM. BANKR. L.J. 221 (1989) (finding creditors' bargain model to be first attempt at unifying theme in bankruptcy); James J. White, *Absolute Priority and New Value*, 8 THOMAS M. COOLEY L. REV. 1 (1991); Derek J. Meyer, Note, *Redefining the New Value Exception to the Absolute Priority Rule in Light of the Creditors' Bargain Model*, 24 IND. L. REV. 417 (1991) (proposing restructuring of new value exception to better accommodate creditors' bargain model).

117. *See* Rusch, *supra* note 56, at 1323 n.51; Rusch, *supra* note 115, at 20.

creditor's bargain theory holds state law contract rights out as sacrosanct.[118] This belief is based upon the idea that the assets of an insolvent company belong to the creditors, and should be distributed to them in the order required by state law.[119]

The concepts of enhanced collective creditor recovery, creditor control, and reverence for state law contract rights favor the undersecured creditor's successful utilization of the classification argument. The undersecured creditor would be the "residual owner" of the asset in a single asset case because of the priority of that claim under state law.[120] The creditor's bargain theorists would assert that the undersecured creditor should be allowed to determine if and how that asset should be reorganized,[121] and that the classification argument is a permissible tool to use to exercise such control.

The loss allocation theory states that Congress created bankruptcies to allocate losses among the parties in accordance with certain values.[122] Since

---

118. Rusch, *supra* note 56, at 1323 n.53; *see* Douglas G. Baird, *Loss Distribution, Forum Shopping and Bankruptcy: A Reply to Warren*, 54 U. CHI. L. REV. 815, 822 (1987) (stating that "nonbankruptcy priority rules distribute losses and will continue to do so regardless of whether a special set of bankruptcy priority rules exist"); Theodore Eisenberg, *Bankruptcy Law in Perspective*, 28 UCLA L. REV. 953, 953-76 (1981) (arguing that Congress should not substitute federal bankruptcy rules for state law). The creditor's bargain theory as a justification for bankruptcy has been attacked as an insufficient reason for altering state law contract rights. *Compare* Barry E. Adler, *Bankruptcy and Risk Allocation*, 77 CORNELL L. REV. 439, 444-55 (1992) (arguing creditors' bargain theory does not justify alteration of state law contract rights) *and* James W. Bowers, *Whither What Hits the Fan?: Murphy's Law, Bankruptcy Theory, and the Elementary Economics of Loss Distribution*, 26 GA. L. REV. 27 (1991) (arguing bankruptcy is inefficient method of collecting debts and primary justification is debtor protection) *with* Charles W. Adams, *An Economic Justification for Corporate Reorganizations*, 20 HOFSTRA L. REV. 117 (1991) (arguing alternatives of chapter 11 may be less efficient and have not been proven less costly than chapter 11 process).

119. *See* Rusch, *supra* note 56, at 1335 n.92.

120. *Id.* at 1323-24 nn.53-54; *see* Baird & Jackson, *Corporate Reorganizations*, *supra* note 116, at 109-21.

121. *See* Rusch, *supra* note 56, at 1324 n.54.

122. *Id.* at 1324 nn.55-57; Rusch, *supra* note 115, at 22-24; *see also* Raymond T. Nimmer, *Negotiated Bankruptcy Reorganization Plans: Absolute Priority and*

Congress chose to promote negotiated reorganizations, the bankruptcy law should be interpreted as providing opportunities and incentives for negotiation.[123] The logical conclusion, then, is that the classification issue should be resolved in a way that promotes negotiated plans. Allowing the undersecured creditor the power to veto any reorganization plan would undermine the negotiation structure.[124] Thus, the loss allocation theorists would argue that the undersecured creditor should not be able to use the classification argument to exercise such absolute power.

Each theory has its deficiencies. The creditor's bargain theory is based upon faulty premises, such as the idea that the undersecured creditor will make the monetary wealth maximizing decision,[125] that the undersecured creditor's decision will be the best decision for all creditors,[126] or that bankruptcy judges are not competent to make decisions about feasibility and valuation in the cramdown process.[127] In addition, the creditor's bargain theory promotes the value of monetary collective creditor wealth maximization as the paramount value in reorganizations.[128] The law, however, could legitimately promote other values as more vital than maximum creditor recovery.[129]

New Value Contributions, 36 EMORY L.J. 1009, 1013-34 (1987) (positing loss is distributed through negotiated bargaining that occurs under framework of legal rules); Elizabeth Warren, *Bankruptcy Policy*, 54 U. CHI. L. REV. 775, 789-93 (1987) (arguing absence of legal scheme to allocate losses would require distribution in some other manner).

123. *See* Rusch, *supra* note 56, at 1324-25 nn.58-59; *see also* Donald R. Korobkin, *Rehabilitating Values: A Jurisprudence of Bankruptcy*, 91 COLUM. L. REV. 717, 762-80 (1991) (illustrating value-based account of bankruptcy law as creating "discourse in which the problem of financial distress may be confronted on its own moral, political, personal, social, and economic terms"); Rusch, *supra* note 115, at 23.

124. *See supra* notes 83-93 and accompanying text (discussing adverse effects of undersecured creditor veto power on negotiation balance).

125. *See* Rusch, *supra* note 56, at 1327-28 nn.67-69; *see also* P. John Kozyris, *In the Cauldron of Jurisprudence: The View From Within the Stew*, 41 J. LEGAL EDUC. 421, 436-37 (1991) (discussing failure of law and economics to account for potential abuse of decision making power).

126. *See* Rusch, *supra* note 56, at 1328-29 nn.69-70.

127. *Id.* at 1329-30 nn.74-76; *see supra* note 90 and accompanying text.

128. *See supra* notes 116-21 and accompanying text.

129. *See* Rusch, *supra* note 56, at 1331-32 nn.78-82; *see also* David G. Carlson, *Philosophy in Bankruptcy*, 85 MICH. L. REV. 1341, 1353 (1987) (arguing

The loss allocation theory is also deficient. This theory does not adequately address what should happen if bargaining between the parties fails, and merely relies upon Congress to make the decision regarding loss allocation when reconciling competing values.[130] Although this theory is a good starting point for analysis due to its focus on value identification, it provides little guidance upon which Congress may base its decisions.

Since the creditor's bargain theory is based upon false and deficient premises, and the loss allocation theory fails to provide sufficient congressional guidance, the question of whether the undersecured creditor should have veto power over a single asset reorganization remains unanswered.

Conclusion

The classification issue, as is the case with many legal questions, involves a balancing of conflicting values based upon a vision of how society should be.[131] The continuous debate over the classification issue reflects the

---

employee creditors may insist on bankruptcy priority for wage claims); Richard E. Flint, *Bankruptcy Policy: Toward a Moral Justification for Financial Rehabilitation of the Consumer Debtor*, 48 WASH. & LEE L. REV. 515, 523-26 (1991) (stating that essence of bankruptcy law is debtor financial relief and such is founded in natural law theory of morality); Korobkin, *supra* note 116, at 340, 343 (arguing economic account ignores aspects of bankruptcy law); Kozyris, *supra* note 125, at 436 (positing that wealth maximization as ultimate premise for law degrades other human values); Warren, *supra* note 122, at 789-93 (bankruptcy law gives "overriding attention to widespread default" based on ability to bear costs and similarities among creditors).

130. *See* Rusch, *supra* note 56, at 1332 nn.83-84. Korobkin has since advocated that the bankruptcy process should accommodate as many of the competing values as possible with some greater consideration given to those who occupy the most vulnerable positions. Donald R. Korobkin, *Contractarianism and the Normative Foundations of Bankruptcy Law*, 71 TEX. L. REV. 541, 584-89 (1993); Rusch, *supra* note 115, at 23.

131. *See* Rusch, *supra* note 115; *see also* Korobkin, *supra* note 116, at 341 (noting court must resolve conflicts between differing values when answering bankruptcy questions); Steven D. Smith, *Reductionism in Legal Thought*, 91 COLUM. L. REV. 68, 73 (1991) (arguing that one of law's functions is promoting desirable social order based upon underlying value judgments).

disagreement reasonable people can have over what values are most important in the reorganization of a single asset debtor. At some point in the debate the lawmaker, in this case Congress, has the ultimate responsibility of deciding what values are paramount, and to structure the law accordingly.[132]

When a single asset debtor encounters financial distress, the following societal values are present: (1) the value of paying existing creditors as much as possible on their claims,[133] (2) the value of placing the risk of failure on the debtor's owners,[134](3) the value of allowing the debtor's owners a second chance to operate the business successfully,[135] and (4) the value of allowing the parties the freedom to negotiate the difficult questions of control and distribution of property.[136] The undersecured creditor does not need the classification argument to promote the first two values and its successful use would undermine the last two values.

The undersecured creditor's use of the classification argument does not advance the value of paying existing creditors as much as possible on their claims. As demonstrated above, the undersecured creditor uses the classification argument because it either wants a better recovery on its claims or it is willing to take more of a loss to be rid of the debtor.[137] The undersecured creditor uses the classification argument to advance its individual self-interest and not to promote the best interests of all of the creditors.[138] Just because the undersecured creditor thinks reorganization is not in its best interest does not mean reorganization is not in the best interest of the other creditors.

The classification argument is not a tool that works to place the risk of business failure on the owners. The undersecured creditor's use of this

---

132. *See* Korobkin, *supra* note 116, at 357 (arguing that choosing among competing values in bankruptcy takes place through rational process and that absolute reductionist standards, like creditor's bargain theory, are not needed to make law and decisions under that law rational).
133. *See* Rusch, *supra* note 56, at 1332-33 nn.84-85.
134. *Id.* at 1330-32.
135. This value is reflected in the emphasis on debtor relief. *See supra* note 102 and accompanying text.
136. This value is reflected in the negotiation structure of the Code. *See supra* notes 83-93 and accompanying text (discussing structure of chapter 11 to encourage negotiation).
137. *See supra* notes 58-61 and accompanying text (providing that undersecured creditors will utilize classification argument to increase payments under plan).
138. *See* Rusch, *supra* note 3, at 197 n.172, 200 n.187, 201 n.196.

argument is unrelated to forcing the debtor's owners to bear the risk of failure, unless one is willing to say that the owners have only one chance to be successful.[139] As long as reorganization is an option, the proper tool for placing the risk of failure on the debtor's owners is the fair and equitable test.[140]

Allowing the undersecured creditor to use the classification argument to block reorganization would negate the last two values, namely giving the debtor a second chance and encouraging negotiation about the distribution of property. This Chapter has argued that both debtor relief and the Code's negotiation structure will be furthered by allowing the debtor to separate the unsecured claim to create an accepting class of impaired claims.[141] Under the current Code structure, successful use of the classification argument would negate the negotiation value and subordinate the debtor's owners' second chance value to the unrestricted whims of the undersecured creditor. Unless a societal consensus[142] is reached determining that these two values should not

---

139. Some commentators advocate abolishing the reorganization concept. *See generally* Michael Bradley & Michael Rosenzweig, *The Untenable Case for Chapter 11*, 101 YALE L.J. 1043 (1992) (arguing increasingly endogenous chapter 11 should be repealed). The debate about the purpose of bankruptcy reorganization is ongoing. *See* Rusch, *supra* note 115.

140. *See* Rusch, *supra* note 56, at 306-08.

141. *See supra* notes 83-93, 102 and accompanying text.

142. *See* GRANT GILMORE, THE AGES OF AMERICAN LAW 109-110 (1977). The author writes:

> As lawyers we will do well to be on our guard against any suggestion that, through law, our society can be reformed, purified, or saved. The function of law, in a society like our own, is altogether more modest and less apocalyptic. It is to provide a mechanism for the settlement of disputes in light of broadly conceived principles on whose soundness, it must be assumed, there is a general consensus among us. If the assumption is wrong, if there is no consensus, then we are headed for war, civil strife, and revolution, and the orderly administration of justice will become an irrelevant, nostalgic whimsy until the social fabric has been stitched together again and a new consensus has emerged. But, so long as the consensus exists, the mechanism which the law provides is designed to insure that our institutions adjust to change, which is inevitable, in a continuing process which will be orderly, gradual, and, to the extent such a thing

be promoted in single asset cases, the classification argument should be resolved in favor of the debtor to allow classification to create one accepting class of impaired claims.

> is possible in human affairs, rational. The function of the lawyer is to preserve a skeptical relativism in a society hell-bent for absolutes. When we become too sure of our premises, we necessarily fail in what we are supposed to be doing.

Id.

CHAPTER VII

CLASSIFICATION OF UNDERSECURED CREDITORS' DEFICIENCY CLAIMS: NO GERRYMANDERING

JACK I. HABERT
PATRICK J. HOEFFNER

The provisions governing the manner in which a debtor may classify adverse claims or interests are contained in section 1122 of the Bankruptcy Code ("Code"). Section 1122 provides:

> (a) Except as provided in subsection (b) of this section, a plan may place a claim or an interest in a particular class only if such claim or interest is substantially similar to the other claim or interests of such class.
> (b) A plan may designate a separate class of claims consisting only of every unsecured claim that is less than or reduced to an amount that the court approves as reasonable and necessary for administrative convenience.[1]

Section 1122(a) makes clear that only "substantially similar" claims may be placed in the same class. The section, however, is not so clear in addressing whether substantially similar claims must be placed together.[2] This lack of

---

1. 11 U.S.C. § 1122 (1994).
2. *See In re* Woodbrook Assocs., 19 F.3d 312, 318 (7th Cir. 1994) (finding separate classification of similar claims not expressly forbidden by § 1122); John Hancock Mut. Life Ins. Co. v. Route 37 Business Park Assocs., 987 F.2d 154, 158 (3d Cir. 1993) (stating § 1122 does not answer question of whether similar claims may be placed in separate classes); *In re* Jersey City Medical Ctr., 817 F.2d 1055, 1060 (3d Cir. 1987) (same); *In re* Gato Realty Trust Corp., 183 B.R. 15, 19 (Bankr. D. Mass. 1995) (finding statute and its

clarity is compounded by section 1129(a)(10)which requires for confirmation that "at least one class of claims that is impaired under the plan has accepted the plan."[3] Debtors' efforts to satisfy the requirements of sections 1122 and 1129(a)(10) have been particularly problematic in single asset reorganizations[4] resulting in an unsettled issue: whether section 1122(a) permits a debtor to classify substantially similar creditors' claims separately to create a single consenting impaired class that satisfies section 1129(a)(10).

A single asset[5] reorganization case generally includes a debtor in possession, a group of general unsecured creditors ("general unsecured

---

legislative history unclear on separate classification issue) (citation omitted); *In re* Krisch Realty Assocs., 174 B.R. 914, 916 (Bankr. W.D. Va. 1994) (finding Code does not contain provision which requires all substantially similar claims to be in same class); *In re* Barney & Carey Co., 170 B.R. 17, 22 (Bankr. D. Mass. 1994) (same); *In re* Bloomingdale Partners, 170 B.R. 984, 989-90 (Bankr. N.D. Ill. 1994) (finding neither express language of § 1122 nor its legislative history "aid . . . in determining the appropriate classification standard"); *In re* S & W Enter., 37 B.R. 153, 157 n.7 (Bankr. N.D. Ill. 1984) (same); *In re* Pine Lake Village Apartment Co., 19 B.R. 819, 829 (Bankr. S.D.N.Y. 1982) (same); Howard M. Neuger, *The Authority of a Debtor to Place Substantially Similar Claims into Separate Classes in order to Cram Down a Reorganization Plan: Should a Bright Line Rule Requiring all Substantially Similar Claims to be Placed into a Single Class Be Adopted?*, 9 BANK. DEV. J. 567, 582-83 (1993) (same); Gregory K. Jones, Comment, *The Classification and Cram Down Controversy in Single Asset Bankruptcy Cases: A Need for the Repeal of Bankruptcy Code Section 1129(a)(10)*, 42 UCLA L. REV. 623, 650 (1994) (stating that § 1122 is ambiguous and that courts have not reached uniform decision on its meaning).

3. Section 1129(a)(10) was amended in 1984 to read that one impaired class must accept the plan as opposed to just one accepting class, presumably because Congress wanted to ensure that at least one class with a stake in the reorganization accepted the confirmed plan. 11 U.S.C. § 1129(a)(10) (1994), *amended by* Pub. L. No. 98-353, § 512(a)(9), 98 Stat. 333, 387 (1984).

4. *See infra* text accompanying notes 5-21; *see also infra* notes 103-12 and accompanying text (discussing how gerrymandering undermines § 1129(a)(10)).

5. *See generally* 11 U.S.C. § 101(51B) (1994), *infra* note 38 (defining "single asset real estate"). This Chapter, however, is not limited to this definition (which has real estate value restrictions) because the arguments advanced apply to any size real estate that has been used to secure credit.

creditors") with recourse against the debtor,[6] and a creditor holding a nonrecourse loan secured by property that has a value less than the balance of the loan ("undersecured creditor").[7] In a typical case, the secured creditor may have loaned the debtor say $10 million secured by a piece of property that has since declined in value to $7 million leaving the secured creditor undersecured by $3 million. The Bankruptcy Code ("Code") addresses this situation in section 506(a), by limiting the lender's secured claim to the value of its collateral.[8] The $10 million loan claim thus becomes a $7 million secured claim. Section 1111(b)(1) (A), in turn, gives the undersecured creditor recourse against the debtor for the $3 million unsecured deficiency claim.[9]

---

6. Jones, *supra* note 2, at 629 (stating trade creditors are generally only ones with recourse); J. Ronald Trost et al., *Survey of the New Value Exception to the Absolute Priority Rule and the Preliminary Problem of Classification, in* FUNDAMENTALS OF CHAPTER 11 BUSINESS REORGANIZATIONS, at 427 (ALI-ABA & Cal. Continuing Educ. of the Bar, 1994) (stating "most general unsecured claims are recourse claims cognizable under state law").
7. *See Woodbrook*, 19 F.3d at 317 n.2 (stating § 1111(b) creates unsecured deficiency claim in amount of lien in excess of collateral's value for undersecured creditor); Lumber Exch. Bldg. Ltd. Partnership v. Mut. Life Ins. Co. (*In re* Lumber Exch. Bldg. Ltd. Partnership), 968 F.2d 647, 648 (8th Cir. 1992) (finding difference between loan and value of collateral created undersecured claim in that amount).
8. 11 U.S.C. § 506(a) (1994); *In re* Thornwood Assocs., 161 B.R. 367, 369 (M.D. Pa. 1993).
9. A deficiency claim is the difference between the amount of debt and value of the collateral. This difference is deemed an unsecured recourse claim, even if under otherwise applicable law the claim is nonrecourse. *In re* 500 Fifth Ave. Assocs., 148 B.R. 1010, 1016 (Bankr. S.D.N.Y.), *aff'd*, No. 93 Civ. 844, 1993 WL 316183 (S.D.N.Y. May 21, 1993); *see also* 11 U.S.C. § 1111(b)(1)(A) (1994). The creditor's deficiency claim is either automatically characterized as an unsecured claim or the creditor may elect, pursuant to § 1111(b), to have its entire claim characterized as a secured claim. *Id.* § 1111(b). If the election is made, the creditor is deemed to have waived the deficiency recourse claim. *Woodbrook*, 19 F.3d at 317 n.2; *In re* Gato Realty Trust Corp., 183 B.R. 15, 16 (Bankr. D. Mass. 1995); David G. Carlson, *Symposium on Bankruptcy: Chapter 11 Issues: The Classification Veto in Single-Asset Cases Under Bankruptcy Code Section 1129(a)(10)*, 44 S.C. L. REV. 565, 588 (1993).

This deficiency claim allows the undersecured creditor to vote among the unsecured creditors on whether to confirm the plan of reorganization.[10]

The deficiency claim is generally greater than the aggregate of all other unsecured claims.[11] As a result of that disproportion, if the undersecured creditor is placed in a single class along with the remaining general unsecured creditors it will alone control the outcome of the class's vote.[12] If the plan is unfavorable to the undersecured creditor it will vote against the plan.[13] This

---

10. 11 U.S.C. § 1111(b)(2) (1994). An undersecured nonrecourse creditor, who elects to be treated as fully secured, is treated as nonrecourse for the full value of its claim, and therefore forfeits its right to vote on the chapter 11 plan as part of the unsecured class. *In re* Barney & Carey Co., 170 B.R. 17, 20 n.3 (Bankr. D. Mass. 1994) (finding "[§] 1111(b) permits creditor with nonrecourse loan to receive recourse status, thereby gaining right to vote in unsecured creditor's class"); 680 Fifth Ave. Assocs. v. Mut. Benefit Life Ins. Co. (*In re* 680 Fifth Ave. Assocs.), 156 B.R. 726, 733 (Bankr. S.D.N.Y. 1993).
11. Boston Post Rd. Ltd. Partnership v. FDIC (*In re* Boston Post Rd.), 21 F.3d 477, 482 (2d Cir. 1994) (noting in single asset bankruptcy cases "the creditor-mortgagee usually has an unsecured deficiency claim, which, if placed in the class containing other unsecured claims . . . will often overwhelm the class"), *cert. denied*, 115 S. Ct. 897 (1995); *Woodbrook*, 19 F.3d at 318 (same); Peter E. Meltzer, *Disenfranchising the Dissenting Creditor Through Artificial Classification or Artificial Impairment*, 66 AM. BANKR. L.J. 281, 304 (1992) (same).
12. *In re* Thornwood Assocs., 161 B.R. 367, 369 (Bankr. M.D. Pa. 1993) (finding § 1111(b) allows substantially undersecured creditor to dominate class and outcome of confirmation vote); *500 Fifth Ave.*, 148 B.R. at 1017-18 (same); General Elec. Mortgage Corp. v. South Village, Inc. (*In re* South Village, Inc.), 25 B.R. 987, 999 (Bankr. D. Utah 1982) (same).
According to § 1126(c) "[a] class of claims has accepted a plan if such plan has been accepted by creditors . . . that hold at least two-thirds in amount and more than one-half in number of the [claims in the class]." 11 U.S.C. § 1126(c) (1994). Thus, an undersecured creditor could ensure that the class of unsecured creditors rejects the plan if it holds a claim greater than one-third of the class's amount. Unsecured creditors would then never obtain the requisite "two-thirds in amount" necessary to accept the plan.
13. The undersecured creditor might do this, among other reasons, to foreclose on the property and salvage whatever is left of its investment. *See* Meltzer, *supra* note 11, at 282 (reasoning when creditor is hostile, plan confirmation may be impossible).

means that the secured class will reject the plan, and if the deficiency claim and the other unsecured creditors are in the same class, the deficiency claim's negative vote will undoubtedly cause the unsecured class to reject the plan.[14] Thus, no impaired class, as required by section 1129(a)(10), will have voted positively and since no plan may be confirmed without an impaired accepting class, the court may not confirm the plan.[15]

In an effort to thwart this outcome, a debtor may attempt to place the unsecured claims in more than one class[16] to create at least one impaired class of general unsecured creditors, such as trade creditors,[17] that might approve the

---

14. *See In re* Overland Park Merchandise Mart Partnership, 167 B.R. 647, 652 (Bankr. D. Kan. 1994) (stating undersecured creditor controls class and forces rejection of plan if jointly classified with unsecured creditors). *But see generally infra* note 96 (discussing possibility that undersecured creditor may not always be able to prevent plan confirmation).

15. 11 U.S.C. § 1129(a)(1)-(13) (1994). Section 1129(a) sets out thirteen requirements that a court must review in order to confirm a plan. *Id.* Section 1129(a)(10) is among those thirteen requirements and requires the acceptance of an impaired class. 11 U.S.C. § 1129(a)(10) (1994). *See* cases cited *infra* note 21 (discussing importance of § 1129(a)(10) to plan confirmation).

16. One Times Square Assocs. Ltd. Partnership v. Banque Nationale De Paris (*In re* One Times Square Assocs. Ltd. Partnership), 165 B.R. 773, 778 (S.D.N.Y.) (finding separate classification necessary to effect cramdown because nonconsenting creditor controlled class), *aff'd*, 41 F.3d 1502 (2d Cir. 1994), *cert. denied*, 115 S. Ct. 1107 (1995); *Thornwood*, 161 B.R. at 369 (same); Trost, *supra* note 6, at 420-21 (noting it is necessary to separately classify undersecured creditor to effect cramdown). Recently, the steep fall in real estate values has caused the mortgagee's unsecured deficiency claim to be much larger than the sum of the other unsecured claims. This has allowed the undersecured creditor to control the class and has resulted in the debtor separately classifying that creditor in order to obtain a consenting class. *In re* D & W Realty Corp., 156 B.R. 140, 144 n.9 (Bankr. S.D.N.Y. 1993).

17. Phoenix Mut. Life Ins. Co. v. Greystone III Joint Venture (*In re* Greystone III Joint Venture), 995 F.2d 1274, 1280 (5th Cir. 1991) (stating trade creditors can be "wooed" to vote in favor of plan by promise of full payment outside of plan), *vacated on other grounds*, 995 F.2d 1284 (5th Cir.), *cert. denied*, 506 U.S. 821 (1992); Meltzer, *supra* note 11, at 305 (stating general unsecured creditors would rather vote to confirm plan because foreclosure would yield them nothing, so they receive more under plan than would receive otherwise); *see also infra* note 68.

plan. By creating this class, the debtor is hoping to ensure satisfaction of section 1129(a)(10)'s requirement.[18] If that threshold requirement is met, then even though the class containing the undersecured creditor's deficiency claim will vote against the plan, thus preventing plan confirmation under section 1129(a), the debtor may be able to convince the court to impose or "cram down"[19] the plan pursuant to section 1129(b).[20] As a result, section 1129(a)(10), has been called the "gatekeeper" to cramdown.[21]

The practice of separately classifying claims solely for the purpose of ensuring that, pursuant to section 1129(a)(10), there will be one impaired class that approves the reorganization plan is commonly referred to as

---

18. 11 U.S.C. § 1129(a)(10) (1994).

19. Section 1129(b) has been called the cramdown provision of chapter 11. "[I]t requires simply that the plan meet certain standards of fairness to dissenting creditors or equity security holders." H.R. REP. NO. 595, 95th Cong., 1st Sess. 413-18 (1977), *reprinted in* 1978 U.S.C.C.A.N. 5963, 6369. Cramdown requires that all the requirements of § 1129(a) be met except for § 1129(a)(8), which requires the approval of all of the classes. 11 U.S.C. § 1129(b)(1) (1994); *see Boston Post Rd.*, 21 F.3d at 480.

20. While § 1129(b)'s "fair and equitable" requirement prevents cramdown if the plan does not adhere to absolute priority regarding the dissenting class, the debtor may still hope for court imposition of a plan through the use of the "new value exception." *Compare* Mark E. MacDonald et al., *Confirmation by Cramdown Through the New Value Exception in Single Asset Cases*, 1 AM. BANKR. INST. L. REV. 65, 67 (1993), *revised in* ch. VIII *infra* at 269, 273 *with* Salvatore G. Gangemi et al., *Note: The New Value Exception: Square Peg In a Round Hole*, 1 AM. BANKR. INST. L. REV. 173, 176 (1993), *revised in* ch. IX *infra* at 309, 315; *see infra* notes 108-12 and accompanying text (discussing implications of new value exception on undersecured creditor).

21. *In re* 500 Fifth Ave. Assocs., 148 B.R. 1010, 1020 (Bankr. S.D.N.Y.), *aff'd*, No. 93 Civ. 844, 1993 WL 316183 (S.D.N.Y. May 21, 1993); *see also Boston Post Rd.*, 21 F.3d at 480 (stating § 1129(a)(10) "makes available a `cramdown' procedure"); *In re* Bloomingdale Partners, 170 B.R. 984, 993 (N.D. Ill. 1994) (finding separate classification would render § 1129(a)(10) "a mere ministerial requirement"); *In re* 266 Washington Assocs., 141 B.R. 275, 286-87 (Bankr. E.D.N.Y.) (noting § 1129(a)(10) "serves a safeguard function"), *aff'd*, 147 B.R. 827 (E.D.N.Y. 1992); Neuger, *supra* note 2, at 568-69 (discussing need for one yes-voting impaired class to confirm plan under cramdown provision of Code).

"gerrymandering."[22] This Chapter maintains that gerrymandering in the context of plan confirmation is improper. This view, however, is not unanimous.[23]

This Chapter begins in Part A by analyzing the legislative history and legislative intent behind the enactment of section 1122. Part B then proceeds to examine the impact of section 1111(b) upon the undersecured creditor's deficiency claim and anomalies within the Code. Part C reviews how gerrymandering circumvents section 1129(a)(10) and reduces judicial economy, as discussed in case law and commentaries. Part D then analyzes the policies in support of a per se rule that prohibits gerrymandering. This Chapter concludes by encouraging the adoption of a per se rule prohibiting gerrymandering.

A. Legislative History and Legislative Intent

1. The Bankruptcy Code of 1978

As previously discussed in the introduction, section 1122 is unclear on whether substantially similar claims may be separately classified for the sole

---

22. "Gerrymandering" is "the process of dividing a . . . territory [or group of claims] into . . . political divisions, but with such . . . arrangement as to accomplish an ulterior or unlawful purpose, as, for instance, to secure a majority . . . where the result would be otherwise if [the territory or group of claims] were divided according to obvious natural lines." BLACK'S LAW DICTIONARY 687 (6th ed. 1990); *see also* Carlson, *supra* note 9, at 566. Carlson writes that the term "gerrymandering" is derived from the "unsavory practice of subdividing voters to produce a preconceived political result." Today the term as used in bankruptcy, applies when a plan proponent, usually the debtor-in-possession, manipulates "the creditors so as to produce a yes-voting noninsider class to get by the requirement of § 1129(a)(10)." *Id.*; Neuger, *supra* note 2, at 568. Neuger writes that the ambiguity in the language of § 1122 has allowed creditors to gerrymander the classes of creditors in order to confirm a plan which might not otherwise be confirmed. *Id.*
23. Linda J. Rusch, *Single Asset Cases and Chapter 11: The Classification Quandary*, 1 AM. BANKR. INST. L. REV. 43, 46 (1993), *revised in* ch. VI *supra* at 179, 186 (concluding debtor should be able to classify claims for purpose of creating impaired accepting class).

purpose of creating an impaired class that will approve the plan.[24] The Code's silence on this issue has created an ambiguity resulting in a continuing controversy regarding section 1122(a)'s proper interpretation[25] and frustrating a possible plain meaning approach to the section's language.[26]

---

24. *See supra*, note 2.
25. *Compare Greystone*, 995 F.2d at 1279 (concluding there was "one clear rule . . . thou shalt not classify similar claims differently in order to gerrymander an affirmative vote on a reorganization plan") *and Boston Post Rd.*, 21 F.3d at 482-83 (following *Greystone*) *and* Meltzer, *supra* note 11, at 298 (concluding that "lender's deficiency claim is substantially similar to trade claims, and that, . . . the only appropriate interpretation of the Code is to prohibit separate classification of the creditors holding those claims") *and* Neuger, *supra* note 2, at 586 (reasoning that "no sound reason exists" for separately classifying substantially similar claims and urging that adoption of rule to prohibit separate classification would "accomplish the underlying objective of [§] 1122: to segregate all substantially similar claims into a single unit") *with In re* ZRM-Oklahoma Partnership, 156 B.R. 67, 68 (Bankr. W.D. Okla. 1993) (stating that proper interpretation of § 1122(a) is "significant issue" in chapter 11 cases and concluding that absent clear direction from Congress debtors should have power to separately classify claims or interests) *and* 5 COLLIER ON BANKRUPTCY, ¶ 1122.03, at 1122-7 (Lawrence P. King ed. 15th ed. 1995) (concluding that, by its terms, Code does not appear to require substantially similar claims be placed together in same class) *and* Carlson, *supra* note 9, at 615 (reasoning separate classification should be allowed) *and* King F. Tower, *"Cram Down" Confirmation of Single-Asset Debtor Reorganization Plans Through Separate Classification of the Deficiency Claim-How* In Re U.S. Truck Co. *Was Run Off the Road.*, 36 WM. & MARY L. REV. 1169, 1200-01 (1995) (finding separate classification of "unsecured claim of undersecured creditor is simply not prohibited by the Code").
26. *See In re* Bloomingdale Partners, 170 B.R. 984, 989 (Bankr. N.D. Ill. 1994) (stating plain meaning of § 1122 is unhelpful); Neuger, *supra* note 2, at 568-69 (finding that "ambiguity of [§] 1122" has resulted in conflict among courts); *see also* United States v. American Trucking, 310 U.S. 534, 543 (1940) (reasoning that where statute's plain meaning leads to absurd, futile or even unreasonable results one should look beyond its plain meaning); *cf.* United States v. Ron Pair Enters., Inc., 489 U.S. 235, 242 (1989) (stating that courts should use plain meaning except where it "`will produce a result demonstrably at odds with the intentions of its drafters'" in which case "the intention of the drafters, rather than the strict language controls"); Varsity Carpet Serv. v.

The silence of the legislative history to section 1122(a) has aggravated the inability of courts to reach a consensus on whether gerrymandering is prohibited.[27] The Historical and Revision Notes ("Notes") following section

---

Richardson (*In re* Colortex Indus.), 19 F.3d 1371, 1375 (11th Cir. 1994) (same); *In re* ZRM-Oklahoma Partnership, 156 B.R. 67, 68-69 (Bankr. W.D. Okla. 1993) (same).

27. *See* Boston Post Rd. Ltd. Partnership v. FDIC (*In re* Boston Post Rd. Ltd. Partnership), 21 F.3d 477, 483 (2d Cir. 1994) (noting that analysis of legislative history of § 1122 sheds little light on its meaning), *cert. denied*, 115 S. Ct. 897 (1995); Bustop Shelters, Inc. v. Classic Homes, Inc., 914 F.2d 810, 813 (6th Cir. 1990) (noting that legislative history of Code provides little assistance in determining limits to segregating similar claims); *In re* Jersey City Medical Center, 817 F.2d 1055, 1060 (3d Cir. 1987) (noting that legislative intent behind § 1122 is inconclusive on whether similar claims may be separately classified); Teamsters Nat'l Freight Ind. Negotiating Comm., Inc. v. U.S. Truck Co. (*In re* U.S. Truck Co.), 800 F.2d 581, 584 (6th Cir. 1986) (concluding that "Congress has sent mixed signals on the issue"); LW-SP2 v. Krisch Realty Assocs. (*In re* Krisch Realty Assocs.), 174 B.R. 914, 917 (Bankr. W.D. Va. 1994) (finding that Code does not contain a provision which requires all substantially similar claims to be placed in same class); *In re* Barney & Carey Co., 170 B.R. 17, 22 (Bankr. D. Mass. 1994) (stating that both plain meaning and legislative history of § 1122 add to confusion of whether all substantially similar claims must be placed together); *In re* S & W Enter., 37 B.R. 153, 157 n.7 (Bankr. N.D. Ill. 1984) (stating that Bankruptcy Code "gives no express guidance" on whether claims may be classified separately); *In re* Pine Lake Village Apartment Co., 19 B.R. 819, 830 (Bankr. S.D.N.Y. 1982) (determining that under § 1122 there is little guidance as to designation of separate classes).

Another reason why the legislative history behind § 1122 may not be particularly helpful is that at the time § 1122 was enacted § 1129(a)(10)'s "requirement of 'at least one accepting class of impaired creditors' [to approve a confirm a reorganization plan] was not yet in place." Neuger, *supra* note 2, at 583; 11 U.S.C. § 1129(a)(10) (1994). Therefore, a debtor could achieve cramdown even though there were no accepting classes. Thus, Congress's failure to address the issue of gerrymandering in § 1122 is irrelevant "since there was no incentive [to gerrymander] for Congress to guard against." *Id.* It may also be argued, however, that since § 1122 codified pre-Code law, § 1122 was presumed to prohibit gerrymandering, so there was no reason to say anything. *See infra* note 33 (discussing pre-Code case law).

1122 in the Code do not aid in clarifying Congress's intentions.[28] The Notes, and both the House and Final Senate Committee Reports,[29] merely quote the statements made in the Report of the Committee on the Judiciary[30] regarding section 1122. It states, section 1122 "**codifies** current case law surrounding the classification of claims . . . . It requires classification based on the **nature** of the claims or interests classified . . . ."[31]

2. Pre-Code Case Law

A review of the pre-Code case law codified in section 1122, however, does lend some clarity.[32] Pre-Code cases state the general rule that "substantially

---

28. 11 U.S.C. § 1122 (1994).
29. H.R. REP. NO. 595, 95th Cong., 1st Sess. 406 (1977), *reprinted in* 1978 U.S.C.C.A.N. 5963, 6362; S. REP. NO. 989, 95th Cong., 2d Sess. 118 (1978), *reprinted in* 1978 U.S.C.C.A.N. 5787, 5904.
30. *Id.*
31. H.R. REP. NO. 595, *supra* note 29; S. REP. NO. 989, *supra* note 29. (emphasis added). The use of the word "nature" is identical to that used in § 597 of the Bankruptcy Act, which was the section on classification of creditors and stockholders. 11 U.S.C. § 597 (1970). Under pre-Code law the judge divided the creditors into classes based on the nature of the claims. Steelcase, Inc. v. Johnston (*In re* Johnston), 21 F.3d 323, 327 (9th Cir. 1994) (stating that to review classification scheme "bankruptcy judges must evaluate the nature of each claim, i.e., the kind, species, or character of each category of claims") (citing *In re* Los Angeles Land & Inv. Ltd., 282 F. Supp. 448, 451 (D. Haw. 1968), *aff'd*, 447 F.2d 1366 (9th Cir. 1971)); *see infra* notes 129-32 and accompanying text (discussing inquiry should be on nature of claims rather than plan proponent's subjective intent in separately classifying claims).
32. It has been argued that pre-Code cases are unhelpful because the decisions depended upon which chapter of the Bankruptcy Act the case fell under. *See* David G. Epstein & Christopher Fuller, *Chapter 11 and 13 of the Bankruptcy Code-Observations on Using Case Authority from One of the Chapters in Proceedings Under the Other*, 38 VAND. L. REV. 901, 924-25 (1985) (stating that "[c]hapters X, XI, and XII . . . the forerunners of [c]hapter 11 [of the Bankruptcy Code] . . . contained differences in their classification provisions that prevent them from being completely analogous to [c]hapter 11"). Nevertheless, in light of the fact that § 1122 is meant to codify pre-Code case law these cases are worth reviewing. *See* Kelly v. Robinson, 479 U.S. 36, 46-50 (1986) (reviewing status of pre-Code case law to determine whether

similar" claims should be classified together.[33] The normal rule of statutory construction is that Congress is presumed to be aware of existing law when it passes legislation,[34] and "that if Congress intends for legislation to change the interpretation of a judicially created concept it makes that intent specific. The Court has followed this rule with particular care in construing the scope of bankruptcy codifications."[35] Therefore, Congress is deemed aware of both the

---

Congress intended to discharge criminal penalties and stating in dicta that Court would have followed pre-Code established judicial trend if had not decided case on other grounds).

33. *Los Angeles Land & Inv.*, 282 F. Supp. at 453. In the context of a single asset reorganization case under chapter X of the Bankruptcy Act, the court stated that the judge classifies creditors in accordance with the "nature" of the claim. *Id.* In addition, an "analysis of the legal character or the quality of the claim" is determinative, but "[g]enerally . . . [a]ll creditors of equal rank with claims against the same property should be placed in the same class." *Id.* (citing Scherk v. Newton (*In re* Rocky Mountain Fuel Co.), 152 F.2d 747, 751 (10th Cir. 1945) (discussing reorganization under chapter X and stating general rule that "[a]ll creditors of equal rank with claims against the same property should be placed in the same class")); Seidel v. Palisades-on-the-Desplaines (*In re* Palisades-on-the-Desplaines), 89 F.2d 214, 217-18 (7th Cir. 1937) (discussing single asset reorganization case under § 77B and stating that courts "should not uselessly increase the number of classifications unless there be substantial differences in the nature of the claims" and proceeding to allow separate classification because of substantial differences among the claims).

34. Miles v. Apex Marine Corp., 498 U.S. 19, 32 (1990) (reasoning that judicial gloss and tradition behind Bankruptcy Act were already in existence and Congress must have been aware of it) (citation omitted); Goodyear Atomic Corp. v. Miller, 486 U.S. 174, 184-85 (1988) (concluding that Congress is presumed knowledgeable of pre-existing law and in "absence of affirmative evidence in the language or history of the statute, we are unwilling to assume that Congress was ignorant of the substantial [precedent already set]"); *see also* John Hancock Mut. Life Ins. Co. v. Route 37 Business Park Assocs., 987 F.2d 154, 158 n.6 (3d Cir. 1993) (stating that neither Code's text nor case law shows that Congress meant to change prior law); *In re* Bloomingdale Partners, 170 B.R. 984, 989 (Bankr. N.D. Ill. 1994) (stating that Code's legislative history does not aid in determining appropriate classification standard); *In re* Barney & Carey Co., 170 B.R. 17, 22 (Bankr. D. Mass. 1994) (same).

35. Midlantic Nat'l Bank v. New Jersey Dep't of Envtl. Protection, 474 U.S. 494, 501 (1986). In that case the trustee sought to abandon property as burdensome

pre-Code case law,[36] and the case law that had developed regarding single

---

to the estate. The City and State of New York objected because it would violate state and federal environmental laws. Section 554 of the Code itself said nothing about the trustee's power being subject to state and federal laws. In discussing § 554 the Supreme Court stated:

> [W]hen Congress enacted § 554, there were well recognized restrictions on a trustee's abandonment power. In codifying the judicially developed rule of abandonment, Congress also presumably included the established corollary that a trustee could not exercise his abandonment power in violation of certain state and federal laws. The normal rule of statutory construction is that if Congress intends for legislation to change the interpretation of a judicially created concept it makes that intent specific.

Id; see also Varsity Carpet Serv. v. Richardson, United States Trustee (*In re* Colortex Ind.), 19 F.3d 1371, 1375 n.2 (11th Cir. 1994). The Eleventh Circuit discussed the proper treatment of an administrative expense following conversion from chapter 11 to chapter 7. The court stated:

> In determining this question of priority we turn first to the Bankruptcy Code itself. Rules of statutory construction dictate that the plain meaning is conclusive, "except in the `rare cases [in which] the literal application of a statute will produce a result demonstrably at odds with the intentions of its drafters.'" *United States v. Ron Pair Enters., Inc.*, 489 U.S. 235, 242 (1989) (quoting *Griffin v. Oceanic Contractors*, 458 U.S. 564, 571 (1982)). "`In expounding a statute, we must not be guided by a single sentence or member of a sentence, but look to the provisions of the whole law, and to its policy.'" *Offshore Logistics, Inc. v. Tallentire*, 477 U.S. 207, 222 (1986) (quoting *Mastro Plastics Corp. v. NLRB*, 350 U.S. 270, 285 (1956) (in turn quoting *United States v. Heirs of Boisdore*, 12 L.Ed. 1009 (1849))). Finally, where a statute is ambiguous, we must analyze whether our interpretation accords with established precedent prior to the enactment of the Code, mindful that "`no changes in law or policy are to be presumed from changes in language in [a statute's] revision unless an intent to make such changes is clearly expressed.'" *Finley v. United States*, 490 U.S. 545, 554 (1989) (quoting *Fourco Glass Co. v. Transmirra Products Corp.*, 353 U.S. 222, 227 (1957)). Silent abrogation of judicially created concepts is particularly disfavored when construing the Bankruptcy Code. *Kelly v. Robinson*, 479 U.S. 36, 47 (1986).

Id. (footnote omitted).

asset real estate bankruptcies and gerrymandering since 1978. In light of this rule of construction, and the ambiguity surrounding section 1122, it may be argued[37] that Congress's failure to clarify section 1122's language in the 1994 revision of the Code[38] may be viewed as an indicia of congressional

---

36. *See supra* note 33.
37. *Contra* Central Bank v. First Interstate Bank, 114 S. Ct. 1436, 1452-53 (1994) (stating Congress's failure to act does not necessarily represent "affirmative Congressional approval" of statute's interpretation) (citations omitted).
38. Presently, § 1122's ambiguity remains because it was neither amended by the most recent overhaul of the Code, the Bankruptcy Reform Act of 1994, Pub. L. No. 103-394 (codified as amended at 11 U.S.C. §§ 101-1330 (1994)), nor was it addressed in the accompanying House Report ("Report"). H.R. REP. NO. 835, 103d Cong., 2d Sess. 32-35 (1994), *reprinted in* 1994 U.S.C.C.A.N. 3340-42. The Report states that this most recent overhaul of the Code attempts to address "conflicting court opinions and uncertainties" in order to "improve the administration of the bankruptcy cases." *Id.* Unfortunately, although Congress made some amendments addressing single asset real estate bankruptcies, Congress did not address whether debtors may gerrymander. The two provisions that Congress did add are:

    1. 11 U.S.C. § 101(51)(b) (1994). This section defines single asset real estate as: "real property constituting a single property or project, other than residential real property with fewer than 4 residential units, which generates substantially all of the gross income of a debtor and on which no substantial business is being conducted by a debtor other than the business of operating the real property and activities incidental thereto having aggregate noncontingent, liquidated secured debts in an amount no more than $4,000,000." *Id.* Note that due to the monetary limits placed in this definition, the requirements of § 362(d)(3) will apply to a limited number of cases, while the majority of single asset real estate cases will not be subject to its 90 day time limit; and

    2. 11 U.S.C. § 362(d)(3) (1994). This section "amends the automatic stay provision of § 362 to provide special circumstances when creditors of a single asset real estate debtor may have the stay lifted if the debtor has not filed a 'feasible' reorganization plan within 90 days of filing, or has not commenced monthly payments to secured creditors." H.R. REP. NO. 835, at 34, *reprinted in* 1994 U.S.C.C.A.N. at 3341. Collier suggests that the purpose of § 362(d)(3) is to assist creditors to lift the stay in certain cases where a plan is not promptly filed or payments not commenced, yet at the same time allow courts to retain the discretion to condition or modify the stay as opposed to terminating it. 2 COLLIER, *supra* note 25 ¶ 362.07, at 362-74.

    A bill presently before Congress would eliminate the $4,000,000

approval[39] of the current judicial trend prohibiting gerrymandering.[40]

---

limitation in the definition of single asset real estate. At the time this Chapter was written, however, no decision had been made. S. 1559, 104th Cong., 2d Sess. § 2 (1996).

39. *Cf.* Varsity Carpet Serv. v. Richardson, United States Trustee (*In re* Colortex Ind.), 19 F.3d 1371, 1375 (11th Cir. 1994).

> [W]here a statute is ambiguous, we must analyze whether our interpretation accords with established precedent prior to the enactment of the Code, mindful that "no changes in law or policy are to be presumed from changes in language in [a statute's] revision unless an intent to make such changes is clearly expressed.

Id; Dutton v. Wolpoff & Abramson, 5 F.3d 649, 655 (3d Cir. 1993). The court stated that:

> When Congress reenacts a whole statute, it may be a useful fiction to assume it has reviewed each provision in the context of the judicial and administrative gloss that has been put on them and decided that the court and agency decisions interpreting and implementing all the statute's provisions are consistent with Congress's intent in reenacting it.

Id. (citing Lorillard v. Pons, 434 U.S. 575, 580-81 (1978)); United Savs. Ass'n v. Timbers of Inwood Forest Assocs., 484 U.S. 365, 371 (1988) (stating court's duty when interpreting Bankruptcy Code is to read statute "holistically"); Midlantic Nat'l Bank v. New Jersey Dep't of Envtl. Protection, 474 U.S. 494, 501 (1986) (accepting bankruptcy statute's pre-Code interpretation absent clear legislative intent indicating contrary); Monell v. Department of Social Servs., 436 U.S. 658, 691 n.56 (1978) (stating that court should not disregard gloss which "life has written upon [the statute]") (citation omitted); Shapiro v. United States, 335 U.S. 1, 31 (1948) (stating that assuming statute is subject to two interpretations, read it to promote rather than impede legislative goal-plain meaning gives way "where its application would produce a futile or an unreasonable result") (citation omitted); St. Laurent v. Ambrose (*In re* St. Laurent), 991 F.2d 672, 679 (11th Cir. 1993) (stating that "`we will not read the Bankruptcy Code to erode past bankruptcy practice absent a clear indication that Congress intended such a departure'"); *In re* Reed, 89 B.R. 603, 606 (Bankr. N.D. Tex. 1988) (reasoning Congress presumed "familiar with the long accepted interpretation of the previous statute" and absent legislative history stating intent to change interpretation, and only stating intent to codify pre-Code case law, interpretation still viable).

40. Granada Wines, Inc. v. New England Teamsters & Trucking Indus. Pension Fund, 748 F.2d 42, 46 (1st Cir. 1984) (prohibiting separate classification

unless difference in legal character of claims exists), *In re* Barney & Carey Co., 170 B.R. 17, 24 (Bankr. D. Mass. 1994) (affirming Granada Wines, Inc. v. New England Teamsters & Trucking Ind. Pension Fund, 748 F.2d 42, 46 (1st Cir. 1984) and stating debtor has burden to establish "non-gerrymandering" reason for separate classification-an independent legal distinction); Boston Post Rd. Ltd. Partnership v. FDIC (*In re* Boston Post Rd. Ltd. Partnership), 21 F.3d 477, 483 (2d Cir. 1994) (prohibiting debtor's attempt to separately classify unsecured claims for sole purpose of creating an impaired assenting class, absent legitimate reason), *cert. denied*, 115 S. Ct. 897 (1995); John Hancock Mut. Life Ins. Co. v. Route 37 Business Park Assocs., 987 F.2d 154, 158 (3d Cir. 1993) (concluding separate classification must be based on legal distinction and merit); Travelers Ins. Co. v. Bryson Properties XVIII (*In re* Bryson Properties XVIII), 961 F.2d 496, 502 (4th Cir.) (reasoning that separate classification requires reason independent from desire to secure assent of an impaired class) (citation omitted), *cert. denied*, 506 U.S. 866 (1992); Phoenix Mut. Life Ins. Co. v. Greystone III Joint Venture (*In re* Greystone III Joint Venture), 995 F.2d 1274, 1279 (5th Cir.) (stating "one clear rule . . . thou shalt not classify similar claims differently in order to gerrymander an affirmative vote on a reorganization plan [unless] for reasons independent of the debtor's motivation to secure [a class's] vote"), *vacated on other grounds*, 995 F.2d 1284 (5th Cir.), *cert. denied*, 506 U.S. 821 (1992); Heartland Fed. Savs. & Loan Ass'n v. Briscoe Enter., Ltd. (*In re* Briscoe Enter., Ltd.), 994 F.2d 1160, 1167 (5th Cir. 1993) (recognizing decision in Phoenix Mut. Life Ins. Co. v. Greystone III Joint Venture (*In re* Greystone III Joint Venture), 995 F.2d 1274, 1279 (5th Cir.), *vacated on other grounds*, 995 F.2d 1284 (5th Cir.), *cert. denied*, 506 U.S. 821 (1992), but nevertheless, in narrow holding, allowing separate classification for good business reason); Bustop Shelters, Inc. v. Classic Homes, Inc., 914 F.2d 810, 813 (6th Cir. 1990) (reasoning that debtor should not be permitted to seek "out a few impaired creditors . . . who will vote for the plan [and then] place them in their own class") (citation omitted); *In re* Woodbrook Assocs., 19 F.3d 312, 318-19 (7th Cir. 1994) (reasoning that although gerrymandering is prohibited, significant legal disparities between claims will justify separate classification); Lumber Exch. Bldg. Ltd. Partnership v. Mut. Life Ins. Co. (*In re* Lumber Exch. Bldg. Ltd. Partnership), 968 F.2d 647, 650 (8th Cir. 1992) (concluding that absent legitimate reason for separate classification, "an attempt to manipulate the vote to assure acceptance of the plan by an impaired class . . . . is improper") (citation omitted); Oxford Life Ins. Co. v. Tucson Self-Storage, Inc. (*In re* Tucson Self-Storage, Inc.), 166 B.R. 892, 897 (Bankr. 9th Cir. 1994) (finding that absent legal distinction, separate classification solely to gerrymander votes

B. Legal Status of Section 1111(b) Claims

Section 1122(a) states that claims that are not substantially similar cannot be classified together.[41] The determination of substantial similarity is a question of fact which recognizes the existence of different creditors' rights.[42] The nonrecourse deficiency portion of undersecured claims automatically becomes an unsecured claim pursuant to section 1111(b).[43] This is referred to as a section 1111(b) unsecured claim. The undersecured creditor has the right

---

is improper); Principal Mut. Life Ins. Co. v. Baldwin Park Towne Ctr., Ltd., (*In re* Baldwin Park Towne Ctr., Ltd.), 171 B.R. 374, 377 (Bankr. C.D. Cal. 1994) (same) (citation omitted); Olympia & York Fla. Equity Corp. v. Bank of New York (*In re* Holywell Corp.), 913 F.2d 873, 880 (11th Cir. 1990) (holding court will not confirm reorganization plan that separately classifies claims to manipulate class voting).

Some bankruptcy courts have allowed separate classification, but based on a perceived difference between an unsecured recourse claim and a § 1111(b) unsecured deficiency claim. *See In re* Overland Park Merchandise Mart Partnership, 167 B.R. 647, 662 (Bankr. D. Kan. 1994); *In re* SM 104 Ltd., 160 B.R. 202, 219 (Bankr. S.D. Fla. 1993) (concluding § 1111(b) deficiency claim and general unsecured claim not "substantially similar" and therefore under § 1122(a) must be separately classified). For reasons that will be discussed, this perceived difference does not justify separate classification and was not intended by Congress. *See* text accompanying notes 40-89.

41. 11 U.S.C. § 1122(a) (1994); *In re* Richard Buick, Inc., 126 B.R. 840, 853 (Bankr. E.D. Pa. 1991) (interpreting § 1122(a) as requiring that all claims classified together must possess substantial similarity); *In re* Hill, 4 B.R. 694 (Bankr. D. Kan. 1980) (discussing "substantially similar" as meaning that nature of claim is determinative of its classification) (citation omitted).

42. Brady v. Andrew (*In re* Commercial W. Fin. Corp.), 761 F.2d 1329 (9th Cir. 1985) (commenting that determination of whether claims are substantially similar is question of fact); Richard F. Broude, *Chapter 11 Reorganization of the Small and Medium Sized Business, in* PLANS OF REORGANIZATION, at 498 (ALI-ABA & U. Wis. Law School 1989) (noting that bank debt and trade debt are not substantially similar); Sharon Youdelman, *Strategic Bankruptcies: Class Actions, Classification & The Dalkon Shield Cases*, 7 CARDOZO L. REV. 817, 837 (1986) (noting that "classification of substantially similar claims has been viewed as the recognition of the existence of different creditors' rights which require different treatment in bankruptcy").

43. *See supra* notes 9-10.

under certain circumstances to elect, pursuant to section 1111(b), to treat its entire claim as secured, thus waiving the conversion of the deficiency to a section 1111(b) unsecured claim as part of its secured claim.[44]

When creditors claim that separate classification is unjustified, debtors often respond by arguing that the legal status of a deficiency claim, created under section 1111(b), is not substantially similar to a "natural" unsecured claim.[45] As a result of this legal difference, debtors contend that separate classification is not only allowed under section 1122(a), but mandated.[46] When

---

44. 11 U.S.C. § 1111(b)(2) (1994).

45. *See In re* Aztec Co., 107 B.R. 585 (M.D. Tenn. 1989). The *Aztec* court notes that the unnatural unsecured deficiency claim exists only by operation of § 1111(b) in a chapter 11 case. The natural recourse claimholders, however, have rights against solvent debtors outside of bankruptcy. *Id.* at 587; *see* Phoenix Mut. Life Ins. Co. v. Greystone III Joint Venture (*In re* Greystone III Joint Venture), 995 F.2d 1274, 1279 (5th Cir. 1991) (holding that Code eliminates legal distinction between nonrecourse deficiency claim and other unsecured claims), *vacated in part*, 995 F.2d 1284 (5th Cir.), *cert. denied*, 506 U.S. 821 (1992); Travelers Ins. Properties v. Bryson Properties (*In re* Bryson Properties), 961 F.2d 496, 502 (4th Cir.) (noting that unnatural claim is Code created), *cert. denied*, 506 U.S. 866 (1992); *In re* Krisch Realty Assocs., 174 B.R. 914, 918 (Bankr. W.D. Va. 1994) (distinguishing natural from unnatural recourse claims based on priorities retained by each, notwithstanding their status as recourse claims in chapter 11); *In re* Dean, 166 B.R. 949, 953 (Bankr. D.N.M. 1994) (noting that to allow debtor to separately classify claim based on creditor's right to make § 1111(b) election would violate Code policy and congressional intent); Michael J. Frankel et al., *Partnership Workouts: Problems and Solutions Under Final Section 704(b) and 752 Regulations, in* PARTNERSHIP & LIMITED LIABILITY COMPANIES: UNIFORM ACTS, TAXATION, DRAFTING, SECURITIES, AND BANKRUPTCY, at 641 (ALI-ABA 1994) (noting that unnatural claims exist only by operation of § 1111(b) and only in chapter 11 case).

46. Boston Post Rd. Ltd. Partnership v. FDIC (*In re* Boston Post Rd. Ltd. Partnership), 21 F.3d 477, 481 (2d Cir. 1994), *cert. denied*, 115 S. Ct. 897 (1995); *In re* Overland Park Merchandise Mart Partnership, 167 B.R. 647, 650-53 (Bankr. D. Kan. 1994) (concluding that "nonrecourse undersecured creditor's § 1111(b) unsecured claim not only can but must be classified separately from claims of recourse unsecured creditors"); *In re* SM 104 Ltd., 160 B.R. 202, 221 (Bankr. S.D. Fla. 1993) (holding that debtor's motive in separately classifying § 1111(b) claims and general unsecured claims is

asserting a difference in the legal status of a claim, the debtor generally argues that the legal status is changed by: (A) the ability to make the section 1111(b) election, (B) the creditors' incentives, (C) the anomalies caused by the nongerrymandering application of section 1111(b).

1. Effect of Right to Make the Section 1111(b) Election

Debtors have successfully argued that the right to make the section 1111(b) election is enough of a difference in legal status that separate classification is warranted.[47] A typical case involves a debtor defending the separate classification of a section 1111(b) nonrecourse deficiency claim from the general unsecured claims by arguing that if the debtor is not within chapter 11 of the Bankruptcy Code then "under state law [the undersecured creditor] has no recourse [with respect to the deficiency claim] against the debtor personally."[48] Under chapter 7 of the Code, the general unsecured creditors would be entitled to their pro rata share of the remaining assets after higher priority creditors were paid off. In sharp contrast, a nonrecourse undersecured creditor would be excluded from collecting anything on its deficiency[49]

---

irrelevant since separate classification is required by § 1122(a)); *In re* D & W Realty Corp., 156 B.R. 140, 141-42 (Bankr. S.D.N.Y. 1993) (debtor arguing that separate classification is not only appropriate, but in fact mandated by Bankruptcy Code and Rules), *rev'd*, 165 B.R. 127 (S.D.N.Y. 1994); Carlson, *supra* note 9, 576-77.

47. *In re* Woodbrook Assocs., 19 F.3d 312, 318 (7th Cir. 1994); *In re* Gato Realty Trust Corp., 183 B.R. 15, 19-22 (Bankr. D. Mass. 1995); *In re* Bjolmes Realty Trust, 134 B.R. 1000, 1003-04 (Bankr. D. Mass. 1991).

48. John Hancock Mut. Life Ins. Co. v. Route 37 Business Park Assocs., 987 F.2d 154, 161 (3d Cir. 1993) (involving classification scheme that separated unsecured claims based on creditor's right to proceed against debtor under state law); *Woodbrook*, 19 F.3d at 318 (same); Phoenix Mut. Life Ins. Co. v. Greystone III Joint Venture (*In re* Greystone III Joint Venture), 995 F.2d 1274, 1279 (5th Cir. 1991), *vacated in part*, 995 F.2d 1284 (5th Cir.), *cert. denied*, 506 U.S. 821 (1992); *In re* SM 104 Ltd., 160 B.R. 202, 218 (Bankr. S.D. Fla. 1993) (noting that courts distinguished general unsecured claims by finding that they are cognizable under state law but § 1111(b) claims only exist under chapter 11).

49. LW-SP2 v. Krisch Realty Assocs. (*In re* Krisch Realty Assocs.), 174 B.R. 914, 918 (Bankr. W.D. Va. 1994) (holding that in chapter 7 § 1111(b) claim loses

because in chapter 7 its claim is limited to the extent of its security.[50] Debtors contend that since outside chapter 11 the deficiency claims are not cognizable,[51] they are legally distinct from natural unsecured claims and, therefore, must be classified separately, pursuant to section 1122(a).[52] This election right has been interpreted to afford the undersecured creditor greater rights than general unsecured creditors and, consequently, make the legal status of those undersecured claims different.[53]

This argument, however, is flawed[54] and, consequently, it has been

---

its "pseudo-recourse status" and is entitled only to extent of its collateral).

50. 11 U.S.C. § 103(f) (1994) ("Subchapter I. . . of chapter 11. . . [, which includes § 1111, applies] only in a case under [chapter 11]"); *Woodbrook*, 19 F.3d at 318; *In re* SM 104 Ltd., 160 B.R. 202, 218 (Bankr. S.D. Fla. 1993); *see* Carlson, *supra* note 9, at 582-83.

51. *In re* Woodbrook Assocs., 19 F.3d 312, 318 (7th Cir. 1994) (noting that a majority of circuits have rejected any legal distinction based on Code); *In re* Aztec Co., 107 B.R. 585, 587 (M.D. Tenn. 1989) (noting that outside of chapter 11 a nonrecourse or deficiency claim could not be pursued).

52. *Woodbrook*, 19 F.3d at 318 (holding limited existence of § 1111(b) claim in chapter 11 significant disparity in legal rights which results in mandatory separate classification); *In re* D & W Realty Corp., 156 B.R. 140, 141-42 (Bankr. S.D.N.Y. 1993), *rev'd*, 165 B.R. 127 (S.D.N.Y. 1994) (holding separate classification mandate); *SM 104*, 160 B.R. at 221 (same).

53. *Woodbrook*, 19 F.3d at 318 (holding that significant disparities do exist between legal rights of holder of a § 1111(b) claim and general unsecured claims which renders claims not substantially similar); *see In re* Gato Realty Trust Corp., 183 B.R. 15, 21 (Bankr. D. Mass. 1995) (holding that right to convert from an unsecured claim to nonrecourse secured claim made it assume "different rank, status, and character than other unsecured creditor claims"); *In re* Overland Park Merchandise Mart Partnership, 167 B.R. 647, 651 (Bankr. D. Kan. 1994) (noting that only nonrecourse creditor is given option of having unsecured claim in chapter 11 that it would not have otherwise); *SM 104*, 160 B.R. at 219 (holding that most obvious difference between general unsecured claim and unsecured deficiency claim created by § 1111(b) is that former exists regardless of what chapter of Code case is under).

54. *See* Meltzer, *supra* note 11, at 299. Meltzer writes that:

> It makes no sense to suggest that a lender's deficiency claim is unique because its recourse right arises only in chapter 11, since all of these issues only arise within chapter 11 in the first place. In other words, the whole concept of a plan of reorganization, and all of the

soundly rejected by several circuits based on section 1111(b)'s elimination of the legal distinction between nonrecourse deficiency claims and other unsecured claims.[55] "Section 1111(b) sets forth the general rule that [nonrecourse deficiency] claims are treated as recourse claims, regardless of whether the claimant had recourse against the debtor under . . . state law."[56] The deficiency claims are, therefore, considered unsecured recourse claims under the Code and it is irrelevant how the claim achieved that status.[57] It is unreasonable to propose that if chapters 7 and 11 were applied to the same fact pattern and the results were inconsistent that it means one of the sets of

---

> confirmation requirements pursuant thereto, including § 1129(a)(10), can only occur within the confines of the chapter 11 universe. The rights of the various parties outside of chapter 11–whether in chapter 7 or outside of bankruptcy altogether–are irrelevant.

Id.

55. *Woodbrook*, 19 F.3d at 318 (noting that majority of circuits have rejected any legal distinction based on Code); John Hancock Mut. Life Ins. Co. v. Route 37 Business Park Assocs., 987 F.2d 154, 161 (3d Cir. 1993) (noting that manner in which claims achieved their status does not alter current character or warrant separate classification); Lumber Exch. Bldg. Ltd. Partnership v. Mut. Life Ins. Co. (*In re* Lumber Exch. Bldg. Ltd. Partnership), 968 F.2d 647, 649 (8th Cir. 1992) (same); Phoenix Mut. Life Ins. Co. v. Greystone III Joint Venture (*In re* Greystone III Joint Venture), 995 F.2d 1274, 1279-80 (5th Cir. 1991) (holding that state law distinction between Code created unsecured deficiency claims and other unsecured claims does not alone warrant separate classification), *vacated on other grounds*, 995 F.2d 1284 (5th Cir.), *cert. denied*, 506 U.S. 821 (1992).
56. *In re* Union Meeting Partners, 160 B.R. 757, 769 (Bankr. E.D. Pa. 1993). The Supremacy Clause of the United States Constitution mandates that federal laws–the Code's reclassification of the deficiency claim to an unsecured recourse claim–are the supreme laws of the land and are, therefore, unaffected by contradictory state law. U.S. CONST. art. VI, § 2.
57. *Lumber Exch.* 968 F.2d at 649 (noting how claim achieved status is irrelevant in classification issue); Travelers Ins. Co. v. Bryson Properties (*In re* Bryson Properties), 961 F.2d 496, 501-02 (4th Cir.) (holding natural/unnatural distinction highly suspect and untenable), *cert. denied*, 506 U.S. 866 (1992); Hanson v. First Bank N.A., 828 F.2d 1310, 1313 (8th Cir. 1987) (same); *Union Meeting Partners*, 160 B.R. at 769 (noting that Congress enacted § 1111(b) to preclude harsh results that occurred in prior case law).

laws should have been applied differently.[58] It simply means that Congress drafted two different chapters because it intended two different results.[59] This becomes even more apparent upon acknowledging that the issue of gerrymandering only arises in a chapter 11 context.[60] Moreover, the "same as if" language of section 1111(b) is explicit evidence of Congress's intent to treat the claims identically.[61] It would be contrary to established rules of statutory interpretation to read into the statute that Congress intended the language to call for the same treatment except in cases of classification.

In addition, the debtor's point of view is dependent on whether the creditor elects to waive his unsecured claim[62] in favor of asserting an augmented secured claim pursuant to section 1111(b).[63] If that election is made, the issue of gerrymandering will not arise and it is irrelevant whether the nonrecourse deficiency claim would have been substantially similar to the general

---

58. *See* Meltzer, *supra* note 11, at 299 (stating that lender's deficiency claims are equivalent to trade claims and, therefore, prohibition of separate classification is only plausible Code interpretation).
59. Of course, § 1129(a)(7) requires that every creditor receive at least what it would have received in chapter 7. The § 1111(b) unsecured claim tends to dilute the assets available for other unsecured creditors in chapter 11. However, this dilution would occur whether or not the deficiency claim is separately classified. Furthermore in the single asset real estate case, where the property is worth less that than the mortgage, there would normally be nothing available for unsecured creditors if the case had been chapter 7.
60. Travelers Ins. Properties v. Bryson Properties (*In re* Bryson Properties), 961 F.2d 496, 502 (4th Cir.) (holding that when unsecured claims receive same treatment in terms of plan distribution, separate classification on the basis of natural versus unnatural claims is highly suspect), *cert. denied*, 506 U.S. 866 (1992); *see* Meltzer, *supra* note 11, at 299 (stating that recourse rights of a lender's deficiency claim arise only in chapter 11).
61. 11 U.S.C. § 1111(b)(1)(A) (1994); *see* Carlson, *supra* note 9, at 582-83.
62. *In re* Gato Realty Trust Corp., 183 B.R. 15, 21 (Bankr. D. Mass. 1995) (concluding that since secured party did not make § 1111(b) election, unsecured deficiency claims retain same legal priority as general unsecured claims); *In re* Barney & Carey Co., 170 B.R. 17, 24 (Bankr. D. Mass. 1994) (same).
63. 11 U.S.C. § 1111(b) (1994).

unsecured claims. If, however, the election is not made, the mere fact that the option is available does not change the claim's legal status.[64]

2. Effect of Creditors' Voting Incentives

The undersecured creditor typically would prefer foreclosing[65] on the secured property rather than allowing the debtor to attempt reorganization.[66] In an effort to terminate the automatic stay and proceed with the preferred foreclosure, the undersecured creditor will often notify the court of its intention to vote against the plan.[67] On the other hand, the general unsecured creditors favor the confirmation of a reorganization plan because of the possibility that they would recover a greater percentage of their claim.[68]

Debtors argue that this difference in voting incentive between the general unsecured creditors and the undersecured creditor is enough of a difference in legal status to separately classify their claims.[69] Debtors base their argument

---

64. *See supra* note 57.
65. *See supra* notes 13-14 and accompanying text (discussing secured creditors preference for liquidation).
66. *In re* Woodbrook Assocs., 19 F.3d 312, 318 (7th Cir. 1994) (noting that even if general unsecured claimant has strong incentive to vote to accept plan, undersecured creditor may foreclose); *John Hancock Mut. Life Ins. Co.*, 987 F.2d at 161 (same); *In re* Gato Realty Trust Corp., 183 B.R. 15, 21 (Bankr. D. Mass. 1995) (same); *In re* Rivers End Apartments, Ltd., 167 B.R. 470, 487 (Bankr. S.D. Ohio 1994); *see also* Meltzer, *supra* note 11, at 297.
67. 11 U.S.C. § 362 (1994); *In re* 266 Washington Assocs., 141 B.R. 275, 281-85 (Bankr. E.D.N.Y. 1992) (holding lift stay motion requires determination whether plan has realistic chance of being confirmed); *In re* 499 W. Warren St. Assocs., Ltd. Partnership, 151 B.R. 307, 310 (Bankr. N.D.N.Y. 1992) (same); *In re* Ashgrove Apartments, 121 B.R. 752, 756 (Bankr. S.D. Ohio 1990) (same).
68. *Woodbrook*, 19 F.3d at 318 (noting that general unsecured creditors may receive nothing upon a foreclosure); *John Hancock*, 987 F.2d at 161 (same); *Rivers End*, 167 B.R. at 487 (same).
69. *Woodbrook*, 19 F.3d at 318 (commenting that trade creditors are usually more willing to agree to reorganization than chapter 7 disbursements); *John Hancock*, 987 F.2d at 161 (same); *Gato*, 183 B.R. at 21 (same); *Rivers End*, 167 B.R. at 487 (same). Trade creditors are usually very willing to confirm a plan because they will at least get a portion of their claim under a chapter 11

on section 1129(a)(10)'s one impaired class approval requirement.[70] They contend that it was not intended to give creditors a veto power, but instead merely to require evidence of creditor support for a debtor's reorganization plan.[71] The intent of section 1129(a)(10), however, was to ensure that the debtor could not saddle all the creditors with a plan that received no acceptance from any impaired class.[72] Further, the voting incentive argument finds no explicit support in the Code and is inconsistent with economic reality.[73] The clear majority of claim holders–whether secured, undersecured, or unsecured–vote in accordance with their overall economic interests and not for the best interests of the creditor pool.[74] "Absent bad faith or illegality, the Code is not concerned with a claimholder's reason for voting one way or the other."[75] Further, it should not be the role of the bankruptcy judge to determine the debtor's voting incentive when it is "the nature of the claims"[76] and not the claimholder that should be in focus.[77]

---

reorganization as compared to the disbursements under § 726 of chapter 7. *See* 11 U.S.C. § 726(a)(2) (1994) (providing that all priority creditors are paid off before general unsecured creditors can be paid).

70. *See supra* note 3.
71. *Woodbrook*, 19 F.3d at 318 (claiming approval requirement of § 1129(a)(10) is just to establish creditor support of plan); *In re* SM 104 Ltd., 160 B.R. 202, 218 (Bankr. S.D. Fla. 1993) (same).
72. *In re* Polytherm Indus., Inc., 33 B.R. 823, 835 (W.D. Wis. 1983).
73. John Hancock Mut. Life Ins. Co. v. Route 37 Business Park Assocs., 987 F.2d 154, 161 (3d Cir. 1993) (rejecting theory of creditor approval through § 1129(a)(10) for good faith).
74. *John Hancock*, 987 F.2d at 161.
75. *Id.*; *In re* 500 Fifth Ave. Assocs., 148 B.R. 1010, 1020 (Bankr. S.D.N.Y.), *aff'd*, No. 93 Civ. 844, 1993 WL 316183 (S.D.N.Y. May 21, 1993) (concluding Code does not turn creditor into fiduciary and creditor is "free to vote [its] . . . self interest").
76. H.R. REP. NO. 595, 95th Cong., 1st Sess. 406 (1977), *reprinted in* 1978 U.S.C.C.A.N. 5963, 6362; S. REP. NO. 989, 95th Cong., 2d Sess. 118 (1978), *reprinted in* 1978 U.S.C.C.A.N. 5787, 5904.
77. Meltzer, *supra* note 11, at 299-301; *see also* 5 COLLIER, *supra* note 25, § 1122.03[1][b], at 1122-28 (discussing role of bankruptcy judge and nature of creditor in chapter 11 proceeding).

3. Imaginary Anomalies

Debtors also contend that classifying undersecured claims with general unsecured claims causes an anomaly in the application of section 1111(b).[78] In order to treat the entire claim of the undersecured creditor as secured, section 1111(b) requires the election to be made by the class of which such claim is a part.[79] Debtors contend that if undersecured deficiency claims and general unsecured claims were classified together, general unsecured creditors would be required to vote on whether the election should be made.[80] This would allow the general unsecured creditors to deny the undersecured creditor the ability to make the election if the general unsecured creditors hold the voting majority within their class.[81] This is a result, debtors argue, that is clearly not what Congress intended.[82]

This argument, however, is untenable. The election under section 1111(b) is not a two step process. Initially, there exists an undersecured claim. At the time the debtor files for bankruptcy, the creditor can elect to have the deficiency portion of the undersecured claim treated as a secured claim *or not*. The deficiency claim does not become unsecured, and thus part of the

---

78. *In re* Woodbrook Assocs., 19 F.3d 312, 319 (7th Cir. 1994) (finding that anomalies exist in application of § 1111(b)); *In re* Gato Realty Trust Corp., 183 B.R. 15, 22 (Bankr. D. Mass. 1995) (noting that where deficiency claim is nonrecourse, enforced classification with other general unsecured claims grants deficiency claim power to block confirmation); *In re* SM 104 Ltd., 160 B.R. 202, 219 (Bankr. S.D. Fla. 1993) (concluding that anomalous result would be obtained because plan could not pass best interests of creditors test).

79. *Woodbrook*, 19 F.3d at 319 (concluding § 1111(b)(1)(A)(i)'s requirement that election be made by members of unsecured creditor class allows general unsecured creditors to block election); *Gato*, 183 B.R. at 21 (same); *SM 104*, 160 B.R. at 220 (same).

80. *Woodbrook*, 19 F.3d at 319 (holding general unsecured creditors ability to block approval of § 1111(b)(2) election makes legal rights of claims substantially different); *Gato*, 183 B.R. at 22 (same); *SM 104*, 160 B.R. at 220 (same). *Contra In re* D & W Realty Corp., 165 B.R. 127, 128 (S.D.N.Y. 1994) (holding right of election belongs to the secured portion of the claim).

81. 11 U.S.C. § 1111(b)(1)(A)(i) (1994); FED. R. BANKR. P. 3014; *Woodbrook*, 19 F.3d at 319; *Gato*, 183 B.R. at 22; *D & W Realty*, 165 B.R. at 128; *SM 104*, 160 B.R. at 220.

82. *Woodbrook*, 19 F.3d at 319; *Gato*, 183 B.R. at 21; *SM 104*, 160 B.R. at 220.

unsecured class, then secured again if the creditor elects. It will simply become unsecured or if the undersecured creditor elects, remain secured. Therefore, the general unsecured creditors have absolutely no control over the section 1111(b) election process.

Additionally, section 1111(b)(1)(A)(i) requires a vote in favor of the election by two-thirds in amount and more than half in number. If the general unsecured creditors could control this vote, it would not make sense to argue it in the first place. The debtor could confirm a plan without separately classifying the section 1111(b) claim and the gerrymandering issue would not arise.[83] Further, section 1111(b)(1)(A), refers to "a claim [that is] secured by a lien on property of the [debtor's] estate."[84] By definition, a deficiency claim is not secured by a lien.[85] Therefore, section 1111(b), refers to the entire claim of the undersecured creditor and is not concerned with the unsecured portion of the secured creditor's claim.[86] Furthermore, the suggestion that Congress intended that a group of unsecured creditors unrelated to the undersecured creditor should be able to decide on whether the undersecured creditor elects a full or recourse claim simply makes no sense.

4. Inconsistency Within Chapter 11

Debtors have also argued that a rule against separate classification of general unsecured claims and undersecured deficiency claims creates anomalies within chapter 11.[87] "Section 1129(a)(7) requires that, for

---

83. 11 U.S.C. § 1111(b)(1)(A)(i) (1994).
84. *Id.* § 1111(b)(1)(A).
85. *In re* D & W Realty Corp., 165 B.R. 127, 128 (S.D.N.Y. 1994). A deficiency claim is the difference in amount of debt and value of collateral. *In re* 500 Fifth Ave. Assocs., 148 B.R. 1010, 1016 (Bankr. S.D.N.Y.), *aff'd*, No. 93 Civ. 844, 1993 WL 316183 (S.D.N.Y. May 21, 1993).
86. *D & W Realty*, 165 B.R. at 128.
87. *In re* Gato Realty Trust Corp., 183 B.R. 15, 20 (Bankr. D. Mass. 1995) (stating that "courts warn that the legal disparities between § 1111(b) claimants and general unsecured creditors could lead to anomalous results when other Bankruptcy Code provisions are implicated"); *In re* Rivers End Apartments, Ltd., 167 B.R. 470, 477 (Bankr. S.D. Ohio 1994) (recognizing inherent difference between chapter 11 and 13 and that § "1122 as incorporated into § 1129(a) is somewhat different from [§] 1322(b)"); David G. Epstein & Christopher Fuller, *Chapter 11 and 13 of the Bankruptcy Code-Observation*

confirmation of a plan where a holder of a claim or interest in an impaired class rejects the plan, each claimant must `receive or retain . . . property of value, as of the effective date of the plan, that is not less than the amount . . . receive[d] or retain[ed] if the debtor were liquidated under chapter 7.'"[88] Therefore, even though the nonrecourse deficiency claim is worthless under chapter 7 of the Code, it is argued that, pursuant to section 1129(A)(7), the undersecured creditor may nevertheless block confirmation unless it receives a payment equal to that of the general unsecured creditors.[89]

This argument, however, assumes that there would have been assets available for distribution in the chapter 7. But, in a single asset real estate case, where the mortgage is greater than the collateral, there would normally

---

on Using Case Authority from One of the Chapter in Proceedings Under the Other, 38 VAND. L. REV. 901, 923 (1985) (contrasting debtor treatment based on classification in chapters 11 and 13). The author recognizes that classification is different and has "greater significance in chapter 11 than in chapter 13 [because in] only chapter 11, a debtor might try to classify claims to manipulate the creditor acceptance process." *Id.* This is in contrast to chapter 13 because creditors do not vote on the plan and judges focus on "individual claims rather than classes of claims." *Id.*

88. 11 U.S.C. § 1129(a)(7) (1994); *Woodbrook*, 19 F.3d at 319 (citing 11 U.S.C. § 1129(a)(7) (1994)); *see also* Meltzer, *supra* note 11, at 299 (noting that confirmation requirements can only occur within confines of chapter 11); Rusch, *supra* note 23, at 49 (detailing § 1129(b) requirements to confirm plan).

89. *Woodbrook*, 19 F.3d at 319. What the court in *Woodbrook* may have been saying is that under § 1129(a)(7), general unsecured claimants must receive, at a minimum, what they would have received under chapter 7, and the addition of a § 1111(b) unsecured claim in chapter 11 only, might reduce the amount available to the other unsecured creditors. Thus, it would be necessary to increase the amount payable to the unsecured creditors in chapter 11 to meet the § 1129(a)(7) requirement. Such a divergence between the creditors in the same class, however, would be prohibited by § 1123(a)(4). This argument, however, assumes that there would have been assets for distribution in the chapter 7. *See In re* SM 104 Ltd., 160 B.R. 202, 220 (Bankr. S.D. Fla. 1993) (reasoning that result derives from § 1123(a)(4) requirement of equality of claims in a class); Carlson, *supra* note 9, at 584-85 (noting § 1129 requires § 1111(b) unsecured claims are entitled to a minimum of zero because that is what they would receive in chapter 7).

be no assets for the unsecured creditors to receive, so there is no reason that they should receive more in a chapter 11 under section 1129(a)(7).

C. Policy Considerations

1. Section 1129(a)(10) and the New Value Exception

Undersecured creditors, in opposition to separate classification, argue that they generally hold the largest claim[90] and should be given a proportionate power in the plan confirmation voting process.[91] To permit gerrymandering, they argue, effectively disenfranchises them of their legislatively created right, under section 1111(b), to vote on the plan as part of the unsecured class.[92]

---

90. *In re* Overland Park Merchandise Mart Partnership, 167 B.R. 647, 653 (Bankr. D. Kan. 1994) (stating that undersecured creditor has significantly larger claim than unsecured creditors); John Hancock Mut. Life Ins. Co. v. Roswell-Hannover Joint Venture (*In re* Roswell-Hannover Joint Venture), 149 B.R. 1014, 1022 (Bankr. N.D. Ga. 1992) (stating that "disenfranchising largest creditor should be carefully scrutinized").

91. *In re* Dean & Carson, 166 B.R. 949, 953-54 (Bankr. D.N.M. 1994) (stating that debtor's largest creditor is disenfranchised because of separate classification and small unsecured creditor is given voting power disproportionate to its interest in bankruptcy estate); *In re* D & W Realty Corp., 165 B.R. 127, 129 (S.D.N.Y. 1994) (recognizing that undersecured creditor has bigger interest in debtor's assets and reasoning that "[t]o give a small group of unsecured creditors voting power that is so disproportionate to their interest . . . does not comply with [§] 1129(b)(1) requirement that a plan does not discriminate unfairly and is fair and equitable"); One Times Square Assocs. Ltd. Partnership v. Banque Nationale De Paris (*In re* One Times Square Assocs. Ltd. Partnership) 165 B.R. 773, 777 (S.D.N.Y.) (stating "creditors with large claims deserve greater voice"), *aff'd*, 41 F.3d 1502 (2d Cir. 1994), *cert. denied*, 115 S. Ct. 1107 (1995); *In re* 266 Washington Assocs., 141 B.R. 275, 286 (Bankr. E.D.N.Y.) (stating that separate classification would disenfranchise debtor's only "meaningful creditor" and would destroy effect of creditor's voting rights), *aff'd*, 147 B.R. 827 (E.D.N.Y. 1992).

92. Boston Post Rd. Ltd. Partnership v. FDIC, 21 F.3d 477, 483 (2d Cir. 1994) (concluding "to disenfranchise the overwhelmingly largest creditor through artificial classification is simply inconsistent with the principles underlying the Bankruptcy Code" and "key premise of the Code is that the creditors holding

They point out that Congress's purpose behind the section 1111(b) conversion was to provide the undersecured nonrecourse creditor with a recourse deficiency claim so that the undersecured creditor could participate in the unsecured creditor class voting process.[93] Allowing separate classification, would, thus, render meaningless the purpose of the deficiency claim.[94]

---

greater debt should have a comparably greater voice in reorganization"), *cert. denied*, 115 S. Ct. 897 (1995); John Hancock Mut. Life Ins. Co. v. Route 37 Business Park Assocs., 987 F.2d 154, 160 (3d Cir. 1993) (same); Phoenix Mut. Life Ins. Co. v. Greystone III Joint Venture (*In re* Greystone III Joint Venture), 948 F.2d 134, 141 (5th Cir. 1992) (stating disenfranchisement of undersecured creditor is "sanctioned neither by the Code nor by case law"); *In re* Dean & Carson, 166 B.R. 949, 953 (Bankr. D.N.M. 1994) (reasoning separate classification of trade creditors and undersecured creditor undermines purpose of § 1111(b), which is meant to allow undersecured creditor to vote among class of unsecured creditors on whether to confirm the plan); *D & W Realty*, 165 B.R. at 129 (separate classification would effectively "disenfranchise" undersecured creditor from their right to vote, in contravention of Congress's intent).

93. *Boston Post Rd.*, 21 F.3d at 483 (§ 1111(b) allows undersecured creditor "to weigh in its vote" with other unsecured creditors); *Greystone*, 995 F.2d at 1280 (stating that Congress did not intend that election under § 1111(b) be "meaningless" and reasoning that undersecured creditor needs deficiency claim as "leverage to persuade the debtor to consider a more reasonable settlement"); Lumber Exch. Bldg. Ltd. Partnership v. Mut. Life Ins. Co., 968 F.2d 647, 649-50 (8th Cir. 1992) (stating separate classification eliminates benefit of recourse status created by Code); *In re* Overland Park Merchandise Mart Partnership, L.P., 167 B.R. 647, 653 (Bankr. D. Kan. 1994) (finding that purpose of treating nonrecourse claim as if recourse is to give "undersecured nonrecourse creditor a share in distributions to unsecured creditors"); *Dean & Carson*, 166 B.R. at 953 (same); Meltzer, *supra* note 11, at 304 (stating that "the primary strategic advantage given to an undersecured creditor by not making the election [and choosing instead to keep its legislatively created deficiency claim]–namely the right to control the voting of the undersecured creditor class–would essentially disappear"); 5 COLLIER, *supra* note 25, § 1122.04 at 1122-24 (discussing § 1111(b) and recognizing that Code protects secured creditors) (citations omitted).

94. *Boston Post Rd.*, 21 F.3d at 483 (holding separate classification nullifies benefit behind § 1111(b)); *Greystone*, 948 F.2d at 139-40 (noting separate

Debtors have responded that requiring joint classification of all substantially similar claims disenfranchises the general unsecured creditors[95] since the undersecured creditor will inevitably control the outcome of the class's vote.[96] The undersecured creditor will reject the plan and the general unsecured creditors will be unable to have their class approve the plan.[97]

In addition, debtors argue that the undersecured creditor is not disenfranchised when separately classified from the general unsecured creditors.[98] The undersecured creditor, initially, retains the power to vote on

---

classification renders right to vote in unsecured class meaningless); *D & W Realty*, 165 B.R. at 129 (same).

95. *See infra* note 97.

96. *See supra* notes 11-14 and accompanying text. *Contra In re* 500 Fifth Ave. Assocs., 148 B.R. 1010, 1020 (Bankr. S.D.N.Y.), *aff'd*, No. 93 Civ. 844, 1993 WL 316183 (S.D.N.Y. May 21, 1993). The court stated, in dicta, that "where the deficiency claim [of the undersecured creditor] is small or where the deficiency claim is not so small, but there are junior mortgagees with claims of a sufficient magnitude [meeting section 1129(a)(10)] would still be possible." *Id.*

97. Teamsters Nat'l Freight Ind. Negotiating Comm., Inc. v. U.S. Truck Co. (*In re* U.S. Truck Co.), 800 F.2d 581, 587 (6th Cir. 1986) (debtor arguing that placing undersecured creditor with general unsecured creditor keeps court from hearing plan that "a significant group of creditors with similar interests have accepted"); *In re* Overland Park Merchandise Mart Partnership, 167 B.R. 647, 651-53 (Bankr. D. Kan. 1994) ("Joint classification" disenfranchises unsecured creditors and allows undersecured creditors to block "consideration under [§] 1129(b) of a plan general unsecured creditors may want to accept."); *In re* Rivers End Apartments, Ltd., 167 B.R. 470, 478 (Bankr. S.D. Ohio 1994) (stating unsecured creditors are disenfranchised through § 1111(b)).

98. *Overland*, 167 B.R. at 652 (noting joint classification would enable undersecured creditor to control class and preclude class from accepting plan). In effect, therefore, the undersecured creditor is being divested of only the power to veto the plan and prevent its confirmation. Principal Mut. Life Ins. Co. v. Baldwin Park Towne Ctr., Ltd. (*In re* Baldwin Park Towne Ctr., Ltd.), 171 B.R. 374, 377 (Bankr. C.D. Cal. 1994) (stating Code does not give creditor veto power over plan simply because of size of claim); *In re* 500 Fifth Ave. Assocs., 148 B.R. 1010, 1020 (Bankr. S.D.N.Y.) (debtor arguing that lumping undersecured creditor's "enormous" deficiency claim with unsecured creditor would effectively give undersecured creditor veto power and preclude confirmation of plan), *aff'd*, No. 93 Civ. 844, 1993 WL 316183 (S.D.N.Y.

the plan within its class. This negative vote for its separate class prevents plan confirmation under section 1129(a) since the debtor is unable to obtain the approval of all the classes.[99] Furthermore, if the debtor then attempts to cram down the plan, pursuant to section 1129(b),[100] over the undersecured creditor's objection, the undersecured creditor will obtain cramdown rights.[101] Section 1129(b) provides the undersecured creditor with protections, it requires that the plan not discriminate unfairly and that it is fair and equitable.[102]

May 21, 1993); *see also Rivers End*, 167 B.R. at 479 (reasoning veto power might discourage beneficial reorganization negotiations).

99. *See* 11 U.S.C. § 1129(a)(8) (1994) (stating that "[w]ith respect to each class of claims or interests–such class has accepted the plan").

100. 11 U.S.C. §§ 1126, 1129(b)(1) (1994) (requiring only one accepting class of claims); *see* Meltzer, *supra* note 11, at 303-04 (discussing § 1129(a)(10) which requires at least one impaired class to approve plan and noting that general unsecured creditors able to become accepting class without considering separately classified undersecured creditor).

101. Heartland Fed. Savs. & Loan Ass'n v. Briscoe Enters., Ltd., II (*In re* Briscoe Enters., Ltd., II) 994 F.2d 1160, 1167 (5th Cir.) (finding requirement that cramdown be fair and equitable), *cert. denied*, 114 S. Ct. 550 (1993); Bustop Shelters, Inc. v. Classic Homes, Inc., 914 F.2d 810, 814 (6th Cir. 1990) (stating that if debtor allowed to separately classify creditor then cramdown provisions apply); *Overland*, 167 B.R. at 652 (reasoning if separately classified undersecured creditors vote against plan, then plan proponent will attempt cramdown); Carlson, *supra* note 9, at 592 (stating that "[b]y voting `no' the [undersecured] creditor obtains cramdown rights, which is the true significance of voting"). For a general discussion of the cramdown procedure and protections afforded the undersecured creditor see MICHAEL T. MADISON & ROBERT M. ZINMAN, MODERN REAL ESTATE FINANCING, A TRANSACTIONAL APPROACH 1094-99 (1991) (discussing undersecured creditor's right to absolute priority or "indubitable equivalent" of its claim before cramdown will be approved).

102. 11 U.S.C. § 1129(b)(1)(A) (1994); Heartland Fed. Savs. & Loan Ass'n v. Briscoe Enters., Ltd., II, 994 F.2d 1160, 1165 (5th Cir.) (stating that Code is primary source of creditor protection), *cert. denied*, 114 S. Ct. 550 (1993); Principal Mut. Life Ins. Co. v. Baldwin Park Towne Ctr., Ltd. (*In re* Baldwin Park Towne Ctr., Ltd.), 171 B.R. 374, 377 (Bankr. C.D. Cal. 1994) (stating plan provides protections); *In re* Overland Park Merchandise Mart Partnership, L.P., 167 B.R. 647, 651 (Bankr. D. Kan. 1994) (same); Madison, *supra* note 94, at 1094-99 (same); Neuger, *supra* note 2, at 582 (reasoning that judiciary

Perhaps, however, the real issue and concern of undersecured creditors is that if a reorganization is permitted to proceed merely because a debtor gerrymandered the classes, various sections of the Code,[103] such as sections 1111(b),[104] 1129(b),[105] and in particular, 1129(a)(10),[106] would be undermined. As a general policy, when interpreting an ambiguous statute that is subject to two interpretations, it should not be read to produce an "unreasonable result."[107] Thus, an interpretation of section 1122 that permits gerrymandering is unreasonable if in the process it undermines sections of the Code.

Undermining section 1129(a)(10) would preclude the undersecured creditor from being able to cut the plan confirmation off prior to a cramdown. This ability is of significant concern to undersecured creditors because although the undersecured creditor would receive protections under section

---

taking it upon themselves to guard against debtor abuse is unnecessary since § 1129 has protective provisions).

103. *In re* D & W Realty, Corp., 165 B.R. 127, 129 (Bankr. S.D.N.Y. 1994) (stating separate classification would undermine "democratic process intrinsic to [c]hapter 11") (citation omitted); *500 Fifth Ave.*, 148 B.R. at 1020 (same); Thomas C. Given & Linda J. Phillips, *Equality in the Eye of the Beholder-Classification of Claims and Interests in Chapter 11 Reorganizations*, 43 OHIO ST. L.J. 735, 765 (1982) (stating that "improper classification may circumvent the voting requirements of [c]hapter 11").

104. *See Boston Post Rd*, 21 F.3d at 483 (stating that chapter 11 may best be served by allowing "the largest unsecured claims to have a significant degree of . . . participation in the reorganization process" also separate classification would undermine 1111(b) election); *In re* Dean & Carson, 166 B.R. 949, 953-54 (stating separate classification "would upset the critical balance of confirmation requirements [and would] . . . undermine the purpose" of § 1111(b)).

105. *See supra* notes 108-12 and accompanying text.

106. John Hancock Mut. Life Ins. Co. v. Route 37 Business Park Assocs., 987 F.2d 154, 159 (3d Cir. 1993) (stating if debtor could gerrymander the classes § 1129(a)(8) & (a)(10) "would be seriously undermined"); *In re* Bloomingdale Partners, 170 B.R. 984, 993 (Bankr. N.D. Ill. 1994) (finding that separate classification would circumvent requirement of § 1129(a)(10) and render it "a mere ministerial requirement"); Meltzer, *supra* note 11, at 302-03 (separate classification allows circumvention of § 1129(a)(10)).

107. United States v. Ron Pair Enters., Inc., 489 U.S. 235, 242 (1989) (citation omitted); Shapiro v. United States, 335 U.S. 1, 31 (1948) (citation omitted); *see also supra* note 35 (discussing rules of statutory interpretation).

1129(b), the new value exception to the absolute priority rule undermines section 1129(b)'s "fair and equitable" requirement.[108] Fair and equitable has been interpreted to require absolute priority,[109] which means that no junior interest or claim may be satisfied before the senior creditors' claims.[110] Pursuant to the new value exception, however, a debtor, generally a junior interest, may retain an interest in property so long as the debtor makes a new contribution of money that is "substantial and constitute[s] reasonably equivalent value,"[111] even though the claims of senior creditors are not being satisfied in full.[112]

2. Review of the Plan Proponent's Motives

A number of courts have not adopted a flat rule prohibiting separate classification.[113] Instead, they have used their discretion and inherent authority

---

108. *In re* Woodbrook Assocs., 19 F.3d 312, 320 (7th Cir. 1994); Steelcase Inc. v. Johnston (*In re* Johnston), 21 F.3d 323, 328 (9th Cir. 1994); Neuger, *supra* note 2, at 584 (stating that obvious purpose of separate classification is to circumvent "absolute priority rule" encompassed in § 1129(b)'s "fair and equitable test").
109. Case v. Los Angeles Lumber Prods. Co., 308 U.S. 106, 114-18 (1939) (recognizing judicial interpretation of "fair and equitable" that requires absolute priority). *See* Hon. Roger M. Whelan & William W. Senft, *The legislative Response to Single Asset Real Estate Bankruptcies: Critical Analysis and Some Suggestions*, 1 AM. BANKR. INST. L. REV. 157, 176-77 (1993) (discussing evolution and definition of absolute priority).
110. *Los Angeles Lumber*, 308 U.S. at 118-19; 11 U.S.C. § 1129(b)(1)(B)(ii) (1994). This section states that "the holder of any claim or interest that is junior to the claims of such class will not receive of retain under the plan on account of such junior claim or interest any property." *Id.*
111. *Woodbrook*, 19 F.3d at 319; *Baldwin Park*, 171 B.R. at 378; MacDonald, *supra* note 20, at 73-74.
112. MacDonald, *supra* note 20, at 69-70.
113. Boston Post Rd. Ltd. Partnership v. FDIC, 21 F.3d 477, 482 (2d Cir. 1994) (stating that separate classification of "substantially similar" claims may be undertaken for reasons independent of motivation to secure vote of impaired class), *cert. denied*, 115 S. Ct. 897 (1995); Phoenix Mut. Life Ins. Co. v. Greystone III Joint Venture (*In re* Greystone III Joint Venture), 995 F.2d 1274, 1279 (5th Cir.) (concluding "[§] 1122(a) permits classification of `substantially

to allow debtors[114] an opportunity to prove that their reasons for separate classification are independent from their motivation to secure a class's vote.[115]

Debtors suggest, for example, that their separate classification is justified if they can show a good business reason.[116] The business reason most often

---

similar' claims in different classes, such classification may only be undertaken for reasons independent of the debtor's motivation to secure the vote of an impaired, assenting class of claims"), *vacated on other grounds*, 995 F.2d 1284 (5th Cir.), *cert. denied*, 506 U.S. 821 (1992); *Briscoe*, 994 F.2d at 1167 (requiring good business reason for separate classification) (citation omitted); Lumber Exch. Bldg. Ltd. Partnership v. Mut. Life Ins. Co. (*In re* Lumber Exch. Ltd. Partnership), 968 F.2d 647, 648 (8th Cir. 1992) (requiring reason other than creating assenting impaired class) (citation omitted); Travelers Ins. Co. v. Bryson Properties (*In re* Bryson Properties), 961 F.2d 496, 502 (4th Cir. 1992) (stating debtor does not have unlimited discretion); Bustop Shelters, Inc. v. Classic Homes, Inc., 914 F.2d 810, 813 (6th Cir. 1990) (reasoning that court must review case to see if trial or lower court abused discretion in rejecting separate classification); Olympia & York Fla. Equity Corp. v. Bank of New York (*In re* Holywell Corp.), 913 F.2d 873, 880 (11th Cir. 1990) (stating there must be some limitation on debtor's ability to classify); Granada Wines, Inc. v. New England Teamsters & Trucking Ind. Pension Fund, 748 F.2d 42, 46 (1st Cir. 1984) (must be a difference in legal character); *Baldwin Park*, 171 B.R. at 376 (most courts look to see if business or economic reason exists to separately classify); *In re* Barney & Carey Co., 170 B.R. 17, 24 (Bankr. D. Mass. 1994) (stating need for legitimate business reason) (citation omitted); *In re* Bloomingdale Partners, 170 B.R. 984, 990 (Bankr. N.D. Ill. 1994) (noting separate classification only where legal difference exists); Oxford Life Ins. Co. v. Tucson Self-Storage, Inc. (*In re* Tucson Self-Storage, Inc.), 166 B.R. 892, 897 (Bankr. 9th Cir. 1994) (concluding that to separately classify need independent reason); *In re* D & W Realty Corp., 165 B.R. 127, 130 (S.D.N.Y. 1994) (same); 5 COLLIER, *supra* note 25, ¶ 1122.03 [4], at 1122-11 (stating that classes may be separately classified if reasonable).

114. John Hancock Mut. Life Ins. Co. v. Route 37 Business Park Assocs., 987 F.2d 154, 162 (3d Cir. 1993) (stating that debtor required to offer reasons behind classification scheme); *Baldwin Park*, 171 B.R. at 377 (same) (citation omitted); *Barney*, 170 B.R. at 24 (same); *Tuscon*, 166 B.R. at 898 (separate classification denied when debtor offered no business or economic justification for separate classification).

115. *See infra* notes 116-22 and accompanying text.

116. *Greystone*, 995 F.2d at 1280 (rejecting "good business reason" because

raised is that the debtor fears that unless the general unsecured creditors (generally suppliers) are paid they will no longer sell supplies to the debtor. Thus, even if the reorganization is successful, it will inevitably fail with no suppliers.[117] Therefore, in an attempt to give the suppliers special treatment, the debtor would separately classify them. Courts, however, have rejected this argument because bankruptcy no longer carries the same stigma that in the past might have indefinitely scarred a business's reputation.[118] To properly support the argument, the debtor would at least have to show that the industry has a "limited market for goods and services"[119] and that the debtor would be unable to receive them if the trade creditors did not receive "preferential treatment under the plan."[120] In addition, the debtor would have to overcome the burden of showing that their plan does not "discriminate unfairly . . . with respect to each class . . . that is impaired under, and has not accepted, the plan."[121]

In addition to the business reason, debtors raise the argument that they have a legitimate reason for separate classification. These legitimate reasons include distinctions, such as section 1111(b), that this Chapter has previously discussed and shown to have been rejected by many courts as insufficient.[122]

---

unsupported); Neuger, *supra* note 2, at 585 (discussing "business purpose").

117. Jones, *supra* note 2, at 634 (discussing maintenance of relationship with trade creditors as a reason debtors have used to justify separate classification); Neuger, *supra* note 2, at 585 (noting that reorganized business will fail without business from suppliers). In single asset cases, however, this fear is not very real since management skills as opposed to suppliers are what is necessary. *See infra* notes 136-37.

118. *Greystone*, 995 F.2d at 1280 (rejecting "good business reason" as support for separate classification); *John Hancock*, 987 F.2d at 162 (rejecting business purpose); Neuger, *supra* note 2, at 585 (stating that bankruptcy is no longer scarlet letter of business world).

119. *Greystone*, 995 F.2d at 1281 (stating that bankruptcy courts finding of "good business reasons for separate classification [is unsupported] and must be set aside as clearly erroneous").

120. *Id.* However, there is no "limited market for goods and services" in a single asset bankruptcy. *See infra* note 136.

121. 11 U.S.C. § 1129(b)(1) (1994).

122. Lumber Exch. Bldg. Ltd. Partnership v. Mut. Life Ins. Co. (*In re* Lumber Exch. Bldg. Ltd. Partnership), 968 F.2d 647, 648 (8th Cir. 1992) (finding that debtor needs reason independent from desire to secure vote of at least one impaired

Even in cases where courts have allowed separate classification based on a legitimate reason, they have been quick to confine their holding to the specific facts of their case.[123] Moreover, courts that have recognized the possibility of a legitimate reason have not defined this nebulous concept and have generally rejected the classification scheme.[124]

Unfortunately, in conducting a subjective review, courts have sacrificed judicial economy.[125] Instead of defining the scope of their review they have

---

class); Travelers Ins. Co. v. Bryson Properties (*In re* Bryson Properties), 961 F.2d 496, 502 (4th Cir.) (stating that § 1111(b) distinction does not justify separate classification), *cert. denied*, 506 U.S. 866 (1992); *see supra* Part B.

123. Heartland Fed. Savs. & Loan Ass'n v. Briscoe Enters., Ltd., II (*In re* Briscoe Enters., Ltd., II) 994 F.2d 1160, 1167 (5th Cir.) (emphasizing narrowness of its holding that separate classification justified where City of Fort Worth shown to have distinct interests from other creditors), *cert. denied*, 114 S. Ct. 550 (1993); Teamsters Nat'l Freight Ind. Negotiating Comm., Inc. v. U.S. Truck Co. (*In re* U.S. Truck Co.), 800 F.2d 581, 587 (6th Cir. 1986) (concluding that separate classification reasonable where debtor showed claims differed substantially because largest creditor, employees' union representative, had different stake in reorganized company's future and had other means of protecting its claim); LW-SP2, L.P. v. Krisch Realty Assocs., L.P. (*In re* Krisch Realty Assocs., L.P.), 174 B.R. 914, 919 (Bankr. W.D. Va. 1994) (finding that parties had, prepetition, contemplated difference among claims so separate classification justified).

124. *Greystone*, 995 F.2d at 1274, 1279 (concluding that separate classification may be undertaken "for reasons independent of the debtor's motivation to" confirm plan, but nevertheless finding that plan "impermissibly classified like creditors"); *Lumber Exch.*, 968 F.2d at 648-49 (recognizing separate classification may at times be justified); *Bryson*, 961 F.2d at 501-02 (same); *Granada*, 748 F.2d at 46 (same); *In re* Barney & Carey Co., 170 B.R. 17, 24 (Bankr. D. Mass. 1994) (same).

125. Bustop Shelters, Inc. v. Classic Homes, Inc., 914 F.2d 810, 812 (6th Cir. 1990) (stating that it is difficult to determine whether the debtor "has used its power to properly classify the claims"); *In re* Bloomingdale Partners, 170 B.R. 984, 996 (Bankr. N.D. Ill. 1994) (reasoning that applying a reasonableness standard leaves more questions unanswered because it is unclear "what aspects of a classification scheme cause it to be reasonable or unreasonable"); *Briscoe*, 138 B.R. at 809 (stating that objective rather than subjective intent should determine whether plan proposed in good faith); 5 COLLIER, *supra* note 25, at 1122-4 (stating that "line of demarcation between a proper and improper

created an environment in which a uniform decision on gerrymandering will never be realized.[126] Courts and commentators have already noted the evolution of different standards of judicial review that are being applied in the bankruptcy courts when issues of separate classification arise.[127] In this type

---

division is not easily drawn") (citation omitted); William Blair, *Classification of Unsecured Claims in Chapter 11 Reorganization*, 58 AM. BANKR. L.J. 197, 210 (1984) (finding that "considerable detail of [§] 1129 suggests that Congress intended the confirmation requirements to rely principally on objective standards").

126. *In re* Woodbrook Assocs., 19 F.3d 312, 318 (7th Cir. 1994). The court stated that, with respect to *Greystone's* rule prohibiting gerrymandering:

> The "one clear rule" is not easy to apply since it is not about "classifying similar claims"; it is about the debtor's purpose. Similarity is not a precise relationship, and the elements by which we judge similarity or resemblance shifts from time to time in bankruptcy.

Id. The court went on to discuss how some courts had allowed separate classification on the basis of the "perceived legal distinction because of § 1111(b). A majority of the circuits, however, have rejected that distinction." *Id.* at 318; *Bustop*, 914 F.2d at 813. The court in *Bustop* stated that they "have noted before the difficulty of determining whether a debtor has used its power to classify claims improperly," and that "the legislative history of the Code provides little assistance in determining what limits there are to segregating claims." *Id.* The court, therefore, concluded that unless there is a requirement to classify similar claims together debtors will continue to find ways to gerrymander. *Id.*; Meltzer, *supra* note 11, at 299 (stating that subjective review leads to inconsistent results); Neuger, *supra* note 2, at 583. Neuger writes that 1122 does not require courts to "guard against debtor abuse" and that courts should not use the silence of § 1122 as an opportunity to create an appropriate standard of review because there are Code created sections, such as 1129, that provide opportunities for review. In addition, it is not judicially efficient for courts to apply a reasonableness standard to issues of gerrymandering on a case by case basis. This method only leaves the "door open for debtors to once again circumvent the rule by uncovering exceptions which will satisfy judicial review." *Id.*

127. *Bloomingdale*, 170 B.R. at 991, 997 (discussing judicially created standards of "restrictive classification" and "flexible classification" and adopting the restrictive classification method as "the appropriate method for evaluating the classification of claims in a chapter 11 plan"); *In re* S & W Enter., 37 B.R. 153, 161 (Bankr. N.D. Ill. 1984) (concluding that application of "reasonable

of uncertain environment, debtors will continue to uncover exceptions which satisfy judicial review.[128]

D. Analysis of Per Se Rule

Section 1122 does not explicitly prohibit separate classification of unsecured claims. Gerrymandering, however, has been shown to run contrary to legislative intent, to create judicial waste, and to undermine provisions of the Code. A per se rule banning gerrymandering would eliminate these problems.[129] Under this rule separate classification merely for the purpose of circumventing section 1129(a)(10) would be prohibited.

The Code itself provides an objective test which focuses on the claims themselves. The test asks whether the claim is "substantially similar" or not; there is only a yes or no answer.[130] The inquiry is thus squarely focused on the nature of the claims[131] in contrast to an inquiry into the plan proponent's subjective intent in separately classifying the claims.[132]

---

and necessary" standard was required); *In re* Kovich, 4 B.R. 403, 407 (Bankr. W.D. Mich. 1980) (proposing four part test "when reviewing debtor's classification"); Neuger, *supra* note 2, at 573 (listing three interpretations of § 1122(a) that have evolved in courts).

128. Meltzer, *supra* note 11, at 302-03 (stating that separate classification "permits easy circumvention of § 1129(a)(10)"); Neuger, *supra* note 2, at 583.

129. Neuger, *supra* note 2, at 585-86. Neuger concludes that "the most sensible interpretation of [§] 1122 is a bright-line rule requiring all substantially similar claims to be placed in a common class . . . . [T]o infer otherwise would be a negative inference with respect to [§] 1122 without any support from the legislative history." *Id.* (footnotes omitted).

130. Steelcase, Inc. v. Johnston (*In re* Johnston), 21 F.3d 323, 327 (9th Cir. 1994) (reasoning that issue to resolve when reviewing classification is whether claims are substantially similar); *Bloomingdale*, 170 B.R. at 996.

131. *Johnston*, 21 F.3d at 327 (stating that to review classification scheme "bankruptcy court judges must evaluate the nature of each claim, i.e., the kind, species, or character of each category of claims"); *see supra* note 31 and accompanying text (quoting legislative history behind § 1122 that requires classification based on nature of claims).

132. *Bloomingdale*, 170 B.R. at 996.

A per se rule would not eliminate a judge's authority to permit separate classification pursuant to section 1122(b)[133] of the Code, it would just focus the scope of judicial review onto whether the classes were separately classified merely to circumvent section 1129(a)(10) or whether a legitimate reason actually exists. Nor would a per se rule overrule those cases that permitted separate classification for legitimate reasons.[134] The per se rule would merely place the burden on the debtor to prove objectively that legitimate reason.

This rule might preclude certain debtors from successfully confirming a plan of reorganization. The Code's legislative history, however, states that the purpose of a reorganization is to allow a business to restructure its finances in order to continue its operations, provide employment, pay its creditors, and earn a return for its stockholders.[135]

A single asset reorganization stands in contrast to Congress's stated purpose of a business reorganization. A single asset reorganization does not involve a real business operation that must be reorganized under its existing management since only "general real estate management skills" are required.[136] There are also typically few employees affected in a single asset case and thus

---

133. A *per se* rule would not prohibit courts from permitting separate classification pursuant to § 1122(b), which allows separate classification of claims if "reasonable and necessary for administrative convenience." 11 U.S.C. § 1122(b) (1994).

134. *See supra* note 122.

135. H.R. REP. NO. 595, *supra* note 29, at 220, *reprinted in* 1978 U.S.C.C.A.N. at 6179.

136. H. Miles Cohn, *Good Faith and the Single-Asset Debtor*, 62 AM. BANKR. L.J. 131, 131 (1988) (stating that "[s]ince the enactment of the Bankruptcy Code in 1978, the single asset debtor has appeared in increasing numbers. . . . [T]he single-asset debtor is typically an investment vehicle . . . formed to purchase . . . a single asset" as opposed to an ongoing business with assets, employees, creditors and customers); Gangemi, *supra* note 20, at 193 (1993) (discussing single asset reorganization as having "few employees, and does not manufacture a product . . . [and that] skills of prior management do not add to going concern value of property" since "general real estate management skills" are all that is required); Mark E. MacDonald, *supra* note 20, at 80 (explaining that "there are typically very few employees and no real business operations to reorganize in a single asset case . . . [except for] the day-to-day management and maintenance of the asset and dealings with potential or current lessees").

no threat of significant job loss.[137] "Congress [never] established as a cardinal rule that reorganization takes precedence over all other policies . . . . [T]here are times when reorganization may not be "fair, possible or desirable. . . ."[138]

Conclusion

This Chapter concludes that, pursuant to congressional intent, the judiciary should impose a per se rule prohibiting the separate classification of claims merely for the purpose of ensuring that there will be one impaired class that approves the reorganization plan. This conclusion is based on both legal and prudential considerations.

The legal arguments in favor of gerrymandering that are based on section 1111(b)'s creation of an unsecured deficiency claim seem to have been clearly refuted by explicit Code provisions and pragmatic case law. Moreover, the argument that general unsecured creditors will be disenfranchised by prohibiting gerrymandering has been shown to be unfounded and contrary to the congressional purpose of giving the undersecured creditor the right to an unsecured deficiency claim.

In addition, the legislative history of the Bankruptcy Code of 1978, while not explicitly calling for a per se rule, contains language indicating that Congress intended to codify the pre-Code case law that required joint classification of substantially similar claims.

Finally, regarding prudential considerations, the courts which have dealt with gerrymandering on an ad hoc basis may be circumventing other sections of the Code and in the process sacrificing judicial efficiency rather than defining and focusing the scope of their review for greater uniformity.

Accordingly, we encourage the adoption of a per se rule prohibiting gerrymandering.

---

137. *See supra* note 136.

138. 5 COLLIER, *supra* note 25, 1122-24 (stating Code does seek to promote interests of secured creditor).

CHAPTER VIII

CONFIRMATION BY CRAMDOWN THROUGH THE NEW VALUE EXCEPTION IN SINGLE ASSET CASES*

MARK E. MACDONALD
SALLY A. SCHREIBER
MARK E. MACDONALD, JR.

Although the absolute priority rule[1] was acknowledged to be the "fixed principle" of bankruptcy law in 1939[2] and was incorporated into section 1129(b) of the Bankruptcy Code[3] (the "Code"), its parameters remain undefined. Much of this imprecision revolves around the new value exception. Among commentators there is no consensus regarding the vitality of this

---

* The authors also thank Daren W. Perkins, co-author of MacDonald and Perkins, *New Developments in the Plan Process: 1992* prepared for the Third Annual Prentice Hall Seminar *Current Problems in Chapter 11 Practice*, and Michael Dorey, co-author of MacDonald, Schreiber, Dorey, and MacDonald, *Reading Tea Leaves: Statutory and Policy Aspects of New Value* presented at the 1992 Spring American Bankruptcy Institute meeting, for permitting such materials to be used extensively in the preparation of this article.

1. *See generally* Walter J. Blum & Stanley A. Kaplan, *The Absolute Priority Doctrine in Corporate Reorganizations*, 41 U. CHI. L. REV. 651, 652-53 (1974) (describing nature of absolute priority doctrine).
2. Case v. Los Angeles Lumber Prods. Co., 308 U.S. 106, 115-16 (1939) (endorsing absolute priority rule as method of assuring "fair and equitable" treatment of creditors).
3. 11 U.S.C. § 1129(b) (1994). Section 1129(b)(2)(B)(ii) states that, with respect to a class of unsecured claims, "the holder of any claim or interest that is junior to the claims of such class will not receive or retain under the plan on account of such junior claim or interest any property." *Id.* The Supreme Court had described this section as incorporating the absolute priority rule. *See* Norwest Bank Worthington v. Ahlers, 485 U.S. 197, 202 (1988).

exception[4] or the proper canons of statutory interpretation or public policy to be employed.[5] In addition, the United States Supreme Court has sent highly conflicting signals as to the interpretive principles that it would apply if presented with a case that fit squarely within the generally accepted standards of the new value exception.[6]

Some courts have suggested that the new value exception is not really an uncodified exception, but rather that it satisfies the Code's "fair and equitable" requirement for confirmation under section 1129(b).[7] Simply stated,

---

4. *See generally* MARK E. MACDONALD & DAREN W. PERKINS, NEW DEVELOPMENTS IN THE PLAN PROCESS: 1992 CURRENT PROBLEMS IN CHAPTER 11 PRACTICE 839 (Prentice Hall 1992); Richard F. Broude, *Cramdown and Chapter 11 of the Bankruptcy Code: The Settlement Imperative*, 39 BUS. LAW. 441, 443 (1984); Richard L. Epling, *The New Value Exception: Is There a Practical, Workable Solution*?, 8 BANKR. DEV. J. 335, 341 (1991) (stating that trend in case law favors adoption of new value exception); Ronald J. Trost & Jerry Bregman, *Preserving Equity's Share of an Insolvent Business Reorganized under the "Cram-Down" Provision of Section 1129(b) of the Bankruptcy Code: Survey of the New Value Exception to the Absolute Priority Rule*, Price Waterhouse National Reorganization & Bankruptcy Conference, 1992; Survey: *Absolute Priority and the Continued Vitality of the "New Value Exception,"* 1 J. BANKR. L. & PRAC. 591, 597-627 (1992) [hereinafter *William and Mary Survey*] (examining cases discussing vitality of new value exception).
5. *See generally William and Mary Survey*, *supra* note 4, at 632-41 (discussing historical perspective of new value).
6. *See generally* U.S. Bancorp Mortgage Co. v. Bonner Mall Partnership, 115 S. Ct. 386, 389 n.1 (1994) (declining to express view on existence of new value exception under Code); *Ahlers*, 485 U.S. at 203 n.3 (refusing to rule on whether "new capital" exception exists).
7. Bonner Mall Partnership v. U.S. Bancorp Mortgage Co. (*In re* Bonner Mall Partnership), 142 B.R. 911, 916 (D. Idaho 1992) (concluding that "fair and equitable" requirement of § 1129(b) is not exclusive; thus, new value exception is not excluded), *aff'd*, 2 F.3d 899 (9th Cir. 1993), *cert. granted*, 114 S. Ct. 681 (1994), *cert. dismissed as moot*, 115 S. Ct. 386 (1994); *In re* SLC Ltd. V, 137 B.R. 847, 851 (Bankr. D. Utah 1992) (noting § 1129(b) "provides certain requirements . . . to the `fair and equitable' concept, but the requirements are not all inclusive nor are they limiting"); Penn Mut. Life Ins. Co. v. Woodscape Ltd. Partnership (*In re* Woodscape Ltd. Partnership), 134 B.R. 165, 169-70 (Bankr. D. Md. 1991) (relying upon *Los Angeles Lumber*, court accepted

the only certainty about the current status of the ability of a single asset debtor to confirm a nonconsensual plan of reorganization that allows equity owners to retain some interest in the debtor in exchange for new value is that there is no certainty. Although practitioners and jurists alike are not particularly comfortable with uncertainty, this uncertainty may ultimately foster the very policies for which the bankruptcy laws were enacted.

A. A Brief History of Absolute Priority and New Value

1. Absolute Priority as Part of the Fair and Equitable Standard

a. General

Prior to the enactment of the Code, bankruptcy law required that a plan of reorganization could only be confirmed if it was "fair and equitable."[8] The fair

---

possibility of plan with stockholder participation to satisfy "fair and equitable" requirement). For a discussion on the survival of the "new value" exception, see Kenneth N. Klee, *Cram Down II*, 64 AM. BANKR. L.J. 229, 241-44 (1990).

8. *See* Act of June 7, 1934, ch. 424, § 77B(e)(1), 48 Stat. 919 (1935) (repealed 1938) ("After hearing such objections as may be made to the plan, the judge shall confirm the plan if satisfied that . . . it is fair and equitable and does not discriminate unfairly in favor of any class of creditors or stockholders . . . ."). Although this requirement was not included in the Bankruptcy Act immediately prior to the adoption of the Code, cases decided when the requirement was present gave rise to a number of interpretations. *See, e.g.*, Northern Pac. R.R. v. Boyd, 228 U.S. 482, 504-05 (1913) (considering whether treatment of all parties is equitable); Louisville Trust Co. v. Louisville, N. A. & C. Ry. Co., 174 U.S. 674, 684 (1899) (noting equity holders' interests are junior to general creditors); James C. Bonbright & Milton M. Bergerman, *Two Rival Theories of Priority Rights of Security Holders in a Corporate Reorganization*, 28 COLUM. L. REV. 127, 130 (1928) (defining "fair and equitable" in terms of "relative priority"); 6A COLLIER ON BANKRUPTCY, ¶11.06, 204-17 (Herzog & King eds., 14th ed. 1977) (discussing genesis of "fair and equitable" rule). Courts interpreting the fair and equitable requirement today acknowledge many of these prior interpretations. *See, e.g.*, Norwest Bank Worthington v. Ahlers, 485 U.S. 197, 202 (1988) (citing cases requiring fair and equitable treatment). The fair and equitable requirement of the Code "had its genesis in judicial construction of the undefined requirement of the early bankruptcy statute that reorganization plans be fair and equitable.'" *Id.*

and equitable requirement was interpreted by the Supreme Court as requiring the preservation of "absolute priority."[9] The absolute priority rule requires that creditors be paid from a bankrupt estate according to an established order before a plan may be confirmed: "Beginning with the topmost class of claims against the debtor, each class in descending rank must receive full and complete compensation for the rights surrendered before the next class may properly participate."[10] First, the plan must satisfy in full the claims of the senior secured creditors before junior secured creditors could receive value; second, the plan must satisfy claims of junior secured creditors before unsecured creditors could receive value; and finally, the plan must satisfy the claims of all creditors before any class of equity interests could receive value.[11] Thus, "fair and equitable" required that no junior class or interest participate under a plan unless full payment was provided for all dissenting senior claims or interests within a class.

Unlike prior versions of the Bankruptcy Act, the Code does not impose a separate "fair and equitable" requirement for plan confirmation if the requisite majorities of each class of claims or interests either accepts the plan or is unimpaired by it.[12] Thus, if a class either accepts a plan or is not impaired by it, the fair and equitable requirement is not imposed.[13]

However, the Code does impose the "fair and equitable" requirement if a plan is to be confirmed under the so-called cramdown provisions of section

---

9. *See, e.g.*, Group of Institutional Investors v. Chicago, Milwaukee, St. Paul & Pac. R.R., 318 U.S. 523, 542 (1943) ("[T]he inclusion of the stock would violate . . . a rule of priority incorporated in § 77(e)(1), as in § 77(b) and Ch. X through the phrase `fair and equitable.'") (citations omitted); Case v. Los Angeles Lumber Prods. Co., 308 U.S. 106, 118-19 (1939) (concluding fair and equitable language of Bankruptcy Act requires that plans conform to absolute priority).
10. 6A COLLIER, *supra* note 8, ¶ 11.06, at 210-11.
11. *Id.*
12. *See* 11 U.S.C. § 1126 (1994) (stating requirements for plan acceptance); 11 U.S.C. § 1124 (1994) (establishing guidelines to determine whether claims or interests are unimpaired).
13. *See* 11 U.S.C. § 1129(a)(8) (1994). *But see Case*, 308 U.S. at 114-16 (holding that creditor approval did not negate need for determination that plan was fair and equitable).

1129(b), which permits a plan to be confirmed despite the presence of a class of impaired claims or interests that does not accept the plan.[14]

b. Statutory Requirements

At least some portion of the absolute priority required by the "fair and equitable" standard was codified in section 1129(b)[15] with respect to secured claims, unsecured claims, and equity interests.[16] However, section 1129(b), as

---

14. 11 U.S.C. § 1129(b)(1) (1994). It should be noted that the fair and equitable requirement applies only to *dissenting* classes that are impaired by the plan. Kane v. Johns-Manville Corp. (*In re* Johns-Manville Corp.), 843 F.2d 636, 650 (2d Cir. 1988). Thus, senior classes can give up value to a junior class so long as no intervening dissenting class is paid less than 100% of its claims. *Id.*
15. Although the House Report indicated that § 1129 was a departure from the absolute priority rule, *see* H.R. REP. NO. 595, 95th Cong., 1st Sess. 413-18 (1977), *reprinted in* 1978 U.S.C.C.A.N. 5963, 6369-74, the section appears to present at least some requirements for absolute priority, even if not identical to those contained under prior law. Norwest Bank Worthington v. Ahlers, 485 U.S. 197, 202 (1988).
16. Section 1129(b) provides as follows:

> (b)(1) Notwithstanding section 510(a) of this title, if all of the applicable requirements of subsection (a) of this section other than paragraph (8) are met with respect to a plan, the court, on request of the proponent of the plan, shall confirm the plan notwithstanding the requirements of such paragraph if the plan does not discriminate unfairly, and is *fair and equitable*, with respect to each class of claims or interests that is impaired under, and has not accepted, the plan.
>
> (2) For the purpose of this subsection, the condition that a plan be fair and equitable with respect to a class includes the following requirements:
>
> (A) With respect to a class of *secured claims*, the plan provides–
>
> (i)(I) that the holders of such claims retain the liens securing such claims, whether the property subject to such liens is retained by the debtor or transferred to another entity, to the extent of the allowed amount of such claims; and
>
> (II) that each holder of a claim of such class receive on account of such claim deferred cash payments totaling at

drafted, has at least three legitimate ambiguities that have given rise to questions concerning its interpretation.

First, section 1129(b) uses the phrase "fair and equitable," which carries with it a substantial amount of judicial baggage left over from the Bankruptcy Act. In *Penn Mutual Life Insurance Co. v. Woodscape Ltd. Partnership (In re Woodscape Ltd Partnership)*,[17] Judge Derby relied on two Supreme Court decisions to interpret "fair and equitable": *Midlantic National Bank v. New*

> least the allowed amount of such claim, of a value, as of the effective date of the plan, of at least the value of such holder's interest in the estate's interest in such property;
>
> (ii) for the sale, subject to section 363(k) of this title, of any property that is subject to the liens securing such claims, free and clear of such liens, with such liens to attach to the proceeds of such sale, and the treatment of such liens on proceeds under clause (i) or (iii) of this subparagraph; or
>
> (iii) for the realization by such holders of the indubitable equivalent of such claims.
>
> (B) With respect to a class of *unsecured claims*–
>
> (i) the plan provides that each holder of a claim of such class receive or retain on account of such claim property of a value, as of the effective date of the plan, equal to the allowed amount of such claim; or
>
> (ii) the holder of any claim or interest that is junior to the claims of such class will not receive or retain under the plan on account of such junior claim or interest any property.
>
> (C) With respect to a *class of interests*–
>
> (i) the plan provides that each holder of an interest of such class receive or retain on account of such interest property of a value, as of the effective date of the plan, equal to the greatest of the allowed amount of any fixed liquidation preference to which such holder is entitled, any fixed redemption price to which such holder is entitled, or the value of such interest; or
>
> (ii) the holder of any interest that is junior to the interests of such class will not receive or retain under the plan on account of such junior interest any property.

11 U.S.C. § 1129(b) (1994) (emphasis added).

17. 134 B.R. 165, 177 (Bankr. D. Md. 1991).

Jersey Department of Environmental Protection,[18] and *United Savings Ass'n v. Timbers of Inwood Forest Associates*.[19] Both cases stand for the proposition that, absent an express and contrary statement of congressional intent in the plain meaning of the statutory language, it is presumed that Congress did not intend to change prior judicial interpretation.[20]

Second, unlike the Bankruptcy Act, which relied on courts to supply the parameters of the "fair and equitable" standard, section 1129(b) comprehensively enumerates the elements of fair and equitable treatment[21] and thus may be read to have intentionally excluded historically applicable parts of the doctrine, whether viewed as exceptions or related concepts. For example, in *Phoenix Mutual Life Insurance Co. v. Greystone III Joint Venture (In re Greystone III Joint Venture)*,[22] Judge Jones argued in her dissent that Congress' refusal to include exceptions to the absolute priority rule at the time it enacted the Code signifies that Congress knowingly codified an unequivocal absolute priority rule.[23]

Third, section 1129(b)(2) uses the word "includes" before the extensive listing, which explicitly means "includes but is not limited to" under section 102(3) of the Code.[24] Creditors may attempt to avoid the force of "includes"

---

18. 474 U.S. 494 (1986).
19. 484 U.S. 365 (1988).
20. *See id.* at 371 (holding that property interest does not include creditor's right to immediate foreclosure); *Midlantic Nat'l Bank*, 474 U.S. at 501 (holding that Congress must clearly express intent to exempt trustee from abandonment law); *see also* Edmonds v. Compagnie Generale Transatlantique, 443 U.S. 256, 257 (1977) (holding Congress must specifically intend change of judicially created concept).
21. 11 U.S.C. § 1129(b) (1994).
22. 995 F.2d 1274 (5th Cir.), *vacated in part*, 995 F.2d 1284 (5th Cir. 1991), *cert. denied*, 113 S. Ct. 72 (1992).
23. *Greystone*, 995 F.2d at 1285.
24. Klee, *supra* note 7. The legislative history of § 1129(b) notes that some factors that are fundamental to the fair and equitable rule were omitted "to avoid statutory complexity and because they would undoubtedly be found by a court to be fundamental to fair and equitable' treatment of a dissenting class." *Id.* at 231 n.14 (quoting 124 CONG. REC. 32,407 (Sept. 28, 1978) (statement of Rep. Don Edwards)). Klee, a noted commentator, has recently identified and explained certain uncodified aspects of the fair and equitable rule: first, no senior class may be compensated more than in full; second, a senior dissenting

by suggesting that the presence of a minimum list can only include more requirements, not provide exceptions that water down the minimum.[25]

2. The "New Value Exception"

a. Historical Evolution Before *Ahlers*

Under the Bankruptcy Act, there existed a judicially created "new value exception" to the absolute priority rule that allowed an equity owner of a debtor's property to retain an ownership interest in exchange for a fresh contribution to the business, notwithstanding the fact that the claims of creditors were not being satisfied in full. This principle was first expressed in *Case v. Los Angeles Lumber Products.*[26] In dictum, Justice Douglas stated:

> It is, of course, clear that there are circumstances under which stockholders may participate in a plan of reorganization of an insolvent debtor . . . . [W]e believe that to accord `the creditor his full right of priority against the corporate assets' where the debtor is insolvent, the stockholder's participation must be based on a contribution in money or in money's worth, reasonably equivalent in view of all the circumstances to the participation of the stockholder.[27]

The court based its decision on policy considerations, noting that "[g]enerally, additional funds will be essential to the success of the undertaking, and it may be impossible to obtain them unless stockholders are permitted to contribute and retain an interest sufficiently valuable to move them."[28] However, despite

---

class must be compensated for its loss of priority relative to a junior class; third, a senior dissenting class may be entitled to be compensated for any right it has to receive postpetition interest before junior classes may participate under a plan; fourth, a senior dissenting class may be forced to take inferior securities if a junior class receives superior securities or cash; fifth, the issuance of "worthless securities" is precluded; sixth, the gratis issuance of reorganization securities to preserve continuity of management is precluded; and seventh, the new value exception survives and is evolving. *Id.* at 231-44.

25. *See Greystone III*, 995 F.2d at 1285.
26. 308 U.S. 106 (1939).
27. *Id.* at 121-22.
28. *Id.* at 117; *see also* Kansas City Terminal Ry. Co. v. Central Union Trust Co.

this policy, Professor Ayer notes that "[t]here appears to be no reported case in the entire period [pre-1978] in which the court expressly permitted the `debtor,' or former equity owners, to retain assets on the strength of a new value contribution and for no other reason."[29]

Given the historical foundations and policy considerations of the new value exception, it is not surprising that most cases decided under the Code before 1988 found that the new value exception still existed,[30] including those decided by several of the circuit courts.[31]

---

of N.Y., 271 U.S. 445, 455 (1926) (making same observation); *In re* Bjolmes Realty Trust, 134 B.R. 1000, 1005 (Bankr. D. Mass. 1991) (noting circumstances under which shareholders may participate in reorganization).

29. John D. Ayer, *Rethinking Absolute Priority After* Ahlers, 87 MICH. L. REV. 963, 1016-19 (1989). *See generally* Jeffery M. Sharp, *Bankruptcy Reorganizations, Section 1129, and the New Capital Quagmire: A Call for Congressional Response*, 28 AM. BUS. L.J. 525, 525-35 (1991) (citing to post-1978 cases applying new value exception); Clifford S. Harris, Note, *A Rule Unvanquished: The New Value Exception To The Absolute Priority Rule*, 89 MICH. L. REV. 2301, 2304-08 (1991) (same); Derek J. Meyer, Note, *Redefining the New Value Exception to the Absolute Priority Rule in Light of the Creditors' Bargain Model*, 24 IND. L. REV. 417, 417-22 (1991) (same). According to one recent article, the language of the *Los Angeles Lumber* case concerning the new value exception was merely dicta because the facts of that case did not warrant application of the exception. *William and Mary Survey, supra* note 4, at 595. Additionally, "no pre-Code court ever adopted the dicta in *Los Angeles Lumber* as its holding." *Id.*

30. *See, e.g.*, Brown v. Brown's Indus. Uniforms *(In re* Brown's Indus. Uniforms), 58 B.R. 139, 141 (N.D. Ill. 1985) (holding stockholders' participation dependent upon fresh contribution of money); *In re* AG Consultants Grain Div., Inc., 77 B.R. 665, 677 (Bankr. N.D. Ind. 1987) (recognizing "new equity" investment); Buffalo Sav. Bank v. Marston Enters. *(In re* Marston Enters.), 13 B.R. 514, 518 (Bankr. E.D.N.Y. 1981) (finding no statutory prohibition barring original shareholders from making substantial necessary capital contribution in consideration for shares of stock in reorganized company); *In re* Landau Boat Co., 13 B.R. 788, 792 (Bankr. W.D. Mo. 1981) (contribution of fresh money entitles shareholders to interest in reorganization).

31. *See, e.g.*, Teamsters Nat'l Freight Indus. Negotiation Comm. v. U.S. Truck Co. *(In re* U.S. Truck Co.), 800 F.2d 581, 588 (6th Cir. 1986) (allowing equity security holder to retain ownership upon payment of $100,000 to debtor company); Official Creditors' Comm. v. Potter Material Serv. *(In re* Potter

b. The Supreme Court's Decision in *Ahlers*

Against this background the Supreme Court decided *Norwest Bank Worthington v. Ahlers*.[32] In *Ahlers*, a creditor moved for relief from an automatic stay, asserting that the plan was not confirmable because it violated the absolute priority rule.[33] The plan proposed that the farm operators would retain an interest in the farm in exchange for a promise to commit labor and expertise to the running of the farm without compensating creditors in full.[34] The Eighth Circuit relied on the language in *Los Angeles Lumber* that permits a contribution to be in "money or money's worth," in holding that "a farmer's efforts in operating and managing his farm [are] essential to any successful farm reorganization, and this yearly contribution is measurable in money or money's worth."[35] The Eighth Circuit further found that, since the going-concern premium could not "be captured for creditors in the event of liquidation, fairness is not violated if [the farmer's] [c]hapter 11 plan leaves that value in [his] hands;"[36] therefore, the debtor farmer "should be entitled to participate in the plan to the extent of this contribution, even though more senior claims are not provided for in full under the plan."[37]

The Supreme Court reversed the Eighth Circuit, noting that the absolute priority rule applies to prevent a debtor from retaining property when a dissenting class of unsecured claims is not paid in full.[38] The Court rejected the Eighth Circuit's conclusion that a promise of future labor could constitute an exception to the absolute priority rule.[39] Finally, the Court noted that its:

> decision . . . should not be taken as any comment on the continuing vitality of the *Los Angeles Lumber* exception — a question which has

---

Material Serv.), 781 F.2d 99, 101 (7th Cir. 1986) (recognizing new value exception).

32. 485 U.S. 197 (1988).
33. *Id.* at 197-98.
34. *Id.* at 200.
35. Norwest Bank Worthington v. Ahlers (*In re* Ahlers), 794 F.2d 388, 402 (8th Cir. 1986).
36. *Id.*
37. *Id.*
38. *Ahlers*, 485 U.S. at 205-06.
39. *Id.* at 204-05.

> divided the lower courts since passage of the Code in 1978 . . . . Rather, . . . even if an "infusion-of- `money-or money's-worth'" exception to the absolute priority rule has survived the enactment of [section] 1129(b), [the debtor's] proposed contribution to the reorganization plan is inadequate to gain the benefit of this exception.[40]

c. Reaction of Courts After *Ahlers*

Despite the Supreme Court's warning that the *Ahlers* "decision . . . should not be taken as any comment on the continuing vitality of the [new value exception],"[41] courts have questioned whether the exception exists.[42] Although some courts have interpreted the *Ahlers* decision as signifying the death of the new value exception,[43] the vast majority of courts that have examined the issue

---

40. *Id.* at 203 n.3 (citations omitted).
41. *Id.*
42. *See* Kham & Nate's Shoes No. 2, Inc. v. First Bank, 908 F.2d 1351, 1360 (7th Cir. 1990) (noting that new value exception may not have survived Code); *In re* Stegall, 865 F.2d 140, 142 (7th Cir. 1989) ("[w]e emphasize, however, that the issue is an open one in this circuit, *Potter* notwithstanding"); *In re* Tara Ltd. Partnership, No. 91-C.574-S, 1991 U.S. Dist. LEXIS 20144, at *9 (W.D. Wisc. Aug. 30, 1991) (finding that *Kham & Nate's Shoes* foreshadows demise of new value exception in Seventh Circuit). *But see* Official Creditors' Comm. v. Potter Material Serv. *(In re* Potter Material Serv.), 781 F.2d 99, 102-04 (7th Cir. 1986) (applying new value exception).
43. *See, e.g., In re* Drimmel, 108 B.R. 284, 288-89 (Bankr. D. Kan. 1989) (concluding that debtors may not retain interest even if they pay its value by providing new capital to business), *aff'd*, 135 B.R. 410 (D. Kan. 1991), *aff'd sub nom.* Unruh v. Rushville State Bank, 987 F.2d 1506 (10th Cir. 1993); Pennbank v. Winters (*In re* Winters), 99 B.R. 658, 663 (Bankr. W.D. Pa. 1989) ("[W]e hold that there is no exception (`infusion of new capital' or otherwise) permitted under 11 U.S.C. § 1129(b)."); *In re* Rudy Debruycker Ranch, Inc., 84 B.R. 187, 190 (Bankr. D. Mont. 1988) (finding no exception to absolute priority rule). In rejecting the notion that shareholders' guarantees of debtor's loans constituted new value justifying retention of equity interests, the Seventh Circuit came close to finding that the new value exception did not survive the enactment of the Code in 1978. *See* Kham & Nate's Shoes No. 2, 908 F.2d at 1360; *see also In re* Maropa Marine Sales Serv. & Storage, 90 B.R. 544, 545-46 (Bankr. S.D. Fla. 1988) (concluding that debtors'

have concluded that the new value exception is still alive today.[44]

d. Requirements of the New Value Exception

The uncertainty surrounding the new value exception's existence has also resulted in uncertainty as to the exact standards that must be satisfied to successfully invoke the exception.[45] *Los Angeles Lumber* indicates that new value must represent a substantial contribution that equals or exceeds the value of the retained interest in the entity.[46] Courts have articulated additional requirements, namely that the contribution be equal to or exceed the value of the retained interest, that the contribution be essential or necessary, and that it does not solely represent a future commitment.[47] However, these terms and

---

contribution is insufficient even if new value exception survives).

44. *See* John Hancock Mut. Life Ins. Co. v. Route 37 Business Park Assocs. (*In re* Route 37 Business Park Assocs.), 146 B.R. 640, 646 (D.N.J. 1992) *rev'd*, 987 F.2d 154 (3d Cir. 1993). The district court in *Route 37* cited to the following courts: Travelers Ins. Co. v. Bryson Properties, XVIII *(In re* Bryson Properties, XVIII), 961 F.2d 496, 504-05 (4th Cir. 1992) (recognizing possibility of limited new capital exception but holding it inapplicable to facts of case), *cert. denied*, 506 U.S. 866 (1992); *In re* E.I. Parks No. 1 Ltd. Partnership, 122 B.R. 549, 557 (Bankr. W.D. Ark. 1990) (recognizing exception to absolute priority if new value given); *In re* Mortgage Inv. Co. of El Paso, Texas, 111 B.R. 604, 618-19 (Bankr. W.D. Tex. 1990) (same); *In re* 222 Liberty Assocs., 108 B.R. 971, 983-84 (Bankr. E.D. Pa. 1990) (asserting that capital infusion exception shall exist notwithstanding *Ahlers*); *In re* Ashton, 107 B.R. 670, 674 (Bankr. D.N.D. 1989) (converting debtor's case to chapter 7 for failure to satisfy absolute priority or new value exception); *In re* Aztec Co., 107 B.R. 585, 588 (Bankr. M.D. Tenn. 1989) (following Sixth Circuit's endorsement of new value exception).

45. *See William and Mary Survey, supra* note 4, at 641-48.

46. *See* Case v. Los Angeles Lumber Prods. Co., 308 U.S. 106, 121 (1939) (validating stockholders' receipt of equity interest equivalent to their "fresh contribution" of capital into the reorganized company); *see also* Consolidated Rock Prods. Co. v. DuBois, 312 U.S. 510, 530 (1941) (same); Elliott D. Levin, *Retention of Ownership Interest Over Creditor Objection — How Intangible and Unsubstantial May the Substantial Contribution Be?*, 92 Com. L.J. 101, 104 (1989) (same).

47. *In re* Future Energy Corp., 83 B.R. 470, 499 (Bankr. S.D. Ohio 1988); *In re* Stegall, 64 B.R. 296, 299 (Bankr. C.D. Ill. 1986), *aff'd*, 85 B.R. 510 (C.D. Ill.

phrases are rarely used with precision. For instance, courts have said that a contribution is necessary if the new value is "essential to the success of the undertaking,"[48] or if the current owners are the *only* or *most feasible* source of financing.[49] Contributions are sometimes found to be substantial when compared with the deficiency claims of the creditors,[50] or with the value of the equity interest retained.[51] However, as long as the contribution amount is not insignificant, the contribution will be considered substantial.[52] Some cases state that the exception requires that an auction be held,[53] while others expressly reject the concept of auction.[54] Some courts require that the new

---

1987), *aff'd,* 865 F.2d 140 (7th Cir. 1989); *In re* Pecht, 57 B.R. 137, 140-41 (Bankr. E.D. Va. 1986).

48. *See, e.g., In re* Eaton Hose & Fitting Co., 73 B.R. 139, 140 (Bankr. S.D. Ohio 1987).

49. *See* Official Creditors' Comm. v. Potter Material Serv. *(In re* Potter Material Serv.), 781 F.2d 99, 101 (7th Cir. 1986) (finding that when unsecured creditors fail to present evidence of a more feasible source, or submit an alternative plan, financing by current owner is most feasible source of new capital); *In re* Jartran, Inc., 44 B.R. 331, 379 (Bankr. N.D. Ill. 1984) (concluding that financing by company that purchased debtor most feasible source of new capital and necessary to successful reorganization).

50. *See, e.g.,* Travelers Ins. Co. v. Olson *(In re* Olson), 80 B.R. 935, 937 (Bankr. C.D. Ill. 1987), *aff'd,* 1989 WL 330439 (C.D. Ill. Feb. 8, 1989) (comparing amount of contribution to amount of unsecured debt due to dissenting class to determine whether new capital contribution is substantial); *In re* Eaton Hose & Fitting Co., 73 B.R. 139, 140 (Bankr. S.D. Ohio 1987) (contribution of new capital equal to 15% of unsecured creditors' claims, plus more, if needed deemed to be substantial).

51. *See, e.g.,* Teamsters Nat'l Freight Indus. Negotiating Comm. v. U.S. Truck Co. (*In re* U.S. Truck Co.), 800 F.2d 581, 588-89 (6th Cir. 1986) (approving district court's conclusion that contribution by former shareholders for shares in reorganized company was well above amount for which shares could have been sold to general public).

52. *See, e.g., In re* SLC Ltd. V, 137 B.R. 847, 855-56 (Bankr. D. Utah 1992) (contribution equal to 3% of total prepetition debt and 5% of total dischargeable debt constitutes substantial contribution under new value plan).

53. *See, e.g., In re* Bjolmes Realty Trust, 134 B.R. 1000, 1010 (Bankr. D. Mass. 1991) (imposing as condition to plan confirmation the sale of equity interest in debtor at public auction in order to ensure proper valuation).

54. *See, e.g.,* Penn Mut. Life Ins. Co. v. Woodscape Ltd. Partnership *(In re*

value be paid out to creditors,[55] while others indicate that the new value contributions must simply ensure the liquidity of the debtor.[56] Whatever the contribution, the plan proponent has the burden of proving the value of the interest being retained.[57]

B. Reading Tea Leaves from The Supreme Court on New Value

The famous *Ahlers*' footnote,[58] which states the Court's decision not to comment upon the continuing validity of the new value exception, has provoked volumes of commentary from the courts and the pundits. The decision can be taken as a classic example of judicial restraint in the face of active lobbying by the Solicitor General to declare the exception invalid. Following the plain meaning approach advanced by Justice Scalia in *Timbers*,[59] the current Court has often preferred to decide bankruptcy issues primarily from an examination of the statutory language, without resort to either legislative history or a determination that a change from pre-Code

---

Woodscape Ltd. Partnership), 134 B.R. 165, 174 (Bankr. D. Md. 1991) (permitting sale of right to future participation in debtor's enterprise but not requiring public auction).

55. *See, e.g., In re* Creekside Landing Ltd., 140 B.R. 713, 719 (Bankr. M.D. Tenn. 1992) (using all "new value" contributed by existing interest holders to retire claims of insiders).
56. *See, e.g., In re* Montgomery Court Apts., Ltd., 141 B.R. 324, 345 (Bankr. S.D. Ohio 1992) (finding new capital contributions necessary to establish an operating reserve and to pay current obligations). *Cf. In re* Sovereign Group 1985-27, Ltd., 142 B.R. 702, 708 (E.D. Pa. 1992) (finding infusion of capital for payment of prepetition debts not necessary to reorganization because debtor's continued relationship with creditors not necessary to ensure successful reorganization).
57. *In re* AG Consultants Grain Div., 77 B.R. 665, 678 (Bankr. N.D. Ind. 1987) (withholding confirmation of debtor's plan for debtor's failure to show value of proposed contribution in relation to a certain class of claims); *In re* Sawmill Hydraulics, Inc., 72 B.R. 454, 458 (Bankr. C.D. Ill. 1987) (holding that "[t]he Debtor had the burden of proving the value of the shareholders' retained interest and failed to do so.").
58. *Supra* note 40 and accompanying text.
59. United Sav. Ass'n v. Timbers of Inwood Forest Assocs., Ltd., 484 U.S. 365 (1988).

practice was intended by Congress.[60] There have been a number of other indications that Justices Thomas and Souter may well favor a plain meaning approach to interpretation.[61] A difficulty with this "tea leaf" is that section 1129(b) has three legitimate ambiguities, as discussed earlier.[62]

Clearly, the strangest case of statutory interpretation in recent years is *Dewsnup v. Timm*.[63] Although *Dewsnup* was a short-term win for secured creditors in denying the right of chapter 7 debtors to strip liens, it was concomitantly a potential long-term disaster for secured creditors in classification and cramdown in single asset chapter 11 proceedings.[64] At the

---

60. *Contra* Union Bank v. Wolas, 502 U.S. 151, 156-57 (1991) (Stevens J., discussing history of § 547). In his concurrence, Justice Scalia agreed with the legislative history and policy arguments made by the majority concerning the scope of ordinary course payments: "[i]t is regrettable that we have a legal culture in which such arguments have to be addressed (and are indeed credited by a Court of Appeals), with respect to a statute utterly devoid of language that could remotely be thought to distinguish between long-term and short-term debt." *Id.* at 163 (Scalia, J. concurring).

    The Supreme Court followed the strict wordsmithing approach in United States v. Nordic Village, Inc., 503 U.S. 30, 34-36 (1992). In *Nordic Village,* Justice Scalia applied a "strict construction" that Justices Stevens and Blackmun believed tortured the clear terms of section 106 and ignored the legislative history in favor of a historically powerful judge-made rule. *Id.* at 41. The net result was that an officer of a debtor-in-possession was permitted to rob the estate in order to minimize his personal tax liability, while the estate was unable to recover the funds from the IRS. *Id.* at 44.

    In Holywell Corp. v. Smith, 503 U.S. 47, 51-54 (1992). Justice Thomas, writing for a unanimous Court, demonstrated the ability to generate a tightly logical interpretation in connection with the duty of the trustee of a liquidating trust for all or substantially all of the assets of a corporate debtor to file returns and pay taxes; instead of looking to policy or legislative history, the Court looked to the plain language of the Code. *Id.* at 54.

61. Scott P. Johnson & Christopher E. Smith, *David Souter's First Term on the Supreme Court: The Impact of a New Justice*, 75 JUDICATURE 238, February-March (1992); Charles Jordan Tabb & Robert M. Lawless, *Of Commas, Gerunds, and Conjunctions: the Bankruptcy Jurisprudence of the Rehnquist Court*, 42 SYRACUSE L. REV. 823 (1991).

62. *See supra* text accompanying notes 16-25.

63. 502 U.S. 410 (1992).

64. A. Miller & J. Tanenbaum, *High Court: Two Cases, Two Directions*, NAT'L

urging of the Solicitor General, Justice Blackmun, speaking for the Court, found that the phrase, "allowed secured claim," does not have the same meaning in section 506(a) of the Code as it does in section 506(d).[65] Further, Justice Blackmun stated in dicta that section 506(d) may not have the same meaning in chapter 7 as it does in chapter 11.[66] This anomalous result was heavily influenced by historical practice under pre-Code bankruptcy law. In dissent, Justices Scalia and Souter pointed out that a concept like "allowed secured claim," that is integral to and used throughout the Code, cannot be given a distinctive meaning without de-stabilizing the entire statute.[67] The dissent's comparison[68] of the opinion to the interpretive principles enunciated in *Midlantic National Bank v. New Jersey Department of Environmental Protection*,[69] *Union Bank v. Wolas*,[70] and *United States v. Ron Pair Enterprises*[71] are required reading for anyone attempting to analyze the ultimate outcome of the new value exception. The creditor bar clearly cannot rely upon Scalia, Souter, or Thomas to vote for property rights, for as judicial conservatives,[72] they believe that bankruptcy issues are a matter of statutory construction, rather than a balancing of creditor's natural rights with debtor rehabilitation.[73]

L.J., May 11, 1992, at 20; F. Jacobson & B. Bentcover, *Secured Creditors Benefit from Dewsnup*, NAT'L L.J., May 11, 1992, at 21.

65. *Dewsnup*, 502 U.S. at 417 (holding that § 506(d) does not allow petitioner to "strip down" lender's lien; therefore "allowed secured claim" has different meaning as compared to § 506(a)).
66. *Id.* at 428-30 (suggesting that an interpretation of 506(a) under chapter 7 which allows a debtor to "strip down" liens would discourage debtors to reorganize under chapters 11, 12 and 13).
67. Id. at 435-36.
68. *Id.* (Scalia, J., dissenting)
69. 474 U.S. 494 (1986).
70. 502 U.S. 151 (1991).
71. 489 U.S. 235 (1989).
72. *See generally* Richard C. Reuben, *Man in the Middle*, CAL. LAW. 35, 37 (Oct. 12, 1992) ("Conservatives hailed Scalia's appointment for his embrace of property rights and strict constructionism, and for his willingness to cast aside any precedent that got in the way of the movement.").
73. *Dewsnup*, 502 U.S. at 435-36. In his dissent, Justice Scalia stated:

> The principal harm caused by today's decision is not the misinterpretation of §506(d) of the Bankruptcy Code. The disposition

Most importantly, the *Dewsnup* decision has been viewed by two district courts as "prescrib[ing] new standards for interpreting the Bankruptcy Code."[74] The same courts noted that "[W]hen Congress amends the bankruptcy laws, it does not write 'on a clean slate.'"[75]

No judge was more surprised by *Dewsnup* than Judge Jones, author of the *In re Greystone III Joint Venture* opinion.[76] In her dissent on the petition for rehearing of *Greystone III*, which withdrew all discussion of new value,[77] Judge Jones stated, "[h]ow one should approach issues of a statutory construction arising from the Bankruptcy Code has been clouded, in my view, by *Dewsnup* v. *Timm*."[78]

C. New Value Exception in Single Asset Cases

Assuming that the new value exception exists under chapter 11, should it be, or has it been, applied in single asset cases differently from other cases?

> that misinterpretation produces brings the Code closer to prior practice and is, as the Court irrelevantly observes, probably fairer from the standpoint of natural justice. (*I say irrelevantly, because a bankruptcy law has little to do with natural justice.*) The greater and more enduring damage of today's opinion consists in its destruction of predictability, in the Bankruptcy Code and elsewhere.

Id. (emphasis added).

74. Bonner Mall Partnership v. U.S. Bancorp Mortgage Co. (*In re* Bonner Mall Partnership), 142 B.R. 911, 916 (D. Idaho 1992) (citing *Dewsnup*), *aff'd*, 2 F.3d 899 (9th Cir. 1993), *cert. granted*, 114 S. Ct. 681 (1994), *cert. dismissed as moot*, 115 S. Ct. 386 (1994).

75. *Id.*; *see also In re* Sovereign Group 1985-27 Ltd., 142 B.R. 702, 707 (D. Pa. 1992) (stating that court is hesitant to read Code as contravening pre-Code practice and thus court will not find new value exception extinguished); *In re* SLC Ltd. V, 137 B.R. 847, 853 (Bankr. D. Utah 1992) (stating court is reluctant to effect a major change in pre-Code practice).

76. Phoenix Mut. Life Ins. Co. v. Greystone III Joint Venture (*In re* Greystone III Joint Venture), 995 F.2d 1274 (5th Cir.1991), *vacated in part*, 995 F.2d 1284 (5th Cir.), *cert. denied*, 506 U.S. 821 (1992).

77. *Greystone*, 995 F.2d at 1285.

78. *Id.*

Many of the cases addressing the viability of the new value exception arise in the context of bankruptcies of debtors who have, in essence, a single asset such as a hotel, apartment building, or complex.[79] A typical single asset case usually involves a secured creditor whose claim dwarfs the claims of other creditors. Yet, the secured creditor is undersecured, so that its claim is bifurcated into a secured portion, based on the value of the collateral, and an unsecured portion, equal to the difference between the total claim and the portion determined to be secured.[80] Additionally, there are few, if any, assets to satisfy the unsecured portion of the claim in full. The plan of reorganization, in such an instance, will provide for the secured creditor to retain a lien on the single asset, equal to the secured portion of its claim, thereby satisfying section 1129(b)(2)(A).[81] Therefore, the single asset debtor is in a worse position than the corporate debtor who may be able to raise sufficient funds to satisfy the absolute priority rule, and fund the working capital needs of the reorganized entity by selling off divisions or assets while retaining its core business. If a single asset debtor sells its single asset, there is no business left to reorganize.[82] Thus, the ability of a real estate debtor to

---

79. *See, e.g.*, Travelers Ins. Co. v. Bryson Properties, XVIII (*In re* Bryson Properties, XVIII), 961 F.2d 496, 498-99 (4th Cir.) (reorganization of complex of three commercial buildings in Omaha), *cert. denied*, 506 U.S. 866 (1992); *In re* Triple R Holdings, L.P., 134 B.R. 382, 384 (Bankr. N.D. Cal. 1991) (condominium unit), *rev'd,* 145 B.R. 57 (N.D. Cal. 1992); *In re* Embassy Enters., 125 B.R. 552, 553 (Bankr. D. Minn. 1991) (hotel); *In re* Lumber Exch. Ltd. Partnership, 125 B.R. 1000, 1002 (Bankr. D. Minn.) (lumber exchange building), *aff'd*, 134 B.R. 354 (D. Minn. 1991), *aff'd*, 968 F.2d 647 (8th Cir. 1992); Pennbank v. Winters (*In re* Winters), 99 B.R. 658, 659 (Bankr. W.D. Pa. 1989) (commercial building and 50% stock of restaurant and tavern on premises).

80. *See* 11 U.S.C. § 506(a) (1994). *See, e.g., In re* Demoff, 109 B.R. 902, 921 (Bankr. N.D. Ind. 1989) (conceding that unsecured creditors after bifurcation have "an opportunity to realize to some extent on their claims"); Regina L. Nassen, Note, *Bankruptcy Code § 1322 (B)(2)'s No-Modification Clause: Who Does It Protect?*, 33 ARIZ. L. REV. 979, 981 (1991) (noting that after bifurcation, "secured claims must be paid in full; unsecured claims, in contrast, may receive as little as ten cents, or even five cents, on the dollar").

81. 11 U.S.C. § 1129(b)(2)(A) (1994) (stating requirements that plan be fair and equitable to one class).

82. *See, e.g.*, Penn Mut. Life Ins. Co. v. Woodscape Ltd. Partnership (*In re*

successfully reorganize frequently depends on the infusion of new capital, either to satisfy the absolute priority rule or to fund working capital post-reorganization needs.[83]

1. Does The New Value Exception Exist in Single Asset Cases?

a. Statutory Analysis

While there may be an economic distinction between single asset real estate cases and other business bankruptcies, as discussed below, this distinction is not reflected in the statutory scheme passed by Congress. The creation of the Code in 1978 was intended to create a single, unified remedy, not only for former chapter X and XI cases, but also for chapter XII cases that involved real estate partnerships typically owning only a single asset.[84] Indeed, the Code's inclusion of section 1111(b) was a response to the perceived abuses of chapter XII's treatment in single asset partnerships.[85]

Woodscape Ltd. Partnership), 134 B.R. 165, 168 (Bankr. D. Md. 1991) ("[S]ince this case involves a single asset of real property, there exists no possibility of reorganization . . . without it.").

83. *Id.* at 177-78. The court in *Woodscape* observed:

> While this court is seeing a greater number of motions for relief from stay against debtors with single real estate assets, the solution is not to make every reorganization of an insolvent debtor into a liquidation by denying equity holders the right of participation. Since few plans of reorganization in today's depressed real estate market could pay unsecured creditors 100% of their claims, refusing to permit equity holders an opportunity to invest destroys any incentive which might exist for capital contribution. Without fresh capital infusion, little hope exists for reorganizing deflated assets in a bad market. Such a result would violate a policy of the Bankruptcy Code to promote reorganization over liquidation where reorganization will preserve on-going business values and materially increase distributions to creditors, while adequately protecting the rights of senior secured creditors.

Id.

84. *In re* Triple R Holdings, L.P., 134 B.R 382, 388 (Bankr. N.D. Cal. 1991), *rev'd*, 145 B.R. 57 (N.D. Cal. 1992).

85. *See, e.g., In re* Pine Gate Assoc. [1977-1978 Transfer Binder], Bankr. L. Rep. (CCH) ¶ 66326 at 76126 (stating that under chapter XII, "value of the debt"

b. Economic Analysis

i. Facilitation of Negotiations

The current bankruptcy scheme can be viewed as a framework for debtor/creditor negotiations.[86] Without this framework, the debtor would have to resort to state law remedies, which are inefficient for several reasons. First, a state law liquidation would force an auction at a time when there was an asymmetrical distribution of information among potential bidders, and when the most knowledgeable of the bidders (the debtor and its owners) were constrained from bidding due to insufficient liquidity.[87] Second, because state law liquidation imposes additional losses in the form of lost going-concern premiums on the marginal creditors and equity holders, these parties may be willing to litigate and thereby attempt to delay the sale to the latest extent possible.[88] Third, a forced sale might depress the value of assets in the relevant market because it will give a false signal regarding the price at which a buyer and a seller would be willing to enter into an exchange.[89] Finally, unless the secured creditor, typically the winner in such auctions, is efficient in managing the property until it is resold, the liquidation sale will probably result in a net loss to society.[90] These economic inefficiencies are no less applicable to a

---

means value of the collateral).

86. *See, e.g.*, Douglas G. Baird & Randal C. Picker, *A Simple Noncooperative Bargaining Model of Corporate Reorganizations*, 20 J. LEGAL STUD. 311, 349 (1991) ("Rules that enhance exit options, such as the new value exception, may have virtues that have been neglected.").

87. *See id.* at 347 (noting that "manager is likely to have better information about the going concern value").

88. *See* Matthew L. Iwicki, Note, *Accounting for Relational Financing in the Creditors' Ex Ante Bargain: Beyond the General Average Model*, 76 VA. L. REV. 815, 819 (1990) (noting state liquidation law encourages individual creditor to "maximize its outcome through a strategy of non-cooperation," including delaying proceedings).

89. *See generally*, Douglas G. Baird & Thomas H. Jackson, *Bargaining After the Fall and the Contours of the Absolute Priority Rule*, 55 U. CHI. L. REV. 738, 743 n.17 (1988) (describing creditor worries in reorganizations)

90. *See id.* at 742 n.13 ("There may be assets that a secured creditor cannot effectively sell. For example, a supplier of unique and valuable input may refuse to deal with new owners.").

single asset debtor. Therefore, the economic rationale for permitting debtors to avail themselves of bankruptcy reorganization mandates that single asset debtors be allowed to utilize the new value exception since, without it, they are effectively denied the right to reorganize. In order to appreciate the relationship between the new value exception and the concept of negotiation, the following analysis is essential.

ii. Preservation of Going-Concern Premium

Most operating businesses have a going-concern premium which signifies that the business is worth more than the cumulative value of its individual assets.[91] This added worth is derived from management's payment of costs associated with hiring and training the work force, locating and acquiring space from which to operate the business, and marketing techniques that generate goodwill for the business and its products.[92] When a business encounters financial distress, this going-concern premium would be lost if creditors sought to enforce their rights through piecemeal liquidation.

According to the "Creditors' Bargain" model espoused by Baird and Jackson, rational and economically-motivated creditors would, but for the costs associated with negotiations, collectively agree to modify their various rights in order to avoid the debtor ever reaching the level of financial distress that could lead to such piecemeal liquidation.[93] Thus, under this model, the bankruptcy laws merely effect a bargaining process in which the creditors themselves should be willing to participate.

If single asset debtors had to base their right to reorganize under the bankruptcy laws on Creditors' Bargain model, they might very well fail, since there is presumably little traditional going-concern premium to protect. In most cases, there are very few employees and no real business operations to reorganize in a single asset case, other than day-to-day management and maintenance of the asset and dealings with potential or current lessees.[94]

---

91. *Id.* at 742-43 (discussing valuation of business as an existing entity versus creditors' concept of its worth).
92. *See id.* at 741 (commenting that previous owner of bankrupt company is better source of supplies and capital).
93. *See id.* at 747-59 (noting that company's value as a single entity considered higher by some creditors than its value as liquidated assets).
94. *See, e.g.*, Brian S. Katz, *Single-Asset Real Estate Cases and the Good Faith*

Nevertheless, because single asset debtors previously had recourse in the bankruptcy courts under chapter XII of the Bankruptcy Act, and because chapter 11 of the Code was enacted to take the place of chapters X, XI, and XII, Congress has granted single asset debtors the right to reorganize.[95]

iii. Common Disaster

If the Creditors' Bargain model does not support the single asset debtor's right to reorganize, then it cannot support the application of the new value exception, which was created to facilitate reorganization by allowing the confirmation of plans which violate the absolute priority rule. However, an expanded Creditors' Bargain model that includes creditors' willingness to share some of the risk of insolvency with equity holders in the case of a "common disaster" does provide a rationale for allowing the application of the exception.[96]

The Common Disaster idea assumes that because a sharing of risks results in modification of the secured creditor's rights, it will only be effected by

---

Requirement: Why Reluctance to Ask Whether Case Belongs in Bankruptcy May Lead to the Incorrect Result, 9 BANKR. DEV. J. 77, 77 (1992) (describing nature of Single Asset corporation). Even these tasks are frequently handled by an entity other than the debtor pursuant to a management contract. However, the entity is usually related to the debtor. *Id.*

95. *See generally*, Barbara E. Nelan, Comment, *Multiple Plans "On the Table" During the Chapter 11 Exclusivity Period*, 6 BANKR. DEV. J. 451, 451 (1989) (discussing the general history of chapter 11 as gleaned from chapters X, XI, XII from the former Bankruptcy Act). *Cf.* Toibb v. Radloff, 501 U.S. 157, 161 (1991) (holding individual may file chapter 11 petition). After *Toibb*, it is clear that there is no requirement that a debtor have an ongoing business in order to reorganize under chapter 11.

96. *See generally* Thomas H. Jackson & Robert E. Scott, *On the Nature of Bankruptcy: An Essay on Bankruptcy Sharing and the Creditors' Bargain*, 75 VA. L. REV. 155, 194-97 (1989) (justifying new value exception as softening of absolute priority rule in order to share risk). This justification is particularly valid "in areas of the country where 'exogenous' forces are responsible for dramatic dips in real estate value and equally dramatic evaporation of alternative sources of credit." Leif M. Clark, *The Single Asset and the Double Bind: Single Asset Real Estate Bankruptcy in the 1990's*, at 3 n.1 (1992) (unpublished manuscript, on file with authors) (commenting on the same).

allowing the creditor to impose higher interest rates on loans.[97] Therefore, although the new value exception circumvents the absolute priority rule, its application can be justified under the Common Disaster model because it represents a loss of value which the secured creditor has agreed to share in exchange for the debtor's payment of higher interest rates.[98]

iv. Absolute Priority Rule

In Baird and Jackson's economic analysis of the bankruptcy process, they depict the absolute priority rule as stemming from the "fair and equitable" requirements of the Code.[99] Simply stated, the absolute priority rule requires that senior classes of creditors be provided a means for payment in full, in

---

97. David A. Skeel, *The Uncertain State of an Unstated Rule: Bankruptcy's Contribution Rule Doctrine After* Ahlers, 63 AM. BANKR. L.J. 221, 234-36 (1989).

98. *Id.* at 240.

99. Baird & Jackson, *supra* note 89, at 764-66; *see also* Douglas G. Baird & Thomas H. Jackson, *Corporate Reorganizations and the Treatment of Diverse Ownership Interests: A Comment on Adequate Protection of Secured Creditors in Bankruptcy*, 51 U. CHI. L. REV. 97, 128-29 (1984) (discussing bankruptcy process); Thomas H. Jackson, *Bankruptcy, Non-Bankruptcy, and the Creditors' Bargain*, 91 YALE L.J. 857 (1982) (same).
The Code's "fair and equitable" doctrine originated under chapter X of the Act, which provided that a plan of reorganization had to conform to this requirement before it could be confirmed. De Forest Billyou, *A Decade of Corporate Reorganization Under Chapter X*, 49 COLUM. L. REV. 456, 480 (1949); DeForest Billyou, *Priority Rights of Security Holders in Bankruptcy Reorganization: New Directions*, 67 HARV. L. REV. 553, 561 (1954). *See also*, Walter J. Blum, *Full Priority and Full Compensation in Corporate Reorganizations*, 25 U. CHI. L. REV. 417, 418 (1958) (discussing fair and equitable doctrine under Bankruptcy Act); Victor Brudney, *The Bankruptcy Commission's Proposed Modifications of the Absolute Priority Rule*, 48 AM. BANKR. L.J. 305, 315 (1974) (discussing potential for change in fair and equitable doctrine); William Polatsek, *The Wreck of the Old 77: A Requiem Review of Equity Interests in Railroad Reorganizations under the Bankruptcy Act*, 34 CORNELL L.Q. 532, 534-35 (1949) (discussing fair and equitable doctrine); Note, *Absolute Priority Under Chapter X—A Rule of Law or a Familiar Quotation?*, 52 COLUM. L. REV. 900, 904 (1952) (same).

order of precedence of each class, before permitting junior classes to participate under the plan.[100] If this rule were as strictly enforced as these advocates desire, the secured creditors would always recover the value of their security, thus, there would be no motivation to negotiate with the debtor.

However, in determining whether the absolute priority rule is strictly satisfied and assuring that each class of creditors gets no more than it deserves, a court will often need to determine the value of the secured assets in question. For instance, the court will have to take into account the value of non-cash assets, the present value of assets received over some future period, the value of the estate's interest in an asset, and the value of an equity interest in the debtor.

Valuing a troubled entity usually involves debate and results in high costs. Current reorganization theories of valuation are based on the fiction that precise values can be ascertained for purposes of determining the allocation of resources.[101] However, practically speaking, a value cannot be expressed in precise terms; it can only be stated within a range.[102] Like the Heisenberg uncertainty principle of physics, it is not possible to measure both the current

---

100. *See* Ayer, *supra* note 29, at 966 (discussing absolute priority rule prior to *Ahlers*).

101. *See* Sandy Ridge Dev. Corp. v. Louisiana Nat'l Bank *(In re* Sandy Ridge Dev. Corp.), 881 F.2d 1346, 1354 (5th Cir. 1989) (concluding that bankruptcy court needed to find a precise value on one particular date, regardless of falling market). The Fifth Circuit noted:

> However, we must reject LNB's argument that the bankruptcy court cannot set the value of property but instead must in all instances require the debtor to abandon that property and let the foreclosure sale market determine its price. . . . Although we recognize that property valuation is not an exact science, it remains an integral part of the bankruptcy process.

Id. (citations omitted).

102. *See, e.g.*, Citibank, N.A. v. Baer, 651 F.2d 1341, 1347 (10th Cir. 1980). Judge Winner valued the debtor as "worth somewhere between $90 million and $100 million as a going concern, and to satisfy the people who want precision on the value, I fix the exact value of the company at the average of those, $96,856,850, which of course is a total absurdity that anybody could fix a value with that degree of precision, but for the lawyers who want me to make that fool estimate, I have just made it." *Id.* (citations omitted).

sales value of an asset if it were sold, and the long-term income stream of the asset if it were retained under existing management.

Historically, under chapter X, the valuation of a debtor did not take into account the actual income stream attributable to the then existing debtor; rather the process contemplated a regularized income stream. Further, the valuation procedure did not utilize a discount rate that represented the then current market, but contemplated a hypothetical fair rate of return. The process of debtor valuation under chapter X blended the regularized stream concept with the hypothetical fair rate of return concept, thereby overvaluing the debtor in order to permit junior classes to participate in the ongoing entity.[103] This was problematic because debtors and creditors, like buyers and sellers within a given market, have different expectations as to the future.[104] Thus, it is not a surprise that one substantial means of permitting each class to continue to participate in the investment was a going-concern value over valuation.

Strict application of the absolute priority rule is inefficient because it eliminates a creditor's incentive to negotiate. Applying absolute priority to various possible values permits each class to receive something, even if the expected value of the entity is such that some classes are "underwater," and would not otherwise be eligible for distribution.[105] In other words, where

---

103. *See* William H. Meckling, *Financial Markets, Default, and Bankruptcy: The Role of the State,* 41 LAW & CONTEMP. PROBS. 13, 35-36 (1977) (discussing valuation under chapter X's absolute priority rule); *see generally* ELIZABETH WARREN & JAY L. WESTBROOK, THE LAW OF DEBTORS AND CREDITORS: TEXT, CASES & PROBLEMS 672, 690 (2d ed. 1991) (discussing chapter X's impact on chapter 11).

104. *See* Donald C. Langevoort, *Theories, Assumptions, and Securities Regulation: Market Efficiency Revisited,* 140 U. PA. L. REV. 851, 858-65 (1992) (discussing inefficiency in market caused by conflicting interests of buyers and sellers); Lynn A. Stout, *Are Takeover Premiums Really Premiums? Market Price, Fair Value, and Corporate Law*, 99 YALE L.J. 1235, 1252 (1990) (commenting on differences in party estimates often depends upon their interests).

105. This process is similar to valuing series of call options because the options retain some value even when the strike price is greater than the current price (an "out-of-the-money" option).
Indeed, one commentator has suggested that by issuing such a series of options, the valuation problem could be avoided entirely. *See* Lucian Arye Bebchuk, *A*

values are ambiguous, the absolute priority rule could be interpreted as requiring a class to receive value even though the expected value of the debtor's assets is less than the claims of prior classes.[106] This result is consistent with the structure of the current chapter 11.[107] This conclusion also supports the decision made in 1978 to integrate chapters X and XI into a single chapter which incorporates the absolute priority rule but permits senior classes to consent to a partial giving up of value to junior classes in order to facilitate a "deal."[108]

New Approach to Corporate Reorganizations, 101 HARV. L. REV. 775, 781-86 (1988) (proposing method of improving reorganization).

106. *See* Mark E. MacDonald, Mark E. MacDonald, Jr., & Camille R. McLeod, *Pictures Are Worth a Thousand Words: Understanding the Chapter 11 Process Through Models and Simulations, in* ADVANCED BANKRUPTCY WORKSHOP 1990, at 468-80 (PLI Commercial Law & Practice Handbook Series No. 526, 1990), *reprinted and expanded as* CHAPTER 11 AS A DYNAMIC EVOLUTIONARY LEARNING PROCESS IN A MARKET WITH FUZZY VALUES, ANNUAL SURVEY OF BANKRUPTCY LAW 1993-1994 (Morton ed. 1993) (discussing absolute priority rule in relation to overvaluing debtor's assets).

107. *See* Peter F. Coogan, *Confirmation of a Plan Under the Bankruptcy Code*, 32 CASE W. RES. L. REV. 301, 321-27 (1982) (discussing reorganization under old chapters X and XI); Kenneth N. Klee, *All You Ever Wanted to Know About Cram Down Under the New Bankruptcy Code*, 53 AM. BANKR. L.J. 133, 145-46 (1979) (discussing impact of valuation in reorganization); Isaac M. Pachulski, *The Cram Down and Valuation Under Chapter 11 of the Bankruptcy Code*, 58 N.C. L. REV. 925, 943-44 (1980) (commenting on effect of valuation in chapter 11); J. Ronald Trost, *Business Reorganizations Under Chapter 11 of the New Bankruptcy Code*, 34 BUS. LAW. 1309, 1309-12 (1979) (same).

108. *See* William J. Boyes & Roger L. Faith, *Some Effects of the Bankruptcy Reform Act of 1978*, 29 J.L. & ECON. 139 (1986) (discussing 1978 revisions which were sparked by desire to modify absolute priority required under Act); Peter F. Coogan, Richard Broude & Herman Glatt, *Comments on Some Reorganization Provisions of the Pending Bankruptcy Bills*, 30 BUS. LAW. 1149, 1153 (1975) (discussing proposed changes in Act, especially concerning absolute priority rule); Klee, *supra* note 7, at 233 (questioning whether courts will allow senior creditors to subordinate claims to receive more value); Sidney Krause, chapter X and XI—A Study *in Contrasts*, 19 BUS. LAW. 511 (1964) (discussing difficulties of absolute priority rule under Bankruptcy Act); Benjamin Weintraub & Harris Levin, *Reorganization or Arrangement: An*

The new value exception tempers the strict absolute priority rule by giving creditors and debtors an incentive to negotiate.[109] Negotiation between the parties is clearly desirable because it avoids the costs, to creditors and to society, of determining the value of the debtor with certainty, usually accomplished only through liquidation. For creditors, the incentive to accept a potentially reduced return instead of demanding "the benefit of their bargain" is that it is collectively less expensive and more efficient to sacrifice part of a claim, than to attempt to value the entity exactly. The results under the old chapter X support this rationale. By not allowing a relaxation of the absolute priority rule, chapter X gave "out of the money" creditors or interest holders an incentive to delay the reorganization, and resulted in proceedings that tended to drag on for years before reaching a resolution.[110] However, the absolute priority rule can be utilized as a starting point for negotiations

---

Analysis of Contemporary Trends in Recent Cases, 37 REF. J. 103 (1963) (commenting on negotiations between creditors to avoid absolute priority); Benjamin Weintraub & Harris Levin, *A Sequel to Chapter X or Chapter XI: Coexistence for the Middle-Sized Corporation*, 26 FORDHAM L. REV. 292 (1957) (discussing further absolute priority rule); Comment: *Drawing a Line Between Chapter X and XI of the Bankruptcy Act—Standard of Reason vs. Strict `Public Securities' Test*, 50 NW. U. L. REV. 761 (1958).

109. It has been argued that the case-created requirements for the new value exception are so vague that the new value exception "introduces an enormously complicating factor in a carefully balanced bargaining structure." Phoenix Mut. Life Ins. Co. v. Greystone III Joint Venture (*In re* Greystone III Joint Venture), 995 F.2d 1274, 1283 (5th Cir. 1991), *vacated in part*, 995 F.2d 1284 (5th Cir.), *cert. denied*, 056 U.S. 821 (1992). Indeed, the inconsistencies found in cases ostensibly applying the exception support the conclusion that the standards are vague. However, it is that very inconsistency that tends to facilitate the bargaining process among the debtor and its creditors. If the outcome is not certain, the parties are more likely to reach a consensus than risk a result based on the vagaries of the new value exception. Furthermore, even if they fail to reach such a consensus, given the requirement that the bankruptcy judge review a plan of reorganization for good faith, fairness, and feasibility, and assuming that the judge uses that power with restraint to encourage bargaining, it is difficult to see what public policy is furthered by a prohibition of new investment from a particular class without the consent of creditors.

110. De Forest Billyou, *Priority Rights of Security Holders in Bankruptcy Reorganization: New Directions*, 67 HARV. L. REV. 553, 565-68 (1954).

because it represents the maximum amount a secured creditor could reasonably expect to receive from the debtor.

Furthermore, the idea that the Code should recognize the various groups of expected claims is not unique. The report of the Commission on the Bankruptcy Laws of the United States recommended that in order to support a plan of reorganization, the court needed only to find a "reasonable probability" that under the plan all creditors would be properly compensated.[111] The economic efficiencies associated with liquidation mandate that single asset debtors be allowed to utilize the new value exception since, without it, they are effectively denied the right to reorganize.

In sum, ambiguity in valuation creates legitimate zones for negotiation among creditors and interest holders. This negotiation could not occur outside chapter 11 as the parties are often facing liquidity constraints. Under this model, the goal of chapter 11 is to create a marketplace in which the previously existing contracts get retreaded or reworked by all of the participants in light of current conditions and future expectations. Thus understood, the judicial reluctance to interpret the "fair and equitable" standard rigidly, so that creditors always get the "benefit of their bargain," becomes more comprehensible. The new value exception both tempers the effect of the absolute priority rule and gives creditors an incentive to negotiate by increasing the range of potential solutions to avoid otherwise costly litigation.

c. Developments Since 1993

The principal appellate level decisions since publication of the earlier version of this article in 1993 have been *Bonner Mall Partnership v. U.S. Bancorp Mortgage Co. (In re Bonner Mall Partnership)*[112] and *In re Woodbrook Associates*.[113] *Bonner Mall* arose in the procedural context of a

---

111. *See* Victor Brudney, *The Bankruptcy Commission's Proposed "Modifications" of the Absolute Priority Rule,* 48 AM. BANKR. L.J. 305, 309 n.9 (1974) (quoting proposed requirements).

112. 2 F.3d 899 (9th Cir. 1993), *cert. granted,* 114 S. Ct. 681 (1994), *cert. dismissed as moot*, 115 S. Ct. 386 (1994). *See* David R. Kuney and Timothy R. Epp, *Aftermath of* Bonner Mall: *Evolution or Regression in the Notion of "New Value"?*, 5 J. BANKR. L. AND PRAC. 11-256 (1996).

113. 19 F.3d 312 (7th Cir. 1994).

motion for relief from stay.[114] Because the secured creditor was undersecured, the debtor asserted that retention of the mall by the debtor was necessary to an effective reorganization and that there was a reasonable possibility of successful reorganization within a reasonable time.[115] After the bankruptcy judge lifted the stay, both the District Court and the Ninth Circuit found that the new value exception was applicable.[116] The Ninth Circuit first utilized the "plain language" of section 1129(b)(2)(B)(ii) to interpret the meaning of that section's prohibition against retaining an interest under the plan by a junior claim "on account of" its junior claim or interest to allow the former owners to participate in the reorganized debtor *on account of* a substantial, necessary, fair new value contribution.[117] *Bonner Mall* suggests that bankruptcy courts should inquire whether a plan that gives stock to former equity holders does so primarily on account of the holder's interests in the debtor or whether the disbursement is for legitimate business reasons.[118] The court phrased the issue as whether, in fact: "old equity is unjustifiably attempting to retain its corporate ownership powers in violation of the absolute priority rule or whether there is a genuine and fair exchange of new capital for an equity interest."[119]

The Ninth Circuit expressly rejected the Fourth Circuit's view[120] as set forth in *Travelers Insurance Co. v. Bryson Properties, XVIII (In re Bryson Properties, XVIII)*,[121] which had suggested that a reorganization plan which gave old equity *alone* the right to obtain an interest in the reorganized debtor in exchange for new value violated the absolute priority rule.[122] Even if the exclusive opportunity to acquire such stock were viewed as property, the Ninth Circuit's approach to interpretation of the phrase "on account of" can still permit exclusive purchase of new equity by old equity for other reasons.[123]

---

114. *Bonner Mall*, 2 F.3d at 902.
115. *Id.*
116. *Id.* at 902-03, 917-18 (remanding to bankruptcy court to determine if requirements of new value exception were met).
117. *Id.* at 908.
118. *Id.* at 909.
119. *Bonner Mall*, 2 F.3d at 909.
120. *Id.* at 910.
121. 961 F.2d 496 (4th Cir.), *cert. denied*, 506 U.S. 866 (1992).
122. *Id.* at 504-05.
123. *Bonner Mall*, 2 F.3d at 910-11.

Examples include the notion that participation of old equity in the new business enhances the value of the business after reorganization, or that additional funding is easier to obtain once the old owners, the most likely investors, know in advance that their partners will all be familiar faces.[124] The court also made a vague assertion that if old equity would not participate without the incentive of an exclusive opportunity, this would be sufficient cause to allow the exclusive opportunity in the Ninth Circuit.[125]

In dealing with the question whether Congress intended for the language of section 1129(b) to change the interpretation of a judicially created concept, the Ninth Circuit relied upon *Pennsylvania Department of Public Welfare v. Davenport*[126] and *Dewsnup v. Timm*[127] to support its finding that specific demonstrated intent would be necessary to change prior law.[128] According to the rules of statutory construction, the fact that section 1129(b)(2) merely includes the general requirements listed in the Code expressly leaves room for additional factors to be considered in applying the principle in other particular circumstances.[129] When certiorari was granted from the Ninth Circuit decision, many in the Bankruptcy Bar believed that the new value issue would finally be settled. Instead, the parties reached a settlement, mooting the appeal.

In re Woodbrook Associates[130] is generally known for its controversial holding permitting classification of section 1111(b) claims separately from other unsecured claims; however, the decision also recognizes the continued viability of the new value exception.[131] In *Woodbrook*, the Seventh Circuit affirmed the denial of confirmation of a new value plan on the grounds of lack of substantial contribution because the plan offered, at most, a new infusion of $100,000, which was approximately 3.8 percent of the total unsecured

---

124. *Id.*
125. *See id.* at 911 (stating that giving equity an exclusive opportunity may satisfy "necessary to the success of the reorganization" requirement) (citations omitted).
126. 495 U.S. 552 (1990).
127. 502 U.S. 410 (1992).
128. *Bonner Mall*, 2 F.3d at 912.
129. *Id.*
130. 19 F.3d 312 (7th Cir. 1994).
131. *Id.* at 320.

debt.[132] It appears, then, that the new value exception is not fatal to creditors. In determining whether the combination was substantial, the *Woodbrook* court relied upon *In re Snyder*.[133] The court in *Snyder* affirmed the denial of confirmation of a plan that provided for the infusion of $30,000 of new capital representing 4.5 percent of the total amount to unsecured creditors.[134] The secured creditor, faced with a new value "offer" which is hedged with conditions, may find comfort in the court's finding that the new value plan was not confirmable because it unfairly discriminated among unsecured creditors.[135]

The decision in *In re Wynnefield Manor Associates, L.P.*[136] is consistent with the new focus upon the substantiality of the contribution rather than the existence of the new value exception.[137] In determining whether a contribution is substantial in the context of a small, closely-held debtor entity, the court examined two factors: 1) whether the proposed payment represents the partner's best efforts, and 2) the amount of the contribution or the percentage of return on claims projected to creditors.[138] The court found that the sum of $25,000, which was 6.08 percent of the secured creditors' unsecured claims, was inadequate in light of testimony that the partners, who owned numerous other real estate holdings, were of substantial means, that the sum was all that they were willing to contribute to this particular enterprise, and that payment only resulted in debtor paying 7.5 percent of its unsecured debt.[139]

By contrast, the same judge confirmed a plan by cramdown in *In re Capital Center Equities*.[140] In that case, based on the partners' limited financial means, a capital contribution that would result in a 30 percent return to unsecured creditors was found to satisfy the substantiality requirement.[141] Similarly, the *Wynnefield Manor* court also rejected consideration of whether

---

132. *Id.*
133. 967 F.2d 1126, 1131-32 (7th Cir. 1992).
134. *Id.*
135. *Woodbrook*, 19 F.3d at 321.
136. 163 B.R. 53 (Bankr. E.D. Pa. 1993).
137. *Id.* at 57-59.
138. *Id.* at 57.
139. *Id.*
140. 144 B.R. 262 (Bankr. E.D. Pa. 1992).
141. *Id.* at 270.

the partners' proposed contribution was proportionate to the value in the debtor that they were retaining, stating:

> We are obliged to consider that the Property has an upside potential as a going concern. If the Debtor's partners wish to savor the benefits of this upside potential, the prospect of which is their only apparent motivation for filing this case and proposing the Plan, then they are obliged to make some reasonable compensation in the nature of protection to the secured creditor in exchange for that creditor's bearing the risk of failure of this upside potential to materialize.[142]

Finally, the court found that the debtor had failed to show that the proposed capital contribution was necessary, since there was no evidence that the new funding was needed, for repairs or otherwise, in the reorganization process other than to make a nominal payment for unsecured creditors.[143]

Similarly, in *Oxford Life Insurance Co. v. Tucson Self-Storage, Inc. (In re Tucson Self Storage, Inc.)*,[144] the Ninth Circuit Bankruptcy Appellate Panel found that a $92,000 contribution was, in reality, a loan, adding another liability to the balance sheet, while bearing no cost, risk, or burden.[145] In *In re Dean*,[146] the court found that a $300,000 contribution by existing owners could constitute reasonably equivalent value and was necessary to make tenant improvements in order to renew a key existing lease.[147] The court however, denied confirmation of the plan on other grounds.[148]

In *Unruh v. Rushville State Bank*,[149] the Tenth Circuit refused to reach the issue of whether the new value exception to absolute priority continues to

---

142. *Wynnefield Manor*, 163 B.R. at 58; *see also* Katherine Kruis, *A Framework for Application of the New Value Exception*, 21 CAL. BANKR. J. 179, 216-25 (1993).
143. *Wynnefield Manor*, 163 B.R. at 58.
144. 166 B.R. 892 (Bankr. 9th Cir. 1994).
145. *Id.* at 899.
146. 166 B.R. 949 (Bankr. D.N.M. 1994).
147. *Id.* at 956.
148. *Id.* at 957. The other grounds included the artificial impairment of the unsecured creditor class, inadequate amortization, and the inadequate rate of return to the secured creditor. *Id.*
149. 987 F.2d 1506 (10th Cir. 1993).

exist, but rather focused on whether the proposed contributions were substantial, necessary to the success of the reorganization, and equal to, or in excess of the value of the retained interest.[150] In *Coones v. Mutual Life Insurance Co.*,[151] the district judge affirmed the dismissal and denied a motion to convert to chapter 12.[152] In so doing, the court deemed the proposed contribution insufficient to save the ranch.[153] *In re BMW Group I, Ltd.*[154] is one example of a court's refusal, notwithstanding its recognition of the new value exception, to permit the debtor-in-possession to exclusively retain the ongoing value if the court "cannot determine from the record that the interest would not bring a higher price if it were offered on the open market."[155]

An unusual wrinkle in the absolute priority rule occurred in *Mutual Life Insurance Co. v. Patrician St. Joseph Partners Ltd. Partnership (In re Patrician St. Joseph Partners Ltd. Partnership)*.[156] The court held that a fully secured creditor did not have standing to challenge the adequacy of a capital contribution where the unsecured class had voted in favor of the plan.[157] The court reasoned that "[t]he absolute priority rule requires [only] that the holder of an unsecured claim must receive the full amount of its allowed claim unless all junior claims and interests will receive no property and retain no interest under the plan."[158] This finding owes much to an earlier decision, *Mutual Life Insurance Co. v. Paradise Springs Associates (In re Paradise Springs Associates)*,[159] in which a less than fully secured creditor, who had elected to treat its unsecured claim as secured, lacked standing to raise the absolute priority rule.[160]

---

150. *Id.* at 1510.
151. 168 B.R. 247 (D. Wyo. 1994), *aff'd*, 56 F.3d 77 (10th Cir. 1995).
152. *Id.* at 260.
153. *Id.* at 255.
154. 168 B.R. 731 (Bankr. W.D. Okla. 1994).
155. *Id.* at 735. The court went further to hold that the plan did not satisfy the fair and equitable requirement under the Code. *Id.*
156. 169 B.R. 669 (D. Ariz. 1994).
157. *Id.* at 682.
158. *Id.*
159. 165 B.R. 913 (Bankr. D. Ariz. 1993).
160. *Id.* at 920-21.

The bankruptcy appellate panel in *Sun Valley Newspapers, Inc. v. Sun World Corp. (In re Sun Valley Newspapers, Inc.)*[161] upheld the bankruptcy court's award of relief from the automatic stay based upon the lower court's finding that there was no prospect of a successful reorganization within a reasonable period of time.[162] The plan attempted to provide "new value" from the cancellation of approximately $23,000 of insider claims, which the bankruptcy court found represented approximately 7 percent of the overall unsecured claims.[163] The bankruptcy panel held that the bankruptcy court had reasonably found that, if confirmed, the reorganized debtor would have assets worth more than $5 million, gross revenues of more than $3.7 million and net income, excluding debt service under the plan, of approximately $840,000.[164] The panel agreed with the bankruptcy court's finding that the value retained was far greater than the proposed contribution.[165] This decision is disturbing because the panel is asserting that a conversion of existing debts to equity cannot constitute new value.[166] The decision is further troublesome because the conversion of existing debt into new equity should be confirmable by cramdown without regard to new value analysis at all. The problem which prevented confirmation of *Sun Valley's* plan was the inadequate amount of debt released, and the release of insider liabilities on guarantees.[167] In a proper situation, if creditors who are also shareholders convert their insider claims to equity, the equity received is based upon the claim, not upon the equity interests. If the insider claim had been subject to equitable subordination so that it was not originally a member of the general unsecured creditor class, the issue might once again involve new value analysis, but only because the specific claim was junior.

In re Dollar Associates[168] is an interesting example of the apparent trend in cases where courts are beginning to focus upon factors other than the existence of the new value exception. In denying confirmation, the court held

---

161. 171 B.R. 71 (Bankr. 9th Cir. 1994).
162. *Id.* at 78.
163. *Id.* at 77.
164. *Id.* at 78.
165. *Id.*
166. *See Sun Valley*, 171 B.R. at 78 (finding contribution by insiders did not constitute infusion of new funds as contemplated by new value exception).
167. *See id.* (stating that main purpose of plan was to benefit insiders).
168. 172 B.R. 945 (Bankr. N.D. Cal. 1994).

that satisfaction of the absolute priority rule was only a minimum requirement for confirmation, and that a plan that did not further goals of reorganization and which undermined statutes prohibiting lien stripping could not be confirmed.[169] Though there was no debate that this was both a substantial and necessary contribution, the court insisted that compliance with absolute priority by new value does not guarantee that a plan is confirmable.[170] The decision outlines a series of factors which would be universally applicable to all single asset real estate partnerships which are undersecured.[171] First, the debtor's plan did not further the recognized reorganization goal of preserving equity of the debtor.[172] Second, the debtor's plan did not further the recognized reorganization goals of preserving jobs and going-concern value and preventing the shrinkage of economic activity resulting from the liquidation of a going business.[173] Third, the debtor's plan did not significantly further the recognized reorganization goal of maximizing distribution to creditors.[174] Fourth, the plan did not further the recognized reorganization goal of discharging debtors or its principals.[175] Fifth, the debtor's plan had been rejected by the overwhelming majority of the claims.[176] Sixth, confirmation would have undermined the congressional determination that a lien should generally not be reduced on the basis of court-determined valuation of the collateral over the lienholder's objection, a concept known as lien stripping.[177]

---

169. *See id.* at 949 (finding plan was not fair and equitable irrespective of whether it satisfied new value exception).
170. *Id.* at 949 (reasoning that under § 1129(b)(2) there are other requirements to be met besides absolute priority rule).
171. *Id.* at 946-52.
172. *Id.* at 949-50 (finding debtor had no genuine economic interest).
173. *Dollar Assocs.*, 172 B.R. at 950 (finding foreclosure would not lead to overall loss of jobs).
174. *Id.*
175. *Id.* at 950-51 (reasoning that secured creditor note was nonrecourse by its own terms).
176. *Id.* at 951 (finding 97.5 percent of unsecured claimants and 99.1 percent of secured claimants rejected debtor's plan).
177. *Id.* (expressing concern regarding possible erroneous valuation and seeking to prevent debtor from retaining exclusive benefit of future appreciation in collateral value).

The *Dollar Associates* decision deals with *Bonner Mall*[178] by suggesting that because the debtor's plan fulfills few, if any, recognized goals of reorganization, confirmation would not constitute a *successful* reorganization.[179] In footnote 14, the court stated:

> I am also inclined not to rely on Gold Coast's argument that Debtor is guilty of "class gerrymandering" and "artificial impairment," because I believe courts often use improper classification as a rationale to deny confirmation in single-asset real estate cases where the court's real concerns are similar to those I have relied upon in holding that Debtor's plan is not fair and equitable in an overall sense. The result of some of those decisions is the creation of classification rules stricter than the language of the Code requires and that may be inappropriate outside the context of a single-asset real estate case.[180]

With this footnote, the discussion of new value as an exception to the absolute priority rule in single asset real estate cases appears to have come full circle. Not only is it unclear whether the new value doctrine exists within a particular circuit, but whether the strong policy views of individual judges redefine the controlling question as the scope of judicial discretion in the event that a debtor's plan meets a narrowly focused analysis of new value.

Conclusion

Based on personal experience as an attorney for secured and unsecured creditors under chapter XI, the senior author of this article has little question that the internal balance of chapter 11 is considerably more creditor-oriented than was chapter XI. The inclusion of the concept of adequate protection, generated from Murphy's leading article on restraint and reimbursement,[181]

---

178. Bonner Mall Partnership v. U.S. Bancorp Mortgage Co. (*In re* Bonner Mall), 2 F.3d 899 (9th Cir. 1993), *cert. granted*, 114 S. Ct. 681 (1994), *cert. dismissed as moot*, 115 S. Ct. 386 (1994).

179. *Dollar Assoc.*, 172 B.R. at 949 (stating that confirmation may not be fair and equitable even if new value exception satisfied).

180. *Id.* at 953 n. 14 (citations omitted).

181. *See* Patrick A. Murphy, *Restraint and Reimbursement: The Secured Creditor in Reorganization and Arrangement Proceedings*, 30 BUS. LAW. 15, 37-38,

generally means that the secured creditor's rights will receive substantial attention while in chapter 11. By contrast, since the chapter 11 judge does possess substantial power, the equitable stretching of powers that was so characteristic of the "Doomsday Principle"[182] under chapter XI has been substantially lessened. In the balance between the unsecured creditors and the debtor, the ability to file a competing plan substantially increases the bargaining power of the unsecured creditors as against the debtor.[183] The debtor's threat under chapter X that it would shoot itself and cause a liquidation often led to plans that paid unsecured creditors a nickel or a dime on the dollar.

By contrast, chapter 11 plans proposing a paltry distribution to unsecured creditors are clearly the exception rather than the rule. The flexibility of chapter 11 in allowing senior classes to consent to the participation of junior classes, coupled with judicial recognition of the new value exception to the absolute priority rule, provides a realistic means by which to shorten the bargaining process in comparison to the chapter X analogue. The resultant shorter process involves substantially lower costs to the participant. Vigorous trading within a market among those having an economic interest is preferable to the decision of an allegedly omniscient third party trustee or judge. This concept is consistent with the modern economic emphasis on market-driven solutions, rather than solutions centrally and bureaucratically imposed.

The Code was not brought down from the mountain on tablets of stone, and thus it is not a matter of natural law, nor was it created for the benefit of University of Chicago economists. The Scalia dissent in *Dewsnup v. Timm*[184] forcibly asserts that point. It is also not a new building without a past; both *Dewsnup* and *Midlantic National Bank v. New Jersey Department of Environmental Protection*[185] view the statute more like an ancient city in

---

43-47 (1974) (concluding that court should have power to protect secured creditor against loss of value in collateral).

182. *See* Paul F. Festersen, *Equitable Powers in Bankruptcy Rehabilitation: Protection of the Debtor and the Doomsday Principle*, 46 AM. BANKR. L.J. 311, 317-23 (1972) (discussing Doomsday Principle).

183. *See* Meckling, *supra* note 103, at 34-35 (stating chapter X may have limited creditor's bargaining power).

184. 502 U.S. 410 (1992) (Scalia, J., dissenting).

185. 474 U.S. 494 (1985) (Rehnquist, J., dissenting).

which the buried layers must be examined for a proper understanding of the present structure.

Finally, the Code must be understood as a political act of highly political legislators who are swayed by populism as well as property rights. One political purpose of chapter 11 in merging the debtor-oriented provisions of chapters XI and XII with the creditor-oriented provisions of chapter X was to create a more flexible system than chapter X with more power than chapter XI. We have suggested in other writings that the result is a mandatory bargaining statute.[186]

The new value exception to the absolute priority rule is a valuable means to promote negotiation, particularly in single asset cases. Additionally creditors are assured that if a bargaining failure results, the Code gives courts the power to effect closure through liquidation.

---

186. *See generally* MACDONALD & PERKINS, *supra* note 4; MacDonald et al., *supra* note 106 (arguing bankruptcy market for "trading for objects and for information" key Code concepts intentionally left undefined to encourage negotiation).

CHAPTER IX

THE NEW VALUE EXCEPTION: SQUARE PEG IN A ROUND HOLE

SALVATORE G. GANGEMI
STEPHEN BORDANARO

Section 1129(b)[1] of the Bankruptcy Code of 1978 (the "Code"),[2] provides for the confirmation of a plan of reorganization over the objections of a class[3]

---

1. 11 U.S.C. § 1129(b) (1994).
2. Bankruptcy Reform Act of 1978 as amended, 11 U.S.C. §§ 101-1330 (1994). The purpose behind the Bankruptcy Reform Act of 1978 was to modernize the bankruptcy laws. H.R. REP. NO. 595, 95th Cong., 2d Sess. 3 (1978), *reprinted in* 1978 U.S.C.C.A.N. 5963, 5965. Prior to 1978, the bankruptcy system was governed by the Bankruptcy Act of 1898. *Id.* The only substantial revision to the Act occurred in 1938, when Congress enacted the Chandler Act. *See id.* at 5966; Chandler Act of July 22, 1938, ch. 575, 52 Stat. 840 (repealed by Pub. L. No. 95-598).
3. *See* 11 U.S.C. § 1122 (1994) (defining classes). Under § 1122, "a plan may place a claim or an interest in a particular class only if such claim or interest is substantially similar to the other claims or interests of such class." *Id.* Courts have allowed debtors some flexibility in classifying claims within a class. *See, e.g.*, Teamsters Nat'l Freight Indus. Negotiating Comm. v. U.S. Truck Co. (*In re* U.S. Truck Co.), 800 F.2d 581, 587 (6th Cir. 1986) (allowing separation of union's unsecured claim based on company's rejection of collective bargaining agreement from other creditors); Steelcase, Inc. v. Johnston (*In re* Johnston), 140 B.R. 526, 529 (Bankr. 9th Cir. 1992) (allowing separate classification of unsecured creditor having security interest from other creditors), *aff'd*, 21 F.3d 323 (9th Cir. 1994); *In re* Aztec Co., 107 B.R. 585, 587 (Bankr. M.D. Tenn. 1989) (stating that debtor may classify recourse claims separately from nonrecourse claims); *In re* A.G. Consultants Grain Div., Inc., 77 B.R. 665, 674-76 (Bankr. N.D. Ind. 1987) (permitting debtor to separate creditors with whom he continued to transact business from all other unsecured creditors). However, courts have struck down plans designed to manipulate classes to

of impaired creditors,[4] provided that the plan is "fair and equitable."[5] It has been labeled the "cramdown" provision.[6] With respect to an unsecured class,

---

insure acceptance of the plan. *See, e.g.*, Phoenix Mut. Life Ins. Co. v. Greystone III Joint Venture (*In re* Greystone III Joint Venture), 995 F.2d 1274, 1279 (5th Cir. 1991) (stating classification scheme should not be approved when classification is done to insure acceptance), *vacated in part*, 995 F.2d 1284 (5th Cir.), *cert. denied*, 506 U.S. 821 (1992); Olympia & York Florida Equity Corp. v. Bank of New York (*In re* Holywell Corp.), 913 F.2d 873, 880 (11th Cir. 1990) (finding debtor's discretion in classification not unlimited); Hanson v. First Bank of S.D., N.A., 828 F.2d 1310, 1313 (8th Cir. 1987) (maintaining that potential for abuse by debtor is significant when classification of claims is done to assure acceptance of plan); Piedmont Assocs. v. Cigna Property & Casualty Ins. Co., 132 B.R. 75, 78 (N.D. Ga. 1991) (requiring, absent valid business reasons, similar creditors to be classified together to prevent discrimination).

4. *See* 11 U.S.C. § 1124 (1994) (describing unimpaired claims). Determining which classes are impaired is important because unimpaired classes are deemed to have accepted the plan. 11 U.S.C. § 1129(a)(8) (1994). Under § 1124, every class is deemed impaired by a plan unless at least one of two conditions are met: first, the plan does not alter "the legal, equitable, and contractual rights" of the creditors or interest holders comprising the class, *Id.* § 1124(1); second, where the plan proposes to cure a "default that occurred before or after the commencement of the [bankruptcy] case," other than a default relating to bankruptcy or insolvency, *Id.* § 1124(2)(A), reinstates the maturity dates that existed prior to default, *Id.* § 1124(2)(B), compensates creditors or interest holders for damages resulting from their "reasonable reliance . . . on [a] contractual provision or such applicable law, *Id.* § 1124(2)(C), and does not alter the rights of a creditor or interest holder in any other way, *Id.* § 1124(2)(D).

5. 11 U.S.C. § 1129(b)(1) (1994). "The Code does not define `fair and equitable.' Congress intended that the contours of this requirement be shaped by pre-Code history, and the individualized review of particular cases." Bruce A. Markell, *Owners, Auctions, and Absolute Priority in Bankruptcy Reorganizations*, 44 STAN. L. REV. 69, 71 (1991). The examples listed in 11 U.S.C. § 1129(b)(2) were not intended to be exclusive. *See* 124 CONG. REC. 17,403, 17,420 (1978) (statement of Rep. Edwards).

6. "Cramdown" is the second of two methods to confirm a plan of reorganization. *See, e.g., U.S. Truck Co.*, 800 F.2d at 583 (considering two means for confirmation of plan). The first method is consensual, requiring the assent of each impaired class. 11 U.S.C. § 1129(a)(8)(A) (1994).

the fair and equitable standard requires adherence to absolute priority.[7] A pre-Code exception to the absolute priority rule permitted equity holders to contribute new capital under a plan of reorganization in exchange for an interest in the debtor equal to their contribution, without having to satisfy senior claims fully.[8] Unlike the absolute priority rule, this "new value exception" was not expressly enacted in the Code; therefore, its viability under

---

Both methods require that the plan be feasible, 11 U.S.C. § 1129(a)(11) (1994); that the plan be proposed in good faith and not contrary to law, *id.* § 1129(a)(3); that at least one impaired class assent to the plan, *id.* § 1129(a)(10); and that each nonassenting creditor and interest holder receive not less than such creditor would receive in a liquidation, *id.* § 1129(a)(7). This latter requirement is often referred to as the "best interests of creditors" rule. BENJAMIN WEINTRAUB & ALAN N. RESNICK, BANKRUPTCY LAW MANUAL, ¶ 8.23[2] (3d ed. 1992) [hereinafter WEINTRAUB & RESNICK].

7. *See* 11 U.S.C. § 1129(b)(2)(B)(ii) (1994) (providing that fair and equitable "[w]ith respect to a class of unsecured claims [means that] the holder of any claim or interest that is junior to the claims of such class will not receive or retain under the plan on account of such junior claim or interest any property."). The meaning given to fair and equitable under the Code was first articulated in Case v. Los Angeles Lumber Prods. Co., 308 U.S. 106, 114-18 (1939). For a discussion of *Case* and the history behind the fair and equitable standard, *see infra* notes 13-21 and accompanying text.

8. *Case*, 308 U.S. at 121-22 (enunciating new value exception to absolute priority rule). *Case* outlined the particular requirements for application of the new value exception as follows: "the stockholder's participation must be based on a [necessary] contribution in money or in money's worth, reasonably equivalent in view of all the circumstances to the participation of the stockholder." *Id.* at 122.

Case's reasoning on new value based its decision dealing with the new value exception on dicta found in Kansas City Terminal Ry. v. Central Union Trust Co., 271 U.S. 445, 455 (1926). *See Case*, 308 U.S. at 114-17. Citing the absolute priority rule, the Court in *Kansas City Terminal Ry.* refused to confirm a reorganization plan that provided shareholders shares in the new corporation without satisfying creditors. *Kansas City Terminal Ry.*, 271 U.S. at 455. However, in dicta the Court stated that "[g]enerally, additional funds will be essential to the success of the undertaking, and it may be impossible to obtain them unless stockholders are permitted to contribute and retain an interest sufficiently valuable to move them." *Id.*

current bankruptcy law has been questioned.[9] This has led to division in the courts, with some finding that the new value exception survived the Code's enactment,[10] and others finding that it did not.[11] The question often arises in

---

9. *See* Norwest Bank Worthington v. Ahlers, 485 U.S. 197, 203 (1988). The Court refused to decide whether the new value exception survived the Code and instead stated that "[*Ahlers*] should not be taken as any comment on the continuing vitality of the [new value] exception . . . ." *Id.* at 203 n.3. Writing for the Court, Justice White interpreted the "money or money's worth" language of *Case* narrowly, and found the promise of future labor not included under the purview of "new value." *Id.* at 206.

Prior to *Ahlers*, many courts had assumed that the new value exception survived the Code's enactment. *See, e.g.*, *Teamsters Nat'l Freight Indus.*, 800 F.2d at 588 (applying new value exception to Code without discussion); Official Creditors' Comm. v. Potter Material Serv., Inc. (*In re* Potter Material Serv., Inc.), 781 F.2d 99, 101-02 (7th Cir. 1986) (stating that new value exception contained within absolute priority of § 1129); *In re* A.G. Consultants Grain Div., Inc., 77 B.R. 665, 677 (Bankr. N.D. Ind. 1987) (finding that Code cases universally apply new value exception); *In re* Sawmill Hydraulics, Inc., 72 B.R. 454, 456 (Bankr. C.D. Ill. 1987) (declaring that long standing principal of law holds shareholder may retain interest in company if invests new capital); *In re* Landau Boat Co., 13 B.R. 788, 792 (Bankr. W.D. Mo. 1981) (holding § 1129(b) to require impaired dissenting class receive full claim over junior interest except when new money is contributed by junior interest); Buffalo Sav. Bank v. Marston Enters. (*In re* Marston Enters.), 13 B.R. 514, 518 (Bankr. E.D.N.Y. 1981) (finding that new value exception as stated in *Case* applies to § 1129(b)).

10. See, e.g., Oxford Life Ins. v. Tucson Self-Storage, Inc. (*In re* Tucson Self-Storage, Inc.), 166 B.R. 892, 899 (Bankr. 9th Cir. 1994) (acknowledging that Ninth Circuit recognizes new value exception); *In re* Sovereign Group 1985-27, Ltd., 142 B.R. 702, 707 (E.D. Pa. 1992) (maintaining that no evidence exists in legislative history to indicate new value exception does not exist under Code); *In re* 222 Liberty Assocs., 108 B.R. 971, 984-85 (E.D. Pa. 1990) (stating new value exception provides debtor with capital necessary to reorganization's success); *In re* U.S. Truck, 47 B.R. 932, 941 (E.D. Mich. 1985) (allowing new value exception), *aff'd sub nom.*, Teamsters Nat'l Freight Indus. Negotiating Comm. v. U.S. Truck Co. (*In re* U.S. Truck), 800 F.2d 581 (6th Cir. 1986); *In re* Rocha, 179 B.R. 305, 307 (Bankr. M.D. Fla. 1995) (holding new value exception survived Code); Penn. Mut. Life Ins. Co. v. Woodscape Ltd. Partnership (*In re* Woodscape Ltd. Partnership), 134 B.R.

cases where a single asset real estate debtor seeks bankruptcy protection in an effort to avoid losing property in a foreclosure proceeding.[12]

165, 175 (Bankr. D. Md. 1991) (finding statutory language does not reject new value exception); *In re* Sherwood Square Assocs., 107 B.R. 872, 887 (Bankr. D. Md. 1989) (assuming without discussion that new value exception survives); *In re* Aztec Co., 107 B.R. 585, 588 (Bankr. M.D. Tenn. 1989) (stating that new value exception is endorsed by Sixth Circuit); *In re* Henke, 90 B.R. 451, 455 (Bankr. D. Mont. 1988) ("proper statutory construction dictates that by using the term 'includes' in § 1129(b)(2), Congress clearly intended that the examples set forth in that section are not limiting, but rather invite an open ended approach, such as the [new value] exception . . ."); *Landau Boat*, 13 B.R. at 792 (assuming without discussion that new value exception is still viable); *Marston Enters.*, 13 B.R. at 517-18 nothing in Code precludes existence of new value exception).

11. *See, e.g.*, Unruh v. Rushville State Bank, 987 F.2d 1506, 1507 (10th Cir. 1993) (holding new value exception nonexistent under Code); Piedmont Assocs. v. Cigna Property & Casualty Ins. Co., 132 B.R. 75, 79 (N.D. Ga. 1991) (finding "the plain language of § 1129(b)(2)(B) and the intent of Congress precludes the existence of any new value exception . . .); *In re* Lumber Exch. Ltd. Partnership, 125 B.R. 1000, 1008 (Bankr. Minn.) (finding that Code does not permit confirmation where new value contribution is provided in plan), *aff'd sub nom*, Lumber Exch. Bldg. Ltd. Partnership v. Mutual Life Ins. Co. of N.Y. (*In re* Lumber Exch. Bldg. Ltd. Partnership), 134 B.R. 345 (D. Minn. 1991), *aff'd*, 968 F.2d 647 (8th Cir. 1992); Pennbank v. Winters (*In re* Winters), 99 B.R. 658, 663 (Bankr. W.D. Pa. 1989) (determining Congress did not mention new value exception in Code as aspect of "fair and equitable" test, thus, it no longer exists).

12. *See, e.g.*, Travelers Ins. Co. v. Bryson Properties, XVIII (*In re* Bryson Properties, XVIII), 961 F.2d 496, 498-99 (4th Cir.) (debtor filed petition after learning of secured creditor's intention to start foreclosure proceeding on commercial property), *cert. denied*, 506 U.S. 866 (1992); *Lumber Exch.*, 968 F.2d at 647 (creditor sought relief from stay after debtor filed petition to halt foreclosure proceeding); Phoenix Mut. Life Ins. Co. v. Greystone III Joint Venture (*In re* Greystone III Joint Venture), 995 F.2d 1274, 1275 (5th Cir. 1991) (debtor defaulted on office building mortgage and secured creditor brought foreclosure action), *vacated in part*, 995 F.2d 1284 (5th Cir.), *cert. denied*, 506 U.S. 821 (1992); *In re* Triple R Holdings, 134 B.R. 382, 384 (Bankr. N.D. Cal. 1991) (debtor filed petition under chapter 11 after secured creditor started foreclosure proceeding on condominium unit), *rev'd sub nom.*, First Republic Thrift & Loan v. Triple R Holdings, L.P. (*In re* Triple R

It is submitted that both statutory interpretation of the Code and an examination of the new value exception's ramifications reveal that, in the absence of Congressional directive, the exception should not apply to single asset real estate reorganizations. Part A of this Chapter will examine the seminal cases which first articulated and defined the new value exception. Part B will discuss how different circuits have addressed the issue. Finally, Part C will focus on why the new value exception is inappropriate for application in single asset reorganizations.

Holdings, L.P.), 145 B.R. 57 (N.D. Cal. 1992).

The typical single asset debtor is a partnership that invested in commercial real estate to enjoy favorable depreciation tax benefits. Brian S. Katz, *Single-Asset Real Estate Cases and the Good Faith Requirement: Why Reluctance to Ask Whether a Case Belongs in Bankruptcy May Lead to the Incorrect Result*, 9 BANKR. DEV. J. 77, 78 (1992) (discussing typical single-asset debtor); H. Miles Cohn, *Good Faith and the Single Asset Debtor*, 62 AM. BANKR. L.J. 131 (1988) (stating single-asset debtor typically investment vehicle). The benefits of such investments was drastically curbed by the Tax Reform Act of 1986. Tax Reform Act of 1986, Pub. L. No. 99-514, 100 Stat. 2085 (eliminating many commercial real estate depreciation benefits); *see also In re* Prince Manor Apts. Ltd., 104 B.R. 414, 416-17 (Bankr. N.D. Fla. 1989) (contrasting tax benefits under old law with changes made in 1986). Additionally, the single asset debtor was hindered by the economic downturn in the real estate industry. *See* Michael L. Molinaro, *Single-Asset Real Estate Bankruptcies: Curbing an Abuse of the Bankruptcy Process*, 24 UCC L.J. 161, 161-62 (1991) (describing how change in tax law and downturn in real estate market caused bankruptcies of many real estate limited partnerships). *See generally* Alan J.B. Aronsohn, *The Tax Reform Act of 1986-Some Selected Real Estate Problems and Possibilities*, 14 J. REAL EST. TAX'N 203, 204-06 (1987) (discussing deleterious effects of Tax Reform Act of 1986 such as higher tax rates on long term capital gains, repeal of real estate exception to at risk rules and reduction in available tax benefits for low income housing); James R. Follain et al., *The Impact of the 1986 Tax Reform Act on Real Estate*, 17 REAL EST. REV. 76, 78-82 (1987) (discussing how new tax law impacts on income producing property and real estate investments made before enactment of Act of 1986).

A. The New Value Exception in the Supreme Court

1. Case v. Los Angeles Lumber Products Co.

Case v. Los Angeles Lumber Products Co.[13] was the first Supreme Court case to recognize the new value exception.[14] Writing for a unanimous Court, Justice Douglas refused to confirm a plan on the grounds that it was not fair and equitable under section 77B[15] of the Bankruptcy Act of 1898 ("the Act").[16] Justice Douglas interpreted the requirement that a plan be fair and equitable as requiring absolute priority.[17] The Court held that the plan violated the

---

13. 308 U.S. 106 (1939).
14. *Id.* at 121-22; *see supra* notes 7-8 and accompanying text.
15. Act of June 7, 1934, ch. 424, § 77B, 48 Stat. 911, 912 (repealed 1938) (concerning corporate reorganizations); *see Case*, 308 U.S. at 119-20 n.14 (discussing new value exception with respect to section 77B).
16. *Case*, 308 U.S. at 119-20. *Case* was decided after Congress had already replaced § 77B through the Chandler Act of 1938. *See* Chandler Act of 1935, ch. 575, 52 Stat. 840, 883-905 (repealed 1978). However, shortly thereafter, the Supreme Court ruled that the meaning of fair and equitable as stated in *Case* was still applicable under chapter X of the Chandler Act. *See* Marine Harbor Properties, Inc. v. Manufacturer's Trust Co., 317 U.S. 78, 85 (1942) (finding fair and equitable applies under chapter X as it did under § 77B).
17. *Case,* 308 U.S. at 117-20. Absolute priority requires that a senior creditor's claims be fully satisfied before any junior interest or claim. *Id.* The *Case* Court pronounced that fair and equitable "had acquired a fixed meaning through judicial interpretations in the field of equity receivership reorganizations." *Id.* at 115. The court based its decision on a line of cases involving the equity receiverships of railroads. *See* Northern Pac. Ry. v. Boyd, 228 U.S. 482, 504 (1913) (stating that general creditors of company can always assert superior rights against equity holders until fully compensated); *see also* Kansas City Terminal Ry. v. Central Union Trust Co., 271 U.S. 445, 454-55 (1926) (requiring shareholders to participate in foreclosure sale if their money is essential to company's success and to ensure all creditor's rights are preserved); Louisville Trust Co. v. Louisville, N.A. & C. Ry., 174 U.S. 674, 684 (1899) (maintaining no arrangements between parties can ever subordinate rights of creditors against equity interest). For additional background on the origin of the absolute priority rule, *see generally* Markell, *supra* note 5 at 74-87 (discussing development of absolute priority rule); Douglas Baird & Thomas Jackson, *Bargaining After the Fall and the Contours of the Absolute Priority*

absolute priority rule because it provided for stockholder participation in the reorganized corporation, without first satisfying the claims of bondholders fully.[18]

The Court in *Case* emphasized that a prior shareholder's participation in a plan of reorganization of an insolvent corporation might be permitted where shareholders contribute "new value" to the plan.[19] Several requirements had to be met, however, for this exception to apply: first, the necessity for new capital must exist; second, the interest retained by the shareholder must be "reasonably equivalent" to the contribution; and finally, the contribution must be tangible and based on "money or money's worth."[20] Based on the facts of *Case*, the Court rejected the argument that the shareholders' continued participation in the management of the corporation fulfilled these requirements.[21]

Rule, 55 U. CHI. L. REV. 738, 739-40 (1988) (discussing absolute priority and its origin and application to receiverships involving railroads).

18. *Case*, 308 U.S. at 115-16. The plan provided that the stockholders would retain a 23% interest in the reorganized corporation. *Id.* at 112. At the time of the plan, the debtor's assets were $830,000 and its liabilities totalled more than $3,800,000. *Id.* at 109, 111.

19. *Id.* at 121. *See supra* note 8 and accompanying text.

20. *Case*, 308 U.S. at 121-22. Courts applying *Case* have generally required that a shareholder's new value contribution be in the form of cash or another tangible asset. *Compare* Official Creditors' Comm. v. Potter Material Serv., Inc. (*In re* Potter Material Serv., Inc.), 781 F.2d 99, 102-03 (7th Cir. 1986) (determining cash and personal guarantee acceptable as new value contribution) *and* Brown v. Brown's Indus. Uniforms, Inc. (*In re* Brown's Indus. Uniforms, Inc.), 58 B.R. 139, 141 (N.D. Ill. 1985) (considering stockholder pledge of security for loan to debtor corporation fresh contribution) *and In re* Landau Boat Co., 13 B.R. 788, 792-93 (Bankr. W.D. Mo. 1981) (declaring combination of cash and loan commitment acceptable new capital contribution) *with In re* Snyder, 967 F.2d 1126, 1131-32 (7th Cir. 1992) (holding cash payment of $30,000 and release of lien on farm equipment worth $20,000 insufficient contribution) *and In re* Stegall, 865 F.2d 140, 142-44 (7th Cir. 1989) (finding future labor and services not acceptable contribution) *and In re* Rocha, 179 B.R. 305, 307-08 (Bankr. M.D. Fla. 1995) (holding mortgage and promise of future earning "not considered new value") *and In re* Pecht, 57 B.R. 137, 140-41 (Bankr. E.D. Va. 1986) (finding promise of future earnings unacceptable as new value contribution).

21. *Case*, 308 U.S. at 122. The consideration given by the *Case* shareholders in

2. Norwest Bank Worthington v. Ahlers

Although the new value exception was not specifically enumerated in the Code, most courts assumed that it was still viable after the Code's enactment.[22] However, the Supreme Court questioned the validity of this assumption in the 1988 case, *Norwest Bank Worthington v. Ahlers*.[23] In *Ahlers*, the debtor-farmers proposed a plan whereby they would retain their farm in exchange for a contribution of new value in the form of their "labor, experience, and expertise."[24] The Eighth Circuit reversed both the bankruptcy court and the district court and found that the farmer's contribution of this "sweat equity" constituted new value.[25]

The Supreme Court reversed the Eighth Circuit,[26] holding that the debtor's promise of future labor, experience and expertise as a farmer did not meet the requirements of new value as stated in *Case*.[27] Despite the overwhelming

---

exchange for shares included the following: first, the company would receive the shareholders' familiarity with business operations, their "financial standing and influence in the community" and "continuity of management;" second, the bondholders were to receive more under the plan than they would in a foreclosure sale (where they would have received less than the appraised value of the property); third, a provision contained in a previous voluntary reorganization plan, which prevented bondholders from foreclosing for a fourteen year period, would be abrogated; finally, because the business would remain in operation, the bondholders would obtain value which outweighed the stock benefits received by the stockholders. The courts below had confirmed the plan because they believed this consideration was sufficient. *Id.* at 112-13.

22. *See supra* note 10 and accompanying text. Until the adoption of the Code there was relatively little controversy surrounding the new value exception. Markell *supra* note 5 at 92-93 (attributing lack of pre-Code litigation to bankrupt's preference for chapter XI filing and inability to prove sufficient value of contribution).
23. 485 U.S. 197 (1988).
24. *Id.* at 201.
25. *Id.* at 200-01. The Eighth Circuit found that the absolute priority rule did not preclude an equity holder from retaining an interest in the property in exchange for a contribution of money or money's worth. *Id.* It held that the farmer's labor, experience, and expertise did fit under this rubric, and therefore confirmed the plan over the creditor's objection. *Id.*
26. *Ahlers,* 485 U.S. at 211.
27. *Id.* at 204-05. The *Ahlers* decision noted that the *Case* decision rejected a

uncertainty surrounding the viability of the new value exception, the Court declined to resolve the issue.[28] The Court stated:

> [O]ur decision today should not be taken as any comment on the continuing vitality of the . . . [new value] exception . . . . Rather, we simply conclude that even if an "infusion-of-'money-or-money's worth'" exception to the absolute priority rule has survived the enactment of § 1129(b), respondents' proposed contribution to the reorganization plan is inadequate to gain the benefit of the exception.[29]

This dictum has caused extensive comment within the legal community[30] and

---

similar argument, and found that stockholders' financial standing in the community and managerial skills were not money's worth, and therefore constituted inadequate consideration. *Id.* The *Ahlers* Court reasoned that a promise of future services is intangible, not readily classified as an asset, and thus can not be exchanged in the current market as "something of value to creditors." *Id.*

28. *Ahlers,* 485 U.S. at 206; Brief for the United States as Amicus Curiae Supporting Petitioners at 17-23, Norwest Bank Worthington v. Ahlers, 485 U.S. 197 (1988) (No. 86-958). The Solicitor General emphasized that:

> [n]othing in the legislative history suggests a congressional intention to maintain the exception discussed in *[Case]*. The House report, in describing proposed Section 1129(b), states: "The general principle of the subsection permits confirmation notwithstanding nonacceptance by an impaired class if that class and all below it in priority are treated according to the absolute priority rule. The dissenting class must be paid in full before any junior class may share under the plan." . . . No exceptions to this rule seem to be contemplated.

Id. at 21.

29. *Ahlers,* 485 U.S. at 203-04 n.3 (citations omitted).

30. *See generally* Douglas S. Neville, Note, *The New Value Exception to the Chapter 11 Absolute Priority Rule*, 60 MO. L. REV. 465, 466-67 (1995) (discussing new value exception after *Bonner Mall*); James J. White, *Absolute Priority and New Value*, 8 COOLEY L. REV. 1, 13 (1991) (discussing how new value exception will invite abuses that fair and equitable rule was meant to prevent); David A. Skeel, *The Uncertain State of an Unstated Rule: Bankruptcy's Contribution Rule Doctrine After Ahlers*, 63 AM. BANKR. L.J.

much division among lower courts.[31]

B. The Current Division Among the Circuits Over the New Value Exception

1. *Bonner Mall Partnership v. U.S. Bancorp Mortgage Co. (In re Bonner Mall Partnership)*

The Ninth Circuit is the only Circuit to have definitively resolved the issue of the new value exception's viability under the Code. In *Bonner Mall Partnership v. U.S. Bancorp Mortgage Co. (In re Bonner Mall Partnership)*,[32] the Ninth Circuit expressly held that the new value exception survived the Code's enactment. The facts of *Bonner Mall* are typical to most single asset real estate reorganizations.[33] In *Bonner Mall*, the debtor's sole

---

221, 224-25 (1989) (suggesting abolition of new value exception due to inherent danger of having it persist); John D. Ayer, *Rethinking Absolute Priority After Ahlers*, 87 MICH. L. REV. 963, 965 (1989) (suggesting that *Ahlers* decision raises issue of whether new value exception exists).

31. *In re* Bjolmes Realty Trust, 134 B.R. 1000, 1005-06 (Bankr. D. Mass. 1991) (*Ahlers* ruling has caused division among the lower courts as to continued vitality of new value exception); *In re* Tallahassee Assocs., L.P., 132 B.R. 712, 717 (Bankr. W.D. Pa. 1991) (noting after *Ahlers*, courts are split on new value exception's viability); *see also supra* notes 9-11 and accompanying text.

32. 2 F.3d 899 (9th Cir. 1993), *cert. granted*, 114 S. Ct. 681, *motion to vacate den. and dismissed by* 115 S. Ct. 386 (1994).

33. *See* Katz, *supra* note 12 at 78.

> The single-asset debtor is normally structured in the form of a corporation or limited partnership, and usually holds a fully mortgaged piece of real estate as its only asset. With few or no employees and little or no cash flow, the single-asset real estate debtor typically falls behind in debt payments, and the secured creditor initiates foreclosure proceedings. In response, the debtor files a chapter 11 petition, obtaining the benefit of the automatic stay.

Id. (footnotes omitted). *See also, In re* F.A.B. Indus., 147 B.R. 763 (C.D. Cal. 1992) (concerning medical and office building complex); First Republic Thrift & Loan v. Triple R Holdings, L.P. (*In re* Triple R Holdings, L.P.), 145 B.R. 57 (N.D. Cal. 1992) (foreclosing condominium); *In re* Waldengreen Assocs., 150

asset was a mall worth approximately $3.2 million.[34] The mall was being used as security for a debt in the amount of $6.3 million.[35] *Bonner Mall's* plan of reorganization provided for, among other things: an infusion of cash in the amount of $200,000 by the partners of the debtor; that the contributing partners would subsidize any deficiency in working capital needed to fund the reorganization during the first thirty-two months after confirmation of the plan; and for a security interest in the mall to guarantee the payment of the property's debts.[36] In exchange for their new value contribution, the partners were accorded a 100% ownership interest in the new corporation.[37]

In its decision, the Ninth Circuit in *Bonner Mall* addressed four related issues. First, the court considered whether the language of the absolute priority rule, as codified, eliminated the new value exception.[38] The Code's absolute priority rule provides in relevant part that (with respect to unsecured claims) "the holder of any claim or interest that is junior to the claims of . . . [a senior] . . . class will not receive or retain under the plan *on account of* such junior claim or interest any property."[39] Bancorp argued that the "on account of" language precludes equity holders from obtaining an interest in the reorganized company without first satisfying debts held by unsecured creditors.[40] The court, however, did not agree. Instead, it supported the debtor's analysis of the new value exception which did not permit equity holders to retain property on account of a prior junior interest, but allowed former owners to participate in the reorganized debtor *on account of* a substantial, necessary, and fair new value contribution.[41] The court reasoned that if the infusion of new capital constitutes a fair exchange for an equity interest, then contributing partners, like third party investors, are not retaining property on account of their prior interest.[42] Furthermore, the court rejected

---

B.R. 468 (Bankr. M.D. Fla. 1993) (involving apartment complex); *In re* One Times Square Assocs. Ltd. Partnership, 159 B.R. 695 (Bankr. S.D.N.Y. 1993) (regarding building in Times Square).

34. *Bonner Mall Partnership*, 2 F.3d at 905.
35. *Id.*
36. *Id.*
37. *Id.*
38. *Id.* at 908-10.
39. 11 U.S.C. § 1129(b)(2)(B)(ii) (1994).
40. *Bonner Mall*, 2 F.3d at 908-09.
41. *Id.* at 909 (emphasis added).
42. *Id.* at 910.

Bancorp's argument that providing the debtor owners an exclusive opportunity to contribute new capital in exchange for an ownership interest in the reorganized company was "on account of" the partners' prior ownership interests.[43] According to the court, a plan of reorganization might provide for the prior owners' exclusive right to contribute based on other factors. Some of the factors include that the participation of old equity will enhance the value of the reorganized business; that it will be easier to obtain additional funding since all the old owners will be familiar with one another, and finally that there mightnot be any other legitimate investor willing to invest in a business just emerging from bankruptcy.[44]

The second issue addressed by the court was whether Congress's failure to expressly include the new value exception in its definition of "fair and equitable" reflects an intent to eliminate the exception.[45] Bancorp contended that it did.[46] The court construed the statute in accordance with the Supreme Court's decision in *Dewsnup v. Timm*,[47] which the court interpreted as standing for the proposition that "[w]here the text of the Code does not unambiguously abrogate pre-Code practice, courts should presume that Congress intended it to continue unless the legislative history dictates a contrary result."[48] Therefore, the court in *Bonner Mall* concluded that nothing in the Code supported a conclusion that Congress intended to eliminate the exception.[49]

The third issue addressed was whether Congress's overhaul of the reorganization process justified a conclusion that the new value exception was abolished.[50] Bancorp had argued that the new value exception was created to temper the Bankruptcy Act's strict confirmation condition which required absolute priority to be applied to individual dissenting creditors as opposed to dissenting classes of creditors, a problem no longer existent under the Code.[51]

---

43. *Id.*
44. *Id.* at 910-11.
45. *Bonner Mall*, 2 F.3d at 911.
46. *Id.*
47. 502 U.S. 410 (1992).
48. *Bonner Mall*, 2 F.3d at 913.
49. *Id.*
50. *Id.* at 913-15.
51. *Id.* at 914. Under the Code a plan of reorganization can be crammed down over the objections of an impaired class. *See supra* notes 1-6 and accompanying text.

Therefore, the new value exception is no longer viable.[52] The court disagreed, reasoning, "it could just as logically be argued that the new value exception was designed to prevent confirmation holdouts, individual or class, from derailing an otherwise `fair and equitable' plan."[53]

Finally, the court noted that the new value exception is consistent with the policies underlying reorganization.[54] More particularly, the court stated that the exception allows control and management of the debtor to remain in the hands of the original owners, "who arguably can best reestablish a profitable business."[55] The court explained that the new value exception's strict requirements prevent prior owners from improperly circumventing the absolute priority rule.[56]

To date, the Ninth Circuit is the first and only circuit to have embraced the viability of the new value exception.[57]

2. *Phoenix Mutual Life Insurance Co. v. Greystone III Joint Venture (In re Greystone III Joint Venture)*

Prior to *Bonner Mall*, the Fifth Circuit had occasion to consider whether the new value exception survived the Code's enactment in *Phoenix Mutual Life Insurance Co. v. Greystone III Joint Venture (In re Greystone III Joint Venture)*.[58] Greystone, a real estate partnership, filed for chapter 11 reorganization in an effort to prevent Phoenix Mutual Life Insurance Company, its nonrecourse lender, from foreclosing on its single asset, an office building.[59] As of the date of the bankruptcy filing, Greystone owed Phoenix approximately $9.3 million, secured by a lien on the office building appraised at $5.8 million.[60] Thus, Phoenix was undersecured by $3.5 million.[61] The plan

---

52. *Bonner Mall*, 2 F.3d at 914.
53. *Id.*
54. *Id.* at 915.
55. *Id.*
56. *Id.*
57. The court in *Bonner Mall* did not, however, rule on whether the requirements of the new value exception had been met. *See supra* note 20 and accompanying text (outlining requirements for new value exception).
58. 995 F.2d 1274 (5th Cir. 1991), *vacated in part*, 995 F.2d 1284 (5th Cir.), *cert. denied*, 506 U.S. 821 (1992).
59. *Id.* at 1276-77.
60. *Id.* at 1276.

of reorganization placed the secured claim of $5.8 million in one class and the unsecured claim of $3.5 million in another class.[62] The plan also created a separate class comprised of trade creditors.[63] The plan impaired Phoenix in that it only proposed to pay less than four percent of Phoenix's unsecured claim.[64] Additionally, the plan provided that Greystone's partners would retain their equity interest in the reorganization in exchange for a $500,000 infusion of new value.[65] Phoenix objected to the plan, and thereby prevented confirmation under section 1129(a).[66] Nevertheless, Greystone was able to get its plan confirmed by a cramdown.[67] On appeal, the district court upheld plan confirmation.[68]

In November 1991, the Fifth Circuit Court of Appeals reversed both the bankruptcy court and the district court.[69] The court of appeals held, *inter alia*, that because the new value exception was not viable under the Code, the plan violated the absolute priority rule and thus could not be confirmed.[70] However, in its February 1992 denial of an en banc rehearing petition, the Fifth Circuit

---

61. *Id.* at 1277.
62. *See id.* Under section 506(a) of the Code, a creditor's claim is deemed a secured claim up to the value of the collateral, and an unsecured claim to the extent that the claim exceeds the value of the collateral. 11 U.S.C. § 506(a) (1994).
63. *Greystone*, 995 F.2d at 1277. As of the date of bankruptcy filing, Greystone owed trade creditors approximately $10,000. *Id.* Those claims were placed in one class. *Id.* Greystone also had tax liabilities of approximately $145,000, which were placed in a second class. *Id.* The plan also provided a separate class for security deposit claims held by tenants. *Id.*
64. *Greystone*, 995 F.2d at 1278. Although the trade creditors would also receive less than four percent of their unsecured claims, the plan provided that upon confirmation the partners would satisfy the balance of those claims. *Id.*
65. *Id.* at 1277.
66. *Id.* at 1278. The class of trade creditors accepted the plan despite the fact they were impaired by it. *Id.* at 1277.
67. *Greystone*, 995 F.2d at 1277; *see also supra* notes 1-8 and accompanying text for a discussion of the "cramdown" procedure.
68. *Greystone*, 995 F.2d at 1277.
69. Phoenix Mut. Life Ins. Co. v. Greystone III Joint Venture (*In re* Greystone III Joint Venture), 948 F.2d 134 (5th Cir.), *modified and republished*, 995 F.2d 1274 (1991).
70. *Id.* at 142-44. The original panel opinion was written by Judge Jones.

withdrew the portion of Judge Jones's opinion which found the new value exception no longer viable.[71]

The redacted part of the opinion addressed many of the same arguments as *Bonner Mall*.[72] However, the *Greystone* court came to different conclusions than the court in *Bonner Mall*. First, the Greystone court determined that the codification of the absolute priority rule eliminated the need for the new value exception.[73] The court reasoned that the increased flexibility of the Code "renders the *Case* exception unnecessary and is certainly a significant distinction from the statutory background to that decision."[74]

Second, in regard to whether the new value exception was incorporated into the Code's definition of "fair and equitable," the *Greystone* court found it to be unlikely.[75] The court found Greystone's argument that once old "equity infuses money into the debtor" it is not retaining its ownership 'on account of'[76] its old equity status to be "mere wordplay."[77]

---

71. Phoenix Mut. Life Ins. Co. v. Greystone III Joint Venture (*In re* Greystone III Joint Venture), 995 F.2d 1274 (5th Cir. 1991), *vacated in part*, 995 F.2d 1284 (5th Cir.), *cert. denied*, 506 U.S. 821 (1992). The court's new opinion refused to confirm the plan on the grounds that the debtor had improperly classified the trade creditors and the unsecured claims of Phoenix separately from other unsecured creditors for the sole purpose of having at least one impaired class assent, *see* 11 U.S.C. § 1129(a)(10) (1994), so that the debtor could attempt a cramdown. *Id.*, 995 F.2d at 1279-81.

    Judge Jones's dissent was limited to the court's withdrawal of that portion of the opinion dealing with the new value exception. *Id.* at 1285. In reaffirming what she wrote about the new value exception in her original opinion, Judge Jones commented on the court's refusal to find the new value exception no longer viable: "I would hope to stand with Galileo, who, rebuffed by a higher temporal authority, muttered under his breath, 'Eppur si muove.' ('And yet it moves')." *Id.* (Jones, J. dissenting).

72. *See supra* notes 32-56 and accompanying text (discussing *Bonner Mall*).

73. *Greystone*, 995 F.2d 1282-83.

74. *Id.*

75. *Id.* Specifically, Judge Jones asserted "that Congress acted knowledgeably in codifying a strict absolute priority rule." *Id.* Judge Jones also argued that the *Ahlers'* decision left the "'equitable powers [of] the bankruptcy courts . . . within the confines of the Bankruptcy Code.'" *Id.* at 1283 (quoting Norwest Bank Worthington v. Ahlers, 485 U.S. 197, 206 (1988)).

76. 11 U.S.C. § 1129(b)(2)(B)(ii) (1994).

77. *Greystone*, 948 F.2d at 1283.

Finally, in response to the debtor's contention that the statute should be interpreted as codifying the new value exception since it neither mentions the new value exception nor contradicts it, the court stated "[t]his position attributes too little weight to the statutory language . . ."[78] The court also pointed out that Congress clearly rejected a proposal by the Bankruptcy Commission to modify the absolute priority rule when it enacted the Code.[79]

Had the Fifth Circuit in *Greystone* not vacated its opinion concerning the new value exception, it would have been the first federal circuit to decide definitively the issue concerning the new value exception's viability.

3. The Fourth, Seventh and Eighth Circuits

In *Travelers Insurance Co. v. Bryson Properties, XVIII (In re Bryson Properties, XVIII)*,[80] the Fourth Circuit intimated that the new value exception might no longer be viable under the Code.[81] The proposed plan of reorganization in *Bryson* allowed the debtor's partners to retain an interest in the reorganized enterprise in exchange for a $625,000 cash contribution and the extension of an $850,000 line of credit, while it failed to provide for satisfaction of the mortgagee's unsecured claim.[82] The plan also provided that if the property were sold within ten years, the proceeds would be used to reimburse the partners for their contribution and extension of credit before it would be applied towards the lender's claim.[83]

---

78. *Id.*
79. *Id.*
80. 961 F.2d 496 (4th Cir.), *cert. denied*, 506 U.S. 866 (1992).
81. *Id.* at 505.
82. *Id.* at 499. The mortgagee holding the unsecured claim was Travelers Insurance Company ("Travelers"). *Id.* at 498. The debtor, a limited partnership, had purchased an office building complex subject to a mortgage held by Travelers. *Id.* At the time of the purchase, the balance of the mortgage amounted to $10.8 million. *Id.* The debtor was able to meet debt service for three years before it defaulted. *Id.*
83. *Bryson Properties*, 961 F.2d at 499. After reimbursing the partners' contribution and line of credit with the proceeds of the sale, the plan provided for "payment to Travelers of any difference in the amount of principal balance shown on the amortization schedule (amortizing original loan amount of $10.8 million at 5.25 percent). . . ." *Id.*

Declining to address the issue of the new value exception's continued viability, the court asked "whether the [plan allows] equityholders [to] receive anything `on account of' their prior interest."[84] In refusing to confirm the plan, the Court found that the debtor's partners' exclusive right to contribute new value constituted property retained on account of a prior interest.[85] Thus, although the *Bryson* court declined to make a defining statement as to the new value exception's viability, the courtemployed a rationale that effectively rejects any plan providing for a new value contribution by former equityholders.[86]

Like the Fourth Circuit, the Eighth Circuit has declined to address the issue of the new value exception's viability. In *In re Blankemeyer*,[87] the plan of reorganization called for the satisfaction of a lender's unsecured claim through interest free payments made over a period of twenty years, and allowed the debtors to retain an interest in the property.[88] Although the Eighth Circuit upheld the district court's refusal to confirm the plan,[89] the court assumed without discussion that the new value exception remained viable.[90]

---

84. *Id.* at 504. The court basically inquired as to whether the plan was fair and equitable to Travelers, i.e., was absolute priority applied to the claims of the dissenting unsecured class. *See id.* at 504-05; 11 U.S.C. § 1129(b)(2)(B)(ii) (1994).
85. *Bryson*, 961 F.2d at 504. The court stated: "the equityholders have given themselves . . . the exclusive right to contribute [and] [t]his exclusive right to contribute constitutes `property' under § 1129(b)(2)(B)(ii), which was received or retained on account of a prior interest." *Id. But see Bonner Mall*, 2 F.3d at 910 ("A proposed equity plan may give old equity the exclusive opportunity to purchase stock in exchange for new capital for other reasons.").
86. *See Bryson*, 961 F.2d at 504-05. In *In re* A.V.B.I., Inc., 143 B.R. 738, 742 (Bankr. C.D. Cal. 1992), the Court views *Bryson* as having definitively decided the issue in the Fourth Circuit. *But see In re* Sovereign Group 1985-27, Ltd., 142 B.R. 702, 707 n.8 (E.D. Pa. 1992) (noting that Fourth Circuit questioned new value exception's viability but had not resolved issue).
87. 861 F.2d 192 (8th Cir. 1988).
88. *Id.*, 861 F.2d at 194.
89. *Id.* The court affirmed the district court finding that the plan was not fair and equitable because it failed to allow the objecting class to receive or retain property of a value equal to the amount of its unsecured claim. *Id.*
90. *Lumber Exch.*, 861 F.2d at 194. The *Blankemeyer* court stated that dissenting unsecured creditors must be compensated in full before junior interests could retain any property under the plan, "unless the junior class contributed

The Eighth Circuit again avoided the issue of the new value exception's continued existence in *Lumber Exchange Building Ltd. Partnership v. Mutual Life Insurance Co. (In re Lumber Exchange Building Ltd. Partnership).*[91] In *Lumber Exchange* the single asset debtor proposed a plan of reorganization whereby the partners would contribute new value to the enterprise.[92] The plan also provided that $200,000 of new value would be shared pro rata by all unsecured creditors including a nonrecourse lender who was undersecured in the amount of $13,877,504.64.[93] Having concluded that the district court was correct in refusing to confirm the plan based on improper classification of creditors, the Eighth Circuit found it unnecessary to address the issue of the new value exception.[94]

The Seventh Circuit responded to *Ahlers* with a line of cases which also declined to definitively determine whether the new value exception was viable. In *In re Stegall,*[95] the court denied confirmation of a plan that would allow the farm debtors to keep their farm in exchange for a promise to work the land[96] without fully satisfying the unsecured lender.[97] Citing *Ahlers*, Judge Posner stated that a promise to work the land could not constitute new value.[98] In

---

something reasonably compensatory and measurable to the reorganization enterprise." *Id.*

91. 968 F.2d 647 (8th Cir. 1992).

92. *Id.* at 648. The partners of the debtor, a limited partnership, proposed to contribute $800,000 under the plan. *See In re* Lumber Exch. Ltd. Partnership, 125 B.R. 1000, 1003 (Bankr. D. Minn. 1991). Out of this amount, $600,000 was to be used for improvements and programs designed to enhance the marketability of the building's leases. *Id.*

93. *Lumber Exch.*, 968 F.2d at 648. The lender in this case had loaned $20 million to the debtor, secured by a mortgage and assignment of all leases and rents on the debtor's sole asset, a building valued at $7 million. *Id.*

94. *Id.* at 650.

95. 865 F.2d 140 (7th Cir. 1989).

96. *Id.* at 142-44. The debtors proposed to contribute new value in the amount of $24,000, out of which $22,000 constituted the value of the crops, planted after the bankruptcy filing. *Id.* at 143. Therefore, only the $2000 constituted the value of two months labor. *Id.*

97. *Stegall*, 865 F.2d at 141. The debtor's principal unsecured creditor was the Federal Land Bank of St. Louis, which held one third of the debtor's unsecured debt. *Id.* The debtor attempted a cramdown after the creditor objected to a plan which proposed to pay only ten percent of the unsecured claim over a period of ten years, interest free. *Id.*

98. *Stegall*, 865 F.2d at 142-43. Even supposing the new value exception still existed, the court found the $2,000 contribution of labor "too little to warrant

addition, the judge noted, even if work could constitute new value, the issue concerning the viability of the new value exception was still unresolved in the Seventh Circuit despite *Official Creditors' Committee v. Potter Material Service, Inc. (In re Potter Material Service, Inc.)*,[99] a pre-*Ahlers* case which embraced the new value exception without discussion.[100]

In *Kham & Nate's Shoes No. 2, Inc. v. First Bank of Whiting*,[101] the Seventh Circuit stopped short of finding the new value exception defunct, but held that a stockholder's guaranty of a loan to the debtor-corporation could not constitute new value.[102] In his opinion, Judge Easterbrook noted that "[t]he language of the Code strongly suggests that [the new value exception is no longer viable], and . . . this language [should be taken] seriously even when it alters pre-Code practices."[103]

---

the drastic remedy of a cram-down." *Id.* at 144. Although the estimated value of the crops, $22,000, was a tangible asset, the court considered the crops already property of the estate. *Id.* at 143-44. Thus, it could not constitute new value. *Id.* at 143.

99. 781 F.2d 99 (7th Cir. 1986).

100. *See id.* at 101-02. The Sixth Circuit also embraced the new value exception without discussion in a pre-*Ahlers* case, Teamsters Nat'l Freight Indus. Negotiating Comm. v. U.S. Truck Co. (*In re* U.S. Truck Co.), 800 F.2d 581, 588 (6th Cir. 1986). Although *U.S. Truck* was decided prior to the Supreme Court's decision in *Ahlers*, several post-*Ahlers* cases have relied on *U.S. Truck* to find that the new value exception is still viable in the Sixth Circuit. *See, e.g., In re* Creekside Landing, Ltd., 140 B.R. 713, 717 (Bankr. M.D. Tenn. 1992) (stating new value exception has been embraced by Sixth Circuit); *In re* Aztec Co., 107 B.R. 585, 588 (Bankr. M.D. Tenn. 1989) (same). *But see In re* A.V.B.I. Inc., 143 B.R. 738, 741 (Bankr. C.D. Cal. 1992) (finding that *U.S. Truck* lacks persuasive value because it predates *Ahlers*).

101. 908 F.2d 1351 (7th Cir. 1990).

102. *Id.* at 1362-63. The *Kham* court found the shareholder guarantees to be "intangible, inalienable, and, in all likelihood, unenforceable." *Id.* at 1362 (quoting *Ahlers*, 485 U.S. at 204). The court reasoned that Illinois state law would not allow shares to be given in exchange for guarantees of loans. *Id.* "Promises inadequate to support the issuance of shares under state law are also inadequate to support the issuance of shares by a bankruptcy judge over the protest of the creditors, the real owners of the firm." *Id.*

103. *Kham & Nate's Shoes*, 908 F.2d at 1361.

In *In re Snyder*,[104] the Seventh Circuit concluded that the new value exception might still be viable,[105] even though it found the debtor's proposal to obtain the release of a lien and to make a contribution of $30,000 not "substantial" enough to qualify for new value.[106] In reaching his conclusion that the new value exception might still be viable, Judge Cudahy referred to *Dewsnup v. Timm*,[107] which he interpreted as stating that absent a showing of clear intent otherwise, "Code provisions must be interpreted in light of pre-Code practices."[108]

More recently, the Seventh Circuit in *In re Woodbrook Associates*,[109] was once again able to avoid resolving the issue of the new value exception's vitality. In *Woodbrook Associates*, the Seventh Circuit held that even if the exception survived the Code's enactment, a cash infusion of $100,000, where the total unsecured debt amounted to $2.6 million, was an insufficient "token" cash infusion which did not amount to new value.[110]

---

104. 967 F.2d 1126 (7th Cir. 1992).
105. *See id.* at 1129-31.
106. *Snyder*, 967 F.2d at 1131-32. As part of their new value contribution, the debtors proposed to have their father release a lien he had over their farm machinery. *Id.* at 1131. The debtors owed their father $126,794, which was secured by vehicles valued at $20,000. *Id.* at 1127. The plan proposed to pay the $20,000 obtained from the release of the lien to unsecured creditors over a five year period. *Id.* The Court likened the debtors' proposal to obtain a release of their father's lien to a promise of future labor. *Id.* at 1131. Both contributions do not constitute "an up-front infusion of money or money's worth." *Id.* In addition, the court found the $30,000 cash contribution relatively insubstantial compared to the amount of the unsecured debt. *Id.* at 1131-32.
107. 502 U.S. 410 (1992).
108. *Snyder*, 967 F.2d at 1129 n.4. The *Snyder* court concluded that "[s]ince there is no other discussion of modifying or eliminating the new value exception in the legislative history, pre-Code practice would appear to control under the standard articulated in *Dewsnup*." *Id.* at 1130.

    Although the opinion in *Snyder* seemed to support the finding of the new value exception's viability under the Code, the court stopped short of stating so, "as [other courts] did in *Kham & Nate's Shoes* and *Stegall*, and as the Supreme Court did in *Ahlers*." *Id.* at 1131 (citations omitted).
109. 19 F.3d 312, 320 (7th Cir. 1994).
110. *Id.* at 320.

C. The New Value Exception in Single Asset Reorganizations

1. Application of the New Value Exception to Single Asset Cases is Not Required by the Plain Language of the Code or **Dewsnup v. Timm**

a. Language of Bankruptcy Code Precludes New Value Exception in Single Asset Cases

The first step in interpreting a statute begins with the language of the statute itself.[111] Where the plain language of the Code is clear, "the sole function of the courts is to enforce it according to its terms."[112] The plain language of the fair and equitable standard as it is codified in section 1129(b)(2)(B) of the Code clearly fails to mention any new value exception.[113] Section 1129(b)(2)(B)(ii) provides that unless unsecured creditors are fully compensated, no junior interest may retain any property "on account of such

---

111. Estate of Cowart v. Nicklas Drilling Co., 505 U.S. 469 (1992). "In a statutory construction case, the beginning point must be the language of the statute, and when a statute speaks with clarity to an issue, judicial inquiry into the statute's meaning, in all but the most extraordinary circumstances is finished." *Id.* at 474. *See also* Demarest v. Manspeaker, 498 U.S. 184, 190 (1991) (stating where statute unambiguous inquiry complete); United States v. Ron Pair Enters., Inc. 489 U.S. 235, 241 (1989) (resolving dispute over meaning of statute begins with statute's language).

112. *Ron Pair Enters.*, 489 U.S. at 241 (quoting Caminetti v. United States, 242 U.S. 470, 485 (1917)).

113. *See* 11 U.S.C. § 1129(b)(2)(B)(ii) (1994) (codifying fair and equitable standard as to unsecured claims); *see also* Travelers Ins. Co. v. Bryson Properties, XVII (*In re* Bryson Properties, XVII), 961 F.2d 496, 504 (4th Cir.) (noting Congressional intent on exemption status remains unclear), *cert. denied*, 506 U.S. 866 (1992); *Kham & Nate's Shoes No.2, Inc. v. First Bank of Whiting*, 908 F.2d 1351, 1361 (7th Cir. 1990) (stating language of Code should be taken seriously); *In re* Outlook/Century Ltd., 127 B.R. 650, 657 (Bankr. N.D. Cal. 1991) (adhering to plain meaning of § 1129(b)(2)(B)); Brief for the United States as Amicus Curiae Supporting Petitioners at 17-23, Norwest Bank Worthington v. Ahlers, 485 U.S. 197 (1988) (No. 86-958); Brief of the American Council of Life Insurance as Amicus Curiae Supporting Petitioners at 4-7, Norwest Bank Worthington v. Ahlers, 485 U.S. 197 (1988) (No. 86-958).

junior claim or interest . . . ."[114] Thus, for the debtor to retain the property without paying the dissenting unsecured creditor class in full, it is necessary to argue that the debtor is not retaining an interest on account of its junior interest, but rather as a third party investor.[115] The new value contribution must, therefore, be viewed as constituting an offer by the debtor to purchase the property subject to the stripped down mortgage, much as a third party might do.[116] The express language of section 1129(b) precludes this argument.

Under section 1129(b)(2)(A)(i), fair and equitable treatment for the dissenting mortgagee's secured claim requires that a lien retained on the property have a face amount equal to the value of the collateral.[117] Value is determined under section 506(a), but is subject to revision for various purposes during the bankruptcy proceeding.[118] Practically speaking, the true test of value is what someone will pay for the property.[119] Where there is only

---

114. 11 U.S.C. § 1129(b)(2)(B)(ii) (1994).

115. *See In re* Mill Place Ltd. Partnership, 94 B.R. 139, 143 (Bankr. D. Minn. 1988) ("In a two-party dispute, the new owner alternative to full payment, provided for in § 1129(b)(2)(B)(ii) would be insufficient to satisfy the fair and equitable test, since the only beneficiaries of its application would be post-confirmation third-party interests of new investors.").

116. *See* Brief of Elizabeth Warren as Amicus Curiae at 4-6, Phoenix Mut. Life Ins. Co. v. Greystone III Joint Venture (*In re* Greystone III Joint Venture), 995 F.2d 1274 (5th Cir. 1991), *vacated in part*, 995 F.2d 1284, *cert. denied*, 506 U.S. 821 (1992).

117. 11 U.S.C. § 1129(b)(2)(A)(i) (1994); *see also* Heartland Fed. Sav. & Loan Assoc. v. Briscone Enters. Ltd., II (*In re* Briscone Enters. Ltd, II), 994 F.2d 1160, 1168-69 (5th Cir. 1993) (stating § 1129(b)(2)(A)(i) requires "the secured creditor retain its lien and receive `deferred cash payments totalling at least the allowed amount of the claim.'"); *In re* Birdneck Apartment Assocs. II, L.P., 156 B.R. 499, 507 (Bankr. E.D. Va. 1993) (determining secured claimholder can "(1) retain its lien; and (2) receive deferred cash payments totaling at least the allowed amount of the claimant's secured claim and a present value equal to the value of their collateral") (citation omitted).

118. 11 U.S.C. § 506(a) (1994). "Such value shall be determined in light of the purpose of the valuation and of the proposed disposition or use of such property, and in conjunction with any hearing on such disposition or use or on a plan affecting such creditor's interest." *Id.*

119. *See, e.g.*, Metrobank v. Trimble (*In re* Trimble), 50 F.3d 530, 531-32 (8th Cir. 1995) (agreeing with Fifth Circuit that retail valuation method is only method that gives full effect to § 506(a)); Associates Commercial Corp. v. Rash (*In re* Rash), 31 F.3d 325, 331 (5th Cir. 1994) (adopting retail valuation method);

one asset, if a third party, or the debtor, should bid more than the stripped down mortgage balance for the property, this would indicate that the property is worth more than previously determined under section 506(a), and that the value and the amount of the stripped down mortgage should be revised upward to the bid price. Because any bid below the amount of the mortgage indebtedness should result in such an increase in the size of the stripped down mortgage, it follows that neither a third party nor the debtor, may acquire the property for less than the debt owed to the holders of secured claims without the agreement of the classes holding those claims. Therefore, the application of the new value exception to single asset cases would appear to be precluded by the precise requirements of section 1129.[120]

The language of the Code precludes the existence of a new value exception for yet another reason. A court is barred from applying pre-Code law in interpreting a Code provision where the provision substantially alters the pre-Code practice on which the pre-Code interpretations were based.[121] In an effort to protect individual dissenting creditors within an accepting class, chapter

---

Huntington Nat'l Bank v. Pees (*In re* McClurkin), 31 F.3d 401, 405 (6th Cir. 1994) (using retail valuation method); Arnette v. General Motors Acceptance Corp. (*In re* Arnette), 156 B.R. 366, 368 (Bankr. D. Conn. 1993) (holding motor vehicle should be valued at price debtor could get for it in market). *But see* General Motors Acceptance Corp. v. Mitchell (*In re* Mitchell), 954 F.2d 557, 560 (9th Cir. 1992) (holding wholesale value is appropriate method); Grubbs v. National Bank of S.C., 114 B.R. 450, 451 (D.S.C. 1990) (same).

120. 11 U.S.C. § 1129 (1994). Indeed, a plan proposed by a single asset debtor under which the debtor will contribute funds in excess of the stripped down amount of the mortgage raises the question whether the debtor, in control of the information relating to the operation of the property and its value, encouraged the initial section 506(a) valuation at below what it knew was the real value of the property in order to facilitate the debtor's retention of the property under the new value exception. *See* 11 U.S.C. § 506(a) (1994). Such a plan also raises the question as to whether such a plan could meet the good faith requirement of section 1129(a)(3). *Id.* § 1129(a)(3).

121. *See* Union Bank v. Wolas, 502 U.S. 151, 160 (1991). Given the substantial changes made to the preference provision, the court chose not to use pre-Code interpretations. The Court reasoned "the fact that Congress carefully reexamined and entirely rewrote the preference provision in 1978 supports the conclusion that the text of § 547(c)(2) as enacted reflects the deliberate choice of Congress." *Id.* (footnote omitted).

X[122] and its predecessor, section 77B,[123] would not confirm a plan without acceptance by the requisite majority of each class and adherence to absolute priority.[124] The result was that a plan could not be confirmed, despite the acceptance by the requisite majorities of each class, unless absolute priority was applied to the claims of individual dissenters within each accepting class.[125] The new value exception emerged to temper this strict application of the absolute priority rule.[126]

When Congress enacted the Code, it relaxed the application of the absolute priority rule by applying it only to the claims of dissenting classes of creditors impaired by the plan, and not to the claims of individual dissenters within an accepting class.[127] By substantially altering the pre-Code law which

---

122. Chandler Act of 1938, ch. 575, 52 Stat. 840, 883-905 (codified as 11 U.S.C. §§ 501-676) (repealed 1978).
123. Act of June 7, 1934, ch. 424, § 77B. 48 Stat. 911, 912, *repealed by* Chandler Act of 1938, Ch. 575, 52 Stat. 840 (1938).
124. *See* Case v. Los Angeles Lumber Prods. Co., 308 U.S. 106, 114-15 (1939) (finding § 77B requires certain percentage of each class to approve plan); Phoenix Mut. Life Ins. Co. v. Greystone III Joint Venture (*In re* Greystone III Joint Venture), 995 F.2d 1274, 1282 (5th Cir. 1991) (stating when *Case* was decided unanimous consent and absolute priority required), *vacated in part*, 995 F.2d 1284 (5th Cir.), *cert. denied*, 506 U.S. 821 (1992); Pennbank v. Winters (*In re* Winters), 99 B.R. 658, 662 (Bankr. W.D. Pa. 1989) (providing under Act, "even though the requisite majority of a class accepted the plan, if a minority dissenting creditor within the accepting class objected, the court could not confirm a plan if the plan did not strictly comply with the absolute priority rule."). *See generally* 6A COLLIER ON BANKRUPTCY ¶ 11.06 (J. Moore et al. eds., 14th ed. 1977) (discussing in depth absolute priority rule under Bankruptcy Act).
125. *See supra* note 124.
126. *See* Case v. Los Angeles Lumber Co., 308 U.S. 106, 117 (1939) (enunciating new value exception); *In re* F.A.B. Indus., 147 B.R. 763, 766 (C.D. Cal. 1992) (stating new value exception "created to rectify problems that arose from strict application of absolute priority"); *In re* Outlook/Century Ltd., 127 B.R. 650, 657 (Bankr. N.D. Cal. 1991) (discussing practical considerations for exception under act); Clifford S. Harris, Note, *A Rule Unvanquished: The New Value Exception to the Absolute Priority Rule*, 89 MICH. L. REV. 2301, 2308 (1991) (discussing history of new value exception).
127. H.R. REP. NO. 595, 95th Cong., 2d Sess. 221-24 (1978), *reprinted in* 1978 U.S.C.C.A.N. 5963, 6181-84; Brief for the United States as Amicus Curiae Supporting Petitioners at 22, Norwest Bank Worthington v. Ahlers, 485 U.S.

led to the creation of the new value exception, Congress eliminated the need for the exception, and thus intentionally omitted it from the plain language of the Code.[128] In fact, had the Code's fair and equitable standard been applied to *Case v. Los Angeles Lumber Products Co.*,[129] which first articulated the new value exception,[130] the plan there would have been confirmed, and the Court would not have had a need to articulate a new value exception.[131]

The court in *Bonner Mall*, however, was not compelled by a similar argument made by Bancorp.[132] The court stated:

> there is no significant difference between the problem that a holdout class poses for confirmation and that posed by a holdout creditor. While Bancorp assumes that the new value exception was intended to

---

197 (1988) (No. 86-958) ("the . . . Code permits a creditor class, by a class vote that overrides the objections of minority members, to assent to a plan that is *not* 'fair and equitable.'"); 5 COLLIER ON BANKRUPTCY ¶ 1129.03[e], at 1129-56-57 (Lawrence P. King. et al. eds. 15th ed. 1979) (describing relationship between § 1129(b) and absolute priority).

128. *Greystone*, 995 F.2d at 1283 (pointing out Congress rejected proposal by Bankruptcy Commission to alter absolute priority rule when it enacted the Code); Kham & Nate's Shoes No. 2, Inc. v. First Bank of Whiting, 908 F.2d 1351, 1361 (7th Cir. 1990) (stating legislative history reinforces notion that new value exception did not survive enactment of Code); *Outlook/Century Ltd.*, 127 B.R. at 656-57 (holding Congress was well aware of exception yet adopted statutory definition containing no new value exception); Piedmont Assocs. v. Cigna Property & Casualty Ins. Co., 132 B.R. 75, 78-80 (N.D. Ga. 1991) (finding plain language of § 1129(b)(2)(B) and intent of Congress precludes existence of new value exception); *Winters*, 99 B.R. at 663 (maintaining Congress purposefully did not use judicial definition of fair and equitable, therefore, new value exception does not exist).

129. 308 U.S. 106 (1939).

130. *See supra* notes 13-21 and accompanying text.

131. *See In re* Outlook/Century Ltd., 127 B.R. 650, 657 (Bankr. N.D. Cal. 1991) (determining any plan that could have been confirmed under *Case* would be confirmed under § 1129(b)(2)(B)); Pennbank v. Winters (*In re* Winters), 99 B.R. 658, 663 (Bankr. W.D. Pa. 1989) (applying facts of *Case* to § 1129(b)(2)(B) and concluding plan would have been confirmed).

132. Bonner Mall Partnership v. U.S. Bankcorp Mortgage Co. (*In re* Bonner Mall Partnership), 2 F.3d 899, 914 (9th Cir. 1993), *cert. granted*, 114 S. Ct. 681, *motion to vacate den. and dismissed by*, 115 S. Ct. 386 (1994).

> solve a no longer existent individual holdout problem, it could just as logically be argued that the new value exception was designed to prevent confirmation holdouts, individual or class, from derailing an otherwise `fair and equitable' plan.[133]

Indeed, in the eyes of the anxious debtor's owners, a holdout class poses the same problems for confirmation as the holdout creditor. However, the Ninth Circuit wrongly downplays the significant fact that Congress, in enacting the Code, chose to apply the absolute priority rule to dissenting impaired *classes* as opposed to dissenting individuals, presumably because it would make plan confirmation less onerous.[134] Thus, Congress saw a difference between the problems caused by a holdout creditor and holdout class.

b. *Dewsnup v. Timm* Does Not Compel the Application of the New Value Exception

In *Dewsnup v. Timm*,[135] Justice Blackmun stated that "[w]hen Congress amends the bankruptcy laws, it does not write 'on a clean slate'."[136] Therefore, the Court must interpret the Code in a way which will not "effect a major change in pre-Code practice that is not the subject of at least some discussion in the legislative history."[137] In accordance with these statements, several courts have been reluctant to conclude that the new value exception is no longer viable under the Code.[138]

---

133. *Id.* (citations omitted).
134. *Id.* ("[T]here is no significant difference between the problem that a holdout class poses for confirmation and that posed by a holdout creditor.").
135. 502 U.S. 410 (1992).
136. *Id.* at 419. *See* Midlantic Nat'l Bank v. New Jersey Dep't of Envtl. Protection, 474 U.S. 494, 501 (1986). The *Midlantic* Court stated that "[t]he normal rule of statutory construction is that if Congress intends for legislation to change the interpretation of a judicially created concept, it makes that intent specific." *Id.*
137. *Dewsnup*, 502 U.S. at 416 ("[T]o attribute to Congress the intention to grant a debtor [a] broad new remedy . . . without the new remedy's being mentioned somewhere in the Code itself or in the annals of Congress is not plausible, in our view, and is contrary to basic bankruptcy principles.").
138. *See, e.g.*, *In re Snyder*, 967 F.2d 1126, 1129 (7th Cir. 1992) (referring to *Dewsnup* in discussing possibility that new value exception might still be viable); *In re* SLC Ltd. V, 137 B.R. 847, 854 (Bankr. C.D. Utah 1992) (stating that *Dewsnup* requires conclusion that new value exception survived Code's enactment). The *Dewsnup* decision has also been cited as having influenced the

However, *Dewsnup* does not compel the conclusion that the new value exception must apply to single asset real estate reorganizations under chapter 11 of the Code. In 1978, the drafters of the Code consolidated chapters X, XI, and XII of the Act into chapter 11.[139] Chapter X,[140] which dealt solely with corporate reorganization, required that plans be fair and equitable, or rather, conform to the absolute priority rule.[141] As stated above, the new value exception arose in response to the fair and equitable requirement of chapter X and its predecessor, section 77B.[142] Under the *Dewsnup* canon of interpretation, because the new value exception was utilized in corporate reorganizations under chapter X of the Act and was, *arguendo,* not explicitly rejected in the plain language and legislative history of the Code,[143] Congress

---

court in *Greystone* to vacate the portion of its opinion dealing with the new value exception. *Snyder*, 967 F.2d at 1129 n.4; *see also* Phoenix Mut. Life Ins. Co. v. Greystone III Joint Venture (*In re* Greystone III Joint Venture), 995 F.2d 1274, 1285 (5th Cir. 1991) (Jones, J., dissenting) ("How one should approach issues of statutory construction arising from the Bankruptcy Code has been clouded, in my view, by *Dewsnup v. Timm.*"), *vacated in part*, 995 F.2d 1284 (5th Cir.), *cert. denied*, 506 U.S. 821 (1992).

139. H.R. REP. NO. 595, 95th Cong., 2d Sess. 5, (1978), *reprinted in* 1978 U.S.C.C.A.N. 5963, 5966 ("The bill consolidates all four chapters into one business reorganization chapter . . . making a business reorganization a quicker, more efficient procedure, and providing greater protection for debtors, creditors, and the public interest.").

140. Chandler Act of 1938, Ch. 575, 52 Stat. 840, 883-905 (codified as 11 U.S.C. §§ 501-676) (repealed 1978).

141. H.R. REP. NO. 595, 95th Cong., 2d Sess. 221-22 (1978), *reprinted in* 1978 U.S.C.C.A.N. 5963, 6181 (citing Case v. Los Angeles Lumber Products Co. Ltd.); *see generally* 5 COLLIER ON BANKRUPTCY ¶ 1129.03, at 1129-76-77 (Lawrence P. King et al. eds. 15th ed. 1995) (discussing absolute priority and chapter X).

142. Act of June 7, 1934, ch. 424, § 77B, 48 Stat. 911, 912, *repealed by* Chandler Act of 1938, Ch. 575, 52 Stat. 840. *See also supra* notes 122-126 and accompanying text.

143. *See* Travelers Ins. Co. v. Bryson Properties, XVIII (*In re* Bryson Properties, XVIII), 961 F.2d 496, 504, n.13 (4th Cir. 1992). Although the legislative history of § 1129(b) contained some discussion of Congress' rejection of a proposal which would have codified the new value exception, it is inconclusive on the issue of the new value exception's viability, because the proposal sought to expand the exception to include noncash contributions. *Id.*

intended it to exist under chapter 11 of the Code.[144] Under the Act, however, real estate reorganizations were dealt with in chapter XII which, unlike chapter X, did not require that a plan conform to the absolute priority rule.[145] Since there was no absolute priority requirement under chapter XII, the new value exception had no application to most real estate reorganizations under pre-Code practice. If a court were to conclude that the new value exception should not apply to single asset real estate reorganizations, it would not be effecting a "major change in pre-Code practice,"[146] and thus would not be in conflict with *Dewsnup*. On the other hand, it might be argued that because chapter 11 applies the absolute priority rule to single asset cases, Congress intended the new value exception to apply to them as well. However, as mentioned earlier, the Code's absolute priority rule is not the same rule that existed under pre-Code practice, and therefore, exceptions to the pre-Code absolute priority rule cannot be implied to exist under the Code.[147] The Supreme Court's decision in *Dewsnup* will therefore allow a finding that the new value exception is not applicable to single asset real estate cases. Accordingly, the ramifications of such application will next be examined.

2. *Application of the New Value Exception to Single Asset Cases Would Frustrate the Purpose of Section 1111(b)*

In order to appreciate the new value exception's effect on single asset cases, it is necessary to discuss the pre-Code case, *In re Pine Gate Associates Ltd.*[148] *Pine Gate* involved the reorganization of a real estate limited

---

144. *Dewsnup*, 502 U.S. at 419-20.

145. *See* Chandler Act, ch. 575, § 472, 52 Stat. 840, 923 (repealed 1978). Prior to the Act's 1952 amendments, the "fair and equitable" standard of chapter X, i.e., the absolute priority rule, also applied in chapter XII. *In re* Pine Gate Assocs. Ltd., [1977-1978 Transfer Binder] Bankr. L. Rep. (CCH) ¶ 66,325, at 76,132 n.15 (N.D. Ga. 1976). However, in 1952, the "fair and equitable" requirement was deleted from chapter XII. Chandler Act Amendments of 1952, ch. 579, § 35, 66 Stat. 420, 433. Since fifty percent of the chapter XII cases filed between 1938 and 1976 were filed between 1970 and 1976, prior practice under chapter XII in actuality did not recognize the absolute priority rule or the new value exception. *See Pine Gate*, [1977-78 Transfer Binder] Bankr. L. Rep. (CCH) at 76,132 n.12.

146. *Dewsnup*, 502 U.S. at 419.

147. *See supra* notes 121-31 and accompanying text.

148. [1977-1978 Transfer Binder] Bankr. L. Rep. (CCH) ¶ 66,325 (N.D. Ga.

partnership under chapter XII of the Act.[149] The partnership defaulted on its mortgage payments and was faced with the threat of foreclosure proceedings.[150] Since the loan had been made on a nonrecourse basis the partners would not have been personally liable for the amount of debt in excess of the value of the collateral.[151] Foreclosure would have resulted, however, in a recapture of accelerated depreciation, giving rise to ordinary income for the partners.[152] To avoid this result, the limited partnership filed for chapter XII in an effort to stay the foreclosure and retain the property.[153] Under chapter XII, a plan of reorganization could not be confirmed over the objection of a class, unless, *inter alia,* that class was paid the value of its debt in cash.[154] Writing for the court, Judge Norton held that the value of a nonrecourse debt is equal to the value of the collateral.[155] At the time of the decision, the *Pine*

1976).

149. *Id.* at 76,121.

150. *Id.*

151. BLACK'S LAW DICTIONARY 1057 (6th ed. 1990) (defining nonrecourse debt as where: "purchaser . . . is not personally liable for [nonrecourse] debt upon default . . . [but creditor may] repossess the related property.").

152. *See In re* Polytherm Indus., 33 B.R. 823, 835 (W.D. Wis. 1983) (finding bankruptcy filed to avert recapture of depreciation as ordinary income); *In re* Barrington Oaks Gen. Partnership, 15 B.R. 952, 969, n.39 (Bankr. D. Utah 1981) (determining petition filed to prevent increased ordinary income due to accelerated depreciation).

153. *Pine Gate*, [1977-1978 Transfer Binder] Bankr. L. Rep. (CCH) at 76,121.

154. Chandler Act of 1938, ch. 575, 52 Stat. 840, 922 (repealed 1978). Section 461 of the Chandler Act was chapter XII's version of the "cramdown" provision. Chapter XII protected dissenting creditors with § 461(11)(c). This section provided that with respect to an "affected" dissenting class, the plan should "provide for . . . adequate protection for the realization by them of the *value of their debts* against the property dealt with by the arrangement and affected by such debts . . . ." *Id.* (emphasis added); *Pine Gate*, [1977-78 transfer binder] Bankr. L. Rep. (CCH) at 76,122 (discussing chapter XII of Act).

155. *Pine Gate*, [1977-1978 Transfer Binder] Bankr. L. Rep. (CCH) at 76,126. Judge Norton reasoned that value of the debts was limited to the appraised value of the collateral because "[section 461(11)] does not say [affected dissenting classes] are entitled to the *amount of their debts.*" *Id.* (emphasis added).

Gate property value had been severely reduced by market conditions existing at that time.[156]

The *Pine Gate* court's rationale led to inequitable results,[157] prompting Congress to enact section 1111(b)(1)(A) of the Code.[158] Section 1111(b)(1)(A) converts a nonrecourse debt into a recourse debt for purposes of claim recognition in bankruptcy.[159] Thus the section 506(a) unsecured claim[160] is transferred into an allowed claim.[161] If not for section

---

156. The mortgage had been for $1.454 million. *Pine Gate*, [1977-78 transfer binder] Bankr. L. Rep. (CCH) at 76,126. At a separate valuation hearing, however, Judge Norton valued the property at $800,000. *In re* Pine Gate Assocs. Ltd., 12 Collier Bankr. Cas. (MB) 607, 629 (N.D. Ga. 1977).

Pine Gate occurred in the mid-1970s, during a recession in the real estate market. *Pine Gate*, [1977-1978 Transfer Binder] Bankr. L. Rep. (CCH) at 76,139. The recession, compounded by an oil embargo, unemployment, and threats of gasoline rationing, caused an increase in the number of chapter XII petitions filed. *Id* at 76,132 n.12. The *Pine Gate* court found a great statistical increase in chapter XII filings. *Id.* For example, while only one chapter XII case had been filed in the Northern District of Georgia from 1938 to 1974, thirty five chapter XII cases were filed in the Northern District of Georgia between March 1974 and June 1976. *Id.* The nationwide increase was similar. *Id.* Approximately one-third of the 2,374 chapter XII cases filed between 1938 and 1976 were filed between 1975 and 1976. *Id.*

157. *See, e.g.*, State Mut. Life Ins. Co. v. KRO Assocs. (*In re* KRO Assocs.), 17 Collier Bankr. Cas. (MB) 658, 676 (Bankr. S.D.N.Y. 1978) (relying on *Pine Gate*, court stripped $6 million mortgage down to $895,000).

In addition to debtors benefitting from the strip down allowed by *Pine Gate*, chapter XII debtors would also enjoy "the appreciation realized in excess of the reduced mortgage if the market rebounded." *In re* Triple R Holdings, L.P., 134 B.R. 382, 387 (Bankr. N.D. Cal. 1991), *rev'd sub nom.*, First Republic Thrift & Loan of San Diego v. Triple R Holdings, L.P. (*In re* Triple R Holdings, L.P.), 145 B.R. 57 (N.D. Cal. 1992).

158. 11 U.S.C. § 1111 (b)(1)(A) (1994); *see* 680 Fifth Ave. Assocs. v. Mutual Benefit Life Ins. Co. In Rehabilitation (*In re* 680 Fifth Avenue Assocs.), 156 B.R. 726, 730 (Bankr. S.D.N.Y. 1993) (stating Congress enacted § 1111(b)(1)(A) in response to *Pine Gate* decision); *see also In re* Aztec Co., 107 B.R. 585, 592 (Bankr. M.D. Tenn. 1989) ("Congress enacted § 1111(b) to alter the result under former chapter XII that a debtor could write down non-recourse notes secured by real estate to the value of the collateral . . . .").

159. 11 U.S.C. § 1111 (b)(1)(A) (1994).

1111(b)(1)(A), the only claim that the mortgagee would be allowed on a nonrecourse debt would be the secured claim, i.e., a claim equal to the amount of the collateral.[162]

Applying the new value exception in single asset reorganizations results in the situation that occurred in *Pine Gate*: the debtor is able to strip down the value of the debt to the value of the collateral simply because prior partners or shareholders contribute new value to the plan.[163] Thus, application of the new value exception in single asset cases effectively eliminates the protection of section 1111(b)(1)(A), and is therefore contrary to the purposes for which the section was enacted.[164]

---

160. Section 506(a) of the Code provides:

> [a]n allowed claim of a creditor secured by a lien on property in which the estate has an interest . . . is a secured claim to the extent of the value of the creditor's interest in the estate's interest in such property . . . and is an unsecured claim to the extent that the value of such creditor's interest . . . is less than the amount of such allowed claim.

11 U.S.C. § 506(a) (1994).

161. *See* 11 U.S.C. § 1111(b)(1)(A) (1994) (providing "[a] claim secured by a lien on property of the estate shall be allowed or disallowed under section 502 of this title the same as if the holder of such claim had recourse against the debtor on account of such claim, whether or not such holder has recourse . . . .").

162. Without § 1111(b)(1)(A), a nonrecourse undersecured mortgagee would not recover the unsecured portion of its claim because § 502(b)(1) disallows claims "when the financing that provides the basis for the claim was advanced on a *nonrecourse* basis." Liona Corp. v. PCH Assocs. (*In re* PCH Assocs.), 949 F.2d 585, 604 (2d Cir. 1991) (emphasis in original).

An alternative to § 1111(b)(1)(A) is the § 1111(b)(2) election. If a creditor elects to have its claim treated under § 1111(b)(2), then "notwithstanding section 506(a) . . ., such claim is a secured claim to the extent that such claim is allowed." 11 U.S.C. § 1111(b)(2) (1994). "By electing under section 1111(b)(2), the claimant sacrifices the right to participate as an unsecured creditor to the extent of any deficiency, but gains protection against a cash out for less than the amount of the entire debt owed." WEINTRAUB & RESNICK, *supra*, note 6, ¶ 8.23[4][a].

163. *See* H. Miles Cohn, *Single Asset Chapter 11 Cases*, 26 TULSA L.J. 523, 543 (1991) (referring to § 1111(b) as imperfect protection since it does not prevent owners from making new value contributions in effort to retain interest in property to detriment of creditors).

164. *See id.* Section 1111 (b)(1)(A) creates a claim for a nonrecourse creditor of a

3. Justification for the New Value Exception Based on the Preservation of the Going Concern Value is Inapplicable in Single Asset Reorganizations

a. Realization of the Going Concern Value in Single Asset Cases

When Congress enacted the Code, one of its primary objectives was to preserve the debtor business as a going concern.[165] Cases have stated that the new value exception is consistent with this objective because it facilitates reorganization by supplying much needed capital, thus avoiding liquidation of the entity's assets.[166] However, liquidation does not mean, in a single asset real estate scenario, that the business will end. The liquidation of the sole asset represents the sale of the entire business. In other words, the single asset debtor's business is the operation of the real estate, which will be continued by the successor if the debtor's business is liquidated. Therefore, the new value exception's application in single asset reorganizations cannot be supported by the possibility that a reorganization will fail absent an infusion of new value. Failure of the reorganization merely prevents the confirmation of a plan under which the debtor would have remained owner of the property.

Although *Bonner Mall* involved a single asset real estate reorganization, the court pointed out that the new value exception "encourages debtors to

---

bankrupt debtor where one was not available before. If prior owners of the real estate give new value (and therefore take a priority interest in the estate property) and the estate is able to pay dissenting classes the lowered value of the collateral to pay off their recourse debt, *see supra* note 162, then the dissenting classes have clearly lost any advantage that section 1111 (b)(1)(A) offers.

165. H.R. REP. NO. 595, 95th Cong., 2d Sess. 220, *reprinted in* 1978 U.S.C.C.A.N. 5963, 6179 ("The premise of a business reorganization is that assets that are used for production in the industry for which they were designed are more valuable than those same assets sold for scrap.").

166. *See* Penn. Mut. Life Ins. Co. v. Woodscape Ltd. Partnership (*In re* Woodscape Ltd. Partnership), 134 B.R. 165, 177 (Bankr. Md. 1991) ("Without fresh capital infusion, little hope exists for reorganizing deflated assets in a bad market."); *In re* Stegall 85 B.R. 510, 513 (C.D. Ill. 1987) (stating benefit of exception is to provide necessary capital from most obvious source), *aff'd*, 865 F.2d 140 (7th Cir. 1989); Case v. Los Angeles Lumber Prods. Co., 308 U.S. 106, 117 (1939) ("Generally, additional funds [are] "essential to the success of the [reorganization].") (quoting Kansas City Terminal Ry. v. Central Union Trust Co., 271 U.S. 445, 455 (1926)).

attempt chapter 11 reorganization instead of liquidating their assets and starting over."[167] However, had the court actually considered the facts of the case in arriving at its conclusion, it would have discovered that its reasoning was wholly inapplicable.[168] The only parties who benefit from avoiding liquidation are the owners of the debtor.[169]

b. Special Skills of Management as Adding to the Going Concern Value of a Single Asset Debtor

Although the chapter 7 liquidation of a single asset real estate debtor preserves the business, it results in a change of ownership. Some might argue that a transfer of ownership is undesirable because prior management might possess special skills and knowledge that add to the entity's going concern value, thus justifying its retention of an interest in the entity equivalent to a contribution of new value.[170] Conversely, it might be argued that the debtor's

---

167. Bonner Mall Partnership v. U.S. Bankcorp Mortgage Co. (*In re* Bonner Mall Partnership), 2 F.3d 899, 916 (9th Cir. 1993), *cert. granted*, 114 S. Ct. 681, *motion to vacate denied and dismissed*, 115 S. Ct. 386 (1994).

168. The court in *Bonner Mall* also noted that "chapter 11 is designed to avoid liquidations under chapter 7, since liquidations may have a negative impact on jobs, suppliers of the business, and the economy as a whole." *Id.* Generally, these are not factors in single asset real estate concerns.

169. Indeed, under a reorganization in which a prior owner has the exclusive right to contribute new value in exchange for an ownership interest it is difficult to see a situation where the plan would satisfy the best interests of creditors rule contained in 11 U.S.C. § 1129(a)(7) (1994). In a liquidation, third parties would compete with one another in bidding on the property. Such competition would result in increased funds, which would go to satisfying the debtor's creditors. Thus, a creditor of a single asset debtor would receive more under chapter 7 than chapter 11.

170. *See* Peter C.L. Roth, Comment, *The Absolute Priority Rule Reasserted—No Equity Participation Without Tangible Capital Contributions—Norwest Bank Worthington v. Ahlers, 108 S. Ct. 963 (1988)*, 23 SUFFOLK U. L. REV. 857, 865 (1989) (stating that "a large part of the value which creditors would enjoy in a reorganization comes directly from the skills and personalities of the owners."). *See, e.g.*, *In re* Snyder 967 F.2d 1126, 1130 (7th Cir. 1992) ("Owners often have valuable information about the enterprise that outsiders lack, and owner participation allows this information to be put to use.") (footnote omitted).

lack of skill was the cause of the enterprise's failure.[171] A "special skills" rationale might more appropriately apply in a multi-asset corporate reorganization, where management's specialized knowledge of the debtor's product can be applied toward the most efficient use of corporation's assets.[172] However, in a real estate limited partnership where the business is composed of only one asset, has few employees, and does not manufacture a product, the skills required of a manager/owner are not generally unique to the particular property.[173] Rather, these skills are general real estate management skills that can be performed by other professional real estate managers of similar property.[174] For this reason, in most single asset real estate cases the skills of prior management do not add to the going concern value of the property.[175] Notwithstanding the foregoing, creditors who believe that owners possess such unique skills are not precluded from proposing or consenting to a plan that will preserve an interest for those owners.

4. Application of the New Value Exception to Single Asset Real Estate Cases Results in a Distortion of the Purposes and Effects of the Exception

The new value exception as employed in single asset real estate cases produces results never contemplated when the exception was devised. As mentioned earlier, the exception developed in multi-asset corporate reorganizations to permit the retention of interests by junior creditors, upon the affirmative vote of senior classes of creditors, notwithstanding chapter X's strict absolute priority requirement.[176] This was permissible because, as the exception was applied, no creditor's interests were diminished.[177] New value

---

171. *See, e.g.*, Fellheimer, Eichen & Braverman, P.C. v. Charter Technologies, Inc., 57 F.3d 1215, 1219 (3d Cir. 1995) (mentioning committee's lack of confidence in debtor's management team and refusal to continue unless they are replaced).
172. Molinaro, *supra* note 12, at 163-64 (comparing differences between multi-asset corporate reorganizations and single asset reorganizations).
173. *Id.*
174. *Katz*, *supra*, note 12 at 85 (suggesting that value of property is unrelated to choice of property manager).
175. Molinaro, *supra* note 12, at 163-64.
176. *See supra* notes 121-31 and accompanying text.
177. Because the contribution did not entitle the junior to an interest in the reorganized company in excess of the amount of the contribution, no creditor's interests were impaired. For example, assume the reorganized company would

contributions merely enlarged the distribution pie and preserved the interests of each existing senior creditor. Junior creditors purchased a participating interest in the new company, increasing its capital and its chance of recovery.

When the new value exception is applied to single asset cases, the result is quite different. This is because theoretically the debtor's property has no value (the mortgage has been stripped down to the property value, leaving the debtor with no equity). Consequently, the new value exception enables the debtor to keep the property, and wipes out the interest of the undersecured creditor with little or no payment on its claim.[178] Thus, a doctrine designed to permit senior classes to agree to include juniors in a plan of reorganization has been distorted, permitting debtors to force their way into a reorganization against the will of senior classes without satisfying the claims of those classes.

Conclusion

Courts and commentators espousing the view that the new value exception continues to be viable fail to take into account the clear language of section 1129 and Congress's codification of an absolute priority rule that is quite different from that which existed under pre-Code practice. In addition, applying the new value exception to single asset cases is not compelled by the Supreme Court's decision in *Dewsnup*, since pre-Code practice under chapter XII of the Act did not require adherence to absolute priority. Moreover, application of the exception to single asset real estate cases leads to the injustice that Congress sought to remedy by enacting section 1111(b)(1)(A) of the Code. Policy considerations also do not support the application of the exception to single asset real estate cases. The new value exception cannot be justified on the grounds that it preserves the going concern value of the debtor by facilitating reorganization. A single asset debtor's going concern value can

---

have assets of $100,000 to be shared among ten unsecured creditors holding equal amounts of debt. Each creditor's interest in the reorganized company would have a value of $10,000. If a junior were permitted to contribute $10,000 to the new company, this would increase the assets of the company to $110,000. As a result, the creditors and the junior would each hold an interest worth $10,000.

178. *See, e.g.*, Phoenix Mut. Life Ins. Co. v. Greystone III Joint Venture (*In re* Greystone III Joint Venture), 995 F.2d 1274, 1277 (5th Cir. 1991) (offering to pay mortgagee less than four percent of claim), *vacated in part*, 995 F.2d 1284 (5th Cir.), *cert. denied*, 113 S. Ct. 72 (1992).

be realized in chapter 7 since, generally speaking, the transfer of a single asset is involved. The special skills of management do not add to the value of most single asset entities and therefore can not justify a prior owner's retention of an interest in the property in exchange for the exclusive right to make a contribution of new value. Finally, the new value exception did not arise in the context of a single asset reorganization, but rather it arose in response to a strict pre-Code absolute priority rule applied to corporate reorganizations. Under such circumstances, the new value exception assisted in rehabilitating the debtor, whereas under current practice, the exception serves as a weapon allowing owners of the debtor to eradicate debt while allowing them to keep their ownership interests in the reorganized entity. In view of these considerations, it is clear that the new value exception is not suited to single asset real estate reorganizations and, in the absence of Congressional mandate, should not be recognized.

CHAPTER X

IMPACT OF BANKRUPTCY ON WORKOUTS AND NEW INVESTMENTS*

JAMES L. LIPSCOMB
ALAN J. ROBIN

Life insurance companies are among the nation's largest and most significant commercial real estate mortgage lenders.[1] In 1993, life insurance companies' net new investment in United States capital markets totaled $143.7 billion, ranking third after mutual funds and commercial banks, among the private domestic capital sources.[2] At the end of 1993, life insurance companies held real property mortgage investments in excess of $229 billion in the United States.[3] Mutual life insurance companies, the largest life insurance companies in the United States,[4] invest for their policyholders, as well as for pension customers that invest for employee retirement funds. In workout discussions, borrowers often express the position that lenders can absorb the impact of investment losses more easily than borrowers. Such a position ignores the economic reality of the sources of the capital which life insurance companies invest and the severity of the impact that investment losses can have on a lender's individual customers.[5]

---

* The views expressed in this paper are those of the authors and do not necessarily represent the views of Metropolitan Life Insurance Company.

1. *See* Joseph C. Shenker & Anthony J. Colletta, *Asset Securitization: Evolution, Current Issues and New Frontiers*, 69 TEX. L. REV. 1369, 1397 (1991) (noting that until 1984, owners of commercial real estate usually financed properties through mortgage loans from large insurance companies).
2. American Council of Life Ins., 1994 LIFE INSURANCE FACT BOOK 85 (1994) [hereinafter ACLI FACT BOOK].
3. *Id.* at 99.
4. *Id.* at 19.
5. In the 1980's, life insurance companies shifted from largely whole life

Although the Bankruptcy Code ("Code") influences workouts of commercial mortgages, the Code also creates many dilemmas for commercial real estate mortgage lenders because of chapter 11 bankruptcy filings by single asset entity borrowers. This Article will describe the nature of these problems, the losses incurred by lenders, and lenders' responses to single asset entity bankruptcies. In addition, Exhibit A summarizes a number of representative single asset bankruptcy cases demonstrating why such concerns exist.

A. Background

The growth in the number and size of commercial real estate mortgage investments in the 1980's was unprecedented in this country's investment history.[6] Unfortunately, during the real estate decline in the late 1980's, the increase in the number of voluntary bankruptcy petitions, particularly chapter 11 petitions, was similarly unprecedented.[7] The "stigma" traditionally associated with formal bankruptcy business reorganization all but disappeared with respect to commercial real estate mortgage investments, which were predominantly single asset entities.

A single asset entity is usually formed solely for the purpose of owning and operating the particular asset.[8] The ownership vehicles are created to

---

nonparticipating polices (where the insurer bears the risk of the investment experience) to participating policies, such as variable life and annuities (where the insured bears the risks of the investment experience). *See* Roger L. Blease, *Participating Whole Life Policy Survey*, *in* BEST'S REVIEW-LIFE-HEALTH INSURANCE 91 (6th ed. 1990) (indicating that sales of participating whole life insurance continued to remain strong through 1989, especially relative to nonparticipating products).

6. *See* Michael Carter, *Uncertainty, Liquidity and Speculation: A Keynesian Perspective on Financial Innovation in the Debt Markets*, 14 J. POST KEYNESIAN ECON. 169 (1991); *Study Suggests Mortgage Backed Securities Could Help Banks Solve Real Estate Problems*, MORTGAGE MARKETPLACE, Dec. 13, 1991.

7. Eugene A. Pinover & Marc Abrams, *Bankruptcy Amendments - BAA Expected to Level the Playing Field in Real Estate Cases*, N.Y. L.J., Jan. 19, 1994, at 5 (stating that decline in real estate values during late 1980s and early 1990s resulted in proliferation of bankruptcy cases, particularly, single asset real estate cases).

8. Single asset real estate is defined as:

encourage investments by passive investors and achieve the objective of limited liability for the investors.[9] In addition, single asset entities facilitate the financing, sale, and if necessary, the reorganization or workout of the property. The first mortgage holder is usually the largest creditor of a single asset entity. Other creditors either do not exist or have de minimis claims in comparison to the amount owed to the primary lender.[10] All too frequently, single asset entity bankruptcies are characterized by (1) a transfer of the property on the eve of filing generally from one single asset entity to another but on occasion from a single asset entity to a multiple asset entity where the borrower concludes that placing the property in a multiple asset entity will create more obstacles to the lender in the bankruptcy proceeding and (2) the recent appearance of a small number of third party creditors, generally trade creditors of accountants, attorneys and other close business acquaintances of the borrower.

In many single asset entity real estate bankruptcies, the lender has fully performed the principal obligation which it agreed to undertake–funding the agreed upon amount of money to the borrower.[11] It is the borrower who seeks to use the bankruptcy process to accomplish what they could not accomplish through bilateral negotiations–rewriting the terms of loan documents to avoid a contractual commitment made to either repay the loan or permit the lender

---

> real property constituting a single property or project, other than residential real property with fewer than 4 residential units, which generates substantially all of the gross income of a debtor and on which no substantial business is being conducted by a debtor other than the business of operating the real property and activities incidental thereto having aggregate noncontingent, liquidated secured debts in an amount no more than $4,000,000.

11 U.S.C. § 101(51B) (1994). The statute has been interpreted to mean "a building or buildings which were intended to be income producing, or raw land." *In re* Kkemko, Inc., 181 B.R. 47, 51 (Bankr. S.D. Ohio 1995).

9. *See* H. Miles Cohn, *Single Asset Chapter 11 Cases*, 26 TULSA L.J. 523, 527 (1991) (describing single asset cases as investment vehicles formed to hold single asset as investment in which investors only risk losing their equity in holding partnership or corporation).

10. *Id.* at 528.

11. *See* RICHARD F. BROUDE, REORGANIZATION UNDER CHAPTER 11 OF THE BANKRUPTCY CODE § 4.05 [2].

to foreclose.[12] Although there are many reasons for this development, none is more important than the manner in which commercial real estate mortgage transactions in the United States are structured to provide limited liability to the constituent members of the borrower.[13]

1. Real Estate Financing

The basic premise of real estate development and investment is that the value of the "business" is equal to the value of the real estate asset. The "business" is providing space to tenants that are "going concerns" involved in providing goods and services to third parties or the public. The value of real estate is determined by appraisal based upon one of three valuation methods: income approach,[14] market approach[15] or cost approach.[16] Mortgage loans are usually made on the basis of market value and an analysis of the expected income after expenses, or net operating income ("NOI").

A majority of first mortgage financing on commercial real estate is on a nonrecourse or limited recourse basis.[17] That is, the borrower does not have a personal obligation to repay the loan, and the lender agrees to look solely to the real estate asset for repayment. Some common exceptions from this

---

12. *Id.*
13. *Id.*
14. This approach is useful only for properties which produce an income stream, such as office buildings, shopping centers or apartment complexes. WILLIAM L. VENTOLO, JR. & MARTHA R. WILLIAMS, FUNDAMENTALS OF REAL ESTATE APPRAISAL 133 (1975).
15. This approach, also known as the "sales comparison" approach, compares similar properties which have recently been sold. *Valuation: General and Real Estate*, 132-3d Tax Mgmt. (BNA) A-2, A-7 (1984). *See, e.g.*, Farmers Home Admin. v. Arnold & Baker Farms (*In re* Arnold & Baker Farms), 177 B.R. 648, 656 (Bankr. 9th Cir. 1994) (using sales comparison approach comparing subject property to similar properties recently sold in same or general area).
16. This approach is based on the appraisal value of the site involved as well as an estimate of the replacement or reproduction cost of the building on the site. VENTOLO & WILLIAMS, *supra* note 14, at 99.
17. *See* J. Philip Rosen et al., *"Travelers" Redux: 2d Circuit Rules on Waste and Nonrecourse Liability in N.Y.*, N.Y. L.J., June 29, 1994, at 5 (stating nonrecourse is "well-established foundation of U.S. real estate financing.").

exculpation from liability are: material misrepresentations, fraud, waste, and losses resulting from environmental contamination. Because the loans are underwritten on the value of the property rather than on the abilities of the constituent members of the borrower to repay the loan, lenders will generally not make a loan that exceeds 75% of the value of the real estate.[18] Nor will a lender generally make a loan where the annual NOI is less than 110% of the required annual debt service on the loan.[19]

An LTV of 75% should not be interpreted to mean that a borrower has invested cash representing the balance of the 25% equity in the property. In many of the commercial loans which are the subject of bankruptcy proceedings, since the appraisal represents the market value of the property, the lender's funding can represent 100% or more of the actual development costs of the property.[20] In such circumstances, the equity resides in the market value of the property based on the leasing of the property at current market rents. This equity can only be realized upon sale of the property or partially realized if the property can be refinanced at a value in excess of the development cost.

The LTV and DCR ("debt coverage ratio") underwriting prerequisites are intended to reduce the lender's risk of loss from an unanticipated decrease in occupancy rates or rental rates by assuring that there is adequate cash flow to pay debt service during the term of the loan, and that the value of the real estate at maturity will be sufficient to repay the principal of the loan.[21] Most

---

18. The percentage determined by dividing the loan amount by the market value of the real estate is commonly called the "loan to value ratio" ("LTV").
19. The annual NOI divided by the annual debt service is commonly referred to as the "debt coverage ratio" (DCR). Investment Dealers Digest, Inc., *Freddie Mac, Driven by Past in Multifamily Policy*, 10 MORTGAGE-BACKED SEC. LETTER, 42 (1995), *available in* WESTLAW, 1995 WL 9893402 (stating that at Freddie Mac, maximum LTV's are 80% and minimum DCR's are 1.25%); Stephen Kleege, *Banks Play More Active Role In Sales of RTC Real Estate*, AM. BANKER, Mar. 17, 1992, at 1 (banks now seek 1.2-to-1.0 DCR on real estate loans).
20. The loan-to-value ratio is defined in the industry as the loan amount divided by the lesser of the sales price or an appraised value of the property in question. Texas Dept. of Hous. & Comm. Affairs v. Verex Assurance, Inc., 68 F.3d 922, 925 n.2 (5th Cir. 1995).
21. Diana G. Browne, *The Private Mortgage Insurance Industry, The Thrift Industry and the Secondary Mortgage Market: Their Interrelationships*, 12

real estate investments are made with the assumption that the LTV will decrease as the value of the real estate increases, and the DCR will increase as the NOI increases as a result of increases in rents. Both lender and borrower are relying on the value of the real estate for a return on their respective investments. However, the borrower benefits from the "upside" in the property if the property appreciates, and the lender either receives a fixed return (the mortgage coupon) or, loses if the value of the property declines below the value of the loan.

2. *Rights and Risks of Parties and Interference By Bankruptcy Courts*

One of the primary misconceptions in bankruptcy is that the borrower and the lender share the same risks. To induce the lender to lend on a nonrecourse basis and accept a fixed return as compensation for the risk, the borrower agrees that if the property does not perform as expected, the lender has the right to acquire ownership of the property through foreclosure.[22] Upon completion of foreclosure, the loan obligation is extinguished.[23] Although the lender underwrites the risks of the market, it does not "price" a nonrecourse loan by accounting for the time, losses and costs associated with a bankruptcy proceeding, which may last from two to four years. Not only is there no pre-agreed second chance for the borrower to create value, but the borrower's consideration for the lender's nonrecourse loan is the right of foreclosure.

This is not to say that borrowers should not have the right to assert any defenses to a foreclosure. To the extent the lender has not performed its obligations under the loan documents or has performed its obligations in an improper manner, the borrower should avail itself to the remedies and defenses under applicable state law. Borrowers also have the right and opportunity to realize any equity in the property at the time of the loan default.[24] It is a

---

AKRON L. REV. 631, 651 (1979) (discussing factors considered by lenders in evaluating risk of underwriting loans).

22. *See* Scott Carlisle, *Single Asset Real Estate in Chapter 11: Secured Creditors' Perspective and the Need for Reform*, 1 AM. BANKR. INST. L. REV. 133, 133 (1993) (describing borrower-lender contract).

23. *See* BLACK'S LAW DICTIONARY 646 (6th ed. 1990) (defining result of foreclosure as "satisfaction of debt").

24. As an economic matter, if the property has a value greater than the amount owed to the lender, the borrower will sell the property before allowing it to

mistaken notion that lenders make a windfall from foreclosing on property and selling it for a profit. No lender wants to foreclose and own distressed property.[25] The true windfall is to borrowers who file for bankruptcy, where bankruptcy court judges substitute their judgement and discretion for the judgement and discretion of the parties to, what is essentially, a bi-lateral agreement.

Unfortunately, in modern times, beginning with the *In re Pine Gate Associates Ltd*[26] decision in 1976 and continuing past the enactment of the Code in 1978, borrowers have turned to the Code and first tier bankruptcy courts to restructure the bi-lateral agreements made between borrowers and lenders.[27] By filing for reorganization under chapter 11, even where the value of the property clearly is less than the amount owed to the lender, borrowers have succeeded in delaying lenders' exercise of their rights under the loan.[28] While the Code seemingly protects the interests of debtors and secured creditors alike, the protection is discretionary,[29] and the exercise of discretion results in protracted delays and significant economic losses to the lender which have generally proved to be unrecoverable.[30]

---

be foreclosed or there will be multiple bidders at the foreclosure sale.

25. *See* Vic Sung Lam, *Avoidability of Foreclosure Sales Under Section 548(A)(2) of the Bankruptcy Code: Revisiting the Transfer Issue and Standardizing Reasonable Equivalency*, 68 WASH. L. REV. 673, 692 (1993) (reasoning that risks associated with distressed properties make them inherently less marketable than other properties).

26. 1977-1978 Bankr. L. Rep.(CCH) ¶ 66,325 (Bankr. N.D. Ga. Oct. 14, 1976) (providing for "cramdown" of principal under chapter XII of Bankruptcy Act enabling debtor to retain ownership of property and any subsequently determined appreciation in value of property).

27. *In re* Anderson Oaks (Phase 1) Ltd. Partnership, 77 B.R. 108, 112 (Bankr. W.D. Tex. 1987) (displaying unsuccessful attempt by debtor to use court to renegotiate loan).

28. *See* 11 U.S.C. § 362 (1994) (imposing automatic stay upon filing of petition).

29. *See generally id.* § 105 (providing court discretion to implement any order necessary to carry out provisions of Code).

30. *See* Hon. Samuel L. Bufford, *Chapter 11 Case Management,* 14 AM. BANKR. INST. J. 35, 46 (1996) (explaining that creditors suffer expenses and losses from delayed chapter 11 cases).

The real estate lenders' concern under the Bankruptcy Act was that chapter XII could be used to achieve a "cramdown" of its principal, allowing the borrower to attribute one value to the property for determining the amount of the lien, while attributing a different value to it for other purposes. When the Code was adopted in 1978, the lending community thought it would no longer be possible for a borrower to retain ownership of real property while the lender was forced to forego the interest and the crammed down principal of its loan. Then along came *Phoenix Mutual Life Insurance Co. v. Greystone III Joint Venture (In re Greystone III Joint Venture)*[31] which resurrected the *Case v. Los Angeles Lumber Products Co.*[32] decision. *Greystone* opened the flood gates for the so-called "new capital exception" cases. Notwithstanding, Judge Jones' thoughtful opinion in the Fifth Circuit's decision of *Greystone*,[33] and the eloquence of Judge Easterbrook in *Kham & Nate's Shoes No. 2, Inc. v. First Bank of Whiting*,[34] the Ninth Circuit affirmed the existence of the new value

---

31. 102 B.R. 560 (Bankr. W.D. Tex. 1989), *aff'd*, 127 B.R. 138 (W.D. Tex. 1990), *rev'd*, 995 F.2d 1274 (5th Cir. 1991), *cert. denied*, 506 U.S. 821 (1992).
32. 308 U.S. 106 (1939) (explaining that if person made new capital contribution to reorganized business plan could provide interest for person in business even though all senior interests had not been paid in full). It is unclear whether this decision survived the adoption of the Code. Salvatore G. Gangemi & Stephen Bordanaro, *The New Value Exception: Square Peg in a Round Hole*, 1 AM. BANKR. INST. L. REV. 173, 187-89 (1993); Gutcho, *The Elimination of the New Value Cram Downs in One Asset Real Estate Bankruptcies*, 10 CAL. PROP. J. 4-1 (1992).
33. *Greystone*, 995 F.2d at 1284 (holding that because new value exception was not viable under Code, plan violated absolute priority rule and could not be confirmed). Although the Court of Appeals unanimously reversed the district court decision in an unusual step, it withdrew and deleted that portion of the opinion which states that the new value exception did not exist. *Id.* Judge Jones, the author of the original opinion, dissented from the action stating, "In reaffirming what I wrote about the 'new value exception'. . . I would hope to stand with Galileo, who, rebuffed by a higher temporal authority, muttered under his breath, `Eppur si muove.' (`And yet it moves.')." *Id.* at 1285.
34. 908 F.2d 1351, 1361-62 (7th Cir. 1990). Judge Easterbrook, writing for the majority, stated his belief that the new value exception may not have survived the codification of the absolute priority rule under the Code. *Id.*

exception to the absolute priority rule in *Bonner Mall Partnership v. U.S. Bancorp Mortgage Co.*[35] The court upheld a bankruptcy court cramdown decision that reduced the lender's secured claim from $6.6 million to $3.2 million while permitting the equity owners of the debtor to contribute $200,000 in exchange for 50% of the reorganized company's common stock.[36]

Real estate lenders have repeatedly asked Congress to amend the Code to remedy the unfairness resulting from the application of the Code to single asset entity real estate cases.[37] Congress passed amendments in 1984,[38] but these amendments did not resolve many of the important issues affecting lenders.[39] Since then, although several bills have been proposed, none have been passed by both houses of Congress until the Bankruptcy Reform Act of 1994 ("1994 Act").[40] Many reforms of the 1994 Act were passed with hasty last minute changes made to provisions that had been the product of years of careful deliberation and debate.[41] Unfortunately, this resulted in a potpourri of

---

35. 2 F.3d 899 (9th Cir. 1993), *cert. granted,* 114 S.Ct. 681, *dismissed as moot,* 115 S.Ct. 386 (1994).
36. *Bonner Mall*, 2 F.2d at 905-07. This is grossly disproportionate to the $3.4 million unsecured claim of the lender. The courts that have supported the new value exception have generally articulated the requirements that the "new value" be 1) new, 2) substantial, 3) money or money's worth, 4) necessary for a successful reorganization, and 5) reasonably equivalent to the value or interest received. *Id.*
37. *See* Frank R. Kennedy, *Involuntary Fraudulent Transfers*, 9 CARDOZO L. REV. 531, 565 (1987).
38. Bankruptcy Amendments and Federal Judgeship Act of 1984, Pub. L. No. 98-353, 98 Stat. 333 (codified as amended at 11 U.S.C. §§ 101 et. seq. (1994)).
39. *See, e.g.*, Jeffery M. Sharp, *Returning Confidence to Prepetition Foreclosure Sales Under the Bankruptcy Code: Scrutinizing Federal Policy and a Vague Statute*, 32 AM. BUS. L. J. 185, 225 (1994) (explaining impact of 1984 amendments).
40. Pub. L. No. 103-394, 108 Stat. 4106 (codified at 11 U.S.C. §§ 101-1330).
41. *See* David G. Hicks, *The October Surprise: The Bankruptcy Reform Act of 1994-An Analysis of Title 11-The Commercial Issues*, 29 CREIGHTON L. REV. 499, 500-02 (1996) (explaining legislative process of Bankruptcy Reform Act).

amendments, many of which did not resolve the critical issues raised by real estate lenders, and in some instances, created greater ambiguities.[42]

One example of the significant shortcomings of the 1994 Act is the section in the bill that was originally introduced to address the delays that had crept into the resolution of single asset entity bankruptcies.[43] As enacted in the 1994 Act, the amendments were narrowed to two provisions, one dealing with the perfection of security interests in rents,[44] and the other designed to speed up reorganization plans.[45] The latter provision in the Senate bill would have amended section 362(d) of the Bankruptcy Code to require that in single asset entity bankruptcies the automatic stay be lifted if the debtor does not either submit a credible plan of reorganization within 90 days of filing or begin to pay lost opportunity costs to the lender.[46] The House changed the definition of single asset real estate to exclude transactions with secured debt in excess of $4 million.[47] Since residential real estate was already excluded under the definition, and the amendment pertained solely to commercial real estate business, it is unclear why the House felt the need for this limitation.

It is clear, however, that the 1994 Act does not alleviate the frustrations that real estate lenders have with commercial real estate bankruptcies. Arguably, the 1994 Act may exacerbate these frustrations if bankruptcy courts decide that since Congress limited these provisions to loans of less than $4 million, it did not intend these provisions or the rationale behind them to be extended to other bankruptcy situations.

---

42. *See* Susan M. Richmond, *Overview of the Bankruptcy Reform Act of 1994*, 67 N.Y. St. B. J. 10 (Nov. 1995) (indicating that 1994 amendments provided little assistance to real estate lenders).
43. *See* S. Rep. No. 168, 103d Cong., 2d. Sess. § 202 (1993).
44. Bankruptcy Reform Act of 1994 § 214, 11 U.S.C. § 552 (1994).
45. *Id.* § 101, 11 U.S.C. § 362(e) (1994).
46. *See supra* note 43 and accompanying text.
47. *See* H.R. Rep. No. 835, 103d Cong., 2d Sess. § 219, at 50 (1994), *reprinted in* 1994 U.S.C.C.A.N. 3340, 3359 (altering definition of "single asset real estate" to property "having aggregate secured debts in an amount no more than $2,000,000."). The enacted version increased this amount to $4,000,000. Bankruptcy Reform Act of 1994 § 218, 11 U.S.C. § 101(51B).

B. Lenders' Experiences in Bankruptcy

It is the shared observation and common experience of many lenders that bankruptcy courts have generally turned a blind eye to the fact that single asset entity bankruptcies are primarily two party disputes.[48] Where there are other creditors, those creditors have generally been created solely for the purpose of disguising the two party dispute. Bankruptcy courts exacerbate the situation by failing to quickly disengage from cases which are, essentially, contractual disputes between two parties.

1. *Purposes of Bankruptcy Code and Inapplicability to Single Asset Real Estate*

The bankruptcy laws of this country were formulated to accomplish specific objectives and demonstrate an approach to business reorganization that reflects important social policies. In her article entitled, *The New Value Exception to the Absolute Priority Rule in Chapter 11 Reorganizations: What Should the Rule Be?*, Professor Linda J. Rusch recites the two fundamental premises of these laws.[49] First, the reorganization of a business, instead of liquidating its assets at a forced sale will often generate more value than its liquidation, and that this value is worth maximizing and preserving.[50] Second is the premise that "a successfully reorganized business, as opposed to a liquidated business, benefits the entire society through production of goods and services, employment, taxes and other contributions."[51] None of

---

48. *See* Charles R. Sterbach, *Absolute Priority and the New Value Exception: A Practitioner's Primer*, 99 COM. L. J. 176, 187-88 (1994) (suggesting most single asset real estate bankruptcies are two party disputes).
49. Linda J. Rusch, *The New Value Exception to the Absolute Priority Rule in Chapter 11 Reorganizations: What Should the Rule Be?*, 19 PEPP. L. REV. 1311 (1992).
50. *Id.* at 1316.
51. *Id.* at 1329. Courts commonly express the benefits of reorganization as: preserving jobs, NLRB v. Bildisco & Bildisco, 465 U.S. 513, 528 (1984) (indicating that fundamental purpose of reorganization is to prevent liquidation and its attendant loss of jobs), retaining a tax base, Northlake Bldg. Partners v. Northwestern Nat'l Life Ins. Co. (*In re* Northlake Bldg. Partners) 41 B.R. 231, 234 (Bankr. N.D. Ill. 1984) (discussing benefit to community if debtor reorganizes rather than liquidates), and protecting the

these policy concerns exist in single asset entity bankruptcies.

First, there is no risk of losing the going concern value of a business. Real estate continues to operate whether the borrower or another investor owns it.[52] A property's performance rarely depends upon the unique contributions of an owning entity.[53] To the contrary, the going concern value of a real estate business may be reduced by the bankruptcy process. The property receives minimal repairs, capital improvements and capital replacements during the bankruptcy.[54] Investing money to repair a property or add value to it during bankruptcy directly conflicts with the borrower's objective of cramming down as much of the lender's loan principal as possible. To the extent that an investment increases the fair market value of the real estate, the amount of principal that can be crammed down decreases and the debtor will be required to pay interest on a greater loan amount after a plan is confirmed. Therefore, finding the necessary new value to make the plan confirmable becomes more difficult for the debtor. Additionally, tenants occupying properties in bankruptcy claim that the property is not maintained as required under the leases.[55] Many existing tenants either negotiate for rent reductions during the pendency of a bankruptcy or abandon the premises entirely.[56] It is difficult to sue these tenants for damages since they have sustainable counterclaims against the landlord for breach of its obligations under the lease.[57] Finally, new

---

community from the losses associated with the closure of a business, *In re* Delta Food Processing Corp. 313 F. Supp. 788, 795 (N.D. Miss. 1970), *aff'd*, 446 F.2d 437 (5th Cir. 1971).

52. *See* Robert L. Lippert, *Determining the Appropriated Cramdown Rate in Single-Asset Bankruptcies*, 24 REAL EST. L.J. 255 (1996).

53. *Id.*

54. See 11 U.S.C. § 503(b)(1)(A) (1994) (giving repairs administrative expense status only when such repairs are *necessary*).

55. *See, e.g.*, Megafoods Stores, Inc. v. Flagstaff Realty Assocs. (*In re* Flagstaff Realty Assocs.), 60 F.3d 1031, 1032 (3d Cir. 1995) (tenant seeking reduction in rent to compensate for repair expenditures made by tenant when repairs were obligation of chapter 11 debtor-landlord).

56. *See, e.g.*, Lovell v. Kevin J. Thornton Enters., Inc. (*In re* Branchaud), 186 B.R. 337, 340 (Bankr. D.R.I. 1995) (tenant abandoned and unsuccessfully claimed constructive eviction).

57. *Id.* (allowing debtor-landlord damages after tenant abandoned premises but subtracted snow removal costs which landlord was obligated to provide under lease).

tenants often negotiate for low rents because of the reputation damage caused because the property has become distressed.[58]

Second, whether the borrower or the lender owns the property does not affect the other societal benefits of a reorganization.[59] The number of employees associated with operating the property will remain the same, and arguably, the sooner the lender is able to foreclose upon the property, the sooner any unpaid taxes will be paid.[60] A distressed property in bankruptcy does not fully contribute to the betterment of the community. Only after a property is no longer subject to the jurisdiction of the bankruptcy courts, can its value be maximized. Even if a lender sells a foreclosed property at a loss, very often that sale is to a company whose purpose in acquiring the property is to rehabilitate it.

According to the authors of the article entitled *Confirmation by Cramdown Through the New Value Exception in Single Asset Cases*,[61] bankruptcy is a framework for debtor/creditor negotiations.[62] The authors conclude that the bankruptcy court is preferable to less efficient state law remedies for four principal reasons: the foreclosure bidding process might not maximize revenues;[63] liquidation may result in additional losses in the form of lost going-concern premiums that would benefit the marginal creditors and equity holders which may result in litigation;[64] a forced sale might depress the value of other properties in the market because it might convey a false notion of market value;[65] and the property may be mismanaged in the transitional

---

58. See Carolin Corp. v. Miller, 886 F.2d 693, 697 (4th Cir. 1989) (dismissing chapter 11 petition because court doubted debtor would attract new tenant without infusion of capital to make property desirable).
59. Ronald S. Orr & James A. McDougal, *The Debtor's View of Chapter 11 in a Case Involving Real Property*, 1993 (PLI Real Est. L. & Practice Course Handbook).
60. American Sav. & Loan Assoc. v. Gill (*In re* North County Place, Ltd.), 92 B.R. 437, 442 (Bankr. C.D. Cal. 1988) (delaying foreclosure allowed unpaid taxes to reach $149,680.56).
61. Mark E. MacDonald et al., *Confirmation by Cramdown Through the New Value Exception in Single Asset Cases,* 1 AM. BANKR. INST. L. REV. 65, 78-80 (1993).
62. *Id.* at 78.
63. *Id.* at 79.
64. *Id.*
65. *Id.*

period when it is owned by a lender thereby resulting in a further loss to society.[66] Because the authors assume that these economic efficiencies are no less applicable to a single asset debtor, they conclude that "the economic rationale for permitting debtors to avail themselves of bankruptcy reorganization mandates that single asset debtors be allowed to utilize the new value exception since, without it, they are effectively denied the right to reorganize."[67]

These arguments do not appear to reflect the reality of single asset entity bankruptcies. First, the fact that a state court may operate inefficiently is no reason why a bankruptcy court should retain jurisdiction over a bi-lateral dispute. Second, in many instances, the resolution of debtor-creditor rights and remedies can be more quickly adjudicated in state court than in bankruptcy court.[68] Using the bankruptcy courts as a forum to encourage dispute resolution between a borrower and a lender does nothing to further the public policy objectives of the bankruptcy laws. Instead, it permits a borrower to designate the bankruptcy courts as a preferred alternative forum to state court foreclosure proceedings. Third, the suggestion that a property may decline in value during the period between foreclosure and resale is contrary to the experience of most lenders who either rehabilitate the property prior to resale or try to market it to a purchaser who will rehabilitate it.[69] Foreclosure reintroduces stability to the property and enables new management to undertake the investment necessary to enhance its market value.[70]

---

66. MacDonald et al., *supra* note 61, at 79.

67. *Id.* at 80.

68. *See* Craig W. West, *Bankruptcy: 'Fresh Start' Policy Cleans Up on State Police and Regulatory Power*, 25 WASHBURN L.J. 552, 554 (1986) (arguing that state courts would handle environmental issues more efficiently than bankruptcy courts) (citing *In re* Charles George Land Reclamation Trust, 30 B.R. 918 (Bankr. D. Mass. 1983) (dismissing case because state court was proper forum)).

69. *See* Kallie Jurgens, *Investors Selecting Proven Managers to Boost Values of Distressed Hotels*, NAT'L REAL EST. INVESTOR, July 1, 1993, at 74 (describing maximization of value by lender of hotels after foreclosure).

70. *Id.* (discussing effects of improved management, marketing and market positioning on hotel's bottom line after revitalization post-foreclosure). After foreclosure, lenders out of fear of liability and desire to maximize value of property may go through great expense to improve property. *See* Marvin Garfinkel, *Real Estate Defaults Investigation Check List for Lender's*

2. *Bad Faith*

Many single asset entity bankruptcies bring into question issues of bad faith.[71] Too often, from the lender's perspective, borrowers turn to bankruptcy courts as an alternative forum to state court litigation to prevent a foreclosure sale from occurring. The Code requires that all plans be filed in good faith.[72] Under section 362, a court may grant relief from the automatic stay for "cause."[73] Since "cause" is not defined, many of the Circuit Courts of Appeals have incorporated good faith into the criteria for determining "cause" to dismiss a bankruptcy or grant relief from the automatic stay.[74] Some courts, however, have not accepted this important principal that prepetition bad faith constitutes grounds for dismissing a bankruptcy proceeding.[75]

Counsel, 1994, at 151 (ALI-ABA Course of Study Real Est. Defaults, Workouts & Reorganizations) (describing necessary steps for lender to protect self from defaulting debtor with distressed property).

71. *See* Brian S. Katz, *Single-Asset real Estate Cases and the Good Faith Requirement: Why Reluctance to Ask Whether a Case Belongs in Bankruptcy Leads to the Incorrect Result*, 9 BANKR. DEV. J. 77, 86 (1992) ("[M]ost courts dismiss single-asset cases from bankruptcy on the ground that the petition initiating the proceeding was not filed in good faith."); Janet A. Flaccus, *Have Eight Circuits Shorted? Good Faith and Chapter 11 Bankruptcy Petitions*, 67 AM. BANKR. L.J. 401, 420 (1993) (stating that "single asset cases are more than 57% of the reported cases of bad faith").
72. 11 U.S.C § 1129(a)(3) (1994).
73. *Id.* § 362(d)(1).
74. Little Creek Dev. Co. v. Commonwealth Mortgage Corp. (*In re* Little Creek Dev. Co.), 779 F.2d 1068, 1072 (5th Cir. 1986); *see also* Laguna Assocs. Ltd. Partnership v. Aetna Casualty & Surety Co. (*In re* Laguna Assocs. Ltd. Partnership), 30 F.3d 734, 737 (6th Cir. 1994) (finding debtor's lack of good faith in filing bankruptcy petition can constitute "cause" for lifting the automatic stay); Carolin Corp. v. Miller, 886 F.2d 693, 699 (4th Cir. 1989) (same); Can-Alta Properties, Ltd. v. State Sav. Mortgage Co. (*In re* Can-Alta Properties, Ltd., 87 B.R. 89, 91 (Bankr. 9th Cir. 1988) (same); Natural Land Corp. v. Baker Farms Inc. (*In re* Natural Land Corp.), 825 F.2d 296, 297 (11th Cir. 1987) (same).
75. *See In re* Victoria Ltd. Partnership, 187 B.R. 54 (Bankr. D. Mass. 1995) (holding that good faith filing doctrine conflicts with Code, "its legislative history, Supreme Court precedent and logic").

Borrowers who create a handful of small debts immediately prior to a bankruptcy filing when the account for the property contains sufficient proceeds to pay these creditors and other projected obligations also enjoy the benefits of the automatic stay. Several of the representative cases fit the "new debtor syndrome" paradigm described in the *Little Creek Development Co. v. Commonwealth Mortgage Corp. (In re Little Creek Development Co.)*[76] This paradigm is a situation in which one property generates all the income, and the property is fully encumbered by a mortgage, leaving the debtor with no equity.[77] Furthermore, there are few trade creditors, each of whom have small claims, and the property has no employees except for the principals.[78] The scenario is compounded where the borrower transfers the property on the eve of foreclosure, after efforts to restructure the loan have failed, to an entity which immediately files bankruptcy.[79]

Yet, in very few instances did a bankruptcy judge grant a lift-stay motion in the early stages of the proceeding. In one case where the lift-stay motion was granted, the judge advised the debtor that it could have filed bankruptcy in a different manner.[80] The debtor then refiled over the lender's objection that the court was allowing the debtor to benefit from its own bad faith by causing further costs and delays to the lender.[81] In another case where a bankruptcy was dismissed for cause, the borrower commenced an appeal, dismissed it and filed a second chapter 11 case.[82] The case was dismissed fifteen months after the second filing. In the decision, the bankruptcy court judge concluded, "reduced to its essence, this case is a two party dispute" and found that the

---

76. 779 F.2d at 1073.
77. *Id.*
78. *Id.*
79. The representative cases are actual experiences of MetLife. During the period 1993-94, one out of every two foreclosures resulted in a bankruptcy filing. With one or two exceptions, all of these cases (58 cases in 15 states, aggregating approximately $750 million) were essentially single asset bankruptcies. In no case did the bankruptcy court judge agree to lift the stay in less than 120 days. The authors do not contend that all bankruptcy judges are pro-debtor. The contention is simply that in single-asset bankruptcies, there is no role for the Code and thus, the egregious situations such as described in the sample cases can be avoided altogether.
80. *See infra* exhibit A, case number 5 pp. 396.
81. *Id.*
82. *See infra* Exhibit A, case number 4 pp. 395.

filing was "simply a tactical maneuver. . . designed to gain more time and distance in an effort to wear down its exhausted secured creditor into some type of settlement submission."[83] The court also recognized that "such antics are an abuse, costing litigants good money, and wasting valuable court time."[84] In another case,[85] the judge did not find that the contribution of twenty-one vacant residential lots in Michigan, on the eve of bankruptcy, into a partnership whose only asset was an apartment complex in Arizona, constituted bad faith.[86] In addition, many bankruptcy courts do not appear to follow the rule enunciated in *United Savings Association of Texas v. Timbers of Inwood Forest Associates, Ltd.*,[87] that a lender should be entitled to relief from the automatic stay where there is lack of equity and the property is not necessary to an effective reorganization under 362, unless the debtor is able to demonstrate that a reorganization is theoretically possible and that there is a reasonable likelihood of a successful reorganization within a reasonable period of time.[88] In many of the representative cases there was no possibility of a successful reorganization within a reasonable period of time. In one case, an empty building remained in bankruptcy for more than one year.[89] The only reason the building emerged from bankruptcy was that the borrower abandoned its plan rather than submit personal financial statements.[90] In another case, the borrower submitted two plans, each of which the court found could not be confirmed.[91] Yet, the court retained jurisdiction over the property for one year to allow the borrower the opportunity to find a purchaser for the property.[92]

In her article on "new value",[93] Professor Rusch concludes that one benefit of the new value exception is that it makes bankruptcy a forum for competing

---

83. *Id.*
84. *Id.*
85. *See infra* Exhibit A, case number 1 pp. 392.
86. *Id.* The borrowers acquired twenty-one lots in Michigan from a friend for a cash investment equal to 2.5% of the purchase price of the lots. *Id.*
87. 484 U.S. 365 (1988).
88. *Id.* at 375.
89. *See infra* Exhibit A, case number 2 pp. 393.
90. *Id.*
91. *See infra* Exhibit A, case number 3 pp. 394.
92. *Id.*
93. Rusch, *supra* note 49, at 1329.

interests to reach an agreement.[94] Presumably, without this exception, too many creditors may not bargain with the owner for a consensual plan because they would be able to defeat it in the bankruptcy confirmation process. However, Professor Rusch ignores the lending community's complaint that the new value exception also allows the debtor to use the bankruptcy process to obtain a lender's consent to a consensual plan which it knows is unworkable but which is better than the specter of the debtor's new value cram down plan.

In her article, Professor Rusch states, "[t]he fear of pro-debtor bias is supported at best by anecdotal evidence and at worst by mere presumption. No proof is available that bankruptcy judges, as a whole, neglect their responsibility to make legally correct and fair decisions."[95] Although the data in Exhibit A of this paper is, admittedly, anecdotal, the authors believe that it is a compelling summary of representative cases based upon the records and filed pleadings from these cases.

The bankruptcy court system does facilitate and coordinate communications between borrowers and lenders which would not otherwise occur without court intervention. However, the utility of the forum diminishes when borrowers file bankruptcy simply as a means of holding lenders hostage. Lenders believe that the proper forum and ground rules for a consensual workout should be determined by the documents governing the relationship between the two parties rather than by the Code. To the extent the Code is used to interfere with the exercise of contractual rights and to require parties in a bilateral dispute to reach a "consensus," the policies of the bankruptcy laws are not furthered. In fact, it is counter-productive in that it not only taxes the resources of the bankruptcy courts but also results in a loss of value to the community. These losses may never be recouped due to a prolonged decline in the condition of the property and the myriad of problems that result from attempting to operate and lease distressed properties.

This is not to say that no single asset entity should be eligible for bankruptcy relief. Rather, the threshold for any single asset entity filing for bankruptcy should be real and significant to the unsecured creditors as well as to the secured lender. Most properties generate sufficient funds to pay all creditors in full except for the secured creditor. Therefore, at the very least, bankruptcy courts should use the good faith requirement as a means of eliminating single asset cases that do not belong in bankruptcy.

---

94. *Id.*
95. *See id.*

C. Impact of The Bankruptcy Code on Workouts

1. General

Realizing that bankruptcy means delay and therefore further loss on the investment, real estate lenders are forced to proceed with private reorganizations or workouts in order to avoid or minimize such losses. Some borrowers, recognizing the lenders' dilemma, try to use the threat of bankruptcy as leverage against lenders to gain concessions under the loan documents.[96] The lenders are forced to deal with these borrowers, who by definition are in default under their loan documents, in order to avoid further losses and erosion of principal through forced participation in a two to four year bankruptcy proceeding. If a workout is successfully negotiated, the lender will require the agreement to provide protection in the event the borrower subsequently files for bankruptcy reorganization.[97]

2. Bad Faith Filing Prohibition

One such protection is a "bad faith" filing provision. Many agreements expressly provide that the workout is itself a "reorganization" between the parties made in lieu of chapter 11 reorganization. Any subsequent filing of a chapter 11 petition is deemed a "bad faith" filing, entitling the lender to immediate relief from the automatic stay.[98] By incorporating these provisions

---

96. *See* James M. Peck & Frederick B. Rosner, *Loan Participants Usually Have Few Legal Rights*, NAT'L L.J., Oct. 21, 1991, at S6 (stating that in order to protect and preserve going-concern value of prebankruptcy collateral on loan, which may suffer sharp decline upon filing of bankruptcy, lenders may be willing to concede to continue financing debtors).

97. This can be accomplished by providing that the lender will be able to apply for relief from the automatic stay and that the debtor will not contest this motion. *See In re* Darrell Creek Assocs. L.P., 187 B.R. 908, 916 (Bankr. D.S.C. 1995) (upholding workout agreement granting lender relief from automatic stay); *In re* Club Tower L.P., 138 B.R. 307, 310 (Bankr. N.D. Ga. 1991) (same); *In re* Hudson Manor Partners, Ltd., No. 91-81065HR, 1991 WL 472592 (Bankr. N.D. Ga. Dec. 31, 1991) (same).

98. *See supra,* note 97. These provisions will also include recitations by the borrower to the effect that it acknowledges that there is no equity in the property and that if a bankruptcy is filed, the borrower will not contest the

into the workout agreement, the lender is seeking to address the concern that concessions in the workout agreement will be the starting point in a subsequent chapter 11 reorganization. Although the enforceability of these provisions is necessarily determined on a case by case basis, many courts give effect to the private reorganization entered into by parties and enforce the "bad faith" provisions.[99] The courts have found these provisions to be enforceable

---

lender's motion for relief from the automatic stay for the purpose of proceeding with a foreclosure.

99. *See, e.g.*, *In re* Cheeks, 167 B.R. 817, 819 (Bankr. D.S.C. 1994) (holding that prepetition forbearance agreement under which borrower agreed not to oppose or reject creditor's motion for stay relief in event of bankruptcy filing was enforceable); *In re* Aurora Investments, 134 B.R. 982, 986 (Bankr. M.D. Fla. 1991) (enforcing provision where parties had stipulated that if debtor filed bankruptcy petition primarily for purpose of delaying foreclosure sale it would be deemed filed in "bad faith"); *In re* Club Tower L.P., 138 B.R. 307, 309-10 (Bankr. N.D. Ga. 1991) (upholding similar provision); *In re* International Supply Corp., Inc., 72 B.R. 510, 511 (Bankr. M.D. Fla 1987) (holding that creditor was entitled to relief from automatic stay in chapter 11 proceeding to enforce rights under prepetition stipulation agreement to evict debtor if debtor filed for bankruptcy); *In re* Citadel Properties, Inc., 86 B.R. 275, 277 (Bankr. M.D. Fla. 1988) (upholding "bad faith" agreement); *In re* Orange Park S. Partnership, 79 B.R. 79, 83 (Bankr. M.D. Fla. 1987) (same); B.O.S.S. Partners I v. Tucker (*In re* B.O.S.S. Partners I), 37 B.R. 348, 350 (Bankr. M.D. Fla. 1984) (holding that absent showing which would justify extraordinary injunctive remedy court would not intervene where debtors entered into agreement with creditor to waive any equitable or legal rights against foreclosure). *But see In re* Jenkins Court Assoc. L.P., 181 B.R. 33, 35-37 (Bankr. E.D. Pa. 1995) (refusing to enforce prepetition waiver of automatic stay absent further development of facts); *In re* Powers, 170 B.R. 480 (Bankr. D. Mass. 1994) (requiring debtor to demonstrate why bankruptcy waiver provision should not be enforced, but denying to automatically grant lift-stay motion); *In re* Sky Group Int'l, Inc., 108 B.R. 86, 90 (Bankr. W.D. Pa. 1989) (finding that involuntary filing was not in "bad faith," even though filing resulted from debtor's representations regarding debtor's inability to pay other creditors if secured party was allowed to exercise foreclosure rights); *In re* Gulf Beach Dev. Corp., 48 B.R. 40, 43 (Bankr. M.D. Fla. 1985) (deciding that debtor cannot be precluded from exercising right to file bankruptcy and that any contrary contractual provision is legally unenforceable).

based upon the following theories: the public policy served by enforcing out of court restructurings;[100] the fact that there was no realistic chance of successful reorganization;[101] and to give effect to a bona fide bargained for exchange between the parties.[102]

3. Springing Liability

As mentioned above, the nature of single asset real estate investment is such that individual developers and investors form single purpose entities, to insulate the individuals from personal liability.[103] Although the individuals that own the entity may have substantial assets, lenders agree not to seek recourse against these individuals and their assets if the property is unable to support the loan in exchange for the right to foreclose upon the property.

Thus, in workouts, lenders usually condition their concessions upon knowing and quantifying the extent to which the individual investors have committed their finances to the property. Commitments to invest money may take many forms. For example, lenders may require funds to be placed in escrow for the use of the property and require that no funds may be withdrawn without its written consent. Lenders may also require personal guarantees of funds if the lender is concerned about the value of property and is otherwise satisfied with the ability of the individual investors to make the required payments.[104] Finally, lenders may hold a letter of credit as additional security to be returned after the borrower has invested an agreed amount of money into the property.[105]

---

100. *In re* Cheeks, 167 B.R. at 819.
101. *See* B.O.S.S. Partners, 37 B.R. at 351; Orange Park S. Partnership, 79 B.R. at 81, Aurora Investments, 134 B.R. at 984-85.
102. *See* International Supply Corp., 72 B.R. at 511.
103. *See supra* text accompanying note 9.
104. *See* Eugene A. Pinover & David Rabin, *Loan Restructurings Both Sides Treat Workout Process as Business as Usual*, N.Y. L.J., June 23, 1993, at 5 (stating that in today's economic environment lenders will seek personal guarantees).
105. *See* Alfred G. Adams, Jr., *The Mortgagees Guide to Single Asset Bankruptcy Reorganizations*, 98 COM. L.J. 350, 360 (1993) ("[L]etters of credit, if obtainable, are particularly valuable as additional collateral because they can be drawn without violation of the automatic stay since their proceeds are not the property of the debtor's estate.").

As part of a private reorganization[106] between a lender and a borrower, lenders may also require a "springing guarantee" to ensure the borrower's pledge not to file for bankruptcy reorganization. This guarantee creates personal liability on the part of the individual constituent members of the borrowing entity if the borrower subsequently files bankruptcy reorganization. Essentially, the right to a private nonbankruptcy modification of the loan terms is predicated on the assurance that the borrower will adhere to the modified terms. To the extent that the borrower seeks to accomplish through bankruptcy what it could not accomplish in restructuring discussions, the loan becomes recourse as to the individual constituents of the borrower. Springing guaranties are intended to have a cautionary effect on single asset entity borrowers by causing them to be more concerned about the ramifications of forcing a lender into being an unwilling participant in a bankruptcy proceeding.

4. The Unsettled Status of Deeds In Lieu of Foreclosure

Lenders have also been concerned about fraudulent conveyances and preferences.[107] In workout situations, accepting a deed in lieu of foreclosure has always been an alternative to a traditional foreclosure action.[108] Some

---

106. The lender and borrower will document the workout agreement as a private reorganization.

107. *See* Scott B. Ehrlich, *Avoidance of Foreclosure Sales as Fraudulent Conveyances: Accommodating State and Federal Objectives*, 71 VA. L. REV. 933 (1985) (describing lenders' concerns).

108. Dennis I. Hellman, *Foreclosure Alternative Available Deeds in Lieu Offer a Number of Advantages*, NAT'L L.J., July 5, 1993, at 25.
In general, prior to accepting a deed in lieu of foreclosure, a lender will require the following items and assurances:
   1) A statement by the borrower that the value of the property is less than the amount of the principal indebtedness owed to the lender.
   2) A release of the claims of all other creditors of the borrower.
   3) Anti-merger provisions in the deed transferring the property to the lender (or entity designated by lender) in order to preserve the lien of the mortgage.
   4) A title policy insuring title in the lender (or entity designated by lender) without exception for creditors' rights.

borrowers prefer giving a deed in lieu of foreclosure because it avoids the adverse publicity of a foreclosure action or allows them to bargain to be relieved of other personal obligations which they might have to the lender.[109] At the same time, some lenders may feel compelled to obtain title to properties as soon as possible to avoid further erosion of value.[110] In jurisdictions where foreclosure may take from one to three years to complete, the lender may wish to acquire title to the property at an earlier date. The result of these parallel motivating factors has been the use of deeds in lieu of foreclosure as part of workout arrangements.

Most lenders, however, disfavor deeds in lieu of foreclosure because of concerns that junior liens and encumbrances will not be extinguished by the conveyance, and that the proscriptions against fraudulent conveyances[111] and preferential transfers[112] may apply to the deed in lieu of foreclosure.[113] As a result, many lenders require transfers by deeds in lieu of foreclosure to be structured in a manner which assures the lender that no objectionable junior liens or encumbrances remain on the property and in a manner which would enable the transfer to withstand an attack in bankruptcy and provide protection for the lender in the event of a successful attack.[114]

---

5) An opinion from the borrower's counsel regarding due authorization and execution of the transactional documents, the validity and enforceability of the transactional documents, and the perfection of the security interests under applicable state law.

Id.

109. *Id.*

110. *Id.*

111. 11 U.S.C. § 548 (1994).

112. *Id.* § 547.

113. *See, e.g.*, Main v. Brim (*In re* Main), 75 B.R. 322, 323 (Bankr. D. Ariz. 1987). The debtors in *Main* gave a deed in lieu of foreclosure to their mortgagees and filed bankruptcy three months later. *Id.* The debtors sought to recover the property on the basis that the transfer was preferential and fraudulent and therefore voidable under the Code. *Id.* The Court held in favor of the debtors. *Id.* While not all deeds in lieu of foreclosure are fraudulent transfers, they may be subject to scrutiny if the transferor files for bankruptcy within the statutory periods. *Id.*

114. *See* Patrick A. Murphy et al., *Lender Liability: Defense and Prevention Real Property Foreclosure* 1990, at 269 (ALI-ABA Course of Study) (discussing pitfalls of deeds in lieu of foreclosure and protective clauses).

A lender that does not accept a deed in lieu of foreclosure, may seek to enter into a consensual foreclosure agreement with the borrower. In such an agreement, the borrower agrees not to contest a foreclosure proceeding.[115] In return, the lender may agree not to seek liability against the individual members of the borrower through an exception to the nonrecourse provision, or, the lender may allow the borrower, under the auspices of a receiver, to continue to manage the property during the pendency of the foreclosure. One benefit of a consensual foreclosure is that the lender may agree to conduct the foreclosure sale at a date which may be advantageous to the borrower in its tax planning.[116]

5. Lockbox Agreements

A lockbox agreement is an agreement between the borrower and lender requiring all the revenues of the property to be placed in one account and limiting withdrawals to operating expenses and debt service.[117] Upon default, the lender has the right to withdraw the remaining proceeds in the lockbox account.[118] The agreement may also establish an escrow account to pay for tenant improvements and other capital items.[119]

Generally the time period in which a lockbox agreement will be in effect is determined by the purpose of the workout. If the workout is to allow for a turnaround in the property, the lockbox arrangement may extend to the

---

115. *See, e.g.*, Banque Arabe et Internationale D'Investissement v. Maryland Nat'l Bank, 850 F. Supp. 1199, 1205 (S.D.N.Y. 1994) (explaining terms of consensual foreclosure agreement), *aff'd*, 57 F.3d 146 (2d Cir. 1995).

116. *See* Davis v. Commissioner, 866 F.2d 852, 856 (6th Cir. 1989) (describing tax consequences of foreclosure).

117. *See, e.g.*, Carl J. Seneker, II, et al., *Loan Workout Documents and Strategies* 1991, at 445 (ALI-ABA Course of Study Real Estate Defaults, Workouts, and Reorganizations) (sample lockbox agreement); *see also* ELIZABETH WARREN & JAY L. WESTBROOK, THE LAW OF DEBTORS AND CREDITORS 447 (2d ed. 1991) (describing lockbox agreement).

118. Herbert F. Fisher, *Collecting Rents and Other Headaches Disturb Commercial Lenders' Peace*, N.Y. L.J., June 14, 1993, at S2 (stating that lender will often reserve right use collected funds to pay principal and interest due under its loan).

119. *Id.* (agreements can provide for borrower to use collected rents to pay operating expenses of property).

maturity of the loan. If the workout allows for the orderly transition of the property to the lender, the arrangement may extend to the next tax year or until the lender completes foreclosure where the lender has declined to accept a deed in lieu of foreclosure. To further protect its rights in the event of the subsequent chapter 11 filing, the lender will require that the lockbox agreement contain provisions granting the lender the right to a cash collateral stipulation upon the filing of a bankruptcy petition and that a copy of the stipulation be attached to the lockbox agreement.[120]

From a lender's perspective, there are several potential concerns with lockbox arrangements which limit their use. First, borrowers might complicate and delay a foreclosure action by claiming that a lender interfered with the management and operation of the property by controlling its receipts and disbursements. Second, in states that have stringent single action[121] and security first rules,[122] where arrangements have not been reviewed by the courts, it is possible that a court would hold that the right of a lender to withdraw money from a lockbox violates these principles, which would jeopardize the lender's ability to foreclose upon the property.

D. Impact of The Bankruptcy Code on New Investments

1. Commercial Mortgage - Backed Securities

In response to the experience of the early 1990's, as lenders return to the real estate market, the structure of loan transactions is being modified to lessen the possibility of a bankruptcy and, in the event of its occurrence, to assure that the lender will be able to protect its investment. One way this is being accomplished is through the development of commercial mortgage-backed securities transactions ("CMBS").[123] These securities are an outgrowth of the

---

120. *See* WARREN & WESTBROOK, *supra* note 117, at 477.
121. *See, e.g.*, IDAHO CODE § 6-101 (1990 & Supp. 1995) (permitting only one action for recovery of debt).
122. *See, e.g.*, CAL. CIV. PROC. CODE § 726 (West 1980 & Supp. 1996) (requiring mortgagee to foreclose security before collecting from debtor's noncollateral assets).
123. *See* C. Wade Cooper, *Commercial Real Estate Securitization: A New Generation of Secured Creditors?*, AM. BANKR. INST. J., Nov. 13, 1994, at 20 (discussing emergence of CMBS).

Resolution Trust Corporation's ("RTC") efforts to sell mortgages which it obtained in its takeover of banking institutions.[124] At the time, because many traditional sources of capital were not investing in real estate, the RTC sought to achieve its sales through the public market.[125] Investment banking firms also enticed developers to structure transactions mirroring the ones being sold by the RTC.[126] As a result, the non-RTC CMBS new issue market has grown from $4.6 billion in 1991 to $18.3 billion in 1995.[127] The total CMBS market is approximately $85 billion and is growing at an accelerated pace.[128] CMBS transactions are rated by the rating agencies and generally require a triple "A" rating in order to be successful.[129] A key element to obtaining a triple "A" rating is the structure of the transaction.[130] The rating agencies may require the borrower to be a "single purpose", "special purpose" or "bankruptcy remote" entity ("SPE").[131]

---

124. *See id.* (stating that emergence of mortgagee-backed securities can be credited to RTC).
125. *See* Peter F. Culver, *The Dawning of Securitization Probate & Property*, Apr. 8, 1994, at 34 (explaining that RTC issue pass-through certificates allowing investors direct ownership in pool of loans).
126. *See id.* (stating that developers have been working with underwriters to securitize their loans as financing vehicle).
127. *1995/1996 Commercial Mortgage-Backed Securitization Survey,* TRENDS AND DEV. (The E&Y Kenneth Leventhal Real Estate Group), 1996, at 4.
128. *Id.* at 3.
129. *See Metropolitan Life Insurance Co. Acquired Close to $500 Million of Commercial Mortgage Securities*, COM. MORTGAGE ALERT, (Harrison Scott Publications, Inc.), Jan. 29, 1996 (explaining that greater risk is involved with CMBS rated lower than double-A); *see also* Richard W. Blanchard, *Introduction to Asset Securitization,* in COM. REAL EST. AND FIN., 427, 433 (Sidney A. Keyles ed. 1993) (providing that demand for highest rated mortgage-backed securities far outweighs demand for lower rated securities).
130. *See* Cooper, *supra* note 123, at 39 (explaining that rating of issue may be enhanced by internal structure of transaction); *see also* Joseph P. Forte, *Real Estate Financing Documentation: Coping With the New Realities* 1995, at 125, 137 (ALI-ABA Course of Study) (stating that transferee must meet credit rating agency criteria as SPE and transfer cannot affect rating of transaction).
131. *See* Joseph C. Franzetti, *Commercial Mortgage Securities Credit Review: Rating Criteria Update* 1989 (PLI Real Est. L. Practice Course). In general,

Standard & Poor's defines an SPE as an entity which is unlikely to become insolvent as a result of its own activities and which is adequately insulated from the consequences of any related party's insolvency.[132] SPE's have been used in securitizations for some time, particularly in pool transactions where the depositor is required to be an SPE.[133] The depositors sole function is to deposit mortgages into a trust which would issue rated securities.[134] The depositor is restricted from engaging in any other activities.[135] One of the concerns that the rating agencies have with transferring loans to a trust is whether the transfer constitutes a true sale under applicable law.[136] If the transaction is deemed not to be a sale, but a financing transaction, then the transaction may be characterized as a pledge of collateral.[137] Under section 541

---

the rating agencies essentially have the same criteria for SPEs. The basic categories are items intended to prohibit the SPE from incurring liabilities (limitations on purpose and indebtedness and prohibition on liquidation, consolidation, merger, etc); items intended to insulate the SPE from liabilities of third parties (separateness covenants and nonconsolidation opinions); items intended to protect the SPE from dissolution risks (prohibition on dissolution and special-purpose bankruptcy remote equity owner); and items intended to protect the solvent SPE from filing a bankruptcy petition (an independent director).

Attached to this paper as Exhibit B is a description of SPE criteria prescribed by Duff & Phelps Credit Rating Co.

132. *Special Purpose Bankruptcy Remote Entities,* REAL EST. FIN. (Standard & Poor's), at 1.

133. *See* Robert M. Elwood, et al., *Many Questions Remain on Applying Market-to-Market Rules to Affiliate Groups,* 82 J. TAX'N 154, 160 (1995) (describing SPE's role in transaction)

134. *See* KENNETH G. LORE, MORTGAGE-BACKED SECURITIES, DEVELOPMENTS AND TRENDS IN THE SECONDARY MORTGAGE MARKET, 11-22 (1994) (explaining that single purpose entities are considered "bankruptcy remote").

135. *See Structured Finance Ratings: Asset Backed Securities Criteria* 1995 (PLI Corp. L. & Practice Course Handbook) (listing factors Standard & Poor's uses when rating mortgage-backed securities).

136. *See* LORE, *supra* note 134, at 9-60 (stating that major concern in pool transaction is whether sale is true sale).

137. *See id.* (explaining that if transaction is not characterized as sale it may be considered financing or pledge of assets).

of the Code the loans would be deemed part of the depositor's estate.[138] Because requiring the depositor to be an SPE and restricting the activities of the SPE makes the depositor "bankruptcy remote", the RTC utilized this pool transaction format.

An outgrowth of pool transactions has been property-specific transactions[139] and credit lease transactions. Developers looking to access lower cost capital than what might otherwise be available from traditional sources have broadened the SPE requirement. In the property-specific transaction, it is important that the borrower not be vulnerable to insolvency.[140] For this reason, the borrower is also required to be an SPE. Where one or more mortgages are deposited in trust, the depositor may also be required to be an SPE if the transfer of the loans to the trust might not be viewed as a sale.

The credit lease transaction involves a lender, a borrower and a rated tenant.[141] The borrower obtains a loan from the lender evidenced by a note and secured by a mortgage and an assignment of the rents payable by the rated tenant.[142] The lender deposits the loan documents in a trust that issues rated securities.[143] Sometimes the borrower issues the notes directly without using a trust.[144] In order to obtain a credit rating for the security, the borrower must be an SPE.[145] It is the credit of the tenant that will determine the rating, but the

---

138. 11 U.S.C. § 541 (1994) (stating with exceptions, that all legal or equitable interests of debtor in property at start of case is property of estate). *But see* LORE, *supra* note 134, at 11-2 to 11-5 (discussing § 541(d) of Code).

139. *See* LORE, *supra* note 134, at 9-3 (explaining that "threshold concern" of ratings agencies is quality of collateral, resulting in emergence of single-family mortgage loans as primary backer of mortgage backed securities).

140. *See Structured Finance Ratings*, *supra* note 133 (discussing danger of insolvency of borrower as factor in rating security).

141. *See* Joseph C. Shenker, *Guaranteed Debt and Miscellaneous Financing Techniques: An Outline of the Principal Structures for Securitized Debt Financing of Individual Commercial Real Properties* 1989, at 135 (PLI Real Est. L. & Practice Course Handbook) (describing structure of credit lease transaction).

142. *See id.*

143. *See id.*

144. *See id.*

145. *See id.*

risk of the borrower's insolvency must be lessened as a source of interference with the income available to pay the securities.[146]

In general, the rating agencies essentially have the same criteria for SPEs. The basic categories are items intended to prohibit the SPE from incurring liabilities; items intended to insulate the SPE from liabilities of third parties; items intended to protect the SPE from dissolution risks; and items intended to protect the solvent SPE from filing a bankruptcy petition. Attached to this chapter as Exhibit B is a description of SPE criteria prescribed by Duff & Phelps Credit Rating Co.

By using SPE's, rating agencies try to assure the investing public that a proposed transaction, as represented in the prospectus, is reliable and that the investors will receive the income stream from the underlying real estate. In the event that the income stream is not adequate to service the loan, the remedial rights under the loan documents can be exercised without the risk of a bankruptcy filing that would materially change the deal. The bankruptcy remoteness of the borrowing entity and other participants are key elements of risk that bear directly upon the pricing for CMBS offerings.[147] For example, the double"A" tranche in a recent property-specific transaction secured by a regional shopping center sold for 98 basis points over 7 year treasuries, while a whole loan on that property would have commanded 135 basis points over 7 year treasuries.[148] A pricing of this type which represents a minimum spread over Treasuries, does not factor in, and simply could not be obtained if there were a risk of a bankruptcy filing. This CMBS market will continue to grow in terms of pooled transactions, property-specific transactions and credit lease transactions as investors look for safety in their investments.

---

146. *See* Shenker, *supra* note 140.

147. LORE, *supra* note 134, at 9-8 (establishing that rating agencies consider risk of bankruptcy in rating CMSB's).

148. Carousel Center Finance, Inc. $208,500,000, 7 year mortgaged collateralized rates, 144A Private Placement, October 10, 1995. The investment safety in the double A tranche resulted in the tighter spread to United States Treasuries. The Bankruptcy remoteness of the borrower entity was essential to the double A return.

2. *Whole Loans*

As institutional real estate lenders return to the commercial mortgage market, they return with many lessons learned from the experience of the late 80's and early 90's. As evidenced by the representative case studies in Exhibit A, lenders lost and continue to lose substantial investment income as a result of bankruptcy petitions filed in single asset entity cases and the dilatory tactics of debtors. Therefore, one of the key considerations in any whole loan real estate investment will be providing adequate assurances against bankruptcy filings.

What assurances can a lender expect to receive? In the underwriting area there will be a stricter correlation between LTV and DCR on the one hand and the loan amount and interest rate on the other.[149] This is expected to impact the number of borrowers who will be able to qualify for a loan to finance or refinance a property. A high LTV and low DCR will require a higher interest rate. Many lenders will not make loans in excess of 75% of the value of the property nor accept a DCR of less than 1.10.[150]

Real estate lenders believe that if the individual investors, as opposed to single-asset real estate entities, have "personal" liability for all or a portion of the loan, it is less likely that the borrowing entity will go into bankruptcy. Such a filing would expose the other assets of the individual investors. Therefore, many lenders are requiring a portion of certain loans to be personally guaranteed and are also requiring "springing" guarantees similar to those used in workout situations.

Conclusion

Clearly, real estate mortgage lenders have found bankruptcy filings to be inconsistent with the basic understandings between the parties at the outset of the transaction. Further, the extraordinary delays in determining the rights of the parties - whether to dismiss a filing, file a plan, lift a stay or confirm a plan - have generally worked more of a hardship on the lender than on the debtor.

---

149. *See* LORE, *supra* note 134, at 9-21 ("[E]mpirical data has shown, for example, that default rates increase dramatically for mortgages with loan-to-value ratios in excess of 80 percent . . . and for mortgages that are not fixed, level payment, 30 year fully amortizing loans.")

150. *See supra* notes 20-21 and accompanying text.

It seems as if the courts are indifferent to the fact that lenders lose money from the time the debtor stops making its contractual payments until there is a resolution of the bankruptcy. The predominant fact of single entity asset bankruptcy, which many lenders believe bankruptcy courts do not appreciate, is that most debtors do not have any equity in the property and merely seek to impair the rights of the lender in order to create an equity position for themselves. What will be the response of the lenders?

One response will be tighter lending requirements. This will translate into less money available to fewer borrowers–not unlike the crisis of the early 90's. Another response will be a greater cost for the money that is available, one that is predicated upon evaluating and assessing the risks and costs of bankruptcy. Another response will be the use of prescribed legal structures for the borrower in order to make the likelihood of bankruptcy remote. A fourth response will be that new investments will be implemented with documents that address the concerns and contain the protections which originated in workout documentation. Finally, net worth maintenance covenants and other covenants common to balance sheet lending will become more the standard in securitized lending. Unfortunately, as a consequence of this additional scrutiny, the loan documentation will become more extensive and the loan closing process will become more expensive, cumbersome and protracted.

The experience of real estate lenders in borrower bankruptcies in the 90's will prove to have a lasting "chilling effect" on the structure of future transactions. Lenders have lost not only billions of dollars in principal and interest, and millions of dollars in legal expenses and consultant fees in bankruptcy proceedings, but also the reinvestment opportunity on those monies. The misconception which appears repeatedly in bankruptcy court decisions is that the losses incurred by lenders do not have an impact outside the walls of those institutions. Insurance companies, as lenders, are investing on behalf of millions of policyholders and public and private pension funds which represent the retirement savings of everyday working people. The losses on real estate investments directly affect the lives of these individuals. Somehow the bankruptcy courts, especially those judges in the first tier of the court system, seem to ignore the fact that real estate lenders are not seeking special treatment under the Code, just fair and equitable treatment in a timely manner.

Exhibit A

SINGLE ASSET BANKRUPTCY FILINGS

The following summary of five representative bankruptcy cases demonstrate the tendency of bankruptcy courts to use the bankruptcy process to coerce lenders and single entity asset borrowers to renegotiate loan terms. These summaries attempt to quantify the unrecoverable costs of bankruptcy, including the costs and expenses of the bankruptcy process as well as the impact of deferred maintenance and loss of leasing opportunities.

1. Garden Apartment Complex Arizona
Loan Amount: $18,000,000
Date of Filing: November, 1992
Date of Resolution: March, 1995
Lender's Attorneys' Fees and Costs: $410,000

Description of Resolution: This matter was settled by a consensual plan after nearly two and one-half years of bankruptcy proceedings. The plan provided that the lender's claim could be satisfied by payment from the debtor of $20 million. If the amount was not paid by a certain date, the stay would be lifted, and the lender could foreclose. There would not have been a plan, and the matter would probably still be in the bankruptcy courts if the debtor had not entered into a simultaneous agreement to sell the property for a profit. Prior to entering into the plan, the debtor had been attempting to cram down the lender by arguing that the value of the property was only $14,000,000.

Comments: This case is an example of how courts may refuse to acknowledge egregious bad faith on the part of the borrower. On the eve of foreclosure, the debtor transferred into the single entity asset twenty-one vacant residential lots in Michigan which the debtor acquired from a friend with nonrecourse financing equal to 97.5% of the purchase price. Debts to other creditors were created solely for the purposes of the bankruptcy filing and were largely either to the borrower's acquaintances or to trade creditors. An unsuccessful attempt was made to explain to the judge that combining the ownership of the Arizona apartment complex with ownership of the residential lots in Michigan served no reasonable business purpose, and that no one could purchase vacant residential lots in a bona fide arms length transaction for a down payment of

2.5% of the purchase price. During the pendency of the proceeding, the debtor rejected several offers on the property which the judge did not require them to pursue. Any of these offers would have yielded several million dollars more in proceeds for the estate than the debtor was claiming the property was worth in its plan. Hearings on the lender's section 362 motion proceeded for many months. The bankruptcy judge conducted hearings one day at a time, with continued hearings scheduled weeks or even months apart. The court determined that the debtor's post filing activities were in good faith and therefore negated an overall finding of bad faith. In order to end the bankruptcy proceeding which had continued for more than two and one-half years, the lender settled for $750,000 less than the amount owed under the loan documents, even though an appraisal showed that the value of the property exceeded the amount owed. There was approximately $1,000,000 in deferred maintenance at the time of the sale. The debtor did not want capital invested in the property because this would have increased its value, preventing the debtor from obtaining the amount of cram down which it sought.

2. Bank Office Building California
Loan Amount: $6,000,000
Date of Filing: September, 1992
Date of Resolution: October, 1993
Lender's Attorneys' Fees and Costs: $225,000.00

Description of Resolution: Confirmation of plan proposed by lender paying unsecured creditors approximately $50,000 in full and borrower's attorneys' fees of approximately $50,000 and foreclosing upon its security. The lender has sold the property for $3,200,000 resulting in a loss of more than $3,250,000.

Comments: The principal issues involved in this matter were the lender's motion for the general partners of the debtor to file financial statements and their refusal to do so. When the judge required these statements, the debtor withdrew its plan and allowed the competing lender's plan to proceed unopposed. Had the debtor not refused to file financial statements with the court, the bankruptcy would have lasted much longer through an evidentiary hearing on the merits. Although lender filed a competing plan which provided for payment of all creditors in full and the borrower's plan impaired several classes of creditors, the judge required a confirmation hearing on both plans. The debtor's plan was not feasible under any circumstances because the property was unoccupied and there were no prospects for leasing sufficient to pay even minimal debt service. At an early stage in the proceeding, the lender filed a motion for an adequate protection payment based upon the fact that the debtor, by its own papers, acknowledged that the property had declined in value during the pendency of the bankruptcy. The judge refused to rule on this motion. If the judge had ruled in favor of the lender, it would have resulted in the discharge of the bankruptcy because the debtor was unable to provide an adequate protection payment equal to the amount that property had declined in value.

The debtor entered into one lease during the bankruptcy. The lender objected to the lease on the grounds that the tenant was not able to pay the rent payments. The court authorized the lease over the lender's objection. The tenant filed bankruptcy prior to the foreclosure of the property and the lender had to expend additional sums evicting the tenant. It was apparent from the first day of the filing that the debtor was unwilling and unable to commit the funds necessary to make reorganization feasible. The judge acknowledged on a number of occasions that it would be difficult to confirm a plan under the circumstances before him; however rather than dismissing the case, the judge retained the property in bankruptcy in the efforts to have the parties reach an agreement. In order to achieve a resolution of the matter, in essence, the lender had to pay the debts of the borrower (including his attorneys' fees) of approximately $100,000.

3. Shopping Center California
Amount of Loan: $29,000,000
Date of Filing: February, 1993
Date of Resolution: April, 1995
Lender’s Attorneys Fees: $340,000

Description of Resolution: The court entered an order in the Spring of 1994 giving the debtor approximately one year in which to sell the property, at the end of which period the stay would automatically be lifted and the lender would be allowed to complete its foreclosure sale. The lender completed its foreclosure sale in April, 1995.

Comments: Although the lender made a motion for relief from the automatic stay, the judge continued both the hearings on the lender's motion for many months and extended the debtor's exclusivity period over the objections of the lender. The bankruptcy court initially permitted the state court receiver to retain possession of the property for a period following the filing of the bankruptcy because of borrower's mismanagement of the property; however, subsequently, the judge appointed a trustee to operate the property and to opine as to whether reorganization was likely. Notwithstanding the fact that the debtor submitted two plans which the judge and the trustee found unconfirmable, the judge retained jurisdiction over the property for a year after granting the lender relief from the automatic stay to provide the debtor with the chance to sell the property. During this time, because of the uncertainty as to who would eventually own the property, minimal expenditures were made to maintain the property, resulting in further physical decline. In addition, because the property was under the jurisdiction of the trustee, all decisions had to be reviewed and approved by the trustee, the debtor, and the lender. Because of this burdensome requirement, the administrative procedures for operating the property were expensive and cumbersome.

As a result of the distressed condition of the property, it is estimated that the value of the property has decreased approximately $1,500,000 since the commencement of the bankruptcy proceeding in February, 1993.

4. Office Building Arizona
Amount of Loan: $2,275,000
Date of Filing: April, 1993
Date of Resolution: September, 1995
Attorney's Fees and Costs To Date: $200,000.

Description of Resolution: Motion to dismiss granted.

Comments: The borrowing entity conveyed its interest in the property to a related single asset entity in April 1993, shortly before the first bankruptcy filing (the "1993 Case"). In December, 1993, the judge orally granted the lender's motion to dismiss. A written order dismissing the case for cause was signed by the bankruptcy judge and entered in February, 1994. The debtor appealed the decision but did not pursue the appeal and did not file a response to the lender's answering brief. The debtor through its counsel threatened to "dismiss the pending appeal and file a new bankruptcy which would further delay your client's return of the property." In June, 1994, the day before the scheduled foreclosure sale and prior to arguments on the appeal of the 1993 Case, the debtor dismissed the appeal and four days later filed a second chapter 11 case (the "1994 Case"). That case was dismissed in September, 1995. A portion of the cash collateral held by the debtor in the first bankruptcy case disappeared between the dismissal of the appeal, including payments to itself and to the debtor's counsel, and the filing of the second chapter 11.

In January of 1995, the lender filed a motion for relief from stay in the 1994 Case combining elements of bad faith in connection with the "chapter 22" double filing, demonstrating debtor's failure to obey the cash collateral order and to account for receipts from the property. The lender argued that there is no possibility of a successful reorganization based upon the similarity of the plan filed by the debtor in the 1994 Case and the plan filed by the debtor in the 1993 Case. In September, 1995, the bankruptcy court judge issued a ruling dismissing the case finding that it was, in essence a two party dispute and the bankruptcy filing was "simply a tactical maneuver, knowing that the court process is lengthy and sometimes slow, designed to gain more time and distance in an effort to wear down its exhausted secured creditor into some type of settlement submission." The court noted that "[s]uch antics are an abuse, costing litigants good money and wasting valuable court time."

5. Business Park California
Loan Amount: $4,750,000.
Date of Filing: May 1993
Date of Resolution: November 1994
Lender's Attorneys' Fees and Costs: $150,000

Description of Resolution: Lender permitted the debtors to retain $25,000 from the cash collateral account, and the debtors stipulated to lender's motion for relief from stay. Lender subsequently acquired the property at the trustee's sale and sold the property to a third party for $3,000,000, resulting in a net loss of interest and principal of approximately $2,250,000.

Comments: The individual borrowers transferred title to the property to a wholly-owned multi-asset corporation shortly before the bankruptcy filing. Although the bankruptcy judge granted lender's motion for relief from stay based on the ground of bad faith filing within five months of the filing date, the judge indicated that the debtors themselves were the proper parties to file bankruptcy. The judge permitted the debtor to transfer the property back to the individuals, one of whom then filed a personal bankruptcy over the objection of the lender. Permitting this transfer and refiling allowed the debtor to benefit from the consequences of actions the court found to have been undertaken in bad faith. The case was finally resolved by stipulation, in part because the constituents of the borrower were concerned that the lender may have recourse claims against them.

Exhibit B

Issuer/SPE Criteria

A nonconsolidation opinion of counsel will generally be required stating that, in the event of a bankruptcy proceeding involving the parent, the assets of the SPE will not be substantively consolidated with those of the parent. The issuer/SPE (or, in the case of pass-through securitization, the seller or depositor) should satisfy certain criteria:

A. The corporate charter, partnership agreement or trust document, as the case may be, should limit the business and operations of the issuer to activities related to acquisition and holding of the specific assets, issuance of the securities and other activities necessary and appropriate to carry out the foregoing.

B. The issuer should be restricted from incurring additional debt unless (1) the debt would not result in a reduction of the current rating, (2) the debt is fully subordinate to the rated debt (provided D&P approves LTV and coverage limits) or (3) the debt is rated at the same or higher level as the existing rated debt and would not impair the current rating.

C. So long as the securities are outstanding, the issuer should not be able to (1) change the limitations set forth in the charter or other governing instrument, (2) dissolve or liquidate prior to payment in full of the securities or (3) merge with any entity, or transfer or pledge any of its property or assets, except under certain limited conditions.

D. SPE and, where applicable, parent or other affiliate, should provide the following "separateness" undertakings:

1) SPE should maintain its books and records separate from its parent and affiliates. It should prepare separate tax returns, or if part of a consolidated group, it should be shown as a separate member.

2) SPE should utilize its own letterhead and telephone and should maintain an office distinct from its parent.

3) All transactions with the parent or any affiliate should be on an arm's length basis and pursuant to enforceable agreements.

4) SPE should be held out to the public by SPE and its parent as a separate and distinct entity. There should be no commingling of assets or funds with any other entity.

5) At least one director of SPE should be an outside director not affiliated with the parent or any of its affiliates.

6) Regular board meetings should be held to approve SPE activities and all transactions with affiliates should be approved by the outside director(s).
7) The transfer of assets to SPE should be adequately disclosed to the transferor's creditors.
8) The parent and identifiable creditors should agree not to voluntarily place SPE into bankruptcy proceedings. SPE should be restricted from filing a voluntary bankruptcy or other insolvency proceeding unless it is approved by all directors, including the outside director.
9) SPE should not guarantee or pay debts or other obligations of the parent or any other entity and the parent should not guarantee obligations of SPE other than indemnification of certain limited obligations to underwriters.

CHAPTER XI

SINGLE ASSET REAL ESTATE IN CHAPTER 11 AFTER THE BANKRUPTCY REFORM ACT OF 1994: SECURED CREDITORS' PERSPECTIVE

SCOTT CARLISLE

"Single asset real estate" is real estate held by an entity as an investment unto itself rather than as part of a business enterprise conducted on that real estate.[1] Such real estate constitutes the sole or primary asset of the entity.[2] Examples of single asset real estate include office buildings, apartment projects, shopping centers, nursing homes, hotels and warehouses.[3] When an entity decides to embark upon a single asset real estate investment, the financing procedure usually adheres to a common scenario. During the construction stage, or when permanent financing is obtained, the owner of single asset real estate borrows from a commercial lender and provides a promissory note secured by a mortgage on the real estate together with, in most instances, an assignment of the owner's interest in any leases and the rents flowing from them.[4] The loan documents provide that in the event of a

---

1. 11 U.S.C. § 101(51B) (1994).
2. *See* H. Miles Cohn, *Good Faith and the Single-Asset Debtor*, 62 AM. BANKR. L.J. 131, 131 (1988) (observing that single asset entity typically was investment vehicle formed to purchase apartment project or office building); *see also* H. Miles Cohn, *Single Asset Chapter 11 Cases*, 26 TULSA L.J. 523, 524-27 (1991) (describing history of single asset real estate cases).
3. *See generally* Cohn, *Single Asset Chapter 11 Cases*, *supra* note 2, at 527 (describing typical single asset case).
4. *See* MICHAEL T. MADISON & ROBERT M. ZINMAN, MODERN REAL ESTATE FINANCING: A TRANSACTIONAL APPROACH 357 (1991) (commenting that most permanent financing is secured by real estate, improvements thereon and project rents).

default by the borrower, either in making the required payments to the lender or in complying with other requirements such as paying taxes or keeping the property insured and free of other encumbrances, the lender shall have the right to take possession of the real estate and to receive the rents in order to satisfy the borrower's obligations.[5] In nearly all instances of default, the lender works extensively with the borrower to preserve the loan and may even agree to a debt restructuring in order to accommodate the borrower's circumstances.[6] The lender also may delay enforcement of its legal remedies in order to allow the borrower to refinance or to obtain additional capital contributions from partners or stockholders.[7]

There are many instances, however, in which a "workout" is not possible due to the particular circumstances leading to default.[8] In these situations, the lender has no way to protect its interest in the loan other than to pursue its contractual rights and legal remedies with regard to the collateral. Typically, this is accomplished by commencing foreclosure proceedings or initiating an action to gain control of the rents.[9] As a result, many borrowers have sought the protection provided by the reorganization provisions of chapter 11.[10]

A. Relief from the Automatic Stay

Prior to enactment of the Bankruptcy Reform Act of 1994 ("BRA"),[11] commercial lenders with mortgages on single asset real estate had some success in obtaining relief from the automatic stay for cause,[12] or for a lack of

---

5. *See id.* at 965 (explaining that repossession of real estate is often lender's only recourse).
6. *See id.* at 965-66 (claiming lender usually makes effort to prevent foreclosure).
7. *See id.* at 966 (commenting that lender may allow limited modification of its legal rights by taking assignment of rents and leases and by appointment of receiver).
8. *See* Alfred G. Adams, Jr., *The Mortgagee's Guide to Single Asset Bankruptcy Reorganizations*, 98 COM. L.J. 350, 350 (1993) (detailing familiar scenario concerning failed attempts at workout).
9. *Id.*
10. 11 U.S.C. §§ 1101-1174 (1994).
11. Pub. L. No. 103-394, 108 Stat. 4106 (enacted on Oct. 22, 1994, effective in cases commenced on or after date of enactment).
12. *See, e.g.*, Sonnax Indus., Inc. v. Tri Component Prods. Corp. (*In re* Sonnax Indus., Inc.), 907 F.2d 1280, 1286 (2d Cir. 1990) (listing twelve factors court

equity combined with the lack of feasibility of a proposed reorganization under sections 362(d)(1) and (2) of the Bankruptcy Code (the "Code").[13] However, obtaining relief from the stay required a substantial investment of time and money, and the results were certainly not guaranteed.[14] The "cause" which merits relief from the stay under section 362(d)(1) may include lack of adequate protection of a lender's interest in a debtor's property.[15] For example, in *United Savings Ass'n v. Timbers of Inwood Forest Associates*,[16] the United States Supreme Court, affirming a decision of the Fifth Circuit Court of Appeals, held that the interest of a lender is not adequately protected if the security is depreciating during the term of the stay.[17] However, the interest

---

should use when determining cause) (citing *In re* Curtis, 40 B.R. 795, 799-800 (Bankr. D. Utah 1984)); *see also infra* note 13 (further discussing "for cause" relief from stay).

13. 11 U.S.C. § 362(d)(1), (2) (1988). The statute provided that:

> (d) On request of a party in interest and after notice and a hearing, the court shall grant relief from the stay provided under subsection (a) of this section, such as by terminating, annulling, modifying, or conditioning such stay–
>
> (1) for cause, including the lack of adequate protection of an interest in property of such party in interest; or
>
> (2) with respect to a stay of an act against the property under subsection (a) of this section, if–
>
> (A) the debtor does not have equity in such property; and
>
> (B) such property is not necessary to an effective reorganization.

Id. See, e.g., Albany Partners, Ltd. v. W.P. Westbrook (*In re* Albany Partners, Ltd.), 749 F.2d 670, 673 (11th Cir. 1984) (upholding relief from automatic stay where debtors lacked equity and had no realistic prospect of reorganization); Sumitomo Trust & Banking Co. v. Holly's, Inc. (*In re* Holly's, Inc.), 140 B.R. 643, 697 (Bankr. W.D. Mich. 1992) (requiring both lack of equity and lack of feasibility for relief from stay).

14. *See generally* ELIZABETH WARREN & JAY L. WESTBROOK, THE LAW OF DEBTORS & CREDITORS: TEXT, CASES & PROBLEMS 212-23 (2d ed. 1991) (discussing difficulties of automatic stay for creditors under chapter 11).

15. 11 U.S.C. § 362(d)(1) (1994).

16. 484 U.S. 365 (1988).

17. *Id.* at 370. The Court stated:

> It is common ground that the "interest in property" referred to by § 362(d)(1) includes the right of a secured creditor to have the

which merits adequate protection in a chapter 11 reorganization proceeding is limited to the value of that lender's collateral at the commencement of the proceeding and does not include a lender's interest in realizing immediately on its collateral.[18]

As a result, undersecured lenders seeking relief from the automatic stay under section 362(d)(1) for cause based upon lack of adequate protection must be prepared to show, by means of an appraisal or other competent evidence, that the value of their collateral is being diminished during the course of the chapter 11 proceeding. This challenging exercise is often accompanied by a battle of appraisers,[19] and is further complicated by uncertainty as to the valuation standard to be applied by a bankruptcy court for purposes of relief from the stay. For example, bankruptcy courts have grappled with the issue of whether to use liquidation value or fair market value.[20]

Another basis for relief under section 362(d)(1) arising in a chapter 11 single asset real estate case is "bad faith filing." In *Little Creek Development Co. v. Commonwealth Mortgage Corp. (In re Little Creek Development Co.)*,[21] the Fifth Circuit found several conditions which illustrate "bad faith" in single asset cases.[22] In addition to providing a basis for relief from the stay,

---

> security applied in payment of the debt upon completion of the reorganization; and that that interest is not adequately protected if the security is depreciating during the term of the stay.

Id.

18. *See id.* at 371 ("[T]he 'interest in property' protected by § 362(d)(1) does not include a secured party's right to immediate foreclosure.").

19. *See, e.g.*, Cheshire Assocs. v. Cheshire Molding Co. (*In re* Cheshire Molding Co.), 9 B.R. 309, 313 (Bankr. D. Conn. 1981) (illustrating conflicting reports of appraisers).

20. *See* Prudential Ins. Co. of Am. v. Monnier Bros. (*In re* Monnier Bros.), 755 F.2d 1336, 1341 (8th Cir. 1985) (finding bankruptcy court's use of market value not inappropriate); *In re* Demakes Enters., 145 B.R. 362, 365 (Bankr. D. Mass. 1992) (using liquidation value).

21. 779 F.2d 1068 (5th Cir. 1986).

22. *Id.* at 1073. The Fifth Circuit listed the following as indicia of bad faith:

> [1] The debtor has one asset, such as a tract of undeveloped or developed real property. [2] The secured creditors' liens encumber this tract. [3] There are generally no employees except for the principals, [4] little or no cash flow, and [5] no available sources of

bad faith also may support dismissal of a case for cause under section 1112(b) of the Code,[23] and relief under both sections is frequently pleaded in the alternative by lenders.

Although bad faith appears to be a particularly appropriate basis for relief from the stay in single asset real estate cases, it does have limitations. Courts have criticized the concept because none of the factors evidencing bad faith in *Little Creek* are dispositive.[24] In addition, although section 1129(a)(3) requires

---

> income to sustain a plan of reorganization or to make adequate protection payments . . . . [6] Typically, there are only a few, if any, unsecured creditors whose claims are relatively small. [7] The property has usually been posted for foreclosure because of arrearages on the debt[,] and the debtor has been unsuccessful in defending actions against the foreclosure in state court. Alternatively, the debtor and one creditor may have proceeded to a stand-still in state court litigation, and the debtor has lost or been required to post a bond which it cannot afford. [8] Bankruptcy offers the only possibility of forestalling loss of the property. [9] There are . . . allegations of wrongdoing by the debtor or its principals.

Id. The Fifth Circuit justified the concept of good faith as part of the process as follows:

> Requirement of good faith prevents abuse of the bankruptcy process by debtors whose overriding motive is to delay creditors without benefiting them in any way or to achieve reprehensible purposes. Moreover, a good faith standard protects the jurisdictional integrity of the bankruptcy courts by rendering their powerful equitable weapons . . . available only to those debtors and creditors with "clean hands."

Id. at 1072.

23. *See* 11 U.S.C. § 1112(b) (1994) (stating courts may convert case under chapter 11 to one under chapter 7 or may dismiss case for cause); *see also* Farley v. Coffee Cupboard, Inc. (*In re* Coffee Cupboard, Inc.), 119 B.R. 14, 17-18 (E.D.N.Y. 1990) (finding lack of good faith grounds for dismissal); *In re* Copy Crafters Quickprint, Inc., 92 B.R. 973, 985 (Bankr. N.D.N.Y. 1988) (stating lack of good faith constitutes "cause").

24. *See In re* Victory Constr. Co., 42 B.R. 145, 149 (Bankr. C.D. Cal. 1984) ("[T]he cases make it clear that [the § 1129(a)(3) good faith requirement] is to be read restrictively."); *see also* Michigan Nat'l Bank v. Charfoos (*In re* Charfoos), 979 F.2d 390, 393 (6th Cir. 1992) (stating that "bad faith is

a finding that a plan "has been proposed in good faith" before it can be confirmed,[25] the Code has no good faith requirement for the filing of a chapter 11 case or as a ground for dismissal. The concept is further criticized because, if, as some courts indicate, the good faith concept is jurisdictional,[26] the bankruptcy court is forced to determine at the outset of a case whether an effective reorganization can be achieved, rather than allowing a debtor time to propose a plan. Section 1129(a)(3), which requires good faith, as a condition of confirmation of a plan, supports the position that the analysis should be postponed until that time. One commentator persuasively argues that courts should give a chapter 11 debtor the opportunity to reorganize even if many of the *Little Creek* factors are present, unless it is clear that the intent of the debtor is not to reorganize, but to avoid the consequences of litigation or foreclosure.[27]

If a debtor lacks equity in the property and the property is not "necessary to an effective reorganization," section 362(d)(2) authorizes relief from the automatic stay for an action against such property, including foreclosure, appointment of a receiver, or an action to enforce an interest in rents.[28] In many single asset real estate cases, there is little or no equity in the property.[29] If there were, the debtor would have a much greater chance of solving its problems by refinancing or obtaining additional contributions from investors. If the lender can win the battle of appraisers and show that there is no equity in the property,[30] the burden shifts to the debtor, pursuant to section 362(g)(2), to establish that the property is "necessary to an effective reorganization"[31]

---

evaluated under flexible and multiple standards").

25. 11 U.S.C. § 1129(a)(3) (1994).
26. *See, e.g.*, Stage I Land Co. v. United States Hous. & Urban Dev. Dep't, 71 B.R. 225, 229 (Bankr. D. Minn. 1986) ("Good faith is a jurisdictional consideration.").
27. *See* Cohn, *Good Faith and the Single Asset Debtor*, *supra* note 2, at 147-48.
28. 11 U.S.C. § 362(d)(2)(B) (1994).
29. *See, e.g.*, *In re* Lake Ridge Assocs., 169 B.R. 576, 578 (E.D. Va. 1994) (noting that debtor had no equity in property); Penn Mut. Life Ins. Co. v. Woodscape Ltd. Partnership (*In re* Woodscape Ltd. Partnership), 134 B.R. 165, 168 (Bankr. D. Md. 1991) (same).
30. *See* 11 U.S.C. § 362(g)(1) (1994) (providing that party requesting relief from automatic stay under § 362(d) has burden of proof on issue of debtor's equity in property).
31. *See id.* § 362(g)(2) (providing that "the party opposing such relief has burden

under section 362(d)(2)(B). The Supreme Court interpreted the phrase "necessary to an effective reorganization" as follows:

> What this requires is not merely a showing that if there is conceivably to be an effective reorganization, this property will be needed for it; but that the property is essential for an effective reorganization *that is in prospect.* This means, as many lower courts, including the en banc court in this case, have properly said, that there must be "a reasonable possibility of a successful reorganization within a reasonable time."[32]

The *Timbers* Court also discussed the timing of the determination of a plan's feasibility:

> The cases are numerous in which [section] 362(d)(2) relief has been provided within less than a year from the filing of the bankruptcy petition. And while the bankruptcy courts demand less detailed showings during the four months in which the debtor is given the exclusive right to put together a plan, see 11 U.S.C. [section] 1121(b), (c)(2), even within that period lack of any realistic prospect of effective reorganization will require [section] 362(d)(2) relief.[33]

Although the Supreme Court has placed new emphasis on a debtor's burden to show a workable plan, the debtor still has added leeway during the four month exclusivity period of section 1121(b).[34] Even in the absence of an "equity cushion,"[35] a lender may have to wait at least four months, and then

---

of proof on all other issues").

32. United Sav. Ass'n v. Timbers of Inwood Forest Assocs., Ltd., 484 U.S. 365, 375-76 (1988) (quoting United Sav. Ass'n v. Timbers of Inwood Forest Assocs., Ltd. (*In re* Timbers of Inwood Forest Assocs., Ltd.), 808 F.2d 363, 370 (5th Cir. 1987), *aff'd*, 484 U.S. 365 (1988)) (emphasis added).
33. *Id.* at 376 (footnotes omitted).
34. *See* 11 U.S.C. § 1121(b) (1994) ("Except as otherwise provided in this section, only the debtor may file a plan until after 120 days after the date of the order for relief under this chapter.").
35. *See* Travelers Ins. Co. v. Plaza Family Partnership (*In re* Plaza Family Partnership), 95 B.R. 166, 171 (Bankr. E.D. Cal. 1989) (stating that "equity

risk a bankruptcy court's subjective reaction to a debtor's projections and assurances, before it receives relief from the stay. This process is simply incongruous in the vast majority of single asset real estate cases in which relief from the stay is ultimately granted to a lender after four to twelve, or more, months of time and expense in fencing with a debtor who has no means of salvation.

For single asset real estate cases, the *Timbers* decision marked the course toward the solution of the automatic stay problems with its discussion of the meaning of "necessary to an effective reorganization" under section 362. Both before and after *Timbers,* courts demonstrated the same concern for the integrity of the chapter 11 process, particularly with respect to single asset real estate; the "bad faith" cases emphasized the abuse of the judicial process when a debtor filed under chapter 11 to gain protection and leverage against a lender rather than as a means to effect a plan of reorganization.[36] Chief Judge Alexander L. Paskay focused on such abuse in several "bad faith" cases involving motions seeking relief from the stay for "cause" under section 362(d)(1)[37] and dismissal for "cause" under section 1112(b).[38] In *In re Southwest Development Corp.*,[39] Chief Judge Paskay explained what may

---

cushion" defined as value in property, above amount owed creditor with secured claim which will shield interest from loss arising from any decrease in value of property during time automatic stay remains in effect); *In re* Lane, 108 B.R. 6, 7 (Bankr. D. Mass. 1989) (discussing equity cushion in light of *Timbers*).

36. *See, e.g.*, Laguna Assocs. Ltd. Partnership v. Aetna Casualty & Sur. Co. (*In re* Laguna Assocs. Ltd. Partnership), 30 F.3d 734, 738 (6th Cir. 1994) (finding bad faith when debtor files bankruptcy at last moment to gain protection); *In re* Washtenaw/Huron Inv. Corp. No. 8, 160 B.R. 74, 79 (E.D. Mich. 1993) (finding bad faith when debtor files bankruptcy merely to frustrate creditor's rights); *In re* Welwood Corp., 60 B.R. 319, 322 (Bankr. M.D. Fla. 1984) (finding bad faith where debtor had no realistic expectation of achieving rehabilitation or establishing feasible plan); *In re* American Property Corp., 44 B.R. 180, 182 (Bankr. M.D. Fla. 1984) (finding bad faith where debtor seeks stay in speculation that asset will increase in value to recover original investment).

37. *See* 11 U.S.C. § 362(d)(1) (1994) (providing that cause includes "lack of adequate protection of an interest in property of such party in interest").

38. *Id.* § 1112(b)(1)-(10).

39. 76 B.R. 196 (Bankr. M.D. Fla. 1987).

constitute "cause" for dismissal under section 1112(b), and found such cause when a corporate debtor filed a chapter 11 petition ten days after a forty-unit apartment complex became involved in a state court foreclosure action.[40]

The Eleventh Circuit went a step further in *Phoenix Piccadilly, Ltd. v. Life Insurance Co. (In re Phoenix Piccadilly, Ltd.)*[41] by affirming the dismissal of a single asset case for "bad faith" even though there was both equity for the debtor and the potential for a successful reorganization.[42] However, the Fourth Circuit, in *Carolin Corp. v. Miller*,[43] held that in order to dismiss a petition for bad faith under section 1112(b), a bankruptcy court must find objective futility as well as subjective bad faith.[44] *Carolin* involved a single asset company which was formed and filed under chapter 11 on the eve of foreclosure in order to delay a creditor's foreclosure sale.[45] The court

---

40. *Id.* at 199. Chief Judge Paskay noted:

> It is now well established that courts are not required to retain cases on their dockets which were not filed to achieve the valid and legitimate purposes designed by Congress through the enactment of the rehabilitative provisions of [c]hapter 11. To do so would be a total disregard of the basic overriding purpose of the system designed by Congress which was to enable a financially distressed debtor to achieve rehabilitation. It is evident from the outset that there is no reasonable expectation that the financial situation of the Debtor can be successfully repaired through the reorganization process and that the case was filed solely to use the bankruptcy forum to hide under the protective umbrella of the automatic stay in order to gain time and prevent secured creditors from enforcing their legitimate claims. This Court is satisfied, therefore, that "cause" exists which warrants a dismissal based on bad faith filing.

Id.

41. 849 F.2d 1393 (11th Cir. 1988).

42. *Id.* at 1395. The court stated:

> We reject the debtor's argument that the bankruptcy court cannot ever dismiss a case for bad faith if there is equity in the property because the presence of equity indicates the potential for a successful reorganization. . . . The possibility of a successful reorganization cannot transform a bad faith filing into one undertaken in good faith.

Id.

43. 886 F.2d 693 (4th Cir. 1989).

44. *Id.* at 700-01.

45. *Id.* at 696. *Carolin* demonstrated what is known as the "new debtor syndrome."

found that these actions demonstrated subjective bad faith on the part of the debtor.[46] The court then considered whether the party seeking relief must meet the objective futility test.[47] After considering decisions dismissing chapter 11 cases for bad faith,[48] the court announced that it agreed with those courts requiring *both* subjective bad faith and objective futility.[49]

In cases that do not merit the protection of chapter 11, United States Bankruptcy Judge A. Thomas Small of the Eastern District of North Carolina has developed a "fast track" procedure in order to expedite the proceedings.[50]

Id. at 696. *See generally* Cohn, *Good Faith and the Single-Asset Debtor*, *supra* note 2, at 134. In such instances, the debtor is formed for the sole purpose of filing bankruptcy, and the only asset transferred to such entity is the property subject to foreclosure. *Id.*

46. *Carolin*, 886 F.2d at 696.

47. *Id.* at 700.

48. *See, e.g.*, Phoenix Piccadilly, Ltd. v. Life Ins. Co. (*In re* Phoenix Piccadilly, Ltd.), 849 F.2d 1393, 1395 (11th Cir. 1988) (affirming bankruptcy court's dismissal for "bad faith"); *In re* Oakgrove Village, Ltd., 90 B.R. 246, 249 (Bankr. W.D. Tex. 1988) (granting relief for bad faith despite possibility of successful reorganization); *In re* McDermott, 78 B.R. 646, 652 (Bankr. N.D.N.Y. 1985) (denying creditor's motion to lift automatic stay but providing that creditor could renew its motion if debtor failed to submit *viable* reorganization plan within 90 days).

49. *Carolin*, 886 F.2d at 701. The court stated:

> This, we think, is the only sufficiently stringent test of justification for threshold denials of [c]hapter 11 relief. Such a test obviously contemplates that it is better to risk proceeding with a wrongly motivated invocation of [c]hapter 11 protections whose futility is not immediately manifest than to risk cutting off even a remote chance that a reorganization effort so motivated might nevertheless yield a successful rehabilitation. Just as obviously, it contemplates that it is better to risk the wastefulness of a probably futile but good faith effort to reorganize than it is to risk error in prejudging its futility at the threshold. We believe that such a stringent test is necessary to accommodate the various and conflicting interests of debtors, creditors, and the courts that are at stake in deciding whether to deny threshold access to [c]hapter 11 proceedings for want of good faith in filing.

Id.

50. *See generally* Hon. A. Thomas Small, *Small Business Bankruptcy Cases*, 1

Noting that chapter 12 requires the filing of a plan within ninety days and chapter 13 within fifteen days, Judge Small found authority to set a deadline for the filing of a plan in chapter 11 under section 1112(b)(4).[51] This section includes among the causes for dismissal or conversion of a chapter 11 case the "failure to propose a plan under section 1121 of this title within any time fixed by the court."[52] Judge Small also pointed to the general power of the court set forth in section 105, which provides that "[t]he court may issue any order, process, or judgment that is necessary or appropriate to carry out the provisions of this title."[53] Under Judge Small's "fast track procedure," in cases deemed appropriate for the expedited process, the debtor is required to file a plan and disclosure statement within sixty to ninety days from the date the petition is filed. The plan and disclosure statement are then reviewed by a bankruptcy administrator, and if accepted, the disclosure statement is sent to creditors, who may then raise objections to the disclosure statement at a preconfirmation hearing.[54]

Judge Small's fast track procedure has been popular among practitioners.[55] Its success and popularity have signaled the need for change in

---

AM. BANKR. INST. L. REV. 305 (1993) (discussing success of fast track approach in Eastern District of North Carolina); John Greenwald, *The Bankruptcy Game*, TIME, May 18, 1992, at 60 (comparing efficiency of fast track cases with other cases); George W. Hay, *Lawyers Overwhelmingly Endorse Judge Small's "Fast Track" 11's*, TURNAROUNDS & WORKOUTS, July 15, 1989, at 1 (discussing reaction to fast track approach).

51. *See* Hon. A. Thomas Small, Comments Concerning Fast Track to Confirmation for Small Chapter 11 Debtors, Annual Meeting of the American Bankruptcy Institute (May 7, 1990) (unpublished manuscript, on file with the American Bankruptcy Institute).

52. 11 U.S.C. § 1112(b)(4) (1994).

53. *Id.* § 105(a).

54. *See* Small, *supra* note 50, at 308.

55. *See* Hay, *supra* note 50, at 308. The author pointed out:

> An overwhelming 82 percent of the attorneys who have filed bankruptcy cases in the Eastern District of North Carolina, a jurisdiction which has adopted a streamlined process for certain [c]hapter 11 cases, recommend that expedited procedures be adopted by the bankruptcy courts, according to a survey by Turnarounds & Workouts. The percentage of those who endorse the use of such procedures rises to 92% if

the Code toward recognizing the important differences that exist among chapter 11 debtors.[56] Judicial decisions are an inadequate solution to the problem because they only can interpret and construe the provisions of the Code itself.[57] In fact, the Supreme Court, in support of its decision in *Timbers*, indicated that the nature of the property meriting adequate protection under section 362(d)(1) is to be determined within the parameters of the Code.[58] Thus, any change in the nature of the property protected under section 362(d)(1) or other changes pertaining to the automatic stay, must be done legislatively.[59]

Prior to the enactment of the Code, the Senate showed insight concerning the changes needed for chapter 11 petitions involving single asset real estate. A proposed version of section 362(d) provided:

> the "No Opinion" answers are eliminated.

Id.

56. *See* Lynn M. Lopucki, *The Trouble With Chapter 11*, 1993 WIS. L. REV. 729, 751-52 (discussing proposed legislation).
57. *See, e.g.*, Chemical Bank v. First Trust, Nat'l Ass'n (*In re* Southeast Banking Corp.), 188 B.R. 452, 469 (Bankr. S.D. Fla. 1995) (discussing courts' ability to interpret statutory language only).
58. *See* United Sav. Ass'n v. Timbers of Inwood Forest Assocs., Ltd., 484 U.S. 365, 371 (1988). In determining whether § 362(d)(1) protects a secured party's right to immediate foreclosure, the United States Supreme Court stated:

> Statutory construction, however, is a holistic endeavor. A provision that may seem ambiguous in isolation is often clarified by the remainder of the statutory scheme—because the same terminology is used elsewhere in a context that makes meaning clear, or because only one of the permissible meanings produces a substantive effect that is compatible with the rest of the law. That is the case here. Section 362(d)(1) is only one of a series of provisions in the Bankruptcy Code dealing with the rights of secured creditors. The language in those other provisions, and the substantive dispositions that they effect, persuade us that the "interest in property" protected by § 362(d)(1) does not include a secured party's right to immediate foreclosure.

Id. (citations omitted).

59. *See Chemical Bank*, 188 B.R. at 469 (discussing Congress's power to change statutory language).

> (d) On request of a party in interest, after notice and a hearing, and for cause, including the lack of adequate protection of an interest in property of such party in interest, the court shall within thirty days after such hearing grant relief from the stay provided under subsection (a) of this section, such as by terminating, annulling, modifying, or conditioning such stay. The court shall grant relief from the stay if the court finds that the debtor has no equity in the property subject to the stay and such property is not necessary to an effective reorganization of the debtor. For the purpose of this subsection (d), property is not necessary to an effective reorganization of the debtor if it is real property on which no business is being conducted by the debtor other than the business of operating the real property and activities incidental thereto.[60]

The Senate clearly envisioned lifting a stay on the ground that property was "not necessary to an effective reorganization" if the property involved was "real property on which no business was being conducted by the debtor other than the business of operating the real property and activities incidental thereto" and if the property lacked equity.[61] The proposal required a value judgment that investment real estate without equity was not entitled to the benefits of chapter 11 which did not survive the legislative process in 1978 and did not become part of the statute as finally enacted. Fifteen years of experience has demonstrated the wisdom of this proposal's analysis.

The BRA[62] provided an additional basis for relief from the stay for single asset real estate by adding a new section, 362(d)(3), as follows:

> (d) On request of a party in interest and after notice and a hearing, the court shall grant relief from the stay . . .
>
> (3) with respect to a stay of an act against single asset real estate under subsection (a), by a creditor whose claim is secured by an interest in such real estate, unless, not later than the date that is 90 days after the entry of the order for relief (or such later date as the court may determine for cause by order entered within that 90-day period)—

---

60. S. 2266, 95th Cong., 2d Sess. § 362 (1978), *reprinted in* APP. 3 COLLIER ON BANKRUPTCY pt. VII, at 354 (Lawrence P. King ed., 15th ed. 1979).

61. *Id.*

62. Pub. L. No. 103-394, 108 Stat. 4106.

> (A) the debtor has filed a plan of reorganization that has a reasonable possibility of being confirmed within a reasonable time; or
>
> (B) the debtor has commenced monthly payments to each creditor whose claim is secured by such real estate (other than a claim secured by a judgment lien or by an unmatured statutory lien), which payments are in an amount equal to interest at a current fair market rate on the value of the creditor's interest in the real estate.[63]

The BRA also added a new section 101(51B), which defines single asset real estate as follows:

> "[S]ingle asset real estate" means real property constituting a single property or project, other than residential real property with fewer than 4 residential units, which generates substantially all of the gross income of a debtor and on which no substantial business is being conducted by a debtor other than the business of operating the real property and activities incidental thereto having aggregate noncontingent, liquidated secured debts in an amount no more than $4,000,000[.][64]

Under section 362(d)(3), the debtor must file a feasible plan within a specific time period in compliance with the *Timbers* standard,[65] but a debtor may remain in chapter 11 beyond such period if it can make payments to the secured creditors; a 90 day extension is available for cause shown before the period expires.[66] Section 362(d)(3) thus recognizes the concerns expressed by the Fourth Circuit in *Carolin* but strikes a balance more appropriate for single

---

63. Bankruptcy Reform Act of 1994, § 218(b), 11 U.S.C. § 362(d)(3) (1994).

64. *Id.* § 218(a), 11 U.S.C. § 101(51B) (1994).

65. *See* United Sav. Ass'n v. Timbers of Inwood Forest Assocs., 484 U.S. 365, 376 (1988) ("[T]here must be 'a reasonable possibility of a successful reorganization within a reasonable time.'") (quoting United Sav. Ass'n v. Timbers of Inwood Forest Assocs. (*In re* Timbers of Inwood Forest Assocs.), 808 F.2d 363, 370 (5th Cir. 1987)).

66. *See* 11 U.S.C. § 362(d)(3)(B) (1994) (providing for relief from stay against single asset real estate *unless* within 90 days debtor has commenced monthly payments to secured creditors).

> asset real estate. The amendment does not restrict a chapter 11 filing involving single asset real estate by "prejudging its futility at the threshold"[67] due to the presence of indicia of bad faith, but rather allows a debtor a period of ninety days to produce a feasible plan.[68] As to a situation in which abuse of the system was common, section 362(d)(3) requires a single asset real estate debtor to come forward with a plan which it can show to be feasible within a reasonably short period of time, rather than requiring a lender to demonstrate "objective futility."[69]

Section 362(d)(3) combats the abuse of the system by decreasing the incentive for single asset real estate debtors to initiate proceedings under chapter 11 when they have no intention or realistic hope of presenting a feasible plan of reorganization. As previously noted, the benefits of chapter 11 are still available for such debtors, but over the past decade, the burden has been placed on the debtor to present a feasible plan within a reasonable period of time. Single asset real estate debtors who are unable to meet the requirements of the provision as revised will be prevented from delaying a secured creditor indefinitely without being willing and able to incur an expense therefor. However, the well-intentioned debtor with a real possibility of an effective reorganization will not be unfairly disadvantaged.

Section 101(51B) limits "single asset real estate" treatment to situations in which a debtor's aggregate contingent, liquidated secured debt does not exceed four million dollars.[70] This limitation, which resulted from political compromise during final conference action on the BRA, significantly undermines the intent of the legislation since the majority of single asset properties have aggregate commercial mortgages in excess of four million dollars. The losses sustained in such ill-conceived chapter 11 proceedings, including loss of time and money for secured and unsecured creditors,

---

67. Carolin Corp. v. Miller, 886 F.2d 693, 701 (4th Cir. 1989).
68. *See id.* "[I]t is better to risk the wastefulness of a probably futile but good faith effort to reorganize than it is to risk error in prejudicing its futility at the threshold." *Id.*
69. *See Timbers*, 484 U.S. at 376 (allowing relief from stay unless debtor presents plan confirmable within reasonable period of time). *Compare with Carolin*, 886 F.2d at 700-01 (stating petition could be dismissed if creditor showed debtor's subjective bad faith and plan's objective futility).
70. 11 U.S.C. § 101(51B) (1994).

deterioration of the property with resultant problems for tenants, retailers and taxing authorities with no coincident benefit for debtors, are more extensive for larger properties. Remedial legislation to remove this arbitrary limitation on secured debt would allow the new provision to operate fairly and achieve its intended purpose.

Since the enactment of section 101(51B), a "single project" has been held to include semi-detached houses owned in discrete blocks by three limited partnerships having a common general partner.[71] On the other hand, a marina which provided boat repair, storage, fuel and food sales, showers and a pool failed to qualify as single asset real estate for purposes of stay relief because it was "more than simply rental of moorings."[72]

Section 362(d)(3) "amends the automatic stay provision of section 362 to provide special circumstances under which creditors of a single asset real estate debtor may have the stay lifted if the debtor has not filed a `feasible' reorganization plan within 90 days of filing, or has not commenced monthly payments to secured creditors."[73] Such payments must be made to all consensual secured creditors but not to holders of judgment liens or unmatured statutory liens, in amounts equal to interest at a current fair market rate on the value of the creditor's interest in the real estate.[74] The timetable for determining value and a fair market rate normally required as part of a confirmation hearing has been accelerated with regard to the single asset real estate debtor. The BRA amended section 362(e) to provide that a hearing on a motion for relief from the stay must be concluded not later than thirty (30) days after the conclusion of a preliminary hearing on such motion, unless such 30-day period is extended by consent of the parties or for a specific time which the court finds is required by compelling circumstances.[75] Since section 362(e) provides that the preliminary hearing must be concluded within thirty (30)

---

71. *See In re* Philmont Dev. Co., 181 B.R. 220, 223-24 (Bankr. E.D. Pa. 1995) (noting under § 101(51B), real property includes "single property" as well as "single projects").
72. *In re* Kkemko, Inc., 181 B.R. 47, 51 (Bankr. S.D. Ohio 1995) (finding marina conducted substantial business "other than the business of operating the real property and activities incidental thereto").
73. 140 CONG. REC. H10,768 (daily ed. Oct. 4, 1994); H.R. REP. NO. 835, 103d Cong., 2d Sess. 50 (1994), *reprinted in* 1994 U.S.C.C.A.N. 3359.
74. 140 CONG. REC. H10,758 (daily ed. Oct. 4, 1994).
75. Bankruptcy Reform Act of 1994, § 101, 11 U.S.C. § 362(e) (1994).

days after the motion has been filed, the determination of value and rate may need to be determined as early as sixty (60) days after the motion for relief from stay has been filed. Should the debtor fail to present adequate evidence of value, it is possible that the court could require that the debtor pay interest on the full amount of the secured debt.[76] Although this provision may increase litigation concerning value and rate, it also will narrow issues and reduce discovery, as a motion to dismiss for bad faith filing will no longer be necessary.

A question may arise as to whether the payments called for by section 362(d)(3) are in addition to adequate protection payments required by section 362 or 363. Under *Timbers*, adequate protection payments are available only to unsecured creditors who show the collateral is declining in value.[77] Section 362(d)(3) makes no reference to adequate protection, nor does it restrict required payments to such situations with regard to single asset real estate.[78] The payments under section 362(d)(3) are required in *all* instances for a single asset real estate debtor to avoid the granting of relief from the stay if a feasible plan has not been filed within the 90-day period.[79] With regard to any possible redundancy of the new provision with the adequate protection required for a debtor's use of rents which constitute cash collateral under section 363, there would seem to be no reason why a creditor's interest in the real estate should not be considered separately, apart from any rents generated by such real estate and the concomitant adequate protection considerations. It is clear that the requirement of payments under section 362(d)(3)(B) will place more pressure upon debtors who have little, if any, cash flow, but the likelihood of successful reorganization for such entities is remote in any event.

At least one commentator has inquired as to whether section 362(d)(3)(B) overrules section 506(b) by entitling an undersecured creditor to receive interest at a current fair market rate.[80] As discussed above, the payments

---

76. Myron M. Scheinfeld, *Small Business and Single Asset Real Estate Bankruptcies*, 41 No. 6 PRAC. LAW. 17, 23 (Sept. 1995).
77. *See* United Sav. Ass'n v. Timbers of Inwood Forest Assocs., Ltd., 484 U.S. 365, 370 (1988) (stating where single asset real estate declines in value, creditor is entitled to cash payments or other security in amount equal to decline).
78. 11 U.S.C. § 362(d)(3) (1994).
79. *Id.*
80. Scheinfeld, *supra* note 76, at 22.

required by section 362(d)(3)(B) are specifically not designated as interest, but as "payments in an amount equal to interest."[81] Some commentators feel that, in the case of an undersecured creditor, if payments are not interest then they should be applied to principal.[82] Since section 362(d) speaks only to the circumstances under which the payments must be made and does not specify the application of said payments by the creditors involved, it seems that such determination has been left to the courts.

B. Facilitating Foreclosure Following Relief from the Stay

The problems encountered by a lender with regard to single asset real estate involved in chapter 11 proceedings do not always cease when relief from the stay has been granted; sometimes a lender must commence foreclosure proceedings in order to enforce its rights as a mortgagee and to gain possession of the collateral. Alternatively, the lender may continue with the proceeding that was interrupted by the application of the automatic stay. The time periods associated with these foreclosure proceedings vary greatly under applicable state and federal laws. The time consumed by a chapter 11 proceeding and the processing of an action to obtain relief from the automatic stay become even more significant when added to the time required for foreclosure. Thus, it seems necessary to revise the Code to allow foreclosure proceedings in single asset estate cases to go forward either nonjudically, or in state or federal court, up to the point of, but not including, a sale, while chapter 11 proceedings are in progress.

The concept of federal bankruptcy courts deferring to other courts to allow important litigation to proceed in those other courts is not new. Although the Bankruptcy Reform Act of 1978 granted original and exclusive jurisdiction over all bankruptcy cases to the United States Bankruptcy Courts,[83] the granting of power to a non-Article III court was held unconstitutional by the Supreme Court in *Northern Pipeline Construction Co. v. Marathon Pipe Line Co.*[84] In response to this decision, 28 U.S.C. § 1334 was amended by

---

81. 11 U.S.C. § 362(d)(3)(B) (1994).
82. 2 COLLIER ON BANKRUPTCY ¶ 362-07, at 362-74 (Lawrence P. King ed., 15th ed. 1995).
83. 28 U.S.C. § 1471 (1978), *repealed by* Bankruptcy Amendments and Federal Judgeship Act of 1984, Pub. L. No. 98-353, §101, 98 Stat. 333 (1984).
84. 458 U.S. 50, 87 (1982). The Court held that bankruptcy judges are not Article

section 101 of the Bankruptcy Amendments and Federal Judgeship Act of 1984[85] to give the federal district courts jurisdiction over bankruptcy cases. Simultaneously, 28 U.S.C. § 157(a) was enacted, which enabled the district courts to pass that jurisdiction on to the bankruptcy courts.[86] This jurisdiction includes the power to abstain from hearing a matter arising in or related to a chapter 11 proceeding which involves state law, or is the subject of a state court proceeding.[87]

For example, courts have held that it is proper for a bankruptcy court to lift the automatic stay and permit a state court to decide the division of marital property in a pending divorce action.[88] Furthermore, a bankruptcy court's decision not to abstain is not reviewable.[89] Although all three bases for abstention provided for in section 1334(c)(1) may apply to a situation involving foreclosure against single asset real estate involved in chapter 11, perhaps "the interest of justice" rationale most accurately describes the justification for the proposed revision.[90] It seems singularly unjust for a lender that is granted relief from the stay in a single asset real estate case to endure the delay incident to the lift stay proceeding in addition to the time otherwise required by state or federal law for a foreclosure proceeding.

Judicial decisions have specifically recognized the importance, from the standpoint of social utility as well as fairness, of allowing a lender to proceed

---

III judges since they sit for a set period of fourteen years and their salaries are not fixed during this period. *Id.* at 60-62.

85. Bankruptcy Amendments and Federal Judgeship Act of 1984, Pub. L. No. 98-353, § 101, 98 Stat. 333 (1984).

86. *See* 28 U.S.C. § 157(a) (1986) ("Each district court may provide that any or all cases under title 11 and any or all proceedings arising under title 11 or arising in or related to a case under title 11 shall be referred to the bankruptcy judges for the district.").

87. *Id.* § 1334(c)(1). "Nothing in this section prevents a district court in the interests of justice, or in the interest of comity with State courts or respect for State law, from abstaining from hearing a particular proceeding arising under title 11 or arising in or *related to* a case under title 11 . . . ." *Id.* (emphasis added).

88. *See, e.g.*, White v. White (*In re* White), 851 F.2d 170, 174 (6th Cir. 1988) (finding that bankruptcy court did not exceed its authority in lifting stay to allow state court divorce action to proceed).

89. *See* 130 CONG. REC. 13,061 (1984) (section-by-section analysis by Sen. Dole).

90. 28 U.S.C. § 1334(c)(1) (1986).

with foreclosure as soon as possible following a determination that relief from stay is appropriate. For example, in *In re Citadel Properties, Inc.*,[91] Judge Proctor, agreeing with Chief Judge Paskay, granted a lender's motion for relief from the stay based upon a prepetition agreement between the debtor and the lender.[92] Under such agreement, the lender would forbear from foreclosing in return for immediate relief from the automatic stay in the event the mortgagor filed a petition for bankruptcy.[93]

In *Sun Valley Ranches, Inc. v. Equitable Life Assurance Society of the United States (In re Sun Valley Ranches, Inc.)*,[94] the Ninth Circuit upheld the district court's denial of a motion under Bankruptcy Rule 8017(a)[95] to stay a decision granting relief from the stay for ten days pending an appeal.[96] The court based its decision on Bankruptcy Rule 7062,[97] which creates an explicit exception to Federal Rule of Civil Procedure 62(a),[98] requiring that a judgment by a district court not be enforced for ten days after its entry.[99] Thus, courts

---

91. 86 B.R. 275 (Bankr. M.D. Fla. 1988).
92. *Id.* at 276. Judge Proctor noted that "Judge Paskay confronted similar issues and determined that pre-petition agreements regarding relief from the stay were enforceable in bankruptcy." *Id.*
93. *Id.* at 275.
94. 823 F.2d 1373 (9th Cir. 1987).
95. FED. R. BANKR. P. 8017 (providing for 10-day stay of judgment after entry).
96. *Sun Valley*, 823 F.2d at 1375.
97. FED. R. BANKR. P. 7062.
98. FED. R. CIV. P. 62(a).
99. *Sun Valley*, 823 F.2d at 1375. The court stated:

> Whether Rule 8017 or Rule 7062 applies, Sun Valley [the debtor] contends that the court's action was an abuse of discretion because it gave inadequate reasons for making the order effective immediately. The policy behind the automatic stay provision is to give debtors a "breathing spell." Because this policy is so important, Sun Valley argues, the court needed to give more reasons for making its order effective immediately. Equitable [the creditor] argues that the district court's reasons for lifting the stay are also reasons for lifting it *immediately*. Those reasons, especially the declining value of the mortgaged property, are adequate to support the district court's decision to make its order effective immediately. The court did not abuse its discretion.

Id.

have recognized the fairness of avoiding delay and proceeding with foreclosure as soon as possible when the lender demonstrates the futility of further protection afforded by the automatic stay.

Senate bankruptcy bill 540[100] added a new subsection (i) to section 362 which allowed a secured creditor the right to request limited relief from the stay in order to continue with foreclosure proceedings up to the point of sale. The compromise bill negotiated with the House did not include proposed section 362(i). The proposed change to section 362 reads, in pertinent part:

> (1) Upon request of a creditor whose claim is secured by an interest in single asset real estate, if the interest has more than de minimis value, the court shall issue an order granting limited relief from the stay provided under subsection (a) to permit the creditor to continue a foreclosure proceeding commenced before the commencement of the case up to, but not including, the point of sale.
> (2) An order under paragraph (1) shall not issue before the date that is 30 days after the date of entry of the order for relief, but thereafter shall issue promptly after such a request.
> (3) A hearing shall not be required for the granting of relief under paragraph (1) unless the debtor files an objection to the request and shows the court extraordinary circumstances requiring such a hearing.[101]

A revision which allows foreclosure proceedings to go forward up to the point of sale may be criticized since it forces a debtor to defend its position against a lender on two fronts simultaneously. Certainly, a portion of a debtor's funds and energies may be diverted to defending a foreclosure action, but that is true in any situation in which a bankruptcy court allows a matter to proceed in another court based upon considerations of state law, comity, or fairness. Moreover, this diversion of funds and energy will apply only if a debtor has a colorable defense or counterclaim to assert against a lender. In such an unusual case, the debtor will undoubtedly make these assertions in response to a lender's motion for relief from the stay and the bankruptcy court will then resolve the matter or defer to the state court. Consequently, it would

---

100. 140 CONG. REC. S14,462 (daily ed. Oct. 6, 1994) (statement of Sen. Grassley); S. 540, 103rd Cong., 2d Sess. § 202 (1994).
101. 140 CONG. REC. S4670 (daily ed. Apr. 21, 1994).

be the exceptional case in which the debtor would actually have to defend on two fronts. Foreclosure normally does not involve significant opposition requiring extensive legal proceedings. Therefore, such a revision would permit limited relief from the stay upon the request of a lender without the necessity of a hearing, and thereby avoid the interruption of a time period that had started to run under state foreclosure laws before the chapter 11 petition was filed. Furthermore, if a debtor has a valid objection, such a revision would allow the court to schedule a hearing and resolve the matter.[102]

C. Treatment of Rents as Cash Collateral

Prior to the enactment of the BRA, an ill-founded chapter 11 proceeding not only delayed a lender's possession of real estate, but also resulted in the loss of rents generated by the property.[103] Section 363, entitled "use, sale, or lease of property," set forth several requirements intended to protect the interests of lenders in certain liquid assets of a debtor, which are defined as "cash collateral,"[104] but such provisions had proven inadequate to protect a lender's interest in rents due to uncertainty that had developed concerning the interplay of other Code provisions. Section 552(a) of the Code, provides that "property acquired by the estate or by the debtor after the commencement of the case is not subject to any lien resulting from any security agreement entered into by the debtor before the commencement of the case."[105] However, if a security interest qualifies under the section 552(b) exception, the creditor may argue that its interest in the rents, for example, continues after the filing of the bankruptcy petition.[106] The question that had arisen was whether a

---

102. *See id.* (applying § 362(i)(3) as written with House into compromise bill).

103. 11 U.S.C. § 362 (1994). Once a borrower has filed a petition, the lender-creditor is stayed from foreclosing on the property. In addition, the rents generated may not be recoverable. *See infra* note 104 and accompanying text.

104. 11 U.S.C. § 363(a) (1994). "[C]ash collateral . . . includes the proceeds, products, offspring, *rents,* or profits of property subject to a security interest as provided in section 552(b) . . . whether existing before or after the commencement of a case under this title." *Id.* (emphasis added).

105. *Id.* § 552(a).

106. *Id.* § 552(b). To qualify as a security interest covered by this section, the security interest had to be based on a security agreement, entered into before the commencement of the case, which applied to property of the debtor

lender had an interest in rents that qualified as "cash collateral" under section 363(a) as a "security interest as provided in section 552(b)."[107] In order to determine whether a lender's interest in rents qualified as "cash collateral," section 552(b) required an analysis of both the security agreement and the applicable nonbankruptcy law.

A lender's interest in rents is typically based upon a provision contained in a mortgage, deed of trust, or separate assignment of rents, which are documents normally recorded in the local registry or clerk's office. The provision in these documents pertaining to rents may be in the form of a security interest or collateral assignment of rents that requires some further action by the lender before it can collect the rents. A variation of this provision, known as an absolute assignment conditional upon default, includes an assignment, effective immediately upon execution of the mortgage, deed of trust, or assignment, to give the lender the right to collect the rents. The lender then grants the borrower a license to use the rents until the right is revoked either upon notice from the lender or automatically upon default. In accordance with the decision of the United States Supreme Court in *Butner v. United States*,[108] state law governs enforcement of an interest in rents.[109] Interpretation by state courts of the provisions ostensibly giving lenders the right to rents had, prior to the BRA, resulted in considerable confusion to the detriment of lenders. This area is not governed by the UCC, which excludes the creation or transfer of an interest in or lien on real estate, including a lease or rents under the lease, from coverage under Article 9.[110] Courts often drew

---

acquired before the commencement of the case, and to the extent provided by the security agreement and by applicable nonbankruptcy law, applied to rents acquired by the estate after commencement of the case. *Id.*

107. 11 U.S.C. § 363(a) (1988). Section 363(a) provided that "'cash collateral' . . . includes the proceeds, products, offsprings, rents, or profits of property . . . subject to a security interest as provided in [§] 552(b) . . . ." *Id.* To qualify under § 552(b) prior to the BRA, the security interest had to be based on a security agreement, entered into before the commencement of the case, which applied to property of the debtor acquired before the commencement of the case and, to the extent provided by the security agreement *and by applicable nonbankruptcy law*, applied to rents acquired by the estate after the commencement of the case. *Id.* § 552(b).

108. 440 U.S. 48 (1979).

109. *Id.* at 56-57.

110. *See* U.C.C. § 9-104(j), 3 U.L.A. 179 (1992); *see, e.g., In re* Bristol Assocs.,

on early common law rules relating to property ownership in determining interests in rents.[111] Under such analysis, a mortgagee fared somewhat better in "title" states, in which mortgagees are deemed to hold legal title to property subject to the right of possession of a mortgagor, as opposed to "lien" states, in which mortgagees are treated as lienholders. A majority of state courts in states which adhere to the pure title theory had held that a mortgagee was automatically entitled to the rents upon default.[112] In lien states, which substantially outnumber title states,[113] a security interest in or a collateral assignment of rents held by a mortgagee is deemed to create an inchoate lien that requires some further action to "perfect" the lien, or make it choate by obtaining actual or legal possession of the property before the holder is entitled to receive the rents.[114] The concept of "perfection," as used in this

---

111. *See* Howard J. Weg, *The Secured Creditor's Rights to Rents From Real Property*, 17 REAL EST. L.J. 29, 32 (1988) ("Essentially, the cases are . . . premised on the same theme . . . [w]hoever has possession or ownership of the real property is entitled to the rents.").

112. *See Butner*, 440 U.S. at 52 ("[T]he mortgagee is automatically entitled to possession of the property, and to a secured interest in the rents."); *see also* Jones v. United States (*In re* Jones), 77 B.R. 981, 983 (Bankr. M.D. Ga. 1987) ("[T]he creditor was not required to take any affirmative act to perfect its security interest in the rents after default."); Eastern Sav. Bank v. Epco Newport News Assocs. (*In re* Epco Newport News Assocs.), 14 B.R. 990, 995 (Bankr. S.D.N.Y. 1981) (relying on *Butner*, finding automatic entitlements available upon mortgagor's default).

113. Lien states include Alaska, Arizona, California, Colorado, Delaware, Florida, Georgia, Hawaii, Indiana, Iowa, Kansas, Kentucky, Louisiana, Michigan, Minnesota, Mississippi, Missouri, Montana, Nebraska, Nevada, New Mexico, New York, North Dakota, Oklahoma, Oregon, South Carolina, South Dakota, Texas, Utah, Washington, Wisconsin, and Wyoming. *See* GEORGE E. OSBORNE ET AL., REAL ESTATE FINANCE LAW § 4.2, at 118 n.13 (1979); ALASKA STAT. § 0.9.45.170-190 (1962); DEL. CODE ANN. tit. 25, § 2106 (1974); HAW. REV. STAT. § 506-1 (1988); MISS. CODE ANN. § 89-1-43 (1972); MO. REV. STAT. § 443.035 (1986). Title States include Alabama, Arkansas, Connecticut, Illinois, Maine, Maryland, Massachusetts, New Hampshire, New Jersey, North Carolina, Ohio, Pennsylvania, Rhode Island, Tennessee, Vermont, Virginia, and West Virginia. *See* RICHARD R. POWELL, 3 POWELL ON REAL PROPERTY ¶ 439, at 37-11 n.7 (1987).

114. *See, e.g.*, Hoelting Enters. v. Trailridge Investors, L.P., 844 P.2d 745, 750 (Kan. Ct. App. 1993) (concluding mortgagee's right to rent and profits vests

context, differs from the U.C.C.'s notion, which creates rights in a lender against third parties by giving them notice of these rights. As it pertains to an assignment of rents, "perfection" is a requisite step for a lender to take in many states to enforce its assignment against a debtor. Under this analysis, although a record dating the mortgage, deed of trust, or assignment of rights is sufficient to give notice of the encumbrance to third parties, something more is required to establish the right of a lender to collect the rents.[115] However, precisely what action is required and when it is deemed effective (1) varies considerably from state to state, (2) often takes considerable time to accomplish, and (3) often entails considerable risk for lenders.

The different methods of perfection or enforcement of an interest in rents are typically set forth by statute, and include, under the guise of actual or constructive possession of the rents or the property: giving notice to tenants to pay rents to the lender; seeking an injunction or temporary restraining order against the debtor for collection of the rents; demanding peaceful possession of the property; taking actual possession of the property; commencing a foreclosure proceeding; filing a petition for appointment of a receiver or sequestration of rents; or requesting the entry of an order for foreclosure,

---

when mortgagee initiates proper legal action); Taylor v. Brennan, 621 S.W.2d 592, 593-94 (Tex. 1981) (concluding that assignment of rentals does not become operative until mortgagee obtains possession); *see also Butner*, 440 U.S. at 52-53 (noting that in most states, mortgagee's right to rent is dependent upon actual or constructive possession of property); *Epco Newport*, 14 B.R. at 995 (stating that majority of states require mortgagee to take some affirmative action to effectuate entitlement to rent).

115. *See* Weg, *supra* note 111, at 33. "[N]otice of ownership rights . . . has basically worked well for determining who owns the real property. Unfortunately it has not . . . solved the problem of determining who has an interest in the separate set of rights relating to the rents derived from the underlying real property." *Id.* Thus, to perfect the right to receive rents, a creditor must obtain possession through foreclosure, obtain appointment of a receiver to collect rents or if in a "lien theory" state, take some affirmative action to obtain possession of the property or rents. *Id.* The filing of a financing statement will not entitle the creditor to immediate possession, but will require some further action. *See* Glenn R. Schmitt, *The Continuing Confusion over Real Property Rents as Cash Collateral in Bankruptcy: The Need for a Consistent Interpretation*, 5 DEPAUL BUS. L.J. 1, 39 (1992).

sequestration of rents, or appointment of a receiver.[116] However, enforcing an interest in rents by taking actual possession of the property can expose a lender to significant risks of liability as a mortgagee in possession, for injuries to person or damage to property subsequently occurring on the property, or for the cost of cleanup under state and federal environmental laws.[117] Prior to the BRA, if a lender had not taken whatever action was required by the applicable state law to "perfect" its interest in rents prior to the filing of a chapter 11 petition, it then might not have been deemed to possess the security interest in rents required under section 552(b) to qualify as "cash collateral" under section 363(a).[118] Unless the rents qualified as cash collateral, the debtor had unrestricted use of them during the pendency of the chapter 11 proceeding and, in most instances, they were lost by the lender.[119]

Courts, in attempting to overcome the "perfection" problem, have adopted several different theories to sustain a lender's interest in rents after the commencement of a chapter 11 proceeding. Some courts held that an absolute assignment of rents, either in trust or with a license back to the borrower conditional upon default, did not require subsequent perfection.[120] In *In re Fry*

---

116. *See* Weg, *supra* note 111, at 33 n.10.

117. Craig B. Welborn & Peter Aitelli, *Lender's Interim and Provisional Remedies: Protecting the Lender's Interest in Rents & Realizing on Collateral Security*, REAL ESTATE WORKOUT & BANKRUPTCIES 1992, at 69 (PLI Real Est. L. & Prac. Course Handbook Series No. N4-4564, 1992).

118. *See* Wolters Village, Ltd. v. Village Properties, Ltd. (*In re* Village Properties, Ltd.), 723 F.2d 441 (5th Cir.), *cert. denied*, 466 U.S. 974 (1984). Since the creditor failed to adequately perfect under the state law requirements, the collateral interest of the creditor was "impotent with regard to rents until it is perfected." *Id.* at 445. The Court rejected the argument that § 363 was intended to preempt state law which traditionally determines property rights. *Id.* Further, if the lender's claim fails to qualify as a security interest under § 552(b), then it will not be successful under § 363. *Id.*

119. *See* Weg, *supra* note 111, at 19-25. When a creditor has failed to perfect, the creditor's collateral interest in the rents can be avoided by a debtor. *Id.* at 19. Thus, the creditor no longer has an enforceable interest in the rental payment, and the debtor has an unrestrained right to use the cash during its bankruptcy. *Id.*

120. *See* Great W. Life Assurance Co. v. Rothman (*In re* Ventura-Louise Properties), 490 F.2d 1141, 1145 (9th Cir. 1974) (finding assignment of rent upon default is not additional security but operates as transfer to mortgagee of

Road Associates, Ltd.,[121] the Bankruptcy Court for the Western District of Texas accepted the argument that when default occurred under an absolute assignment of rents as recognized by Texas law, the rents were no longer assets of the debtor and therefore were not collateral of any kind—cash or otherwise.[122] The actions of the debtor could be interpreted as a surrender, and consequently, the debtor could not use the rents for operating expenses. Many courts, however, viewed this analysis as based on a distinction without a difference because the documentation was provided to collateralize a loan.[123] In addition, an absolute assignment could be deemed to create an agency relationship between the lender and debtor which could lead to unwanted obligations of the lender to the debtor and third parties.[124]

Faced with the problems encountered in trying to sustain a lender's interest in rents in a chapter 11 situation, some courts considered whether certain postpetition actions could sustain this interest in the face of the automatic stay. In *Wolters Village, Ltd. v. Village Properties, Ltd. (In re Village Properties,*

---

mortgagor's right to collect upon happening of some event); *In re* Gould, 78 B.R. 590, 592-93 (D. Idaho 1987) (same); *see also* Vienna Park Properties v. United Postal Sav. Ass'n (*In re* Vienna Park Properties), 976 F.2d 106, 113 (2d Cir. 1992) (holding rent assignment clause under Virginia law qualifies as security interest even though absent actual possession); FDIC v. International Property Management, Inc., 929 F.2d 1033, 1034-35 (5th Cir. 1991) (concluding borrower under absolute assignment immediately transfers title to rents, but retains right to collect until default).

121. 64 B.R. 808 (Bankr. W.D. Tex. 1986).

122. *Id.* at 809.

123. *See In re* Polo Club Apartments Assocs. Ltd. Partnership, 150 B.R. 840, 850 (Bankr. N.D. Ga. 1993) ("[I]f an absolute conveyance by security deed does not convey an absolute estate as to title, an absolute conveyance by assignment of rents arising from the same property does not convey an absolute estate in the rents."); Northwestern Nat'l Life Ins. Co. v. Metro Square (*In re* Metro Square), 93 B.R. 990, 996 (Bankr. D. Minn. 1988) (concluding assignment was for collateral purposes as additional security), *rev'd*, 106 B.R. 584 (D. Minn. 1989); *In re* Prichard Plaza Assocs. Ltd. Partnership, 84 B.R. 289, 298 (Bankr. D. Mass. 1988) (holding mortgagee must take possession of property in order to have right to collect rents even if mortgagee has assignment of rents).

124. *See* Weg, *supra* note 111, at 35.

Ltd.),[125] the Fifth Circuit held that a lender's filing of a motion for relief from the stay was insufficient, without more, to perfect an interest in rents.[126] Subsequently, in *Casbeer v. State Federal Savings & Loan Ass'n of Lubbock (In re Casbeer)*,[127] the mortgagee filed motions for relief from the stay on several of Casbeer's properties and, before the hearing on the motions, filed additional motions seeking a temporary restraining order and temporary and permanent injunctions to prevent the debtor from using the rents from properties on which the mortgagee held deeds of trust containing rental assignment clauses.[128] The Fifth Circuit did not say which, if any, of the motions would be sufficient if filed alone, but found a basis for a mortgagee to perfect its assignment of rents under section 546(b).[129]

If "perfection" of an assignment of rents was deemed to qualify for protection under section 546(b), perfection could be accomplished postpetition by the mere filing of notice with the bankruptcy court. As a result, a lender would receive the benefit of section 362(b)(3), which provided that the filing of a petition does not operate as a stay "under subsection (a) of this section, of any act to perfect an interest in property to the extent that the trustee's rights and powers are subject to such perfection under section 546(b) of this title . . . ."[130] The issue then became whether state law pertaining to perfection

---

125. 723 F.2d 441 (5th Cir.), *cert. denied*, 466 U.S. 974 (1984).
126. *Id.* at 445-46.
127. 793 F.2d 1436 (5th Cir. 1986).
128. *Id.* at 1438.
129. *Id.* at 1442-43. Prior to the BRA, § 546(b) read:

> (b) The rights and powers of a trustee under sections 544, 545, and 549 of this title are subject to any generally applicable law that permits perfection of an interest in property to be effective against an entity that acquires rights in such property before the date of such perfection. If such law requires seizure of such property or commencement of an action to accomplish such perfection, and such property has not been seized or such action has not been commenced before the date of the filing of the petition, such interest in such property shall be perfected by notice within the time fixed by such law for such seizure or commencement.

11 U.S.C. § 546(b) (1988) (current version at 11 U.S.C. § 546(b) (1994)).
130. 11 U.S.C. § 362(b)(3) (1988). *See also* 4 COLLIER, *supra* note 82, ¶ 546.01.

of assignments of rents is the type of "generally applicable law" entitled to protection from section 546(b).

Reliance upon section 546(b) was challenged by a minority of courts and commentators who stressed that applicable state law did not specifically entitle "perfection" of an interest in rents to "relate back" to the time the interest was created.[131] These minority courts agreed that section 546(b) was intended to apply only to the UCC's concept of perfection and was designed to affirm the validity of certain UCC provisions that specifically allow retroactive effect, such as UCC section 9-301(2) concerning purchase money security interests.[132] At least one commentator expanded on this idea by pointing out that: (1) the purpose of section 546(b) was to remove certain actions from the trustee's power to avoid unperfected and postpetition transfers, and (2) the legislative history discusses these exceptions in terms of U.C.C. perfection that would necessarily occur when the assignment of rents was recorded, rendering section 546(b) inapplicable.[133]

If a lender could not protect itself by an absolute assignment of rents, by giving notice under section 546(b), or by taking other action to perfect its interest in rents postpetition, the lender had to endure the time-consuming and expensive process of seeking relief from the stay. During such time, the lender was deprived of its interest in the rents as "cash collateral" and, thus, these

---

131. *See, e.g.*, *In re* Multi-Group III Ltd. Partnership, 99 B.R. 5, 9 (Bankr. D. Ariz. 1989) (Arizona law); Northwestern Nat'l Life Ins. Co. v. Metro Square (*In re* Metro Square), 93 B.R. 990, 999-1000 (Bankr. D. Minn. 1988) (Minnesota law), *rev'd*, 106 B.R. 584 (D. Minn. 1989); *In re* TM Carlton House Partners, Ltd., 91 B.R. 349, 354-56 (Bankr. E.D. Pa. 1988) (Pennsylvania law); *In re* Association Ctr. Ltd. Partnership, 87 B.R. 142, 146 (Bankr. W.D. Wash. 1988) (Washington law); *In re* Prichard Plaza Assocs. Ltd. Partnership, 84 B.R. 289, 300-01 (Bankr. D. Mass. 1988) (Massachusetts law); Exchange Nat'l Bank v. Gotta (*In re* Gotta), 47 B.R. 198, 202 (Bankr. W.D. Wis. 1985) (Wisconsin law).

132. *See, e.g.*, Drummond v. Farm Credit Bank (*In re* Kurth Ranch), 110 B.R. 501, 507 (Bankr. D. Mont. 1990) (concluding § 546(b) was designed to affirm validity of statutes such as 9-301(2) of UCC); *TM Carlton House*, 91 B.R. at 355 (stating § 546(b) was to extend to narrow class of parties within scope of § 9-301(2) of UCC); *Prichard Plaza*, 84 B.R. at 301 (stating § 546(b) refers to concept of perfection such as that employed by UCC).

133. *See* LAURENCE D. CHERKIS, COLLIER REAL ESTATE TRANSACTION AND THE BANKRUPTCY CODE ¶ 2.03[1] (1989).

sums were often consumed by the debtor. Fortunately, there were several judicial decisions which approached the assignment of rents problem from a different perspective and showed the way toward a solution. A district court, in *New York Life Insurance Co. v. Bremer Towers*,[134] broke a stalemate between two previous bankruptcy court decisions in its district, and held that New York Life, as assignee of the mortgage and assignment of rents, had an interest in rents that qualified as cash collateral simply because its assignment was recorded in the public records.[135] The debtor asserted that the interest in rents was unperfected and inchoate because New York Life had failed to obtain the appointment of a receiver or take any other affirmative action to gain possession of the property.[136] The district court agreed with the decision in *In re Pavilion Place Associates*[137] and held that affirmative conduct was not necessary and that the requisite perfection had occurred at the time of recording.[138]

The *Bremer Towers* court correctly emphasized that a lender has a security interest in rents by virtue of an original agreement with the debtor. Upon recording, the interest is perfected in order to give notice to the world. A bankruptcy trustee or chapter 11 debtor-in-possession is deemed to have notice of such interest.[139] However, despite a perfected interest, the creditor must still take action to enforce its interest in the rents.[140] The court recognized the essential distinction between perfection in the *establishment* of an interest and perfection in the *enforcement* of an interest.[141] The distinction denies a debtor the fortuitous opportunity, presented when a chapter 11 petition is filed, to obstruct a lender's reliance upon an existing interest in rents under the guise

---

134. 714 F. Supp. 414 (D. Minn. 1989).
135. *Id.* at 419. "[T]he court finds that upon recordation of the mortgage and assignments of rents, New York Life perfected its security in the rents of Bremer Towers." *Id.*
136. *Id.* at 416.
137. 89 B.R. 36, 38-39 (Bankr. D. Minn. 1988) (holding that security interest is perfected upon recording).
138. *Bremer Towers*, 714 F. Supp. at 418-19.
139. *Id.* at 418.
140. *Id.*
141. *See id.* (noting that creditor's right to enforcement is stayed pending court's confirmation of perfected interest).

of preventing the creation of that interest.[142] Ten years earlier, the Supreme Court, in *Butner v. United States*,[143] held that enforcement of an interest in rents must be done in accordance with state law and alluded to the virtue of seeking "to prevent a party from receiving a 'windfall merely by reason of the happenstance of bankruptcy.'"[144] Although the Court did not favor the enforcement of rights which would not be available to a mortgagee but for the filing of bankruptcy, it also recognized the importance of a mortgagee's state law security interest.[145]

Following the *Bremer Towers* decision, *Capital Realty Investor Tax Exempt Fund Ltd. Partnership v. Greenhaven Village Apartments of Burnsville Phase II Ltd. Partnership (In re Greenhaven Village Apartments of Burnsville Phase II Ltd. Partnership)*,[146] held that a properly recorded assignment of rents was superior to the rights in rents acquired by a trustee or a chapter 11 debtor-in-possession in its status as a bona fide purchaser, or a judicial lien creditor at the commencement of the case. The interest in rents qualified as "cash collateral" under section 363(b) unless the interest was actually avoided by the trustee or debtor-in-possession through an adversary proceeding commenced for that purpose.[147] Other courts followed in recognizing the distinction between perfection and enforcement of a security interest, and placing a lender in the same relationship with the debtor concerning the rents that existed before the bankruptcy proceeding was commenced.[148]

---

142. *See id.* at 418 (commenting that creditor's efforts to perfect security interest can be easily frustrated by debtor's filing bankruptcy petition, thus triggering automatic stay preventing completion of requisite acts by creditor).
143. 440 U.S. 48 (1979).
144. *Id.* at 55 (citing Lewis v. Manufacturers Nat'l Bank, 364 U.S. 603, 609 (1961)).
145. *Id.* at 56 ("At the same time, our decision avoids the opposite inequity of depriving a mortgagee of his state law security interest when bankruptcy intervenes.")
146. 100 B.R. 465 (Bankr. D. Minn. 1989).
147. *Id.* at 471.
148. *See* Sears Sav. Bank v. Tucson Indus. Partners (*In re* Tucson Indus. Partners), 129 B.R. 614, 618-19 (Bankr. 9th Cir. 1991) (stating that upon filing petition debtor may not use rents unless request made to court and secured creditor is adequately protected), *dismissed as moot*, 990 F.2d 1099 (9th Cir. 1993); Midlantic Nat'l Bank v. Sourlis, 141 B.R. 826, 835 (D.N.J. 1992) (stating that

The states of California, Florida, Kansas, Maryland, North Carolina, Tennessee, Virginia, Washington, Nebraska, Louisiana, South Carolina, and Indiana enacted statutes declaring that the recording of an instrument which purports to assign an interest in rents fully perfects the interest in the assignee without requiring any further action.[149] Such statutory reform addressed the problem from the right direction, but there were variations among the states.[150] Even if an attempt had been made to enact a uniform state law, it is likely that significant differences would have existed among the states, and moreover, such statutes would have been subject to varying judicial interpretations.

In view of the problems encountered by the courts in dealing with the existing Code provisions and the difficulty in resolving such problems by amending or enacting state statutes dealing with perfection of an interest in

---

creditor with perfected lien may still have to take affirmative action to enforce lien); SLC Ltd. V v. Bradford Group W., Inc. (*In re* SLC Ltd. V), 152 B.R. 755 (Bankr. D. Utah 1993) (explaining difference between perfecting and enforcing security interest); *In re* Brandon Assocs., 128 B.R. 729, 732 (Bankr. W.D. Va. 1991) (indicating that mortgagor is entitled to rents until mortgagee obtains receiver or takes possession of property); *In re* KNM Roswell Ltd. Partnership, 126 B.R. 548, 552 (Bankr. N.D. Ill. 1991) (noting that filing perfects inchoate lien on rents); *In re* Rancourt, 123 B.R. 143, 147 (Bankr. D.N.H. 1991) (noting that creditor can enforce right to rents in several ways); *In re* Foxhill Place Assoc., 119 B.R. 708, 711-12 (Bankr. W.D. Mo. 1990) (noting distinction between perfection and enforcement).

149. CAL. CIV. CODE § 2938 (West 1995); FLA. STAT. ANN. § 697.07 (West 1995); IND. CODE ANN. § 32-1-2-16.3 (West 1995); KAN. STAT. ANN. § 58-2343 (1994); MD. REAL PROP. CODE ANN. § 3-204 (Michie 1994); NEB. REV. STAT. § 52-1704 (1994); N.C. GEN. STAT. § 47-20(c)-(d) (Michie 1994); S.C. CODE ANN. § 29-3-100 (Law Co-op. 1993); TENN. CODE ANN. § 66-26-116(a) (1995); VA. CODE ANN. § 55-220.1 (Michie 1995); WASH. REV. CODE ANN. § 7.28.230(3) (West 1995).

150. *See, e.g.*, LA. REV. STAT. ANN. § 9:4401:A(1)-(3) (West 1995) (indicating that assignment is perfected upon filing but enforcement requires notice to debtor); MICH. COMP. LAWS § 554.232 (West 1995) (perfecting interest upon recording but requiring additional acts for enforcement); *see also In re* Cadwell's Corners Partnership, 174 B.R. 744, 750-52 (Bankr. N.D. Ill. 1994) (requiring affirmative acts in addition to recording to perfect security interest otherwise interest is cash collateral which may be used by debtor for reorganization); *In re* Sansone, 126 B.R. 16, 19 (Bankr. D. Conn. 1991) (stating that mortgagee's right to rents is perfected at recording of mortgage).

rents, revision of the Code became the most logical solution to the problem. Support for that approach could be found in *Butner v. United States*,[151] in which the Court adopted the position taken by a majority of the Circuit Courts of Appeal, that the right to rents is determined by reference to state law.[152] However, the court further stated that Congress had the constitutional authority, though unexercised, to enact a statute defining a mortgagee's interest in rents and profits earned by property in a bankruptcy estate.[153] Significant and confusing differences had arisen among the states which detracted from the efficiency of a single federal statutory scheme such as the Code, and it was time for Congress to create a uniform rule that would rectify the inequity between lenders and debtors.

The BRA amended section 552 of the Code by dividing subsection (b) into two parts: Part (1) addresses the postpetition effect of security interests flowing from property of the debtor; Part (2) focuses on the postpetition effect of a creditor's interest in rents.[154] While the two parts are substantially similar in construction, the omission of "applicable nonbankruptcy law" in part (2) removes the necessity, for purposes of section 552, that a creditor meet various state law requirements related to legal possession of rents, or "perfection" in the enforcement (rather than notice) sense. Therefore, as long as the requirements of section 552(b)(2) are met, rents can qualify for treatment as cash collateral under section 363.[155] With the deletion of "applicable nonbankruptcy law," Congress has left it to the provisions of a security agreement, mortgage or trust agreement executed by a debtor to determine whether an interest in rents has been adequately identified in order to qualify for treatment as cash collateral.[156] By eliminating from consideration many of the vagaries of state law, Congress has moved to standardize the treatment of rents in bankruptcy proceedings. The effect of decisions such as *In re Multi-Group III Ltd. Partnership*[157] which required that a lender obtain legal

151. 440 U.S. 48 (1979).
152. *Id.* at 54.
153. *Id.* at 54 (citing U.S. CONST. art. I, § 8, cl. 4).
154. 11 U.S.C. § 552(b) (1994).
155. *See id.* § 363(a) (defining cash collateral).
156. *See id.* § 552(b) (providing that absent applicability of other Code sections security agreement controls).
157. 99 B.R. 5 (Bankr. D. Ariz. 1989).

possession of property by the appointment of a receiver,[158] and *In re Prichard Plaza Associates Ltd. Partnership*[159] which required actual possession of the property by entry thereon[160] has been lessened without ignoring the concerns of the *Multi Group* and *Prichard Plaza* courts regarding the harm to a debtor if rents are accorded treatment as cash collateral.[161] The final limiting phrase of original section 552(b) "except to any extent that the court, after notice and a hearing and based on the equities of the case, orders otherwise" has been retained so that a court is expressly empowered to balance the interests of a creditor against other interests, including a debtor's possible rehabilitation, the preservation of jobs, and the payment of taxes.[162] Section 552(b)(2) has also retained the original prefatory language granting exceptions for the provisions of sections 363, 506(c), 522, 544, 545, 547 and 548,[163] which offer protection for the debtor.

Under section 363, rents which qualify as cash collateral may be made available for use by a debtor with the consent of a lender *or* approval by the court conditioned upon "adequate protection" for a lender.[164] In a typical case, the court may permit a debtor to use rents to cover operating expenses and maintenance of the property with any remaining balance paid to the lender or held in a segregated account pending the outcome of the reorganization proceeding.[165] The reference in section 552(b)(2) to section 506(c), which permits recovery from property held as collateral of the reasonable and necessary costs and expenses of preserving that collateral, creates the

---

158. *Id.* at 7 (stating that appointment of a receiver is one method of enforcing assignment of rents).
159. 84 B.R. 289 (Bankr. D. Mass. 1988).
160. *Id.* at 301 (holding that because bank did not take possession of property, security interest was inchoate).
161. *Multi Group*, 99 B.R. at 7; *Prichard Plaza*, 84 B.R. at 293 (noting that debtor may not use rents characterized as cash collateral unless each entity with an interest consents; thus, debtor's reorganization may be impaired if left without access to rents).
162. 11 U.S.C. § 552(b) (1994).
163. *Id.* § 552(b)(2).
164. *Id.* § 363(a), (e).
165. *See, e.g.*, McCombs Properties VI, Ltd. v. First Tex. Sav. Ass'n (*In re* McCombs Properties VI, Ltd.), 88 B.R. 261, 267 (Bankr. C.D. Cal. 1988) (allowing debtor to use cash collateral for maintenance of property with any excess going to secured creditor).

possibility of deducting from the rent the cost of utilities, repairs, payroll and other operating expenses of a debtor.[166] The reference to section 522 means that certain property of the debtor which is exempted from the bankruptcy estate cannot be adversely affected by the treatment of rents as cash collateral.[167]

The remaining sections referenced in section 552(b)(2), enable a trustee to use its avoiding powers under certain circumstances. Section 544,[168] which gives a trustee or debtor the rights and powers of a judicial lien creditor as of the commencement of the case, may enable the avoidance of a security interest in rents created by a security agreement, mortgage or deed of trust which has not been perfected by recording in the appropriate public office.[169] In addition, the trustee also retains the power to avoid statutory liens,[170] preferences,[171] and fraudulent transfers.[172] Retention of these powers should preclude unfair treatment of a debtor which would result from the recording of any security instrument as a preferential or fraudulent transfer prior to the commencement of a bankruptcy proceeding.

The argument that inclusion of section 544 may enable a return to state law whereby a debtor may retain rents which have not been "perfected" in the enforcement sense, or for purposes of determining whether a security interest "extends to property" under revised section 552(b), should be rejected. The legislative intent underlying section 552(b), and the balancing of interests enacted into such provision clearly demonstrates that lenders may have valid security interests in postpetition rents for bankruptcy purposes, notwithstanding their failure to have fully perfected their security interest under applicable state law.[173] Section 552(b) has levelled the playing field between debtor and creditors by preventing a debtor from avoiding a creditor's

---

166. 11 U.S.C. § 552(b)(2) (1994).
167. *See id.* § 522 (delineating exemptions).
168. *Id.* § 544.
169. *See supra* note 140 and accompanying text (discussing perfection of interests in assignment of rents when properly recorded).
170. 11 U.S.C. § 545 (1994).
171. *Id.* § 547.
172. *Id.* § 548.
173. H.R. REP. NO. 835, 103d Cong., 2d Sess. 49 (1994), *reprinted in* 1994 U.S.C.C.A.N. 3340, 3357-58 (stating that amendment to § 552 would apply to lenders with secured interests in underlying property and postpetition rents).

bargained for interest in rents, but it does not allow a creditor to summarily wrest control of the rents from the debtor.

The BRA made another significant change with its enactment of section 552(b)(2) by extending its coverage beyond rents to "the fees, charges, accounts, or other payments for the use or occupancy of rooms and other public facilities in hotels, motels, or other lodging properties."[174] The same phrase was added to section 363(a) in order to expand the definition of "cash collateral" to include such interests.[175] These amendments were necessitated by judicial decisions declaring that postpetition hotel revenues were not rents entitled to treatment as cash collateral in accordance with the provisions of sections 552 and 363, but rather were personal property accounts, subject to the state law perfection requirements of the UCC and were unenforceable postpetition pursuant to section 552.[176] A split arose as to whether hotel revenues were rents to be treated as "cash collateral" under section 363.[177] Since the revenue generated by a hotel is an essential component of the value of a hotel as collateral for a lender, decisions that such revenues were not rents had a disastrous effect upon hotel financing. Congress again sought to recognize and respect the interests of both the debtor and its creditors.

These revenue streams, while critical to a hotel's continued operation, are also the most liquid and most valuable collateral the hotel can provide to its financiers. When the hotel experiences financial distress, the interests of the hotel operations, including employment for clerks, maids, and other workers can collide with the interests of persons to whom the revenues are pledged.

---

174. 11 U.S.C. § 552(b)(2) (1994).

175. *See id.* § 363(a) (utilizing same language as § 552(b)(2)).

176. *See, e.g., In re* Majestic Motel Assocs., 131 B.R. 523, 526 (Bankr. D. Me. 1991) (holding motel revenues are not rents, but profits derived from incidental services furnished to guests).

177. *See In re* Corpus Christi Hotel Partners, Ltd., 133 B.R. 850, 854 (Bankr. S.D. Tex. 1991) (holding hotel revenues are not rent); Kearney Hotel Partners v. Richardson (*In re* Kearney Hotel Partners), 92 B.R. 95, 99 (Bankr. S.D.N.Y. 1988) (same). *Contra* T-H New Orleans Ltd. Partnership v. Financial Sec. Assurance, Inc. (*In re* T-H New Orleans Ltd. Partnership), 10 F.3d 1099, 1105 (5th Cir. 1993) (holding hotel revenues are rents), *cert. denied*, 114 S. Ct. 1833 (1994); *In re* Churchill Properties VIII Ltd. Partnership, 164 B.R. 607, 608-09 (Bankr. N.D. Ill. 1994) (same); *In re* S.F. Drake Hotel Assocs., 131 B.R. 156, 160-61 (Bankr. N.D. Cal. 1991) (same), *aff'd*, 147 B.R. 538 (N.D. Cal. 1992).

Section 215 of the House Report recognizes the importance of this revenue stream for the two competing interests and attempts to strike a fair balance between them.[178]

Thus, all of the safeguards discussed above, including the "equities of the case" provision in section 552(b)(2),[179] use of cash collateral with adequate protection under section 363,[180] payment of operating expenses under section 506(c),[181] and the avoiding powers of sections 544, 545, 547 and 548 are available to a hotel borrower.[182]

At least one court has focused on the language used to define hotel revenues in sections 552(b)(2) and 363 and in dicta found "convincing" a debtor's argument that any interests not specifically included have been deliberately left out.[183] In view of the clear legislative intent to balance the interests of the debtor and its creditors and the safeguards included in section 552(b) to accomplish that end, it would seem inappropriate to upset that balance by such a restrictive reading of the language used by Congress to define hotel revenues.

Conclusion

The BRA amendments discussed in this Chapter have been intended to reduce, in a manner which balances the interests of all of the participants in a chapter 11 reorganization proceeding, the costly and harmful delays resulting from futile single asset real estate cases and from debilitating contests over a lender's interest in rents.

Prior to the amendments, lenders often endured a lengthy and expensive process to gain relief from the automatic stay in order to enforce their rights as holders of secured interests in single asset real estate in cases wherein there was no possibility of a successful reorganization. The amendments to section 362 removed inequities in the system which had prolonged the process to the detriment of all parties involved, by adopting a pragmatic approach to the critical determination of whether a reorganization proceeding is worthwhile.

---

178. H.R. REP. NO. 835, *supra* note 173, *reprinted in* 1994 U.S.C.C.A.N. at 3358.
179. 11 U.S.C. § 552(b)(2) (1994).
180. *Id.* § 363.
181. *Id.* § 506(c).
182. *Id.* §§ 544, 545, 547 and 548.
183. *In re* Brandywine River Hotel, Inc., 177 B.R. 10, 15 (Bankr. E.D. Pa. 1995).

Under section 362, as amended, a single asset real estate debtor is allowed a reasonable but finite period of time to propose a feasible plan of reorganization, and may not further delay the process without making compensatory payments to secured lenders in order to continue to receive the protection afforded by the automatic stay.

The amendment to section 522(b) brought much needed certainty and uniformity to a situation in which inconsistent state laws and judicial decisions often confused requirements for the establishment as compared to the enforcement of a lender's secured interest in rents, and engendered costly legal conflicts which only hindered any possibility of a successful reorganization. The amendment removed inequities in the system by recognizing, and preventing a bankruptcy debtor's avoidance of, a bargained for interest in rents contained in a security agreement, while retaining the debtor's ability to utilize the rents within the constraints which the Code accords to "cash collateral."[184]

Changes such as those embodied in the amendments discussed in this Chapter, are necessary if the Code is to deal effectively with the increased number and variety of chapter 11 reorganization proceedings in order to retain the confidence of the participants in the utility and fairness of the bankruptcy process.

---

184. *See generally* 11 U.S.C. § 362 (1994) (defining "cash collateral").

CHAPTER XII

THE LEGISLATIVE RESPONSE TO SINGLE ASSET REAL ESTATE BANKRUPTCIES: AN UPDATED CRITICAL ANALYSIS AND SOME SUGGESTIONS

HON. ROGER M. WHELAN

The introduction of section 211 of the Omnibus Bankruptcy Reform Legislation marked the beginning of single asset real estate cases.[1] The bill, originally sponsored by Senators Heflin and Grassley,[2] unanimously passed the United States Senate on June 17, 1992.[3] Because of House opposition,

---

1. S. 1985, 102d Cong., 2d Sess. (1992).
2. *See* 137 CONG. REC. S17,047 (daily ed. Nov. 19, 1991).
3. *See* 138 CONG. REC. S8331-59 (daily ed. June 17, 1992). The original provisions of § 211 of S. 1985 represented the desire of the United States Senate to force single asset real estate cases on to a fast-track basis in order to prevent economic prejudice to the secured creditors' when attempting to liquidate collateral after the debtor's default. The original proposed amendments to the Bankruptcy Code regarding single asset real estate cases began with the following definition to § 101(54):

   > "single asset real estate" means real property, other than residential real property with fewer than 4 residential units, which generates substantially all of the gross income of a debtor and on which no business is being conducted by a debtor other than the business of operating the real property and activities incidental thereto[.]

   S. 1985, 102d Cong., 2d Sess. § 211(a)(2) (1992) (version #2 May 7, 1992).

   Amendments to 11 U.S.C. § 362 added specific grounds for relief from the automatic stay. One such suggested amendment stated:

   > (3) with respect to a stay of an act against real property under subsection (a), if the property is single asset real estate, and the debtor has not, within 90 days after the filing of a petition under [§]

section 211 was deleted from S. 1985 after an expedited House-Senate conference meeting during the week of October 5, 1992, and the revised Senate Bill which passed the Senate on October 7, 1992 did not include the single asset amendments.[4] Due to the pressure of election year concerns, and because of a dispute respecting amendments dealing with retiree benefits, the House adjourned on October 8, 1992 without any substantive bankruptcy legislation having been passed.[5] Subsequently, the Senate introduced S. 540

> 301 or [§] 302 of this title, or the entry of an order for relief under [§] 303 of this title, filed a plan of reorganization which has a reasonable possibility of being confirmed within a reasonable period of time, or the debtor has commenced payment to the holder of a claim secured by such real property of interest on a monthly basis at a current fair market rate on the value of the creditor's secured interest in such property. The court may extend such 90-day period only for cause and only if an order granting such an extension is entered within such 90-day period[.]

Id. § 211(b)(1)(C).

Finally, 11 U.S.C. § 362 would have been amended to add a provision allowing limited continuation of foreclosure proceedings in the postpetition period as § 362(i):

> (i) Upon request of a party in interest in a case under this title in which the property of the estate is single asset real estate, the court, with or without a hearing, shall grant such limited relief from a stay provided under subsections (a)(1), (a)(3), and (a)(4) of this section, as is necessary to allow such party in interest to proceed during the pendency of the case under this title with a foreclosure proceeding, whether judicial or nonjudicial, which had been commenced before a petition was filed under this title, up to but not including the point of sale of such real property.

Id. § 211(b)(2).

4. *See* S. 1985, 102d Cong., 2d Sess. (1992).

5. For a discussion of the concern over retirees' health care benefits, see 138 CONG. REC. S18,250-602 (daily ed. Oct. 8, 1992); *see also* Jane Lee Vris, *Recent Development in Single Asset Cases*, *in* CURRENT DEVELOPMENT IN BANKRUPTCY AND REORGANIZATION 1993 (PLI Com. L. & Prac. Course Handbook Series, 1993), *available in* WESTLAW, 656 PLI/Comm 527, *63-63 (commenting that Omnibus Bankruptcy Reform Legislation Bill almost passed in final hours of 1992 Congressional session, but was defeated because

which again reintroduced the single asset provisions originally set forth in S. 1985.[6] However, although the substance of the new provisions tracked the predecessor bill, the definition of "single asset real estate" was further clarified by adding the words "constituting a single property or project."[7] The House did not take up consideration of S. 540 until late in September 1994 and again the provisions dealing with single asset real estate cases faced strong opposition.[8] The original House Bill, H.R. 5116 (superseding S. 540), further limited the definition of single asset real estate cases by limiting the provisions to those debtors having "aggregate noncontingent, liquidated secured debts in an amount up to $2,000,000."[9] In addition, while the remaining sections of H.R. 5116 tracked S. 540, any order for relief from the stay could not be entered by the court until at least 30 days after the entry of the order for relief in such a single asset case.[10] In addition, the relief from stay motion, when filed, could have been granted without the necessity of a hearing, unless the debtor objected and set forth "extraordinary circumstances requiring such a hearing."[11] Furthermore, the provisions permitting continuation of foreclosure proceedings in the postpetition period were deleted.[12] As a result of final meetings between the House and Senate committee staff, the final version of the single asset provisions emerged.[13]

---

of adverse response to last minute amendment granting retiree health benefits priority over creditors of chapter 11 debtors).

6. S. 540, 103d Cong., 1st Sess. (1993).
7. *Id.* § 202(a).
8. 140 CONG. REC. S14,461-64 (daily ed. Oct. 6, 1994).
9. *See* H.R. REP. NO. 835, 103d Cong., 2d Sess. 50 (1994), *reprinted in* 1994 U.S.C.C.A.N. 3340, 3359.
10. *Id.*
11. *Id.*
12. The single asset provisions were then set forth as § 219 of Title II - Commercial Bankruptcy Issues, in the newly introduced H.R. 5116. H.R. 5116, 103d Cong., 2d Sess. § 219 (1994).
13. The legislation was then forwarded to the White House and President Clinton signed "The Bankruptcy Reform Act of 1994" into law on October 22, 1994. Bankruptcy Reform Act of 1994, Pub. L. No. 103-394, 108 Stat. 4106. The provisions pertaining to the single asset real estate provisions then became applicable to all such cases as defined on October 22, 1994, and thereafter. *Id.* Section 101(51B) now reads as follows:

    (51B) "single asset real estate" means real property constituting

A review of the original legislative history may be helpful in discerning the general purpose of this legislation. Senate Report 102-279 states:

> Section 211 would create a statutory definition for "single asset real estate," that is limited to investment property of the debtor. Further, residential real estate with fewer than four units is excluded from such definition. Such "single asset real estate" must be held by an entity, whether an individual, partnership, or corporation, as an enterprise conducted at least in part on the real estate, and constitutes the sole or primary asset of that entity.[14]

This provision amends section 362(d):

> to provide for the termination of the automatic stay 90 days after the commencement of a chapter 11 proceeding involving single asset real

---

> a single property or project, other than residential real property with fewer than 4 residential units, which generates substantially all of the gross income of a debtor and on which no substantial business is being conducted by a debtor other than the business of operating real property and activities incidental thereto having aggregate non-contingent, liquidated secured debts in an amount no more than $4,000,000.

11 U.S.C. § 101(51B) (1994). Additionally, there were changes made to the automatic stay provisions. Section 362(d)(3) now reads:

> [W]ith respect to a stay of an act against single asset real estate under subsection (a), by a creditor whose claim is secured by an interest in such real estate, unless, not later than the date that is 90 days after the entry of the order for relief (or such later date as the court may determine for cause by order entered within that 90-day period)–
>
> (A) the debtor has filed a plan of reorganization that has a reasonable possibility of being confirmed within a reasonable time; or
>
> (B) the debtor has commenced monthly payments to each creditor whose claim is secured by such real estate (other than a claim secured by a judgment lien or by an unmatured statutory lien), which payments are in an amount equal to interest at a current fair market rate on the value of the creditor's interest in the real estate.

11 U.S.C. § 362(d)(3) (1994).

14. S. REP. NO. 279, 102d Cong., 2d Sess. 37 (1992).

estate if the debtor has not filed a feasible plan of reorganization, or in the alternative, the debtor may commence payment of interest at a fair market rate on the value of the real property held as collateral. This amendment ensures that the automatic stay provision is not abused, while giving a debtor a reasonable opportunity to create a workable plan of reorganization.[15]

While this legislation is clearly a significant step in the right direction with respect to the myriad of problems associated with single asset real estate bankruptcy cases,[16] unfortunately, the legislation as finally passed creates far too many problems. Therefore, the amendments may only be marginally beneficial in addressing the problems confronting the nation's courts with respect to single asset cases. This Chapter will examine some of the problems which are likely to arise in filings, some of which have already been confronted by the bankruptcy courts.

A. Preliminary Issues

1. Eligibility

Initially, based on the language employed in section 101(51B),[17] issues of eligibility have already arisen as to whether or not a given type of business operation is subject to the single asset real estate provisions.[18] In the first

---

15. *Id.*
16. *See In re* Philmont Dev. Co., 181 B.R. 220, 224 (Bankr. E.D. Pa. 1995) (holding limited partnership's series of semidetached houses constituted "single project" within definition of single asset real estate); *In re* Kkemko, Inc., 181 B.R. 47, 50-51 (Bankr. S.D. Ohio 1995) (holding that marina was "business" as compared to "real estate held for income," and therefore not entitled to "single asset real estate" treatment); CMF Loudoun Ltd. Partnership v. Nattchase Assocs. Ltd. Partnership (*In re* Nattchase Assocs. Ltd. Partnership), 178 B.R. 409, 416 (Bankr. E.D. Va. 1994) (finding single asset debtor's egregious behavior constituted "cause" for relief from automatic stay).
17. 11 U.S.C. § 101(51B) (1994).
18. *See, e.g., In re* Oceanside Mission Assocs., 192 B.R. 232, 234-35 (Bankr. S.D. Cal. 1996) (interpreting § 101(51B) to exclude raw undeveloped land which generates no income but stated in dicta that language is ambiguous).

reported decision dealing with this issue, *In re Kkemko, Inc.*,[19] the court determined that the debtor's marina business was not the type of business operation intended to be dealt with as a "single asset real estate" case.[20] The judge's ruling was predicated on the fact that the marina had other sources of income from storage fees, repairs and the sale of gas which were not directly related to the operation of the real property.[21] In other words, where a significant source of income is derived from sources independent of the real property, the "single asset" sections are not likely to apply. As a result, farming operations, hospitals and related type businesses which will often be based on "real property constituting a single property or project"[22] will not be eligible within this definition because there will be "substantial business . . . being conducted by a debtor other than the business of operating the real property . . . ."[23]

An additional issue will naturally arise because of the debt limitation inserted in the definition which limits the substantive provisions of the single asset real estate case to those debtors "having aggregate noncontingent, liquidated secured debts in an amount no more than $4,000,000."[24] The initial question arises as to whether the $4,000,000 figure relates to an aggregate

---

19. *Kkemko,* 181 B.R. at 49-50. Another interesting development concerning the interpretation of the definition set forth in § 101(51B) can be found in *Philmont.* In *Philmont* the debtor argued that its assets, which consisted of partnership interests in three limited partnerships and two other undeveloped building lots, did not constitute a "single asset real estate" case. *Philmont,* 181 B.R. at 224. The court overruled the debtor's contention because of the words "single property or *project.*" *Id.* at 223-24 (emphasis added). The court held that the definition would include either single properties or single projects even though the houses in this case were semi-detached homes operated by each limited partnership. *Id.* at 224-25.
20. *Kkemko*, 181 B.R. at 51.
21. *Id.*
22. 11 U.S.C. § 101(51B) (1994).
23. *Id.*; *see Kkemko*, 181 B.R. at 51 (noting common meaning of single asset real estate as "a building or buildings which were intended to be income producing, or raw land" was intended by Congress).
24. 11 U.S.C. § 101(51B) (1994). In February, 1996, a technical amendment bill, S. 1559, was referred to the Senate Judiciary Committee which would delete this monetary limitation. *Sens. Grassley, Heflin, Introduce Bankruptcy "Technical Corrections" Bill*, BNA BANKR. L. DAILY, Feb. 15, 1996, at D4.

total of secured debt of no more than $4,000,000, or whether the $4,000,000 relates to the secured claim or claims as customarily treated and defined under section 506(a) of the Code.[25] In the event that bankruptcy courts adopt the latter interpretation, an evaluation hearing of some type will be required in order to ascertain the value of the real property at issue.[26] In applying the plain language of the statute, the reference to "secured *debts*"[27] would seem to indicate that the former approach of looking to the aggregate total of secured debt, is the correct and more practical one to follow in determining whether the aggregate secured debt is "no more than $4,000,000."[28]

2. Relief from Stay

Another issue likely to arise concerns the right of secured creditors to file a motion for relief from stay prior to the expiration of the initial 90-day period after commencement of the order for relief.[29] In other words, is the secured creditor limited to seeking relief from the stay only after 90 days from the commencement of a voluntary case, or after entry for an order for relief in an involuntary case? It would appear from a complete review of the applicable provisions set forth under section 362(d)(3) that a motion for relief from the stay may be filed at any time within the 90-day period, but is subject to the express conditions set forth under (A) and (B) of section 362(d)(3).[30] At any

---

25. 11 U.S.C. §§ 101(51B), 506(a) (1994); *see In re* Philmont Dev. Co., 181 B.R. 220, 223 (Bankr. E.D. Pa. 1995) (implying that court would look to aggregate secured debt if necessary).
26. FED. R. BANKR. P. 3012 (establishing that court may determine value of secured claim); *In re* Pourtless, 93 B.R. 23, 25 (Bankr. W.D.N.Y. 1988) (noting valuation hearing of secured property is anticipated by court under 11 U.S.C. § 506(a)).
27. 11 U.S.C. § 101(51B) (1994) (emphasis added).
28. *Id.*
29. *Id.* § 362(d)(3) (stating that relief from stay will be granted to secured creditor of single asset real estate so long as 90 days from entry of order for relief has elapsed).
30. *Id.* § 362(d)(3)(A), (B). The statute generally provides that relief from the stay shall be granted to a secured creditor with a secured interest in the asset of a single asset real estate. *Id.* If however, the debtor filed a plan of reorganization that is likely to be approved, or has begun monthly payments to all creditors, then relief from stay will not be granted. *Id.* There is no express statutory

rate, where the secured creditor is confronted with a situation involving "irreparable damage" (e.g., waste by the debtor, failure to maintain insurance, etc.) to the interest of an entity in property, relief may always be obtained pursuant to section 362(f).[31]

The essence of the new single asset real estate provisions is set forth in section 362(d)(3).[32] The amended statute provides the debtor with a 90-day time period within which to file a plan or to commence monthly payments on the secured claim associated with the real property held by the debtor.[33] Clearly, the new amendments to section 362(d) evidence an intention by Congress to expedite the plan process in a single asset real estate bankruptcy case, or to compensate the secured creditor for the use of the real property during the case.[34] This legislation signals real improvement over what was previously section 362(d); however, in attempting not to shift the balance of power too far in favor of the secured creditor, and by imposing a monetary limit which has no real significance, in addition to other delay factors present in this legislation, the single asset real estate provisions are not likely to achieve fully the stated legislative goal. These distinct problems relate to the ability of the debtor to secure delay beyond the stated 90-day time period. The legislation is ambiguous because of reference to "monthly payments . . . in an amount equal to interest at a current fair market rate on the value of the creditor's interest in the real estate."[35] The context of a single asset real estate bankruptcy case under the new amendments will ultimately depend upon the debtor's ability and/or desire to pay interest (or some other compensatory

---

language in the new subsection (3) which states when a motion for relief from stay may be filed. *Id.*

31. *Id.* § 362(f) (allowing ex parte relief from stay if irreparable harm would otherwise result from stay). However, "it is unlikely that *ex parte* relief will be necessary in any but the most infrequent cases." 2 COLLIER ON BANKRUPTCY ¶ 362.09 (Lawrence P. King ed., 15th ed. 1995).

32. 11 U.S.C. § 362(d)(3) (1994).

33. *Id.* § 362(a)(3)(A), (B); *see* H.R. REP. NO. 835, *supra* note 9, at 50, *reprinted in* 1994 U.S.C.C.A.N. 3340, 3359.

34. *See* H.R. REP. NO. 835, *supra* note 9, at 32-34, *reprinted in* 1994 U.S.C.C.A.N. at 3340-42 (noting goals of proposed bill was to "increase efficiency of bankruptcy process and resolve some uncertainties regarding application of the Code," and more specifically to expedite hearings concerning automatic stay).

35. 11 U.S.C. § 362(d)(3)(B) (1994).

payment) on the secured claims against the single asset real estate project. The following discussion will address how litigation might unfold in the context of single asset real estate bankruptcy cases where the debtor has the intention and ability to pay interest, and in instances where the debtor lacks such intention or ability.

B. Cases Where the Debtor Lacks Ability and/or Intention to Pay Interest on Secured Claims

Much of the frustration created by single asset real estate bankruptcy cases is due to the secured creditor's perception that the debtor, through the use of chapter 11, can significantly delay foreclosure proceedings without offering any meaningful compensation to the secured creditor for the use of collateral pending such delay.[36] Often the secured creditor finds itself in an undersecured position, entitled to no interest or other form of adequate protection except upon a showing that the property is declining in value.[37] Moreover, the secured creditor may or may not be entitled to the rental income stream as cash collateral, even with the increased protection available under the provisions of section 552(b)(2) because in many instances the court, "based on the equities of the case," will order that the rents be applied to meet the continued maintenance needs of the asset. [38]

---

36. *See* 9281 Shore Rd. Owners Corp. v. Seminole Realty Co. (*In re* 9281 Shore Rd. Owners Corp.), 187 B.R. 837, 852-65 (E.D.N.Y. 1995) (reversing bankruptcy court decision granting relief from automatic stay and recognizing equitable nature of chapter 11 proceedings); *In re* Clinton Fields, Inc., 168 B.R. 265, 270-71 (Bankr. M.D. Ga. 1994) (holding chapter 11 proceeding filed in good faith would not be dismissed even though commenced on eve of creditor starting foreclosure); *In re* Mitan, 168 B.R. 326, 329-30 (Bankr. E.D. Mich. 1994) (finding chapter 11 proceeding commenced with intention to stall foreclosure proceedings thereby dismissing for bad faith). The court looked to the purpose of chapter 11 reorganization which is to provide debtor with a fresh start, not "to forestall the creditors' efforts to collect their debts." *Id.* at 330.
37. *See* United Sav. Ass'n v. Timbers of Inwood Forest Assoc., 484 U.S. 365, 370 (1988) (holding undersecured creditor entitled to postpetition interest only to extent that creditor's interest in property is declining in value).
38. 11 U.S.C. § 552(b)(2) (1994); *see In re* Creekstone Apartments Assocs., L.P., No. 92-04511, 1995 Bankr. LEXIS 552, at *80-81 (Bankr. M.D. Tenn. Sept.

Meanwhile the secured creditor may not be able to obtain relief from the stay because the real estate is essential to the debtor's reorganization. Thus, the secured creditor would not be able to demonstrate that there is a sufficiently low likelihood that the debtor can confirm a plan of reorganization in order to justify the court's effectively terminating the debtor's reorganization efforts by lifting the automatic stay.[39] The secured creditor may also find itself

---

18, 1995) (allowing rents to be reinvested in building); 5028 Wisconsin Ave. Assocs. Ltd. Partnership v. Copy King, Inc. (*In re* 5028 Wisconsin Ave. Assocs. Ltd. Partnership), 167 B.R. 699, 706 (Bankr. D.D.C. 1994) (recognizing debtors limited right of access to rents to operate and maintain building).

39. See 11 U.S.C. § 362(d)(2) (1994). In *Timbers*, the Supreme Court addressed the rights of an undersecured creditor in a single asset real estate bankruptcy case in the context of a motion to lift stay for lack of adequate protection under 11 U.S.C. §§ 361, 362(d)(1). *Timbers*, 484 U.S. at 365. In the process of determining that the undersecured creditor was not entitled to interest on its secured claim during the pendency of the case, the Court also considered the consequences of its decision on stay litigation in single asset real estate bankruptcy cases. *Id.* at 375-76. If the undersecured creditor cannot prove that the single asset real estate collateral is declining in value and is denied the ability to demand interest as compensation for delay, the creditor is powerless in seeking relief from the stay under § 362(d)(1). *Id.* at 371 (noting that although Code was amended, relevant statute remains unchanged). Further, since the single asset real estate unquestionably is "essential for an effective reorganization," relief from the stay would not be available under § 362(d)(2). *Id.* at 375-76. Thus, the secured creditor would have no ability to liquidate its collateral except through contesting plan confirmation or seeking conversion to chapter 7 or dismissal of the bankruptcy case. Experience teaches that this process could take a year or longer. The Court recognized this dilemma and sought to adjust the debtor/creditor balance of power in the bankruptcy case by adding a gloss to the "necessary to an effective reorganization" language in § 362(d)(2). *Timbers*, 365 U.S. at 376. The Court noted that the stay should be lifted to allow an unsecured creditor to foreclose on single asset real estate collateral where there is no plan in prospect, meaning that there is no "reasonable possibility of a successful reorganization within a reasonable time." *Id.* It is interesting to note that this language has been incorporated almost verbatim into § 362(d)(3). 11 U.S.C. § 362(d)(3) (1994). As such, that aspect of the proposed § 362(d)(3) is merely a codification of the current interpretation of § 362(d)(2). *But see Mitan*, 168 B.R. at 329-30 (granting

in the position of holding an oversecured claim where the court will deny payment of interest on its claim, finding that the equity in the property is sufficient adequate protection for the creditor's secured claim.[40] Situations where the debtor has no desire or ability to pay interest frequently arise when the single asset real estate involved is raw land,[41] property with a vacant commercial development,[42] or property on which there is construction in progress.[43] The amendments to section 362(d)(3) seek to ameliorate these situations by requiring the debtor to pay interest in order to obtain delay through a chapter 11 proceeding.[44]

A careful reading of section 362(d)(3) raises a question as to whether the referenced monthly payments due to the secured creditor are "interest at a

---

creditor relief from automatic stay because of bad faith filing of chapter 11 petition by debtor).

40. A significant number of cases have held, where property is not declining in value, an oversecured creditor has no interest in preserving the equity cushion and is not entitled to payments to offset accruing interest which erodes the equity cushion. Rather the equity cushion alone is "adequate protection" and even if payments are made by the debtor, such payments should be offset against the amount of equity cushion existing at any given time in order to ensure that the secured creditor does not, under any circumstances, receive postpetition payments in excess of the value of its collateral. *See* Westchase I Assocs., L.P. v. Lincoln Nat'l Life Ins. Co. (*In re* Westchase I Assocs., L.P.), 126 B.R. 692, 694-95 (W.D.N.C. 1991); *In re* Senior Care Properties, Inc., 137 B.R. 527, 528-29 (Bankr. N.D. Fla. 1992); *In re* Belmont Realty Corp., 113 B.R. 118, 121 (Bankr. D.R.I. 1990); *In re* Lane, 108 B.R. 6, 8-9 (Bankr. D. Mass. 1989); *In re* Chauncy St. Assoc. Ltd. Partnership, 107 B.R. 7, 8 (Bankr. D. Mass. 1989); McCombs Properties VI, Ltd. v. First Tex. Sav. Ass'n (*In re* McCombs Properties VI, Ltd.), 88 B.R. 261, 265-66 (Bankr. C.D. Cal. 1988).

41. *See, e.g.*, First Am. Bank v. Monica Rd. Assocs. (*In re* Monica Rd. Assocs.), 147 B.R. 385, 386 (Bankr. E.D. Va. 1992) (granting relief from stay for single asset debtor involving "raw land").

42. Humble Place Joint Venture v. Fory (*In re* Humble Place Joint Venture), 936 F.2d 814, 815 (5th Cir. 1991) ("would-be commercial development" chapter 11 case).

43. *See Monica*, 147 B.R. at 388-89 (discussing costs required to complete development of property).

44. 11 U.S.C. § 362(d)(3) (1994) (requiring that stay be lifted unless debtor filed plan or has begun to make monthly payments to secured creditors).

current fair market rate" or payments "in an amount equal to interest at a current fair market rate."[45] Consequently, a dilemma is created because of the holding in the *Timbers* case which expressly prohibits the payment of interest to an undersecured creditor.[46] Ironically, if this is deemed to be an interest payment, a secured creditor with a claim less than $4,000,000 will receive interest, even where such creditor is undersecured, whereas a secured creditor with a claim greater than $4,000,000 will not be entitled to interest payments, assuming they are in an undersecured position.[47] The legislative history is not entirely clear because the original statement set forth in the Senate Report 102-279, states that: "the debtor may commence *payment of interest at a fair market rate* on the value of the real property held as collateral."[48] Ironically, the House Congressional Record merely states as follows: "[i]t amends the automatic stay provision of section 362 to provide special circumstances under which creditors of a single asset real estate debtor may have the stay lifted if the debtor has not filed a `feasible' reorganization plan within 90 days of filing, or has not commenced *monthly payments to secured creditors*."[49]

In response, secured creditors are likely to argue that the monthly payments required to be made are not interest payments, but rather monthly payments to compensate the secured creditor for the delay occasioned by the debtor's failure to file a feasible plan within the initial 90-day time period.[50] At any rate, if the court determines that these are interest payments, for which the undersecured creditor is entitled, there still remains the continuing legal issue as to how the interest payments will be applied.[51]

---

45. *See id.*
46. United Sav. Ass'n v. Timbers of Inwood Forest Assocs., 484 U.S. 365, 372 (1988) (stating value of creditor's interest in property that merited protection is value of collateral).
47. 11 U.S.C. § 101(51B) (1994).
48. S. REP. NO. 279, *supra* note 14, at 37 (emphasis added).
49. H.R. REP. NO. 835, *supra* note 9, at 50, *reprinted in* 1994 U.S.C.C.A.N. at 3359 (emphasis added).
50. Conversely, if the payments are considered interest, and the claims exceed $4,000,000, the secured creditor is not entitled to the payments.
51. In other words, an inevitable question will arise as to whether the postpetition interest payments will be credited directly against the secured claim, or whether they will be treated as a separate form of income collateral which will not effect the amount of the secured claim. A discussion of the so-called "substraction and addition" theories is set forth in the well reasoned decision, *In re* Union

Consider, however, how litigation is likely to be conducted under the new section 362(d)(3) where the debtor has no intention and/or lacks the ability to pay interest. The debtor's first tactic in creating delay will be to seek an extension "for cause" under the terms of section 362(d)(3).[52] Certainly, the statute provides ample room for a debtor-oriented court to give as much latitude to the debtor as currently may be available through extensions of exclusivity for filing a plan contained in section 1121.[53] Hopefully, in light of the expressed intent set forth in section 362(d)(3), which is to prevent unnecessary delay in a single asset real estate case,[54] courts will be reluctant to extend the 90-day period. The section's requirement that if an order extending the 90-day period is entered, such an order must be entered during the 90-day period, will prevent the filing of a motion to extend the 90-day period on the 89th day. However, if debtor's counsel is diligent in filing a motion for extension of time well before the 90th day, the requirement that an order be entered within the 90-day period usually can be accommodated. It must be recognized, however, that the mere opportunity for an extension of time "for cause" will give rise to litigation and particularly where court dockets are heavy, extensions can be expected.

Moreover, a serious question of exclusivity will arise in those chapter 11 cases where the court has ordered the appointment of a trustee pursuant to

---

Meeting Partners, 165 B.R. 553 (Bankr. E.D. Pa. 1994), *aff'd*, 52 F.3d 317 (3d Cir. 1995). Finally, the bankruptcy courts will have to confront the question as to what constitutes interest "at a current fair market rate on the value of the creditor's interest in the real estate." This determination is clearly in no way limited by the interest or discount rate set forth in the mortgage or deed of trust, but rather will require the bankruptcy court to determine a prevailing "fair market rate" based on the secured creditor's claim against the subject real estate. *See* United Sav. Ass'n v. Timbers of Inwood Forest Assocs., 484 U.S. 365 (1988).

52. *See* 11 U.S.C. § 362(d)(3) (1994).

53. *See id.* § 1121(d) ("[T]he court may for cause reduce or increase the 120-day period or the 180-day period referred to in this section."); *id.* § 1121(e)(3)(B) ("[T]he court may . . . increase the 100-day period . . . if debtor shows that the need for an increase in caused by circumstances for which the debtor should not be held accountable.").

54. S. REP. NO. 279, *supra* note 14, at 15 (1992) (stating intent of § 362(d) was to ensure "that the automatic stay provision is not abused, while giving a debtor a reasonable opportunity to create a workable plan of reorganization").

section 1104.[55] In other words, an argument will be raised, because of the rights available to a trustee under section 1121(c), that the right to file a plan may extend beyond the debtor's initial 90-day period for filing a plan.[56] However, in view of the overall intent to avoid delay, it is unlikely that the bankruptcy courts will construe section 1121 as conferring any rights other than those already set forth under subsections (A) and (B).[57] The statute could be improved through either the deletion of this provision or mandating that specific conditions be met as a prerequisite to receiving an extension of the exclusivity period.[58]

Assuming that the 90-day period has not been extended, the debtor who has no desire to pay interest will likely file a simple plan of reorganization on the 90th day.[59] The secured creditor will respond with a motion to lift the stay stating that there is no reasonable possibility that the plan can be confirmed within a reasonable period of time. Anticipating this, the debtor will have taken advantage of the current interpretation of chapter 11 which allows liquidation as an acceptable form of reorganization.[60] Thus, the debtor might

---

55. 11 U.S.C. § 1104 (1994) (providing for appointment of trustee for cause or if "best interests" of parties). Under § 1106(5), if a trustee is appointed, they must file a plan in compliance with § 1121. *Id.* § 1106(5).

56. *Id.* § 1121(c)(3). The trustee would argue that the 90-day period required to lift stay motions should be extended in order to allow the trustee to file a plan. *Id.*

57. *Id.* § 1121(a), (b) (providing right of debtor to file plan and that only debtor is entitled to file plan during 120 days after date of order).

58. *See The Bankruptcy Amendments Act of 1993: Hearing on S. 540 Before the Subcomm. on Courts and Admin. Practice of the Comm. on the Judiciary U.S. Senate*, 103d Cong., 1st Sess. (1993). William J. Pearlstein made a statement at the hearing before the Subcommittee on Courts and Administrative Practice of the Committee on the Judiciary of the United States on March 31, 1993, wherein Mr. Pearlstein suggested that where the debtor is unable to make current interest payments on the current value of the property, the debtor should be compelled to file a liquidating chapter 11 plan. *Id.* at 159. In addition, the suggestion is made that there should be only one additional 90-day extension. *Id.*

59. *See* 11 U.S.C. § 362(d)(3) (1994). If the debtor has filed a plan within the 90-day period, the stay can not be lifted in a single asset real estate case. *Id.* § 362(d)(3)(A).

60. Sandy Ridge Dev. Corp. v. Louisiana Nat'l Bank (*In re* Sandy Ridge Dev.

file a plan which calls for the property to be liquidated within some short period of time, perhaps 12 to 18 months. Knowing that the plan can always be amended prior to a confirmation hearing, the debtor filing such plan will attempt to test the court's limits by proposing a plan which essentially requests a short period of time to liquidate the property in lieu of allowing the property to be sold for what may be perceived as an unreasonably low value at a foreclosure sale.[61] In light of the general perception that a foreclosure sale will bring a drastically reduced price for the property, most courts would be amenable to a short term plan of reorganization allowing the debtor some time to sell the property through normal, but aggressive marketing efforts.[62] The debtor will support its claim that it has a genuine desire to sell the property within a reasonable time frame by employing a broker to assist in the sale of the property.[63] The greatest prejudice to the undersecured creditor lies in

---

Corp.), 881 F.2d 1346, 1352 (5th Cir. 1989) (noting Congress did contemplate liquidating reorganizations in Code); *In re* Conroe Forge & Mfg. Corp., 82 B.R. 781, 784-85 (Bankr. W.D. Pa. 1988) (noting concept of reorganization includes liquidation); *In re* Naron & Wagner, Chartered, 88 B.R. 85, 89 (Bankr. D. Md. 1988) (stating liquidation plans authorized under chapter 11); *In re* All Am., Inc., 40 B.R. 104, 106 (Bankr. N.D. Ga. 1984) (holding no per se prohibition against chapter 11 liquidation where creditors receive more than in chapter 7 liquidation); *In re* WFDR, Inc., 10 B.R. 109, 110 (Bankr. N.D. Ga. 1981) (finding no prohibition against liquidation in chapter 11); *In re* Alves Photo Serv., Inc., 6. B.R. 690, 694 (Bankr. D. Mass. 1980) (finding liquidation permissible in chapter 11). *But see In re* Lyons Transp. Lines, Inc., 123 B.R. 526, 529-34 (Bankr. W.D. Pa. 1991) (finding provisions allowing reorganization of assets intended to accommodate financial restructuring do not authorize liquidation under chapter 11 where debtor's initial intent is liquidation).

61. *See, e.g., In re* Snider Farms, Inc., 79 B.R. 801 (Bankr. N.D. Ind. 1987). The court stated that "what needs to be protected is the value of the property, not the value of the creditor's 'interest' in property." *Id.* at 808. Further, "[e]ven if a foreclosure sale is conducted properly, a court may reject the price realized at the sale as too low to be a true liquidation value." *Id.* at 815; *see In re* Independence Village, Inc., 52 B.R. 715, 728 (Bankr. E.D. Mich. 1985) (explaining that sudden foreclosure sale might get creditors quicker payment but it would be lower than if property was prudently marketed).

62. *See supra* note 14.

63. *See, e.g.,* Daniel v. AMCI, Inc. (*In re* Ferncrest Court Partners, Ltd.), 66 F.3d 778, 780 (6th Cir. 1995) (allowing debtor to hire broker to sell property for

situations where the property, for whatever economic reason, is not likely to produce a price that will, at a minimum, equal the balance of the secured claim as of the commencement of the case.

If the debtor files such a plan, the court will hold a preliminary hearing on the secured creditor's motion to lift the stay.[64] At this hearing, the court will be reluctant to lift the stay unless the secured creditor clearly demonstrates that no possibility exists for the debtor to confirm a plan of reorganization.[65] This might be the case where the debtor has only one secured creditor holding undersecured debt with a deficiency claim[66] large enough to control the class of unsecured claims, and where no other class of claims exists which could accept the debtor's plan for the purpose of cramdown under the Bankruptcy Code section 1129.[67] The debtor may not be able to create the necessary accepting class of claims through separate classification of the unsecured creditor's deficiency claim in view of the current trend of case law.[68] In such

---

more than expected from foreclosure sale).

64. 11 U.S.C. § 362(d) (1994). Section 362(d) provides for a hearing before a party in interest can have the stay lifted. *Id.*

65. *Id.* Section 362(d)(3) provides that a stay can be lifted with respect to actions against single asset real estate unless "the debtor has filed a plan of reorganization that has a reasonable possibility of being confirmed." *Id.* § 362(d)(3)(A). Furthermore, the Code suggests that the party opposing the motion has the burden of proof with respect to the feasibility of the plan. *Id.* § 362(g)(2).

66. *Id.* § 506(a). Section 506(a) creates a secured claim up to the value of the collateral and an unsecured claim for any excess for an undersecured creditor. *Id.*

67. *See id.* § 1129(a)(10) (stating that, "[i]f a class of claims is impaired under the plan, at least one class of claims that is impaired under the plan" must accept plan); Travelers Ins. Co. v. Bryson Properties, XVIII (*In re* Bryson Properties, XVIII), 961 F.2d 496, 501 n.8 (4th Cir.) (finding priority tax claimants not able to accept plan under § 1129), *cert. denied*, 506 U.S. 866 (1992); *In re* Perdido Motel Group, Inc., 101 B.R. 289, 294 (Bankr. N.D. Ala. 1989) (holding priority tax claims were not class able to accept plan).

68. *See, e.g.*, *In re* Woodbrook Assocs., 19 F.3d 312, 318 (7th Cir. 1994) (stating "thou shalt not classify similar claims differently in order to gerrymander an affirmative vote on reorganization") (citation omitted); Boston Post Rd. Ltd. Partnership v. FDIC (*In re* Boston Post Rd. Ltd. Partnership), 21 F.3d 477, 484 (2d Cir. 1994) (noting that unsecured creditor cannot be segregated from

cases the stay should be lifted at a preliminary hearing, since the bankruptcy case is the kind of dispute which has given rise to bad faith filing litigation in connection with motions to dismiss bankruptcy cases.[69]

In situations where the debtor has a class of non-insider, unsecured, or other claims which are not controlled by the secured creditor, and the possibility exists that the debtor can obtain the acceptance of an impaired class of claims for the purposes of cramdown, and where the debtor proposes a plan merely requesting a short period of time to sell property, the bankruptcy court will probably not lift the stay at the preliminary hearing stage of stay litigation.[70] Considering the crowded nature of most bankruptcy court dockets and the fact that, under section 362(d)(3), stay litigation turns upon whether or not the debtor can confirm a plan of reorganization, the court most likely will attempt to consolidate a final hearing on the secured creditor's motion for relief from stay with a confirmation hearing on the debtor's proposed plan.[71] In doing so, the court may have real difficulty reconciling the statutory notice requirements for the approval and circulation of a disclosure statement before voting and confirmation of a plan with the statutory requirement that a final hearing in connection with a motion to lift stay be held within 30 days of the

---

other unsecured creditors for no legitimate reason other than cramdown), *cert. denied*, 115 S. Ct. 897 (1995); John Hancock Mut. Life Ins. Co. v. Route 37 Business Park Assocs., 987 F.2d 154, 161 (3d Cir. 1993) (holding that debtor had no justification for classification scheme); *Bryson Properties*, 961 F.2d at 502 (holding that purpose of particular classification was to manipulate voting); Phoenix Mut. Life Ins. Co. v. Greystone III Joint Venture (*In re* Greystone III Joint Venture), 995 F.2d 1274, 1281 (5th Cir. 1991) (rejecting debtor's classification in plan), *vacated in part*, 995 F.2d 1284 (5th Cir.), *cert. denied*, 506 U.S. 821 (1992); Olympia & York Florida Equity Corp. v. Bank of New York (*In re* Holywell Corp.), 913 F.2d 873, 880 (11th Cir. 1990) (finding that there is limit on debtor's power to classify creditors).

69. *See, e.g.*, Little Creek Dev. Co. v. Commonwealth Mortgage Corp. (*In re* Little Creek Dev. Co.), 779 F.2d 1068, 1072 (5th Cir. 1986) (discussing lack of good faith as "cause" for lifting stay); Albany Partners, Ltd. v. Westbrook (*In re* Albany Partners, Ltd.), 749 F.2d 670, 674 (11th Cir. 1984) (dismissing petition because it was not filed in good faith); *In re* North Redington Beach Assoc. Ltd., 91 B.R. 166, 167 (Bankr. M.D. Fla. 1988) (denying motion to dismiss based on lack of good faith argument).

70. *See supra* note 65 and accompanying text.

71. *See* 11 U.S.C. § 362(e) (1994).

conclusion of the preliminary hearing.[72] It has been the author's experience, however, that most counsel will waive the section 362(e) requirement to accommodate the court's calendar. Therefore, section 362(d)(3) clearly places pressure upon the court to expedite the plan confirmation process, but does not, as a practical matter, prevent the court from giving the debtor a shot at confirming a plan before the stay would be lifted.[73] It should also be noted that in cases where the single asset real estate does not generate sufficient income to offer a secured creditor any debt service, thus forcing the debtor to file a liquidation plan, current law indicates that a court most likely will hear a secured creditor's motion to lift stay concurrently with a confirmation hearing on the debtor's plan.[74] As such, the legislation will not significantly accelerate the plan confirmation process.

Pending a confirmation hearing, the debtor undoubtedly will engage in efforts to procure outside financing or investment to enable the debtor to propose a plan of reorganization with a longer term.[75] If the debtor is

---

72. *See id.* §§ 1125, 1128; FED. R. BANKR. P. 3017(a), (d) (requiring 25 days notice of disclosure statement hearing and of confirmation hearing); *see also* 11 U.S.C. § 362(e) (1994) (requiring final hearing on motion to lift stay within 30 days after conclusion of preliminary hearing).

73. *See* 11 U.S.C. § 362(d)(3) (1994) (providing that court can lift stay if the debtor fails to file plan that has reasonable chance of confirmation within 90 days).

74. Under § 362(d)(2) of the Bankruptcy Code a court must consider whether the property in question "is necessary to an effective reorganization" before they decide whether to lift a stay with respect to a particular piece of property. *Id.* § 362(d)(2)(B). The Supreme Court suggested that for something to be "necessary for an effective reorganization" would require that there is "a reasonable possibility of a successful reorganization." *In re* 499 W. Warren St. Assocs., Ltd. Partnership, 151 B.R. 307, 310 (Bankr. N.D.N.Y. 1992) (quoting United Sav. Ass'n v. Timbers of Inwood Forest Assoc., 484 U.S. 365, 375-76 (1988)). "The definition of 'effective reorganization' articulated by the Supreme Court in the *Timbers* case necessarily implicates . . . consideration of the plan confirmation standards under [§ 1129]." *In re* 266 Washington Assocs., 141 B.R. 275, 281 (Bankr. E.D.N.Y. 1992).

75. For an example of a debtor attempting to obtain outside pre-confirmation financing, see *In re* Krypton Broadcasting, 181 B.R. 657, 661 (Bankr. S.D. Fla. 1995) (discussing debtor's failure to obtain financing). However, where the debtor needs outside financing, it must be clearly in sight. *In re* Great Am.

successful in procuring such financing or investment, they can be expected to file an amended plan, and the court, in addressing the secured creditor's motion to lift the stay under section 362(d)(3), will be forced again to consider confirmation of the debtor's plan.[76] If the debtor's efforts to procure outside financing or investment are successful in obtaining a bona fide commitment, the court will most likely give the debtor an opportunity to confirm such a plan.[77] Generally, a bankruptcy court will reward efforts by the debtor to produce constructive results. Courts are reluctant to terminate the chapter 11 process where the debtor appears to be making real progress.[78] The amendments to section 362(d)(3) should have no impact on the courts' current approach. The proposed test for relief from the stay, incorporating a determination of whether a plan proposed by the debtor has a reasonable possibility of being confirmed within a reasonable period of time, therefore, does not significantly alter the status quo in bankruptcy cases where the debtor acts diligently.[79]

The statute does make a difference, however, in a good number of cases where the debtor lacks the ability and/or intention to pay interest on secured claims. This is because the statute focuses on the debtor's ability to reorganize and eliminates the need for a secured creditor to demonstrate that its claim is undersecured in obtaining relief from the stay.[80] Thus, where the debtor cannot or will not pay interest, the stay can be lifted if the debtor absolutely cannot confirm a plan of reorganization, because then there is no class of impaired

---

Pyramid Joint Venture, 144 B.R. 780, 792 (Bankr. W.D. Tenn. 1992) (stating that plan "must be more than a nebulous speculative venture").

76. Section 362(d)(3)(A) requires the court to deny the motion to lift the stay where the debtor has filed a plan that has a reasonable chance of being confirmed. 11 U.S.C. § 1127 (1994).

77. *See id.* § 1127(b) (allowing reorganized debtor to modify plan if circumstances warrant it and court, after notice and a hearing, confirms it).

78. *See id.* § 1112(b) (enumerating causes to dismiss or confirm chapter 11 plan).

79. *See id.* § 1129 (in order to be confirmed, plan must be made in "good faith"); *In re* Sound Radio, Inc., 93 B.R. 849, 853 (Bankr. D.N.J. 1988) (explaining only test of "good faith" of proposed reorganization plan is whether plan can succeed), *aff'd*, 103 B.R. 521 (D.N.J. 1989), *aff'd*, 908 F.2d 964 (3d Cir. 1990); *see also* 11 U.S.C. § 362(d)(3)(A) (1994) (plan of reorganization has to have reasonable possibility of confirmation within reasonable time).

80. *See* 11 U.S.C. § 362(d)(3) (1994) (focusing on debtor's ability to reorganize).

claims to accept the plan for the purposes of cramdown.[81] To the extent that the statute gives bankruptcy courts clear authority to lift the stay in such cases, without regard to whether a debt is over or undersecured, the statute represents a real improvement upon current law. Prior to the enactment of section 362(d)(3), under section 362(d)(2), in addition to proving that the debtor cannot reorganize, a secured creditor had to prove that its claim was undersecured in order to get relief from stay in a single asset real estate bankruptcy case.[82] Additionally, if relief under section 362(d)(2) was not available, a creditor could have requested relief from the stay `for cause' under section 362(d)(1), but usually did not obtain relief from the stay when there was equity in the property, unless the secured creditor could demonstrate that the property was declining in value and that the debtor could not offer adequate protection for such decline.[83]

C. Cases Where the Debtor Has the Ability and Intention to Pay Interest On Secured Claims

Under interpretations of section 362(d)(1) and (2) applicable to cases pending prior to the effective date of the Bankruptcy Reform Act of 1994, in a single asset bankruptcy case where the property is not declining in value, the debtor generally could have successfully defended a motion to lift the stay simply by paying the secured creditor a market rate of interest on its secured claim.[84]

---

81. *See supra* notes 65-68 and accompanying text.

82. *See* United Sav. Ass'n v. Timbers of Inwood Forest Assocs., 484 U.S. 365, 375 (1988).

83. *See* 11 U.S.C. § 362(d)(1) (1994) (stating relief from stay will be granted "for cause, including the lack of adequate protection of an interest in property of such party in interest"). Section 361 attempts to define adequate protection. *Id.* § 361. For example, adequate protection may be satisfied by requiring the trustee to make cash payments to the extent necessary to compensate for any decrease in value of the interest of the party making the request. *See id.* § 361(1); 2 COLLIER, *supra* note 31, ¶ 362.07[1].

84. As was expressed in *Timbers*, where a secured creditor receives a market rate of interest on its secured claim and its collateral is not depreciating, the Code should not "provide relief [from the stay] for such an obstreperous and thoroughly unharmed creditor." *Timbers*, 484 U.S. at 375.

In this situation nothing has been changed by the addition of section 362(d)(3).[85] What has changed, however, is the manner in which litigation may proceed in single asset real estate bankruptcy cases with respect to the payment of interest. A debtor who has some ability and intention to pay interest is likely to file a motion shortly before expiration of the 90-day period requesting that the court determine the value of the creditor's "secured interest" in the real estate and the "current fair market rate" of interest.[86] Such a motion might not even allege the debtor's position regarding these figures. The motion simply could state the debtor's intention to take advantage of the interest payment provisions of section 362(d)(3). If litigation is allowed to proceed in this manner, the debtor is likely to obtain delay beyond the 90th day of the case without payment of interest.[87] Having obtained such delay, shortly prior to a determination of value and market interest rate (assuming, of course, that the court treats the "monthly payment" as an interest payment and not some form of compensation for delay or as a form of "adequate protection"), the debtor could then oppose the lifting of the stay by filing a plan of reorganization under section 362(d)(3)(A).[88] This would also relieve the debtor from any obligation to pay interest except as might be required in connection with the secured creditor's request for adequate protection,[89] or pursuant to

---

85. Section 362(d)(3)(B) provides that relief from the stay will be granted, unless within 90 days after the order for relief the debtor has commenced monthly payments to secured creditors in an amount equal to interest at a current fair market rate on their claims. *See* 11 U.S.C. § 362(d)(3)(B) (1994). "It should be noted that the payments are not necessarily payments of interest," but are equal to that amount. 2 COLLIER, *supra* note 31, ¶ 362.07[3].

86. *See* 11 U.S.C. § 362(d)(3)(B) (1994). Section 506 of the Code governs the determination of a person's secured status. *Id.* § 506. It provides, essentially, that a creditor is secured only to the extent of either the value of their claim or the value of the collateral whichever is less. *Id.* § 506(a).

87. *See id.* § 362(d)(3). Additionally, it should be noted that this 90-day grace period may be extended for cause by an order entered within that 90-day period. *Id.*

88. *Id.* § 362(d)(3)(A) (providing that if debtor files plan lift stay will not be granted).

89. *See, e.g., In re* Suarez, 98 B.R. 76 (Bankr. M.D. Fla. 1989) (requiring payment of interest on oversecured claim as condition to continuance of stay). *But see supra* note 40 (discussing interest payment when creditor oversecured).

section 1129(b)(2)(A).[90]

A debtor might also proceed by paying interest on the 90th day, based on an assumed market rate of interest and an assumed value of the creditor's secured claim.[91] The creditor most likely will counter with a motion to lift the stay stating that the interest being paid is not a market rate and that the amount of the secured claim is not proper.[92] The debtor probably will not proceed in this manner unless it is forced to. This is because the debtor would not want, in the early stages of the case, to commit itself to a valuation of the property or to a market rate of interest on the creditor's claim which may eventually bind the litigant with respect to a proposed plan of reorganization. However, if the debtor does choose this course, the court must, at a hearing on the creditor's motion to lift stay, determine the market rate of interest and the amount of the secured claim.[93] Again, the debtor could avoid the early determination of an interest rate by filing a plan.[94] Invariably, a motion to avoid the lifting of a stay, based upon the filing of a plan, will be continued in order to give the parties ample time to present a case to the court regarding whether or not such a plan has a reasonable possibility of being confirmed within a reasonable period of time.

The aforementioned tactics demonstrate that if the debtor is crafty, it may take advantage of the provisions of section 362(d)(3) in procuring delay. In order to make section 362(d)(3) work as its drafters intended, it should be supplemented by a federal rule of bankruptcy procedure.

---

90. 11 U.S.C. § 1129(b)(2)(A)(i)(II) (1994) (providing that secured creditor receive payment of full amount of claim plus interest).

91. Because § 362(d)(3)(b) does not set forth what "an amount equal to interest at a current fair market rate" is or how it is determined, a debtor may choose what he or she thinks an appropriate rate should be. *See id.* § 362(d)(3)(b) (referring ambiguously to current "fair market rate"). A debtor may also, due to ambiguity of § 362(d)(3)(b), choose a value of the creditor's secured claim, which suits his or her purpose. *Id.*

92. FED. R. BANKR. P. 9014 (providing that relief in contested matter under Code be requested by motion).

93. *See* 11 U.S.C. § 362(d) (1994). Subsection (d) states that a court can lift the stay only "after notice and a hearing." *Id.*

94. *See id.* § 362(d)(3)(A). The filing of a plan within 90 days of filing makes it possible to oppose the motion to lift the stay without presently committing to making interest payments and having to determine the market rate of interest. *Id.*

D. Proposed Remedy

The author proposes a rule stating that, pending a hearing on the amount of interest to be paid pursuant to section 362(d)(3)(B), the debtor must pay the rate of interest provided in the loan documents evidencing the debt secured by single asset real estate. Such a rule will prevent the debtor from adjusting creatively the valuation of the property at the outset of the case. Often, single asset real estate debtors claim an unduly inflated value of property in schedules filed at the outset of the case, thus discouraging a motion to lift stay under section 362(d)(2). Later, the debtor often files a plan in which, the value of the property has suddenly dropped, creating a deficiency claim, and the debtor will then attempt to bifurcate the secured creditor's claim, thereby easing the burden of plan confirmation under section 1129(b)(2)(A) of the Code.[95]

If the debtor chooses to take advantage of the interest payment provisions of section 362(d)(3)(B), a rule requiring the debtor to make such payment based upon the lesser of the full amount of the creditor's claim, or the value of

---

95. Section 506 provides that a creditor's claim is secured to the extent of the value of the property in which they hold a lien. 11 U.S.C. § 506 (1994). However, § 506(a) requires a bifurcation of an undersecured claim into separate secured and unsecured components. *Id.*; 3 COLLIER, *supra* note 31, ¶ 506.04[1], at 506-15. The bifurcation process plays a significant role in the confirmation of a plan because § 1129 requires that the debtor's plan pay to parties holding secured claims the full amount of such claim. 11 U.S.C. § 1129(b)(2)(A) (1994). In order for a plan to be feasible, the debtor must demonstrate that such payments can be made. *See In re* Sound Radio, Inc., 103 B.R. 521, 523 (D.N.J. 1989) (requiring finding that debtor able to make all payments), *aff'd*, 908 F.2d 964 (3d Cir. 1990); Mutual Life Ins. Co. v. Patrician St. Joseph Partners Ltd. Partnership (*In re* Patrician St. Joseph Partners Ltd. Partnership), 169 B.R. 669, 676 (Bankr. D. Ariz. 1994) (citing Federal Land Bank v. Cheatham (*In re* Cheatham), 91 B.R. 377, 379 (E.D.N.C. 1988)). In many cases, it is profitable for the debtor to understate the value of the collateral because it will result in understating the amount of the secured claim. *See* 11 U.S.C. § 1129(a)(9) (1994) (providing that debtor must propose plan which calls for full segment of secured claims). Maximizing the creditor's deficiency claim through the above tactic, the debtor can propose a much longer term payout of the unsecured portion of the creditor's claim, thus further easing the short term burden on the debtor to make payments.

the collateral stated in the schedules, would force the debtor to take a much harder look at the value it places on collateral in their schedules. This may reduce some delay in single asset real estate bankruptcy cases if it forces the debtor to choose a position in its schedules that the secured creditor's debt is undersecured.[96] The proposed rule will also eliminate the debtor's ability to obtain delay through litigation over the amount of the secured claim and market rate of interest.

Assuming that the debtor chooses to litigate the proper market rate of interest and secured claim valuation, one must consider whether such findings would be binding in connection with a proposed plan of reorganization.[97] Litigation over the value of collateral and market rate of interest invariably involves expert testimony and can be time consuming.[98] Therefore, a court in a bankruptcy proceeding will likely attempt to avoid litigating these issues more than once. If a court determines the value of collateral and market interest rate during stay proceedings, it is likely that the outcome will be determinative of the outcome of plan confirmation litigation.[99] For instance,

---

96. If the secured creditors debt is undersecured the court will grant relief from the stay, under 11 U.S.C. § 362(d)(1) (1994). In that instance, the time consuming tactics of the crafty debtor will be avoided.
97. This market rate may become important since it may ultimately determine what the secured creditor gets paid under the plan. *See* 11 U.S.C. § 1129(b)(2)(A)(i)(II) (1994) (providing that secured party must receive deferred cash payments equal to amount of claim).
98. For examples of use of expert testimony, see Metropolitan Life Ins. Co. v. Monroe Park (*In re* Monroe Park), 17 B.R. 934, 939 n.2 (Bankr. D. Del. 1982) (using expert witnesses to measure property appreciation); Heritage Sav. & Loan Ass'n v. Rogers Dev. Corp. (*In re* Rogers Dev. Corp.), 2 B.R. 679, 682 (Bankr. E.D. Va. 1980) (using expert real estate appraiser to determine adequate protection under § 362(d)(2)).
99. Strictly speaking, a determination of the value of property for the purposes of stay litigation is not binding on either the debtor or the secured creditor in later plan confirmation litigation. Also, neither the debtor nor creditor will be collaterally estopped from arguing different values at the various hearings or plan confirmation. *See* 11 U.S.C. § 506(a) (1994); Ahlers v. Norwest Bank Worthington (*In re* Ahlers), 794 F.2d 388, 398 (8th Cir. 1986), *rev'd*, 485 U.S. 197 (1988); *In re* Krueger, 66 B.R. 463, 466 (Bankr. S.D. Fla. 1986); S. REP. NO. 989, 95th Cong., 2d Sess. 68 (1978), *reprinted in* 1978 U.S.C.C.A.N. 5787, 5854. In fact, courts have uniformly recognized that the

in considering a plan of reorganization which proposes a long-term payout of such claims, the court most likely will give great deference to the earlier determination of applicable interest rate and collateral value, and consider only whether such payout is feasible. Since litigation over the market rate of interest and the amount of a secured claim is likely to have a significant impact on issues in connection with confirmation of a plan, it is unlikely that the debtor would risk an adverse determination on these issues early in the case.[100] Accordingly, there may be very few cases in which the debtor will seek to take advantage of the interest payment option under the new section 362(d)(3).

Also, in applying the interest payment provision of section 362(d)(3),[101] one must consider the interplay with section 1111(b).[102] Query, if a secured creditor makes the 1111(b) election, whereby it will have its' entire debt treated as nonrecourse, will such election be binding upon the creditor with regard to the payment of interest mandated by subsection (d)(3)? Section 362(d)(3) provides that interest should be paid on the "value of the creditor's interest."[103] The question is whether the "value of the creditor's interest" is the same as the creditor's "secured claim."[104] Under section 506(a), a creditor's

---

value of the secured property may change during the course of a bankruptcy case. 3 COLLIER, *supra* note 31, ¶ 506.04[2], at 506-26 (citing Bray v. Shenandoah Fed. Sav. & Loan Ass'n (*In re* Snowshoe Co.), 789 F.2d 1085, 1088-89 (4th Cir. 1986)). However, as a practical matter, the debtor's or secured creditor's credibility with the court will be severely strained if significantly different values are argued at a later plan confirmation hearing.

100. *See supra* text accompanying notes 91 & 92.

101. 11 U.S.C. § 362(d)(3) (1994).

102. *Id.* § 1111(b). Part of the reason for the § 1111(b)(2) election "is to provide additional protection to a partially secured creditor when the secured creditor believes that the collateral has been undervalued." 5 COLLIER, *supra* note 31, ¶ 1111.02[5], at 1111-39.

The § 1111(b)(2) election allows the undersecured creditors to be regarded as having a secured claim for the full amount of the allowed claim, regardless of the value of the property. *Id.* However, the secured creditor loses its right to a later deficiency claim. *Id*; *see also* 4 COWANS BANKRUPTCY LAW AND PRACTICE § 20.26, at 123 (4th ed. 1994).

103. 11 U.S.C. § 362(d)(3)(B) (1994).

104. While S. 540 substantially tracked the language of S. 1985's version of § 362(d)(3), reference in S. 540 and its successor bill H.R. 5116, refer solely to the "creditor's interest in the real estate," rather than "the creditor's *secured*

secured claim is defined generally as "the value of such creditor's interest in the estate's interest in such property . . ." (the secured creditor's collateral).[105] If the secured creditor's section 1111(b) election establishes the creditor's property interest by securing its entire claim for the purpose of determining the amount of its secured claim for use in calculating interest to be paid under section 362(d)(3), then by reason of such election, the creditor could, as a practical matter, eliminate the debtor's ability to take advantage of the interest payment provisions under section 362(d)(3).[106] In other words, it is not likely that the debtor would be able to pay interest on the full amount of the creditor's claim, because if the section 1111(b) election is made, the amount of the interest to be paid would be determined without regard to the value of the property.[107] In many cases it is not in the secured creditor's best interest to make the section 1111(b) election. In addition, because any payments made must relate to the underlying value of the property, it is likely that a correct court determination will construe the mandated payments under subsection (d)(3) consistent with "cramdown" principles set forth in section 1129(b).[108]

---

interest in such property." H.R. 5116, 103d Cong., 2d Sess. § 218 (1994) (emphasis added). While attorneys are bound to argue and attach significance to this omission, the reference in subsection (d)(3)(B) to "whose claim is secured" and "creditor's interest in the real estate" strongly supports, if not conclusively, the argument that the creditor is entitled to payment of interest based solely on the value of the real estate. Of greater importance is the House amendment, H.R. 5116, which added the excepting language in subsection (3)(B) of § 362(d) for judgment liens and unmatured statutory liens. *See* Bankruptcy Reform Act of 1994, Pub. L. No. 103-394, § 218(b)(3), *reprinted in* 1994 U.S.C.C.A.N. 3340, 3358. Therefore, any judgment lien creditor or statutory lien creditor, whose lien has not matured as of the date of bankruptcy, will not be entitled to receive any form of interest payment.

105. 11 U.S.C. § 506(a) (1994).

106. *Id.* § 362(d)(3).

107. *See supra* note 103 and accompanying text.

108. 11 U.S.C. § 1129(b)(2)(A)(i)(II) (1994) (requiring that secured claimants receive full present value of claim from plan). For excellent and in depth discussion of problems likely to arise with respect to a § 1111(b) election, see generally Kenneth N. Klee, *Cram Down II*, 64 AM. BANKR. L.J. 229 (1990) (discussing 1129(b)(2) "fair and equitable" standards during "cramdown" proceedings); James A. Pusateri et al., *Section 1111(b) of the Bankruptcy Code: How Much Does The Debtor Have To Pay And When Should The*

Conclusion

For the most part, the enactment of the single asset real estate provisions should send a clear message to real estate debtors that, in the absence of the ability to formulate a feasible plan of reorganization, the courts will deal with such cases on an expedited basis. What will be the ultimate impact of these significant legislative amendments, is hard to assess at this time–not only because of the unrealistic cap on the amount of secured debt, but because of the other problems of interpretation and construction that are likely to arise. The existing case law generated under *Timbers*,[109] has not generated fair results in most single asset bankruptcy cases. *Timbers* prevents an undersecured creditor from obtaining interest on its secured claim as compensation for the delay in the secured creditor's ability to liquidate its collateral. Also, due to the fact that the stay cannot be lifted unless it can be demonstrated that there is no realistic prospect of reorganization,[110] undersecured creditors have suffered real economic prejudice due to the frequent extensions of exclusivity that courts have often granted. *Timbers* has generally been viewed as discouraging the lifting of the automatic stay on undersecured claims so long as the debtor is still within the 120-day exclusivity period under section 1121.[111] But through extensions of the exclusivity period, debtors successfully have argued that a court should not find that the debtor failed to file a plan within the exclusive period *because such exclusive period may have been extended.*

In so many single asset cases, particularly those involving unimproved real estate, the debtor has little, if any, unsecured debt and few, if any, non-insider

---

Creditor Elect?, 58 AM. BANKR. L.J. 129 (1984) (discussing both § 1111(b) election and "cramdown" proceedings); Dale C. Schian, *Section 1111(b)(2): Preserving the In Rem Claim*, 67 AM. BANKR. L.J. 479 (1993) (discussing § 1111(b) elections).

109. United Sav. Ass'n v. Timbers of Inwood Forest Assocs., Ltd., 484 U.S. 365 (1988).

110. *Id.* at 376.

111. Section 1121(b) provides that "only the debtor may file a plan until after 120 days after the date of the order for relief under this chapter." 11 U.S.C. § 1121(b) (1994). During this 120-day exclusive period, the bankruptcy courts demand a less detailed showing on the part of the debtor with respect to § 362 relief. *Timbers*, 484 U.S. at 376.

employees. Even in those cases where the real estate is income producing, the income stream itself is insufficient to service the debt load or to provide for required repairs or improvements to the real estate. Such a situation creates a "no-win" situation for the lender who has financed the project based on a calculated loan to value ratio and, accordingly, delay exacts a heavy toll for such a lender.

The single asset amendments clearly evidence a desire on the part of Congress that exclusivity not be extended in single asset real estate cases. Also, in those cases which merit an extension, that the secured creditor receive some form of compensatory monthly payment to account for the delay and enforcement of the secured creditor's rights. If our nation's courts respond to the will expressed in the new single asset provisions and refuse to extend the 90-day period (except in those truly meritorious cases where an extension would be warranted) the legislation will be a success. It will force the debtor to either compensate the secured creditor for delay through the monthly payment of interest or, if the debtor has no ability to pay such interest, at least force the debtor to propose a plan of liquidation. The hope that springs eternal in every debtor's breast had now better be tempered by the congressional mandate that "a plan of reorganization . . . has a reasonable possibility of being confirmed within a reasonable time."[112] However, for the time being, this message is limited to only those single asset cases involving less than $4,000,000 in secured debt.

112. 11 U.S.C. § 362(d)(3)(A) (1994).

CONTRIBUTORS

Catherine V. Battle • Associate with Mineola law firm Bee, Eisman and Ready. Ms. Battle was a former editor of the *American Bankruptcy Institute Law Review* and a 1993 graduate of St. John's University School of Law.

Stephen Bordanaro • 1993 graduate of St. John's University School of Law. Former editor of *American Bankruptcy Institute Law Review.*

Albert J. Cardinali • Partner in the Tax Practice Group of Thacher, Proffitt and Wood. Mr. Cardinali attended the City University of New York where he received his B.A. in 1955. He received his LL.B. from Columbia University in 1958 and his LL.M. in Taxation from New York University in 1965. Mr. Cardinali is a former Chairman of the Committee on Banking and Saving Institution of the Tax Section of the American Bar Association.

Scott Carlisle • Counsel in the Legal Department of UNUM Life Insurance Company of America ("UNUM"). A graduate of Philips Exeter, Dartmouth College and the University of Virginia Law School, Scott practiced law in Portland, Maine from 1970 with a concentration in bankruptcy work. Since joining UNUM in 1987, he has spent a significant amount of time working with commercial real estate mortgages involved in foreclosure and bankruptcy proceedings. Scott presently chairs the Subcommittee on Federal Bankruptcy Legislation for the American Council of Life Insurance and the Investments Section of the Association of Life Insurance Counsel. He is a member of the American Bar Association, Maine Bar Association, and the American College of Mortgage Attorneys. He has contributed articles to the *ABA Real Property, Probate and Trust Journal* and the *American Bankruptcy Institute Law Review*, and served as a panelist for the recent ABI Symposium "Should the Automatic Stay Be Abolished."

Lisa Hill Fenning • United States Bankruptcy Judge, Central District of California, Los Angeles Division since 1985. Judge Fenning is a 1974 graduate of the Yale Law School and received her B.A. with honors from Wellesley College in 1971. Judge Fenning currently serves on the Board of Governors of the American Bankruptcy Institute, on the Board of Regents of the American College of Bankruptcy, and on the Board of Directors of the National Conference of Bankruptcy Judges Endowment for Education. She is also a member of the ABA Standing Committee on Federal Judicial Improvements, having previously served as a founding member of the ABA Commission on Women in the Profession. She was elected a Fellow of the American Bar Association in 1992.

SALVATORE G. GANGEMI • Partner of Gangemi and Mango, LLP in New York City. Mr. Gangemi is a former Executive Articles Editor of the *American Bankruptcy Institute Law Review* and a 1993 graduate of St. John's University School of Law.

WILLIAM R. GREENDYKE • United States Bankruptcy Judge, Southern District of Texas. Judge Greendyke graduated from Baylor Law School *cum laude* in 1979.

KAREN GROSS • Professor of Law at New York Law School. Prior to her entry into academia in 1984, Professor Gross practiced bankruptcy/corporate law in Chicago and New York. She is the author of numerous articles and is a contributing editor to Collier on Bankruptcy (15th ed.). Professor Gross is currently co-chair of the ABA's Task Force on Abuse in chapter 11. She received her B.A. from Smith College and her J.D. from Temple University Law School, having spent her third year of law school at the University of Chicago.

JACK I. HABERT • Mr. Habert is an associate in the New York City firm of Zalkin, Rodin & Goodman, LLP. He is a former editor of the *American Bankruptcy Institute Law Review*. Mr. Habert graduated *cum laude* from St. John's University School of Law in 1996.

WILLIAM C. HILLMAN • United States Bankruptcy Judge, District of Massachusetts. Judge Hillman received his LL.M. from Boston University as well as his J.D. While attending law school, Judge Hillman was an editor and secretary for the *Boston University Law Review*.

PATRICK J. HOEFFNER • 1996 graduate of St. John's University School of Law. Mr. Hoeffner was Executive Publications Editor of the *American Bankruptcy Institute Law Review*.

JAMES L. LIPSCOMB • Senior Vice President in the Real Estate Investment Department of Metropolitan Life Insurance Company. Mr. Lipscomb received his B.A. *cum laude* from Howard University in 1969; his J.D. from Columbia University School of Law 1972 and his LL.M. from New York University School of Law in 1977. Mr. Lipscomb is a member and former governor of the American College of Real Estate Lawyers and is currently a member of the Executive Committee of the Association of the Bar of the City of New York.

JOHN P. MCNICHOLAS • Bankruptcy associate at the law firm of Windels, Marx, Davies & Ives in New York City. He is a former law clerk to the Honorable Conrad B. Duberstein, Chief United States Bankruptcy Judge for the Eastern District of New York. Mr. McNicholas is a 1993 graduate of St. John's University School of Law and a former editor of the *American Bankruptcy Institute Law Review*.

MARK E. MACDONALD • Partner in the Dallas, Texas office of Baker & McKenzie. He received his B.A. degree from Northwestern University with honors in 1964 and his J.D. degree from Northwestern University with honors in 1967, graduating Phi Beta Kappa and Order of the Coif. He is currently subcommittee chair of the Chapter 11 Subcommittee of the ABA Business Bankruptcy Committee and is formerly subcommittee chair of its Secured Creditor and Executory Contract Subcommittees. He is a fellow of the American College of Bankruptcy and a former director of the American Bankruptcy Institute.

MARK E. MACDONALD, JR. • Senior consultant in the corporate Recovery practice at Price Waterhouse LLP. He received his B.A. degree *summa cum laude* from University of Pennsylvania in 1989, his J.D. degree *cum laude* from Northwestern University School of Law in 1993, and his M.M. degree with distinction from J.L. Kellogg Graduate School of Management in 1993. Contributing author to *Advanced Chapter 11 Bankruptcy Practice*, 1993 edition.

ROBERT A. MARK • United States Bankruptcy Judge, Southern District of Florida since November 1, 1990. Prior to his appointment, Judge Mark was a partner in the Miami law firm of Stearns Weaver Miller Weissler Alhadeff & Sitterson. He received his undergraduate degree in economics from

Brandeis University graduating *magna cum laude* and his J.D. from Boalt Hall School of Law (University of California of Berkley) in 1978. Following graduation, he clerked for United State District Judge Sidney Aconovitz.

DAVID. C. MILLER • Chairman of the Tax Practice Group at Thacher, Proffitt & Wood. Mr. Miller received a B.A. from the University of Michigan in 1971 and a J.D. from the University of Michigan in 1975. He obtained an LL.M. in Taxation from New York University in 1978.

CAROLLYNN H.G. PEDREIRA • Attorney at the firm of Willkie Farr & Gallagher. Ms. Pedreira is a 1994 graduate of St. John's University School of Law and a former Associate Managing Editor of the *American Bankruptcy Institute Law Review*.

ALAN J. ROBIN • Associate General Counsel of Metropolitan Life Insurance Company responsible for real estate investments and developments. Mr. Robin is a graduate of Swarthmore College and New York University School of Law and is a member of the New York and California State Bar Association. He is a member of the Council of the Real Property, Probate and Trust Law Section of the American Bar Association and is also the Editor of the Books and Media Group for the Section. Mr. Robin is a member of the American College Real Estate Lawyers where he serves as Chair of the Publications Committee. Mr. Robin is also on the Advisory Board of the John Marshall Law School (Chicago, Illinois) LL.M. Program in Real Estate Law and is an Adjunct Faculty member of the law school.

LINDA J. RUSCH • Professor of Law at Hamline University School of Law in St. Paul, Minnesota. Professor Rusch received her B.A. from Augustana College, Sioux Falls, S.D., and her J.D. from University of Iowa College of Law. She is the vice-chair of the Task Force on Article 2 Revisions of the ABA Business Law Section UCC Committee and is the co-editor of the Commercial Law Newsletter. She is also chair of the Book Development and Editorial Board of the ABA Business Law Section Publications Committee.

SALLY A. SCHREIBER • Shareholder in the Dallas, Texas law firm of Munsch Hardt Kopf Harr & Dinan, P.C. She is a graduate of the University of New Mexico, B.B.A., 1973, and Stanford University, J.D., 1976. Ms. Schreiber is a member of Texas State Bar Committees on Corporation Law, Partnership

Law, Legal Opinion, and Limited Liability Companies. She serves as Director, Fellow and Secretary of the Texas Business Law Foundation.

ROGER M. WHELAN • Senior Counsel in the Washington, D.C. firm of Shaw, Pittman, Potts & Trowbridge. Judge Whelan received his B.A., *cum laude* from Georgetown University in 1959 and his J.D. from Georgetown University Law Center in 1962. He served as a U.S. Bankruptcy Judge for the District of Columbia from 1972-1983. Judge Whelan is a member of the Federal Bar (past Chairman Bankruptcy Litigation Section), the American Bankruptcy Institute (Director, Chairman Legislative Committee; Regional Chairman of Membership Committee), American College of Bankruptcy (Board of Regents (1990-1996); Board of Directors), Master, Walter Chandler American Inn of Court, and Distinguished Lecturer, Columbus School of Law (1975).

DEBORAH D. WILLIAMSON • Shareholder in the San Antonio, Texas firm of Cox & Smith Incorporated. She received her B.A. with honors from University of Texas, El Paso and her J.D. degree from University of Houston Law Center, *cum laude*. She is Vice President - Publications, a Director and a member of the Executive Committee of the American Bankruptcy Institute and Executive Editor of the *American Bankruptcy Institute Journal*. She is a former Vice President of the San Antonio Bankruptcy Bar Association.

ROBERT M. ZINMAN • Professor of Law at St. John's University School of Law and President of the American Bankruptcy Institute. Professor Zinman also serves as Senior Counsellor to the firm of Thacher, Proffitt, & Wood in New York City. He retired in 1988 as Vice President and Investment Counsel at Metropolitan Life Insurance Company. A former Governor of the American College of Real Estate Lawyers and Supervising Council Member of the ABA Section of Real Property, Probate and Trust Law, Professor Zinman serves as a member of the Joint Editorial Board for the Uniform Real Property Acts and as an Adviser for the Restatement of Property (Third) Security. He is a co-author of Michael T. Madison and Robert M. Zinman, MODERN REAL ESTATE FINANCING--A TRANSACTIONAL APPROACH, published by Little, Brown & Co. (1991). He holds a J.D. degree from Harvard Law School and an LL.M. from New York University School of Law.

About the American Bankruptcy Institute

The American Bankruptcy Institute is a multidisciplinary, nonprofit research and educational organization devoted to issues relating to insolvency. Its membership, which is now over 5200, is composed of judges, academics, attorneys, accountants, turnaround specialists and leaders in fields affected by bankruptcy who are dedicated to the improvement of the nation's bankruptcy machinery.

Among its activities, the ABI publishes a monthly Journal and semiannual Law Review, sponsors educational programs, and participates in legislative initiatives. For information about membership and other ABI activities please contact Samuel Gerdano, Executive Director, 44 Canal Center Plaza, Alexandria Virginia 22314.

About St. John's

St. John's University School of Law is particularly suited for its participation in the production of this book because of its strong real estate orientation, offering eight advanced courses in real estate and environmental law in addition to a full-year basic property course. In recent years, St. John's has moved into prominence in the field of bankruptcy education, with its students publishing the *American Bankruptcy Institute Law Review* and, in connection with the ABI, hosting the annual Judge Conrad B. Duberstein National Bankruptcy Moot Court Competition.

For further information contact Dean Rudolph C. Hasl, St. John's University School of Law, 8000 Utopia Parkway, Jamaica, New York 11439.

Index

C